D1519180

THE THEATRICAL CAST OF ATHENS

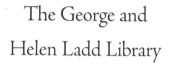

THE
THEATRICAL
CAST OF
ATHENS

*Interactions between Ancient Greek
Drama and Society*

EDITH HALL

OXFORD
UNIVERSITY PRESS

Great Clarendon Street, Oxford OX2 6DP

Oxford University Press is a department of the University of Oxford.
It furthers the University's objective of excellence in research, scholarship,
and education by publishing worldwide in

Oxford New York

Auckland Cape Town Dar es Salaam Hong Kong Karachi
Kuala Lumpur Madrid Melbourne Mexico City Nairobi
New Delhi Shanghai Taipei Toronto
With offices in

Argentina Austria Brazil Chile Czech Republic France Greece
Guatemala Hungary Italy Japan Poland Portugal Singapore
South Korea Switzerland Thailand Turkey Ukraine Vietnam

Oxford is a registered trade mark of Oxford University Press
in the UK and in certain other countries

Published in the United States
by Oxford University Press Inc., New York

British Library Cataloguing in Publication Data

Data available

Library of Congress Cataloguing in Publication Data

Data available

Typeset by SPI Publisher Services, Pondicherry, India
Printed in Great Britain
on acid-free paper by
Biddles Ltd., King's Lynn

ISBN 0-19-929889-0   978-0-19-929889-1

1 3 5 7 9 10 8 6 4 2

Acknowledgements

Since some of the essays in this book have been germinating for two decades, the number of friends and colleagues to whom I am indebted for intellectual, practical, or other help has grown uncontrollably. I have tried throughout to thank the individuals who have helped me on specific details, with the provision of information and offprints, and by commenting on individual chapters. But there are several people who have earned special gratitude, and whose input has been all-pervasive. Robin Osborne and Froma Zeitlin, who provided the reports for OUP, were extraordinarily generous in the dispensation of wise advice and detailed suggestions. I have been more or less continuously in dialogue for years with Pat Easterling, Peter Brown, Helene Foley, Fiona Macintosh, Pantelis Michelakis, Christopher Rowe, and Oliver Taplin. Emma Bridges, Amanda Wrigley, Chris Weaver, Leanne Hunnings, Ranja Knöbl and Rosie Wyles all helped by tracking down recalcitrant references and items of bibliography. Peter Heslin came to the rescue on images and software. Hilary O'Shea supported the project enthusiastically; Jenny Wagstaffe was a calm administrator; Tom Chandler was a superb copy-editor. Esther McGilvray and Christine Flowers tirelessly printed out the seemingly endless new drafts of all the chapters. Richard Poynder thought up the title and makes the best cup of tea in Britain.

This book is dedicated to the memory of Margot Heinemann.

Contents

List of Illustrations

Abbreviations

In addition to those listed below, other abbreviations of modern and classical works follow those listed in the *Oxford Classical Dictionary*, 3rd edition (1996).

ARV²	J.D. Beazley, *Attic Red-Figure Vase-Painters²*. Oxford (1963).
CIL	T. Mommsen et al. (eds.), *Corpus Inscriptionum Latinarum*. Berlin (1872–1953).
D–K	Hermann Diels and Walther Kranz (eds.), *Die Fragmente der Vorsokratiker*. 3 vols. Dublin and Zurich (1966).
FgrH	Felix Jacoby (ed.), *Die Fragmente der griechischen Historiker*. Leiden (1923–).
IEG	M.L West (ed.), *Iambi et elegi graeci ante Alexandrum cantata*. 2nd edn., 2 vols. Oxford (1989–92).
K–A	R. Kassel and C. Austin (eds.), *Poetae Comici Graeci*. Berlin (1983–).
LIMC	*Lexicon Iconographicum Mythologiae Classicae*, Zurich and Munich (1981–99).
LSJ	Henry George Liddell and Robert Scott, *A Greek–English Lexicon*, 9th edn., revised and augmented by Henry Stuart Jones, with a revised supplement ed. P. G. W. Glare. Oxford (1996).
MNC³	T. B. L. Webster, *Monuments Illustrating New Comedy*. 3rd edn., revised and enlarged by J.R. Green and A. Seeberg. London (1995).
M–W	R. Merkelbach and M. L. West (eds.), *Fragmenta Hesiodea*. Oxford (1967).
PLF	Edgar Lobel and Denys Page (eds.), *Poetarum Lesbiorum Fragmenta*. Oxford (1955).
PMG	Denys Page (ed.), *Poetae Melici Graeci*. Oxford (1962).
SH	H. Lloyd-Jones and Peter Parsons (eds.), *Supplementum Hellenisticum*. Berlin and New York (1983).

S–M   Bruno Snell and Herwig Maehler (eds.), *Pindari Car-mina cum Fragmentis* Pars II, *Fragmenta. Indices.* Leipzig (1975).

TgrF   Bruno Snell and Richard Kannicht (eds.), *Tragicorum Graecorum Fragmenta.* Göttingen (1971–2004).

1

Introduction

THEATRICAL ART AND REALITY

One of the most important interpretative problems presented by classical Athenian drama is the nature of the relationship it bore to Athenian social reality. Since the 1970s, which ushered in a reaction against reading the Greek tragic texts primarily as masterworks of timeless aesthetic genius, this relationship has been scrutinized and reformulated by scholars operating within multifarious theoretical models. These have ranged from the influential Marxist-inflected structuralism of Vernant and Vidal-Naquet, to the ritual-anthropological approaches of Foley, Lissarrague, Sourvinou-Inwood, and Seaford; the psychosocial arguments of Griffith; the contextualization of theatre's interests and content within the intellectual and cultural tendencies of the classical period associated with, for example, Goldhill, Zeitlin, Hesk, Wilson, and Ford; to the more specifically historicist readings of Podlecki, Sommerstein or Rosenbloom.[1] The metaphors used to describe this relationship have been numerous; they have included restatements of the ancient proposition that what is on stage 'mirrors' or 'reflects' reality; that it 'refracts' or 'mediates' it; that it 'fertilizes', 'shapes', 'conditions', 'affects', 'influences', 'determines', 'produces', or '*re*produces' it.

---

[1] See e.g. Vernant and Vidal-Naquet (1988); Foley (1981*a*), (1985), (1993), (2001); Lissarrague (1990a), (1990b); Sourvinou-Inwood (1994), (2003); Seaford (1984), (1994), (2003); Griffith (1995), (1998), (2002); Goldhill (1984), (1986), (2004); Zeitlin (1980), (1981), (1985), (1991), (1993), (1994), (1996), (2003); Hesk (1999), (2000), (2003); P. Wilson (1996), (1999–2000), (2000*b*); Ford (2002); Podlecki (1999); Sommerstein (1977), (1996*a*), (2002); Rosenbloom (2002), (2005).

Other language became popular in the 1990s: the Athenian play-scripts and Athenian society mutually 'problematized', 'interrogated', 'subverted', and 'deconstructed' one another.

The volume proposes that a problem with almost all the metaphors used to describe the classical Athenian world–stage relationship is that the relationship that they have posited between the fictions represented on stage, and the world inhabited by its spectators, is fundamentally binary—one reflects the other, etc. But the relationship, this book contends, was never so straightforward: many of the spectators had once performed in dramatic choruses themselves, and may often have been watching their own sons and grandsons participating. Moreover, the fictions of drama were written and performed by poets and actors who were also, at least in the fifth century, almost all Athenian citizens. Drama did not simply 'reflect' social reality in a one-to-one process; members of the social cast of Athens, its acting families, poets, and amateur chorusmen, collaboratively created fictions in their communal spaces that in turn had a dialectical impact, whatever metaphors we use to define it, not only on themselves but throughout their community—the real, social beings who gathered together to watch them in the theatre. The degree of excitement the performance generated affected the way in which the audience reacted, and the audience's own vocal performance of applause or denigration (on which see Ch. 12, pp. 363–6), itself became a key element in the total experience at the drama competitions, by affecting the judges' decisions determining which playwright would win.

In *Frogs* Aristophanes tries, albeit humorously, to define the core of the complicated psychological process by which theatrical stories related to reality. Aeschylus says that, as a tragic playwright, (i) his imagination had 'cast' his heroes Teucer and Patroclus from a 'mould' shaped by a real-world Athenian general (1039–40), and (ii) that watching his warlike heroes made his real-world citizen spectators manly and eager for war (1041–2). Whatever generalizing claims Aristophanes may put in the mouths of his staged playwrights, however, not all Athenian audiences will ever have reacted in identical ways: although they will have shared a vast amount of ideological common ground, they each manifestly had their own personal history, experiences, tastes and psychological individuality (see especially Ch. 7, pp. 197–211). But the tension between shared and entirely disparate individual reactions is and always has been a hallmark of theatre; one of the reasons why theatre is such a privileged and illuminating arena in which to conduct cultural history is precisely because its spectators are situated on the very cusp between the public, communal, and ideological on the one hand, and the private and subjective on the other.

Important strides have been taken in recent decades by performance-focused classicists such as Russo and Taplin, and by theorists and historians of the ancient theatre; Sifakis, Stephanis, J. R. Green, Handley, Wiles, Wilson, Csapo, and Slater, for example, have immeasurably enhanced our understanding of its place in ancient Greek society, its personnel, venues, performances spaces, financial basis, and contributions to the classical Athenian liturgical system, tribal competitions, and civic calendar.[2] This book is profoundly dependent upon their work, but its underlying contention is that the complicated dialectic between the infrastructure underlying theatrical fictions and the impact they had on society can only be fully understood by approaching them from 'both sides of the curtain' simultaneously—reading the fictional roles and stories enacted in drama from a wide enough angle to accommodate the presence of both their creators and their spectators.

If one thing is clear from the collective scholarly endeavour of the last few decades, moreover, it is that no one model, metaphor, or theory can ever be sufficiently nuanced to offer a complete understanding of the complex status of ancient dramatic texts as social documents. The project constituted by this book therefore eschews grand theory in favour of sustained studies of individual phenomena—specific roles or role types, formal theatre conventions, or social arenas beyond the theatre that themselves became theatricalized. Different theories or methodological approaches have been used eclectically whenever they seemed to be helpful (see further the Afterword). The book is an attempt to enrich, by small increments, our understanding of the interface between classical Athenian society and its theatrical fictions by looking in detail at a series of revealing world/stage *interactions*—that is, at a series of ways in which phe-

---

[2] e.g. Russo (1994); Taplin (1977), (1978); Sifakis (1967), (1971*a*), (1971*b*), (1979); Stephanis (1988); J. R. Green (1994); J. R. Green and E. W. Handley (1995); Wiles (1997), (2000), P. Wilson (2000*a*); Csapo (1997), (2002), (2004*a*), (2004*b*); Csapo and Slater (1995).

nomena manifested in the fictional world of the stage, and phenomena in the world that produced that stage, were engaged in a process of continuous mutual pollination. In order to further this aim, reference is made at times to theories, models, methods, disciplines, and parallels drawn from as diverse fields as cognitive psychology, social anthropology, medical obstetrics, plaster casting, medieval French lexicography, Renaissance rhetoric, Jacobean allegory, eighteenth-century theatrical anecdotes, Mozart studies, Romantic aesthetics, Existentialist phenomenology, the recent poetry of Rita Dove or Tony Harrison, Saddam Hussein's propaganda campaigns, and press responses to contemporary productions deriving from ancient playscripts. Indeed, the sole criterion for inclusion in this volume is that the evidence potentially throws some light on a dimension of the ancient experience of drama within its original performative and social context.

DRY ICE AND IDEOLOGY

This is not to say that the questions asked here are not ultimately derived from the intellectual model first proposed in *The German Ideology* (1846) by Karl Marx and Friedrich Engels, according to which all activities of the human consciousness are informed by the material world underlying them. The metaphors favoured by these two titans of cultural history belong to the realms of textile production and the physical sciences: the creation of ideas and consciousness is 'interwoven' (*verflochten*) into material reality, and constitutes an 'efflux' (*Ausfluß*) of actual human life processes; the images in the human minds are like inevitable chemical 'sublimates' (*Sublimate*) of empirical reality,[3] an image which brilliantly captures the unceasing transformations of the 'solid' material environment into the 'vaporous' presences psychically apprehended within the realm of the imagination, *and vice versa*. Dry ice, which is frozen carbon dioxide,

---

[3] Marx and Engels (1956–68), iii. 26. Many thanks to Felix Budelmann for discussing the German metaphors with me.

can be transformed into a vapour (and appropriately enough, this transformation often takes place at exciting moments in the theatre). But that sublimate is equally susceptible to being frozen in order to create another batch of dry ice. Life in classical Athens informed every detail of the stage fictions it enacted; but those stage fictions informed in turn the way that Athenian life was itself conducted.

The ancient literary critics were nevertheless surely correct in emphasizing that one of the two great goals of art, along with usefulness to humankind (*to ōphelimon*) is pleasure (*hēdonē*); as an avid consumer of theatre, movies, and TV drama, always shamelessly motivated by the desire for pleasure rather than for moral or political instruction, I have long felt that Marxist theory, and all the schools of socially contextualizing literary criticism that derive from Marxism (New Historicism, Gender Studies, Postcolonial theory), have tended to underplay people's need for sheer *enjoyment*. No genre or medium of art will ever last for long—certainly not the hundreds of years for which tragedy, comedy and mythological pantomime were enjoyed on the stages of antiquity—if people don't actually *like* it. Glimmerings of the pleasure people derived from theatre can be seen through the truly superstar status of popular actors by the last decades of the fifth century; evidence of this has survived through the fragmentary anecdotal tradition which lasted throughout pagan antiquity, preserving memorable stories about these performers' charisma, glamour, technical skills, and fabled capacity for arousing emotions.[4]

Dionysus may move in Aristophanes' *Frogs* from a position where he simply reports how much pleasure he derived from certain tragedies and particular speeches and scenes within them (e.g. 1028) to a position where he acknowledges that tragedy should also edify and civically enlighten (1433–6). But in doing so the god of theatre was anticipating the recent new wave of Lacanian Marxist theorists, above all Slavoj Žižek, who insists that political ideas work most effectively

[4] The historian Rufus, for example, who was working in the second half of the first century AD, compiled a *Dramatikē Historia*; according to Photius, who refers to extracts from this preserved in Sopatros' *Eklogai Diaphoroi* bk. 4, it contained 'many strange and incredible stories, and the various deeds, words, and interests of tragic and comic actors, and other such things' (*Bibliotheca* no. 161, 103b12–15 ed. Bekker (1824–5)). Thanks to Nigel Wilson and Leofranc Holford-Strevens for help in tracking down this important reference.

when they elicit the psychological responses of enjoyment and desire.[5] Fantasy dressed up in fiction or performed mimesis offers gratification, and by thus *appealing* to its consumers as subjects of desire and pleasure reinforces their status as *political* subjects. It is in the intersection between our capacity for enjoyment—aesthetic and/or libidinal—and our political subjectivity as citizens, that fantasies and fictions find by far their most effective sphere of action (see especially Ch. 7, pp. 191–2).

PSYCHIC RETENTION

Fictions that are enacted in theatre leave a distinctive quality of impression on the human memory. Far from being finite and ephemeral, vanishing without trace, a gripping theatrical experience can instantaneously leave an ineradicable mark on the human psyche (a phenomenon which the myth scholar Joseph Campbell was to term 'aesthetic arrest'),[6] and an immanent presence within it, of a different kind even from the printed word or painted image. One of the most significant examples in intellectual history is Sigmund Freud's psychic retention of the great tragic actor Jean Mounet-Sully's realization of the role of Oedipus at the Comédie-Française in Paris in 1885–6.[7] Four decades earlier, Søren Kierkegaard had attempted to provide a theoretical account of the aesthetic categories by which the human memory selects and prioritizes types of experience, and in particular the cognitive and emotional power of the experience of performed language and music (in his case, Mozartian opera). Kierkegaard suggested that the immediacy of 'the Moment' of apprehension of a performance transcends time, for the images it leaves on the mind are uniquely powerful and indelible. This moment is in one sense lost forever, but it can also be held in remarkable detail in the consciousness until death.[8]

---

[5] See Žižek (1994) and (2002).   [6] See Campbell (1968), 66.
[7] See further E. Hall (2004), 69.
[8] See Kierkegaard (1987), 42, 68, 117–18, 239, 486–7.

It can also be held in the subconscious mind. Freud was convinced of the affinity between the world of the theatre, which intertwines verbal and visual semiosis, with the complex imagery of dream-scapes,[9] and in Mediterranean antiquity people experienced theatrical dreams just as they do today. Demosthenes was said to have dreamed that he was an actor, competing in a tragic competition with Archias ([Plut.] *Life of Demosthenes* 28–9). Before the battle of Arginusae, one of the Athenian admirals dreamt that he and his six colleagues were playing the roles of the Seven against Thebes in Euripides' *Phoenician Women*, while the Spartan leaders were competing against them as the sons of the Seven in his *Suppliant Women* (Diodorus 13.97–8).[10] The dream interpreter Artemidorus of Daldis cites numerous examples of theatre-related dreams (see below, pp. 17–18).

In writing about the slightly different form of mimesis involving actors that is constituted by cinema, Fredric Jameson formulates ideas that illuminate the impact any performance with a visual dimension has on the human psyche. To Jameson,

movies are a physical experience, and are remembered as such, stored up in bodily synapses that evade the thinking mind. Baudelaire and Proust showed us how memories are part of the body anyway...or perhaps it would be better to say that memories are first and foremost memories of the senses, and that it is the senses that remember, and not the "person" or personal identity.[11]

Memory is primarily sensual, and it is the senses that can so often 'jog' a memory of a long-forgotten film (or theatrical performance) years after the event; but Jameson proceeds to describe superbly, in relation to film, how visual images saturate the psyche immediately after they are watched,

in the seam between the day to day; the filmic images of the night before stain the morning and saturate it with half-conscious reminiscence, in a way calculated to raise moralizing alarm; like the visual of which it is a part, but also an essence and a concentration, and an emblem and a whole program, film is an addiction that leaves its traces in the body itself.[12]

---

[9] See further E. Hall (2004), 73.   [10] See further Easterling (2002), 336–9.
[11] Jameson (1990), 1–3.   [12] Jameson (1990), 2.

Jameson's meditation on what makes the filmic experience so special is also at least suggestive for anyone trying to understand the importance of what happens in a theatre. It is Susan Sontag, in her essay 'Against interpretation', who has in relatively recent times most eloquently emphasized the intellectual importance of the sensuous dimension of theatre, and advocated the avoidance of reducing it to a 'meaning' that can be apprehended without consideration of its *physically* apprehended impact.[13]

ORIGINS

The Theatrical Cast of Athens has been germinating for nearly twenty years, since I first began research into ancient Greek literature—specifically, into the representation of non-Greeks in the archaic and classical periods—as a doctoral student at Oxford University in the mid-1980s. It has grown alongside my conviction that while other ancient cities and eras had other genres—epic, lyric, biography, fiction—it was in the theatre that the classical Athenians encountered many of the roles through which they imagined themselves. Drama has the status of a unique conceptual instrument, a special kind of social practice. Thinking in detail about the theatrical cast that peopled the Athenian stage also offers a valuable access road to the Athenian psyche. Theatre may be an 'aesthetic detachment' from everyday life, but it is an unusually revealing one.[14] Athenian culture came to be 'cast' (in another sense of the word) directly through theatre, as it was moulded, and continuously remoulded itself, in identifiably 'theatrical' ways.

Most of the book is organized in groups of chapters revolving around types of theatrical role defined to a significant degree by gender, ethnicity, and styles of vocal performance. Chapters 2 to 4,

---

[13] This essay, originally published in the early 1960s in *Evergreen Review*, is most accessibly republished in Sontag (1994). See her indictment of our contemporary culture, 'whose already classical dilemma is the hypertrophy of intellect at the expense of energy and sensual capability' ((1994), 7), and also her remarks in an interview published in Marranca and Dasgupta (1999), 2–9 at p. 7.

[14] Wilshire (1982), p. ix.

which have not been published before, have nevertheless been evolving over many years of teaching (and indeed watching productions of) ancient drama. Chapter 2 addresses the concept of the dramatic role in classical Greece from a series of perspectives: the author's, the actor's, the audience's, and that of the wider society beyond the immediate performance context. It argues that although there was no equivalent of the term 'role' in ancient Greek, in this absence lies a clue to the extraordinary strength of the conflation of the actor with his represented character at the time of performance, and to the deep cultural penetration of such important stage roles as Clytemnestra, Oedipus, or Pasiphae. The third chapter, 'Childbearing Women: Birth and Family Crisis in Ancient Drama' focuses on a particular category of theatrical role, the woman who gives birth at around the dramatic moment that the play is set; birth plots appeared in all the ancient genres of drama, in both Greek and Latin. The discussion asks why dramatists were so attracted to childbirth as a theme, how the male actors dealt with the requirement to look pregnant or feign labour pains, and how these phenomena fitted with the clear reluctance, at least of classical Athenian men, to discuss obstetric matters in public on any occasion whatsoever.[15]

The fourth chapter, 'Visible Women: Painted Masks and Tragic Aesthetics,' has been more than eighteen years in gestation (it was first delivered at the University of Oxford in 1987). It addresses the frequent comparison of figures in tragedy, especially women, with painted or sculpted artworks; it argues that these comparisons were stimulated by the transvestite convention which required male actors to wear plaster-cast masks painted to resemble female faces.

---

[15] This chapter was read as a paper at Columbia, Durham, and Pennsylvania Universities, the Scuola Normale Superiore di Pisa, and (originally) at a seminar on the ancient Greek household at Cambridge University, run by Paul Cartledge and Lene Rubinstein in the autumn of 1998 (appropriately enough, just six weeks into the unprecedented domestic chaos created by the birth of my first child). Pantelis Michelakis was a supremely helpful respondent and Ruth Bardel provided essential support of other kinds. I would like to thank my hosts for extremely useful feedback, as well as all the following people for help or suggestions: Victoria Amengual, Rebecca Armstrong, Deborah Beck, Eric Csapo, Pat Easterling, Helene Foley, Richard Hamilton, Eric Handley, Angela Heap, François Lissarrague, Martin Ostwald, Ralph Rosen, Brunhilde Ridgway, Francesca Schironi, Brent D. Shaw, Oliver Taplin, Carine Weicherding, and Froma Zeitlin.

Moreover, it was through such verbally constructed analogies that the tragedians could theorize the relationship between the visual dimension of theatre and the aesthetics peculiar to tragedy, without resorting to the type of overt 'metatheatre' that scholars of late have been rather too keen to detect in the closed-off and elevated heroic world represented in Athenian tragic drama.[16]

The subsequent two gender-related chapters have, however, both been published before. The kernel of Chapter 5, 'Horny Satyrs and Tragic Tetralogies', was first delivered at a seminar in the University of Oxford in 1990, and was published in a collection of essays that Maria Wyke edited under the aegis of the journal *Gender and History* in 1998.[17] It examines what can be reconstructed of the female roles in satyr drama, and how its nymphs and shipwrecked princesses were harassed by the ubiquitous chorus of priapic satyrs. The argument is that too little attention has been paid to the deeply masculine psychological and somatic orientation of satyr drama, which throughout the fifth century and some of the fourth was the compulsory final element in the tragic tetralogies enacted at the City Dionysia. At a deep psychosocial level, the satyr play functioned to affirm a group identity founded in homosocial laughter and the libidinal awareness of its male, citizen audience.[18]

---

[16] This chapter has also been read as a paper in vastly different versions, over an embarrassing number of years, at venues including the Universities of Exeter (1990), Reading (1990), Konstanz (1994), Oxford (1995), Durham (2001), and Harvard (2002). Enlightening comments were made on some of those occasions by Richard Seaford, Peter Wiseman, Tessa Rajak, Martin Hose, Denis Feeney, Don Fowler, Gregory Hutchinson, and C. J. Rowe.

[17] 'Ithyphallic males behaving badly: satyr drama as gendered tragic ending', in Wyke (ed.), *Parchments of Gender: Deciphering the Body in Antiquity* (Oxford, 1998), 13–37. The paper was also read at the University of Reading's research seminar in 1993, and St Anne's College Classics Society, Oxford in 1997. I am very grateful to Tessa Rajak, Maria Wyke, Christopher Pelling, Gregory Hutchinson, and Peta Fowler for comments that they made on those occasions.

[18] This interpretation is in many places strikingly similar to some of the contents of Mark Griffith's brilliant, psychoanalytically inflected, discussion of satyr drama (2002), with special reference to Aeschylus' *Proteus*, the satyr play concluding the *Oresteia*. Since Griffith has drawn my attention to the fact that he wrote that study without any knowledge of my article, which had been published four years previously, it is fascinating to read the two essays in conjunction with one another, since their arguments, arrived at wholly independently, are both mutually supportive and complementary.

'Female Personifications of Poetry in Old Comedy', the sixth chapter, was first delivered at a conference held at the Institute of Classical Studies in 1996, under the joint auspices of the University of Wales Institute of Classics and Ancient History and the London Classical Society.[19] It explores the way in which the poets of Old Comedy—Cratinus and Pherecrates as well as Aristophanes—required actors to impersonate literary abstractions that were gendered feminine, such as Poetry and Comedy. The world–stage relationship took on an extremely concrete, vivid, and self-conscious form in a theatrical genre where actors playing 'real' members of the community, such as dramatists and other poets, abused other actors playing anthropomorphic feminine symbols of art. Poetic and theatrical innovation are visibly figured as sexual depravity and sexual violence.

The most recent chapter in this volume to have been conceived is 'Recasting the Barbarian' (Ch. 7), which was written in January 2005 after I had considered, only to reject, a suggestion that I produce a revised edition of *Inventing the Barbarian*, the book that emerged in 1989 from my doctoral thesis. This chapter attempts to update the issues and bibliography presented in the monograph, while arguing that the new global context must entail very different third-millennial scholarly responses to the Hellenocentric bias of Athenian tragedy from those which were published during the final stages of the Cold War.

It was two whole decades previously, in the year 1985, that saw the original version of the next essay on the theatrical treatment of ethnicity, 'The Scythian Archer in Aristophanes' *Thesmophoriazusae*' (Ch. 8). After being delivered at an Oxford postgraduate seminar on Aristophanes run by Angus Bowie and Laetitia Parker, it was published in what was still (just) the East German journal *Philologus* in the same year as *Inventing the Barbarian* (1989).[20] The version

---

[19] It was first published in the volume which resulted from that conference, David Harvey and John Wilkins (eds.), *The Rivals of Aristophanes: Studies in Athenian Old Comedy* (London, 2000), 407–18. I am extremely grateful to David Harvey for his comments at the conference and suggestions for ways in which to improve the argument; Eric Handley provided some important references; Peter Brown read the manuscript with his usual meticulous eye for detail and provided many helpful comments.

[20] The original version, published in *Philologus* 133 (1989), 38–48, was entitled 'The archer scene in Aristophanes' *Thesmophoriazusae*'. I remain very grateful to Angus Bowie and Laetitia Edwards for their kind and incisive comments all those

reproduced here has been considerably revised and updated to take
account of the spate of recent analyses of this important comedy.[21]
The third essay with a focus on the representation of ethnicity,
'Drowning Act: The Greeks, Swimming, and Timotheus' *Persians*'
(Ch. 9), was also published in an earlier version arising out of a
conference, organized by Alan Sommerstein in Nottingham.[22] But it
has been extensively revised in the light of recent scholarly
commentaries on the text as well as some extremely important new
work on what Timotheus' New Music meant in terms of the radical
shifts in aesthetics and culture in Greece during the later part of the
fifth century and the early decades of the fourth.[23]

   The last three essays all deal with aspects of vocal performance,
opening with Chapter 10, 'Singing Roles in Tragedy'. The issue is not
so much the techniques and experience of the singing actor himself
(a topic I have discussed at length in another volume[24]), but what the
formal structure of Greek tragedy, rhythmically and musically, has to
do with its ideological meaning. The approach taken owes much in
its broad approach, although not in any specific detail, to the work of
Fredric Jameson on the relationship between a text's patent external
form and its latent 'political unconscious'.[25] The essay argues that the
aural and musical form of Athenian tragedy—especially the points at
which solo song and speech intersected one another—is what Marx
would have called a 'sublimate' of the social structure and aspirations

years ago, and to Peter Rhodes, Rita Dove, Deborah Roberts, and the late Nan Dunbar
for supplying me much more recently with further information and references.

   [21] See especially the essays collected in Gamel (2002*a*).

   [22] 'Drowning by nomes: the Greeks, swimming, and Timotheus' *Persians*,' Nottingham Classical Literature Studies 2 (1993), 44–80; this volume was edited by H. A.
Khan under the title *The Birth of the European Identity: The Europe–Asia Contrast in
Greek Thought 490–322 BC* (Nottingham, 1994). I am grateful to the editors of NCLS
for granting permission to publish a revised version. The original paper had been
read at several venues, including the University of Pennsylvania at Philadelphia,
Columbia University in New York, and a seminar at the University of Cambridge,
and I am grateful to my hosts for many useful comments and suggestions. Numerous
other people provided me with other help; besides the individuals named in the
footnotes, I am most grateful to Mary Beard, Andy Ford, Martin Hose, Richard
Jenkyns, Helen Morales, Robin Osborne, Tessa Rajak, Ralph Rosen, Charles Sprawson, Andrew Wallace-Hadrill, and Rosemary Wright.

   [23] See esp. van Minnen (1997); Csapo (2004*b*); Peter Wilson (2004).

   [24] E. Hall (2002*a*).

   [25] See Jameson (1971) and (1981).

of the Athenian democracy. Tragic form was partly characterized by patriarchal and ethnocentric notions, even to the point of making its women and barbarians express themselves in vocal media distinguishable in large measure from those adopted by free Greek male characters in their prime. This chapter is only a lightly revised version of the original article, published in the volume which arose from a conference devoted to the performance culture of classical Athens, which was organized at Cambridge by Simon Goldhill and Robin Osborne.[26]

'Casting the Role of Trygaeus in Aristophanes' *Peace*' (Ch. 11), in contrast, has not been published before, although it has been evolving since it was first delivered at a Classics Faculty seminar in Cambridge in 1988.[27] It examines what was required of the actor who played Trygaeus, and shows that although the role entailed some uniquely acrobatic displays upon the theatrical crane, it also made extreme vocal demands. The actor (who seems to have been named Apollodorus) not only had to sing tragic lyrics while ascending on his dung-beetle, but to recite tragic anapaests, display a command of Stesichorean lyric, and latterly extemporize in hexameters from cues like a rhapsode at the Panathenaea. The name *Trygaeus* suggests a relationship with what Aristophanes termed *Trugedy*, comedy with a message and an affinity with tragedy; this trugedic performer therefore needed not only to score points off his bellicose adversaries in the manner expected of a canny comic hero, but to assume the role of Bellerophon and subsequently of Silenus in a satyr play. Eventually he

[26] 'Actor's song in tragedy', in Simon Goldhill and Robin Osborne (eds.), *Performance Culture and Athenian Democracy* (Cambridge, 1999), 96–122. The paper had previously been delivered at an interdisciplinary conference organised at St Cross College, Oxford by Patricia Fann in 1990, as well as at the Cambridge conference which gave rise to the publication. Several people provided invaluable help when I presented both early drafts. Important references are owed to Helene Foley, Simon Goldhill, Peter Wilson, and Oliver Taplin. I would also like in particular to thank Chris Collard, and above all Pat Easterling for her perceptive criticisms and abundance of references, and Eric Csapo for his encouragement.

[27] Another early draft was delivered as one of a seminar series on Old Comedy organized at Corpus Christi College, Oxford by Ian Ruffell and Martin Revermann. I am very grateful for their comments and those of several others who were present on these occasions, including Maria Wyke, John Henderson, Ewen Bowie, Oliver Taplin, and especially Peter Wilson. Paul Cartledge also read the typescript and made many helpful points.

had even to transform himself into a scion of Hesiod in a humorous dramatization of the *Contest of Homer and Hesiod.*

The final chapter in the volume, 'Lawcourt Dramas: Acting and Performance in Greek Legal Oratory', takes the argument out of the theatre and into the lawcourts, one of the contexts which most clearly reveals the increasingly theatrical tenor (or 'cast') of Athenian society at large and of its public discourses. In a survey of the corpus of legal oratory from classical Athens, the essay argues that the analogy between a trial and a theatrical performance was close and multi-layered. There were strong similarities between the writing of roles for a play and the composition of speeches for delivery in court; there was a considerable degree of overlap between what was expected of tragic actors and litigants in terms of vocal performance. This essay is a heavily revised version of a paper originally delivered at a London University seminar series on law at Athens convened by Lin Foxhall and Andrew Lewis, and subsequently published in *BICS* (1995).[28]

All of the chapters therefore study interactions between Athenian reality and the theatrical cast—the *dramatis personae*—that inhabited the Athenian theatre and imagination, whether the prime focus is a particular category of role, an individual role in a specific play, or role-playing and mimetic performance in genres closely allied to drama such as citharodic arias or lawcourt speeches, delivered from a platform in front of an audience of citizens. Some of the chapters begin with a consideration of a formal and aesthetic element within theatre (mask, tetralogy, monody), before asking what relationship this element may bear to its social and ideological context. A third continuous strand traces the way that Greek drama itself came to meditate, with varying degrees of explicitness, on its own relation-ship with reality. Tragedy created rhetorical tropes that meditated on its status as spectacle; comedy impersonated poetic abstractions, and in Aristophanes' *Peace*, performed at what seemed like a pivotal moment in Athenian and Greek history, a comic hero established an ideologically charged taxonomy of poetic media and genres. But

---

[28] 'Lawcourt dramas: the power of performance in Greek forensic oratory', *BICS* 40 (1995), 39–58. The paper had also been delivered at the Universities of Yale and Princeton. Several people helped me enormously to improve it, including Victor Bers, Christopher Carey, Paul Cartledge, James Davidson, Lin Foxhall, Josh Ober, Bob Sharples, Stephen Todd, and Froma Zeitlin.

these separate threads, although weaving in and out of the fabric of the book, wind together in the direction of a single fundamental objective: they illustrate the relevance to classical Greek theatre of the extraordinarily profound insight, commonly attributed to Oscar Wilde, that the stage 'is not merely the meeting place of all the arts, but is also the return of art *to life*.'

2

The Theatrical Roles of Athens

WHAT'S IN A ROLE?

When the members of an ancient audience left the theatre after the performance of a play, with all its costumes, special effects, music, and variegated poetry, what features left durable marks on their memories? According to a character in a fourth-century comedy by Timocrates, it was the afflictions suffered by the leading characters: conscious thought about individuals suffering worse cases of their own problems can benefit audience members. Thus an indigent spectator is comforted by the extreme poverty of Telephus; a sick one by the ravings of Alcmaeon; one with bad eyesight by the blinded sons of Phineus; one whose child has died by Niobe (fr. 6.5–19 K–A).[1] Even the ancient *sub*conscious seems to have been impressed by individual figures in tragedy. A modern psychoanalyst will scrutinize the fictional characters with whom a client identifies; in the second century AD, the dream interpreter Artemidorus of Daldis was already convinced that his science required understanding of the stories 'about Prometheus and Niobe and all the heroes of tragedy', because they were 'well-known and believed by most people' (4.47). Agave made an impression on one mother, who killed her own three-year-old son after dreaming that she was a Bacchant, 'for such is the story of Pentheus and Agave' (4.39). Another domestic tragedy was caused by the replication of the relationship between the two leading roles in Euripides' *Andromache*, when a slave woman

---

[1] The fragment actually seems to derive from Euripides' *Syleus* (see (65) Eur. fr. 687 *TgrF*) rather than *Andromache*, demonstrating the extent to which verses by the famous tragedians were inherently transferable between their plays.

dreamt that she recited the part of the Trojan captive: her jealous mistress, like Hermione in Euripides' play, subjected her to cruel mistreatment (4.59).[2] Artemidorus also records a man who 'dreamt that he played a character named *Androgynos* in a comedy (*Androgunon kōmōidein edoxe tis*, 4.37). His penis became diseased...the dream became true because of the name'. Artemidorus concludes that if anyone dreams that he acts in either a comedy or a tragedy, *and he remembers his role*, then the experiences undergone by that character will happen in reality to the dreamer.[3]

The residual presence of Agave, Andromache, Hermione, and Prometheus in the subconscious minds of Artemidorus' clients represents a late stage in the long journey undergone by such roles. Cognitive psychologists argue that the origins of such archetypal roles as these—persecutory mother, victim, rival, and martyr—lie deep in our species' collective subconscious, are manifested in the imaginative repertoire of every human culture, and that infants must learn to recognize and participate in their enactment.[4] Yet it was inside a playwright's psyche that each specific Greek dramatic role germinated, fertilized by earlier art and poetry; it was shaped into new verses (predominantly iambic trimeters), learned by an actor, recited publicly with the aid of props and gestures, and thence became engraved upon the collective memory. Impressive roles also came to inform other types of ancient text and artifact, and familiarity with them did not necessarily require seeing them in a theatre; the theatrical cast first invented in Athens came to inhabit not only dream books, but historiography, legal speeches, philosophical dialogues, love elegy, erotic novels, public sculpture, and the interior décor of private houses. This book discusses a series of examples of the circulation of roles within the ancient imagination; each role moved from the mind of a dramatist to his audience and beyond via the mind, body, and voice, of the actor who performed it.

---

[2] See also Antiphanes fr. 189 K–A, which implies that the broad outlines of the stories of Oedipus and Alcmaeon were universally familiar.

[3] In his discussion of the phenomenal number of different positions in which ancient men apparently dreamed about having sex with their mothers (1.79), Artemidorus' text recalls one of the most memorable of all ancient roles.

[4] On alternative 'universal' psychological taxonomies, with several references to the casts of ancient Greek drama, see Landy (1993), 163–255.

Artemidorus' clients dreamed roles before they lived them; Athan-
asius of Alexandria, who grew up to be no friend of theatre's false
images, as a child took the playground role of Christian bishop long
before he lived it (Rufinus, *Hist. Eccl.* 10.15); in the fourth century BC,
the tragic actor Polus inverted the regular chronological relationship of
role to real-life experience by handling the urn containing his son's
remains in order to express authentic sorrow when assuming the role of
Electra (Aulus Gellius 6.5). A different articulation of the nature of role
assumption occurs in the earliest surviving comedy, Aristophanes'
Acharnians. Once the hero Dicaeopolis has acquired the ragged costume worn by the leading role in Euripides' *Telephus*, he quotes that
play in explaining to the audience, 'Today I must appear to be a beggar;
I must *be* who I am, but *seem* not to be' (440–1).[5] Although the picture
is complicated by Dicaeopolis' own status as a fictional character
impersonated by an actor, and because the role of Telephus he assumes
itself involved disguise and role-playing, the fundamentally triangular
nature of theatre is here lucidly expressed. For according to the most
rudimentary definition, theatre is a situation in which *A* impersonates
B before *C*, or, to use the Dicaeopolis-actor's words, *A* 'must appear to
be' *B* in the eyes of those he is addressing. In this triangular process, two
parties exist and are present: *A* (the actor) and *C* (the spectator). But
B—the role—is a *conjured* presence. *B* is not present at all. Unlike the
actor and spectator, moreover, *B* may be an animal, a symbol, a satyr, or
a god. *B* may be dead, as yet unborn, or fictional. *B* may be an invented
citizen of Athens or a mythical princess of Argos. *B* can disappear at any
time if the actor's 'mask slips'; the breathing actor is present alongside
the imminent *absence* of the assumed identity should the 'electric
current' charging the performance fail.[6] Yet live performance, although
an essential condition of theatre, is an insufficient definition. Listening
to an after-dinner speaker deliver a live oration in his or her 'real'
persona does not offer the same engagement as a theatrical performance. What is most essential to theatre, therefore, is the live-ness of the

---

[5] *einai men hosper eimi, phainesthai de mē* (= Euripides 67 fr. 698 *TgrF*). The
importance of this passage in the ancient exploration of what it meant to be a
dramatic actor has been well analysed by Lada-Richards (2002), especially 396–7. It
is Triclinius on whose authority the lines are said to have been taken from Euripides'
Telephus: see the discussion of Olson (2002), 189 with references.
[6] Hornby (1986), 98–9.

representation of the *fictive identities* and the manner in which they are sustained.[7]

This book is about aspects of the triangle that constituted the ancient theatre, in particular about element '*B*'. It addresses roles that were impersonated in pagan Greece: women in childbirth, satyrs, literary personifications, despotic, drowning, or obtuse barbarians, singing heralds, and peasant farmers—some of the more colourful members of the 'virtual community' residing in the Athenian imagination. The underlying assumption, and argument, is that acting out gendered or ethnically inflected roles is a process in which the histrionic, pleasurable and fictional is transformed into the ideologically and socially cogent. This chapter concentrates on the concept of the role from several perspectives, from its imaginative creation to the moment it transcended the moment of performance to become in its own right an active ideological influence on public discourses beyond the theatre.

It has not lately been fashionable to stress the centrality of *B*—the role played—to the experience of theatre. It is regarded by many drama theorists as a relic of the neoclassical theatre's narcissistic star system. It is held in suspicion by both the experimental avant-garde and the traditional left wing, which, since Brecht, has seen the domination of theatre by individual roles and their actors as a bourgeois, decadent betrayal of the rightfully collaborative status of the medium. Individual roles interest neither those who see performances as events or 'happenings', nor advocates of ensemble acting. In Classics, too, the notion of the theatrical role has been oddly recessive. With some outstanding exceptions, the conjured identities that peopled the Greek theatre, along with the achievement of the actors who conjured them (and who by the 420s were becoming virtuosic stars), attracted surprisingly little attention during the last three decades of the twentieth century.[8] One strand in the scholarship

---

[7] Ibid.; see also E. Hall (2004), 74–7.

[8] An important exception is the study of role-playing in Euripides' *Orestes* by Zeitlin (1980), especially the remarks about role-models, identity, and the shifting of social/emotional roles between actors and characters on pp. 55 and 69; Macintosh (2000) sees Medea's repertoire of theatrical roles as her defining characteristic; Gellrich (2002) offers a subtle study of the way that in *Medea* 'Euripides exploits the insight that the dramatic agent is first and above all an actor with a variety of

has indeed been reinstating the ancient plays as performance scripts, and assessing the impact of individual actors' and performers' entrances, actions, and exits. But even this approach tends to look at roles from the perspective of the seeing spectator rather than from 'both sides of the curtain', and often neglects the aural dimension of drama, in particular vocal delivery.[9] The other major trend, from the late 1970s onwards, entailed returning the texts to the sociological and religious contexts in which they were first produced,[10] and in this work the multiplicity of individuals peopling a drama was often of less importance than its nature as a homogeneous narrative.[11] The same can be said of the work of scholars examining, from an anthropological viewpoint, the structural patterns that reflected ritual,[12] or the lyric consciousness embodied in the dancing chorus;[13] even studies of the visual dimensions of theatre—its relationship with painting and sculpture, or its ramifications for the development of cognitive science, epistemology, and aesthetics—have not been concerned with the central roles and the men who acted them.[14] These late twentieth-century questions have recently been displaced by the postmodern obsession with self-referential aesthetics: metatheatre, imprecisely defined, has threatened to displace theatre (see Ch. 4, pp. 105–11).

Centuries before theatre had come into existence, however, many of its aspects had been anticipated. There had been mimetic elements not only in the performance of epic,[15] but in rituals with

histrionic postures at his disposal, a theatrical being intent upon fulfilling the freedom that comes from playing roles' (p. 319). There are some valuable insights into role-playing, both literal and metaphorical, in individual Sophoclean tragedies in Ringer (1998), although his definition of 'metatheater' is problematically imprecise.

[9] See e.g. Seale (1982). Analyses of likely role distribution in individual Aristophanic plays can however be found in Russo (1994); see also, for both tragedy and comedy, Pickard-Cambridge (1988), 138–55. For recent studies that have concentrated on the audiences of Greek drama and their responses, see especially P. Wilson (2000*b*); Griffith (1995), (1998), and (2002).

[10] See above all the essays collected in Vernant and Vidal-Naquet (1988).

[11] For examples of this approach see the influential essays contained in Winkler and Zeitlin (1990) and Easterling (1997*a*).

[12] See, purely *exempli gratia*, the approach of Sourvinou-Inwood (2003).

[13] e.g. Henrichs (1994–5); Stehle (2004).

[14] See Ch. 4, pp. 112–19.

[15] For the most extreme presentation of the case that the performance of epic was as dramatic as the performance of drama, and virtually indistinguishable from it, see Else (1957), 34–5.

mythological and narrative dimensions, for example thunderous and clattering noises in enactments of the epiphany of chthonic gods.[16] Archaic choruses, such as the Delian maidens in the cult of Apollo, had long played with alternative identities, expressed fluctuating and mutating subjectivities, and incorporated mimetic elements into their gestures.[17] The possibility of a poem being spoken in an identified persona had been explored in the Archilochean iambics uttered in the voice of Charon the carpenter (*IEG* 19);[18] choral lyric could be composed in dialogue form, without framing narrative in the third person, as Bacchylides 18 alternates the voice of Aegeus and that of an Athenian chorus. What made theatre distinctively *theatrical* when it was invented in the late sixth century was the moment that an actor assumed a role by masking his identity and speaking in the voice of Pentheus or Tiresias;[19] even scholars who downplay the distinction between theatre and archaic poetry's mimetic elements—indeed its embryonic role performance—concede that drama, as 'primary' mimesis, has a major claim to innovative status:[20] Dionysus' relationship with tragedy is partly to be discovered in its newness, and its material epiphanies.[21] Theatre happened on the cusp between the empirically discernible world and the imaginary world of the play, at the moment the actor brought to life his fictive identity. Theatre can be theatrical without much happening, but *A* must impersonate *B* before *C*.

Yet ever since Aristotle insisted on the priority of plot, while conceding that some plays were indeed determined by the nature of an individual character (*Poetics* 1456^{a}1–2), there has always been atension in dramatic theory between these two fundamental

[16] See Hardie (2004), 16–18, with the bibliography in notes 28 and 18; Nielsen (2002), 816; Horn (1972), 76 even speaks of 'die Pantomime in den Mysterien'; for Dionysiac cult see also Ricciardelli (2000), 265–82.

[17] See e.g. Lonsdale (1993), 62–70.

[18] See Hdt. 1.12.2 and Ar. *Rhet.* 3.1418^{b}30 with Ford (2002), 147.

[19] The argument here is much in accordance with that of Wise (1998), 61–2; see also Seaford (1994), 277–8; Nielsen (2002), 79–80.

[20] Nagy (1996), 80: 'There is in fact a staggering variety of roles to be played out in all the various performance traditions of ancient Greek song-making, whether they are overtly dramatic or otherwise… Still, it is justifiable to consider drama, with its ritual background, as a primary form of mimesis.'

[21] See Vernant in Vernant and Vidal-Naquet (1988), 181–8; Halliwell (1993), 197; Marshall (1999), 197.

notions.[22] Do people who have seen Euripides' *Medea* primarily remember the actor playing the role of Medea? Or are their recollections conditioned by the series of events—the complexities of the plot, with its eight ancillary roles? The answer seems to be the figure of Medea plus an emblematic action; what is taken away in the imagination is indeed the scary woman, but it is the scary woman who killed her children. Although playwrights subsequent to Euripides could change the story by making Medea send her children away rather than murder them, as Carcinus did in his fourth-century *Medea*, the child-killing still inescapably informed Carcinus' conception of her role: he made her argue that it would have been irrational to kill the children while leaving Jason alive (Aristotle, *Rhet.* 2.23.28 $1400^b = 70$ Carcinus II fr. 1e *TgrF*). In Athens this tension between story and role affected the development of theatrical practice, and the shape of tragedy. Acting out narratives in intermissions between choral dancing may have been the way theatre began. But as it evolved, the individual actor challenged the dominance of the chorus;[23] what was expected of star actors then affected the way in which plays were composed.

In Aeschylus' earlier works, the balance between the size and the significance of the roles remains fairly equal and no one figure, at least until Clytemnestra in *Agamemnon*, stakes a claim psychologically to dominate the action of a single play;[24] Clytemnestra, moreover, yields her central position over the course of the trilogy to Orestes. It is significant that a tragic actor's prize was not added to the

---

[22] Not just drama theorists: psychologists and sociologist also tend to prefer to analyse people's subjective accounts of themselves in terms of one of these two models: (i) fictional narratives and plot types (see e.g. J. Hillman's *Healing Fiction* (1983)), with the use, for example, of the thirty-one universal plot elements identified by the structuralist folklore analyst Vladimir Propp (1958); (ii) shifting identification with a repertoire of roles. The latter perspective was developed by J. L. Moreno in his *Psychodrama* (1946), which in turn informed Erving Goffman's seminal *The Presentation of Self in Everyday Life* (1959). Others recognize the fusion of the two approaches: see Landy (1993), 24–6.

[23] See especially Csapo (2004a), 52–6.

[24] Herington (1985), 143 and 271 n. 72, is to be commended when failing to be impressed by attempts to make Eteocles in *Septem* commensurate with the towering monolithic heroes of Sophocles or *PV*. A factor which even Herington does not mention is that Eteocles' speeches are threatened with being upstaged by the full and florid narratives delivered by the actor playing the soldier and the herald.

Lenaea festival until the late 430s, and possibly not until 423 BC.[25] By the 420s, tragedies were more likely to revolve around a titanic personality who rarely leaves the stage, for example in Sophocles' *Oedipus* or Euripides' *Hecuba*. By the time of Aristophanes' *Thesmophoriazusae* a decade or more later, the tragic poet Agathon distinguishes between composing 'female dramas' and 'male dramas' (148–58). The process is presented, albeit comically, as role-driven in a way that the audience seem to have understood;[26] Agathon proposes that play composition is directly affected by the sex of the central role he is creating (see further Ch. 5, pp. 153–4). Much of the discussion of tragic composition in *Frogs* centres on the roles and role types to be associated with Aeschylus and Euripides respectively (e.g. 1039–44, courageous men like Patroclus and Teucer, libidinous women like Phaedra and Stheneboea). Subsequently, when Plato's Socrates evicts theatre from his republic, he objects less to the narratives retold in dramatic plots than to the idea of theatrical impersonation, in particular the roles of sexually motivated women, women giving birth, and women upbraiding their husbands (3.395d5–e3, see below, pp. 67 and 164). It was partly in order to circumvent Plato's objections that Aristotle claimed that the characters involved in tragic drama were less important than plotlines (1450^{a}15–26), and that acting could be dispensed with altogether since a cogent plot could take effect if recounted without theatrical enactment (1453^{b}3–8). But Aristotle was bucking the inexorable trend in the theatre of his day, which the craze for star actors like Theodorus had taken in the opposite direction: this nonpareil travelled between farflung engagements and festival contests, where he upstaged all his fellow performers in realizations of great roles in the repertoire, including Antigone, Electra, and Hecuba.[27]

---

[25] The precise date depends on reconciling the evidence from several inscriptions, for a discussion of which see Csapo and Slater (1995), 227–8.

[26] See Muecke (1982), 53: *gunaikeia dramata* here 'are plays the heroines of which are women, rather than plays with a female chorus, the explanation offered by the scholia'. In n. 88 she draws attention to the opposition at Plutarch, *Cleom.* 39 between a *gunaikeion* and an *andreion drama* in the sense that the protagonists of the metaphorical drama being enacted are first women, and then later men. For a recent discussion of this scene from the perspective of the actors' costumes and ithyphalloi, see Stehle (2002), 281.

[27] The evidence is assembled in Stephanis (1988), no. 1157.

In the twentieth century, theatrical roles became a notoriously politicized issue. At the Moscow Art Theatre a hundred years ago, Constantin Stanislavski focused on the actor's conviction in the naturalistic realization of a role.[28] But his critics always urged that this school produced self-regarding actors, who erected a wall between themselves and the voyeuristic audience: quintessentially bourgeois theatre.[29] Brecht insisted that the actor destroy the role in order to present it as a manufactured entity, enabling the maintenance of critical distance. And for Dario Fo, acting means 'recounting': the actor must find the story rather than the character. Fo has urged that inherent in 'the people' is a collective dimension different from the individualizing tendencies of the bourgeoisie; this consciousness is supposedly expressed in 'popular' entertainment forms that require actors to enter into dialogue with the audience, rather than to display themselves for inspection.[30]

The problem with Fo's approach is that it is too grown-up. It requires an intellectual effort on the part of the spectator *not* to look for an individual with whom to identify. Theatre produced with Fo's agenda risks defeating its own political purpose by becoming an elite, esoteric art form. Most 'ordinary' people enjoy plays which offer dominant roles: spectators aspiring to improve their lot have always found psychological encouragement in identification with the fictive heroes furnished by theatre. As Northrop Frye once wisely said, princes and princesses can be wish-fulfilment dreams as well as social facts.[31] The *primary* intuitive drive in the human psyche, moreover, is to think in terms of identifiable individuals, rather than event sequences, collective nouns, or abstractions. Such are the conclusions of research into children's play, the content of which is surprisingly universal. Gender and cultural differences inevitably introduce variants,[32] but recent comparisons of children in the USA, China, and Argentina have identified substantial universal

---

[28] For the classic exposition of his ideas on role creation, see Stanislavski's unfinished *Creating a Role* (1961), the third volume of his planned trilogy on training an actor.

[29] Farrell and Scuderi (2000), 11.

[30] Fo (1974), 33.

[31] Frye (1965), 146.

[32] Bornstein et al. (1999).

aspects, reflecting 'species-general developmental processes'.[33] Hui-zinga's seminal *Homo Ludens* (1938) argued that mimetic play is genetically hardwired in the newborn human's psyche, and many experts now believe that the requirement to produce *roles* is similarly innate.[34] Fantasy play begins in the second year of life,[35] but children of three start to move beyond a solitary pretence of drinking from toy teacups in their 'own' persona; they embark on playing roles (invari-ably those of parents and children) interactively with each other.[36] In this earliest role play, children do not say, if asked the name of their game, that they are playing 'marriage' or 'families'; the title of their drama is always 'mummies and daddies'; another favourite early game, which older children might call 'hospitals', is originally 'doc-tors and nurses'.[37] However profound Aristotle's perception that in sophisticated adult tragedy storyline takes precedence over other constituents, including character, for humans in their infancy it is the character—the role, the *prosōpon*—that is universally prior.

Moreover, for theorists of child development, it is the dramatiza-tion not of events but of *self* and *other* that is crucial to maturation. The seminal works on identity have all stressed that it is through dramatization of roles that children and teenagers develop their self-images, thus expanding their control over reality,[38] even if they do not do it so explicitly as the children whom Epictetus observed, around the end of the first century AD, pretending to be figures in tragedies as well as wrestlers, gladiators, and trumpet-players (*Encheiridion* 29). The process underpins an independent identity and remains necessary throughout adulthood; it is nurtured by all kinds of storytelling. Psychologists agree that cultural materials that allow the vicarious experience of roles, identities, and the emotions appropriate to them—materials that include literature and drama—make a significant contribution to selfhood,[39] 'as the mimetic

---

[33] Haight et al. (1999); Bornstein et al. (1999); see also Piaget (1967).

[34] See Mauss (1985); Landy (1993), 17–18, with bibliography.

[35] McArdle (2001); Pellegrini and Boyd (1993); Pellegrini and Perlmutter (1989).

[36] Miller and Garvey (1984).

[37] See the discussion of Rubin and Wolf (1979); L. R. Goldman (1998), 32, on recent research into the developing ability of children as they get older to sustain and indeed switch roles across complex narratives.

[38] Erikson (1963), 222.

[39] Smith-Lovin (2002), 131.

impulse transforms identity'.[40] This has always been the case: empathizing with the individuals in epic or the theatre—or alternatively fearing and hating them—was essential to the creation of the individual ancient Athenian's identity. Perceptions of others have always been mediated by the experience of their dramatic substitutes in a culture's collectively experienced 'cast' of characters.[41] Audiences today experience the roles and relationships of the theatre as resembling and revealing our own 'mimetically conditioned and imitative relationships offstage or those with which we are acquainted'.[42] Moreover, we are affected offstage by our perception of what roles *others* expect of us: how should we act at a parent's funeral? At our wedding?[43]

A great role well acted can actually add a whole new individual permanently to a culture's functional 'cast'. Drama radically affects the way people behave, especially in unusual circumstances of which they have no experience *except* through staged enactment (and its modern equivalents, which are often screened). It may be difficult to believe the claims of Aristophanes' Aeschylus that his Patroclus and Teucer 'inspired every male citizen to live up to their example whenever he heard the trumpet sound' (*Frogs* 1041–2), but war offers stark examples of people taking comfort in dramatic role models under extreme circumstances, as witnessed by this American veteran of World War II:

Combat as I saw it was exorbitant, outrageous, excruciating and above all tasteless, perhaps because of the number of fighting men who had read Hemingway or Remarque was a fraction of those who had seen B movies about bloodshed. If a platoon leader had watched Douglas Fairbanks, Jr., Errol Flynn, Victor McLaglen, John Wayne, or Gary Cooper leap recklessly about, he was likely to follow this role model.[44]

Analysing any culture gains from studying its shared cast of characters—its equivalents of the role of Patroclus or those played by John Wayne; much public discourse assumes not only acquaintance with this cast, but familiarity.

---

[40] Postlewait and Davis (2003), 10.   [41] Bentley (1964), 36.
[42] Wilshire (1982), p. xiv.   [43] Wilshire (1982), xv.
[44] Manchester (1979), 83, quoted in Hornby (1986), 22.

During the fifth century, the Athenians' experience of theatre and its roles infiltrated other social practices and forms of communication: the visual arts, the collective memory, lyric poetry, and the courts of law (see Chs. 4, 7, 9, and 12 respectively). By the early fourth century, the metaphor of acting appears in psychology; according to Xenophon, Socrates suggested that his son Lamprocles could control himself in the face of his mother's abuse by remembering that her insults and threats were no more real than those exchanged by actors (*hupokritai*) in the tragic theatre; there was a contradiction between her acted behaviour and her true stance towards her son, whose best interests she had at heart (*Mem.* 2.2.8–9). Another fine example occurs in the historiography of Thucydides, which ancient literary critics were already aware was intensely dramatic,[45] and in which more recent scholars have noted the presence of tragic plot patterns.[46] Even the conception of individuals and the roles they played in the narrative of Athenian history is affected by pre-existing theatrical role typologies. The first scholar to appreciate this fully was Francis Cornford, who in 1907 (six years before the word 'role' appears in a sense transferred from the theatre in the social sciences), identified Thucydides' account of Pausanias' career (1.128–35) as a response to a familiar type of theatrical role. 'Pausanias... boasts of his power... can no longer live like ordinary men; behaves like an oriental... and displays a harsh temper. We know all these symptoms well enough, and we foresee the end.'[47] The answer to the implicit question of *how* we know the symptoms is offered in Cornford's next paragraph: 'the story is a drama, framed on familiar lines, and ready to be transferred to the stage.'[48] The 'facts' about Pausanias' death were 'shaped by imagination on the model of preconceived morality and views of human nature. The mould is

---

[45] Plutarch saw how Thucydides turned his readers into spectators by making his narrative 'like a painting', especially by the 'vivid representation of emotions and characters' (*Are the Athenians More Famous for War or for Wisdom?* (= *Mor.* 347a).

[46] See e.g. MacLeod (1982); Pelling (2000), chs. 2, 4–6 contains important discussions of the rhetorical and explanatory strategies shared by the tragedians and the Greek historians. For intellectual manoeuvres that reflect cross-fertilization between Euripides and Thucydides, see J. H. Finley (1967), ch. 2.

[47] Cornford (1907), 135–6.

[48] Ibid. 136.

supplied by drama'.[49] Cornford deduces that Thucydides 'learnt his psychology from the drama, just as we moderns... learn ours, not by direct observation, but from the drama and the novel'.[50] The cast of Athenian historiography was becoming recognizably theatrical.

So were Athenian lawsuits. If an Athenian woman was indicted for murdering her husband, it created an opportunity to claim that she had been acting out the role of Clytemnestra (Antiphon 1.17). When Demosthenes wanted to undermine the popularity of Aeschines, a former tragic actor, he implied that playing the role of the tyrant Creon in Sophocles' *Antigone* had rubbed off on his rival.[51] Evidence for the priority of the notion of role permeates ancient discourses, from Dicaeopolis' assumption of the role of Telephus (see above), and his delight in Euripides' invention of the sophistical slave role (*Ach.* 398–401), to controversies over the legitimacy of theatre conducted between Christians and pagans more than eight centuries later (see Ch. 3, pp. 67–8). Yet every one of these cultural presences, each canonical role, was first realized in performance by a male actor, usually at Athens. In the cases of neither Clytemnestra nor Creon do we know the name of the actor who 'created' the role. We often know the names of actors who played the important roles in subsequent revivals or in new plays on old themes: the earliest identifiable individual to have played the role of Medea, for example, was a fourth-century actor appropriately named Androsthenes; he was followed by a tragic singer named Canopus in Claudius' day, and later, perhaps, by Augustine (*Conf.* 3.6, 4.2).[52] In only a very few instances can we attach an actor's name to the actual première of a role (the first protagonist of Euripides' *Orestes* was called Hegelochus (Σ *Or.* 729)). But the other fifth-century actors have not disappeared altogether. A few names are recorded, such as that of Oeagrus, renowned for his delivery of speeches from a tragic *Niobe* (*Wasps* 579–80). Sophocles cultivated an actor by the name of

[49] Cornford (1907), 137, who also notices that Thucydides identifies Cleon's type 'as though on a play-bill: "Cleon, the most violent of the citizens"... Pericles is introduced in the same way'.

[50] Ibid. 147.

[51] See Demosthenes 18.129, 19.247, and the references in Easterling (2002), 338 with n. 41.

[52] Androsthenes played in Theodorides' *Medea* and *Phaethon* at the Lenaea of 363 BC. See Stephanis (1988), no. 182. On Canopus see Cockle (1975); on Augustine, E. Hall (2002a), 3.

Tlepolemus (*Σ Clouds* 1266), although sadly we do not know whether we can associate this name with the creation of such outstanding roles as Oedipus, Ajax, or Electra.

The surviving classical Greek tragedies and Aristophanic comedies, which all date from the fifth and early fourth centuries BC, were first performed in the theatre of Dionysus at Athens in Attica during drama competitions held at one of the festivals of Dionysus. These were the Lenaea (held in the equivalent of January–February) and the much larger City Dionysia (held in the equivalent of March–April), at which visitors from allied states were welcomed. Current scholarship estimates that the total population of Attica during this period was in the region of quarter of a million, but that the large proportion of resident foreigners ('metics') and slaves meant that only perhaps thirty thousand inhabitants were adult male citizens.[53] The major theatrical contests, which seem to have been extremely popular, may have accommodated a little more than 50 per cent of this citizen body; it is unlikely that the theatre of Dionysus could have seated significantly more. The audience at premières of the plays is therefore likely to have been dominantly (some scholars argue almost exclusively) free, Athenian or allied to Athens, and male.[54] Yet when considering the impact that these plays had on their audiences, it is crucial to remember that the more popular and successful were revived, with increasing frequency, from at least as early as the 460s; the venues included not only smaller neighbourhood theatres in some of the 140 demes of Attica, but cities as far afield as Sicily, southern Italy, and Macedon. Scholars have recently been stressing the likely diversity of the audiences of theatrical performances in deme theatres and far beyond the borders of Attica; in such venues it becomes more hazardous to make assumptions about the sex, status, or ethnicity of the spectators.[55]

---

[53] See the judicious remarks in the account of Cartledge (1997), 6 and 16.

[54] The evidence for the constitution of the audiences is conveniently assembled in Eng. trans. in Csapo and Slater (1995), 286–305, although some of the inferences they derive from it are controversial. For other important contributions see Pickard-Cambridge (1988), 263–78; Winkler (1990); P. Wilson (2000*b*); Revermann (forthcoming); and (especially on the issue of women in the audience), Goldhill (1994), with bibliography.

[55] On revivals and performances in deme theatres and beyond Attica, see Taplin (1999); Revermann (1999–2000); Csapo (2004*a*) and (forthcoming); E. Hall (forthcoming *a*) and (forthcoming *b*).

Recent scholarship has also considered in depth the actual people, besides the audiences, involved in the collaborative effort that created the première of an Athenian play, and the traces that they left on the transmitted texts. They include the priests and orphans involved in the pre-dramatic displays, the administrators of the competition, the *chorēgoi* who funded the performances, the musicians, the chorusmen, and even (speculatively) the women of the city.[56] Some aspects of the actor's contribution have also begun to receive concerted attention: his professional family, his impact on the shape taken by drama, the physical demands made on him by mask and costume change, his subjective experience of acting, his increasing stylistic realism and virtuosity towards the end of the fifth century, his economic position, his presence as a figure of glamour or authority in the public imagination, and so on.[57] But one element bears closer examination: his enacted *role*.

A MATTER OF LANGUAGE

The idea of the role was a significant factor in the development of philosophical aesthetics; the earliest attested uses of the word *mimēsis* meaning something approximating to 'representation in literary art' still retain the early connotation of dressing up in order to act a theatrical role.[58] The role was equally important in the invention of

[56] See e.g., for pre-dramatic festival displays, Goldhill (1987); competitive administration: R. Osborne (1993); *chorēgoi* and chorusmen: P. Wilson (2000*a*); Foley (2003*b*), 2–5; musicians: P. Wilson (2002); Csapo (2004*b*); women: O'Higgins (2003), esp. ch. 5; for a fascinating discussion of the way that prayer in cult, including exclusively female cult, affected the content of choral odes in tragedy, see Stehle (2004). Women certainly participated, along with metics, in the grand procession that opened the Dionysia: see Susan Guettel Cole (1993), 28; Sourvinou-Inwood (1994), 270; Goldhill (1994), 356–7; and below, Ch. 7, pp. 196–8.

[57] Acting families: Sutton (1987); the actor's impact on the shape taken by drama: Slater (1990); role distribution and change: Damen (1989), Pavloskis (1977), Jouan (1981), Marshall (1994); the actor's subjective experience: Lada-Richards (2002); developments in style: Valakas (2002); realism: Csapo (2002); actors' economic position: (Csapo, forthcoming); actors' authority: Easterling (2002). See also recently the collection of essays edited by Hugoniot, Hurlet, and Milanezi (2004); on the Hellenistic 'Artists of Dionysus', Le Guen (2001) and Lightfoot (2002).

[58] Aristophanes, *Thesm.* 156; *Frogs* 109. See Else (1958), 81; Muecke (1982), 55; Sörbom (1966), 31.

political theory and sociology: it provided the prerequisite identification of a type of individual with a particular appearance, name,
and set of expected behaviours—a 'social role'.[59] The connection was
analysed by Ralf Dahrendorf in a classic essay, '*Homo sociologicus*',
which argued that the concept of social role, like that of the atom, is a
self-evident category; the point at which man is born as a social being
is when he accepts or rejects the responsibilities which society prescribes for him. With this decision, according to Dahrendorf, man
assumes his appearance on 'the stage of life' which Cicero called his
persona, Marx his 'character mask' (signifying e.g. the Bourgeois or
the Capitalist), Shakespeare his 'part', and sociologists his 'role'.[60] The
basic context of all these terms—*persona, character mask, part, role*—
is the theatre, which is thus a prerequisite of any self-conscious
theory of society. Without the communal fictive laboratory—the
virtual world created by theatre—in which social subjects watch
characters enact roles, they can not gain sufficient perspective on
their collective organism in order to analyse how it functions.[61]
Without the roles enacted in the Athenian theatre there could have
been no Protagorean political theory, no Platonic Republic, no
Aristotelian Ethics.

It was in his work on the self that the philosopher G. H. Mead had,
by 1913, become the first to use the metaphor of role assumption to
describe the process by which the subject empathetically adopts
another person's outlook; two decades later the metaphor was
adopted in the analysis of the 'roles' of spouses.[62] But the role

[59] The proposal of the evolutionary universality of the idea of the 'person' as a
human mental category, supported by arguments from the terminology of masking
and theatrical practices that have evolved in many different societies, was first
developed by Marcel Mauss in 1938, an essay available in English translation as
Mauss (1985).

[60] Dahrendorf (1998), 129. The history of the terms *prosōpon* and *persona* is traced
by Nédoncelle (1948), 278–81 and 296–8 respectively. For Cicero's *personae*, inherited
from the *prosōpa* defined by the Stoic philosopher Panaetius in the 2nd cent. BC, see
above all Gill (1988), 173–6, 179–82, 187–96.

[61] On the long history of the 'stage of life' metaphor, see also E. Burns (1972);
Burke (1965).

[62] Mead (1913), 377: 'This response to the social conduct of the self may be in the
rôle of another—we may present his argument in imagination, and do it with his
intonations and gestures.' Roles of spouses: Lumpkin (1933), discussed in e.g.
Rocheblave-Spenlé (1962), 17.

concept effectively infiltrated mainstream social sciences with Linton's textbook of anthropology *The Study of Man* (1936), which argued that, while a cluster of rights and obligations could constitute a person's *status*, a role needed to be *dynamic*. It is only when someone 'puts the rights and duties into effect' that 'he is performing a role'.[63] A theatrical role, analogously, is much more than that which is represented on a theatrical mask (sex, age, kinship group, ethnicity, status), since it is the *dynamic aspect* of that *prosōpon*. As Aristotle was to say about the representation of character in tragedy, it is only through seeing someone *do* something that the character becomes subject to moral assessment (*Poet.* 1450ª15–22). In a revealing passage, Plutarch distinguishes between the 'kingly name and mask' (*onoma basileōs kai prosōpon*) worn by the ineffectual Macedonian monarch Aridaeus, and his role—what he actually *did* when wearing that mask. His role was analogous to that of a 'mute spear-carrier' on stage (*epi skēnēs doruphorēma kōphon, Mor.* 791e).[64] Aridaeus' kingly *prosōpon* did not match his lowly role.

If it is important to distinguish between static mask and dynamic role, it is essential to distinguish theatrical and social roles. Dahrendorf sees the immanent connection between them as lying in an analogy 'between prescribed behaviour patterns' for actors and 'socially defined' behaviour norms for persons in given positions.[65] Indeed, in the language of modern sociology, those who reject the social role they have been prescribed are not social role-players, but *deviants*. Dahrendorf's example is a Shakespearean lover who neither sighs nor makes a woeful ballad to his mistress's eyebrow. On this argument a large number of the characters in ancient tragedy, although they constitute roles in the theatrical sense, are social beings who *reject* their role, and thus become deviants: women who leave their husbands are deviant wives; men who are bad leaders are deviant kings. This is a crucial difference between the way that sociologists and dramatic theorists discuss roles: dramatic theorists would discuss the 'role' of an adulterous wife, a tyrannical king, or a

---

[63] Banton (1965), 25.

[64] = *Whether an Old Man Should Engage in Public Affairs* 14.

[65] Dahrendorf (1998), 128, from his own translation into English of his German text, first published in 1958.

disobedient daughter, whereas in sociology really bad wives, tyrannical kings, and disobedient daughters are precisely *rejecting* their roles.

The word *role* derives from the term *rotula* in thirteenth-century medieval French, which evolved into *role*. *Rotula* is itself a diminutive form of the classical Latin *rota*.[66] The primary designation of a *rotula* was something physically 'rolled up', a roll of parchment; the notions of a catalogue ('roll call') or a theatrical part ('role') are both later, metonymic extensions. The *role* appears first in the sphere of law: a parchment *role* was something on which, in the fifteenth century, a notary would inscribe a judgment relating to contractual obligations, or the notification of a case for someone to take to tribunal. A litigant might be given his own *role*, in the form of a legal document pertaining to his rights, duties, or possessions. Law still protects our rights and prescribes our social roles, and some types of professional status, at least, are still officially bestowed in the form of certificates ornamentally rolled and beribboned for the ceremony at which they are awarded. But by 1538 the term appears in theatrical context, designating the speeches, inscribed on a parchment roll, to be delivered by an actor in a particular part;[67] in subsequent sixteenth-century French texts its meaning becomes less attached to the actor's physical role and more suggestive of the psychological process, the part played by the actor impersonating an *impératrice*, for example.

At this time the regular word used in English for an actor's written-up words, and by extension his role on stage, was 'part': in 1495 the roles of knights and demons in the Coventry Mystery Plays are called their 'partes',[68] and in *As You Like it* (1600), Jacques famously says that during his lifetime each man 'playes many parts' on the stage that is all the world (II.vii.142, see further Ch. 4, pp. 105–6). The term *role* was not used in English until the early seventeenth century, when Samuel Gardiner saw God as assigning the Evangelist the 'rowle' which 'inioyned him, to prepare the way of the Lord'; here

---

[66] The word *rota* is itself connected with an ancient Indo-European root, which also gave rise to the Sanskrit *ráthaḥ*: see Rey (1995), ii. 1837. *Rotula* also produced the similar terms *rolle* in Provençal, and *rolde* in Spanish.

[67] Rey (1995), ii. 1821.

[68] 'Payd for copying of the ij knyghts partes, & demons' (Sharp (1825), 6).

the association seems, as in medieval French, to relate to a contractual obligation.[69] It is not until the late eighteenth century that the
fully theatrical sense of the term *role* is adopted into English, at
exactly the same time as the elaborate notion of the actor's 'creation'
of a role begin to be manifested in French (*créer un rôle*).[70]

There is no single ancient Greek word which precisely translates
the term *role*. The term *prosōpon* is the strongest candidate, but it
lacks almost all sense of the dynamic aspect of a role—its verbal 'part'
and associated actions. Semiotically speaking, a mask can denote a
role in a synchronic, static medium, such as painting or relief sculpture: see, for example, fig. 2.1, an extraordinary stele which probably
came from an actor's grave, found on Salamis in the early 1970s: it
depicts a young man gazing at the female tragic mask he holds before
him.[71] But a mask is less likely to be able to denote the words and
gestures that are learned, the aural dimension of a role, or the
dynamic development of an actor's part through performance time.
The generic vase-paintings in which groups of theatrical performers
are seen donning costumes and masks, with the performers who have
completed their disguise beginning to assume the gestures required
by the role they are playing, constitute an attempt to express the
dynamic aspects of a role in relation to the mask.[72] But the ancient
Greek language never discovered a term that embraced both aspects.

The explanation might lie in the language actually used by classical
Greek theatregoers in passages where it is tempting for a translator to
introduce the term 'part' or 'role'. A standard way of saying one was
acting a role, at least from the fourth century, seems to have been to
use the verb *hupokrinomai* plus the accusative of the individual being

---

[69] See also L'Estrange (1692), 281: 'The methods of Government and of humane
Society must be preserved, where every man has his roll, and his station assigned to him.'

[70] The *OED* cites a letter dated 1790 or 1791 to Charles Sharpe, in which Robert
Burns uses, alongside one another, the old English word 'part' and the new French
term 'role': 'I admire the several actors in the great drama of life, simply as they act
their parts... As you, Sir, go through your rôle with such distinguished merit.' See
also Byron, *Don Juan* 16.96: 'Juan, when he cast a glance | On Adeline while playing
her grand role.'

[71] For a detailed description and discussion, see Slater (1985*a*), 340–4 with plate 2.

[72] See below, fig. 5.1 (chorusmen dressing as satyrs), and the Attic pelike by the
Phiale Painter in the Boston Museum of Fine Arts (98.883–11), depicting two
chorusmen dressing as women, reproduced in Csapo and Slater (1995), pl. 7b and
E. Hall (1998), 248.

F<small>IG</small>. 2.1   Grave stele in the Piraeus Museum

impersonated: to act Antigone or the beggar was *hupokrinesthai tēn Antigonēn*, or *ton alētēn*.[73] Hopes are raised by the case of Aristotle's *Politics* 5.1314ᵃ40, where 'to play [sc. the role of] the king' is *hupokrinesthai ton basilikon*. If the assumed noun described by the adjective *basilikon* was really in the masculine accusative, it cannot have been the neuter *prosōpon*, as at e.g. Plut. *Mor.* 785c, where old men are said to 'put off the political *prosōpon*'.[74] But a

---

[73] See e.g. Epictetus/Arrian, *Dissertationes*, fr. 11 ed. Schenkl (1916), ll. 7–9 on playing the role of Oedipus the *tyrannos* or of Oedipus the itinerant beggar. See also, in Aristotle, *hupekrinonto tas tragōidias* (*Rhet.* 3.1403ᵇ23); actors can be intransitively *hoi hupokrinomenoi* (*EN* 7.1147ᵃ23); *hupokrisis* can mean just 'acting' (*EN* 3.1118ᵃ8).

[74] *apotithesthai to politikon prosōpon* = *Whether an Old Man Should Engage in Public Affairs* 4.

manuscript variant indeed supplies the alternative, neuter *to basili-kon*, a reading which removes altogether the necessity to supply a masculine noun meaning 'role'.

A fairly close equivalent to our word 'role' in contexts that are not explicitly about role-playing in a theatre seems to have been *schēma*. This is the word used, for example, in Plato's *Symposium*, where Alcibiades is describing the difference between Socrates' 'outer casing' and his true internal nature. Socrates has the *schēma* of a sculpted silen, and this can also mean his physical appearance. But it is also possible to have a non-material, behavioural *schēma* (216d2–7); Socrates' *schēma* includes professed agnosticism (216d3–4) as well as his supposed erotic feelings towards beautiful people.[75] Towards the end of the speech, even disavowal of knowledge has become a silenic characteristic; the 'role' Socrates feigns is likened to a theatrical costume—the leather hide worn by a hubristic satyr (*saturou dē tina hubristou doran*, 221e1–2). This extended analogy between the theatrical role assumed by an actor playing a satyr, and the behavioural *schēma* which Socrates adopts, is of course set in the context of the Alcibiades scene; this generically calls to mind satyr drama, with its homoerotic and sympotic interests (see Ch. 5).[76] Yet the *schēma* here is not a 'role' consisting of speeches, but a set of unchanging attributes, an attitude, a demeanour. It is almost as static as a *prosōpon*.

In a fragment of the comic poet Strattis (8 K–A), someone voices the complaint that Euripides' *Orestes* had been wrecked by the individual responsible for 'hiring' the tragic actor Hegelochus 'to speak the most important lines' (*Hēgelochon... | misthōsamenos ta prōta tōn epōn legein*). This suggests that one way of referring to 'the leading role' in a play was as the sum of the protagonist's speeches, *ta prōta tōn epōn*. But it is not unreasonable to hope that Aristophanic comedy might offer more sophisticated terms meaning 'role', if only because its heroes often temporarily assume familiar tragic ones. In *Peace* there is a telling phrase: Trygaeus' daughter pleads with him not to fall off his beetle, 'be lamed, provide a plot for Euripides, and

---

[75] See the discussion in Usher (2002), 217–18.
[76] Usher (2002), 219–23, although the connections he draws specifically between *Cyclops* and the *Symposium* are less than convincing.

become a tragedy' (*chōlos ōn Euripidēi* | *logon parascheis kai tragōidia genēi*, 147–8).⁷⁷ As a lamed character Trygaeus would potentially *provide* a plot and himself 'become' a tragedy. Here the identification of a lame *identity* with the whole play is close indeed. But there is no word for 'role'. In *Thesmophoriazusae*, when the kinsman is about to begin the parody of *Helen*, he says 'I know; I'll act the new *Helen* (*tēn kainēn Helenēn mimēsomai*). I've got the female costume on, anyway' (850–1). Here the term the would-be actor uses for acting is *mimeisthai*;⁷⁸ but the meaning of 'the new *Helen*' is ambiguous. At first it seems that he means just the Euripidean tragedy; but the following line, explaining that he already has the female costume, implies that 'the new *Helen*' means the novel characterization of that heroine in Euripides' recent play, which in turn means 'the [role of the] new Helen' (no italics). An actor could therefore indicate his role by simply saying that he was about to *mimeisthai* a proper name in the accusative case. In the parody of *Andromeda* that follows, the language is even less ambiguous: here the kinsman says that Perseus has signalled that he must 'become Andromeda (*hoti dei me gignesth' Andromedan*). I've got the bonds, anyway' (1010–13). So an actor could use the verb *gignesthai* in order to say that he actually 'became' the character he was acting.

   The language used in comedy to express what we call 'playing a role' thus describes a direct and binary relationship between the actor and the concrete individual he actually 'becomes', rather than a more complex triangular relationship including the mysterious, abstract additional entity we now call the 'role' of the impersonated individual. But other, more elaborate metaphors crop up in philosophical prose. In Plato's *Republic* Adeimantos argues that seeming (*to dokein*) to be virtuous is more profitable than virtue: 'For a front (*prothura*) and an assumed demeanour (*schēma*) I need to draw round myself a shadow-outline (*skiagraphian*) of virtue, but drag in my wake the fox of the most sage Archilochus, shifty and avaricious.'⁷⁹ Archilochus'

---

⁷⁷ On this passage see also Ch. 11, pp. 339–40.

⁷⁸ Muecke (1982), 55; see also Sörbom (1966), 78, 27–9.

⁷⁹ *prothura men kai schēma kuklōi peri emauton skiagraphian aretēs perigrapteon, tēn de tou sophōtatou Archilochou alōpeka helkteon exopisthen kerdalean kai poikilēn* (2.365ᶜ2–6).

proverbially cunning fox becomes the 'real' actor beneath the role, which is apparently expressed in the language of stage illusion—the portico, the *schēma* and perspectival scene-painting.[80] The entrance of the actual actor onto the intellectual stage of the *Republic* follows a little later. In a healthy state, says Socrates, certain things are superfluous: 'the entire class of huntsmen, and the *mimētai*, many of them occupied with figures and colours and many with music—the poets and their assistants, rhapsodes, actors, chorus-dancers, contractors, and the manufacturers of equipment, especially those that have to do with the adornment of women.'[81] The metaphorical stage-illusionist, who earlier was said to fake an appearance of virtue, here slides almost imperceptibly into the *professional* visual illusionist and then the poetic illusionist, along with those at his service—performers of epic, actors, choral dancers, and the suppliers of props and costumes, especially female attire.

In Socrates' discussion of *oratio recta* in book 3, the notion of 'assuming a role' or 'playing a part' is expressed by the verb 'to be'. When Socrates is speaking of Homer's narrator, he asks: 'But when he delivers a speech as if he were someone else (*hōs tis allos ōn*), shall we not say that he then assimilates thereby his own diction as far as possible to that of the person whom he announces as about to speak?' (3.393b–c). Subsequently, Socrates uses both the phrases 'to liken one's self to another' (*to homoioun heauton allōi*), and 'to imitate' (*mimeisthai*), in ways that are well translated 'to act the role of': 'And is not likening one's self to another in speech or bodily bearing (*schēma*) an imitation of him to whom one likens one's self?' (3.393c). These three phrases—'as if being' someone else, 'making one's self like' someone else, and 'imitating someone else' are all, implicitly, very much stronger than the English phrase 'take on a role'; if we are told that an actor has 'taken on a role', something of his double identity is retained in our mind's eye. He has not *become* anyone else, or made his own *self* like someone else; he is still *he*, a he who has assumed a role, whether that role is imagined textually as a

[80] On the stage origins of these metaphors, see Steven (1933), 149; Keuls (1975) and (1978), 84.
[81] *polloi men hoi peri ta schēmata te kai chrōmata, polloi de hoi peri mousikēn, poiētai te kai toutōn hupēretai, rhapsōidoi, hupokritai, choreutai, ergolaboi, skeuōn te pantodapōn dēmiourgoi, tōn te allōn kai tōn peri ton gunaikeion kosmon* (2.373[b]5–c1).

physical script (a roll of paper on which is inscribed a 'part'), or materially as a second, false, different face. Plato, however, exploits the power of the ancient apprehension of the fusion of actor and part, indicated by the actual lack of a term for 'role', in furthering his argument against theatrical mimesis. For Plato, acting goes beyond the idea of role-playing to the *shaping* of nature itself: youngsters must not be allowed to act, because 'imitations, if continued from youth into life, settle down into habits *and nature* in the body, the speech, and thought' (3.395d). There is no such thing as assuming a role: *A* does not impersonate *B* before *C*, but temporarily—and in due course permanently—turns into *B* in nature.[82]

GREEKS IN THEIR PARTS

In David Garrick's Georgian theatre, the actors' parts were often called their 'lengths'; when it was necessary to calculate how long a play might take to perform, the length was the unit multiplied. A physical sense of what the word 'length' meant to the actor handed one to prepare emanates from the description supplied in Garrick's published correspondence: 'Take half a sheet of foolscap paper and divide it, the two sides are called a length by the players; and in this form their parts are always written out by the Prompter or his clerk'.[83] If the ancient Greeks did not have a word exactly equivalent to 'role', a semantic gap exploited by Plato in his critique of theatre, did they have one for the 'roll', the (presumably) rolled-up material on which a character's 'part' was written out for him to learn off by heart?

---

[82] A little later yet, the metaphors for this type of shaping again call into play the creation of visual artworks: Socrates argues that a good man will not want to liken himself seriously to someone inferior (*spoudēi apeikazein heauton tōi cheironi*), and one reason for this is that he 'shrinks in distaste from moulding and fitting himself to the types that are baser' (*hauton ekmattein te kai enistanai eis tous tōn kakionōn tupous*, 3.396d7–e1). See further Ch. 4, pp. 102–3. For a stimulating study of Plato's body-centred and politically charged objections to acting, see Bassi (1998), 99–143.

[83] Boaden (1831–2), i. 120 n.; see T. Stern (2000), 253 and n. 61.

There exist approximately forty-five representations in Attic vase-painting of papyrus rolls in educational and musical contexts, including the famous scroll on which a line of epic is inscribed on the fifth-century Douris kylix; the poem is being taught to a schoolboy (Berlin F 2285). Every single papyrus roll on a vase, even when not actually inscribed, appears in a context where it suggests a book of poetry. But there is no classical image of the writing out, or learning of, a line from a dramatic text.[84] Theatre's dependence on the written word is implied by the scroll held by the personification of the stage (*SKĒNĒ*) in a Hellenistic marble relief sculpture in the Istanbul Archaeological Museum; in her other hand she holds a tragic mask of Heracles, which she is passing to a seated Euripides in the presence of Dionysus (fig. 2.2). But in classical art related to theatre it is only on the Pronomos vase (Naples H 3240) that a seated figure labelled 'Demetrios' holds an unopened scroll, with a larger one, also unopened, resting against his seat (fig. 2.3); he is probably the author of the tetralogy celebrated by this performance, and his scrolls may be intended to suggest to the vase's viewer parts of a written version, at least of the satyr play.[85] There is also a mysterious figure towards the rear of the scene depicted in one of the theatre-related Pompeii mosaics, which are probably modelled on Greek prototypes. In the scene several actors are preparing for the performance of a play that looks like a satyr drama; in the centre is the musician, already dressed, and playing his pipes. An older man sits, amidst the actors, in the lower right section of the picture; two actors are already in costume: a third is being helped into his by a smaller assistant. But between the two pillars at the back there stands a man who is reading from a text (fig. 2.4); it could be an actor's 'part', a version of the complete play, or the words to go with the melody that the piper is practising.

---

[84] The images are collected by Immerwahr (1964), supplemented by Immerwahr (1973), in a considerable advance on Birt (1907); see also Lissarrague (1987), 130–2; Ford (2002), 195; J. R. Green (1995*a*).

[85] Immerwahr (1964), 36, suggests that the larger roll might be the 'part' for chorus. Equally, the larger roll, if it is not simply an empty container, might represent a papyrus containing the whole play, and the smaller one an individual actor's 'part'. Even a relatively long tragedy such as *Orestes* could have been accommodated on a single roll of about 700 cm in length, to judge from preserved papyri: see Donovan (1969), 35, and the fascinating suggestion of Macleod (1983).

Fɪɢ. 2.2   Hellenistic marble relief sculpture honouring Euripides (centre)

Fɪɢ. 2.3   Detail of the 'Pronomos vase', Attic volute-krater of *c.* 400 BC

Fɪɢ. 2.4   Mosaic from 'House of the tragic poet' at Pompeii

Several papyri have long been identified, by marginal sigla indicating changes of speaker, as likely to have been used in later antiquity
during rehearsals of Greek tragedy for performance.[86] The most
important example contains six fragments of Euripides' *Cresphontes*
(*POxy* 2458); the marginal notations indicate not changes in speaking

---

[86] Occasional attempts are made to argue that the very existence of substantial
numbers of papyri of tragedy, especially Euripides, is indicative not just of a vital
tradition of reading and studying his plays in much later antiquity, but of regular
theatrical performances. See esp. Pertusi (1959).

role, but rather the several parts in the play assumed by a single actor.[87] Recently, however, the publication of a new papyrus (*POxy* 4546) has thrown unprecedented light on the ways in which individual actors prepared themselves, a process which has always remained obscure, except for the anecdote in which Plutarch describes Euripides training a chorus; here the word used is *hupolegō* plus dative (*De Audiendo* 46b). This probably means that Euripides is using an antiphonal teaching technique.[88] But the new papyrus shows that actors could be given texts of their own lines in a play. Dated to between 100 BC and AD 50, it contains the thirty lines spoken by Admetus in Euripides' *Alcestis* 344–82, but excludes the lines delivered in the stichomythia by his interlocutors—the actor playing Alcestis (seven lines: 344, 346, 347, 348, 355, 357, 376), and the chorus (two lines: 369–70).

Marshall's study suggests that no other criterion for the selection of these lines fits the form taken by the text in the papyrus.[89] It is unlikely to be part of an anthology of the kind mentioned by Plato in the *Laws*, which consisted of excerpted oratorical highlights and individual speeches (7.811a1–5). Nor does it contain the type of collection represented by existing papyrus fragments of anthologies, since it contains neither a series of quotations with gnomic or sententious potential, nor a selection of excerpts linked by a theme (e.g. evaluations of womankind). Nor does it provide a parallel with those papyri that contain a group of tragic songs to be delivered by a *tragōidos* (perhaps a recital programme),[90] or the iambic portions alone from the opening of *Hippolytus* (see *PSorb* Inv. 2252), which may suggest a reduced version to be performed without chorus or musician. Nor does it resemble the papyrus reproducing excerpts from different parts of Menander's *Kolax* (*POxy* 409 + 2655). It is

---

[87] Two actors are indicated, suggesting that one of the actors had made an appearance previously. Turner (1962*a*), 76 concludes that 'this papyrus represents an acting copy…presumably…used for actual representation in the theatre of Oxyrhynchus'. See also Donovan (1969), 76–8.

[88] See Marshall (2004), 27, and Plutarch *Mor.* 790e–f (= *Whether an Old Man Should Engage in Public Affairs* 12): 'just as teachers of letters or of music themselves first play the notes or read to the pupils and thus show them the way' (*autoi proanakrouontai kai proanagignōskousin huphēgoumenoi tois manthanousin*).

[89] Marshall (2004).

[90] See e.g. the odes from *IA* with music in *PLeid* Inv. 510, with E. Hall (2002*a*), 12–14.

unlikely to be a schoolboy exercise in copying out, unless its ultimate purpose was performance-related. It is not, like the fragmentary 'Charition Mime', a musician's copy.[91] The large handwriting is designed to be easily read, perhaps by an actor who needed to practise movements as well as oral delivery.[92]

What, however, did the tragic actor who learnt the role of Admetus from *POxy* 4546 call that piece of papyrus, or indeed what he learned from it? If the part was small, requiring only one sheet of papyrus, the word might have been *chartē*;[93] but in the case of Admetus' substantial speaking part, the more likely candidate seems to be *biblion*. This is generally used in the fifth and fourth centuries to designate a strip of *bublos* made from glued-together sheets; it can also mean a document, including the dramatic *biblion* which the chorus of *Frogs* claims every member of the audience can now consult (*Frogs* 1114, see also Hdt. 1.123, 3.238; Ar. *Birds* 974; Plato *Ap.* 26d).[94] Remoter possibilities include *grammateion*, which is found in the sense of a written document (Aeschines 1.165) as well as a contract or account book (Ar. *Clouds* 19). A word meaning 'papers' or 'documents' in legal oratory is *ta grammata* (Antiphon 1.30, Lys. 32.14), a plural which actually means a piece of writing—an epistle—in Euripides' *IT* 594 (see also Herodotus 1.124). Lucian uses the plural *ta iambeia* to denote the sections of tragedy in the iambic metre (Lucian, *Salt.* 27), and it is just possible that actors saw themselves as in some sense memorizing their 'lines' or *stichoi*, which, when they did not mean lines of soldiers, could mean lines of verse (*Frogs* 1239; Plato, *Laws* 12.959a1).[95] In Aristophanes fr. 158 K–A, the words spoken by the tragic actor Sthenelus seem to be called his *rhēmata*; this would be more plausible than the term *rhēseis*. In the singular a

---

[91] See Ch. 8, p. 228.

[92] See Obbink (2001), 19, and the discussion in Marshall (2004), 28–9 and n. 5.

[93] See Cockle (1983), 149.   [94] See Flory (1980), 20.

[95] See also the phrase *epeōn stiches* ('rows of words') which Pindar uses for Medea's prophetic speech in *Pythian* 4.57; at Aeschylus' *Persians* 430, after describing the battle of Salamis, the messenger says that he could not give the queen 'a full narrative about the plethora of disasters even if I took ten days to go through it line by line' (*stoichēgoroiēn*). The metaphor here is playing on the parallel between military files and inscribed lines of words; when the messenger first arrived, similarly, both he and the queen used the metaphor of 'unfolding' the full extent of the casualties (254, 294), which metaphorically, at least, suggests a document containing a catalogue.

rhēsis can denote a [long] 'speech' in (or excerpted from) a tragedy (Aesch. *Suppl.* 273, Ar. *Nub.* 1371), but it is difficult to believe it can ever have denoted written-out lines of stichomythia. The term most commonly in use for longish speeches learned from a script was probably similar to *ho ek tou bibliou rhētheis* [*logos*]—'the speech read from the papyrus roll' in Plato's *Phaedrus* (243c).[96]

The idea of learning a speech from a roll would certainly have been familiar to the fifth-century litigant, whose speeches were written out for him to learn before delivery, as in Aristophanes' *Knights* the Sausage-Seller is said to study his prosecution speeches, wearying his friends with incessant rehearsals (347–9; see Ch. 12, p. 370).[97] Although the families that produced professional actors could presumably hand down knowledge of important speeches across generations,[98] it is counter-intuitive to assume that all the roles ever delivered by actors in the fifth century—certainly at the pre-mières of the plays in question—were learned without the aid of writing.[99] The scholars who have most ardently defended the

[96] This is to discount such unusual terms as *skutalē*, the scroll with a message in some kind of code with which Pindar compares a song at Olympian 6.90–1; see Ford (2002), 119 with nn. 28 and 29. On Pindar and writing see esp. Segal (1986), 9–11, 153–61.

[97] There is, however, insufficient evidence to determine why the verb *hupokrino-mai*, which in Homeric Greek can mean either 'expound' (*Il.* 12.228) or 'answer' (e.g. *Il.* 7.407, see also the Homeric *Hymn to Apollo* 172–3), came to be used in the terminology both of acting and of rhetorical delivery, even though the debate about this issue extends back to the mid-19th cent. For the most comprehensive discussion of the ancient evidence (albeit with a perverse conclusion) and bibliography see Else (1959), esp. 75 n. 4; Pickard-Cambridge (1988), 126–7 with n. 5; see also Nagy (1989), 60–1; Gellrich (2002), 315–17. The noun *hupokritēs* already means 'actor' in Aristophanes' *Wasps* 1279, and *hupokrisis* is certainly by Aristotle's day the accepted term for rhetorical delivery in an actorly manner (*Rhet.* 3.1413b23), regard-less of whether its apparent appearance in Pindar (*ere-|thizomai pros aütan | haliou delphinos hupokrisin* fr. 140b 13–15 S–M) really denotes human imitation of a dolphin's cries. It was only later that the word *hupokrisis* acquired the negative overtones it still bears today and which underlie, for example, Artemidorus' advice to his readers against believing dreams containing certain kinds of people: 'Actors and players who mount the stage are obviously not to be believed by anyone, since they play parts' (*dia tas hupokriseis pasin apistoi*, 2.69).

[98] On theatrical families see Sutton (1987); the important study of whether 5th-cent. family traditions were preserved in Athens orally or with the aid of documents by R. Thomas (1989), 100–8, unfortunately does not address the question of the transmission of knowledge of playscripts within theatrical households.

[99] On the collective learning of choral poetry, see J. R. Green (1995a), 83, who offers a detailed bibliography (84 n. 21). Thoroughgoing oral composition of all parts

possibility of orally composed and memorized tragedy have tended
not to draw a sufficient distinction between the learning of songs
by the amateur chorusmen (which could easily have been effected by
time-honoured methods of response and repetition dating from far
earlier than writing), and the composition and memorization of
parts by the specialist—and increasingly professionalized—actors.
Each year the actors in the tragic competition at the Dionysia alone
had to memorize many hundreds of lines; where technology exists to
expedite challenging tasks, it tends to be exploited. It is therefore
almost inconceivable that there was not a word in currency to denote
the actual written 'part' from which an actor might learn his lines. Or,
as Wise has trenchantly put it, in 'a literate world, performers were
suddenly able to memorize a story written from start to finish by
someone else, and to do so conceivably overnight'.[100]

The earliest surviving papyrus from Greece is said to be a roll
found in 1981, along with a male skeleton, a bronze pen with split nib
and the remains of a tortoiseshell lyre, in a tomb on Vouliagmeni (the
road out of Athens to Sounion); it has been suggested that the dead
man was a singing actor or poet.[101] And there has been renewed
scholarly enthusiasm lately for the relationship between literacy
and the Athenian theatre. J. R. Green has revived interest in an
early fifth-century vase which depicts Hermes, carrying a writing
tablet and stylus, in the act of introducing two chorusmen to
Dionysus; this must suggest that the vase's viewer understood that
writing—at least in the temporary medium of the tablet—played a

---

of tragedy was defended by Havelock (1982), 261–313, but bracingly questioned by
Segal (1982), 131–54 and (1984), 42, where he firmly states that although tragedy is
an oral performance, it is 'one controlled by a written text', and that the role of writing
in the composition of tragedy affected its contents. For extensive bibliography on the
status of a written text in a predominantly oral culture, see Gentili (1983). Ford
(2002), 153 with notes 84–5 offers useful discussion, and his overall argument at
155–7 suggests that he sees writing as having a great impact on both poetry and
literary criticism by the late 5th cent.

[100] Wise (1998), 65. Robb (1994), 186–8, acknowledges that, in the 5th cent.,
writing made the practice of memorizing and performing epic verse 'more efficient'
in the educational contexts seen in vase-painting, but does not comment on whether
writing was used in preparation for performing drama.

[101] See Cockle (1983), 147, citing an article in *The Times* 25 May (1981). The grave
apparently remains unpublished.

role of some kind in theatrical performances.[102] Some have argued that the theatre encouraged literacy in its Athenian audience;[103] others have seen the relationship as working the other way round, and that theatre was actually one of the products made possible by the assimilation of literacy into public life at Athens.[104] Wise has argued that the sources of ancient Athenian theatre lay in literate activities, including the writing down of epic, school 'textbooks', legal speeches, and inscriptions on coins and tombs.[105] But the writing out of actors' lines may also have affected the nature of classical drama; it is almost certainly connected, for example, with the remarkably uninhibited way in which the tragedians import examples of writing and metaphors connected with it into their heroic world.[106] Writing is probably implied by the metaphor used in connection with the tragedian Agathon which adopts the *koll-* ('glue') stem to describe 'glueing' pieces of poetry together, like sections of papyrus glued together to make a roll (Ar. *Thesm.* 54).

Recent work on the type of texts available to actors of English-language medieval and Renaissance drama has focused on texts equivalent to the Alcestis papyrus, designed to help actors learn their speaking parts.[107] Between the sixteenth and the eighteenth centuries, when new plays were put on every few days, much time and effort was spent by individual actors committing to memory their 'parts', sometimes called 'parcells'.[108] The parts consisted of a written version of the lines to be delivered by the individual actor, with cues consisting of the last few words delivered by the previous speaker. Parts learned in this way could produce a first performance that had *never been rehearsed by the full cast*

---

[102] J. R. Green (1995*a*), esp. 81–4, with pl. 1. The significance of the writing tablet on the hydria, which is by the Pan Painter and now in the Hermitage Museum in St Petersburg (B 201; St. 1538), was first appreciated by Schmidt (1967), 78–9; but she thought that it signified something to do with the recording of the names of men selected to perform in a Dionysiac chorus; 'Die Rolle eines Organisators würde besonders gut zu dem wendigen Gotte Hermes passen.'

[103] Svenbro (1990); see also, more tendentiously, de Kerckhove (1979).

[104] See e.g. Burns (1981).

[105] Wise (1998).

[106] See Aristophanes fr. 656 K–A and the references in Ford (2002), with notes 95 and 96; references to writing within tragedy are assembled and analysed by Easterling (1985), 3–6.

[107] For a detailed account, see Palfrey and Stern (forthcoming).

[108] T. Stern (2000), 10; (2004), 62–90, 124.

before, with each actor listening out for cues before delivering his own role, prepared in isolation.[109]

The ramifications of such 'part-based' theatre are complex. Authors under pressure of time must often have written parts, or at least substantial monologues, in isolation from the rest of the play. Actors had a free hand in altering parts to their own tastes. Star actors could influence less important cast members if they did not like the dialogue when they did finally put the play together. Well-known plays were subject to actors' attempts to stamp their personal signature on roles, entailing extensive alterations.[110] Some Renaissance and Early Modern actors always seem to have adapted whatever roles they played to conform with one or two stereotypical character types, associated with their own offstage personalities in their audience's minds (which calls to mind the famous Hellenistic Tegean actor who was so drawn to play mythical boxers and strongmen, discussed below p. 55). The types of character in which an actor specialized, and to which he adapted any role that he took on, were known as his 'lines' (as in retail lines) or his 'casts' of playing: Garrick had an unusual range, excelling 'in every Cast of Playing'—kings and clowns, rakes and fops, footmen and gentlemen.[111] These phenomena are all suggestive for the relationship between actor, script, and role that must have been manifested in different venues and times across the thousand years of antiquity in which the dramas of classical Athens continued to inspire different types of live performance.

CREATING A ROLE: AUTHOR AND ACTOR

In fifth-century Athens a theatrical role seems to have begun with the author's choice of subject-matter to dramatize at an upcoming festival. At some point mid-century, protagonists began to be allocated to the tragic poets whose plays were selected for

[109] Such an eventuality, indeed, was far from unknown during the period in question: see T. Stern (2000), 12.

[110] T. Stern (2000), 98–112, 148–57.

[111] The *List of All the Dramatic Authors* attributed to John Mottley and appended to Whincop (1747), as quoted in T. Stern (2000), 152.

performance at a festival, a development probably connected with the increasing importance of star actors.[112] But even if the poet was allocated an actor arbitrarily, the 'role' could presumably continue to develop during the rehearsal process, in response to the actor's capabilities.[113] Moreover, there is no evidence that the second and third actors were allocated, and some roles that look as though they were written around a particular individual's talents are not ones taken by the protagonist (see below). The total number of actors available during most of the fifth century was not enormous; actors came from theatrical families, often the same families as the playwrights, and were trained from childhood.[114] There will have been opportunities for playwrights to learn about the available talent. Certain actors became known for their particular delivery techniques: if Sophocles or Euripides knew that they might be writing a role for the stellar Nikostratos, they would have been wise to write him a passage of tetrameters to deliver to aulos accompaniment, or a striking messenger speech (Xen. *Symp.* 6.3; Zenobius 1.42).[115] But if they were writing for Callippides, it would have been advisable to produce a role like that of Telephus, which entailed pretending to be a humble porter, or one requiring the impersonation of a lower-class woman (Aristotle, *Poetics* 1461^{b}26–1462^{a}14).[116]

The ancient *Life of Sophocles* reports, on the authority of one Ister, that Sophocles wrote his dramas to suit the 'natures' (*phuseis*) of his actors and chorusmen,[117] and some parts certainly look as though they were written with specific thespian expertise in mind. Sophocles' *Thamyris*, for example, required the leading actor to play the cithara, and another actor to dance ecstatically on stage in the role of Thamyris' mother. The actor who played her, Aeschylus' son Euaion, was an admired dancer.[118] Whoever took the role of Echo in

---

[112] See Slater (1990), 391.

[113] See Slater (1990), 389, who sensibly points out (ibid. n. 11) that texts 'in a working theatre are never written in stone'; on last-minute alterations to a tragedy, see J. R. Green (1990).

[114] Sutton (1987); Sifakis (1979).

[115] See the testimonia collected by Stephanis (1988), no. 1861.

[116] See also Aristophanes, *Women Pitching Tents* fr. 490 K–A and the other evidence in Stephanis (1988), 1348.

[117] This passage in the *Life* is discussed well in Slater (1990), 388–9.

[118] See E. Hall (2002*a*), 9–10 with fig. 1.

Euripides' *Andromeda* must have been a fine vocal mimic; in *Orestes* the actor playing both Electra (who sings at a high pitch) and the singing Phrygian eunuch also took the part of Menelaus, whose gait was said to have become soft and unmanly during his sojourn in the East (349–51). These features suggest an actor with a high tessitura specializing in female and effeminate male roles.[119] What we do not know is whether Euripides had this epicene actor in mind before he originally decided on the subject-matter of his play, its cast, or perhaps just the details of the musical sequences. Furthermore, an overlooked task of all playwrights is that s/he must invent not just a 'character', but a role.[120] Each role has, in practical terms, to be playable; the sequence in which the character receives information has to be plausible; his or her actions and linguistic registers need to be acceptably consistent; the entrances and exits (and, in the case of ancient drama, mask and costume changes) have to be carefully scripted, with sufficient time allowed to render them executable. But the author is not just writing the parts for a single actor: in the case of the ancient tragedians there were three.

The actor in the earlier years of the fifth century, when drama was still in its experimental infancy, would have been advised to keep an open mind about the type of role he might be expected to realize. The earlier playwrights' love of exotic roles has been explored by Herington.[121] Some of them diverged widely from the authorized male 'self' who ran the Athenian polis; tragic and satyric dramas alone required the representation of the ontologically other (ghosts), the supernatural beings central to satyr drama (Silenus, Proteus, Polyphemus), metamorphosed characters (the semi-bovine Io), the ethnically other (Persians and other barbarians), the hormonally other (beautiful maidens, women in childbirth), and so on. Comic actors were from early days required to impersonate animals and abstract personifications in addition to gods, heroes, and politicians.

Common sense suggests that an actor would always have been able to alter his role during the rehearsal process, if only in detail rather than in large-scale intervention; one of the musical papyri

---

[119] See the references in E. Hall (2002*a*), 10 n. 26.
[120] Bentley (1964), 170–1.   [121] Herington (1985), 103–3.

suggests that accomplished singing actors had considerable room for creative input when performing the lyrics sung by a character such as Cassandra.[122] By the fourth century there is explicit evidence for the actor Theodorus demanding that the character he was playing as protagonist be given the prologue, on the ground that audiences always sympathize most with the first voice that they hear (Arist. *Pol.* 7.1336[b]27–31); since Theodorus specialized in reviving canonical masterpieces by Sophocles and Euripides, this must in practice have meant that new prologues needed to be created hastily and prefixed to favourite plays in the repertoire. Such thespian input explains why, for example, *Iphigenia in Aulis* has two prologues, a more drastic intervention in the text than the standard 'actor's interpolation' (e.g. the addition of two trimeters expanding a rhetorical argument).[123]

In the case of the 'part' for an actor playing Admetus discovered on papyrus (see above), the process can actually be seen at work by which the script developed in performance: the famous figure by which Admetus says he will have a statue of Alcestis 'stretched out' in the marriage bed becomes altered to 'painted in' the bed (see Ch. 4, p. 128). When Lycurgus arranged for the texts of the fifth-century tragic masterpieces to be collected and held for the benefit of the public (*en koinōi*, [Plut.], *Lives of the Ten Orators, Lyc.* 841F), probably in the Athenian Metröon where documents of public interest had been archived since the late fifth century, his scribes may have faced a paper jungle.[124] The papyri are likely to have included star actors' individual 'parts', rival versions of prologues and epilogues, and probably libretti with musical annotation for the lyric sections. However irritating 'actors' interpolations' may be to critics aspiring to the holy grail of textual 'authenticity', they are welcome evidence of the flourishing performance tradition, and creative actors elaborating famous roles for the edification of stage-struck audiences.

---

[122] *TgrF* adesp. 649 = *POxy* 2746; see Coles (1968); Hall (2002a), 18.

[123] See E. Hall (forthcoming *b*), and the rather different approach of Gurd (2005).

[124] See the fascinating remarks of R. Thomas (1989), 38–40, and 48–9, although she does not discuss the wide variations in acting versions that scribes conducting Lycurgus' recension will presumably have faced.

THE IMPACT OF ROLES ON THEATRICAL
LITERATURE

When it comes to the playscripts of ancient Greece, it is important to retain a sceptical response to the contemporary fashion for arguing that the dominant interest of the ancient tragedians was not in poetry, or metaphysics, or society, or aesthetic beauty, but in constantly remind-ing the theatrical audience that they were in a theatre—that is, in 'metatheatre' (see Ch. 4, pp. 105–11). The undoubted impact of the experience of theatre on the nature of ancient Greek drama can, however, be analysed using slightly different and less imprecise terms. One of the most subtle recent discussions of drama argues that the one thing everyone *always* 'recognizes' in a play is this: *the presence of acting*.[125] Even the most extreme method actors, trained to erase their own selves, never completely disappear. If actors really did disappear, the audience would no longer be watching a play: they would be hallucinating.[126] At the heart of drama is the process by which an actor creates and projects an identity—the relationship between *A* and *B*, enacted before *C*.

The 'uncanny' power of drama is mysteriously connected with this actor–role identification.[127] Indeed, the recognition scene in tragedy, which often involves a return from the dead (whether the recognized individual was believed to be dead or about to be mistakenly exe-cuted), can be seen as a synecdoche of the theatrical experience; dramatic recognition 'resonates with the unease' which audiences feel in the presence of actors acting.[128] In *The Birth of Tragedy*, when Nietzsche was pondering the origin of enactment, it was not a Dionysiac myth to which he turned, but the spine-tingling moment when Admetus in *Alcestis* sees the veiled figure, a semblance of his dead wife, the woman who has expired before him, being led back into his presence. This encounter is comparable, Nietzsche suggests, to the experience of the members of the Athenian audience appre-hending a tragic actor in his role.[129]

---

[125] Goldman (2000), 8.   [126] Cavell (1969), 327–30.
[127] Goldman (2000), 8–10.   [128] Ibid. 23.
[129] What the spectators saw was a 'Visionsgestalt'. In Admetus' uneasy apprehen-sion of the image of the woman that so resembled his wife, 'haben wir ein Analogon

As if taking their cue from the presence of actors, who offer substitutes for the identities of others, dramatists ancient and modern have often used the notion of 'standing in', of substitution, of surrogacy, in the construction of their plots—Oedipus substitutes for Laius, Hamlet steps into his father's shoes, Electra is her dead father's advocate, Antigone her dead brother's.[130] Playwrights have been fertile in the invention of storylines involving internal role-playing, deceit, disguise, and mistaken identity.[131] Questions of the perception of identity lie at the heart of Old Comedy, and are obvious in the fragmentary satyr plays (see Ch. 5); they are also a pronounced feature of Greek tragedies, in more than two-thirds of which the audience consciously watches a 'strong' form of role-playing by one of the characters. In the most obvious type of internal 'role-playing' the audience is made to collude with one character and/or with a conspiratorial chorus as they play roles or tell lies in order to deceive another character. This category includes the deception of Agamemnon in *Agamemnon*, of Clytemnestra and Aegisthus in *Libation-Bearers* and Sophocles' *Electra*, of Philoctetes in *Philoctetes*, the false speech of Lichas in *Women of Trachis*, the magisterial acting of Medea in her second scene with Jason in *Medea*, of Hecuba to Polymestor in *Hecuba*, of Helen to Theoclymenus in *Helen*, of Iphigenia to Thoas in *IT*, of Electra in *Orestes* or of Agamemnon to Clytemnestra in *IA*. In *Rhesus*, remarkably, a god temporarily plays the role of another immortal (something even the skilled impostor Dionysus of *Bacchae* does not attempt).[132] Sometimes such internal 'parts' are unelaborated, and merely entail reporting false information. But others involve ambitious role-playing, such as Electra's impersonation of a newly parturient mother in Euripides' *Electra* (see Ch. 3, pp. 77–80), or Helen's of a mourning widow in his *Helen*.

Another form of internal role-playing occurs in those tragedies which revolve around a character whose whole life is an unwitting 'act'—Oedipus and Ion. Others involve a character whose own perceptions become so distorted that they force other characters

---

zu der Empfindung, mit der der dionysisch erregte Zuschauer den Gott auf der Bühne heranschreiten sah': Nietzsche (1972 [1872]), 59–60, ch. 8.

[130] See Wilshire (1982), 43, 45.

[131] Hesk (2000) relates the tragedians' fascination with deception scenes to another type of narrative—the protocols of cunning and deceit in the Athenian democracy.

[132] *Rhes.* 637–67: Athena pretends to be Aphrodite in order to trick Alexander.

into false roles, as Heracles' children 'become' the children of Eurystheus in the eyes of the maddened hero of Euripides' *Heracles*; in *Heraclidae* the ageing Iolaus' self-casting as vigorous hoplite stems from a milder form of god-sent delusion; in both *Trojan Women* and *Suppliant Women* young women under the extreme psychological pressure of bereavement assume the entirely inappropriate roles of happy brides.[133] In one tragedy, *Bacchae*, nearly every role entails either disguise, costume adjustment, or delusional misperception of another character's identity. Yet amongst the few remaining plays which feature none of these three strong types of internal 'acting', two are Aeschylus' earliest tragedies *Persians* and *Seven against Thebes*. Although literature directly involving Dionysus may always have been likely to exploit themes of disguise, appearance, and transformation, Aeschylus' early plays do not suggest that elaborate play with perception of identity was necessarily an aboriginal feature of tragedy (the conclusion to which many studies of *Bacchae* have come). It may as well have been an innovative development in response to the evolving experience of theatre during the earlier fifth century.[134]

ROLES AND UNITY: AMPHITRYON IN EURIPIDES' *HERACLES*

Soon after theatrical texts began to become obsessed with role playing, and at around the same time as the emergence of plays which are clearly vehicles for a star actor, the idea seems to have been conceived that a single role can hold a tragic drama together; from the date of its earliest surviving example, *Acharnians* (425 BC) the same is already true of comedy. This pattern can be seen reflected in the difference between Aeschylean tragedies, and *Medea*, *Oedipus*, or *Hecuba*. Several such plays, unperformed for centuries after the Renaissance, seemed

[133] Eur. *Her.* 967–85; *Hcld.* 680–747; *Tro.* 307–41; *Suppl.* 990–1071.
[134] In Aeschylus' undated *Lycurgus*, the first play in his *Lycurgeia* tetralogy, the titular Thracian king certainly questioned Dionysus, who may have been in disguise, about his peculiar appearance (frags. 59–61 *TgrF*): see Rau (1967), 109–11; E. Hall (1989), 127; Austin and Olson (2004), 99–100.

disastrously episodic to the critics who only read them: A. W. von Schlegel's influential indictment on the ground of disunity of the then unacted *Trojan Women* was to ensure that it was derided for decades subsequently.[135] Yet, when theatrically performed, *Trojan Women* suddenly made sense. It became obvious that one character—Hecuba—visually supplied the axis around which every emotion and encounter revolved.[136] Whatever has been written about dramatic 'unity', a play in performance is inevitably bounded and therefore 'unified' by the nature of the relationship it bears to its audience,[137] and the conduit for this relationship is often an individual role.

Another example is provided by Euripides' *Heracles*, of unknown date but probably first performed not long before or after *Trojan Women* in 416. This play was already causing controversy in antiquity.[138] The role of Heracles was certainly one conceived in a particular way, and a favourite of certain kinds of actor: on a third-century inscription at Tegea an anonymous actor-athlete's victories are recorded:

At the Great Dionysia at Athens in Euripides' *Orestes*. At the Delphic Soteria in the *Heracles* of Euripides and the *Antaeus* of Archestratos. At the Alexandrian Ptolemaia in men's boxing. At the Heraia in Euripides' *Heracles*, and Euripides' *Archelaus*. At the Naia at Dodona in Euripides' *Archelaus* and Chaeremon's *Achilles*.[139]

This strongman was a specialist in the roles of muscular male heroes, including mythical boxers like Antaeus, which exploited his reputation as boxing champion. Euripides' *Heracles* was still familiar half a millennium later (see Philostratus, *Imagines* 2.23), and has subsequently had important admirers, including the Brownings: in *Aristophanes' Apology* (1875) Balaustion introduces the play as 'the

---

[135] English translation in von Schlegel (1840), 136.

[136] Bates (1930), 200–1, reports his own Damascene experience on seeing a performance of *Trojan Women*. Suddenly a play which had struck him as a concatenation of laments took on extraordinary coherence and power.

[137] Hornby (1986), 110; see E. Hall (2004), 70–1.

[138] The story is recorded in a papyrus that Euripides was prosecuted by Cleon for showing Heracles going mad in a play at the Dionysia. The story is almost certainly untrue, but reveals something of antiquity's impression of the drama. *POxy* 2400, vol. 24, 107–9, lines 10–14.

[139] Stephanis (1988), no. 3003; see also no. 238, which suggests that the boxing actor may have been an Arcadian named Apollogenes.

consummate Tragedy'.[140] The advanced ethics of the play have been appreciated by its more sophisticated readers, including D. W. Lucas, who argued that it 'poses in the most challenging form the problem of undeserved suffering.'[141] More recently, Burkert has identified the play as the clearest single example of the radical epistemic shift marking the late fifth century.[142]

Conversely, neo-Aristotelian critics, ever since von Schlegel (again) in the early nineteenth century, have complained about the play's two movements, calling it 'diptychal', 'broken-backed', or worse. They have proposed different solutions to this alleged problem. Some point to themes which are central to the whole play,[143] or argue that Heracles' madness is prefigured in the way he is presented in the first half.[144] Cropp sees the play's unique structure as 'a response to the unique significance of its mythical subject . . . the mythical biography and personality of Heracles drew a particularly fine line between mortality and divinity'; this 'called for presentation in peculiarly stark terms'. But despite this promising proposal, ultimately Cropp reveals that (like nearly everyone else), he is dissatisfied with the opening scenes. They are, he writes, sufficiently separated from the main action to entail 'the cost of some banality in the deployment of plot and ethos before the crisis.'[145] Foley's ritual-anthropological analysis is more persuasive; Heracles' heroic *aretē* and *kleos*, the topic of the first half, can only exist 'at the cost of the family's or community's survival. What place can such firebrands command in a fifth-century democracy, in which ideally the exploits of the individual

---

[140] See Riley (2003) and (2004), 138–207; it was in the same humanist tradition that Verrall (1905), 134–98, wrote his contentiously brilliant defence of the play.

[141] Lucas (1950), 198–9.

[142] Quoting Heracles' view at 1307–8 and 1341–6, Burkert (1985), 317–18 writes: 'That Heracles with these words calls his own existence into question, that tragedy loses its foundation with the annihilation of myth, is what makes Euripidean drama so problematic and perplexing.'

[143] e.g. Chalk (1962). See also the interpretation of Burnett (1971), 160–1, who hears an extremity of negative and ominous resonances everywhere at the beginning of the play.

[144] Ruck (1976), 53–5. For a useful summary of the structural obsessions of critics two decades ago, see Barlow (1982). Important recent approaches, quite different from the one presented here, include Dunn (1997) and Kraus (1998).

[145] Cropp (1986), 188–9.

contribute to the glory and survival of the group?'[146] The first half is required to establish the picture of the archaic hero's definition of excellence that the democracy, represented by Theseus, will latterly need to accommodate.

But it was the maverick Arrowsmith's interpretation that long did most justice to the first half; in *Heracles* 'two savagely different actions, one conventional and the other set in a world where tradition is dumb and conduct uncharted, are jammed harshly against each other, and the collision of their values is stressed by the most violent peripety in Greek tragedy'. Arrowsmith notes that the terms hitherto appropriate to the Heracles of tradition are transformed, a process by which 'Amphitryon becomes Herakles' "real" father, not by the fact of conception, but by the fact of love, *philia*'.[147] And the lucidity of this insight has been borne out during the series of professional productions of *Heracles* since the late 1990s.[148]

In the responses to these performances, it is clear that reviewers with no preconceived idea that the unity of the play was supposed to present a problem failed to discern it as such. Moreover, the role of Amphitryon was generally perceived to be every bit as important as that of Heracles. Thus a review of a production at The Gate in Notting Hill typically commends 'the strong, unostentatious performances, particularly from Kevin Costello as Amphitryon and Alistair Petrie as Herakles. Both men are visibly brought to their knees by the terrifying forces of irrationality that lurk in the human heart.'[149] A scholar who was indeed familiar with the orthodox critique of the play was struck by the importance of Amphitryon's contribution in Simon Armitage's version of the tragedy, *Mister Heracles*, which played at the West Yorkshire Playhouse in Leeds in 2001: 'Amphitryon's reactions, as the man whose tragedy is to have survived the slaughter, are impressively conveyed ... At breaking

---

[146] 'The crazed Heracles of the peripety can be said to represent a whole class of epic heroes whose violent achievement of *kleos* (fame) comes at the cost of the family's or community's survival. What place can such firebrands command in a fifth-century democracy, in which ideally the exploits of the individual contribute to the glory and survival of the group?' (Foley (1985), 150).

[147] Arrowsmith (1968), 34–5. For a very different aspect and rather less fortunate aspect of Arrowsmith's critical legacy, see below, Ch. 8, pp. 253–4.

[148] See Riley (2004).

[149] *Time Out* 1456 (15/7/98), 137.

point, but able to "see it out", he is "overwhelmed with pity for the
son whom he must confront with the knowledge of his crimes" '.[150]

The importance of Amphitryon in the memory of these and other
reviewers must give pause for thought. Amphitryon's role needs to be
reappraised from the perspectives of the actor and of the audience with
whom he must communicate. Unlike the actor playing Heracles, whoever acted Amphitryon did not change mask, but delivered all his 313
lines (to Heracles' 271) in the same role. For Heracles' 'adoptive' father
is on the stage at the beginning, and at the end, and is rarely absent from
it: the exceptions are only between lines 348–450 (i.e. the ode recounting the labours of Heracles) and lines 733–1041 (the crisis within the
palace). Amphitryon is the aged survivor who loses everything, even his
beloved son (to Athens), but must live on so that Heracles can remain
innocent at least of parricide (this probably explains Athena's intervention at 908), and organize the Theban funerals of his daughter-in-law
and grandsons. He is the 'true' father to Heracles; even more than
Theseus, he represents the force of *philia* which does not depend on
blood-kinship. His role is central to the advanced ethics of the play
noted by its distinguished admirers, but it demands more versatility
from an actor than that of Heracles: it is also surprisingly physical,
entailing such important gestures as the supplication of Heracles
(1206), and the disrupted embrace in the final moments.

Amphitryon delivers the prologue, which establishes his major claim
on the audience's sympathy and invites them to adopt his perspective in
their viewing of events (see above on Theodorus). The actor needs a
command of rhetorical technique, since he has to deliver an epideictic
defence in the archery *agōn* with Lycus (170–235). He also performs
the 'luring scene' in which Lycus is persuaded to enter the house (701–
33), an act of collusive engagement with the audience elsewhere associated with Euripidean protagonists (Helen in *Helen* and Iphigenia in
IT). Almost certainly it is Amphitryon who delivers the offstage cries
which mark the death of the children (886–908). His is also the only
singing role in the play, required to vocalize the complex dochmiac
dialogue (*kommos*) with the chorus (1042–88). He must break the news
to Heracles and support him as it sinks in (1109–62). The success of this
play in performance—as well as its philosophical examination of the

---

[150] Riley (2001).

transcendental power of *philia* between men who are not even biologically related—therefore depended to a great degree on the sustained
presence of the actor who assumed the role of Amphitryon, which on
an emotional and intuitive level provided all the structural 'unity'
which critics have denied to the play altogether.

THE THEATRICAL CAST OF ATHENS

This chapter has moved to a close by beginning to concentrate on the
physical and vocal work of a particular ancient actor in bringing to
life the words composed for him by the poet—in discharging his
role—and to see how this analytical trajectory can alter our reading
of the way that an ancient play worked on the minds of its original
spectators. Although most of this chapter has considered the ancient
way of thinking about theatrical roles from the perspective of the
men who actually created the theatrical fictions in Athens, the rest of
this book attempts to watch those fictions interacting with their
audiences' expectations of theatre, and responses to it, during the
unceasing creative dialectic by which social meaning was generated
in the most pleasurable possible way. The student of classical drama
needs to deploy a wide enough camera angle on the synchronic plane
of classical Athens to accommodate everyone involved in the première of the great dramas, from the authors and performers to the
thousands of spectators crammed into the Theatre of Dionysus. But
by being open to accounts of the way that any particular play was
received and revived in later antiquity, and indeed by very recent
spectators during contemporary revivals at the dawn of the third
millennium, the *Heracles* case study has implied that there can
sometimes be invaluable insights to be gained by panning with that
camera diachronically. It is by keeping in mind the possibility of time
travel through theatre history, as well as the importance of seeing the
Athenian theatrical experience as inseparable from the members of
the wider community who created and enjoyed it, that the studies of
individual dimensions of that experience will now proceed.

3

Childbearing Women:

Birth and Family Crisis in Ancient Drama

INTRODUCTION

Overheard labour, obstetric arias, fake pregnancies: this chapter addresses ways in which ancient Greek actors played out one of the most important moments in family life by performing the roles of childbearing women. The Roman theatre extended the range to include puerperal prostitutes, balletic parturition, Alcumena's twin-size bump, and Poppaea's gravid nightmares. Yet outside drama, discussing obstetrics was usually regarded as embarrassing. According to Theophrastus, a way of inferring that a man has poor taste (*aēdia*) is that he takes his baby from its wet-nurse to pet it, chews its food for it, uses baby-talk, and even asks his mother in front of servants such unseemly questions as 'Tell me, Mummy, what [kind of] day was it when you were in labour with me and giving birth to me?' (*hot' ōdines kai etiktes me, Char.* 20.5–8). The relationship of this example of tasteless conduct to ancient Greek 'reality' can of course be conceived in contrasting ways. Theophrastus may be *describing* a form of indecorous behaviour which was so widespread as to be instantly recognizable, or *proscribing* an example of poor breeding so extreme as to revolt a cultivated audience. Yet either way his baby-oriented man still supports one fundamental proposition: the domestic protocols for leisure-class Greek men of his period, at least as formulated for public consumption, discouraged them from openly discussing childbirth.

A different perspective is offered by a legal speech of the earlier fourth century. The logographer Isaeus composed a case against the defendant Dicaeogenes, accused of failing to hand over to his female cousins and their offspring the estate that was their due. Dicaeogenes' behaviour, it is said, has alienated his own mother, and we hear the plaintiff claim that 'everyone saw his mother seated in the shrine of Eileithyia, and charging him with acts which I am ashamed to mention but he was not ashamed to commit' (5.39). Isaeus assumed that the audience in the courtroom would see the shrine of the goddess of childbirth as an appropriate—indeed emotionally charged—setting for a maternal arraignment of a son. This forensic scene is not dissimilar in impact to the occasions in which women in 'fictional' literature—Hecuba, Clytemnestra—mention childbirth or suckling in rhetorical appeals to *their* refractory sons (*Iliad* 22.80, Aesch. *Choeph.* 896–8).

Theophrastus' tasteless man and Dicaeogenes' high-minded mother represent two different manifestations of a single prob- lem—how were the men of classical Greece to cope emotionally with the explosive issue of childbirth? These two pieces of evidence share another significance in that they are rare. Despite the much- studied funeral monuments,[1] it is notoriously difficult to access the fifth-and fourth-century Greek psyche when it comes to the impact of childbirth on the immediate family. Since Mycenaean times preg- nant women had worshipped Eileithyia all over the Greek world,[2] and there is substantial evidence for the material offerings (clothes, terracotta figures, replica uteruses, votive reliefs) which they dedi- cated in her shrines or those of other birth-related divinities such as Artemis, the nymphs, and Asclepius.[3] At Cyrene, newly wed and

---

[1] These are collected in Vedder (1988). See e.g. the stele found at Oropus (on the Attic/Boeotian border) for Plangon and Tolmides, on which one of the legs of the contorted seating woman is sticking up awkwardly (Athens, National Archaeological Museum NM 749, reproduced as Demand (1994), pl. 6). See also the visibly distorted pregnant woman on the early Hellenistic stele in Alexandria, reproduced in Vedder (1988) as pl. 23.2.

[2] See esp. Willetts (1958).

[3] See van Straten (1981), 99–100, with bibliography in notes 172–3; Neils (2003), 145; Dillon (2002), 228–32, with fig. 7.3 (the 6th-cent. BC painted plaque discovered

pregnant women, unusually, were required by state legislation to sacrifice to Artemis.[4] Yet women's subjective voices on what must have been a terrifying ordeal, even when it ended safely in the birth of a healthy child, are virtually inaudible.[5] The sources for men's feelings—even at Athens—are also recalcitrant.

The evidential problem is connected with the circumstances surrounding the birth of Athenian babies. The events of the first hazardous days after parturition, at least until the night-long feast on the tenth day (*dekatē*, actually the ninth since the Greeks counted inclusively), were virtually excluded from public discussion. Plato's Alcibiades attests to a view he had heard expressed in comedy, that not even neighbours are aware when a baby has been born (*Alcibiades* 121d). This lack of immediate excitement about a baby's arrival, at least beyond the household, was in turn connected with the pollution supposedly operative for several days after childbirth (which may have functioned more as a form of quarantine protecting mother and baby from infection). At Cyrene in the fourth century BC, a sacred law decreed that the period of pollution was only to last for three days and could not communicate itself to anyone who had not actually been under the new mother's roof.[6] Indeed, it is debatable how far this type of miasma was in practice taken seriously by new fathers: not only was the period of pollution considerably shorter than those observed in, for example, the ancient Babylonian and Jewish worlds,

at Pitsa in the Peloponnese depicting women sacrificing to the nymphs), 250–1. Several essays in a new collection on birth and infancy in the ancient Mediterranean edited by Dasen (2004) are relevant; see esp. Morizot on the 4th-cent. Achinos relief depicting a mother dedicating a newborn, and Pirenne-Delforge (2004) on the Athenian application of the epithet *kourotrophos* to female divinities.

[4] See Rhodes and Osborne (2003), 499, no. 97.83–105; R. Parker (1983), 345; Dillon (1999), 67.

[5] Their silence contrasts starkly with the recent literary exploration by women of the subjects of pregnancy and birth, for a discussion of which see Adams (1994).

[6] Rhodes and Osborne (2003), 495, no. 97.16–20: 'the woman who gives birth pollutes the house. She pollutes anyone within the house, but she does not pollute anyone outside the house, unless he comes inside. Any person who is inside will be defiled for three days, but he will not pass the pollution to another, no matter where this person goes.' As Rhodes and Osborne suggest (p. 502), the wording here implies that the pollution is linked to the physical place and is not acquired by kinship with the new mother. Interestingly, the decree specifies that if a woman miscarries and the baby is not yet 'distinguishable', the pollution is as for childbirth rather than death: ibid. no. 97.106–8.

but it is a sign of Theophrastus' *excessively* superstitious man that he will not go near a childbed for fear of being polluted (16.9).[7]

The evidence for the religious activities during the first few days of a baby's life is notoriously sparse and confused, although it included a sacrifice (likely recipients included Artemis or Eileithyia, Artemis as Eileithyia or Lochia,[8] or the nymphs), and some running either by midwives or family members, *possibly* including fathers, around the domestic hearth (*amphidromia*).[9] Some feminists have reacted indignantly to the lack of evidence: Keuls, troubled by the difficulty of ascertaining how many women died in childbirth, declared that 'Athenian male society had rung down a curtain of secrecy and disgust over everything that had to do with pregnancy, birth, and death, which they relegated to the sinister domain of their sequestered women'.[10] Speculative reconstructions of the *amphidromia*, which have been as elaborate as those for the alleged Roman ritual designated by the term *tollere liberum*,[11] have not superseded Hamilton's incisive examination of the evidence: he concluded that the first few days were indeed almost exclusively a female affair, with private rituals extending only to the inner circle of the family, leading to preparation for a feast, accompanied by drinking, at which the nine-day-old baby (at least if it was a boy) was formally named and accepted by its father and wider circle of male relatives and friends.[12] The *dekatē* may have involved the convention (rare enough in Athens) of a choral performance by women: a fragment of Eubulus' fourth-century comedy *Alcylion* involves an injunction to some women to dance all night

---

[7] On the Ancient Near East see Stol (2000), 205–6. Eur. *IT* 382–3 and *Auge* fr. 266 *TgrF* provide contentious but significant evidence that some Greeks, at least, thought that the pollution concern was illogical.

[8] See e.g. the two sets of statues dedicated to Artemis Eileithyia at Chaironeia (*IG* 7.3410 and 3411); the cult of Artemis Lochia is attested at e.g. Thespiai. See Schachter (1981), 98 and 105 n. 2.

[9] For an excellent discussion of the ancient evidence for male involvement in birth, from a practical and medical point of view, across antiquity, see Hanson (1994).

[10] Keuls (1985), 140.

[11] Shaw (2001), 32–56, argues plausibly that the evidence for this alleged Roman rite is insubstantial. See also the recent discussion of the whole process by which the arrival of babies was marked in Roman Italy in Rawson (2003), Part 2 ch. 2, 'Welcoming a Child'.

[12] Hamilton (1984).

for a baby's *dekatē*.[13] These festivities were far more private than the rituals marking either death or marriage: a relationship between men which entailed mutual invitations to *dekatē* parties is seen in a fourth-century lawcourt oration as indicating noteworthy intimacy (*sundekatizontas*, [Demosthenes] 58.40).

Silences are usually significant. We should not be misled by the inaccessibility of the Athenians' experience of new babies in the *oikos*. Childbirth is inevitably disruptive, whatever the beliefs and practices surrounding it, in whatever human community. It jeopardizes maternal life; it creates new financial responsibilities, social identities, psychological tensions, and affective ties. In ancient Athens it was arguably more transformative of the family than either death or the other great rite of passage, marriage, for marriage was a *process*, extending from betrothal through to its climax, the birth of the first child.[14] Childbirth affected two families—both cognate and agnate—with social concerns about the child's legitimacy, legal concerns about its sex and status as heir, medical concerns about the mother's life and the baby's viability, and religious concerns relating to pollution.[15] Childbirth marked violent transitions for everyone involved, a first child especially turning the mother from *parthenos* to *gynē*,[16] the father into the head of his own nuclear family, and sometimes the previous generation into grandparents for the first time.

The near-secrecy surrounding the days after childbirth, the private nature of the festivities even by the 'tenth day', and the masculine civic protocols excluding expressions of interest in obstetric matters, have occluded one type of emphatically public activity in which pregnancy, birth, and the first few days after it played a significant role: the theatre. The very time period which is inscrutable if approached from the angle of documents dealing with 'reality' was the precise moment at which numerous ancient plays—both tragedies and comedies—were set. This

---

[13] Eubulus fr. 3 ed. R. Hunter (1983), preserved in Athenaeus *Deipn.* 15.668d. Sifakis (1971a), 423–4, has suggested that this is an invocation to the chorus to perform its first interlude; Hunter thinks the lines may have been spoken by a character who, on entering the stage from the house, speaks backwards into it (R. Hunter (1979), 35 n. 62). Either of these explanations suggests that a baby had recently been born.

[14] Vernant (1988), 55–77.

[15] See the excellent remarks of Hanson (1994), 180.

[16] King (1983).

disjunction would instantly attract the attention of any Phenomeno-logical analyst of theatre, for whom theatrical mimesis has a special claim to truth value. Such critics, who trace their approach to Edmund Husserl, the founder of Phenomenology, stress the importance of *visible* manifestations or symptoms of underlying social structures, the forms taken by their appearances on the surface of life. To Bruce Wilshire, an influential Phenomenological theorist of theatre, it 'is a disciplined use of the fictionalizing imagination which can discover... aspects of actuality'.[17] Theatre is a privileged source for documenting psychosocial 'reality' precisely because it is so obviously artificial, and its characters so unreal. This results in a potential to reveal the truth free from the mendacious tendency of discourses, genres, and media which stake false claims to veracity. Untrue, partial, or distorted historiog-raphy, oratory, funerary monuments and medical textbooks can all 'masquerade' as truth, but theatre can never masquerade as the truth because it *is* masquerade. If there is incommensurability between accounts of a particular topic rendered by the documents recording 'reality' and by the fictions enacted within the theatre enjoyed within that reality, it is likely to be significant.

This chapter developed in response to Nancy Demand's *Birth, Death and Motherhood in Classical Greece* (1994), which takes ac-count of most previous work on the medical and iconographic evidence, supplemented by a few literary sources. Yet she seems unaware of the popularity of parturition and neonate scenes in the ancient theatre, scenes which can be handled so as supplement our understanding of the way in which the ancient imagination pro-cessed its thoughts about childbirth. It is not that the childbirth motif in the ancient theatre has been neglected. When it comes to tragedy, attention has been paid to the metaphorical notion of male 'sowing' of the female body, and the biological dimension of the rival paternal and maternal claims in *Eumenides*.[18] Johnston's work on ancient Greek demons who threatened parturient women and their offspring has connected them with the myth enacted in Euripides' *Medea*, a key text also in Pache's study of baby and child heroes.[19]

---

[17] Wilshire (1982), 11; see further E. Hall (2004*c*), 67–8.
[18] See e.g. P. DuBois (1988); Demand (1994), 135.
[19] See Johnston (1995) and Johnston (1997); Pache (2004), 9–19.

Nosologists have speculated about the medical identity (malaria?) of the 'Fever-god' causing women's 'barren pangs' in the plague-beset Thebes of *Oedipus Tyrannus*.[20] Loraux's study of the conceptual equivalence between men who died on the battlefield and women who died in childbirth included discussion of dramatic texts, especially Medea's preference for standing three times by her shield rather than giving birth once (Eur. *Med.* 248–51).[21] Athena's announcement at the end of *IT*, that the clothes of women who died in childbirth will be dedicated to Iphigenia at Brauron (1462–7), has attracted attention both because of the availability of inscriptions listing garments donated to Artemis at Brauron,[22] and because Athena's ordinance misrepresents known cult practice.[23] In *Ion* Creusa's memory of her lonely labour has been shown to be implicated in the Athenian myth of autochthony; the first stasimon has been shown to violate the female language of prayer for good birth associated with Athenian cult.[24]

Comedy has been sifted for evidence: a fragment of Theopompus says that Eileithyia is constantly flustered 'as a result of the pleadings of women' (Theopompus, *Teisamenos* fr. 60 K–A); Praxagora escapes from her husband in *Ecclesiazusae* on the pretext of going to help a friend in labour (526–50). In *Thesmophoriazusae* a woman describes a wife who faked labour and introduced a supposititious baby into the household (502–16). This has been used to argue that Athenian men knew more about a normal labour than we might suppose.[25] Scafuro has applied a legal perspective to many of the plays which will feature shortly in this chapter, extrapolating what they reveal about attitudes to rape and disputes relating to it; Heap has recently argued that in Menander the new baby takes over the role of the saviour-hero whose arrival resolves apparently insoluble problems.[26] This chapter, however, investigates something different: the curious cultural phenomenon which entailed male enjoyment of theatre in which

[20] Jones (1909), 43 and n. 1.   [21] Loraux (1981), 197–253.

[22] See esp. *IG²* 1514.7–18, with Linders (1972); Foxhall and Stears (2000); van Straten (1981), 99.

[23] See Hamilton (1992), 119, quoting a paper delivered by Christian Wolff which was published as Wolff (1992).

[24] Loraux (1981); Stehle (2004), 140–4.

[25] Hanson (1994), 178.

[26] Scafuro (1997), 238–78; Heap (2002–3).

other men actually pretended to be women pregnant, giving birth (if only by screaming for help from Artemis or Eileithyia from backstage), faking childbirth, cuddling their babies, or indeed alternatively acting out the emotions undergone by the husbands, lovers, relatives, and slaves of these parturient women.

CHILDBIRTH PLOTS IN TRAGEDY

It will be seen later that poetic narratives about divine and heroic birth and babies were no *invention* of the theatre, since they are found in the Homeric *Hymns* and lyric poetry. Scholars ancient and modern have, however, always associated childbirth primarily with drama, or rather with the New Comedy of Menander. But in the fourth century AD the Greek rhetorician Libanius, in his treatise in defence of the danced tragedy constituted by pantomime, coupled two types of theatrical performer. He is responding to standard rhetorical examples of the degradation of the theatre adduced by those (including Christians) who opposed it on moral grounds: one is the tragic actor (*tragōidos*) who impersonated Pasiphae and her bizarre sexual passion, and the other is the comic actor who portrayed 'the women who give birth in Menander'.[27] Libanius' reference to the tragic Pasiphae reminds us that it was not New Comedy that invented the theatre's fascination with acting out childbirth plots: the theatrical mimesis of 'a woman in labour' is already one of the most pernicious forms of acting in the opinion of Socrates in Plato's *Republic* (*ōdinousan*, 3.395e2). From Clytemnestra in *Agamemnon* (1417–18) through to Euripides' *Medea* (248–51) and onwards, appealing to the pain of childbirth had been a rhetorical marker of the emotionally disturbed tragic woman: in *Hippolytus* the more discreet chorus women consider that certain ailments—probably gynaecological ones—are 'unspeakable' and must be treated by women rather than referred to male doctors (293–6).

---

[27] Libanius *Or.* 54.73 in the Teubner edn. of Richard Foerster: *hina mē tragōidos eiselthōn Pasiphaēn mimēsetai tēn exokeilasan eis allokoton erōta mēd' au komōidos tas peri tōi Menandrōi tiktousas.*

Although Euripides fleetingly raises the possibility that Clytemnestra might be pregnant in his iconoclastic *Electra* (see below), there is not one pregnant character in extant Greek tragedy to stand beside Alcumena in Plautus' *Amphitryo,* Poppaea in the pseudo-Senecan *Octavia* or indeed Juliet in Shakespeare's *Measure for Measure.*[28] By the last third of the fifth century, however, childbirth had become a significant concern of tragedy. The baby-plays of Euripides form an important group which was decisively to influence the course taken by comedy in the late fourth century, and indeed, via two indirect routes (the eleventh of Ovid's *Heroides* and, once again, *Octavia*), the shape of Jacobean tragedy in England.[29] That the baby-plays formed a recognized category of tragedies is shown by the way that the collective concept of tragic birth-plots is addressed in Aristophanes' *Lysistrata.* When one woman seeks to escape from the Athenian acropolis, she feigns labour, crying out, 'O Lady Eileithyia, hold back my labour until I can get somewhere where it's sanctioned to give birth' (742–3). She insists that she is about to give birth *immediately* (*autika mal' texomai,* 743), and begs to be allowed home to find a midwife (746). But Lysistrata discovers that it is

[28] Alcumena, about to give birth to twin boys, one of whom was the prodigiously strong baby Heracles (*magnust et multum valet,* 1103), ought to have been very large indeed at the moment of the play's action: this may be one of the points of the jokes at 667–8 and 681, where she is described as *saturam, gravidam,* and *pulcre plenam.* See Sedgwick (1960), 106–7; Phillips (1985); and Baier (1999*b*), 216 n. 44. The pregnancy of Poppaea, who appears briefly in *Octavia* in order to perform a sacrifice after being terrorized by dreams (756–60), is what has precipitated the crisis in this tragedy, by eliciting Nero's resolve to marry his pregnant mistress. Octavia complains about the pregnancy at 181–2. Poppaea was actually pregnant with a short-lived girl child who was named Claudia; see Ballaira (1974), 34; her pregnancy in the face of Octavia's alleged sterility was, according to Tacitus (*Ann.* 14.60), Nero's justification for replacing one wife with another. For an interesting discussion of the way that in *Measure for Measure* Shakespeare plays off men's uses of metaphorical pregnancy of the intellectual or spiritual kind against the manifest pregnancy of Juliet, see Crane (2001), esp. 159 and 167.

[29] Canace's pregnancy in *Heroides* 11 inspired one of the most important Renaissance attempt at imitating Greek tragedy, Sperone Speroni's *Canace* (1546), and thence several sibling-incest tragedies including John Ford's masterpiece *'Tis Pity She's a Whore* (1633). The pregnancy of Poppaea in the *Octavia* attributed to Seneca ensured the popularity of illicit pregnancies in Jacobean tragedy. Many Jacobean heroines are disruptively pregnant during their plays: the only crime of the heroine of John Webster's *The Duchess of Malfi* (1613–14) is to produce sons by her lower-class husband Antonio, during the drama, against the wishes of her natal family; the carnage in Beaumont and Fletcher's *The Maid's Tragedy* (1610–11) is caused entirely by Evadne's decision to marry Amintor when actually pregnant by the King.

Athena's helmet, not 'a male child' (*arren paidion*), that is creating the apparent bulge in her belly (748–751). Here the male actor playing the escapee had to play not a parturient woman, but a woman who was deliberately *pretending* to give birth (the first of several such roles we will encounter shortly). The subsequent scene in *Lysistrata* between Myrrhine and Cinesias also revolves around their unweaned baby (879, 881). But this obstetric theme had been set up in the opening scene, when Lysistrata had sighed that it is hardly surprising that tragedies are made about women, when they are nothing but 'Poseidon and a tub' (*ouden gar esmen plēn Poseidōn kai skaphē*, 138–9). As the scholiast remarks (at 138–9), this means 'copulation and childbirth', *ouden esmen ei mē sunousiazein kai tiktein*. Lysistrata is referring to a lost tragedy by Sophocles, one of his two *Tyro* plays, which dealt with the story of Tyro's intercourse with Poseidon, the birth of her sons Pelias and Neleus, their exposure in a skiff, rearing by shepherds, and eventual reunion with their mother.[30] Although this tragedy took place at the time of the reunion, when the tub-cradle was a recognition token (Aristotle, *Poetics* 1454^{b}25), Tyro's confinement must have been mentioned.

Lysistrata's remark shows that the equation of tragic women with childbirth was a familiar enough formula by 411 BC to raise a laugh in comedy.[31] It is intriguing that the tragedy to which Lysistrata alludes is by Sophocles, because most sources suggest that the childbirth motif was usually associated, rather, with Euripides. One of the many accusations levelled at Euripides by Aeschylus in *Frogs* is that his plays featured 'women giving birth in sanctuaries' (*tiktousas en tois hierois*, 1080), where it was sacrilegious to deliver a baby, as the woman feigning pregnancy in *Lysistrata* averred (742–3). According to a scholion on the *Frogs* passage there was a Euripidean tragedy in which a woman did just that: in *Auge* the heroine, a priestess of Athena impregnated by Heracles, had given or actually gave birth to Telephus in the sanctuary of Athena (*hē Augē hē thugatēr Aleou hiereia d' Athēnas en tōi hierōi gennai ton Tēlephon* (= Euripides

---

[30] Sophocles frr. 648–69a *TgrF*. See esp. A. C. Pearson (1917), ii. 270–4.

[31] It may also be relevant that in the parody of Euripidean monody sung by Aeschylus in Aristophanes' *Frogs*, the singer whose identity he assumes concludes by asking her little child to fling its arms around her (1322). This may reveal awareness of the new mothers in Euripidean tragedy, unless it is an exclusive reference to Opheltes, the baby whom Hypsipyle was attending in *Hypsipyle* (see Ch. 10, p. 305).

(14) *Auge* T iii *TgrF*). She complained that it was unfair that Athena should enjoy seeing her temple housing lethal weapons stripped from corpses, while objecting to her own priestess giving birth there (fr. 266 *TgrF*, quoted from Clement of Alexandria, *Strom.* 7.841–2).

The fragments suggest that the birth may have happened during the play, with Auge screaming for help from Artemis or Eileithyia from backstage, but this is not certain.[32] The horror felt at the pollution caused by childbirth in a sacred enclosure is reflected in the inscriptions recording miraculous cures experienced in the sanctuary of Asclepius at Epidauros. These attest to women who incubated at the shrine in the hopes of finding relief from their difficult pregnancies, but were compelled to dash to the edges of the sacred area in order to deliver their offspring: Ithmonika of Pellene had asked the god for help in conceiving a daughter, then returned to the sanctuary as a suppliant because her pregnancy lasted for three years: 'After this she left the Abaton hurriedly and when she was outside the sanctuary gave birth to a daughter.'[33] Pausanias says that the local people resented the plethora of births (and deaths) occurring on their land (2.27.7). When 'baby-plays' were performed in theatres adjacent to sanctuaries of Asclepius frequented by pregnant women (at Corinth, for example, as well as Epidaurus), they must have been imbued with a special emotional cogency.

Perhaps Euripides was the first tragedian to replace the standard offstage death cries with an actor's imitations of the screams of a labouring woman.[34] Menander and his colleagues in New Comedy may have found the striking effect of the pregnant woman's formulaic plea to Eileithyia in their tragic forerunner.[35] The action of *Auge*

[32] See Moses Choronensis, *Progymnasmata* 3.3, and the discussion of Katsouris (1975), 160–1.

[33] Text and translation: Rhodes and Osborne (2003), 533–5, no. 102.9–21. The case of Cleo, pregnant for five years (ibid. 533, no. 102.3–8), is even more miraculous; as soon as she had left the Abaton 'and was clear of the sanctuary she bore a son who, immediately he was born, washed himself in the fountain and crawled around beside his mother'. See also LiDonnici (1995), 84–7.

[34] He certainly created a shocking (and probably new) effect with the offstage death cries of children interrupting a choral lyric in *Medea* (1270–81), on which see the wise remarks of Segal (1997), 167–72.

[35] Rosivach (1998), 43–4, discusses the extent of the influence exerted by the rape motif of *Auge* on New Comedy in general.

certainly dealt with events immediately after the birth; a plague (resulting from the defilement of the temple?), the baby's discovery, the decree
of Auge's father that she be drowned, and Heracles' rescue of both
mother and child.[36] The story—besides being imitated by the tragedian
Aphareus in his *Auge* (341 BC)—influenced Menander (see especially
Epitrepontes 1121–6), and became popular on the comic stage. One of
the two fragments of Philyllios' late fifth- or early fourth-century *Auge*
(fr. 3 K–A) describes the conclusion of a female-only feast (which is
suggestive given the apparent female domination of the first days of the
rituals after a birth); the comic poet Eubulus also composed an *Auge*
which included a description (fr. 14 K–A) of a lavish feast.[37] A stunning
fourth-century vase of the type which used to be associated with
'phlyax' drama portrays a scene including Heracles apparently leaving
Auge after an encounter with her (fig. 3.1); this may be related to either
Philyllios' or Eubulus' comedies. So may a delightful set of seven Attic
terracotta figures of the second quarter of the fourth century which
include a Heracles, an old woman carrying a baby, and an apparently
embarrassed young woman.[38]

  Euripidean specialists have long recognised that *Auge* was perhaps
the last in a gallery produced by this tragedian crammed with what
were once accurately described as 'women with irregular babies'.[39] In
Skyrioi Lycomedes' daughter Deidamia, who had been impregnated
by Achilles, is likely to have given birth (a story narrated in Apollodorus' *Bibliotheke* 3.74). In one fragment her father is told that she is
dangerously ill (*hē pais nosei sou kapikindunōs echei*, (64) *Skyrioi* fr.
682.1 *TgrF*).[40] The present tense implies that she is either about to
give birth, or has done so extremely recently. A neonatal theme was
certainly developed in the form of Pasiphae's particularly 'irregular'
baby in *Cretans*. In a dialogue preserved on papyrus one interlocutor

---

[36] See Webster (1967), 239. In Euripides' *Telephus* the eponymous hero explained
that Eileithyia had helped his mother's labour pains (Eur. (67) fr. 696.6–7 *TgrF*).

[37] The Philyllios fragment is quoted in Athenaeus *Deipn.* 9.408e; the Eubulus in
Athen. *Deipn.* 14.622e. Machon may also have written a play with this title: see R.
Hunter (1983), 103–4.

[38] Trendall and Webster (1971), 136–7 with pl. IV.24 and 126–7 with pl. IV.9.

[39] Webster (1967), 240.

[40] The fragment is quoted as relating to Deidamia by Sextus Empiricus 671.2. That
the play included the moment of birth, and probably offstage labour cries, was argued
in detail by Körte (1935).

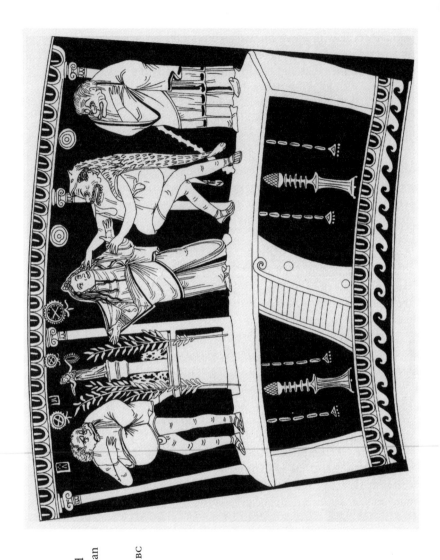

FIG. 3.1 Scene depicting Auge and Heracles on a Sicilian kalyx-krater of the Manfria Group in Lentini, c. 340–330 BC

(perhaps Minos) asks the other whether the monstrous baby is suckled by its human mother or by a wetnurse-cow, and the answer seems to be in the present tense.[41]

Most of the socially disruptive pregnancies in Euripides are 'unrealistic' insofar as the babies are fathered by gods (especially Zeus and Poseidon), for example in *Alope*. That in this play gender-based invective was prominent is indicated by (8) *Alope* fr. 108 *TgrF* ('somehow it is natural that a woman be an ally to another woman'), and also by fr. 111, which asserts that even 'well-brought up women' wreck households more than those who have not been properly supervised. This tragedy, like Carcinus' emotional fourth-century play of the same name, dramatized the secret birth of Alope's son Hippothoon to Poseidon and the baby's exposure.[42] Yet, paradoxically, pregnancies such as Auge's were in one sense 'realistic' in that they provoked harsh mistreatment of the unmarried mothers by their angry fathers: if we knew of such a case involving a daughter of one of the spectators at the Great Dionysia we might know better just how 'realistic' the harsh treatment was.[43] In effect, most of Euripides' tragic childbirth plays were about the reactions of *maternal grandfathers* to the appearance of baby *grandsons*. In *Alope* the heroine exposed the baby for fear of her father Cercyon. In Euripides' *Danae*, in which the baby boy was Zeus' son Perseus, one fragment speaks of the delight which a newborn child brings to the childless ((20) *Danae* fr. 316.5–7 *TgrF*). But the grandfather Akrisios punished both mother and son terribly. In *Wise Melanippe* the heroine had borne twins whom her father wanted to have burnt. In *Auge* the heroine likewise incurred the wrath of her father, although Heracles, the baby's father, was presented as a saviour who rescued the baby from exposure and intervened on behalf of the mother with her father.

---

[41] *POxy* 2461. This is (41) *Cretans* fr. 472bc.38–9 *TgrF*; it is also fr. 2.21–2 in Cozzoli (2001), who discusses the identity of the interlocutors in detail on pp. 93–4. See also Collard, Cropp and Lee (1995), 71.

[42] *Alope Cercyonis filia formosissima cum esset, Neptunus eam compressit, qua ex compressione peperit infantem, quem inscio patre nutrici dedit exponendum—* Hyginus *fab.* 187. On Carcinus' *Alope*, in which Cercyon's psychological pain as the father of Alope was a major focus (70 F 1b *TgrF*), see Xanthakis-Karamanos (1980), 36–7.

[43] Scafuro (1997), 273–4, discusses the scanty evidence, and suggests that Greek fathers may have been more compassionate in such cases than the sources imply.

In these baby-plays, the babies were sired by half-divine heroes, gods, or the inhuman bull of Pasiphae. This casts the scandalous nature of perhaps Euripides' most notorious tragedy, *Aeolus*, into relief, for the illicit (and incestuous) pregnancy was created by two humans of equivalent status. First staged in 423 or earlier, *Aeolus* was quickly parodied in Aristophanes' *Peace* (114–19—see Eur. (2) *Aeolus* frr. 17 + 18 *TgrF* and below, Ch. 11, p. 340); it probably inspired his comedy *Aeolosicon*. In the fourth century it gave rise to two comedies in which the incestuous sex was explained by the effects on Macareus of alcohol (Antiphanes fr. 19 K–A, and Eriphus fr. 1 K–A).[44] In the Euripidean prototype Macareus, son of Aeolus, impregnated his own full sister Canace, and delivered a notorious speech defending his right to marry her on the radically relativist ground that no action is inherently shameful—it only becomes so if it is so deemed (fr. 19 *TgrF*, *ti d' aischron ēn mē toisi chrōmenois dokēi?*). This speech outraged the old-fashioned Strepsiades of *Clouds* (see 1371–2). According to tradition, it also so infuriated Socrates that he rebuked Euripides, declaring that 'what is shameful is indeed shameful, whether so deemed or not!'[45]

Canace's relationship with her brother may have been the peg on which Euripides the philosopher could hang a rhetorical presentation of the case for extreme moral relativism. But in dramatic terms it was the baby's arrival that caused domestic catastrophe. A papyrus hypothesis (*POxy* 2457) makes the action fairly clear (= Eur. (2) *Aiolos* T ii.21–34 *TgrF*):[46]

Aeolus received from the gods the administration of the winds, and settled in the lands opposite Etruria, having begotten six sons and the same number of daughters. The youngest of them, Macareus, fell in love with one of his sisters and seduced her. She became pregnant and hid the birth by pretending sickness (*hē d' egkuos genē[theisa] ton tokon ekrupten*, 25–26). The young man persuaded the father to marry his daughters to his sons, and the latter, falling in with the plan, appointed a marriage ballot for all. The instigator of the scheme failed in the draw, since the lot fell out for the girl he had seduced to become another's wife. Running together... the nurse about the baby... (*to men gennēthen hē trophos...*)

---

[44] On parodies of *Aeolus* see MacCary (1973), 198–200.

[45] Serenus in Stobaeus, *Flor.* 5, 82: *aischron to g' aischron, kan dokēi kan mē dokēi*. See also Plutarch, *De Audiendis Poetis* 12.33c, where the rebuke is attributed to Antisthenes, and Athenaeus 13.582d.

[46] Translation adapted from Turner (1962*b*).

It looks likely that Canace killed herself with a sword sent by her father; her brother may have followed suit on discovering her corpse.[47] A late fifth-century Lucanian hydria (fig. 3.2) gives pride of place to Canace, lying on a couch, holding the suicide weapon, her hair and clothing loosened (often a sign of recent labour), dishevelled and 'drooping in death'.[48] There is no sign of the baby, who in most versions of the story had been discovered by her father and exposed by the time of Canace's death (e.g. Ovid, *Her.* 11.66–86). Behind Canace stands her father Aeolus, hurling insults across her limp body at her brother; also present is the nurse, her grey head covered; she has been arrested. She may have been involved in attempting to smuggle the newborn out of the house (see e.g. Ovid, *Her.* 11.66–74) in addition to conniving in the concealment of the pregnancy.

Euripides' portrayal of the death of Canace indelibly marked the ancient imagination. Besides being parodied in comedy,[49] the tragedy led to the scene of Canace's death being famously painted by Aristides of Thebes (Pliny, *NH* 35.99). A fresco in the Vatican displays Canace alongside other erotic tragic heroines (Pasiphae, Phaedra, etc.).[50] If, as several scholars believe, Ovid's *Heroides* 11 drew extensively on the play, then the traumatic birth undergone by Canace will have been somehow narrated during its course, or possibly her labour cries overheard from behind the scenes.[51] Ovid's Canace writes to her brother in detail that the agonizing pain of labour had brought her to the verge of death, and even Lucina had denied her assistance.[52]

---

[47] See [Plut.], *Parallela Graeca et Romana* 28 = *Mor.* 312c–d. This source also reports an almost identical Roman tale involving the baby born to Papirius Romanus and his full sister Canulia. See also Stobaeus *Flor.* 4.20–71, and the discussion of the sources of Ovid's Canace epistle in Knox (1995), 258.

[48] Trendall and Webster (1971), 74. It has been argued that, in the visual arts, loosened hair or clothing as well as limp position and supportive attendants can be indications that the woman is undergoing or has recently experienced birth: a group of such scenes on about a dozen Attic or Atticizing lekythoi and stelai, mostly late 4th-cent. or Hellenistic, is published by Vedder (1988), and discussed in Demand (1994), 121–7.

[49] See Berger-Doer (1990), 951.

[50] Berger-Doer (1990), 951. The definitive prose account of the story seems to have been written in the 1st-cent. BC *Tyrrhenica*, by a scholar named Sostratus.

[51] See Reeson (2001), 57–64; Verducci (1985), 213.

[52] '*Mors erat ante oculos, et opem Lucina negabat*' (*Her.* 11.55).

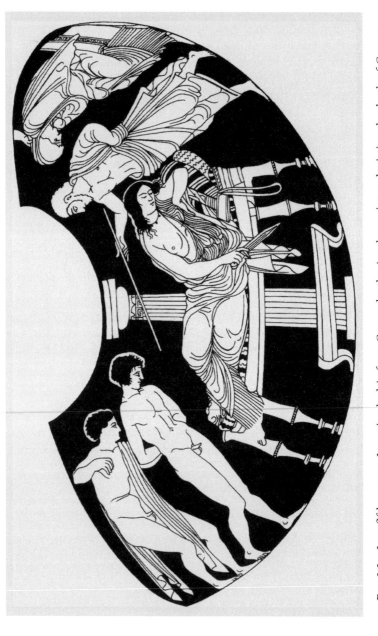

FIG. 3.2 Late fifth-century Lucanian hydria from Canosa by the Amykos painter, depicting the death of Canace

FAKING NEW MOTHERHOOD IN EURIPIDES'
ELECTRA

In *Aeolus* Euripides interlaced a childbirth plot with the scandalous
motif of sibling incest. Some of the other baby-tragedies (certainly
including *Cretans* in 438 BC) must have preceded his *Electra*. This is
the sole 'baby-play' where the impact of the theme on the entirety of
the drama can be appreciated; it is also, perhaps, the most intriguing,
in that it may show the author playing with his own fixation on
childbirth plots by inserting into Electra's story the motif of the baby
that never was. This tragedy required its male leading actor to display
the female character he was playing at a moment when she was
pretending to be a newly delivered woman in front of a person
intimately acquainted with her physiology and temperament: her
own mother.[53] Euripides thus invited his audience to engage in a
tragic version of the procedure which also marked the 'escape' scene
of the fraudulently pregnant woman in *Lysistrata*: they were to watch
his Electra faking a woman close to the time of birth, a role not
dissimilar to that which he several times asked his own leading actors
to assume 'genuinely' in other plays where the disruptive mythical
childbirth being enacted was not counterfeit at all.

The purpose of the fictional baby is to lure Clytemnestra into the
lowly cottage Electra shares with her husband, a peasant residing in
the Argive countryside. Electra tells the old *paidagōgos* to inform
Clytemnestra that her daughter Electra is 'confined with a male child's
birth', which allegedly took place ten days previously (652).[54] When

[53] See the perceptive remarks of Foley (2001), 234–5 on the way that Euripides'
version of the tragedy confronts the two women in a non-civic, rural setting, while
preventing Orestes from speaking directly to his mother 'or confronting the full
power of her body' until he actually kills her.
[54] The other two tragedians both made striking use of fiction in their versions of
Electra's story. In *Libation-Bearers* Orestes and Pylades gain entrance by disguising
themselves as strangers and falsely reporting Orestes' death; Sophocles' *Electra* features its remarkable deceitful 'messenger speech', delivered by Orestes' *paidagōgos*,
fraudulently narrating Orestes' death at the Pythian games. We do not know whether
Euripides' *Electra* preceded or followed Sophocles' version. But there is a feigned
death in both Aeschylus and Sophocles and a feigned *birth* in Euripides, a subversive
half-equivalence which looks not untypical of Euripides' sense of humour.

Clytemnestra arrives Electra confirms that she has given birth, and continues: 'Please make the tenth-night sacrifice for this, according to custom. I do not know how to myself. I am inexperienced, this being my first child.' Clytemnestra objects that the 'tenth night' sacrifice was conventionally performed by the woman who had delivered the baby (1128),[55] but Electra has an answer ready: 'I was my own midwife and bore my baby alone' (1129). And so, commiserating with Electra's loneliness and dishevelment, Clytemnestra enters the cottage, thinking that she is about 'to sacrifice to the gods for the child's completed term' (1132–3).

The audience is introduced to the idea of Electra bearing a child in the prologue (22–42), where they learn that Aegisthus feared that if she married a nobleman she might 'bear a son to avenge Agamemnon'. The folkloric notion that a father-figure might be afraid of his daughter's offspring is instantiated in Greek myth by the story of Danae, Perseus, and Acrisius (Perseus is depicted on Achilles' shield in the first stasimon of *Electra*, 458–63). Herodotus relates another example in his tale of Astyages, king of the Medes in Asia, Mandane, and her baby Cyrus, who deposed his grandfather to become the first king of a united Medo-Persian empire (1.107–8). It was stories such as these which Euripides had in mind when he invented Aegisthus' fear of Electra bearing a child who would one day take vengeance upon his wicked step-grandfather. From there it was a short step to give Electra a fictional baby. The childbirth motif perhaps suggested in turn the play's temporal location at the start of the 'Heraia', the festival of Hera, tutelary deity of Argos, the importance of which to the tragedy has been demonstrated by Zeitlin.[56] Hera was worshipped under a series of cult titles reflecting different stages in women's lives, and was responsible for the transitions between them. She was 'Hera the Maid' and also 'Hera the Bride' (*Numpheuomenē*), the divinity in charge of women's social transitions from girl to bride to wife. As 'Hera the Fulfilled' (*Teleia*) she oversaw women's fulfilment in marriage, which included giving birth.[57]

---

[55] See Hamilton (1984), 244–6, who argues that this is cogent evidence for the female domination of the rituals soon after childbirth.

[56] Zeitlin (1970).

[57] For Hera under both these titles at e.g. Plataea, see Schachter (1981), 242.

The invented baby certainly opens up opportunities for theatrical irony. Electra had earlier ordered the servants to conceal Aegisthus' corpse inside the cottage (959–61). Clytemnestra thinks that it contains a newborn boy: it houses, instead, the cadaver of a newly slain husband. The baby motif appears in the form of infancy images in the choral odes, which stress the presence of the nymphs, so often involved in childbirth sacrifices (e.g. 447). There is a delicate description of Achilles, 'Thetis' offspring', being brought up by Cheiron; Achilles' shield included an engraving of Perseus in company with Hermes, 'the rustic child of Maia' (462–3); even the golden lamb was brought down by Pan 'from its *tender mother* in the Argive mountains' (699–705). The baby theme also illuminates the references to the infancy of earlier members of Electra's family. Clytemnestra herself had once delivered a firstborn child, Iphigenia (1002–3); Orestes was rescued while still little by his *paidagōgos*; the same man had even raised Agamemnon from babyhood, 'holding him in his arms' (506).

Electra's invention of the baby expresses a psychological insight. She envies her mother's status as fulfilled wife and mother: the fictiveness of the baby thus adds to the tragedy of her own existence. And her virginity is stressed by both the peasant and Electra (44, 255): since he does not have sexual intercourse with her, Electra can never bear a child.[58] Orestes, like his sister, has babies on the brain. Clytemnestra and Aegisthus have had 'new' children (62–3), who enjoy the palace life of which Electra and Orestes have been deprived. When Orestes hears that Aegisthus is to sacrifice to the nymphs, he assumes that the ritual is connected either with rearing these children or with an anticipated birth (*pro mellontos tokou*, 626)—raising at least the suspicion in his audience's heads, nowhere contradicted, that Clytemnestra may be pregnant again.

The baby creates a focus on the physical way Orestes talks about his relationship with his mother. As Clytemnestra's carriage approaches the cottage, he has his first pang of doubt: 'how will I kill her, who raised me and who gave birth to me?' (*hē m' etrepse kateken*, 969). After the deed is done, Orestes can hardly bear to remember how his mother, in her death throes, 'bared and showed her breast

---

[58] See the sensitive remarks of Zeitlin (2003), 265–6.

outside her clothes... sinking to the ground upon the limbs that bore us' (*pros pedōi | titheisa gonima melea*, 1207–9). Electra, whose doubts only begin after the murder, shares the awareness of the physical bond she has violated by collaborating in her mother's murder: 'I am to blame', she announces. 'I burned with my ruthless hatred for my mother here, who gave me, her daughter, birth' (*ha m' etikte kouran*, 1182–4). Even the chorus join this primal theme, saying to Orestes that they understand the 'pain' Orestes experienced when he heard the death cry of the mother who bore him (*has' etikten*, 1211); the word for his pain is *odunas* (1210), the standard word for labour pains.[59]

By revealing the tender side of Clytemnestra herself, the imaginary baby also complicates the emotional impact of the play. He proves that Clytemnestra does care about Electra's welfare, at least a little bit. When Electra first divulges the 'baby' ruse to the *paidagōgos*, she is quite certain that her mother will come when she hears that her daughter is in childbed; when the *paidagōgos* responds by asking if Clytemnestra really cares that much about her daughter, Electra simply says 'yes' (658). And Clytemnestra is tolerant indeed of Electra's hostility, memorably confessing to her, 'I am not so very pleased, my child, with the things I have done' (1005–6). The word for 'child' here (*teknon*) is etymologically so close to the verbs meaning 'give birth' such as *teknoomai* and some tenses of *tiktō*, used so often by Clytemnestra's children in the play (see above), that the audience is forced to recall that the older woman in front of them once actually laboured to bring the younger into the world as a baby.[60] And Clytemnestra's baby, so Clytemnestra thinks, has in turn just had *her* first baby: it is difficult for an audience to be enthusiastic about reciprocal bloodletting when the victim thinks that she has just become a grandmother.

---

[59] This is a play set in Argos in which a male actor played a woman pretending to be pregnant, and a male character's grief reminds the chorus of labour pains: it is difficult not to be reminded of the sex role inversions at the Argive festival called the Hybristika, at which the women dressed as men and the men as women, in an ancient transvestite ritual (Plutarch, *On the Bravery of Women*, 245f).

[60] On the tight bonding of words with similar beginnings, endings or rhythm within the mental/cognitive lexicon, see Aitchison (1994), 142.

NEW COMEDY AND NEW MATERNITY

The motif of the fictional baby in Euripides' *Electra* suggests just how much subtle and serious psychological drama has been lost in his other baby-plays. But *Electra* may have had a more light-hearted dramatic afterlife in Greek New Comedy, if Plautus found the idea for Phronesium's fake baby—the theatrical heart of his *Truculentus*—in a Greek prototype. Although no such play has yet emerged from the papyri, some scholars have argued that Plautus must have had an archetype produced in the first few years of the third century BC.[61] In the Roman play the author subjects the ancient interest in the theatrical impersonation of a pregnant woman to a fascinating in-spection. The (male) actor playing the *meretrix* Phronesium, who smuggles in an exposed baby in order to pretend that she has herself borne a child to Stratophanes, needs to act not a parturient woman, but (like the male actors in Aristophanes' *Lysistrata* and Euripides' *Electra*) a woman *acting the part* of a parturient woman. This is no easy role. Phronesium may be by far 'Plautus's most outrageous *femme fatale*', and a persuasive actress;[62] she has nevertheless failed to convince one of her three lovers, Dinarchus, that she is pregnant, whether because her acting is inadequate, or because he would obviously have noticed earlier if his lover had been expecting a baby: 'Did she suppose she could hide it from me, if she had been with child?' he indignantly asks the audience (*an me censuit | celare se potesse, gravida si foret*? 89–90).

Phronesium's rehearsals have been elaborate. She has even coached her maidservant in her supporting role, for Astaphium corroborates her story and improvises sensational detail: 'Poor me, I shudder every time that childbirth's mentioned, since it was nearly the end of Phronesium!' (285–6). Her mistress, meanwhile, who in order to appear attractively recovered arranges the timing so that it is the fifth day after the supposed birth (424), is awarded a show-stopping scene.

---

[61] Nixon (1938), p. viii; Hueffner (1894), 33. Enk (1964), 64, the author of a substantial edition of the play, believed that the author was a pupil of Menander. See also Moore (1998), 141 and n. 2.

[62] See Moore (1998), 140.

Dressed in an ornamental nightgown suited to puerperal convalescence (463–4, 475), she arranges herself on a couch to receive the 'father'. She rehearses the complaints a new mother might be expected to utter ('The anxiety and the torments we mothers endure!', 449–50), and the fears for the new baby's life (454–5). Maids bring the props necessary for a sacrifice to Lucina, complete with myrrh to throw on the fire (476). Phronesium takes up the prostrate position of a *puerpura* (478), removes her sandals and asks for a blanket. When the supposed new father Stratophanes finally arrives, he is informed that the baby looks just like him (512–55). The whole dialogue between them is unique in ancient literature: it is marked by hilarious jokes about the way the baby already takes after his father's military deportment, Phronesium's complaints about the pain she is still in, and Stratophanes' pride in new paternity.

Plautus was responding to a central concern of New Comedy. Indeed, even Middle Comedy had been interested in obstetrics: besides Eubulus' burlesque of Euripides' *Auge,* and a taste in his era for plots dramatizing the birth of gods,[63] Nicomachus wrote a play entitled *Eileithyia.* Alexis composed a play entitled *Wet-Nurse(s)* (*Tithē or Titthai,* frags. 228–9 K–A),[64] and a dialogue in his *Stratiōtis* involved two speakers squabbling about who should take responsibility for an unwanted infant (*paidarion,* Alexis fr. 212 K–A);[65] the deictic *touti* (line 2) suggests that the baby was physically present on stage. Antiphanes' *Misoponēros* included a discussion of midwives and wetnurses (Antiphanes fr. 115 K–A). Artemis' sanctuary at Brauron was the setting of the play from which Diphilus fr. 29 K–A derived, and his *Foster-Children* (*Syntrophoi*) mentioned a baby prone to wetting its swaddling-bands (fr. 73 K–A).

Yet in New Comedy, as in *Aeolus,* the focus was generally on the relationship between father and son. The most famous 'baby-play' of Menander is probably his *Samia,* in which the identity of the parents of Plangon's still unweaned baby is the central theme. This comedy gives a stronger sense than any other ancient text of the physical

---

[63] See Lindberger (1956), 25–6.

[64] For other plays with this title see R. Hunter (1983), 207, who also assembles references to wet-nurses from Aristophanes' *Knights* 716–18 onwards.

[65] On this fragment see Arnott (1996), 607.

reality of living with the incessant crying and demands for rocking and physical contact to which new babies subject households (see especially Demeas' account of the nurse who rescued the screaming baby from the couch where it had been dumped, and the physical fight over the on-stage baby at 568–75). Yet birth itself does not constitute the climax of *Samia*, whereas there was undoubtedly a stock scene-type in New Comedy during which an unmarried maiden, whose pregnancy has been kept secret from the men in the plot, goes into labour backstage. Her cries are heard through the *skēnē*, precipitating familial crisis. Aulus Gellius describes the contents of such a scene (later imitated in Latin by the dramatist Caecilius) in the introduction to a quotation from Menander's *Plokion* (fr. 298 K–A): the slave who delivered the fragment stands outside the doors, at first ignorant of the young woman's pregnancy, but 'he hears the groans and prayers of the girl labouring in childbirth; he expresses fear, anger, suspicion, pity, and grief' (*gemitum et ploratum audit puellae in puerperio enitentis: timet, irascitur, suspicatur, miseretur, dolet*, 2.23.18).

Accidents of transmission mean that it is from Roman drama, which enthusiastically adopted the childbirth motif, that the precise contents of such scenes are clearest. Familial chaos is precipitated in Plautus' *Aulularia* by Phaedria's offstage labour cries as she begs her nurse and Juno Lucina to alleviate her pain (*'Perii, mea nutrix. Obsecro te, uterum dolet. | Iuno Lucina, tuam fidem!'*, 691–2). In *Adelphi* the labour of Pamphila, who fears for her life, is announced by her similar cry *'miseram me, differor doloribus! | Iuno Lucina, fer opem! Serva me, obsecro!'* (486–7). In *Hecyra*, whose model was largely a play by Apollodorus, Pamphilus is shattered to discover that his wife Philumena is in labour backstage, since he believes that the baby cannot be his;[66] much of the drama explores the issues of exposure, feigned miscarriage, the time required for gestation, and the difficulties inherent in attempting to conceal a pregnancy, a birth, or a noisy newborn for any length of time. In Terence's *Andria* the birth is precipitated by the conversation between Mysis and the midwife Lesbia about the pregnant Glycerium. Their conversation is overheard by Davos and Simo (the new paternal grandfather), who

---

[66] For a sensitive account of the way that in this play knowledge of a pregnancy psychologically splits the hero in two, see Slater (1988), 254–5.

remains sceptical about the authenticity of the pregnancy even after the women enter the house and Glycerium's agonized cries are heard at 473. Glycerium uses the standard Latin appeal, *Juno Lucina, fer opem, serva me, obsecro* ('Juno Lucina, Help! Save me, I implore you!'), on which Donatus commented, 'Menander Dianam appellet' ('Menander calls her Diana'), which probably implies that this line was in the Greek original, and that the goddess was there named as Artemis.[67]

We have lost direct access to this conventional scene-type of the Greek theatre, which certainly appeared in comedies other than *Plokion*, probably including the so-called *Fabula Incerta* 1 found on *PCair* 43227; this addressed the theme of pre-marital sex and offered the information that the young man Moschion 'has now produced a baby'.[68] In *Farmer*, too, it is possible to discern that the stability of two neighbouring families is threatened by the birth of a child to one of them.[69] In one house live Myrrhine and her adult twins (a youth and a young woman); the daughter, at the opening of the play, is apparently nine months' pregnant by the young man who lives next door. On returning from Corinth he discovers that he has been betrothed by his father to his step-sister. Although there are complications relating to the identity of the twins' father, the central crisis is caused by the arrival of Myrrhine's grandchild. Had this baby never been conceived, the sexual encounter between its parents would not have led them to be married. The picture is complicated by the news that Cleainetos (the 'farmer' of the title) has offered to marry Myrrhine's daughter (63–83). But this marriage of convenience, like the other, is prevented by the pregnant woman's labour, heard from off-stage, summoning the aid of Artemis (*tēn Artemin*, 112). The baby is denoted as *to paidion* (116), the standard term for newborns in the Hippocratic corpus.[70]

The biological parents of the baby will have married, preventing the two other marriages planned in the course of the scenes preceding the arrival of the baby. Since in the concluding act Cleainetos may

---

[67] See Katsouris (1975), 158 and n. 1; Shipp (1979), 160 points out that in Catullus' hymn to Diana 34.13.14 'Juno Lucina' operates as a title of Diana.

[68] *Fabula Incerta* 1. 55 in Arnott (2000).

[69] Gomme and Sandbach (1973), 111.

[70] Demand (1994), 142–3.

have been discovered to have been the father of the twins, and thus of the new mother, the arrival of the baby may have prevented a disastrously incestuous father-daughter union; the marriage planned for the baby's father—to his step-sister—would also have been an intra-familial affair. The arrival of the baby thus creates the possibility of bond based on affection (the young man calls the pregnant maiden his *philtatēn* at line 15), and a fresh new alliance between two previously unrelated households. *Farmer* was typical of childbirth plots in New Comedy in that the birth, while initially threatening familial relationships, nevertheless led to idealized solutions which erased the problems caused in 'reality' by unmarried motherhood and illegitimacy. New Comedy appropriated childbirth to its strategic portrayal of the foundation or consolidation of the family. In the utopian world of New Comic endings, the potentially catastrophic disruption caused by unauthorized pregnancy is always contained and defused. In passing, however, other (far from ideal) scenarios are fleetingly envisaged, which illuminate the thought-world of the Athenian society which produced the plays.

THE GRANDFATHER'S TALE

Childbirth, then, was perceived as a familiar—even conventional—plot pivot in both the tragedy and New Comedy of Athens. That not a single Greek play staging childbirth survives in entirety may perhaps be partly a result of the sometimes censorious judgments of those who decided what texts would be transmitted. But the fragmentary nature of the evidence should not prevent us from addressing *the reasons* why the Greeks staged childbirth plays when they were so coy about talking about women giving birth in other public discourses. A sociological explanation would stress that the baby-plays are tied up with the procedures which marked the beginning of a citizen son's developmental cycle under his father's legal authority. The Athenian father had the right to reject a newborn child altogether, at least up until the moment of the naming ceremony in the second week of the baby's life, when the father made it clear that he accepted the child as his own and as a member of his *oikos* (i.e. his biological family).

Before the baby was accepted by the father it could be rejected or exposed. The crises enacted in the ancient baby-plays mostly presuppose precisely the 'limbo' time around and/or shortly after the birth but before 'official' acceptance into the family. Strauss emphasizes how quick the Athenian father had to be in deciding a child was his own or rejecting it as a bastard.[71] He could not change his mind later. The decisions taken in the baby-plays over accepting the newborn are thus of momentous importance, and the plays are set at a moment of decision-making which would prove critical for all concerned.

For ultimately all the baby-plays are *male* psychodramas. The illegitimate pregnancy legitimized in the course of such plays is the cultural product of a society obsessed with policing women's sexuality, if we see most of New Comedy in terms of David Konstan's study of *Epitrepontes*, as expressing anxiety about female behaviour.[72] The very repetitiveness of the plots of New Comedy 'provides important evidence for what was most culturally important. Why, after all, did audiences need the same plots, over and over?'[73] The baby-plays are also part of Athenian society's need to represent the father–son relationship (what Susan Lape has called 'the father–son romance'),[74] a need which Strauss argues has been central to all patrilineal societies until very recently indeed: 'The uncertainty (before the modern technology of verification) of paternity makes it necessary for a culture and the individuals within it to construct, discursively, the ties that bind father and son.'[75] Those ties are both more complex and more fragile than the patently physical bond between birth mother and infant. The baby-plays of the Greek theatre were one arena in which to affirm the ties that bind the *oikos* across the generations of *men*. As Fowler has succinctly put it when discussing ancient Greek genealogical thinking: 'In patrilinear societies the male line is cohesive and extends ideally in both directions forever.'[76]

[71] Strauss (1993), 98.
[72] Konstan (1993); see also the excellent study of *Samia* by Heap (1998).
[73] Lape (2004), 17 n. 51. On the notion of the formulaic happy ending as an escapist 'correction' of reality, see also Préaux (1957), 88 and Rosivach (1998), 9–10.
[74] Lape (2004), 137–41.
[75] Strauss (1993), 22. For a collection of references to suppositious babies supposedly imposed on unsuspecting men, see Austin and Olson (2004), 163.
[76] R. Fowler (1998), 5.

Unlike tragic childbirth plots, which often featured angry fathers of the pregnant women, most of the new mothers of New Comedy do not seem to have fathers; they are usually dead, absent, or not mentioned at all.[77] Almost all of New Comedy's babies are really catalysts for creating and solving disputes and conflicts between one of the baby's parents (i.e. the man's), and *his* father.[78] In New Comedy the babies of the sons put extreme pressure on these father–son relationships. The young man, himself becoming a father in acknowledging the baby as his own, undergoes a rite of passage which creates both a new *oikos* and a new bond between two existing ones. As Strauss observes, the independent nuclear household, rather than the extended family, dominated the architecture and economy of classical Athens.[79] It is against this background that we need to understand the predominance of the nuclear *oikos* in classical Athenian ideology and therefore also in the theatre. The importance of the *grand*father—apparent in the scrutiny of candidates for citizenship and the archonship ([Arist.] *Ath. Pol.* 52–5)—and the continuity of the intergenerational male line, are repeatedly problematized and re-enacted in the birth scenes of ancient drama.

DIONYSUS' BABIES

Addressing the baby-plays from the perspective of religion would involve stressing, in the case of tragedy, that some are explicable in terms of this genre's pervasive aetiological function. In most of the plays the father is a god, and the core of the plot, at least, is inherited from catalogue poetry and geneaologies. Burkert groups the myths of

---

[77] See Gomme and Sandbach (1973), 33. See also the introduction to Dedousi (1965). An exception is *Samia*, where although the father was absent during his daughter's pregnancy and birth, he does return during the play, and his anger is potentially dangerous to both daughter and seducer. If at the conclusion of *Farmer* Cleianetos was indeed revealed as the pregnant girl's father, the plot would have been exceptional, but would still have avoided the presence of the father of a problematically pregnant unmarried woman.

[78] See Saller (1993), 99.

[79] Strauss (1993), 35, 43, 73.

Auge, Danae, Tyro, and Melanippe together as some of a whole Greek nexus of myths he collects under the label 'The girl's tragedy'. These myths explain the genealogy of heroes and ethnic groups by recounting the structurally similar stories of their mothers, who are separated from their families, secluded, raped, subjected to trials, but rescued as a prelude to the emergence of a hero.[80] In addition to ethnographic aetiologies the Euripidean 'baby-plays' certainly enacted myths closely related to childbirth cults and rituals, similar to that prescribed at the end of *IT*: there may well be a connection with Euripides underlying the Tegean conflation of Auge *en gonasin*, Auge 'on her knees', with the childbirth goddess Eileithyia herself (see Pausanias 8.48.7). In Euripides' fragmentary *Hypsipyle*, the death of the Nemean royal baby Opheltes was implicated in the foundation myth of the Nemean Games.[81] But even aetiology can not provide a full explanation of the phenomenon of the enacted birth.

It is also *a priori* likely that the motif is at some deep religious and psychosocial level connected with Dionysus, the 'twice-*born*' god, the god who emerged violently from his mother Semele's body, appeared in the visual arts as a baby himself,[82] and whose birth from Zeus's thigh was a particularly popular image;[83] this scene (together with an attendant Eileithyia) actually ornamented the *frons scaenae* of the theatre at Perge.[84] Birth brings out into the open—makes known and physically visible—subversive, illicit, and secret sexual acts which might otherwise have passed unnoticed. If one of the oneirocritic Artemidorus' clients saw a midwife in their dream, it signified that

[80] Burkert (1979), 6–7; see also Scafuro (1990). The second most common familial motif in heroic cult, after the heterosexual pair, is the combination of son and mother: see Larson (1995), 89–91.

[81] See Neils (2003), 143–4; Pache (2004), 99–103.

[82] See e.g. Schöne (1987), 63, 81, 83–4. I am grateful to Oliver Taplin for drawing my attention to a late Apulian volute-krater found at Arpinova (near Foggia), which shows Semele being blasted, with Hermes below holding the baby Dionysus, and about to hand him over to the nymphs of Nysa. To the right of the nymphs is a figure dressed in what is obviously the *costume* of a papposilen (his knees and part of his navel are exposed), which implies a theatrical connection. The vase is in Trendall and Cambitoglou (1983), no. 28/96, discussed on pp. 924 and 926, with pl. 362.

[83] Pingiatoglou (1981), 14–19. On Zeus's involvement with unusual conceptions and parturitions, see also Boardman (2004).

[84] Olmos (1986), 691–2, who also points out that the birth of Apollo and Artemis was an ornament at the theatre of Hierapolis in the late 3rd cent. AD.

'secrets will be revealed because midwives search for what is secret and concealed' (3.32). Of course, if the 'Cologne Archilochus' is anything to go by, countless ancient liaisons must have escaped attention, if men like the speaker in that fragment deliberately avoided ejaculating inside their lovers (fr. 196a *IEG*). But Dionysus was god of arrival, explosive manifestation, revelation, of rendering the unseen seen, of violent individuation: pregnancy and birth are essentially visual, theatrical types of action, staging an unquestionably unique type of epiphany. Pausanias said that it made sense for the statue of Eileithyia in her ancient sanctuary at Aigion in Achaea to hold a torch, not 'because the birth-pangs of women are like fire, but... on the ground that she brings children into the light' (7.23.5). Childbirth, moreover, not only makes public an earlier, private act, but creates a disruptive moment of crisis in the wider community, enabling a dramatist to unravel in the compressed time of drama the whole past and the future of an individual *oikos*.

Babies, moreover, are inherently part of the Dionysiac sphere, the repertoire of images related to this god's myths, cults, and poetic narratives, for example in the description of the neonate Theban mothers who leave their houses, their breasts bursting with milk, for the mountainsides in Euripides' *Bacchae* (699–702). There was at least one Dionysiac festival at Athens in which not only small children but babies who were still at the crawling stage (i.e. less than thirteen months or so) seem to have featured prominently, the Anthesteria.[85] Dionysus has a close affinity in art with very young children,[86] and babies are important in the playful world of his attendant satyrs.[87]

Even more significantly, birth and babies seem to have been a fundamental theme from Aeschylus' day (rather than Sophocles' or Euripides') in satyr *drama*, from which, according to Aristotle, tragic

---

[85] On the 182 choes and squat lekythoi associated with this festival which portray crawling babies, many of whose realistically large heads are festively crowned, see Hamilton (1992), 57, 65, 67 n. 14, 71–3, 98–9, with fig. 7, with the additional remarks of Neils (2003), 145–6. It may be relevant that the part of the festival known as the *Chytroi* included choruses and spectacles, perhaps even dramatic performances: Hamilton (1992), 38–42; more speculatively, Maurizio (2001).

[86] See esp. Shapiro (2003), 89; Schöne (1987), 54.

[87] See Lissarrague (1990*a*), and esp. Lissarrague (2003); E. Hall (forthcoming *a*).

drama had originally evolved (*Poet.* 1449ª20). This interest may
have been connected with the *topos* of divine birth and infancy
characteristic of archaic hymns, especially in the cases of Zeus's
children Hermes, Apollo and Artemis.[88] The two longest fragmentary
satyr dramas—Aeschylus' *Dictyulci* ('*Net-Fishers*') and Sophocles'
Trackers—both prominently feature babies (a hero and a god respectively), born in the temporal location of the early mythical time
beloved of this genre, the era when famous heroes were little and
which saw important technological inventions (see Ch. 5, p. 155). In
Dictyulci Silenus and the satyrs drag up a chest from the sea-shore
and discover Danae and her baby Perseus (fr. 47a.786–813 *TgrF*); in
Trackers the baby Hermes is only a few days old and his mother Maia
is still recovering (fr. 314.267–82 *TgrF*).[89] The world of theatrical
satyrs indulged its on-stage babies: witness the tender words of
Silenus in *Dictyulci* to the baby Perseus, ogling his smiles and his
hairless little head (fr. 47a785–8 *TgrF*). The divine birth theme was
adopted by comedy in the fifth century (in, for example, Hermippus'
Athenas Gonai),[90] and in the fourth century the birth of gods
appeared under a new generic guise, the mythological *theōn gonai*
burlesques favoured by Philiscus;[91] the tone of these dramas must be
reflected in Plautus' only 'mythological' comedy, *Amphitruo*, in
which the grossly padded actor playing Alcumena retires from the
stage to give birth (with miraculous ease) to both Zeus' child Her-
cules and Amphitruo's baby son (1061–70).[92]

One unscholarly-sounding reason why there are tiny babies in
drama may be simply that they are charming, and likely to facilitate
a prize-winning theatrical coup. At the risk of making universalizing
claims about the human psyche, in reality babies of the desired sex
born to the right people at the right time have always made them
incredibly happy; in the case, at least, of comedy, waiting for the
semi-formulaic screams of the parturient woman backstage, and
subsequently, perhaps, for a glimpse of the newborn (probably a
swaddled doll rather than a real baby) must have given vicarious

[88] See Janko (1981), 13, 16, 19–20.
[89] These are discussed further below pp. 158–60 and in E. Hall (forthcoming *a*).
[90] Pingiatoglou (1981), 80–1.
[91] See the important remarks of Nesselrath (1995), 27; Benz (1999), 53.
[92] Alexis, for example, wrote a *Birth of Aphrodite* (frr. 57–8 K–A).

pleasure, similar to the more modern dramatic and cinematic protocols of the request for towels and hot water, the cigar-smoking father
anxiously pacing the hospital corridor, and relief at the eventual cries
of the newborn. Some lines in *Thesmophoriazusae* suggest that
fathers would rejoice at the midwife's announcement that 'it's a
boy, a real lion of a boy and the image of his dad' (507–16). The
pleasure offered by the new baby was articulated in Euripides' *Auge*,
probably by Heracles, the proud father of Telephus (Eur. (14) *Auge* fr.
272 *TgrF*, and also (probably) fr. 272a *TgrF*, in which Heracles says he
likes to play, *paizein*). Later antiquity did not forget the baby-plays,
either: Euripides' *Auge* is represented in a Roman imperial mural
from Pompeii and also in a Hadrianic marble relief sculpture from
the Villa Borghese.[93]

Hellenistic mime also had a taste for human infants, although it is
not clear whether Praxinoa's baby in Theocritus' 'Adonia' idyll is
preverbal, or a tiny toddler (15.13–14, 41). Similarly, the speaker in
a fragmentary mime by Herodas asks for the baby or small child—*to
paidion*—to be brought to the breakfast table (9.1, *Aponēstizome-
nai*).[94] The Hellenistic consumers who purchased souvenir artefacts
associated with the theatre certainly had a penchant for terracotta
figurines of child-minding dramatic satyrs, nurses, or slaves holding
babies (fig. 3.3).[95] As late as the third century AD figures holding
babies appear in several scenes illustrating New Comedy: the Myti-
lene mosaics, found in a late Roman villa, display Chrysis holding the
baby in a *Samia* scene, and a small female figure holding the baby in a
scene from *Epitrepontes*.[96]

The poetic tradition shows the popularity of the theme of women
with babies. If the Simonidean poem featuring a lyrically lactating
Danae (fr. 543 *PMG*) was ever performed by a monodist, he would
have been required to sing solo in her persona.[97] By the end of the
fifth century even women in labour were impersonated by the

[93] See Bauchhenss-Thüriedl (1986), 50, with nos. 31 and 32, and Sen. *Herc. O.*
366–8.
[94] On children and Hellenistic taste see B. Fowler (1989), 17–18, 97–9, 126–7.
[95] See Neils and Oakley (2003), 227; *MNC*[3], vol. ii, and 149; London, BM 1842.7–
28.751 (no. 736 in Higgins (1954), vol. i).
[96] See Charitonidis, Kahil, and Ginouvès (1970).
[97] On which see above all Rosenmeyer (1991).

FIG. 3.3   Terracotta satyr holding a wrapped baby, fourth-century BC

citharodic poet Timotheus, whose recitals were marked by a mimetic realism. His poems included imitations of individuals undergoing extreme psychosomatic disturbance such as the drowning barbarian in his *Persians* (70–96), Ajax mad in *The Madness of Ajax*, and probably the monstrous Scylla's mauling of mariners in *Scylla*.[98] One of his poems was *The Birth-Pangs of Semele*. A famous wit quoted in Athenaeus says that Timotheus' Semele 'could not have made more noise if she had given birth to a stage carpenter instead of a god' (*PMG* fr. 792 = *Deipn.* 8.352a).[99] It is in such a tradition of histrionic impersonation by men of women in labour that we can place not only the brilliant ruse of the feigned childbirth in Plautus' republican Roman *Truculentus*, but the information handed down by Suetonius and Cassius Dio that one of the emperor Nero's favourite roles was *Canace Parturiens* (Suetonius, *Nero* 21; Cassius Dio 63.10,2)—whether in Latin or Greek, this may have been an adaptation of part or all of Euripides' *Aeolus*. Canace was also the subject of a pantomime, perhaps the danced *Aeolus* elsewhere attested.[100] This genre also included other titles which suggest an obstetric interest, for example *Danae*, *Epaphos*, *Birth Pangs of Leto*, and *Pasiphae*.[101] Pregnancy, labour pains and birth may have offered interesting opportunities to the transvestite skills of the athletic star dancers of this popular imperial entertainment.[102]

CULTURAL COUVADE

Such sensational drag roles represent an extreme form of 'playing the other', to use Zeitlin's memorable phrase:[103] extreme because they meant playing the naturally, *biologically* other, rather than imitating behaviours and traits considered 'feminine' culturally. Childbirth is one of the few things men simply cannot do. When in Plato's *Cratylus* the biological difference between men and women is essentialised

---

[98] Herington (1985), 153–4.   [99] See Csapo (2004*b*), 213–16.
[100] See *AP* 11.254, and P. Knox (1995), 258.
[101] See Wüst (1949), cols. 847–9.
[102] On which see further Lada-Richards (2003).   [103] Zeitlin (1985).

through etymology, the word for 'man' is connected with abstractions such as courage, upward movement, and opposition to injustice, while the words for 'woman' are associated exclusively with terms signifying biological reproduction and lactation (*gunē / gonē, thēlu / thēlē*, 414a1–5). But in the theatre men pretended to be undergoing the experiences from which they were *in nature* debarred. The school of psychoanalysis founded by Arthur Janov, post-Freudian inventor of the primal scream, and author of *Imprints: The Lifelong Effects of the Birth Experience* (1983), would argue that it was the psychological and physical trouble caused by the intact unconscious memory of their own birth traumas—the experience of the one and only birth in which they had physically participated—that underlay this bizarre cultural phenomenon.[104] Janov's argument could also apply to the parallel male expropriation of the experience of pregnancy encountered in the myths of Zeus and in the obstetric metaphors developed in Plato's Socratic dialogues, above all the *Theaetetus*.[105] But the psychology of theatrical childbirth can be approached from a different angle: dramatic enactment of the effect of births on the *oikos*, whether with tragic or comic consequences, constituted a form of collective social *couvade*.

Couvade—the 'hatching' syndrome—is a word now used of men's tendency to produce symptoms mimicking pregnancy—weight gain, tooth problems, and gastrointestinal pain—during their partners' pregnancies.[106] In modern men living under advanced capitalism its manifestations are sometimes asomatic: acute anxiety, emotive dreams. In more traditional societies *couvade* takes ritualized forms, in which men act out childbirth, practise sympathetic self-mutilation, follow diets, or avoid using weapons during their wives' pregnancies. Ritual couvade in Polynesia and Africa has fascinated anthropologists since the nineteenth century.[107] But more recently a pervasive correlation has been identified between the tribal practice of couvade,

[104] See Janov (1983), 237, 239, and Adams (1994), 3–4.
[105] On Socratic midwifery see Halperin (1990*b*), 117–18 and the bibliography in Pender (1992), 72 n. 1.
[106] See Figes (1998), 146 and especially Bogren (1989).
[107] For a recent view see Douglas (1975). Couvade was explained in the 19th cent. by anthropologists such as J. J. Bachofen as a residual ritual marker of the supersession of matriarchy by patriarchy. See the bibliography in Köves-Zulauf (1990), 91 n. 333.

weak definition of marriage, and a strong interest on the part of husbands in asserting their claims to a particular wife and child.[108]

This might explain why in classical Greece, which had (in anthropological terms) an unusually 'strong' definition of marriage and interest on the part of husbands in *dis*claiming any child of suspect paternity, there is little evidence for couvade—whether medical, psychological, or ritual. There was no word for it. According to Diodorus, who was probably drawing on the late fourth- or early third-century Greek historian Timaeus of Tauromenium in Sicily, something like couvade was practised by the native men of Corsica.[109] The labouring woman was neglected, while her husband took to his bed for the birth (*locheuetai*), 'as if his body were the one suffering the pains' (*hōs tou sōmatos autōi kakopathountos*). The custom of vicarious male labour was a *topos* of Greek ethnography, located amongst non-Greek tribes when authors are suggesting that some barbarian women were unusually courageous or powerful: in Apollonius it is the Tibareni of the Black Sea, where the husbands of parturient women 'groan and collapse in bed, with bandages on their heads' (*stenachousin eni lecheessi pesontes,* | *kraata dēsamenoi*, 2.1011–14). For Strabo it is the Iberian women, who 'when they have given birth to a child, instead of going to bed, put their husbands to bed and minister to them' (3.4.17).

Yet in Greece there was at least one ritual in which men acted out labour pains. Plutarch's *Life of Theseus* (20.2–4) attributes to an author named Paion an account of rites performed in honour of Ariadne in his city, Amathous in Cyprus. Ariadne had gone into labour on Cyprus after Theseus had put her ashore, heavily pregnant, during a storm. He had been driven back out to sea. She died before the child was born. Theseus returned, was devastated, and commanded the foundation of rites in her honour. At the annual sacrifice 'one of the young men lies down and imitates the cries and gestures of women in travail' (*kataklinomenon tina tōn neaniskōn phtheggesthai kai poiein haper ōdinousai gunaikes*). Leitao has stressed that the single ritual actor who performed the substitute labour was young rather than fully adult.[110] He argues that the men involved

---

[108] See Douglas (1975), 64–5.

[109] Diodorus 5.14.2, see *FgrH* 3B 566, F 164.272–74 and Hanson (1994), 158.

[110] Leitao (1998). He also suggests that he was thus dis-identified with the 'father', Theseus, but Theseus at this stage in his adventures is still himself ephebic.

in the ritual, while wishing to experience the magical properties of childbirth, had difficulty in imagining a male body which could give birth without ceasing to be male. The myth and ritual at Amathous, on this argument, enacted an appropriation of female potency, but needed to promote enough 'misrecognition' to tone down the effeminizing aspects of the male birth fantasy. This may be the case, although no account of the obviously Dionysiac reverberations of Ariadne's pregnancy is taken in Leitao's analysis, any more than they are in Plutarch's (although they do feature briefly in a fine recent discussion by Deborah Lyons[111]). But it is indeed suggestive that it is in a context involving a bride of the theatre god that the sole known example of *Greek* mimetic couvade occurs.

Pregnancy causes psychological upheaval in men, and this must have been even greater in a society where pregnancy was so threatening to the mother's life. The Hippocratic *Diseases of Women* describes the agony of protracted labour, and the mortal danger presented by complications such as breech presentation. Inscriptions record the dangers of childbirth and the threat they posed to maternal life.[112] Dean-Jones suggests that when a doctor does attend a female patient in the Hippocratic texts, he usually refers to her by her relationship to a man: a third of the women in the case histories are suffering from complications of pregnancy and childbirth, 'perhaps reflecting the occasion on which men of the household insisted on involving themselves in the question of a woman's treatment'.[113]

It was precisely in atypical, dangerous labour that male family members were most likely to become involved.[114] Husbands appear alone as dedicators of gifts to Artemis in this capacity, along with married couples acting together, exemplified in a statue base at Tanagra dedicated by a husband and wife to Artemis Eileithyia in the fourth or third century BC.[115] Fathers' dedications to Artemis and

---

[111] See Lyons (1997), 125–6, who intelligently notes (126) that in this rite 'we find again the exchange of gender roles that permeates the cult of Dionysos. At the same time the myth and the ritual both emphasize the dangers of childbirth, a theme already apparent in the myth of Semele.'

[112] Lefkowitz and Fant (1992), 263–4.

[113] Dean-Jones (1994), 34.

[114] Hanson (1994).

[115] *IG* 7.555, discussed in Schachter (1981), 102; for other examples see Pingiatoglou (1981), 102–30.

Eileithyia suggest that they suffered anxiety about their daughters; brothers must have felt similar concern.[116] Watching other men imitate childbirth, whether in the Cypriot cult of Ariadne or the mass collective arena of a metropolitan theatre, was a social phenomenon functioning as what we might well call ideological *couvade*.[117] By theatrically playing the pregnant 'other', the fears surrounding birth were processed in ways that conventional silence impeded in other genres and media.

CONCLUSION

At the conclusion of her classic article on the role played by men in 'real' ancient childbirths, Hanson introduced a theatrical metaphor: 'Birthing was a family matter and a stage on which the dynamics of a household played themselves out.'[118] This chapter has argued something complementary: the stage was a place on which birthing could legitimately and pleasurably become a *social* matter. The ancient baby-plays—however fragmentary and elusive—constitute an important dimension of ancient collective psychology. Their existence needs to be acknowledged alongside the traditional 'sources' for childbirth (dedications to birth goddesses, funerary monuments, and medical writings), since none of these reveals much about the impact of childbirth on the *family*. The protocols of the theatre admittedly avoided certain unpleasant scenarios: both tragedy and comedy never apparently confronted maternal death in childbirth (acknowledged at the end of *IT* but not enacted), the neonatal death

---

[116] See the evidence for fathers' dedications to Eileithyia or Artemis at Athens and Anthedon cited in Pingiatoglou (1981), 43, 100, 103. Cf. the evidence of brotherly concern in letters from Oxyrhynchus discussed in Winter (1933), 56, 91; at Rome the heartbreaking testimony of Pliny the Younger on the fate of the Helvidiae, two sisters who both died in the bloom of youth, giving birth to daughters, leaving a lonely brother (*Letters* 4.21).

[117] In his book on Roman birth rituals, Köves-Zulauf (1990), 91, uses the notion of 'ideologische Couvade' to illuminate the psychological processes underpinning the ritual performed by the Roman father which was denoted by the phrase *tollere infantem.*

[118] Hanson (1994), 198.

of a *citizen* baby (as opposed to the death of the non-citizen Chrysis' own baby in *Samia*), the *successful* exposure of an infant, or for that matter the birth of a girl-child.[119] New Comedy never even portrays unmarried girls with unexplained pregnancies, unmarried women *willingly* having illicit sexual liaisons leading to pregnancy, men divorcing or failing to marry women they have impregnated, or the children of incestuous unions. But the fictive 'correction' of reality, and the utopian thinking underlying such generic evasions, render them ultimately far more telling about the ancient collective psyche than the actual stories which *were* enacted.[120] The new babies whose arrival transformed ancient households yell very loudly indeed from the remains of the playscripts of the theatre.

[119] For insightful remarks on the scant evidence surrounding the births of female children, see Foley (2003*a*), 114–17.

[120] Lape (2004), 15–17, discusses New Comedy's avoidance of violating any of the laws or ideologies pertaining to Athenian citizen membership.

4

Visible Women: Painted Masks and Tragic Aesthetics

PAINTED FACES

A portrait of the Alexandrian scholar Aristarchus was once painted by his student Dionysius of Thrace. Aristarchus was depicted wearing a robe on which was embroidered the figure of Tragedy, an image within a painted image.[1] Paint and tragedy are closely allied in other sources. Ovid's personified *Tragoedia* is imposing in her elaborate coiffure, trailing robe, sceptre (13–14) and *painted* boots (*pictis …cothurnis, Amores* 3.31).[2] Plutarch imagined Tragedy as a rich woman accompanied by famous actors, who act as her costumiers and stool-bearers: 'let them follow on as though they were painters and gilders and dyers of statues' (*De Glor. Athen.* 348e–f).[3] Tragedy resembles a statue beautified by the application of paint. By the time of the Byzantine Michael Psellus, she was not only 'painted' by her actors, but was colourfully ornamented, made *poikilē*, by the variety of metres she displayed.[4]

A similar association of tragedy and decorative arts appears in the ancient biographical traditions which link all three canonical tragedians with either sculpture or painting. Aeschylus reportedly

---

[1] Dionysios Thrax T 6 b in the edition of Linke (1977). Thanks to Francesca Schironi for help on this.

[2] For a discussion, see Schrijvers (1976), 416–18.

[3] Translated by Babbitt (1936), 512–13 (slightly adapted).

[4] *Essay on Euripides and George of Pisidia* 21–4, ed. Dyck (1986). For detailed accounts of the evolution of personifications of Tragedy, see Kossatz-Deissmann (1997); E. Hall (forthcoming *a*).

discussed the relationship between archaic statues and those contemporary with him. It is the ancient reaction to his own works that the remark attributed to him reveals: the earlier, simply made examples retained a spark of the divine, whereas the more polished and intricate later statues had lost that unearthly air (Porph. *De Abstin.* 2.18e). Euripides was said to have practised as a painter, a *zōgraphos*, whose pictures (*pinakia*) could be inspected in the city of Megara.[5] Sophocles, meanwhile, was thought to have theorised the relationship between poetry and painting; the poet Ion reported that Sophocles had distinguished the representation of colour in poetry and in visual art. One example Sophocles supplied is the term 'rosy-fingered': a poet can describe a female's fingers as rosy, but if a painter tried to create the same effect, 'he would produce the hands of a purple-dyer and not those of a lovely woman' (Athen. *Deipn.* 13.603e–604d).[6]

It was not until Lessing's seminal essay *Laocoön* (1766) that the difference between poetic and visual mimesis was understood in temporal terms: Lessing's view was that art is static but permanent, arresting its object at a particular instant, whereas literary mimesis (especially the ephemeral art of theatre) represents its objects as moving through time, between presence and absence.[7] For the ancients, however, the most important difference—expressed in the Sophocles anecdote—was not temporal but *sensory*: visual art may make no sound, but poetry in isolation offers nothing material to see. Lessing's criterion of permanence would have made little sense, in any case, to a culture convinced that poetry shared with funerary monuments the function of conferring immortality, but that paintings soon fade: as the Athenian says in Plato's *Laws*, the work that goes into a painting is ephemeral; the colours must be touched up constantly in order to prevent deterioration (6.769c3–8). In the ancient

---

[5] *Life of Euripides* 17–18. Other ancient testimony to the biographical tradition suggests that Euripides had *originally* been a painter, but had given up visual art in favour of poetry after studying philosophy (*Suda*, s.v. 'Euripides' E 3695.4' = Kovacs (1994), 10–11, no. 2).

[6] Sophocles T 75 *TgrF* = Ion fr. 392 *FgrH*; see von Blumenthal (1939), 11–13; and Leurini (1992), 144–8. For an excellent analysis of the significance of this passage in the history of ancient literary criticism, see Ford (2002), 190–3.

[7] *Laocoön* has been published repeatedly in English translation since Lessing (1836); for discussions of these concepts see Park (1969), Bryson (1981), p. xvi, Wendy Steiner (1982) and (1988), 1–8.

imagination painting and writing are more often allied than polarized: both were designated by the root term *graph-*; in the earliest references to inscribed marks (e.g. the murderous signs that Proteus engraved (*egrapsen*) on the tablet he sent with Bellerophontes to Lycia), it is not clear whether pictures or letters are meant.[8]

One factor in the association of tragedians with visual art must have been the convention by which actors wore beautiful painted masks (the grotesque masks of Old Comedy are a different matter). Halliwell has argued that it is to connections with painting and sculpture rather than Dionysiac rituals that we need to look for the aesthetics that shaped the experience of the tragic mask.[9] The mask was less a ritual hangover, according to this argument, than a marker of the mimetic nature of theatre. Many scholars have observed the similarities between the beautiful visages of classical Greek sculpture and those of tragic characters represented in the visual arts. Like the statues contemporary with them, the facial contours of the masks worn in tragedy seem to have been softly rounded, rather than using sharp angles and planes to represent three dimensions.[10]

Masks, however artistic in effect, were material objects made out of everyday materials, more perishable than marble, bronze, or terracotta, if not quite as impermanent as the paint that decorated them or as a theatrical performance.[11] They often came with hair attached, and may have been fixed to felt caps (it is probably to actor's equipment that Demosthenes refers when he speaks of Aeschines' skull-cap (*pilidion*) in

---

[8] *Iliad* 6.168–9; see D. Steiner (1994), 10–13. On the complementarity and equivalence of painting and sculpture, see also Webster (1939).

[9] Halliwell (1993), 201–2.

[10] I have benefited greatly from discussions of ancient masks with Chris Vervain, a theorist and practitioner of theatrical mask-making, and with David Wiles. Wiles (1991), 82, perhaps overstates the difference between the art of the mask-maker and other sculptors.

[11] In a Hellenistic epigram attributed to Callimachus, a comic actor from Rhodes by the name of Agoranax dedicates a mask in commemoration of a victory (no. 47 in Gow and Page (1965), i. 64 = *AP* 6.311). The recondite point being made about the mask in the second couplet *may* be implying that it has become dark and wrinkled with age. The character that the mask represented was named Pamphilus (a typical name in New Comedy for a youthful male romantic lead), but the mask looks like a sun-burned, dessicated fig. For this and other possible explanations of the difficult language, see Gow and Page's commentary (1965), ii. 183–5: the interpretation proposed by Wiles (1991), 103 and 113 with n. 241 seems to me more difficult to extract from the Greek.

On the False Embassy 255). The evidence for the manufacture of masks largely comes from later antiquity.[12] Most sources say that they were made of fabric rags (Suda s.v. Thespis),[13] soaked in plaster (Σ *Frogs* 406, Isidore of Seville *Origines* 10.119). Attempts by modern mask-makers to recreate examples in which it is feasible to speak, sing, and dance have shown that linen soaked in plaster (the equivalent of the 'stuccoed linen' used to make medical casts), or stiffened with glue and coated with plaster, can be moulded over what is called a former (a basic convex form of the mask, made in clay or wood, which can be moulded or carved into smooth contours); alternatively, it can be built into a negative, concave mould of the former. That these procedures would have presented little challenge to the advanced ancient techniques of casting from moulds is evidenced in the mass production of pieces in terracotta and bronze. Aristophanes' Aeschylus is almost certainly referring to this process when he says that he used the historical figure of Lamachus to provide the mould 'from which his own intellect had cast' (*hothen hēmē phrēn apomaxamenē*) the images of virtue constituted by his Patroclus and Teucer (*Frogs* 1039–40). In Plato's *Republic* a different figure of speech with the same root verb *massein* or *mattein* probably refers to mask-making.[14] Socrates is arguing that a good man would be unwilling to mimic characters inferior to himself: he 'shrinks in distaste from moulding and fitting himself into the baser types' (*ekmattein te kai enistanai eis tous tōn kakionōn tupous*, 3.396d7–e1). The word for 'types', *tupoi*, is a standard term both for former/mould and for the images cast from it; Plato's metaphors conflate the distortion of a man's real character with two processes: smearing the wet substance of which plaster casts were made (*ekmattein*) onto the positive former or into the negative former, and subsequently fitting facial features into the mask.[15]

[12] Pickard-Cambridge (1988), 191–2.

[13] See Halliwell (1993), 202 with n. 22; Webster (1995), i. 3; Marshall (1999), 188–90 with the refs. in n. 8.

[14] Slater (2002), 17, suggests that the reference to 'the rags' of the old woman's face (*tou prosōpou ta rhakē*) at Aristophanes *Wealth* 1065 'subtly plays on the fact that masks were made of painted linen', while conceding that 'it could simply be a metaphor for the ravages of age'.

[15] The verb certainly implies wiping or smearing a wet or greasy substance: Soph. *El.* 446 (wipe off stains from a head); Eur. *HF* 1400 (wipe off blood); it is often used of wiping something dry with a sponge, greasing statues, or applying an ointment to the anus (e.g. Artemidorus 2.33, 5.4).

The face painted on the dried rags-plaster laminate, once dried and removed from the mould, could vary in appearance—as Helen says in Euripides' *Helen*, you could wipe the paint off a beautiful inanimate visage and replace it with paint depicting ugly features (262–3).[16] A single former could be used repeatedly if a whole chorus needed similar masks, if one actor found a particular former produced masks that enhanced his performance, or if there was a requirement for a likeness between two individuals (see Cratinus fr. 275). A probable example occurs in Euripides' *Electra*, and is indicated by one of the rare instances in tragedy where the face compared with a manufactured image is *male* (see below). The old man is scrutinizing the disguised Orestes. Orestes asks Electra why he is doing so (559), 'as if examining the bright impress (*charaktēr*') on a silver coin. Is he finding in me a likeness to somebody else?'

Actors are likely to have encouraged their mask-makers to re-use the same 'former' when one had been developed that produced masks that were comfortable; the science of fit, when it came to moulded items of personal equipment, was advanced. In Xenophon's *Memorabilia* Socrates conducts an enquiry into what Goldhill has called 'the politics of looking',[17] in the course of which he visits a painter, a sculptor, and then an expert armourer Pistias (3.109–15). Pistias explains that his breastplates are superior because of the way that they fit (*harmottei*) the body of the man who commissions them. A well-fitting breastplate, proportioned in relation to the individual wearer, does not chafe and feels lighter to wear. It 'may almost be called an accessory (*prosthēma*) rather than an encumbrance (*phorēma*)'. Presumably the mask-makers aimed at making a mask fit the actor, and thus feel to him like an 'accessory' rather than an 'encumbrance'.

---

[16] For other metaphorical uses of the term for erasing the paint (*exaleiphein*), see D. Müller (1974), 188–9. Removing the paint and re-applying it may be the procedure underlying a (probably rather corrupt) passage in Hyperides' speech in defence of Euxenippus. Polyeuctus is said to have been ordered by Zeus of Dodona to embellish the statue of Dione, and to have made a face (or 'the face') as beautiful as possible (25). For a discussion of other possible interpretations, see Whitehead (2000), 226. Pausanias 3.16.1 reports that the daughters of a Spartan priestess of Apollo, whose names were Hilaeria and Phoebe, ornamented one of the cult statues with facial features in a style that looked too contemporary.

[17] Goldhill (1998), 111.

The visual arts become more prominent in fifth-century poetry. More than a thousand allusions to art objects have been counted in tragedy alone,[18] which also adds references to paintings, almost unknown in the earlier surviving Greek literature.[19] There are, for example, several instances of a rhetorical figure in which characters say that they have learned what they know about a particular topic from its depiction in paintings—the claim Hecuba makes about ships in *Trojan Women* (686–7), Hippolytus about sexual intercourse (*Hippolytus* 1004–5) and Ion about Erichthonios and Cecrops' daughters (*Ion* 271). This chapter explores a different phenomenon: on about twenty occasions in the extant and fragmentary tragedies characters are *compared* with works of visual art. They are said to look like a painting, a figure in a painting, or a sculpture; alternatively, they are described in metaphors that suggest such a resemblance. These comparisons were collated long ago,[20] and have attracted so much critical interest since the early 1990s that revisiting them may at first seem superfluous. But their specific relationship to the *theatrical* medium of the tragic genre in which they appear has not been comprehensively investigated. It is on the work of Segal, Zeitlin, and Steiner that this chapter therefore builds in order to derive a series of propositions from such figures.[21] First, they are in some senses the precursors of the metatheatrical tropes common in Renaissance tragic theatre. Second, the material form in which tragedy was presented allowed it to play a crucial role in the establishment of this type of imagery in the western literary canon. The comparison between an individual and an artwork became a familiar trope in later Graeco-Roman literature, for example Anacreontic poetry and the novel. In consequence, it has been a dominant conceit in western literature.[22] Yet, with a couple of revealing exceptions, it is unprecedented in pre-theatrical poetry. It was in tragic drama that it

[18] By Golder (1992), 327.

[19] See Xanthakis-Karamanos (1980), 74. Two fragments of Xenophanes may possibly suggest 'a sense that both singers and painters or sculptors provided images, at least where the gods are concerned' (Ford (2002), 98, a very perceptive discussion): Xenophanes B 15.1–2, 4 DK and 16 DK with the context where it is quoted, Clement, *Stromateis* 7.22.

[20] Kinkel (1872); Huddilston (1898).

[21] Segal (1993); Zeitlin (1994); D. Steiner (2001).

[22] See e.g. Park (1969); Wendy Steiner (1988), 1–3, 8; Frye (1976).

first proliferated, on account of theatre's *visual dimension*, in particular the masking convention, which portrayed characters precisely as painted sculptures. Third, the contexts in which these figures appear are significant: they almost all involve death, erotic allure, or the emotions of pity or terror; moreover, it is in different contexts that women and men are compared with artworks. Lastly, the figures can be read as important markers of the nature of tragic theatre—of the elements that in combination constituted its *generic difference* from other literature, even other drama.[23]

'METATHEATRE'

The first proposition requires a brief excursus into the difference between Greek tragic and Renaissance theatrical self-consciousness. An important non-equivalence between the imagery of Greek tragedy and of Renaissance theatre is instantiated in Cassius' command to his fellow-conspirators to wash themselves in Caesar's blood:

> How many ages hence
> Shall this our lofty scene be acted over
> In states unborn and accents yet unknown?
>
> (*Julius Caesar* iii.i.111–13)

As Homan puts it, 'these Romans anticipate a Globe audience in 1599 watching a stage representation of their deed'.[24] In Renaissance and Jacobean drama, an obvious form such self-consciousness takes is the explicit comparison of the world to a stage, and people to actors in the drama of life: the motto of the Globe Theatre itself was 'all the world plays the part of an actor' (*totus mundus agit histrionem*).[25] The most

---

[23] The absence of generic distinctions between the way artwork analogies are handled in theatre and in other media is my only ground of complaint in reference to Deborah Steiner's brilliant study of statues in archaic and classical Greek literature (2001); I wholly concur with her elegant formulation (p. 120), that poets, historians, and philosophers all used the statue 'as a vehicle for focusing an audience's thoughts on the divergent relationship between visible appearance and internal reality'.

[24] Homan (1981), 11–12.

[25] Chambers (1930), ii. 278.

famous example is Jacques's account of the human life cycle in *As You Like It*, beginning (II.vii.139–43),

> All the world's a stage,
> And all the men and women merely players;
> They have their exits and their entrances,
> And one man in his time plays many parts,
> His acts being seven ages.

Yet the trope was given its most metaphysical formulation by Pedro Calderón in *El Gran Teatro del Mundi* (*c.*1648), a sacramental drama in which God himself is not only demiurge but dramaturge; as author, he creates the world, and declares that mortals are to enter as his actors until they make their exits 'by a tomb'.[26]

The ancient sources for such comparisons are Cynic and Stoic philosophy, above all Ciceronian and Senecan prose, rather than Greek or even Senecan tragedy.[27] As Anne Righter argued in a neglected study of the play metaphor, the image of the *world* as a stage 'was associated almost entirely with non-dramatic literature'.[28] What made possible the elaboration of the world-stage equation in the *drama* of the Renaissance was a unique moment at which discrete traditions collided: the ancient philosophical habit of figuring the world as a stage met the explicit discussion of the nature of enactment that had been developed in the secular Morality plays of the late fifteenth and early sixteenth centuries.[29] It is also to ancient Roman *discussion* of theatre that allusions to individual named actors must be traced, for example King Henry's comparison of himself, when under threat of assassination, with the Republican Roman actor Roscius: 'what scene of death hath Roscius now to act?' (*King Henry VI* Part III.v.vi).[30] There are also references to the creation

[26] Postlewait and Davis (2003), 9.

[27] See C. Edwards (2002), esp. 378–9; Postlewait and Davis (2003), 8–11. There is a comparison of the world with a stage and life with a performance found in the collection of sayings under the name 'Democrates' in Stobaeus' anthology; but its attribution to the presocratic Democritus by Diels and Kranz (68 B 115) was incorrect. For a fascinating Senecan exception see below, pp. 110–11.

[28] See Righter (1962), 65.

[29] Righter (1962), 23–65.

[30] On references to Roscius in English literature, and their Roman sources, see Garton (1972), 203–29; E. Hall (2002*b*), 420–1.

of a theatrical illusion within the Shakespearean playhouse: the chorus delivering the prologue to *Henry V* talks of the spirits who have dared to bring forth such important scenes as Agincourt 'on this unworthy scaffold', 'this cockpit' and 'this wooden O'. Such open references to the stage building may find parallels in Greek Old Comedy, above all in *Peace* (see Ch. 11). But it is inconceivable under the terms of the cognitive contract between Greek tragic author, actor, and audience.

Numerous plays are acted within plays in the drama of Shakespeare and his contemporaries, from *The Revenger's Tragedy* and *Hamlet* through to Philip Massinger's Jacobean *The Roman Actor*, but the ancient sources implicated in these elaborate scenes are biographers and historiographers—Plutarch, Dio Cassius, and Suetonius. When Hamlet discusses what Hecuba might mean to Claudius after the players have performed at the court (ii.ii), he is not thinking about Euripides' *Hecuba* even in its Erasmian translation. His source is, rather, an anecdote he had found in Sir Thomas North's English translation of Jacques Amyot's French translation of Plutarch's *Life of Pelopidas*; it concerned the ancient actor Theodorus, whose emotive performance in *Trojan Women* had made a vicious tyrant weep.[31]

For information on the fashionable topic of metatheatre, students are currently sent down a bibliographical path that began with the concepts elaborated in Righter's foundational *Shakespeare and the Idea of the Play* in 1962, and which entered mainstream discussion when shortly thereafter labelled 'Metatheatre' by Abel.[32] But the canonical study remains Hornby's *Drama, Metadrama, and Perception* (1986), which slices through the morass of alleged instances by distinguishing five essential categories: plays within plays, generic self-reference, performed rituals, role playing within roles, and self-conscious intertextual allusion.[33] While in Greek tragedy there are manifold examples of the performance of ritual, some of overt role-playing within roles (e.g. when characters appear in disguise), and a few of indisputable intertextual allusion, the two primary types of

[31] See E. Hall (2002*b*), 423; Plutarch, *Life of Pelopidas* 29.4–6.
[32] Righter (1962), esp. ch. 3; the term 'metatheatre' seems to have been invented by Abel (1963). See Hornby (1986). Slater (2002), 1–21 is a sensible, brief survey of 'metatheatre' scholarship as it has developed in relation to Aristophanes.
[33] Hornby (1986), 32–5.

metatheatre—plays within plays and overt generic self-reference—do not occur. Taplin was correct in identifying ancient Greek tragedy's lack of overt self-referentiality as one of its definitive differences from Old Comedy.[34] More recently, Easterling has cautioned that the quest for 'self-consciousness' is only useful insofar as it elucidates the serious and dangerous issues which are really at stake in tragedy.[35] Yet there has been a recent tendency in discussion of Athenian tragedy to use both the term 'self-consciousness' and 'metatheatre' (with its cognates) far too imprecisely.[36]

No terminology which is exclusive to *theatrical* literature, poetry, or performance conventions appears in Greek tragedy. Terms for dramatic genres are never used: tragedy is not named, nor comedy, nor satyric drama. Nor are there found in tragedy the words for dramatic actor—*tragōidos, kōmōidos, hupokritēs*. The word for theatre (*theatron*) does not appear, nor the theatrically specific technical terms that are found in Old Comedy referring to props, stage machinery, orchestra, entrance routes, and even rows of audience benches.[37] The word by the fourth century used for stage (*skēnē*) means, in extant tragedy, a tent in a military encampment or at a religious festival, or a curtained caravan on wheels (Eur. *Hec.* 1289, *Ion* 808; Aesch. *Pers.* 1000). The word for 'face' (*prosōpon*), which

---

[34] Taplin (1986).

[35] She shows how *Philoctetes* uses its status as theatre to underline its exploration of deceit, but what 'is important here is that the ironic play with the dramatic medium is intimately related to the central issues'; 'in the end the most important point must be that the plays were about real issues' (Easterling (1997c), 170, 172).

[36] Taplin (1996) himself modified his earlier position, preferring to talk in terms of the degrees of intensity and explicitness of self-referentiality rather than of its presence or absence (p. 189). But the wider and vaguer the definition of 'metatheatre', the less useful it becomes as an analytical tool: see e.g. Bierl (1990), whose otherwise excellent study of *PKöln* VI 242 A = *TgrF* fr. 646a adesp. is compromised by his reluctance to define what he means by 'metatheatrical'; Ringer (1998), 7, for whom both metatheatre or metadrama mean 'drama within drama as well as drama about drama' (it would be very difficult to deduce from Ringer's introduction that there was actually no explicitly and exclusively theatrical vocabulary in Sophocles); similarly, see M. Puchner (2003), 133–5. Gellrich (2002) is, however, a very subtle analysis of a certain type of self-consciousness in Euripides' *Medea*; her study is partly so effective because she consciously reflects on the *differences* between Greek tragic and Renaissance theatrical self-consciousness (see especially p. 326). There are some intelligent remarks on this topic in relation to New Comedy in Gutzwiller (2000).

[37] See the examples collected in Slater (2002), 15–20.

certainly by the fourth century can also mean 'mask' or *'dramatis persona'*, is perhaps the best candidate for the bearing of explicit metatheatrical meaning, above all in *Bacchae*. Here the ambiguity of the term *may* have been exploited by Euripides if Pentheus' character mask was indeed used to represent his decapitated head in the Agave scene: at 1277 Cadmus asks her, 'And whose face (*prosōpon*) are you carrying in your arms, then?'[38] But the term never exclusively means 'mask', let alone 'theatrical mask', in extant Greek tragedy. The moment where arguably the material presence of the actor's mask is with most force brought to the audience's conscious attention does not involve the word *prosōpon* at all, but rather the notion of paint overlaid on a three-dimensional, sculptural image: in *Helen,* the loveliest woman in the world, desired by Menelaus, Paris, and now Theoclymenus, blames her suffering on her beauty. She wishes that, as on a statue, the paint which made her lovely could be obliterated, and replaced by ugly features (262–3).

The exception may come in satyric drama, which was indeed part of the tragic production in the fifth century and some of the fourth.[39] In Aeschylus' *Theoroi* the satyrs dedicate 'likenesses' of themselves (*eikous*) in the temple of Poseidon Isthmios; the portraits may be by Daedalus himself, are painted (*kalligrapton*), and said to reproduce the satyrs' features exactly (fr. 78a.6–17 *TgrF*). These images may have been painted sculptures representing satyr masks, of the kind that were sometimes used as antefixes and placed along the cornices of temples.[40] They are likely to have resembled the theatrical masks worn by the satyrs, and thus to have drawn closer attention to the masking convention than any surviving passage in tragedy.[41] But appreciating the remoteness and elevation of the heroic world which the dramatists sought to create in their tragic plays involves

[38] Foley (1985), 251–2; see D. Steiner (2001), 177 and n. 168.
[39] *IG* II^2 2319–23. The implications of the detachment of the satyr play are well brought out in Easterling (1997*d*), 214–16; see also below, Ch. 4 *passim.*
[40] Lloyd-Jones (1983), 543; Fraenkel (1942), 244. For further references and bibliography see Krumeich, Pechstein, and Seidensticker (1999), 135.
[41] Sophocles seems to have written a satyr drama, perhaps called *Talos*, in which Daedalus' gigantic bronze robot, familiar from Apollonius' *Argonautica* (4.1638–88), may have been executed by Medea: see Krumeich, Pechstein, and Seidensticker (1999), 389–90. Another satyr-drama, Euripides' *Eurystheus*, included a discussion of Daedalus' marvellous lifelike *agalmata* ((25) Eur. fr. 372 *TgrF*).

acknowledging their generic *avoidance* of overt reference to the theatre, whether as a social institution, a physical location, a material presence, or an aesthetic experience. This avoidance must result in part from a desire to avoid anachronism—the playwrights, aware of the relative newness of their medium, were staging the heroic world portrayed in epic and archaic lyric narrative, which know nothing of theatre.[42] But if the tragedians had wanted to discuss explicitly the role that the heroic stories they dramatized would one day play in the theatre, they could have found ways to do so: in the final act of *Antony and Cleopatra* the Egyptian queen fears that one day she and Antony will be staged by 'quick comedians', who

> Extemporally will stage us and present
> Our Alexandrian revels. Antony
> Shall be brought forth, and I shall see
> Some squeaking Cleopatra boy my greatness
> I' th' posture of a whore.   (v.ii)

There was no formal impediment preventing a Greek tragedian from making, for example, a god predict that one day the story being acted would end up in a drama. Indeed, at the end of *Hippolytus*, Artemis comes within an inch of so doing, but stops short of mentioning future theatrical realizations in favour of what is apparently choral lyric—the 'muse-inspired' songs she plans that Hippolytus will receive from maidens (*parthenōn*, 1428–9).[43]

The Greek tragedians' avoidance of overt metatheatre can be appreciated by comparing a scene in Euripides' *Hecuba* with a similar one, partly dependent upon it, in the Senecan *Troades*. In *Hecuba* the herald Talthybius describes Polyxena's defiant arrival at the sacrificial venue (558–61): 'Taking hold of her gown, she tore it from her shoulders to her waist beside the navel, and showed her breasts and her torso, most beautiful, like those of a statue' (*hōs agalmatos*). At the moment of her death, both internal and external audiences are

---

[42] See Easterling (1985), 6, who rightly stresses that the avoidance of modern-sounding theatrical vocabulary was connected with the playwrights' desire to preserve the dignity and solemnity of their artistic mode.

[43] For an interpretation of the *Oresteia*'s references to dance and music as providing an implicit aetiology for the tragic *choros*, see Taplin and Wilson (1993).

asked to think of Polyxena as a beautiful artwork, but not explicitly as a *theatrical* one. In contrast, when the Senecan messenger is setting the scene for his description of the sacrifice of Polyxena, which follows the death of Astyanax, he reports:

When the boy fell headlong from the lofty walls and the Greek crowd had wept for the wickedness it had committed, the same people turned back to another wicked act and the tomb of Achilles. The Rhotean waters beat on its far side with gentle breakers; a plain fringes the near side, and a valley grows, rising with an easy slope and enclosing a central space, *like a theatre* (*clivo levi | erecta medium vallis includens locum | crescit theatri more*). The numerous throng filled the whole shore... (1120–6).[44]

Polyxena enters the scene, and although her face 'glows' and her beauty emanates brilliance (*fulget genae, | magisque solito splendet extremus decor*, 1137–8), she is not likened to an *agalma* as she was in the equivalent narrative in Euripides. Instead, the simile, by which we are invited to view her as entering a space 'like a theatre', is verging on explicit metatheatre.[45]

GREEK TRAGEDY AS VISUAL MEDIUM

Greek tragedy found ways to evade its own proscription on theatrical terminology. One was to discuss dancing (*choros, choreuein*), as the self-referential chorus of *OT* examines the role its dancing plays in cult.[46] Another was to talk, like Artemis in *Hippolytus*, about *songs* and *singers*, using such lexical items as *molpai, humnoi*, and *aoidoi*, or their cognate verbs; so the chorus of Euripides' *Ion* discuss, for example, the male domination of the poetic representation of women (1090–8).[47] There is, nevertheless, little in such passages to

[44] Translated by Fantham (1982).

[45] Fantham (1982), comment on 1121–5, compares the natural (amphi)theatre for the Sicilian games in the *Aeneid* (5.288), '*mediaque in valle theatri | circus erat*'. She and other critics regard the greatest change as making Polyxena silent, and have not been particularly struck by the transformation of the analogy with a statue into an analogy with a theatre. As late as Quintus of Smyrna's epic version of the fall of Troy, Polyxena is still an artefact; her tear-drops glisten on flesh 'like costly ivory' (14.270–1).

[46] For discussions in Euripides of song, see especially Peter Wilson (1999–2000).

[47] Henrichs (1994–5).

demarcate theatrical poetry from epic or archaic lyric. Indeed, the
tragedians went out of their way to avoid even using the words 'poet',
'poetry', and 'compose a poem' (*poiētēs, poiēsis, poiein*) which, certainly by Herodotus' day, were the standard terms in prose and
comedy for composing verse.[48] Another possibility, this chapter
contends, was to talk about visual perception *through discussion of
the visual arts.* In one passage of Euripides' *Hippolytus* these two types
of self-reference are strikingly conjoined. The nurse argues along
vaguely Empedoclean lines that Cypris is a positive force in the
universe. She cites Zeus and Eos, libidinous divine role models
whom students of visual arts and poetry would recognize (451–6).[49]
Here the analogy between paintings and poems is explicit; they are
two parallel sources of knowledge about dangerous liaisons in myth.[50]

In functional terms, artwork tropes in tragedy fall into two categories: those that construe as artworks a character who is physically
present, and those which operate by creating an image of a character
as an artwork in the audience's mind's eye (Polyxena in *Hecuba*). With
the exception of the way that Orestes is construed in Euripides' *Electra*
as an image printed on a coin (see above), all those that encourage the
audience to think of a character visibly present before them are in
reference to females. The earliest occurs in Aeschylus' *Suppliant
Women*, when the Argive King Pelasgus gazes at the fifty Egyptian

[48] See the excellent discussion of Ford (2002), 132–8. He points out that there is
one exception, the much-quoted fragment of Euripides' *Stheneboea* (61 fr. 663 *TgrF*),
'Eros teaches anyone to be a poet, even if he had not previously cultivated the Muses'.
Euripides also occasionally uses *-poios* in compound adjectives such as
mousopoios (*Tro.* 1188–9), and *humnopoios* (*Suppl.* 180–1).
[49] For poetic opinions in the mouth of another nurse, see Eur. *Med.* 199–200. The
winged and therefore decidedly super-human Eos is, in fact, the only female pursuer
of young men (Tithonus and Cephalus) who appears in classical art: see the fascinating discussion of the reasons for her singularity in R. Osborne (1996), 67 and 78 n.
14, with Weiss (1986), esp. section III.
[50] Barrett (1964), 242, argues that *graphai* here does not refer to pictures because
of the adjective *palaiterōn*: 'What old paintings would there be in a private house in
Euripides's day? (we must think presumably chiefly of vase-paintings; and of these
wear and tear, if not taste as well, would have little but contemporary red-figure)'. But
there were numerous visual images of love affairs between gods and mortals with
which Euripides' audience could have been familiar (see above n. 49). The requirement that they be either old or exclusive to private houses seems superfluous. Yet
Barrett's note is cited by those who want these *graphai* to be examples of writing
rather than painting (e.g. Ford (2002), 154 and n. 90).

maidens encamped in a precinct. His words direct the audience to join him in viewing the theatrical masks representing the beautiful black faces of these visitors. They look, says Pelasgus, more like Libyan or Egyptian women than like Argive women: a Cyprian impress (*charaktēr*) distinguishes them, 'like that which has been stamped on female forms (*en gunaikeois tupois | peplēktai*) by craftsmen' (282–3). Pelasgus' metaphor may be drawn from casting from moulds, including plaster masks. Or it could primarily have brought to mind the hammering of bronze plates over a three-dimensional wooden former so that the flexible metal surface takes on the underlying shape.[51] It could be a direct reference to a recognizable type of statue of Aphrodite, or of statue type associated with Cyprus.[52] Or it may designate the striking of coins from dies with Aphrodite's image upon them.[53] But whatever the exact meaning of the 'Cyprian impress', the young women, marked by similarity to Aphrodite, are metaphorically construed as artworks with erotic appeal.[54] Their beautiful faces, depicted by masks, are brought to the forefront of the audience's consciousness, a phenomenon closely mirrored in Euripides' *Phoenician Women* more than half a century later. Here, again, the chorus consists of barbarian women, exotic in their behaviour (they perform prostration before Polynices, 293) and presumably in the appearance of their masks and clothing. They have arrived in Greece to serve as hierodules at Delphi, and invite the audience to see them as the equivalents of votary statues in a precinct (220–1): 'like gold-wrought *agalmata* I am in the service of Phoebus.'[55]

Such metaphorical language is linked to casting from moulds and painting—technologies also central to the production of masks for

[51] Kranz (1933), 73; Marenghi (1959), 320–1.

[52] Kranz (1933), 73.

[53] See Johansen and Whittle (1980), ii. 223. For the technological process, e.g. Carradice (1995), 11–14.

[54] When Pollux discusses the typical mask of the stage *korē*, worn by young female characters, he gives as an example the sort of mask 'a Danaid would wear or another girl' (*paidiskē*, 4.141).

[55] At first sight this phrase looks similar to Euripides' *Autolycus* (15/16) fr. 282.10–11 *TgrF*, where young athletes are said to be 'brilliant in their youth' and 'ornaments' to their city (*lamprōi d' en hēbēi kai poleōs agalmata | phoitōs'*). But these metaphorical *agalmata* are not concretized by being associated with gold; moreover, the rhetoric of the situation raises the question whether such parasitical members of the polis represent any kind of asset at all.

theatrical performances. The linguistic metaphors of the visual image, the impression like a goddess on statue or coin, are uttered through mouths scarcely visible through apertures in artificial faces that have been moulded and painted like the faces on statues. Technology and ephemeral matter have thus left their everlasting traces on the frail semblance of the total theatrical performance we have inherited in printed books. Rags, plaster, and paint transmute into similes crafted in poetic verse. For the tragic mask is the most potent symbol of the mimetic nature of tragedy, whatever its other functions.[56] Such metaphors are also culturally specific in another sense; they are symptomatic of the aesthetic training undergone by the Athenian. In an influential article Zeitlin argued that it was the Athenian theatre which raised the topic of the partnership between the representational modes of drama and the visual arts to prominence; the development of the figurative arts themselves in the fifth century was virtually coextensive with the evolution of drama. The theatregoer was trained in a stylized mode of viewing which not only aroused his affective responses, but also engaged his cognitive skills in evaluating and interpreting the 'visual codes' of what he saw.[57] Theories of art and cognition were stimulated; Democritus wrote a treatise on painting (*peri zōgraphias*, 68 A 33 DK), and Hippias's discussions included both painting and statue-making (*peri zōgraphias kai peri algalmatopoiïas*, 86 A 2 DK).[58]

Yet Pelasgus' reaction to the Danaids, composed as early as the 460s, indicates that even pre-sophistic tragedies could display their own affinity, as performed *spectacles*, with the visual arts. Tragedy was aurally innovative in its introduction to Greek poetry of the

[56] These of course include estrangement, the masking of actors' gender, age and unattractiveness, the demarcation of the boundary between the real and the unreal, between life stages, and between life and death. Amongst the large bibliography on these interpretations, the most influential items recently include e.g. the ritualist trajectory of the essays collected in Vernant and Vidal-Naquet (1988), on which see E. Hall (1990); the structuralist semiotics of Calame (1986); the analysis of the depiction in vase-painting of theatrical masks in contexts other than within scenes from drama by J. R. Green (1995*b*); the expert theoretical summary of Wiles (2000), 147–53.

[57] Zeitlin (1994), 140–1.

[58] On Democritus' treatise see Lanata (1963). Other treatises on the visual arts which some ancient sources ascribed to the 5th cent. include Polycleitus' *Canon* (on sculpture) and Agatharchus' study of perspective (*skēnographia*); see Pollitt (1974), 14–22.

dochmiac metre and its synthesis of contrasting genres in variegated metres.[59] But one of its most revolutionary features was that it offered audiences visual representation *simultaneously* with poetry. Dramatic poetry was the earliest artistic medium which not only made its poetry visual but also gave voice to its pictures—painted sculptures worn by men. The poetry composed for them was radically affected by the introduction of this new visual dimension: in Sophocles' lost *Tereus* the raped Philomela, whose tongue had been pulled out, communicated with her sister Procne by means of a woven textile called a 'patterned gown' (*poikilon pharos*, fr. 586 *TgrF*). Although *Tereus* survives only in meagre fragments, its recognition device clearly made an impact. A papyrus which contains what is almost certainly the hypothesis states that when Philomela 'was unable to speak her misfortune, she revealed it by a piece of weaving' (*di' hupho*[*us*], *POxy* 3013); Aristotle's views on tragic recognition included, moreover, a reaction to the ruse he calls 'the voice of the shuttle' (*Poet.* 1454^{b}30 = Sophocles fr. 595 *TgrF*).[60]

MASK AND INTERTEXT

One of the most complicated moments of overt metatheatre in Shakespearean drama is when Julia in *The Two Gentlemen of Verona* (a boy actor playing a girl currently in disguise as a boy) invents the story of a pageant in which s/he had acted the 'lamentable part' of Ariadne, 'passioning | For Theseus's perjury and unjust flight' (iv.iv). Indeed, s/he acted the part 'so lively' that she had forth tears in her

---

[59] E. Hall (2002*a*), 8; below, Ch. 10, pp. 299–301.

[60] The suggestion that the recognition was produced by means of an ekphrasis, dramatized by Procne's reading (on-stage or reported) of pictures or writing woven into the *pharos* by her sister, may perhaps be supported by the prominence of the ekphrasis in later versions of the story. In Ovid, *Met.* 6.576–86, Philomela weaves purple signs into the white background of her 'barbaric' web; the robe with pictures woven in is itself depicted within a painting described and interpreted in Achilles Tatius' *Leucippe & Clitophon* 5.3 and 5.5. Sophocles' ingenious device also suggests that the assumption that Sophocles was not interested in the connection (see e.g. Huddilston (1898), 3) results from the unrepresentative nature of the surviving evidence. In *Trackers* Silenus calls the satyrs, terrified into inaction by the noise of the lyre, 'damnable figures moulded from wax' (fr. 314.146 *TgrF*); see also Sophocles fr. 35 *TgrF.*

mistress Julia (i.e. in herself). The reference may have nudged the
Shakespearean audience into recalling some actual piece about Theseus and Ariadne which they had previously seen enacted. And this
passage reminds *us* that the audience of Greek tragedy may often
have been reminded of previous tragic performances, and not only by
verbal echoes.[61] Shakespeare's Julia raises the possibility that some
references to works of visual art may be more specific than it is now
possible to prove. Athenian tragedy may sometimes have alluded, as
comedy did, to statues and paintings familiar to the audience, and
indeed not far away from the theatre: in *Lysistrata* the chorus of old
men liken themselves to the famous statue of the tyrannicides, and
the women to Micon's Amazons (633–4, 678–9).[62] A reference to
painted figures could, moreover, be the theatrical equivalent of an
inter-textual reference: it could refer to a previous *performance*.

In Aeschylus' *Eumenides* the Pythian priestess is describing the
repellant appearance of the supernatural creatures who have occupied
her shrine. They are not women, she says, 'but Gorgons; | nor indeed
shall I compare them to images (*tupoi*) of Gorgons|...|once before
now I saw some painted female creatures | carrying off Phineus's meal'
(*eidon pot' ēdē Phineōs gegrammenas | deipnon pherousas* 48–51).
Athough there may be a missing line here, it is clear that the Pythia's
memory provides her with images of sculpted gorgons,[63] and then of
painted harpies. In the cultural encyclopedia of her audience there
were certainly various harpy images, for example on the Kypselos
chest (Paus. 5.7.11), on Apollo's throne at Amyklai (Paus. 3.8.15), and
in archaic vase-painting.[64] But there are several vases portraying
harpies dating from around 470, include a fascinating red-figure
amphora in London (E 302 = ARV^2 652.2; see fig. 4.1); here not

---

[61] Examples of indisputable verbal references to previous plays include Eur. *El.*
524–37, which must be commenting on Aesch. *Choeph.* 164–210, and Eur. *Phoen.*
1090–140, which bears a relation to Aesch. *Septem* 422–652.

[62] See also *Ach.* 991–2 with scholion (Zeuxis's 'Aphrodite and Eros'); *Birds* 670
(Pheidias' Athena Parthenos); *Thesm.* 940, with Austin and Olson (2004), 298 (a jibe
at the Athenian painter Pauson). For a possible reference in *Peace* to Polygnotus'
painting of the sack of Troy, see below, Ch. 11, pp. 346–7.

[63] On this and other references in tragedy to the terrifying impact of carved
gorgons, see D. Steiner (2001), 176.

[64] e.g. a 6th-cent. black-figure amphora in the British Museum (BM 1894.
11–1.161), and a Hydria in the Getty Museum (85 AE 316). See Kahil (1988).

FIG. 4.1   Phineus and a Harpy on an Attic red-figured neck-amphora by the Nikon painter, 470–450 BC

only is Phineus presented wearing what is almost certainly a mask (there is a discernible line connecting beard to ear), but beneath the harpy wings are youths, labelled *kalos* by the painter, which could 'refer to the young men who play the parts'.[65] This vase-painting, along with others of similar date, is likely to be connected with the painted harpies of another kind who had appeared in a previous tragedy by Aeschylus, his *Phineus*, performed in 472 as the first play in the prizewinning group comprising *Phineus, Persians, Glaukos Potnieus*, and a satyric *Prometheus*.[66]

In *Phineus*, the harpy incident seems to have been an important focus. In three of the four fragments of the play, the harpies and the

---

[65] Trendall and Webster (1971), pl. III.1, 25.
[66] Kahil (1988), 449; Kahil (1994), 388; E. Hall (1996a), 10–11.

stolen meals provide the subject-matter. One reports 'and many a deceitful meal with greedy jaws did they snatch away amid the first delight of appetite' (fr. 258 *TgrF*); a second that 'hungry wailing does not stand aloof', and a third refers to seizing with hands (258a, 259a). The fourth, which concerns footwear, may well refer to the Boreads who pursued the harpies (fr. 259). Harpy roles would be consonant with Aeschylus' ancient reputation for having been the first to stage 'terrifying masks painted with colours' (*prosōpeia deina chrōmasi kechrismena*, Aeschylus T 2 *TgrF* = Suda s.v. αι 357). The terrifying masks worn by the Erinyes that the audience were about to glimpse, when the Pythia compared them with painted harpies, may therefore have resembled those which Aeschylus' harpies had worn fourteen years previously, in his *Phineus*. An allusion to works of visual art may well 'mask' a specific inter-performative reference.[67]

THE AESTHETICS OF TRAGIC THEATRE

Artwork analogies also offered the potential for abstract meditation on specifically theatrical aesthetics. In a discussion of a passage in Euripides' *Hecuba* (see further below), Segal saw that an artwork comparison in which a painter beholds 'at a distance a scene of suffering can also suggest the mixture of pain and pleasure *of the tragic spectacle as a whole*'.[68] Segal thus identified, fleetingly, the special impact of this artwork analogy as saying something important about the visual dimension not just of theatre in general (which would include comedy), nor of tragic drama (which would include the possibility of reading the text rather than witnessing it in performance), but exclusively of *tragic theatre*. The reason why this is so significant is that there were few advanced literary critical concepts with which to analyse tragedy available during most of the fifth

---

[67] For some examples of the way that later tragedies visually reminded their audiences of earlier tragic spectacles, see Easterling (1997c), 168–9 (on the relationship between the recognition scene in *Libation-Bearers* and its counterparts in the *Electra* plays of Euripides and Sophocles).

[68] Segal (1993), 178 (my emphasis).

century BC. Although the Aristophanic phenomenon of paratragedy eventually enabled the Athenian audience to reflect on some of the stylistic and visual effects peculiar to tragedy,[69] the emergence of an awareness of what it might be as a generic entity emerges late. An influential article by Most argues that tragedy received the 'poetological prerogative' of being theorized earlier than any other genre.[70] He is correct when it comes to Plato, but there is little developed intellectual analysis of the tragic in the fifth century,[71] certainly according to the analytical, tonal, and qualitative aesthetic criteria which emerged in the fourth.[72]

This is not to say that the earliest theatre did not make an extraordinary impression. Indeed, from the perspective of the early twenty-first century, the actor's assumption of another identity is so much a part of our cultural environment that it can be difficult to recreate the enormity of its original impact, just as the soaking of our own third-millennial culture in celluloid, videotape and digital images means that we will never experience the excitement felt by the earliest cinema audiences. The Greek tragic actor or chorus member superimposed upon his own features a mask depicting another individual, and impersonated that individual's speech and movement. In numerous roles this entailed shedding a masculine identity and substituting a female one. The actors' physical assumption of the

---

[69] Silk (1993).　　[70] Most (2000), 18–19.

[71] The candidates are (i) Sophocles in his apocryphal treatise on the chorus (attested only by the *Suda*): Ford (2002), 189, remarks, 'there is not a trace of any critical idea it may have contained' anywhere in later literature, and (ii) Gorgias' *Encomium of Helen*. This involves nothing which could not apply to the effect of Homeric epic; its points of contact with the Helen scene in Euripides' *Trojan Women* are the persuasive force of verbal rhetoric and physical beauty (8–19), rather than anything exclusive to theatre. Moreover, Ford argues that, far from an embryonic model of tragedy, Gorgias' *Helen* develops a scientific understanding of language which synthesises the perspectives of natural philosophy, including Democritean materialism and Anaxagorean theory of Mind (Ford (2002), 176–80). Although Gorgias did famously say that tragedy entails deceit (82 B 23 DK), a superior witness in Most's defence would be the anonymous author of the somewhat later *Dissoi Logoi*, who draws a parallel between the fictive power of painting and tragedy (90 B 3.10 DK, 'In composing tragedy and in painting, he is best who deceives by making things most resemble the truth'). For the emergence of a theory of the Tragic in the 4th cent., and the developments in performance context which made it possible, see further E. Hall (forthcoming *a* and *b*).

[72] Nightingale (1995), 193–5 argues that it took Plato's agonistic conception of the relationship between discourses to elicit embryonic notions of genre.

personae of women was a practice that probably sent shockwaves through early Athenian audiences. Indeed, despite the speculations surrounding the appearance of maenads in the vase-painting of Peisistratus' times, there is little reason to suppose that the preponderance of female characters and choruses in the extant tragedies was even a traditional and aboriginal feature of the genre.[73] The notice under the name of Phrynichus in the *Suda* (φ 762) claims that he was the first tragedian to introduce a female *prosōpon* into tragedy (= 3 *TgrF* T1). Phrynichus had certainly made use of both female characters and choruses, since the titles of his plays include an *Alcestis* as well as a *Phoenician Women*. But the titles attributed to Thespis, the only tragedian certainly known to have been working before Phrynichus, are *Funeral Games of Pelias*, *Priests*, and *Pentheus*, none of which requires us to imagine a female character or even chorus, since even encounters with maenads do not have to be enacted visibly: they could conceivably be reported (as they are in Euripides' *Bacchae*) and lamented by men. Tragedy, then, far from being a genre *ab initio* preoccupied with the feminine, may have evolved into this, even as late as Phrynichus' heyday in the first third of the fifth century. Watching actors impersonate females, with the concomitant phenomenon of the sculpted female mask, may still have been recent developments in Aeschylus' early manhood.

In Athenian tragic theatre the tragedian is often a male 'maker' (*poiētēs*) of women to be viewed by men. The conflation of the craftsman and the poet was becoming standard by the early fifth century: it is already apparent in Aeschylus' older contemporary Pindar, who called epic poets 'wise craftsmen' (*tektones sophoi*, *Pyth.* 3.113). In a striking figure constructing himself as a sculptor, Pindar suggests that he set up a 'monument whiter than Parian marble' for Callicles, by singing in his honour (*Nem.* 4.81).[74] The seminal and specific role of *drama* in altering Greek views on the nature of poetic activity, by elevating *technē* in the concepts of the poet and poetry over the role of inspiration, has recently

[73] Carpenter (1986), 90; Seaford (1994), 270–4; for a wide-ranging discussion of ritual transvestism in Dionysiac worship, see Csapo (1997), 261–4. But explanations of the nature of tragedy that lie in its synchronic *function* rather than its occluded diachronic *origins* are almost invariably to be preferred.

[74] See the fine discussion of D. Steiner (2001), 148–9.

been stressed by Finkelberg.[75] The epic singer, the *aoidos*, became a *poiētēs*, and inspiration was replaced by skill.

The poet, moreover, created poetry that another skilled individual, the actor, needed to memorize rather than improvise: relative to rhapsodic or rhetorical performances, at any rate, tragic poetry was decidedly unspontaneous. According to some later Greeks (e.g. Dio Chrysostom, *Or.* 19.5), this was one of the most important differences between the delivery of poetry and of oratory.[76] It is suggestive to find memorized speech being likened to a lovely artwork by the early fourth century: Gorgias' pupil Alcidamas argued that the distinction between extempore speech and memorized scripts is analogous to the difference between real human bodies and beautiful statues. Extempore speech and real bodies are plain, but potent and versatile. Statues, however lovely, are like the predetermined word, which can only ever offer 'an image of speech' (*De Soph.* 27–8).[77] From this perspective, the function of the artwork analogy goes beyond drawing attention to the visual dimension of theatre: it actually contributes to the process by which tragedy reveals its own understanding of itself as consisting of moving statues which reproduce previously crafted poetic *speech*. As Feeney has put it, responding to any kind of fiction requires a hermeneutic 'duality'; a bifurcated response offers 'one way of trying to come to terms with the apprehension that art is something crafted *and* emotionally compelling or immediate. Even the most enthralling documents of mimetic art may call attention to their own crafted status.'[78] When a Greek tragedian introduces a comparison with a work of visual art, the apprehension of the highly wrought nature of the poetry, as well as the masks, is heightened in the audience's consciousness. But another aim of these analogies was to heighten the emotional impact of the immediate theatrical moment. This emerges from an analysis of the psychological and emotional situations in which they occur: sex, death, pity, and fear.

---

[75] Finkelberg (1998), 176–7.   [76] E. Hall (2002*a*), 17–18.

[77] Ford (2002), 234–5 n. 14, discusses the possibility that it was the rhetorical doctrines of Theramenes, perhaps parodied at *Frogs* 536, that lie behind Alcidamas' notions of the contrast between dynamic extemporization and static recitation from memory.

[78] Feeney (1993), 238. Feeney was himself discussing the theory of 'duality' proposed in connection with fiction by Newsom (see e.g. Newsom (1994)).

SEX AND DEATH

In Menander's *Dyskolos*, Sostratos describes how difficult it was for him not to kiss Cnemon's daughter during the attempt to rescue her father from the well into which he had fallen (686–9). Sostratos is in love. The audience has previously learned that the maiden is distressed, fearful that her 'beloved papa' (648) will die; now her suitor recalls that she 'was tearing her hair, weeping, and vehemently beating her breast'—in fact, behaving exactly like a woman in a tragedy (673–4).[79] Sostratos reports how this vision of distressed loveliness transfixed him, and his language reinforces the comparison with a scene from a tragedy in which an aristocratic woman bewails her lot in the presence of her old attendant (675–8): he stood 'near her, just like a nurse' (*trophos*), supplicated her repeatedly (*hiketeuon*), 'and gazed on that exquisite statue' (*emblepōn agalmati | ou tōi tuchonti*). A young man in love gazes upon a young woman reacting like a Greek tragic heroine to a potentially lethal situation; what more conventionally suitable moment could there be for a comparison with an artwork?

It has often been remarked that several artwork analogies in the tragic corpus imply an erotic element in the gaze directed at the woman, for example the figure of Andromeda, chained to her rock, as perceived by her husband-to-be Perseus when he flew into Ethiopia in Euripides' *Andromeda* (fr. 125 *TgrF*): 'Well, what hill is this I see, with sea-foam flowing around it? And what image of a maiden, chiselled from the very form of the rock itself, a statue made by a skilled hand?'[80] But this category of artwork analogy needs to be connected with the medium in which it was verbalized. The sexual allure of the acted character is bound up with live theatre's distinctive performance aesthetics, above all its dependence on the human body. Even painting and sculpture, which can be intensely focused on eliciting sexual responses, maintain a restraint foregone by the

---

[79] On some other ways in which *Dyskolos* uses references to tragic convention, see Gutzwiller (2000), 117.

[80] *parthenou d' eikō tina | ex automorphōn laïnōn tuchismatōn, | sophēs agalma cheiros.* This play was dramatized in 412, in the same group as *Helen*, another play where the heroine is likened to a work of art (see above).

theatre, in that no flesh lies beneath their manufactured surfaces. 'Only theatre thrusts at its audience the supreme object of sensual thoughts: the human body. And while in the theatre it will ... seldom be naked, its clothing is the more erotic in its double function of concealing and revealing, canceling and enhancing, denying and affirming.'[81] The mysterious somatic power of theatre—its fundamental exhibitionism—'transcends all degrees of costuming and concealment'.[82] Yet where actors wear painted and sculpted masks, the form taken by that somatic power is equivocal and complex. The charismatic presence of the live actor is paradoxically both obscured and *emphasized*. When it is the painted face of a lovely woman, the effect is startling: the power of the male physique and indeed voice are not cancelled, but merely transformed and apprehended through the chiselled features of the heroine. The actor is both the dynamic, fleshy converse of a painting or statue and a visual artwork himself. The ancients believed that the face of the gorgon could not be viewed, and yet it was ubiquitously represented in the inherently viewable material media of metal, clay and paint:[83] by a similar paradox the mask of tragedy, moulded and artistically painted, was a visibly present sign denoting a character who was entirely absent.

The visual art analogy operates in tragedy as a prompt to what Zeitlin calls 'hyper-viewing', stimulating spectators to become conscious of their own contemplation of the masked characters before them.[84] There is an analogous phenomenon in classical Greek vase-painting, in the selective use of frontality in the depiction of certain types of figure. Frontisi-Ducroux has examined the instances of female frontality, an eye-catching technique which invites the viewer of the vase into immediate communication with the figure in question.[85] Frontality can mark psychological or physical transition or heightened experience: death, ecstasy, sleep, and music-making are some of the states in which characters of *both* sexes are depicted

---

[81] Bentley (1964), 153. See D. Steiner (2001), 197, who writes elegantly of the way the image comparison, in the presence of an audience, 'directs its often fetishizing scrutiny to the body-object on display'.

[82] Bentley (1964), 153.

[83] See the brilliant discussion by Mack (2002), esp. 574–5.

[84] Zeitlin (1994), 145.

[85] Frontisi-Ducroux (1984), (1995), and (1996), 88–90.

frontally. A dying Amazon may be turned to address the vase's viewer, just like her male counterparts, dying warriors. But frontally depicted women tend to offer the viewer erotic appeal. Sleeping maenads and Ariadnes are often approached sexually by figures within the vase; their frontality invites the vase's viewer to respond to them as well. In contrast, the frontal convention for sleeping men is confined to non-citizens: giants, barbarians, and children. In scenes of sexual pursuit, frontality marks women such as Oreithyia, pursued by Boreas; they seem vulnerably alluring to the viewer of the vase. In contrast, when youths are being pursued by female divinities, for example in scenes where Cephalus is pursued by Eos, they never gaze out at the viewer.[86] This use of female frontality has similarities with some of the artwork comparisons in tragedy.

A fragment of the fourth-century tragedian Chaeremon, who was renowned for his descriptive powers, preserves a close poetic equivalent to this type of frontality in vases. A sensuous description of sleeping maenads extends the familiar fifth-century comparison woman/artwork analogy to encompass an entire landscape with sexually suggestive figures (fr. 14 *TgrF*):

One was lying in the pale moonlight, her shoulder strap relaxed to disclose her breast; another girl's left flank was loosened to view as she danced; naked to the sight of the sky, she looked like a living picture (*zōsan graphēn ephaine*), while the colour of her skin, white to the eyes, gave off a radiance which contrasted with the effect of the dark shadows . . . and the crocus imprinted on the woven texture of their robes was a sun-like image of shadow (*skias eidōlon*).

In another of his fragments the precise, tactile effect of the texture of curled hair on a waxwork becomes, for the first known time in tragedy, the point of comparison with some beautiful woman, perhaps Alphesiboea (the titular heroine of the play from which the fragment (1) derived):[87] 'Radiant and magnificent, her white skin shone resplendent in the vision of her body, yet modesty tempered

---

[86] See also the comments on Frontisi-Ducroux (1995) by Mack (2002), 577: 'it is a complex exploration of the dialectic of looking that frontal faces catalyse.' For a discussion of such vases showing Eos in pursuit, see R. Osborne (1996), 66–72 with figs. 27 to 30B.

[87] These figures anticipate the Hellenistic taste for intricate ekphrasis, on which see Manakidou (1993).

the gentle blush with which she covered the brightness of colour; her long tresses, curls and all, as of some statue fashioned of wax (*kēro-chrōtos hōs agalmatos | ... ekpeplasmenou*), were tossed about luxuriantly in the humming breezes'.[88] The detail here foreshadows many later descriptions of artistic representations, for example in Callistratus' *Ekphraseis* 2.3, a description of the statue of a Bacchant.

Edgar Allan Poe in 1833 wrote the poem that gave the world the phrase 'the glory that was Greece' (*To Helen*), in which he likened the mythical Helen to a statue erected in a window-niche. In 1845 he saw a professional production of Sophocles' *Antigone* which attempted a 'sculptural' aesthetic in its setting and costumes.[89] A year later he proposed that 'The death of a beautiful woman is, unquestionably, the most poetical topic in the world.'[90] While many have bridled at the apparent misogyny here, Bronfen argues that Poe had seen something essential about femininity and aesthetics.

> By dying, a beautiful woman serves as the motive for the creation of an art work and as its object of representation. As a deanimated body, she can also become an art object or be compared with one... Because her dying figures as an analogy to the creation of an art work... the 'death of a beautiful woman' marks the *mise en abyme* of a text, the moment of self-reflexivity, where the text seems to comment on itself and its own process of composition.[91]

Certainly, in the case of Polyxena, the girl who in death has been rendered a permanent image in the mind, the artwork trope correlates to the process by which tragedy turns horror and somatic suffering into art. But Bronfen's primary focus is art history, and the force of her argument, at least in relation to literature, depends on the genre. It often makes sense for Greek tragedy, but needs

[88] On Chaeremon's imagery, see Collard (1970). 33; Xanthakis-Karamanos (1980), 74, 79–82. The root verb *plassein*, which occurs in several of the artwork analogies, in Greek could metaphorically imply the creation of falsehood; it thus draws attention to the connection between the 'fictive' and deceptive nature of the character represented on a sculpted *prosōpon* and the process by which it had been materially produced. On *plassein* and its cognates in ancient literary criticism, see Hose (1996).

[89] See Hall and Macintosh (2005), ch. 12.

[90] Poe (1846), 201.

[91] Bronfen (1992), 71. On the notion of the literary *mise en abyme*, see below, pp. 137–8.

qualification when it comes to epic, where it is the male body that is typically aestheticized.

A simile in the *Odyssey* likens Odysseus' divinely rejuvenated beauty to the work of a craftsman in fine metal (*Od.* 6.228–35, the last part of which is repeated at 23.159–62): the subliminal force here is erotic rather than death-focussed, since the context is Odysseus' arrival at the court of Nausicaa's father. In the *Iliad* Menelaus' blood, streaming from his wounded thigh, is compared with the purple dye with which a Maeonian or Carian woman stains ivory to decorate the cheek-piece of a bridle (4.140–7), and the context not only stresses the beauty of Menelaus' legs, but equates his gore-smeared skin with a valuable adornment (*agalma, kosmos*).[92] Yet the most important moment in the *Iliad* from the perspective of its own awareness of its aesthetics is in Priam's appeal to Hector, delivered from the wall of Troy, which partly takes the form of a proleptic exploration of the sack of Troy (22.71–6):

It is in every respect becoming for a young man, when he is slain in war, to lie dead, mangled by the sharp bronze. Even though he is dead, everything looks beautiful, whatever part of him is seen (*panta de kala thanonti per, hotti phanēēi*). But when dogs work dishonour on the grey head and grey beard and the genitals of an *old* man who is slaughtered, this is indeed the most piteous thing that can happen to wretched mortals.

At this programmatic moment, the *Iliad* seems aware of its premise, that young men, slain in war, are things of beauty.[93] The *Iliad* creates beauty out of what is actually disgusting—the process by which flesh is mangled, and the life is driven out of healthy young male bodies by weapons and violence on the battlefield. Priam articulates this: young male cadavers, even those rent by bronze weapons, look attractive from any angle.

Greek literature elsewhere gives thought to the processes by which particular sights can simultaneously repel and fascinate. In Plato's *Republic* these conflicting impulses illustrate the way that discrete elements in the soul combat one another, using the example of an individual named Leontius. On walking past the dead bodies lying

[92] See Philipp (1968), 4–5, 15; Ford (2002), 115–17.
[93] See the rather different readings of this passage in Vernant (1982), 58–62 and D. Steiner (2001), 218 with the bibliography in n. 111.

near the place of Athenian public execution, he 'felt at the same time a desire to see them and a repugnance and aversion'. In the end he gazed his fill, but felt angry with himself for so doing (4.439e7–440a3).[94] It may have been thinking about this issue that led Aristotle to his remarkable insight in the *Poetics* into the aesthetic process by which repulsive sights are alchemically transformed through art into something not only bearable, but actually enjoyable and legitimate to contemplate. In arguing that the desire to imitate is innate in humans, he introduces the analogy of learning from works of visual art: 'We feel pleasure in looking (*chairomen theōrountes*) at the most exact portrayals of things that give us pain to look at (*ha…lupērōs horōmen*) in real life, the lowest animals, for instance, or corpses' (4.1448^{b}10–12). This statement articulates the process by which the pain of material reality is aestheticized by art, transformed into something not only bearable to contemplate, but *pleasurable* and instructive. This sentence partly explains why the art galleries of the West are crammed with pictures of individuals undergoing combat, assault, rape, and torture. It also suggests how tragedy can be understood. The misery undergone in tragedy is not something we would elect to see another individual suffer in reality, but in the theatre we can 'feel pleasure in looking' at it.

In Aeschylus' *Agamemnon* the chorus famously describes Iphigenia at the moment before she was killed (239–43): 'shedding to earth her yellow-dyed robe, she struck each one of the sacrificers with piteous eyes, looking as if she were in a picture (*prepousa th' hōs en graphais*), yearning to speak'. The two most striking visual details— the yellow robe flowing to the ground and the beseeching eyes—are emphasized by the poet's request that his audience imagine the scene as a painting. The silence of painted figures became a standard *topos* in ancient literature, especially in full-scale *ecphrasis*.[95] But in this, the earliest surviving instance, the pathos of the moment is

---

[94] For a detailed exploration of the implications of this anecdote, see von Reden and Goldhill (1999), 257–8.

[95] In Apollonius' *Argonautica*, for example, the narrator says that Phrixus and his ram were so vividly portrayed on Jason's cloak that it was tempting to keep silent in the vain hope of hearing their words (1.763–7). In Catullus 64.132, the poet plays on this convention when he makes his wretched Ariadne launch into a first-person speech from the coverlet on which she is portrayed. On the topos of the voiceless statue, see Kassel (1983) and especially D. Steiner (2001), 136–7.

immeasurably heightened by the frustration of the gagged Iphigenia, *forcibly* silenced. Moreover, the participle *prepousa* may bear the connotation 'standing out conspicuously', thus encouraging the audience's internal eye to focus even more sharply on the tragic girl's plight: as Fraenkel says, this passage is 'our earliest evidence for the clear definition of the individual figures being regarded as an essential quality in painting'.[96]

Some instances of the artwork analogy draw attention simultaneously to the erotic attractions of the female in question, and to her death—actual or impending. In *Andromeda* (see above) the analogy may have asked the audience to think in terms of the voyeuristic delight offered by contemplating not only the aesthetic beauty of the desirable maiden, but her vulnerability to mortal danger. Death with an erotic frisson is also provided by the much-discussed passage in *Alcestis*, when Admetus tells his dying wife that a likeness (*eikasthen*) of her body will be made by the skilled hands of craftsmen, and stretched out upon their bed (*ektathēsetai*) for him to fall upon and embrace (348–52).[97] The effect here is identical to a simile in that it makes the audience imagine Alcestis as a work of art; it may well be connected with the practice of interring sculpted images of the dead person in their graves, attested by archaeological discoveries in Thera and Italian Locri.[98] In performance, artwork images seem to have been susceptible to elaboration by actors: the recently published *POxy* 4546, the scripted 'part' for the actor playing Admetus discussed in detail in Chapter 2 (above pp. 51–2), seems to have read not *ektathēsetai* but *engraphēsetai*: thus Admetus proposed to commission a likeness of Alcestis which would be 'painted in' his bed, rather than stretched out upon it.

With the recent return of *Hecuba* to the contemporary theatrical repertoire,[99] an increasingly familiar example is the equation of Polyxena with a statue in that play (see above).[100] The sacrifice of

[96] Fraenkel (1950), ii. 139.

[97] Amongst a huge recent bibliography on this passage, see in particular the aesthetic approach of Segal (1993), and the more historical approach of Slater (2000), 117–19.

[98] See D. Steiner (2001), 5–6.

[99] See Stothard (2005); Hardwick (2005).

[100] The term *agalma* used in reference to Polyxena had specific connotations within the reciprocal exchanges between humans and immortals in Athenian religion. Statues

Polyxena was portrayed in archaic vase-painting, and had remained a popular theme in the visual arts, for example in the Pinakotheke of the Athenian Propylaea (Paus. 1.22.6). But theatre could explore the effect of such a scene on its viewers. Talthybius, the Euripidean speaker recounting the event, is male, as are the other onlookers (Neoptolemus and the massed Greeks at Troy). Yet the immediate internal audience of the eyewitness account is Hecuba, asked by Talthybius to imagine her dying daughter as a beautiful work of art. This is clearly a context where feminine death is one of the factors that have prompted the use of the artwork analogy, and on this critics are agreed. Pucci, for example, argues that the rhetoric is primarily one of pathos: it is pity for the girl and her bereaved mother that builds in Talthybius' language 'a consoling moment': 'The shivering that should grasp everyone at the mortal stroke to the poor body of Polyxena is replaced by an image that evokes already restitution, honour, and immortality… The monument is erected before the sacrifice; the restitution is given before the loss, the immortality is evoked before destruction.'[101] Pucci seems to be operating within similar parameters to the seminal theorization of Pushkin's sculptural aesthetic by Roman Jakobson, for whom there was a paradoxical sense in which the image of a statue always 'evokes the *opposite* of image of rigidified people', whether or not it involves 'actual dying

of both young men and young women were erected as votive offerings. The term used for the young male statues was *kouros*, and at Athens no example exists labelled *agalma*; Osborne has shown that in contrast the term most often used for a female statue was not *korē* but *agalma*; he suggests these types of statue related humankind to the gods in different ways. In identifying *korai* as *agalmata* the inscriptions beneath them situate them in a world where women were the prime source of symbolic capital, and with whom capital was exchanged in the course of commerce between men. It was Gernet who argued that even in the classical period such precious works as *agalmata* still retained a mythic notion of value: 'through the choice of material, formal beauty, and the perfection of workmanship, the creation of the craftsman was seen by the person who commissioned it as a testimony of wealth, power, and success' (see the Eng. trans. of 'La notion mythique de la valeur en Grèce antique' (1948) in Gordon (1981), 111–46; see also Kurke (1991), 163–94). The concrete *agalmata* mark a system of exchange between mortals and immortals. This can illuminate the sense in which young women are figured as *agalmata* in tragedy; Alcestis' life is exchanged for Admetus'; Polyxena's life is exchanged for the goodwill of the semi-divine Achilles.

[101] Pucci (1977), 168.

and death. Here the boundary between life and immobile dead matter is deliberately obliterated.'[102]

The image at the moment of Polyxena's death also, however, has nuptial overtones. Athens was packed with funeral monuments for very young women which drew on nuptial imagery, and tragedy conflates the rituals of marriage and death.[103] Polyxena's execution is in one sense her wedding, since she has been demanded by the shade of Achilles. Moreover, the passage has voyeuristic connotations of mass sexual excitement that can not be ignored; Hecuba's response to Talthybius articulates her fear that the Greeks will violate her daughter's corpse (604–8).[104] The audience today is made painfully aware that it is taking pleasure in listening to a narrative in which a nubile young woman appears semi-naked before thousands of men; the reaction in one influential production was to make the audience uncomfortably aware that they were colluding in (to use today's language) something little short of sadistic pornography.[105] There is no reason to suppose that there were not members of Euripides' original audience (which might even have included Plato's Leontius, apparently an historical figure) who felt a similar mixture of pity, excitement, and awareness of their own pleasure in looking at death.

Although it is just possible that Euripides' *Protesilaus* included the motif of a woman's devotion to a statue made in the image of her dead husband, erotic appeal is not the point of any of the few extant Greek tragic tropes in which a *man* is compared to an artwork.[106]

[102] Jakobson (1987), 326 (written in 1937).

[103] Foley (1985), 65–105; Rehm (1994), esp. 84–96.

[104] Any sexual connotation is denied by Mossman (1991), 105–6 and Mossman (1995), 143–5 and 159. But see Marshall (2001), 131 and the overview of interpretations of the image in Gregory (1999), 112–13. For the popularity of scenes of sexualised assault against women in another artistic medium designed for male consumption, the paintings on symposium pottery, Zweig (1992), 83, and below Chs. 5 and 6, pp. 169 and 180–3.

[105] See E. Hall (1992).

[106] According to a scholion on Aristides (p. 671–2), Euripides' *Protesilaus* portrayed Laodamia's plea to the gods to be allowed one more day with her dead husband, the first Greek casualty at Troy. The question is whether Euripides' version already included the motif, known from later authors (e.g. Ovid, *Her.* 13.151–8), which had Laodamia keeping a likeness of her husband in her bedroom. Euripides' play was reconstructed along lines suggested by the versions in Hyginus' *Fabulae* 103 and 104 by von Wilamowitz-Moellendorff (1929), followed by at least one distinguished editor of *Alcestis* (Dale (1954), 79), and D. Steiner (2001), 191 (although at

This is one of the distinctive aspects of the tragic use of such tropes.[107] A feminist reading of the Polyxena passage would be likely to emphasize that the female body has been routinely sexualized in western culture, and that the male-dominated history of theatre and cinema has fixed the female body as the object of the (implicitly male) viewing subject.[108] If a theorist such as Laura Mulvey had written about these analogies in the 1980s, she would probably have seen them as symptoms of the hierarchical duality marking western culture's pleasure-in-looking (Freud's *scopophilia*), which has overwhelmingly made the male active and the female passive; it has objectified the female in the eyes of a subject assumed to be a heterosexual male.[109] But it is here more helpful to ask whether the ancient men who created tragic drama and its artwork analogies thought that works of visual art could be erotically arousing. The answer to this question is affirmative.

In *Agamemnon* the chorus recall the reaction in Argos to the departure of Helen, and quote the palace seers' description of Menelaus' desperate longing for his absent wife: 'the charm of beautifully formed statues is hateful to him, and in the absence of eyes there is no Aphrodite [i.e. sexual desire]'.[110] The fourth-century comic poet

193 n. 31, she is much more cautious). In *Fabula* 103, 'Protesilaus', we hear that Laodamia was allowed to be reunited with her husband for three hours, but could not endure her grief when he died again: in no. 104, 'Laodamia', she makes a bronze likeness of him, but a slave sees her in the act of embracing it. Her father Acastus first thinks that she has taken a lover, but subsequently has the statue burnt; Laodamia throws herself on the pyre built for her husband's likeness. These stories—especially the uncanny motifs of the revenant lover and the erotic icon—have an air of *Alcestis* about them, and might have originated in satyric (or prosatyric) drama, especially since *Alcestis* and the Protesilaus myth share a Thessalian connection. But a tragic *Protesilaus* involving a woman embracing a statue of her dead spouse would have been a very remarkable play; not one of the ten or so fragments that have survived actually mentions an image of the husband. It is equally likely that the words of Euripides' bereaved Admetus in *Alcestis* suggested the new development in the story of Laodamia, similarly bereft, to some ingenious post-Euripidean re-worker of myth.

107 The comparison of young men with artworks that can arouse erotic responses is of course widespread in other genres, such as Platonic dialogue: see D. Steiner (2001), 198–200. But the relationship between *genre* and gender in these instances has received insufficient attention.

108 See e.g. Mulvey (1975), 13; de Lauretis (1987), 13.

109 Mulvey (1989), 16, 19.

110 416–19: *eumorphōn de kolossōn | echthetai charis andri; | ommatōn d' en achēniais | errei pas' Aphrodita*. At the time of the *Oresteia* the term *kolossos* probably

Alexis composed a play entitled *The Painting* (*Graphē*), in which the story was related of Cleisophus of Selymbria. He conceived a passion for a maiden made of stone (fr. 41 K–A). In a pathbreaking article, Osborne argued that sculpted women were often designed to elicit a response in the male viewer.[111] This phenomenon can certainly be traced back to the classical period, in the Victory leaning over to fiddle with her sandal in the temple of Athena Nike, and in Praxiteles' Aphrodite. Later authors compiled anecdotes proving the sexual power of images of desirable females: Athenaeus, who preserved the Cleisophus story, also reported that a bull once tried to mount the bronze cow of Priene, and that a dog, a pigeon, and a gander had all

designated not size but a style in which the statue's legs were tightly held together or replaced by a pillar (see Benveniste (1932); Roux (1960), 34; Ducat (1976)). Fraenkel (1950), ii. 219 and n. 1 thinks that Aeschylus may have meant statues of young women like those of the late 6th-cent. Attic *korai*. The statues have been thought by some scholars to be portraits of Helen at which Menelaus can no longer bear to look: see e.g. Huddilston (1898), 5, or Lloyd-Jones's translation (1979), 39–40: 'And the charm of her beautiful statues | is hateful to her husband.' But this is overly specific, since statues of beautiful young women (and men) were believed to be erotically inflammatory. The text refers to unspecified beautiful statues, which might normally be expected to arouse Menelaus, but can have no effect on the depressive cuckold now. The other controversy relates to the owner of the eyes. The options are (i) that it is the statues (e.g. D. Steiner (1995*b*), 179). But statues always lack 'real' eyes, and yet were universally thought in antiquity to stimulate the viewer, and indeed it was their eyes that were thought to be the most beautiful of all a statue's features (Plato *Rep.* 4.420c; see also *Hipp. Maj.* 290b). (ii) Menelaus. See Smyth's Loeb translation, 'In the hunger of his eyes all loveliness has departed'. On this view, Aphrodite (i.e. sexual passion) is missing because Menelaus 'has no eyes' for anyone any more. But *en achēniais* must mean a want or absence of something, and the eyes that are actually missing are those of Helen. (iii) The third hypothetical owner of the eyes is indeed Helen. See Lloyd-Jones's translation: 'and in the absence of *her* eyes, gone is all the power of love.' There is, however, a further possibility (iv), suggested by George Thomson (1966), 41, but routinely ignored: the nearest parallel to the form and thought expressed here is a proverb attributed to the Orphic thinkers: *cheirōn ollumenōn erren poluergos Athēnē* ('Without hands there is no Athena, goddess of handicrafts'; Orphic fr. 347 ed. Kern (1922), quoted by Orion *Etymolog.* 163.23). This means 'No hands, no handicraft'. In the Aeschylus passage the thought could be equally proverbial: 'No eyes, no sex'. The ancients were clear that sexual attraction emanated from the eyes and passed into the smitten party through their eyes. In Hesiod, Eros flows from the Graces' eyes with their glance (*Theog.* 910–11); in *Hippolytus* Eros distils desire upon the eyes (525–6). Menelaus and Helen can't see each other any more; the chorus's elliptical expression is gnomic and ambiguous. Without the eye contact between loved and beloved there can be no sexual desire.

[111] R. Osborne (1994).

approached painted females (*Deipn.* 13.605–6). In his polemic against idolatry, Clement of Alexandria fulminates against a man who desired the Aphrodite of Knidos (*Protr. pros Hellēnas* 4.51).[112] The sexual aura emanating from a charismatic actor wearing the mask of a beautiful woman, a painted sculpture, may have filled spectators with especially uneasy pleasure.

PITY AND TERROR

One of the emotions often named in these analogies is pity. Pity was central to the agenda of characters in early tragedy, who attempt to elicit it in their onlookers (e.g. *Persae* 931, 1046), and to all classical attempts to theorize the genre.[113] In *Hecuba*, when the Trojan queen is entreating Agamemnon, she produces the artwork analogy in which Segal saw that nothing less than the aesthetics of the entire 'tragic spectacle' might be at stake (see above). 'Pity me: standing back like a painter look at me and scrutinize my plight' (806–7). The Greek here could be heard by the audience as meaning that Hecuba was a living model for Agamemnon the artist to examine while he painted. There are certainly reports in antiquity of the use of female models by artists, such as Socrates' encounter with Theodote in his enquiry into vision in Xenophon's *Symposium* (3.11), whom he came upon 'posing for a painter' (*zōgraphōi tini parestēkuian*, 3.2).[114] In the case of *Hecuba*, the old queen implies that Agamemnon has the power to affect the type of picture in which Hecuba will appear: his decision in relation to Polymestor will be affected by contemplating her as a living example of a pitiable woman. The advantage of this interpretation is that Hecuba does not liken herself to a painted figure devoid of sensibility, but to a living human being who has become the topic of art. Yet antiquity preferred the more obvious meaning, that Hecuba invites Agamemnon to look at her as if she was a figure in a pre-existing painting, depicted in

---

[112] For medieval Christian stories where the statue becomes an object of erotic devotion, see Warner (1985), 230.

[113] See Plato, *Phaedrus* 268c.

[114] For Theodote from the perspectives of the nude in art and political theory, see respectively Havelock (1995), 30, and Goldhill (1998), 113–24.

a manner designed to maximize pity in the viewer. The ancient scholiasts interpreted it thus, probably influenced by the popularity in visual art of the suffering of the women of Troy.[115] On this reading, Euripides' formulation construes this woman as an icon of grief; she is analogous to the image he and his actor and mask-maker have collaboratively conjured out of words and her painted mask. But perhaps the ambiguity should be left unresolved, in which case the figure demonstrates what is stake here for Hecuba: a deadly struggle over the status of subject and object in this episode. Hecuba is offering herself as object to Agamemnon (and the audience's) subjective gaze, in order to further her own agenda—to assume the role of not only subject but *agent* in pursuit of Polymestor.

When a man is the object, the emotional register is different. In Euripides' *Phoenician Women* the young Antigone, watching the enemy army from the walls of Thebes, screams on seeing Hippomedon. She compares his appearance to 'an earthborn giant in paintings' (128–9): he looks *terrifying* (*phoberos eisidein*, 127). This comparison is one of those that works in the audience's 'mind's eye', assisting them to *imagine* the scene that lies in the teichoscopic view of Antigone. Her emotional response—terror—differs from any of those in Greek tragedy where a mortal woman's appearance is under discussion, resembling only the emotion elicited in Aeschylus' priestess of Apollo when she contemplated the Erinyes. Terror, of course, is one of the two emotions the Greeks felt were most characteristic of, and proper to, tragedy. But the context of the comparison of Hippomedon with a figure in a painting also differs from those in which women are compared with artworks: Hippomedon is not dying, nor alluring nor eliciting pity: he is a military aggressor.

Such a context is shared by a rare Aeschylean comparison of a man with an artwork. In *Agamemnon* the chorus prepare to greet their king: he may or may not himself yet be visible. They meditate on the scene in Aulis long ago (799–801). 'Then, when you were marshalling the army for Helen's sake (I will not hide it), in my eyes you were depicted most inartistically (*kart' apomousōs ēstha gegrammenos*)'.

---

[115] See D. Steiner (2001), 51 and n. 148, who compares Lucian's *Pro eikonibus* 12, where Polystratus gains improved perception of an *eikōn* by looking at it from a distance.

Agamemnon cut an *unattractive* or *badly painted* figure. The analogy prompts the audience to visualize a scene at Aulis—perhaps the identical scene in which Iphigenia had been remembered, gagged in her yellow gown. The instance is unique in that it explicitly requires imagining an inartistic picture which does not bestow pleasure. It has sometimes been argued that *gegrammenos* here means not 'painted' but 'written'—Agamemnon is 'inscribed' upon the memory.[116] It was once even suggested that the metaphor is an unusually transparent reference to the circumstances of the tragic competitions external to the world of the play, and that it alludes to the judges writing down their verdicts (as at Lysias 4.3, *egrapse men tauta eis to grammateion*): Agamemnon's conduct at Aulis was judged by his Argive chorus to have been the work of a 'bungler' at the tragic art.[117] Yet an interlinear gloss on the passage reads *ezōgraphēmenos*, which unequivocally means 'painted', suggesting how antiquity understood the metaphor.

There is one Sophoclean example. In *Women of Trachis*, Hyllus is describing how the robe Deianeira sent to Heracles turned out to be lethally doctored (765–9): 'But when the bloodshot flame from the sacred offerings and from the resinous pine blazed up, the sweat came up upon his body, and the thing clung closely to his sides, as a craftsman's tunic might [or, 'like the effect a sculptor can create'], at every joint (*kai prosptussetai pleuraisin artikollos, hōste tektonos, chitōn hapan kat' arthron*).' Heracles is perhaps to be imagined looking like a workman who is sweating so heavily that his tunic sticks to his bones and muscles, defining them; it is more likely, however, that the passage means that the fabric is adhering to his skin, making him look like a chiselled sculpture.[118] This interpretation makes the hyper-male Heracles the only masculine figure in extant tragedy to be talked about in his dying moment—like Iphigenia or Polyxena or Alcestis—as a work of visual art. In one sense this is the exception that proves the rule, since the 'feminization' of Heracles in this play, defeated by a woman, is a prominent issue.[119] But it must be noted that the passage differs from

[116] H. J. Rose (1958), vol. ii, 58–9.   [117] Petersen (1911).

[118] Easterling (1982), 168–9, discusses a range of possible interpretations, and prefers to see the simile as suggesting that 'Heracles is as firmly stuck in the robe as if it were some artefact made by a carpenter'.

[119] See above all, 'Herakles: the supermale and the feminine', published as ch. 7 of Loraux (1995).

those which occur at the moment of women's expiry in that it is emotionally not directive. Hyllus is not *explicitly* prompting either pity or aesthetic awe. The comparison is arguably more macabre than ornamental. It must be conceded that in Euripides' *Electra* it is possible that Orestes' facial beauty is one point of the reference to an image on a coin (see above). But the major difference between the male and female artwork figures in tragedy is underscored by comparison with the use of such figures in other genres; in Plato, for example, it is young *men* who are likened to statues to be gazed at with erotic longing: Charmides was so beautiful that all who beheld him desired him, and 'gazed at him as if he were a statue' (*agalma*, *Charmides* 154c; see also *Sophist* 239d).

ARTWORKS AND AUTHORIAL POWER

In the majority of the poetic figures discussed here, the artwork is evoked in a comparison with a woman or women: the creator of the artwork, if mentioned, is either an anonymous male craftsman or a named individual (Agamemnon characterized as Hecuba's painter). Since the situation in which the female victims find themselves is often created by the men in the play, the artwork can be seen as a moment in which agency of the man and the sexual appeal or victimhood of the woman are acknowledged on the level of imagery. Yet the last section has shown that there were exceptions. Moreover, no two artwork comparisons are formally identical. Some constitute comparisons with paintings (Iphigenia), some with carved or moulded figures (the Phoenician Women, Andromache), and some with both (Helen in *Helen*). The figures may be on stage (the Danaids, Orestes), about to arrive (the Erinyes), have already departed (Polyxena), or never appear (Hippomedon, Iphigenia). If present to the spectators' eyes, the figure may draw the comparison herself (Hecuba) or themselves (the Phoenician Women)—in the surviving texts it is never himself—or it may be drawn by another character (Pelasgus in *Suppliant Women*). There may be an internal audience involved other than the chorus. The tropes reveal the restless, creative agenda of the poets, experimenting with the new effects they could create by implementing what had swiftly become a conventional weapon in their artillery of images. What these comparisons have in common, therefore, is not formal qualities. It is an intense relationship with the complex, multimedial performance art which their role is partly to *define*.

Gide invented the extraordinarily influential notion of the literary *mise en abyme*—a picture within an artwork of the process of its own composition—after discovering heraldry.[120] By his definition, an exact *mise en abyme* in tragic drama would involve an account of a playwright at work: this does occur in fifth-century plays, but they are comedies—*Acharnians, Thesmophoriazusae*.[121] An equally precise *mise en abyme* in a tragic drama might be a picture of performers in rehearsal, and here there is a close equivalent—the 'dressing-up' scene in *Bacchae* (914–76), which nevertheless differs from a picture of theatrical performers at work: Pentheus is unaware of the actual role that has been predetermined for him. A nearer approximation to a scene depicting 'actors' preparing themselves is supplied, again, by comedy: Aristophanes' female infiltrators of the assembly do rehearse speeches; indeed, it is from this passage that we know the Greek verb meaning 'to rehearse' (*promeletan, Eccl.* 117).[122]

Creators of art within any artwork tend to operate as authorial surrogates. In texts they can be emblematic of the author's power over all the figures in the narrative. Characters who actually voice artwork tropes can be interpreted as attempting to control their fates. Thus, in a striking instance in Euripides' *Andromache*, it is as a monument to bereaved motherhood that Andromache tries to 'fix' her destiny; in the conclusion of her lament, before the statue of Thetis, she says that she is dissolving in grief like a gushing libation in rock. She imagines

---

[120] Journal entry for 9 September 1893, in Gide (1996), 171.

[121] See especially Muecke (1982).

[122] For a recent reading of this rehearsal scene as comic metatheatre, see Slater (2002), 209–16. Phenomena in tragedy 'suggestive' of the theatrical process (e.g. the humiliation of Ajax by Athena in *Ajax*, watched by Odysseus) can alternatively be understood as a type of dramatic writing which could only develop because of the Athenians' experience of theatre. Sophocles could write a scene in which *A* tortures *B* before internal spectator *C* because of the introduction of the third actor, which allowed the possibility of an articulate solo witness (as opposed to a chorus or mute attendants) to others' dialogue, a scene type which can *always* be described as 'metatheatre' on a weak interpretation of that term. On the other hand we could describe it as a brilliant dramaturgical development which had internalized the tragic audience in the new phenomenon of the third actor.

herself as petrified in eternal tears (116–18), a phrase which must have
brought to mind the Iliadic Niobe.[123] Andromache also invokes the
real statue as ally when she tells her adversary Hermione that the
statue is gazing at her reprovingly (246). But Hermione (the only
female in tragedy to apply an artwork trope to another woman)
orders her to leave the altar where she sits as a suppliant. Even if she
were fixed, says Hermione, on that spot, by a base of molten lead (i.e.
by the means by which a statue would be normally be planted in a
hollow in the plinth on which it sat), she (Hermione) would make her
move (266–8). Hermione wants control over Andromache's destiny—the equivalent of authorial power. This confrontation thus
involves adversarial claims to write the 'script' of the play through
rival imagery of petrification and the uprooting of a statue; will it be a
Niobe tragedy composed by Andromache, or a revenge plot in which
Hermione is both agent and author?

In *Hecuba*, the desperate Trojan queen uses several art images, as if
trying to negotiate the status of the work in which she is the principal
figure. Having likened her enslaved self to a mere 'deathlike shape'
(*nekrou morpha*, 191), and 'a feeble *agalma* of the dead' (192), she
subsequently tries to take charge of the plot. In the same speech
where she figures Agamemnon as painter, she also expresses the wish
that she had a tongue in her arms and hands and hair and feet, by the
art of Daedalus or some god, with which to supplicate Agamemnon
(836–40).[124] While, as a female, she is still the created image, the
product of a male craftsman, her fantasy of acquiring agency paradoxically entails being refashioned as a rhetorical automaton whose
supernatural powers of speech are irresistible. The carefully crafted
rhetoric of Hecuba is implicitly likened to an artwork, in a trope
whose upshot is not dissimilar to Alcidamas' equation of written
speeches with statues (see above).

Yet, at least until Euripides, the Greeks were always challenged by the
portrayal of female subjectivity. This fact of ancient Greek poetic life is
connected with the prevalent concept of the female as a material
artifact, an insentient commodity, like the robotic golden handmaids

---

[123] For an alternative interpretation of the functions of the artwork figures here,
see Golder (1992), 328.
[124] See above all D. Steiner (2001), 142–3.

Hephaestus has created to attend upon him in the *Iliad* (18.417–20).[125]
The medical writers' view of the female body tends, similarly, to
construct it as material content, providing in the reproductive process
the clay-like substance to be shaped by masculine *form*. Aristotle's
theory of reproduction in *De Generatione Animalium* states that during heterosexual intercourse, the function of the male is to 'fashion by
the movement in the semen the mass forming from the material
supplied by the female'. The male is the craftsman (*dēmiourgei*),
while the female is the material (*hulē*) upon which the craftsman
works. Aristotle assumes that 'while it is necessary for the female to
provide a body and a material mass (*sōma kai ogkon*), it is not necessary
for the male, because it is not within what is produced that the tools or
tool-maker (*ta organa ... oute to poioun*) must exist' (2.4.738^{b}10–13,
20–28). This conceptual complex was given early articulation in the
story of Pandora, Hesiod's aetiology for womankind. In *Works and
Days* (60–82) and the *Theogony* (578–89), she is constructed out of
earth and water by Hephaestus, and the other gods endow her severally
with erotic charm, finery, gold, flowers, a human voice, a face like a
goddess, skill in weaving, and the evil arts of cunning and deceit. She
is notoriously *not* invested with the ability to suffer herself, in contrast
to the subjectivity granted to Eve, who must suffer in childbirth, in the
Judaeo-Christian tradition.[126] In this narrative *all* women trace their
origins from the woman/artwork made from crude matter; and at least
one misogynist in a tragedy likely to have been by Euripides derived his
figure of speech from this story. If woman is 'the creation (*plasma*) of
one of the gods, then be sure that he is the greatest craftsman of evils
and hostile to mankind' (Eur. fr. inc. 1059.6–8).

Hippolytus is appealing to the same rhetorical tradition when he
tells the nurse in Euripides' play (631–3) that the man who takes a
bride into his home 'rapturously decks his hateful *agalma* with fair
ornaments and gowns, the poor wretch, wasting his family fortune'.
Excluded from consideration is any notion that this lovely manne-
quin might herself have the capacity to feel within her manufactured
and ornamented presence (a subjectivity which the masked male

---

[125] See the discussion of D. Steiner (2001), 117.
[126] For the classic articulation of this issue, see Arthur (1973); see also Loraux
(1981), 84–6; Zeitlin (1996), 53–86.

playing the male poet's creation, Phaedra, has, paradoxically, just been revealing to the audience). And, as we shall see in the next chapter, Pandora may have been created on stage during at least one fifth-century satyr play, Sophocles' *Hammerers*.

ART AND METAPHYSICS

The artwork analogies of *Agamemnon* have haunted this chapter as Iphigenia, the subject of one of the most memorable of them, haunts the play itself. At its climax, when Cassandra is about to enter the palace and certain death, an artwork analogy is turned to bold effect. It is as deeply implicated in the theorization of tragedy as any of the others, but its focus is not on pity, fear, gender, sex, agency, female materiality, nor even the audience's experience of Cassandra's specific death: it is metaphysical. Cassandra meditates on the fragility of life (1327–9). 'Alas, for human fortune! In prosperity, one may liken it to a sketch, but in disaster, the stroke of a wet sponge obliterates the picture'.[127] Cassandra, played by a man behind a painted mask, compares human life, as well as her own particular living self, to a painting about to be erased as watercolour paints dissolve when water is applied to them.[128] Her words were reformulated by a character in Euripides' *Peleus* (55 fr. 618 *TgrF*), who remarked that prosperity (*olbos*) is something that god can erase (*exaleiphei*) even more easily than a painting (*graphē*). It is in these two meditative applications of the artwork trope that the ambition of the figure of the world as a stage, delivered by Shakespeare's Jacques, is most

---

[127] H. J. Rose (1958), 95 is almost alone in interpreting Cassandra's words here as referring to the erasure of writing rather than painting (see also above n. 117), and suggests that the metaphor suggests wiping out rough notes with lamp black and water, as in Suet. *Aug.* 85.

[128] To become impervious to water, painted figures needed to be applied using encaustic techniques (Plato, *Tim.* 26c, *hoion egkaumata anekplutou graphēs*). The process to which Cassandra refers is also illuminated in Plutarch, *De Fortuna* 99a–b: an artist once painted a horse, and could not achieve the result he wanted in portraying the froth and foam-flecked breath coming from the animal's mouth. After many failed attempts, he flew into a rage and threw his sponge, full of wet paint, at the easel. The desired effect was achieved.

nearly approached. Yet rather than liken the world to an artwork, they make the more profound metaphysical point, which comes closer to Calderón's figure of God as tragic dramatist in *El Gran Teatro del Mundi*, that all human existence is as fragile as a painting, and as easily obliterated.

5

Horny Satyrs and Tragic Tetralogies

Throughout the fifth century BC, and well into the fourth, the chorusmen's last change of costume during tragic performances at the Dionysia required them to put on the masks and accoutrements made of leather, wool, and fur that befitted semi-naked satyrs. Only hours and minutes earlier they had been dressed in one of the three rather different outfits, required by the preceding plays in the tetralogy, suitable for the women, men, or supernatural females[1] who constituted the choruses of all extant tragedies. In contrast, it was attired in masks and elaborate garments indistinguishable in textile and style from those of tragedy that the actors who had been impersonating mythical aristocrats in heroic drama returned, to consort with the satyrs in a light-hearted recasting of the atmosphere of mythical time.

Hundreds of classical satyr plays were produced, yet only Euripides' *Cyclops* survives in its entirety, together with a substantial part of Sophocles' *Trackers* (*Ichneutae*). One of the few certainties about this enigmatic genre is that its gender orientation was more profoundly male than that of tragedy and comedy. Like them it was produced by male poets and performed by male actors, in front of a largely male audience. Yet unlike the choruses of tragedy and comedy, which could represent either females or males, the chorus of satyr drama by convention consisted of male satyrs with conspicuous phalluses.[2]

---

[1] e.g. the Erinyes in *Eumenides* and the Oceanids in *Prometheus Bound*.

[2] That the satyr chorus was invariable is supported by the interchangeability of the plural noun 'satyrs' (*saturoi*) with the term '*saturikon* (or *silēnikon*) *drama*': see Ar. *Thesm.* 157; Brommer (1937), 4; Hedreen (1992), 10 n. 1. Aristotle's pupil Chamaeleon wrote a treatise on satyr drama, a companion piece to his *On Comedy*, entitled *On Satyrs* (*peri Saturōn*): see Werhrli (1969), 60, 85. The case for satyr-free satyr

Satyr plays served as the conclusions to performances of tragedy, in which the audience had often been identifying with female characters and reacting with emotions often socially constructed as 'feminine'. This chapter argues that one function of satyr drama was to reaffirm in its audience at the end of the tragic productions a masculine collective consciousness based on libidinal awareness.[3]

In *Trackers* the actor taking the role of the mountain nymph Cyllene said to the satyrs, 'You always did behave like a baby. You're a full-grown man with a beard. But you are as saucy as a goat among the thistles. It's time that bald skull stopped fluttering with ecstasy' (fr. 314.366–8).[4] For the satyrs, like their divine master Dionysus, confounded most of the polarities by which the Greeks organized their conceptual grasp of the world.[5] They were almost human, yet both slightly bestial and marginally divine. They were childlike and yet their bald heads suggested that they were simultaneously old. They lived in the untamed wild and yet in myth were present at the dawn of technology and the arts of civilisation. They were innocent yet knowing, often stupid yet capable of cunning. They were pugnacious yet timorous and oddly charming. The single social and psychological boundary they emphatically did *not* confuse or challenge is that between male and female. Biologically they were exaggeratedly male. They were culturally and behaviourally masculine and homosocial, by which I mean that they were represented as preferring to live with members of their own sex, and to share with them in performing exclusively masculine activities (for example, hunting and athletics). The satyrs are also by biology exaggeratedly male. Their extreme male libidinousness was visually represented in their frequent state of erection, represented by the actors' costumes (See fig. 5.1). When Cyllene said that the satyrs' bald heads were

drama has nevertheless occasionally been made since Décharme (1889). Yet the title of the Aeschylean *Nurses* (*Trophoi*) *of Dionysos* is irrelevant, for the satyrs will have been the nurses in that play, as they almost certainly were in Sophocles' *Dionysiskos*. The other alleged evidence for female choruses more likely suggests satyric transvestism: see below n. 40.

[3] On the similarities between some of this chapter and Mark Griffith's discussion of satyr drama (Griffith (2002)), see Ch. 1 p. 10 n. 18

[4] Translated by Page (1952), 51. The bald head to which Cyllene refers is probably a euphemism for the conspicuous satyric phallus: see below.

[5] On Dionysus' capacity for dissolving polarities, see above all Segal (1978).

Fɪɢ. 5.1　Chorusmen dressing as satyrs, on an Apulian bell-krater by the Tarporley painter

fluttering with ecstasy, a sexual *double entendre* is probably intended, for the satyrs often had rounded, bald or balding heads, pictorially represented thrusting forwards, thus offering a second, imitation phallus-tip (see fig. 5.2): it must have been difficult to avoid hearing a pun created by the similarity between the Greeks word for 'phallus' (*phallos* and *phalos*), and for 'bald' (*phalakros*).[6] The satyrs' hairiness and other enlarged bodily extremities—they had tails, upwardly pointing animal ears, and sometimes hoofed feet—completed the picture of a hyperbolic maleness, a caricatured male carnality.

---

[6] See the suggestion of Lobel discussed in Lloyd-Jones (1983), 538.

Fɪɢ. 5.2   Satyr and Maenad on a late fifth-century red-figured oinochoe

Satyrs are attested in ancient art and literature from archaic Greek epic until the later Roman empire. Their reputation as 'good-for-nothings' was already established in their earliest literary manifestation (Hesiod fr. 123.2 M–W), but thereafter their identity was fundamentally defined by their sexual appetite:[7] all satyrs are potential rapists. In satyr drama they are obsessed with their genitals (*Ichn.* fr. 314.151); a medicinal herb which enhanced sexual desire and performance in men was named after them (Hesychius, s.v. *saturion*). At its most anodyne the satyrs' lust is directed at their mythical female companions, the nymphs or maenads: an early mention of the silens (equivalents of the satyrs), in the *Homeric Hymn to Aphrodite* (262–3), depicts them making love to nymphs. Centuries later the satyr which Sulla's army allegedly captured was found asleep in a grove of the nymphs (Plut. *Vit. Sull.* 27). But the nymphs in the sixth century had been conflated with the maenads, and in the classical

[7] See the hilariously thorough documentation by Lissarrague (1990*a*).

period the female figures being chased by satyrs on most vases are maenads rather than nymphs.

When the satyrs' desires were directed at humans they became more frightening. Some people believed that satyrs really might assault women, at least in remote parts of the world. Pausanias tells the story of the Carian Euphemus, whose ship was driven to islands inhabited by satyrs. The satyrs ran down to the ship and grabbed at the women passengers; the frightened sailors tossed them a barbarian woman, 'and she was raped by the satyrs not only in the usual place but all over her body' (1.23.7). Similarly, when the mystic and philosopher Apollonius was dining in an Ethiopian village in the first century AD, his biographer Philostratus reports that he was surprised by the cry of the village women. The men grabbed clubs and stones and shouted for their friends as if they had caught an adulterer. It transpired that the village had for nine months been visited by 'the apparition of a satyr', which 'was mad for women and had already killed the two it apparently desired most' (Philost. *Vit. Apoll.* 6.27).

The satyrs' literary and theatrical heyday was the fifth century, coincident with Athens' greatness as a democratic imperial power. The subject-matter of satyr drama is heroic myth; favoured plot motifs are servitude and escape, hunting, athletics, drinking, eating, and sex. Athletics in particular offered possibilities for raucous fun with the ligature and associated practices which athletes used for controlling their penises during competitions; in Aeschylus' *Theoroi*, Dionysus comments that the satyrs have prepared for competing in the athletics events at the Isthmian games by bobbing their ithyphalloi, with the result that they look like mouse tails (fr. 78a.29). The temporal location is an early stage in mythical time: satyr drama often portrays the infancy of gods and heroes or the invention of technologies such as wine or musical instruments. While both tragedy and comedy choose the civic settings of public spaces or citizens' homes, satyr drama usually reflects the imagined life of the pre-urban (even neolithic) male by locating itself outside mountain caves or on remote seashores.[8] *Trackers*, for example, is set on Mount Cyllene in Arcadia; it portrays the enslaved satyrs tracking the stolen cattle of

---

[8] The Roman architect Vitruvius recommends that the scenery for satyr drama be decorated 'arboribus, speluncis, montibus reliquisque agrestibus rebus' (5.6.9).

Apollo, before arriving at the cave where the nymph Cyllene is nursing the newborn Hermes, and the baby's invention of the lyre.

Satyr drama shared with tragedy most of its conventions (its heroes' costumes, metrical structures, and avoidance of explicit audience address). Yet the genre's jocularity, and its obsession with bodily functions, betray a closer affinity of ethos with comedy than with tragedy.[9] In Euripides' *Cyclops* cooking, eating, farting and belching were central jokes (see e.g. 325–8, 523), and in Aeschylus' satyric *Lycurgus* the titular mythical king staggered around, drunk on beer (fr. 124). Satyr drama was also much rowdier than tragedy: satyrs danced and pranced continuously, and used more 'shouting noises' (*epiphthegmata*).[10] The satyrs in Sophocles' *Trackers*, for example, yell to the audience, '*u u, ps ps, a a*' (fr. 314.176).

Euripides' *Cyclops* offers insights into the homosocial and sexually focused world of the satyr. It takes the incident of Odysseus' escape from the one-eyed giant Polyphemus from *Odyssey* 9, and introduces into the plot a chorus of satyrs who have been shipwrecked on Sicily and are currently the Cyclops' slaves. After drinking wine Polyphemus seizes Silenus, whom he mistakes for Ganymede, the Trojan boy Zeus loved. He staggers into his cave to rape the ageing satyr, thus allowing Odysseus and the others to blind him and subsequently escape. Polyphemus' sexual preferences, as he states, are homoerotic (583–4): he prefers this 'Ganymede' to the other satyrs, whom in his alcoholic confusion he identifies with the (female) Graces. *Cyclops* thus dramatizes a boisterous all-male plot involving drinking and morally uncomplicated violence enacted against a villain who also happens to be a homosexual rapist. But there are hints, even in this exclusively male world, of the satyrs' notion of the function of the female sex. Before Odysseus' arrival Silenus laments the absence of wine on the island: he longs to drink in order to get an erection, for it is a satyric *topos* that drink enhances ithyphallicism.[11] In the third *Eclogue* of the Carthaginian poet Nemesianus (third century AD), the inspiration for which is likely to have been Sophocles' satyric

---

[9] See Seidensticker (1979), 247.
[10] Browning (1963), 67–81, at 70 para. 9. For the huge variety of different leg movements that satyrs are shown performing on Attic vases, see Seidensticker (2003), 111–17, with excellent illustrations.
[11] See Seaford (1984), 135, for further examples.

Dionysiskos, the satyrs yearn sexually for nymphs after drinking the
newly invented wine (3.18–65).[12] In *Cyclops* Silenus also fantasizes
about what he would do if there were any females available: he wants
to pull at breasts, and to handle 'depilated meadows' (169–71). The
meadow is a euphemism for the female pubic area; this form of
sexual assault by satyrs is illustrated on several vases.[13]

The views on women expressed by this satyric chorus are confined
to their desire for Helen of Troy. In tragedy the people of both Troy
and Greece blame Helen for the Trojan war and would like to see her
killed (e.g. Eur. *Tro.* 874–9). But the satyrs of *Cyclops* have a different
punishment in mind when they ask Odysseus what the Greeks did
with her (179–87):

When you caught that woman, didn't you all 'knock her through' one after
the other, since she takes pleasure in sexual intercourse with many men? The
traitress! When she glimpsed the man [Paris], with his embroidered baggy
trousers around his two legs and a golden chain around the middle of his
neck, she got so excited that she left Menelaus, the best of fellows. It would be
a good thing if the race of women did not exist—except for a few for me![14]

Three aspects of the presentation of the satyrs' lechery here deserve
attention. First, multiple rape is their fantasy. All satyrs would obviously want to rape Helen (Aristides 2.399 suggests that they may
actually have attempted to 'gangbang' her in Sophocles' *Marriage of
Helen*). But they conceive it as a *collective* activity. The Cyclops'
uncontrolled sexuality is portrayed as the impulse of an autarkic,
tyrannical individual who in threatening Silenus threatens the whole
community of satyrs. In contrast the satyrs' eroticism, however
rampant, is presented as fun rather than as dangerous partly because
it is unindividuated, even egalitarian. Secondly, sexual *double entendre* is a preferred mode of satyric discourse, for the 'neck' in
Greek suggests an erect penis,[15] and the baggy trousers may therefore
imply testicles.[16] Helen is imagined by the satyrs as becoming

[12] See Krumeich, Pechstein, and Seidensticker (1999), 256–7.
[13] ARV² 117.2 (Berlin Inv. 3232); ARV² 188.68 (Musée des Antiquités de Rouen,
Inv. 538.3). For a discussion of how these scenes may have been read by their
Athenian viewers, see R. Osborne (1996), 72–6.
[14] My translation.
[15] J. Henderson (1975), 114 and 171.
[16] Seaford (1984), 139; see also J. Henderson (1975), 27.

sexually aroused by eyeing Paris's private parts. Thirdly, the dream of
a world without the 'race' of women is a misogynist commonplace,
expressed by men in Euripides' own tragedies (see e.g. *Hipp.* 618–24).
But the satyrs, typically, undercut their own rhetorical seriousness
with a comic clause exempting themselves from any ban on females:
the peripatetic critic Demetrius after all defined satyr drama as
tragōidia paizousa, 'tragedy at play' (*De Eloc.* 169).

SATYR DRAMA AS TRAGIC CLOSURE

Throughout tragedy's heyday in the fifth century, satyr plays were an
intrinsic part of the theatrical experience of watching tragic performances. At this time most tragedies were first performed at the City
Dionysia, the largest annual Athenian festival of Dionysus, according
to a regular formula of three-plus-one: three tragic poets competed
against one another over three days with a programme of four plays
each, three tragedies plus a satyr drama, performed in that order
sequentially.

We do not know how the tragic competition came to be formulated as a contest between groups comprising three tragedies plus a
satyr play. Aristotle may be correct when he proposes that tragedy
developed out of a chronologically anterior satyr drama (*Poetics*
4.1449ª19–24): alternatively, truth may lie behind Horace's view
that satyr plays were added to the drama competitions after tragedy
had become established in them (*AP* 220–1). But regardless of the
evolutionary process, in the fifth century satyr drama was treated as
an intrinsic part of the tragic performances, as fundamentally inseparable from the foregoing tragedies: Easterling suggests that it may
help to recall the tradition that the dramatist Ion of Chios criticized Pericles on the ground that virtue, like a complete 'tragic
production' (*tragikē didaskalia*), needed a satyric element (Plut.
Pericles 5).[17] The three-plus-one formula did not last for ever: at
some point in the fourth century, before 341 BC, the programme was
altered so that only a single satyr play preceded the entire drama

[17] Easterling (1997*b*), 40.

festival.[18] The nature of satyr plays may have changed, and become more like comedy, as a result of being performed in isolation from tragedy; examples are subsequently attested in various performance contexts until the second century AD,[19] including Python's sensational fourth-century *Agen*, in which Alexander the Great's administrator Harpalus was apparently depicted attempting a necromancy in order to summon from the underworld his dead *hetaira* Pythionike.[20] But the current argument is concerned with the fifth-century satyr play's function as the final component of a composite performance of four dramas.

In earlier tragedy, particularly in Aeschylus, the satyr drama was sometimes connected in subject-matter with the tragedies which had preceded it, forming what the Alexandrian scholars called a *tetralogy*. To close the *Oresteia* tetralogy, for example, the satyric *Proteus* treated Menelaus' journey home from Troy: the first preceding tragedy, *Agamemnon*, had dramatized his brother's homecoming in a more sombre manner. Other Aeschylean tetralogies included the *Oedipodeia* (the satyr drama was *Sphinx*), the *Danaides*, and the *Lycurgeia*. But Aeschylus also sometimes presented four plays without any obvious connection in subject-matter, for example the group *Phineus*, *Persae*, *Glaukos Potnieus*, and the satyric *Prometheus Firekindler*.[21] Little illumination, however, is to be gained from exploring connected tetralogies, since neither *Cyclops* nor any of the more substantial fragments is known to have been part of any extant *tragikē didaskalia*.[22]

Since the satyr play functioned for decades as the conclusion to, and culmination of tragic performances at the City Dionysia, it must have been perceived in that context to be aesthetically,

---

[18] *IG* 2². 2319–23. The implications of the detachment of the satyr play are well brought out in Easterling (1997c), 214–16. See also Collinge (1958–9), 28; Pickard-Cambridge (1988), 79. The apparent exclusion of satyr plays from the contest when tragedies were introduced at the smaller Lenaea festival in the 430s may have prefigured the 4th-cent. abandonment of the three-plus-one model. Perhaps that is also how we should see Euripides' pro-satyric experiment with *Alcestis* during the same decade (438 BC).

[19] See Seidensticker (1979), 228–31, and the 'Introduction' to the edition of the fragments of the minor authors of the genre by Cipolla (2003).

[20] See Snell (1964), chs. 5–6.

[21] On possible links between these plays see E. Hall (1996a), 10–11.

[22] On the exiguous remains of Aechylus' *Amymone* (the satyr drama which concluded the *Danaids* tetralogy) see below.

psychologically, emotionally, and socially appropriate, even indispensable: the two genres were fundamentally and dialectically interdependent.[23] Discussions of the relationship between them goes back even beyond Demetrius (see above), but it has not been a prominent scholarly concern to explore the gender dynamics of the interface.

In the Renaissance (besides regularly being confused with satire), satyr drama was viewed as an intermediate genre, and 'imitated' in the form of pastoral tragicomedy: *Cyclops* played an important role in the discussion of mixed genres in general.[24] Satyr drama was first properly understood by Isaac Casaubon in 1605, but his treatise *De Satyrica Graecorum poesi, & Romanorum satira libri duo* still bears traces of this 'mixed' or 'middle' genre theory.[25] In the nineteenth century three new concepts entered the critical discourse: first, at a time when burlesques and burlettas of highbrow plays and operas were a staple of the western European popular theatre, the notion of tragic 'burlesque' (or 'travesty' or 'parody') becomes prominent. Secondly, A. W. von Schlegel's famous lectures introduced the functionalist idea of satyr drama as providing psychological 'release', 'relaxation', or 'resolution' of tragic conflict.[26] Thirdly, aesthetic disapproval is expressed: commentators began to see satyr drama as a regrettably primitive 'after-piece' of no intrinsic merit or pertinence to the foregoing tragedies: 'the practice of terminating a trilogy with a satyric play... may seem questionable to modern taste, and can hardly be defended upon artistic grounds.'[27] Throughout the twentieth century, many scholars continued to draw on the 'parody', 'release', and 'inferior after-piece' paradigms. The last two are fused, for example, in the introduction to a Penguin translation of *Cyclops* and *Trackers* in 1957:

---

[23] The first scholar fully to understand the dialectical interdependence of the two genres was Brommer (1959), 5: 'The satyr play in its heyday is unthinkable without tragedy, but so is tragedy unthinkable without satyr drama.'

[24] Herrick (1955), 7–14.

[25] Casaubon (1605), reproduced in facsimile with an introduction by Medine (1973), 130–1: *Satyrica est poëma dramaticum, tragœdiae adnexum, chorum e Satyris habens, personarum illustrium actionem notabilem, partim seriam, partim iocosam exprimens, stilo hilari, exitu plerunque læto.* On the passion for burlesques of serious tragedy in 19th-cent. Paris and London, see Hall and Macintosh (2005), chs. 12–15.

[26] See von Schlegel (1840), i. 189.

[27] Haigh (1889), 25.

Thus we have the unique example of a primitive drama continuing to exist side by side with the highest literary achievement; of the greatest dramatists writing what are almost folk-plays as well as their great tragedies... It is almost as if Shakespeare had written a *Punch and Judy* to be presented as an *after-piece* to *Romeo and Juliet*... By the time of Sophocles and Euripides the most obvious function of the satyr play was to supply a *release* from the tragic tension of the preceding plays.[28]

More adventurous conceptions of the genre have appeared, but gender has never figured prominently in their formulation: satyr drama has been thought to offer the tragic playwrights a chance to abandon heroics and write more realistically,[29] or to make explicit references to contemporary politics.[30] Luigi Campo's triple division of satyr dramas into those with a 'heroico', 'parodico', or 'amoroso' plot failed to perceive that the 'amorousness' of the genre is, in contradistinction to tragedy, apparently a male monopoly.[31] Indeed, the level of most critics' awareness of gender issues at that time can be inferred from the fact that a prominent expert on satyr drama argued in print as late as 1980 that 'the general psychological principle is self-evident. Who of us has not received the advice that when going for an interview with a superior one should imagine *him* clad in his underwear?'[32]

Recently, however, critics have rightly been focusing on the religious and Dionysiac aspects of the genre. The poet Tony Harrison sees the physical conditions of the Athenian drama festivals, which united 'sufferer and celebrant in the same light', as the basis of the dialectical relationship between tragic and satyric drama.[33] Vase-paintings show that entourages of satyrs had been associated with the worship of Dionysus since well before the establishment of drama festivals; Easterling therefore argues that the identity of the satyr chorus indicates that they enact something with much more to do with Dionysus and his cult than either of the other genres.[34] Lissarrague's formulation

---

[28] R. L. Green (1957), 11.   [29] Pohlenz (1954), 134.
[30] C. T. Murphy (1935); Lassere (1973).   [31] Campo (1940), 221–61.
[32] D. F. Sutton (1980), 4.   [33] Tony Harrison (1991), p. xiv.
[34] Easterling (1997*b*), esp. 38, argues that the satyr play is a *culmination*, in which the performers of the tragic tetralogy ultimately approach their nearest approximation to their cultic role as Dionysus' worshippers. See also Wiles (2000), 36: 'For the dancers who had reached the end of a long and draining process, the satyr uniform must have helped them experience possession by the god, with all feeling of ego gone.'

defines the Dionysiac function of the satyrs as playing the same serious social issues as tragedy 'in a different key':[35]

we may say that satyrs reproduce the 'normal' values of Greek males by transforming them, *according to a set of rules that are never random* . . . Tragedy poses fundamental questions about the relation between mortals and gods, or it reflects on such serious issues as sacrifice, war, marriage, or law. Satyric drama, by contrast, plays with culture by first distancing it and then reconstructing it through its antitypes, the satyrs.

This anthropological interpretation is currently canonical, and invites further questions as to the way satyric drama plays with the 'serious issues' on which tragedy reflects. The economic and social implications of the encounter between man, monstrous giant, and satyr in *Cyclops* have been analysed by David Konstan; he argues that the contrast ultimately serves to present 'the human community . . . as the positive realization of social relations', in contrast with both the monadic Cyclops and the unindividuated satyric collective.[36] It would be interesting to ask whether the motifs of slavery and release, and the communistic utopianism of the satyrs' group ideology, function as fanstasy-correctives to the class-ridden city-state of Athens, founded on slave labour. But the question in hand is the relation between the satyrs' exclusively masculine viewpoint and the quite different perspective of tragedy, for satyr drama has been analysed by the male-dominated history of classical scholarship in a characteristically male-determined way—that is, by overlooking its gender dynamics altogether.

SATYR DRAMA'S MASCULINE FOCUS

Aristophanes' *Thesmophoriazusae* (411) testifies to the early currency of a theory concerning dramatic representation, according to which a writer's own habits and perceived gender orientation influenced the characters he created. A 'womanish' man is thus more likely to create convincing parts for women characters than a 'masculine' one: even

---

[35] Lissarrague (1990*b*), 235–6.   [36] Konstan (1990), 227.

adopting the dress and behaviour of women will help in writing tragedies about them. The interlocutors are the notoriously effeminate tragedian Agathon and a conspicuously 'butch' relative by marriage of the more famous tragedian Euripides (148–58):[37]

AGATHON   I change my clothing according as I change my mentality. A man who is a poet must adopt habits that match the plays he's committed to composing. For example, if one is writing plays about women, one's body must participate in their habits.

INLAW   So when you write a *Phaedra*, you mount astride?

AGATHON   If you're writing about men, your body has what it takes already, but when it's a question of something we don't possess, then it must be captured by imitation (*mimēsis*).

INLAW   Ask me over then, when you're writing a satyr-play,[38] so I can collaborate with you, long and hard, from the rear.

The inlaw's second joke illumines the psychosexual orientation of satyr drama. To write a satyr play Agathon will need to be in the process of being buggered. The transvestite Agathon's gender is ambivalent: he is as effeminate as the Greek comic imagination could conceive a man to be. He is a man-woman who, the joke suggests, will collaborate in a satyr drama with the lustily masculine inlaw while being anally penetrated by him. The success of the joke depends on the audience's assumption that the viewpoint of dramatic satyrs was pointedly masculine, characterized by a hyperbolic sexual appetitiveness, and permitted both heterosexual and homosexual expression.

Do the remains of satyr drama substantiate Euripides' inlaw's view? Certainly Agathon's cross-dressing points to what seems to have been a regular satyric motif, for there is evidence for transvestite satyrs on vases.[39] There were also transvestite roles in satyr plays such as Ion's *Omphale*, where both Heracles and the satyrs, enslaved to the

---

[37] Translation taken from Sommerstein (1994), 33–5. There is a detailed appraisal of this scene, from the perspective of the actors' costumes and the likely appearance of their ithyphalloi, in Stehle (2002), 378–87.

[38] The Greek text literally says 'when you are doing (or 'making') satyrs' (*hotan saturous toinun poieis*): see above p. 142 n. 2.

[39] See Brommer (1959), nos. 118 and 118a.

powerful queen Omphale, seem to have donned women's attire.[40] Certainly the satyrs, unlike male characters at least in extant tragedy, are not exclusively heterosexual. Indeed, in Sophocles' *Lovers of Achilles*, in which eros was a topic of discussion generally (fr. 149.8–9 *TgrF*), Phoenix upbraided the satyrs for having turned from homoerotic to heterosexual ways, specifically for desiring women rather than boys (*ta paidika*, fr. 153 *TgrF*). The homosexual tendencies of the satyrs are also implied in Achaeus' *Linos* (fr. 26 *TgrF*), and documented on vases.[41] But the satyrs also despise effeminate males, for they taunt Dionysus himself with looking like a woman in Aeschylus' *Theōroi* (fr. 78a.68 *TgrF*). In *Trackers* Silenus boasts of the martial achievements of his youth, when he hung up trophies in nymphs' caves as evidence of his *manly* valour (*andreia*, fr. 314.154 *TgrF*).

One of the typical interests of the genre was invention, and even this motif was associated with (male) sexual arousal. Stage satyrs were privileged to be present at the introduction of fire to the terrestrial domain in Aeschylus' *Prometheus Firekindler*; in a fragment from it they envisage their domestic sex games now occurring in comfortable warmth (fr. 204b.2–5 *TgrF*): '[Throw down] your bright cloaks by the unwearying light of the fire. Often shall one of the naiads, when she has heard me tell this tale, pursue me by the blaze within the hearth…' The life-transforming arrival of fire allows the satyrs to fantasize that for once it will be they who are the objects of erotic pursuit. The satyrs also tasted the first ever wine in Sophocles' *Dionysiskos* (of which one of the few fragments, Soph. frr. 171–2 *TgrF*, is a masculine singular participle meaning 'drunk'), and the wine seems to have made them horny.[42] In another

---

[40] The female vocative plurals in Ion's *Omphale* ('maidens' and 'Lydian harp-women', frr. 20, 22 *TgrF*), almost certainly apostrophize the satyrs temporarily dressed, like Heracles in service to Omphale, as women. In Euripides' *Skiron* the satyrs may either have dressed as women, or pursued female companions of Theseus (*The Oxyrhynchus Papyri* 27 (1962), 57). Actors could put on additional (female) clothing over their satyric costumes: for a parallel see the goatskins in *Cyclops* 80; Seidensticker (1979), 233; Steffen (1971), 207–8.

[41] Lissarrague (1990*a*), 64–5. On *Lovers of Achilles* see the comments in Krumeich, Pechstein, and Seidensticker (1999), 234–5.

[42] For further references to drink enhancing sexual appetite in satyrs, see above pp. 147–8.

Sophoclean play the satyrs actually participated in the invention of womankind. In a fragment of his *Pandora* one individual (Hephaestus?) is instructed by another to 'begin to manipulate the clay in your two hands' (fr. 482 *TgrF*). This leaves little doubt that Pandora, the first woman, was actually constructed in the Athenian theatre, as she had been in Hesiod's accounts (*Theog.* 578–89, *Op.* 60–82). Other evidence links the satyrs with Hephaestus in the role of his workmen,[43] and the play had an alternative title, *Sphyrokopoi*, 'Hammerers', which indicates that the satyrs were involved. They either helped to craft Pandora, or hammered on the ground to release her from it, an interpretation perhaps supported by a vase-painting likely to have been inspired by this play, in which scene Pandora appears to be depicted in the process of rising from the earth (fig. 5.3).[44]

If the satyrs enjoy witnessing the creation of Woman, they also desire to win women as prizes in athletics. In a satyric dialogue probably composed by Sophocles, someone called Oineus or Schoineus converses with the chorus. [Sch]oineus has apparently announced that his daughter will be given to the victor in an athletics competition; when he asks the satyrs who they are, they deliver a manifesto of satyrdom (fr. 1130.6–18 *TgrF*):

You will learn everything. We have come as bridegrooms, but are the children of nymphs, devotees of Bacchus, and neighbours of the gods. Every worthwhile art is embodied in us: fighting with spears, wrestling matches, horsemanship, running, boxing, biting, testicle-twisting; in us you will find musical song, knowledgeable prophecy with no fakery, discriminating knowledge of medicine, measuring of the heavens, dance, and discussion of the underworld. Hey, is my erudition not to bear fruit? If you give me your daughter, you can take whichever of my skills you desire.

This play therefore combined two of the satyrs' favourite activities: the pursuit of women and athletics. The princess's opinion, of course, is unlikely to have been taken into account.

The fragments suggest that in satyr plays it was not only the satyrs but the leading roles who participated in the sexual pursuit of

---

[43] See A. C. Pearson (1917), i.110, ii.9, 136.

[44] An Attic red-figured volute-krater in Ferrara (T.579), dating from around 450. For a discussion and illustrations of the rest of the painting see Trendall and Webster (1971), 33 and pl. II.7. For more recent comments, see Krumeich, Pechstein, and Seidensticker (1999), 378–9.

Fig. 5.3   Scene from the neck of an Attic red-figured volute-krater in Ferrara, c. 450 BC

females. Euripides' *Syleus* seems to have concluded with Heracles chasing Syleus' daughter (Xenodoke or Xenodike), through Syleus' vineyard.[45] Aeschylus' *Amymone* was the satyr play concluding his *Danaids* tetralogy, whose central topic had been the repudiation of marriage by Danaus' fifty daughters. The satyr play is likely to have enacted a marriage-related story preserved in Apollodorus (*Bibl.* 2.1.4), in which the Danaid Amymone was looking for water after a drought struck Argos. A satyr was about to rape her, but was disturbed by the arrival of Poseidon, who then had sex with her himself and revealed a spring to her: one of the only three fragments (fr. 13 *TgrF*) has a male saying to a female that it is fated that she marry (or 'mate with'—*gameisthai*) him.[46]

From Sophocles' *Trackers* there survive about 180 lines of an altercation between the satyrs and the nymph Cyllene, who certainly fears their violence and shouting (fr. 314.251–5). She is nursing the baby Hermes, borne by Atlas' daughter to Zeus (fr. 314.267–76), but the satyrs are convinced that her cave conceals Apollo's cattle. They make no explicitly sexual threats against her, which may suggest that theatrical satyrs treated nymphs with more respect than human women. In Aesch. *Theōroi* fr. 78a.14–17 the satyrs seem to have a strong maternal attachment, and their mothers are always nymphs. But the scene in *Trackers*, equally, may have concluded with an assault, since the dialogue is turning into angry stichomythia just as the papyrus becomes unintelligible (fr. 314.390–404 *TgrF*).

The best example of heterosexual harassment in satyr drama is in Aeschylus' *Dictyulci*, which dramatized the story of the baby Perseus. His mother Danae was impregnated by Zeus (disguised as a shower of gold), locked up in a chest with the baby by her wicked father, and pushed out to sea. Eventually the chest arrived at the island of Seriphos and was hauled up in a fishing-net. The surviving scene involves an encounter between mother, baby, Silenus,[47] and the satyrs, in which Silenus plans to marry Danae despite a (human) rival called Dictys. The text contains holes, but it is clear that Danae responds in horror to Silenus, calling on her ancestral gods to prevent

---

[45] *The Oxyrhynchus Papyri* 27 (1962), 57–8.

[46] See Sutton (1974).

[47] Lloyd-Jones's case that Danae's interlocutor in fr. 47a (765–72, 786–820) must be Silenus is overwhelmingly convincing: see Smyth (1957), 33–5.

her from being 'violated' (*lumanthēsomai*) by the bestial satyrs (*knō-dalois*, fr. 47a 765–85 *TgrF*). Her register of speech is distinctly tragic, in comparison with the more colloquial and obscene vocabulary of the satyrs, which suggests that differentials in elevation of diction may have sometimes functioned in satyr drama to distinguish feminine from masculine speech.[48] Danae contemplates suicide by the conventional female tragic means of hanging.[49] Her fears are justified: even her child is at risk of sexual assault. For Silenus replies that her baby is smiling at his 'bald head'. Since the Greeks are likely to have drawn aural connections between their words for 'bald' and for 'phallus' (see above), this is probably a euphemism for the tip of Silenus' phallus. He adds that 'the little one' is clearly a 'penis-lover' (*posthophilēs*). An innocent critic once took this scene as evidence that Aeschylus 'loved and knew infants intimately'.[50] But Lissarrague much more plausibly draws attention to the equivalence between a baby satyr and a phallus carried by two satyrs on the two sides of an amphora in Boston.[51] In the male and highly sexualized world of the satyr, bald heads and babies thus become virtually indistinguishable from satyrs.

The papyrus' quality now improves. The satyrs envisage that Danae will marry Silenus rather than the rival Dictys, and believe her to be in need of 'a good seeing to' (fr. 47a 799–832 *TgrF*):[52]

SILENUS   If I don't rejoice [at the sight] of you. Damnation take Dictys, who [is trying to cheat] me of this prize [behind my back]. Come here, my dearie!

Don't be frightened! Why are you whimpering? Over here to my sons, so that you can come to my protecting arms, dear boy—I'm so

---

[48] It has been proposed that male heroes and satyrs used two different stylistic levels—i.e. that heroes had the same elevated diction as in tragedy, while the satyrs spoke in a more demotic register: see Schmid (1934), 83 n. 7. But Odysseus in *Cyclops* uses poetic diction with no obvious differences from that used by Silenus. For further discussion see Krumeich, Pechstein, and Seidensticker (1999), 15–16.

[49] There is no justification for the view of Lobel (1941), 12, that Danae's phrase, 'Shall I then knot myself a noose', is slang-influenced: see Sophocles' *OT* 1374, Eur. *Hel.* 299. Her other allegedly untragic phrase, 'You have heard all I have to say' has a direct parallel at Aesch. *Ag.* 582.

[50] Howe (1959), 163.

[51] Lissarrague (1990*a*), 58.

[52] Translation by Lloyd-Jones in Smyth (1957), 537–41. Square brackets enclose conjectural supplements.

kind—and you can find pleasure in the martens and the fawns and the young porcupines, and can make a third in bed with your mother and with me your father. And daddy shall give the little one his fun. And you shall lead a healthy life, so that one day, when you've grown strong, you yourself—for your father's losing his grip on fawn-killing footwork—you yourself shall catch beasts without a spear, and give them to your mother for dinner, after the fashion of her husband's family, amongst whom you will be earning your keep.

CHORUS Come now, dear fellows, let us go and hurry on the marriage, for the time is ripe for it and without words speaks for it. Why, I see that already the bride is eager to enjoy our love to the full. No wonder: she spent a long time wasting away all lonely in the ship beneath the foam. Well, now that she has before her eyes our youthful vigour, she rejoices and exults; such is the bridegroom that by the bright gleam of Aphrodite's torches...

Here the papyrus breaks off, but even this brief sequence is of unique importance as the sole example of the satyrs of satyr drama in direct colloquy with an object of their sexual desire. Danae is indistinguishable in this scene from a tragic heroine, but the pathos of her fear of rape is undercut by the humorous presentation of the libidinousness of the satyrs. The ageing Silenus' intentions towards Danae may be more domestic than erotic, and he seems to be more interested (in this scene, anyway) in the baby Perseus than in his mother. But the satyrs themselves have only one thing in mind: the delightful prospect of collective sexual intercourse with the woman before them. In the event Danae was almost certainly spared the actual ordeal of multiple rape, and instead married Silenus' rival. But the intentionally comic fantasy of the satyrs speaks volumes about the psychosexual dynamics underpinning their audience's group identity.[53]

THE FEMININITY OF TRAGEDY

Satyr drama, therefore, was characterized by an unapologetic obsession with male sexuality, visually represented in the satyrs' costumes,

[53] I have quoted *Net-Fishers* at length partly because antiquity held Aeschylus to have been by far the best writer of satyr dramas: Paus. 2.13.6; Menedemus (Hellenistic philosopher), quoted at Diog. Laert. 2.133.

and a masculine, *homosocial* consciousness manifested in and articulated by its chorus of satyrs. The next stage in the argument requires establishing a distinction between this gender alignment and that of tragedy. First, some symbolism: on the rare occasions when the ancients represented the relationship between the two genres in visual or allegorical form, satyr play was certainly conceived as masculine in contrast with 'feminine' tragedy. On a vase from the last third of the fifth century a sexually excited satyr creeps up on a sleeping maenad significantly name-labelled 'Tragedy', thus formulating the genre relationship of satyric to tragic drama as one of covert sexual assault.[54] As Robin Osborne has argued, this scene is one of a group of similar vase-paintings depicting satyrs' covert sexual assault on sleeping maenads—scenes which themselves, though not explicitly theatre-related, undeniably play out libidinal dramas often involving a third party in the form of an additional spectating satyr.[55] Another image is the matronly Tragedy in Horace's *Ars Poetica* (231–3): 'Tragedy does not deserve to blurt out trivial lines, but she will modestly consort a little with the forward satyrs, like a respectable lady dancing because she must on a feast day.'[56]

Female characters and choruses are extremely prominent in Athenian tragedy. Only one extant tragedy, Sophocles' *Philoctetes*, contains no women; female tragic choruses in the surviving plays outnumber male by no fewer than twenty-one to ten; some plays are named for their memorable female choruses (Aeschylus' *Suppliant Women*, Euripides' *Bacchae*). Numerous tragedies were named for a

[54] See fig. 5.2 above. It is just possible that the female figure holding a mask to the right of Ariadne on the 'Pronomos Vase' is a personification of satyr play (see Csapo and Slater (1995), 69 and pl. 8), but I have argued elsewhere that she is, rather, *Tragōidia*, a personification of Tragedy herself, presiding over the celebration of a tragic tetralogy concluded by the satyr drama of which the chorusmen are painted on the vase: E. Hall (forthcoming *a*).

[55] R. Osborne (1996), 73–7.

[56] *effutire leves indigna Tragoedia versus* | *ut festis matrona moveri iussa diebus,* | *intererit Satyris paulum pudibunda protervis*, lines which formed part of Wiseman's famous hypothesis (1988) that Horace had himself attempted to compose satyr plays. Allegorical conceptions of tragedy as an imposing female are of course customary: see e.g. Plutarch's picture of Tragedy as an ornamental rich woman, with famous tragic actors serving her like beauticians and stool-bearers (*De Glor. Athen.* 349; see Ch. 4, p. 99). For a detailed discussion of the ancient personifications of Tragedy, both literary and visual, see E. Hall (forthcoming *a*). They begin in about 440 BC.

female role (*Antigone*), or had a female protagonist,[57] a phenomenon replicated amongst the titles and remains of the lost plays.[58] Many plays named for a female chorus also had an important individual female role.[59] Even in many plays named for a male protagonist or chorus, the character on stage for the longest, or with the largest or most memorable part, may nevertheless be a woman (the Queen in *Persians*, Clytemnestra in *Agamemnon*, Phaedra in *Hippolytus*). The ancients already sensed the female domination of tragedy: the satirist Lucian commented that 'there are more females than males' (*De Salt.* 28, see also Ach. Tat. 1.8). The assertiveness and articulacy of tragic women caused offence throughout antiquity: Aristotle recommends that women should not be depicted as clever or brave (*Poet.* 1454ᵃ23–4), Plutarch complains that tragedy represented women as adept rhetoricians (*De Aud. Poet.* 28a), and the Christian Origen criticized Euripidean women for inappropriately expressing philosophical opinions (*Contra Celsum* 7.36.34–6).

Many reasons have been proposed for women's prominence in tragedy. Some are based on women's role in religion, their perform-ance of funeral lamentation, and the phenomena of maenadism and transvestism in Dionysiac cult. Some draw on anthropological sym-bolism's findings that patriarchal cultures use the figures and bodies of women to imagine abstractions and think about their social order. Others point to the construction of women as more susceptible to invasive passions such as eros and daemonic possession.[60] Zeitlin has importantly argued that theatrical representations of women, socially constructed as more emotionally expressive than men, offered a medium through which the Athenian male could legitimately explore a full range of emotions (including those denied socially to the 'ideal' self-restrained man), by watching his fellow citizens 'playing the other' in the theatre.[61] We know from an invaluable fifth-century source that the Athenian audience was once reduced *en masse* to tears

---

[57] The two *Electras, Medea, Hecuba, Andromache, Helen, IT,* and *IA*.

[58] e.g. Choerilus' *Alope*, Phrynichus' *Alcestis*, Aeschylus' and Sophocles' *Niobe*, Sophocles' *Phaedra*, Euripides' *Melanippe* plays, *Hypsipyle, Auge,* and *Andromeda*.

[59] *Libation-Bearers, Eumenides, Women of Trachis, Trojan Women, Suppliant Women, Phoenician Women*.

[60] For overviews and bibliography see e.g. Foley (1981*a*); E. Hall (1997*b*), section 3.

[61] Zeitlin (1996), 341–74.

by a tragedy, Phrynichus' *Sack of Miletus* (which almost certainly included female lamentation).[62] Reports attest to the emotive effect of tragic scenes on spectators, most of which relate to actors' performances in poignant female roles—Polus as Electra, Theodorus in *Trojan Women* (see Ch. 10, pp. 312–13).

In Aristophanes the femininity of tragedy is consciously associated with Euripides and Agathon. In *Frogs* Aeschylus formulates the contrast between himself and Euripides primarily in terms of gender, and in particular of the active sexuality of Euripides' women. Aeschylus says that his heroes made every 'citizen man' (*andra politēn*) warlike, and that he never created 'whores' (*pornas*) such as Phaedra or Stheneboea, nor ever portrayed a woman driven by erotic passion (*erōsan...gunaika*, 1041–4). Aeschylus claims that the poet has a special duty to conceal what is immoral, rather than dramatizing it. For while little children are taught by whomsoever addresses them, 'young men' (*toisi d' hēbōsi*) are taught by poets (1054–5). This juxtaposition of the objection to the sexually driven woman (*erōsa gunē*) in tragedy with the responsibility of poets to the moral education of youths adumbrates Socrates' objections to tragic mimesis in Plato's *Republic*.

The 'femininity' of tragedy is deeply implicated in its banishment by Socrates from the ideal polity. A function of poetry should be to make men brave (*andreioi*—literally, 'manly'): all lamentations and expressions of pity by men of note should therefore be excised from 'Homer and the other poets' (3.387d1–2). Since the good man in reality grieves as little as possible when he loses 'a son or brother or anything like that', in literature, likewise, the laments attributed to notable men should be removed, and given to women (but not to serious women), and to cowardly men (3.387e9–388a3). This applies to poetry in general, and several of the examples supplied suggest that the author is thinking as much of the gloomier parts of epic as of tragedy.

But Socrates subsequently focuses on drama, which he regards as particularly psychologically dangerous since it consists entirely of

---

[62] Hdt. 6.21.1. Phrynichus' women must have been striking, for a tradition developed holding him responsible for the introduction of female characters into tragedy (*Suda* φ 762); see Ch. 4, p. 120. On the paradox whereby Athenian tragedy depicted forms of lamentation actively discouraged at Athens, see Foley (1993).

direct speech. First he establishes that the future guardians must not imitate anyone except brave, self-controlled, righteous and free men, lest they become that which they imitate (3.395c2–d3). The first type of person whom they must never imitate is, 'given that they are men, a woman' (*gunaika mimeisthai andras ontas*). Socrates then specifies types of activity typical of tragic women which he deems absolutely unsuitable for imitation: reviling a husband, boastfully competing with the gods, being overtaken by misfortune, mourning or lamentation, illness, lust (*erōsan*), or childbirth (3.395d5–e3, on which see above, Ch. 2).

Socrates next proscribes the imitation of slaves, bad men, cowards, the foul-mouthed, and madmen (3.395e5–396a4). Yet the impersonation of women has taken overwhelming priority in his list of *dramatis personae* banned because they are felt to damage spectators as well as actors.[63] And gender differentials speedily resurface when Socrates later focuses more specifically on the audience. He is discussing the emotional impact made by performances of Homer and tragedy (10.605c10–d5):

When the best of us hear Homer or some other tragic poet imitating a hero in mourning, delivering a long speech of lamentation, singing, or beating his breast, you know how we feel pleasure and give ourselves up to it, how we follow in sympathy and praise the excellence of the poet who does this to us most effectively?[64]

On the other hand, says Socrates, we pride ourselves on the opposite reaction—on enduring the pain in silence when suffering a real bereavement, 'because the latter is the reaction of a man, and the former is the reaction of a woman' (*hōs touto men andros ōn, ekeino de gunaikas*, 10.605d7–e1). The archaic poet Archilochus had long before defined grief as a womanish (*gunaikeion*) emotion to be avoided (fr. 13.9–10 *IEG*). But in Plato it has become a reprehensibly 'womanish' thing even vicariously to undergo the experience of a grieving hero.

Plato's objections to tragedy thus reveal that even the classical Athenians were already aware that the theatre paradoxically licensed and even encouraged men to undergo emotional reactions, especially

---

[63] P. Murray (1996), 176.
[64] Translation by Lindsay (1976), 309.

grief and lamentation, which in 'reality' would be disparaged as 'feminine';[65] as Zeitlin puts it, 'theater uses the feminine for the purposes of imagining a fuller model for the masculine self, and "playing the other" opens that self to those often banned emotions of pity and fear'.[66]

MALES BEHAVING BADLY

Fifth-century Athenian tragedy seems actually to have preferred female choruses and is rich in important female roles. Comedy, likewise, offers many examples of both choruses and characters assuming female identities.[67] But two of the defining features of satyr drama were its satyr-chorus, and probably the individual character of Father Silenus.[68] These features suggest that the genre included an obligatory and highly sexed masculine voice and viewpoint. A survey of the remains of the genre has not cast doubt on this inference; on the contrary, rape fantasies and the harassment of females have been found to be generic staples. Whatever conclusions are to drawn from this startlingly gendered perspective must take into account satyr drama's function as the culmination of a quadruple tragic production at the City Dionysia, which, as late twentieth-century scholarship demonstrated, functioned sociopolitically as a celebration of collective *male* Athenian citizenship.[69]

Unfortunately it is impossible to discuss the configuring of gender in satyr drama further without speculation. The *Odyssey* was a regular source for satyric plots, yet we know neither whether Penelope

---

[65] In the *Laws* it is speculated that the people in a hypothetical community who would regard tragedy as the most pleasurable genre would be 'the more educated' of the women, very young men, and the common herd (2.658c10–d4), a passage which may reflect the increasing diversity of venues in which tragedy was performed in the fourth century, and of the spectators who regularly enjoyed it. See Ch. 7, pp. 197–8 and E. Hall (forthcoming *b*).

[66] Zeitlin (1996), 363.

[67] Aristophanes' *Clouds*, *Lysistrata*, *Thesmophoriazusae* and *Ecclesiazusae*; the phenomenon is replicated amongst the fragments of Old Comedy.

[68] Collinge (1958–9), 29.

[69] e.g. Winkler (1990), Zeitlin (1996); E. Hall (1989), 201–10.

appeared in Aeschylus' *Ostologoi*, nor how Circe was presented in his *Circe*. Witches featured, yet we know nothing of the extent of Medea's involvement in Sophocles' *Daedalos* (or *Talos*). There may have been a satyric *Iambe* by Sophocles, representing a mythical female comedian, the personification of scurrilous iambic lampoon.[70] Supernatural or superhuman females appeared in Aeschylus' *Sphinx* and *Proteus* (Eidothea),[71] Achaeus' *Moirai* and Aristias' *Kēres*. The evidence for female divinities is present but frustratingly slight:[72] Sophocles wrote a *Krisis* which *may* imply the presence of Hera, Athena, and/or Aphrodite; there was *probably* a satyr play in which Athena competed with Marsyas on the aulos; Hera was *apparently* humiliated in Achaeus' *Hephaistos*; the popular vase-painting motif in which the satyrs sexually assault Iris *may* suggest a plot for Achaeus' *Iris*.[73]

Yet despite the loss of so many texts, an attempt to decode the gender dynamics of satyr drama is crucial to our understanding of the total emotional experience undergone by the fifth-century spectator of tragedy. The protagonist of satyr drama is really its satyric chorus,[74] and the chorus consists of males quite incapable of regulating their own sexual appetites; in Freudian terms, the satyrs are all male id and no superego.[75] Eros is central also to tragedy, in which the plots are frequently motivated by inappropriate or excessive

[70] See further Ch. 6, p. 176.
[71] Ussher (1977), 290.
[72] In his edition of *Trackers* R. J. Walker (1919), 575 argued (in the course of a speculative reconstruction of Aeschylus' *Proteus*), that Apollo was 'more fitted' than Athena 'to be brought, without offence, into the satyric atmosphere'. I cite this here only to show the extent to which scholars used to allow their own prejudices about gender roles to colour their work on satyr drama.
[73] For further discussion of all these plays, including useful bibliography but highly speculative reconstructions, see Sutton (1980).
[74] Seidensticker (1979), 179.
[75] Psychoanalysts would be interested to learn that ancient men dreamt about satyrs. In the *Interpretation of Dreams* by Artemidorus, dreaming about any attendants of Dionysus, including the satyrs, is diagnosed as 'signifying great disturbance, dangers, and scandals'. Dreaming of actually dancing in honour of Dionysus 'is inauspicious for all but slaves. For most men, it foretells folly and harm because of the *ecstasies* of the mental processes and the frenzy' (2.37, translated by R. J. White (1975), 118). See also the pseudo-Callisthenic *Alexander Romance*, in which Alexander 'saw in his sleep a satyr, one of the attendants of Dionysus, offering him a cheese made from milk' (35).

erotic impulses which ultimately threaten to destabilise not only the individual family but the entire community. The sexually motivated character in tragedy is particularly dangerous if she is a woman: although Aristophanes regarded the *erōsa gunē* as an identifiably Euripidean phenomenon, she is anticipated by Aeschylus' Clytemnestra and Sophocles' Deianeira. But in satyr drama, rather than afflicting disturbed individuals of either sex, eros is a permanent attribute of the (male) choral collective.

At least one post-hippie critic has read the satyrs' sexuality as a Rousseauesque idealization of the innocent desires of Man in Nature before the restrictive social regulation of sexual relations in marriage: 'the satyr exists harmoniously with himself, with Nature, with Dionysus. He is the supreme embodiment of health. Although he is less than human, he embodies a kind of wisdom: he represents what Man can and should be.'[76] Besides the gender-blindness of this reading, which assumes the entire human race under the sign of 'Man', its assumption that the satyrs represented an enviable model of freedom from psychosexual repression is wholly anachronistic. A diametrically opposite view diagnoses the satyrs as a sign of the Athenian male's negation of his own sexuality:

Greek satyrdom is an expression of a basically misogynous outlook. In the vase-painting of the mid-fifth century—and undoubtedly on the stage—Greek satyrs are characterised as profoundly anti-female. By inventing the satyr to personify his fear, or disapproval, of natural sexuality—and by banishing him to the category 'animal'—the Greek is representing nature as incompatible with culture. He does not wish to be reminded that he is a sexual animal.[77]

While correctly appreciating the underlying misogyny of satyr drama, this reading surely overstates the ancient ambivalence towards male sexuality. Nearer to the mark is Konstan's interpretation of *Cyclops*,[78] in which both the satyrs' primitive communitarianism, and Polyphemus' anarchically monadic self-sufficiency, function as antitypes to the human community. Satyr drama thus sanctions humanity's internal relations (including its sexual mores and institution of marriage). To push this view to its limit, one function of the

[76] Sutton (1980), 179.   [77] Hoffmann (1977), 3–4.
[78] Konstan (1990), 227.

satyrs' pre-polis wantonness is to legitimize the regulation of wantonness in the polis.

Yet the most satisfactory definition of satyrdom available is Lissarrague's notion that it reproduces the values of ancient Greek males
by distancing them from their cultural norms, and systematically
transforming them according to a precise set of rules.[79] The only
problem with this illuminating description lies in its *emotional neu-
trality*: it would be impossible for any female reader, let alone a
conscious feminist, to contemplate the remains of satyr drama without a degree of emotional alienation. Lissarrague's 'rules that are
never random' included the rule that male sexual aggression was a
phenomenon to be riotously celebrated. This 'rule' poses an even
greater problem to the *constructionist* feminist, who believes that the
majority of gender role distinctions, including those defining sexual
behaviour, are products of culture rather than of nature. For to her
the genre must ultimately be seen to legitimize male sexual appetitiveness by *construing* it as embedded in nature, and to valorize it by
theatrically tracing it in a special and hilarious form of quasi-aetio-
logical charter to mythical prehistory. 'We were all satyrs together
once, and wasn't it fun?', the plays seem to me to shout noisily to the
men of Athens.

Satyr drama certainly used pleasure in order 'to parade the boundaries of what men may acceptably be seen to do':[80] by masturbating,
assaulting women, and screaming in fear, the satyrs entertainingly
helped to define the protocols which governed correct male public
conduct in their spectator, who no doubt felt some satisfaction in the
knowledge that he was himself better able to regulate his appetites
and control his emotions. Yet satyr drama also sends the male
spectator out of the theatre not only laughing rather than crying,
but reassured of his place in the *male* collective. Tragedy has served
one of its purposes by offering the assembled citizens of Athens an
opportunity to indulge emotions socially constructed as feminine.
But playing satyr drama's childlike, carnal, homosocial 'other' brings
the spectator back into the psychological gender orientation appropriate to the City Dionysia, by substituting a joyous collective
male consciousness physically centred on the phallus. A much-cited

[79] Lissarrague (1990*b*), 235–6.   [80] R. Osborne (1996), 65.

definition suggests that in satyr play tragedy subverts itself, 'and thereby effects insurance against the surfeit of the painful passions which it has unleashed'.[81] I would like to modify this definition so as to emphasize the gendered basis of the genre dichotomization: satyr drama offers the insurance of a reaffirmed sense of unindividuated masculinity, based in libidinal awareness, in order to protect against the painful 'feminine' emotions which tragedy has unleashed.

It might be objected that the satyrs do not apparently fulfil their sexual desires in satyr drama;[82] they are suspended in a state of eternal sexual excitement. While tragedy traces the consequences of dangerous sexualities through to their bitter end, satyr drama seems to have controlled the satyrs by foreclosing on its own invitation to sexual licence. But whatever the ideological implications of the apparently infinite deferral of theatrical satyrs' sexual gratification, the last and loudest voices heard whooping at the tragic competitions were male, uncouth, and lecherous. Satyr drama sent the Athenian male away from the tragic productions, to parties where he drank wine from cups frequently adorned with scenes illustrating sexual violence against women,[83] only after edifying him with at least an hour's worth of ithyphallic males behaving badly.

---

[81] '[U]nd erwirkt sich dadurch Indemnität für das Übermass der leidvollen Affekte, die sie entfesselt hat': Schmid (1934), 82.

[82] Seidensticker (1979), 244–5; Werre-de Haas (1961), 73.

[83] Zweig (1992), 83.

6

Female Personifications of
Poetry in Old Comedy

In the heyday of the court masque in England, actors impersonated
poetic abstractions with some regularity. In his Jacobean *The Lord's
Masque* (1613), Thomas Campion distributed poetry's features and
functions amongst three anthropomorphic figures. The Spirit of
Music was represented by the musician Orpheus, and Poetry's Usefulness to Mankind was embodied in mankind's patron, Prometheus.
But the abstract notion of the 'Phoebean Brain' of poetic inspiration
was represented by a personification, Entheus. The audiences under
Charles I became increasingly sophisticated in their appreciation of
such self-referential commentary on poetry, music, and the arts,
offered to them by the poets of the masque. Ben Jonson dramatized
in his *Masque of Beauty* the welcome given to the poets and poetry of
ancient Greece on their arrival in England; in his *Chloridia* Fame was
supported by figures including Poesy and Sculpture.[1] Ben Jonson, of
course, knew his Aristophanes well;[2] perhaps he had noticed the
personified abstractions in Old Comedy, which required male actors
to dress in the costumes and masks appropriate to such specific social
notions as the right to attend festivals at international cult centres
(in *Peace*, see Ch. 11), and political ideas such as Reconciliation (in
Lysistrata), in addition to literary entities such as the Muse of Euripides (see below, pp. 173, 305). Whether or not such figures ultimately
lie behind Jonson's allegorical cast members, the early seventeenth-
century interest in the theatrical impersonation of specifically *poetic*

---

[1] Kogan (1986), 75–6, 112, 118.
[2] See Gum 1969; Steggle (forthcoming) with bibliography.

abstractions serves well to introduce another period when such complex metapoetic theatre and metapoetic personifications was enjoyed—the late fifth century BC.

This chapter was originally inspired by the configurations of gender in the parabasis of Aristophanes' *Clouds*. The chorus consists of Athenian citizens costumed and masked as female Clouds, who temporarily assume the voice of the male poet who had created their own comedy (528–37):

> Years ago I won your applause in this very theatre with *The Bugger and the Prude*—and I may say it's always a pleasure to present a play to you, successful or not—well, since I was still a virgin girl, and so could not bring it up myself, I gave it to another girl to adopt; and then you very generously looked after it and fostered it with your applause … Now here comes this present comedy, to look for an audience equally discerning. She's just like Electra in that play; she'll recognise the lock of her brother's hair if she sees it. And you can see what a modest girl she is.[3]

In this striking passage, whatever it signifies about Aristophanes' earliest career as a playwright, the poet uses gender and metaphor in a series of related images. He imagines himself as a young unmarried mother, and his play as her baby. He also conceptualizes the present comedy, *Clouds*, as a young woman, a sister, and a tragic heroine, Electra. It is clear from this passage that Old Comedy's tendency to offer metapoetic comment on itself and its creators, and these creators' capacity for talking about their own history and their rivals, found in the discourse of gender, the female body, and sexuality a rich seam of metaphor, allegory, and personification.[4]

Aristophanes' images in the parabasis of *Clouds* belong to the same broad category as the configurations of literary *mimēsis* in *Thesmophoriazusae*, which have been shown by Froma Zeitlin to be inseparable from their context in the discussion of the representation of gender.[5] More particularly, the images in *Clouds* prefigure *Frogs*,

---

[3] Translation adapted from Easterling and Easterling (1962).
[4] Much has been published on the blurred distinction between allegory and personification. Following e.g. Maresca (1993), this chapter seeks to avoid confusion by henceforwards using only the term 'personification' and avoiding 'allegorical figure'.
[5] Zeitlin (1996).

where Aristophanes again uses a female figure and her body, this time to represent the personified art (*technē*) of the tragic poets through medical metaphors. Euripides says that he took the *technē* over from Aeschylus in an overweight state, and had to put her on a diet and slim her down by applying quasi-medical treatments including walks, learning, and monodies (939–44).[6] This personification of the tragic art as a woman in some non-mimetic sense still functions visually, by making the abstraction appear concretely before the mind's eye.[7] Personifications in literature are always particularly rich in societies where gods are conceived anthropomorphically, and which enjoy highly developed symbolic codes of visual representation in painting, sculpture, coins, and especially in the theatre.[8] Personification has fascinated modern literary theorists: it is defined as a form of literary anthropomorphism, which is more extreme than most forms of figurative language, since it posits as given 'an identification at the level of substance'.[9] But however extreme as instantiations of figurative language, Aristophanes' personifications neither in *Clouds* nor of the tragic art are physically represented, like Campion's Entheus or Jonson's Poesie, by a dramatic actor. They are better understood as comic equivalents of Sir Philip Sydney's Lady Poesie, or Alexander Pope's notion of the genre of opera, conceptualized 'in Harlot form'.[10]

The apparent dearth of females figures *physically* representing literary abstractions in extant Old Comedy is intriguing given that a female representative of a type of speech or argument may have appeared in the theatre, represented by a male actor in drag, as early as the Sicilian Epicharmus' comedy *Logos kai Logina*.[11] It is even more surprising when we consider Aristophanes' celebrated taste for

[6] See further Newiger (1957), 130–3.

[7] Warner (1987), 82.

[8] See Petersen (1939), 63–72 on Hellenistic personifications; Chapin (1955), 57–9 on 18th-cent. literature; Paxson (1994), 13 on drama's relationship with rhetorical *prosōpopeia*.

[9] See de Man (1984), 241.

[10] Chapin (1955), 120, 129.

[11] Very little is known about this intriguing title, but see Cassio (2002), 69–70 for a fascinating discussion of the possible reverberations of the ancient Greek feminine termination in *-ina*.

introducing actors representing social, political, or quasi-religious abstractions into his plays. Female roles of this kind include those created for *Opōra* and *Theōria* in *Peace*,[12] *Diallagē* in *Lysistrata*, and *Penia* in *Wealth*; these figures belong to the spheres of cult, agriculture, or political theory. Yet literary concepts are, with one exception, not physically personified in Aristophanes' extant comedies. The sole exception is the Muse of Euripides in *Frogs*. She appears and apparently remains in view, perhaps dancing continuously, throughout Aeschylus' parody of Euripidean choral lyric and monody (1304–64). 'Someone bring out a lyre,' says Aeschylus, but then cancels this request, asking for 'that female who rattles potsherds (*ostraka*)'. By the rattling of the potsherds (1305) he probably means to remind his audience of the castanets or rattle (*krotala*) with which Hypsipyle had entertained the baby Opheltes as she sang to him in her name-play by Euripides. This is especially likely since *Hypsipyle* is quoted in *Frogs*, and was performed only a very few years before it.[13] 'Come here, Muse of Euripides,' Aeschylus instructs this mute character, adding that she is a suitable accompanist for the forthcoming songs.[14]

Little else can be inferred from the text about this startling comic creation, except whatever is to be understood by Dionysus' comment that she was not the sort of female to *lesbiazein* (1308). This line is open to different interpretations. B. B. Rogers innocently saw Dionysus as protesting that so dignified and noble a figure as a Muse could not possibly be a 'harlot';[15] more plausibly, it might mean that she was not like the great poets from the past who hailed from Lesbos (Arion, Terpander, Alcaeus, Sappho), or that 'she never sang in Lesbian modes like those of Terpander imitated by Aeschylus',[16] or, indeed, that she never performed fellatio. Even this last possibility does not secure the appearance and demeanour of the Muse: the comment could be sarcastic and mean the opposite of its apparent significance, implying that she is *exactly* the sort of woman who

---

[12] See Cassio (1985), 122–6, 140.

[13] Fr. I ii 9–16, in Cockle (1987), 59, = *Hypsipyle* fr. 752 *TgrF*, which is quoted at *Frogs* 1211–13. *Hypsipyle* was performed between 412 and 407, for a scholion to *Frogs* 53 says it was performed with *Phoenissae* and *Antiope*. See further Ch. 10, p. 306 n. 70.

[14] See further Rau (1967), 127–36; E. Hall (1998).

[15] Rogers (1902), 199.

[16] J. Henderson (1991), 183.

performs fellatio: Barker fantasizes, on little solid evidence, that she was 'a naked, dancing houri'.[17] It could therefore be a remark on her obvious profession as prostitute or, conversely, on her obvious *lack* of sexual talent or appeal. Her costume and mask might represent her as an ugly old woman, a scruffy young one, or as a vulgar prostitute, but we can at least be sure 'that she is neither dignified nor attractive'.[18] Her social status, at least currently, is clearly not high, which thus makes the Muse of Euripides consonant with the *Frogs'* overall picture of this tragedian as a purveyor of unheroic individuals, domestic plots, colloquial speech and a 'democratized' type of tragedy in which women and servants speak on a par with male heads of the household (e.g. 949–52, 959, 978–9).[19]

Thus an extraordinary feature of the Muse of Euripides is that she is, to borrow a term from Narratology, 'focalized' from Aeschylus' perspective. She is not just a personification of something upon whose nature there was universal agreement. Rather, she is Euripides' Muse as conceived from the perspective of Aristophanes' Aeschylus. She is therefore a personification of a *qualitative aesthetic evaluation,* which is indeed a refined concept for a mute actor in a comedy to signify, and a peculiar role for him to play. She is a physical manifestation of the newly sophisticated theory *and practice* of informed poetic judgement, which had been nurtured by the comic poets in their complex responses to poetry in Athens in the fifth century BC.

Muses also appeared in the comedy by Phrynichus which competed against *Frogs* in 405 BC. Phrynichus' play was named for its chorus: *Mousai.* We know virtually nothing about this comedy, although speculation has resulted from the title, which suggests that Phrynichus' offering shared with *Frogs* a pronounced metapoetic focus. The exiguous fragments confirm this hypothesis: one is a famous encomium of Sophocles, who is said to have lived a happy life and to

---

[17] Andrew Barker (2004), 199, who argues that the effect of the scene was similar to that created in the hoopoe scene in *Birds.* In his appealing but extremely speculative account, Procne in *Birds* is portrayed as a degraded slave-*aulētris* who doubles as a prostitute, and is a personification of the controversial New Music: at 665, 'Enter the figure of Music incarnate, probably dressed in nothing to speak of apart from her golden ornaments, with pipes in her mouth, shimmying provocatively at Euelpides' (p. 198).

[18] Dover (1992), 351–2.

[19] On which see further E. Hall (1997*b*).

have written many beautiful tragedies (fr. 32 K–A); a trial or competition between poets similar to that in *Frogs* is further suggested by
another fragment showing that some kind of judicial decision
was taken in the course of the play (fr. 33 K–A). But of the Muses
themselves nothing is known—not their number, role, appearance,
nor even whether they constituted a transvestite disguise for male
poets themselves.[20]

If we revert to *Clouds*, or at least to the competition in which its
original version was produced in 423 BC (hypothesis to *Clouds*, =
Pytine T 1 K–A), we encounter perhaps the most stunning personified metapoetic abstraction of them all. The play which was victorious in that year was actually Cratinus' *Pytinē*. This comedy was
significant for many reasons,[21] not least that when Aristophanes
called *his* comedy a virgin girl (see above), he may have been asking
his audience to contrast her with Cratinus' (presumably much older)
matronly Comedy-wife. But from the point of view of the current
discussion, the most remarkable feature of *Pytinē* was simply its
adoption of Comedy herself as one of the leading members of the
cast. It is difficult to imagine a more sophisticated metapoetic
phenomenon than the personification of the genre currently being
performed appearing in it herself, except perhaps the personifications of comic *productions* which seem to have appeared in another
Cratinan comedy, the *Didaskaliai*.

The testimonia to *Pytinē* include the information that in it Cratinus attacked himself for his own drinking, and that Comedy was
married to Cratinus. She was portrayed as wanting to divorce him
and so filing a suit against him for cruelty (Σ Ar. *Eq.* 400a = *Pytine* T
ii K–A). Comedy explains to friends that Cratinus had of late been
writing no comedies, devoting himself instead to drinking; she
pleaded her case to them in a fragment the scholiast responsible for
this description quotes. It is a heavily corrupt fragment of four and a
half lines, but it is just about clear that Comedy in the past had not
been concerned if Cratinus turned to 'another woman', but
that factors including his old age (*gēras*, 4) meant that the current
situation was for her now intolerable (fr. 193 K–A). One fragment
seems to be a characterization of his excessive drinking habits (fr. 195

---

[20] See the discussion of Harvey (2000).   [21] See e.g. Rosen (2000).

K–A); another is a female voice saying 'I used to be his wife, but am not now' (fr. 194 K–A). In another Cratinus apparently says that he is dying for a drink (fr. 196 K–A).

It would be good to know what visual means Cratinus used to characterize Comedy. There are fewer than a dozen images of Comedy listed in *LIMC*: they include Aëtion's lost painting of Dionysus, Tragedy, and Comedy from the middle of the fouth century (Pliny, *NH* 35,78), and solemn relief sculptures, a mosaic, and a terracotta from later Hellenistic and Roman times. In the fifth century BC, Comedy appears on three vases, always as a maenad in a *thiasos*, and sometimes in company with another maenad representing Tragedy.[22] One of them depicts Hephaestus accompanied by Dionysus, Marsyas, and Comedy, holding a kantharos and thyrsos.[23] But there is no evidence in the fragments of *Pytine* that Cratinus' abandoned wife was represented as a maenad. This play raises two important questions about comedy's distinctive capacity for self-reference. First, despite the Muse who appears in the *Rhesus* attributed to Euripides, it is unthinkable that an ancient tragedy could feature personifications of literary genres, let alone Tragedy herself. It is just possible that Sophocles included the female figure Iambē in a satyr play named for this female personification of scurrilous lampoon: in the *Homeric Hymn to Demeter* Iambē cheered Demeter with racy jokes when she was mourning the loss of Persephone (202–5). There is evidence that Iambē was an aetiological figure representing the obscene jesting of women celebrating the Thesmophoria (Apollodorus, *Bibl.* 1.5.1). But this play is only mentioned by a single ancient grammarian,[24] and anyway the elusive genre of satyr drama seems to have admitted all kinds of features which seem to have been alien to tragedy.

Secondly, in staging *Kōmōidia* Cratinus incarnates his genre, and in a suggestive metaphorical construction of his own relationship with poetic production, presents it as a marriage. But still he is the maker—the *kōmōidopoios*—while she is the abstraction, the creation,

---

[22] Kossatz-Deissmann (1997), 92–4; see further E. Hall (forthcoming *a*).

[23] Kossatz-Deissmann (1997), 92; *ARV²* 1037, 1.

[24] The lone fragment of *Iambe* (Sophocles fr. inc. 731 *TgrF*) has also been attributed to *Triptolemus*: see Pearson (1917), iii. 1. On Iambē see Foley (1994), 45–6, and above p. 166.

the genre itself—*hē kōmōidia*. Such gendered antinomic pairings of active with passive, creater with created, form provider with content provider, concrete with abstract, or agent with activity, are found everywhere in ancient thought. The gendered active-passive antinomy informs ancient thinking in general. Hephaestus creates Pandora (*Erg.* 70–82, *Theog.* 570–89); Aristotle conceives mammalian reproduction in terms of creative semen giving form to the shapeless matter provided by the female (*De Gen. An.* 2.4. 738^{b}20–8); musicologists saw rhythm as a masculine force which shaped formless feminine sound into music (Aristides Quintilianus 1.19). The specific agent–action duality has been connected with the prevalent tendency of the Greek and Latin languages to use masculine nouns for the agents of its verbs, and feminine nouns for the actions or spheres of activity which those verbs describe (e.g. *poein, poiētēs,* and *poiēsis,* or *ago, actor,* and *actio*).[25] This gendered duality informs numerous images of artistic production, from the Hesiodic pictures of the male singer (*aoidos*) being inspired with song (*aoidē*) by the Muses (*Theog.* 22–34), to Ovid's encounters with female personifications of Elegy and Tragedy (*Amores* 3.1.7–68), and Plutarch's portrayal of Tragedy as a rich woman, attended by a train of actors (*De Glor. Athen.* 349; see Ch. 4, p. 99). The extant and fragmentary remains of Old Comedy show that, likewise, its metapoetics not only tended to construct poets and performers (especially those set in the 'contemporary' world, rather than those treating dead poets of the past) as male agents, but also to represent the abstractions denoting their spheres of activity as feminine characters.

The plays and fragments attest to the relative frequency with which poets, whether we know their names or not, physically appeared in the genre. Euripides, Agathon, and Aeschylus appeared in Aristophanes' *Acharnians, Thesmophoriazusae,* and *Frogs*; Aeschylus appeared in at least one other Aristophanic comedy, in which he commented on the dance movements in his *Phrygians* (fr. 696 *TgrF*); the ghost of Aeschylus also appeared in Pherecrates' *Krapataloi.*[26] There were poets in Aristophanes' *Birds* and *Gērytades,* in the comic poet Plato's *Poiētēs* and *Laconians* or *Poiētai,* and probably Phrynichus' *Tragōidoi.*

---

[25] Warner (1987), 67–8; Paxson (1994), 173–4.
[26] Pherecrates fr. 100 K–A. Thanks to Ian Ruffell for this reference.

Yet the nearest thing to a masculine poetic abstraction in Old Comedy is probably the brilliant poetic performer Trygaeus in *Peace*, whose identification with *trugedy* (comedy with the same social utility and didactic force as tragedy, see e.g. *Ach.* 599–600) is closer than has usually been allowed (see Ch. 11, pp. 328–35). Trygaeus could be seen as virtually a personification of socially useful Comedy.[27] There is also the figure of Aigisthos on the '*Chorēgoi*' vase, dated to about 380 BC, who Taplin suspects is not simply a character playing a tragic part, but somehow 'representative of tragedy'.[28] In another example, a single naked youth labelled *tragōdos* is painted on a late Apulian krater, the reverse of which portrays a comic mask, thus opposing the two major dramatic genres.[29] But none of these phenomena comes close to the abstraction constituted by Cratinus' dramatic character Kōmōidia.

Indeed, the gendered agent/action duality does fundamentally inform the poetics of Old Comedy, especially when the plays are set in the world of contemporary Athens. The female poet Sappho, of course, was an exceptional figure in every way, and does seem to have been a popular character in comedies of both the fifth and fourth centuries, including the comic poet Plato's *Phaon*.[30] Ameipsias, Aristophanes' rival, composed a *Sappho* of which sadly little is known (fr. 15 K–A); in Diphilus' *Sappho* the Ionian poets Archilochus and Hipponax were her *erastai* (fr. 70 K–A). Other fourth-century *Sappho* comedies are credited to Amphis (fr. 32 K–A), Ephippus (fr. 20 K–A), Timocles (fr. 32 K–A), and Antiphanes, whose

---

[27] See Taplin (1983); E. Hall (forthcoming *a*).

[28] See also the so-called 'Goose play vase' (New York, MMA 24.98.104). Taplin (1993), 62 and fig. 10.2 argued that the label *tragōidos* was attached to the small, half-naked boy, painted on a higher plane than the figures in comic costume; he may have represented a jibe at tragedy from the perspective of those keen to promote comedy. But Schmidt (1998), 26–8 has pointed out that the label can not refer to this boy, who is of a type which on vases conventionally represents the attendants of naked men at the palaestra such as the man on the bottom left of the painting. Whom or what the label 'tragode' designates therefore remains a mystery, although Schmidt recognizes that the scene must nevertheless juxtapose tragedy and comedy in a fairly sophisticated manner. Thanks to Oliver Taplin for help on this point.

[29] Trendall and Cambitoglou (1983), 122, 22/563d, with pl. 22.6; see Taplin (1993), 62 n. 19.

[30] See Athenaeus, *Deipn.* 10.450e–451b, 13.572.c. Dover discusses Sappho in Greek comedy in Dover (1978), 174.

Sappho propounded riddles on stage (fr. 194 K–A). There is just one other lost comedy, Cratinus' *Kleoboulinai*, which may have featured a female poet other than Sappho: Kleoboulina, interestingly, was also associated with riddles. Diogenes Laertius reports that Kleoboulina had been a poetess (*poiētrian*), of riddles in hexameters, and that she was named in Cratinus' play (1.89 = Cratinus T i). Unfortunately the fragments (91–101) are uninformative. Otherwise, in the world of fifth-century comedy, poets are male (as they were, of course, in the 'real' world of classical Athens) and poetry is female. Moreover, there is much more negotiation with this relationship, taking the form of the physical representation of metapoetic concepts as female characters, than the surviving plays of Aristophanes suggest. If Cratinus' wife Comedy is the most self-referential character in all Old Comedy, she was not the only speaking—indeed litigating—poetic personification of which we know. There seems to have been an exciting species of Old Comedies in which the primary focus was literature, and this group had a genus in which female figures representing Poetry or Music, usually wronged by male poets, were with some regularity involved as characters.

One possible candidate is provided by Aristophanes' *Gērytades*, a play whose metapoetic importance was first fully appreciated by Michael Silk. He describes it as the sole 'Aristophanic comedy which had a permanent interest in art or literature, but was not centred on tragedy'.[31] In *Gērytades* a delegation of poets of trugedy (see Ch. 11, pp. 328–55), tragedy, and cyclic hymns had been to the underworld, a trip which was described in the course of the play (fr. 156 K–A). The purpose of the expedition, unfortunately, is not made explicit: there is a strong possibility, however, that the poets' task was to visit, or retrieve from the underworld, a female divinity such as *Poiēsis*.

This inference is drawn from an anonymous commentary on a play by Aristophanes which *may* be his *Gērytades*; the commentary includes a lemma whose contents are explicitly compared with an expression in Aristophanes' *Peace,* concerning a female *daimōn* whom the speaker has 'led up' (*anēgagon*) and somehow established in the agora (Aristophanes fr. 591.84–6 K–A, see *Peace* 923, 925). If

[31] Silk (1993).

this female *daimōn* who has been 'led up' is Poetry, and if the play is a
commentary on *Gērytades*, then there was indeed a wonderful Aristophanic plot featuring poets of various genres bringing back Poetry
herself from chthonic exile, self-imposed or not, on the lines of
Trygaeus' rescue of Peace from her subterranean cave. But Peace
was represented on stage by an inanimate statue, a feature of the
comedy for which Aristophanes was criticized by two of his rivals:[32]
there is no reason to think that if Poetry appeared in *Gērytades* she
was not a speaking character.

Fortunately there is a surer case of a 'retrieval' plot featuring a
poetic personification, in Aristophanes' *Poiēsis*. This is known from a
Yale papyrus fragment (Aristophanes fr. 466.3–17 K–A = *PTurner* 4),
which is proved to be from this metapoetic comedy because of the
coincidence of two of its lines with a book fragment attributed to
Poiēsis by Priscian (lines 4–5). As the first editor of the papyrus saw,
the text contains a dialogue between one person and a plural group,
perhaps a chorus of poets, in which it is stated that a female figure is
being sought 'throughout all Greece' (*hapasēs Hellad*[*os*, line 3);[33]
this, too, is reminiscent of the pan-Hellenic recovery of Peace, under
Trygaeus' direction, in *Peace*. Lloyd-Jones argues that there is no
certain evidence in this papyrus fragment for a chorus of poets in
the manner of *Gērytades*, and that the scene from which it derives
feels similar to the typical opening dialogue in Aristophanes, some
way into which 'one of the speakers turns to the audience and
explains the situation'.[34] At the beginning a single individual is
addressed (*p*]*ara se*, 5), but the plural 'to you' (*humin*) at line 12
suggests that the individual a little later responds to the group,
strongly implying dialogue. This individual gives specific details
about the female figure, who has apparently been ill-treated in
some way (*adikoum*[, *adikoumenē*, 14, 16). Since we know securely
that this play was the *Poiēsis*, it would be perverse to identify the
mistreated object of the quest as anyone but an Aristophanic personification of Poetry herself. It is probably important that the other
fragment (467 K–A) refers to singing songs to the seven-stringed lyre.

---

[32] Eupolis fr. 54 K–A; Plato fr. 81 K–A. See further Cassio (1985), 47–50, and
below, p. 349 and n. 114.
[33] Stephens (1981).
[34] Lloyd-Jones (1981).

In the fourth century Antiphanes followed Aristophanes by producing a comedy called *Poetry* (*Poiēsis*). In the single fragment,
quoted by Athenaeus, the speaker claims that tragedians are more
fortunate than comic poets, because the basic facts about tragedians'
characters are already familiar to their audiences. Moreover, they also
enjoy the expedient of the machine to help them resolve their plots
(Athenaeus 6.222 = fr. 189 K–A). Conversely, argues the speaker, 'to
us (*hēmin*) these advantages do not apply, but everything has to be
invented' (189.17–18). The identity of the speaker depends entirely
on how 'to us' is understood. Although it would be pleasant to be
able to believe that the speaker was indeed Comic Poetry, it seems
more obvious to infer that it is a comic poet, perhaps in a scene
where he confronts the claims of a tragedian.

Another close parallel with the quest for missing Poetry in Aristophanes' *Poiēsis* is provided by Pherecrates' *Cheiron*, which contains
perhaps the most elaborate of all the metapoetic fragments of Old
Comedy. Here the wronged female is not Kōmōidia nor Poiēsis, but
Mousikē herself, the divine personification of music. She has been
outraged by a series of poets, and is explaining the injustices she has
suffered to the female divinity Dikaiosunē. Dikaiosunē is herself a
fascinating figure to have appeared on the comic stage, reminiscent
of the appearance of Justice (who names herself), in the papyrus
fragment of Aeschylus' so-called 'Dikē-play' (Aeschylus fr. inc.
281a.15 *TgrF*).

We owe the passage from Pherecrates' *Cheiron* to Plutarch's *On
Music* 30, which explains that Mousikē was introduced 'in the guise of
a woman whose whole person has been brutally mauled' (*en gunaikeiōi
schēmati, holēn katēikismenēn to sōma*). When Justice asks her how she
came to suffer such an outrage (*lōbē*), Mousikē[35] replies that she will
give an answer with pleasure (Pherecrates fr. 155 K–A). Melanippides,
she says, was the first to injure her, by introducing twelve strings.
He was followed by Cinesias, who introduced innovations into the

[35] The Greek text of Plutarch actually says *tēn Poiēsin* here, but most editors have
assumed that this is a slip for *tēn Mousikēn*. The unreliability of the text must also cast
some doubt on its statement at the end of the Pherecratean fragment, to the effect
that Aristophanes also portrayed Mousikē in one of his plays, making her say
something about Philoxenus' musical innovations in cyclic choruses (Aristophanes
fr. 953 K–A).

dithyramb, and by Phrynis with his twelve modes on five strings. Music had acclimatized herself to the various injuries each of them had done to her. But, she explains to Justice, when it came to that red-haired Timotheus of Miletus, with his wriggling music like ant-runs, she has been so abominably mistreated that recovery is impossible (19–20). Music concludes that if Timotheus happens upon her when she is out walking alone, he strips and undoes her with his twelve strings (24–5).

It is certain that many of the different innovations introduced by the lover-poets are open to sexual interpretation. The Phrynis section probably contains *double entendres* relating to sexual positions, while the characterization of Timotheus as rapist could scarcely be more explicit. Musical innovation is thus overtly formulated in terms of male–female sexual assault: as Lloyd-Jones interprets it, Mousikē speaks 'as a hetaira might describe her maltreatment by a succession of lovers'.[36] She is thus yet another mistreated female poetic abstraction. Cratinus was a poor husband to Comedy, Dionysus derides Euripides' Muse in sexual terms, and Timotheus is but one of a whole series of men who have sexually abused Music herself.[37]

In conclusion, studies of both gender in Old Comedy and literary criticism in the fifth century should perhaps take more serious note of these feminine literary abstractions, impersonated by male actors; the roles demonstrate more clearly than any other feature of the genre its ability to meditate upon its own poetics. Naked or semi-naked female bodies (whether represented by 'real' women or costumed men) were routinely exposed, suggestively discussed, and roughly man-handled in Aristophanic comedy: examples that crop up elsewhere in this volume include Elaphion the dancing prostitute in *Thesmophoriazusae* and the feminine abstractions *Opōra* and *Theōria* in his *Peace* (see below pp. 328 and 337).[38] The female body—virginal or pregnant, overweight or slimmed down, performing fellatio or supposedly too ugly to have sex with, married, serially sexually abused, or raped by Timotheus—was something which the poets of Old Comedy discovered was good to think with when it

---

[36] Lloyd-Jones (1981), 25.

[37] For a long discussion of the Pherecratean passage see Dobrov and Urios-Aparisi (1995).

[38] See esp. Zweig (1992), 74–81.

came to understanding poetry and its relationship with poets.[39] More than just good to think with, poetry was good to *stage*. Cratinus, Aristophanes, Antiphanes, and Pherecrates all offered the Athenian public memorable feminine metapoetic figures, in the form of male actors dressed as Muses, Comedy, Poetry, and Music: was this an area in which Aristophanes and his rivals, like the poets of the court masque under James I and Charles I, consciously competed?

---

[39] Eupolis in his *Poleis* and Aristophanes in his *Nēsoi* presented their audiences with female personifications of the Athenians' subject states, thus making similar use of the metaphorical resonances of the male–female relationship. See Rosen (1997*a*).

7

Recasting the Barbarian

THICKENING THE PLOT

One day in the early fifth century BC, the imaginary figure of the barbarian despot, gorgeous and sensual within his luxurious court, arose from his golden throne. He minced in his soft slippers from the Athenian stage and directly into the ancient imagination. There he was to remain, one of the most familiar fixtures in the cultural repertoire, throughout the long centuries of pagan antiquity. He appeared in nearly every genre—historiography, biography, satire, epic, philosophy, mime, rhetorical exercises, and the ancient novel. Some principles in his delineation remained virtually unchanged across time.[1] All the ancient sources agree, for example, that the guiding principle of the Persian élite was *pleasure*. 'Lend yourselves to pleasure (*hēdonēn*) every day, despite the current difficulties, since wealth is of no use to the dead at all,' Darius enjoins the chorus in Aeschylus' *Persians*, as he returns into the Stygian gloom (840–2); it was pleasure that the fifth-century medical tradition already regarded as the ruling principle of Asiatic communities (Hippocr. *De Aër.* 12.40–4); in Heraclides Ponticus' fourth-century philosophical dialogue *On Pleasure* the Persians were regarded as the most luxurious of all barbarians;[2] it is still Xerxes to whom Cicero alludes when

---

[1] See Clough (2004), and the Introduction to Bridges, Hall, and Rhodes (2006). For an analysis of the sources of all the early appearances of each element in the stereotypical picture—awnings, peacocks, eunuchs etc.—see Tuplin (1996), 132–77.

[2] Heraclides Ponticus fr. 55, quoted by Athen. *Deipn.* 12.512a, in Wehrli (1953), 21–2; see further Tuplin (1996), 156–7 and n. 55.

discussing the absurdity of the notion that man's highest aim in life was the pursuit of pleasure (*De Finibus* 2.111–12; see also *Tusc. Disp* 5.20).

The sheer staginess of the barbarian tyrant offers another thread of continuity. The entertainments on offer during the Second Sophistic, for example, included dramatic enactments of the arrogance and frivolity of the barbarian character, delivered during the course of showcase declamations. The sophist Scopelianus of Clazomenae, a renowned declaimer, had a particular talent for speeches involving Darius and Xerxes (probably including the *Xerxes* composed by his own teacher of rhetoric, Nicetes); these histrionic enactments involved 'lurching around like a Bacchant' (Philostratus, *Lives of the Sophists*, 519–20).[3] This era also retained a clear visual picture of Darius, Xerxes, and their ilk: the Philostratean description of a painting of Themistocles calls its subject a 'Greek among barbarians, a man amongst non-men' (*Hellēn en barbarois, anēr en ouk andrasin*). Themistocles is lecturing the Persian king and his eunuchs, who are theatrically posed before him, iridescent in gaudy costumes against an opulent palace setting (*Imagines* 2.31).[4]

A new understanding of the longevity, within Graeco-Roman antiquity, of the politically potent images of the Oriental monarch has been one factor in making ethnic difference in theatrical performance become of late a more, rather than less, pressing issue. Another reason is that the ethnically charged confrontations in Greek tragedy have struck such a chord with global audiences at a time when race, statehood, and religion are at the forefront of international politics. This is connected with the stress that has been placed on ethnic stereotypes in contemporary cinema, theatre, and television programmes by cultural critics committed to civil rights

---

[3] For an excellent discussion of the mimetic elements in the performances of the orators of the second sophistic, and their attraction to themes from the glory days of the classical Athenian past, see Conolly (2001), esp. 84–5.

[4] The Persian king, in tiara and *kandys*, sits on his golden throne; other traditional details include the imposing arms of his guards, and the burning of costly myrrh and frankincense. The *ekphrasis* professes to describe a painting on private display in a Roman villa in Italy, but probably derives from a familiar scene in Greek art. For detailed discussions see Borchhardt (1983), 213–14 and Gabelmann (1984), 73.

and anti-colonial movements;[5] stereotypes have come under such scrutiny that interest in their cultural ancestry has inevitably been attracted back to their archetypes in ancient theatre.[6] Imagining how Greek tragedy worked on the cusp between collective ideology and individual subjectivity can also be enhanced by consulting recent work in Film Studies, where there have been some sophisticated demonstrations of how cinema trains ethnic consciousness at a 'middlebrow' level.[7]

A further factor has emerged from the scrutiny of the ancient dramatic texts by performance-oriented scholars, whose founding fathers were, in the case of comedy, Solomos and Russo in the early 1960s, and in tragedy, Taplin in the 1970s.[8] Subsequent to these foundational studies, there has been far greater interest in precisely those material, histrionic, and choreographical aspects of Greek theatre which most reveal its exoticism, spectacle, and the elaboration of its mimesis. Tragedy, especially, was a genre which revelled in decorative clothes, crowns, sceptres, and the staging of fantastic royal courts; in studies of tyranny, powerful women, and sexual deviance; in musical modes of exotic provenance; in extravagant chariots, retinues, and rituals of prostration before royalty; even in characters whose gait and vocality were represented as ethnically inflected. The fancy dress of Greek stage tyrants, at least by the end of the fifth century, became difficult to distinguish from the costumes worn by stage barbarians. This fascination almost certainly had something to do with Dionysus. If I were to rewrite *Inventing the Barbarian*, which was completed in early 1988 and published the year after, it would

---

[5] See e.g. MacKenzie (1995), 176–99 on Orientalism in the theatre; Hallam and Street (2000) on ethnicity in mass media; Coyne (1998) on American identity and ethnicity in 'westerns'; Ignatieff (1998) on the heroic ethnic minority warrior in popular culture; Basinger (2003) on World War II combat movies, including discussions of the ethnic stereotyping within them.

[6] See Favorini (2003); Hall, Macintosh, and Wrigley (2004), esp. the Introduction and the chapters by Hardwick and Hall.

[7] Christina Klein's analysis of Rodgers and Hammerstein's *The King and I* (1956) is particularly stimulating for those studying the ancient texts involving visitors to fabled eastern courts, from Herodotus and Ctesias to the ancient novel (Christina Klein (2003), 191–222). See also N. Z. Davis (2000), an exemplary study of the representation of slavery in the cinema.

[8] Solomos (1961); Russo (1994 [1962]); Taplin (1977) and (1978).

now explore the Dionysiac dimension of the fifth century's delight in representing ethnic alterity. It is partly a result of the insatiable appetite for research into Dionysus that scholars have now become fascinated by ancient Greek tragedy's fascination with otherness.[9] The stage barbarian had always been central to this dynamic.

The ideological content of Athenian tragedy was inevitably conditioned by the historical society that produced it. But I have become less certain about the exact nature of the antitype at stake in Athenian dramatic discourse surrounding the barbarian. Tragedy's content is undoubtedly peculiar to Athens, in the sense that the Athenians saw the tragic competitions as a medium through which they displayed, indeed advertised, their polis to the larger Greek world.[10] Moreover, in its 'myth-napping' of important non-Athenian heroes, tragedy reads the archaic Greek myths from a profoundly Athenocentric perspective.[11] The Athenian promulgation of the image of the barbarian offers a contrast to the thought-world of the Spartans who did not even use the term *barbaros* (Hdt. 9.11.12);[12] presumably the Athenians' outlook on the world differed, likewise, from the way that the citizens of any other polis defined their own ethnic identity and those who did not share it.[13] The barbarian bolsters the notion of Panhellenism, which was a crucial part of the system of ideas by which the Athenian empire expanded and maintained itself; the barbarian is therefore undoubtedly an imperial image; moreover, the classical Athenian image of the barbarian may furnish an example of what has recently been described as 'pre-colonial' discourse, an ideological project by which a foreign territory is subdued in the colonizer's imagination prior to actual military subordination, as it

[9] Bibliography in Zeitlin (1993), 152.

[10] A point well brought out by Carter (2004), 11–12, in his careful response to Goldhill (1987).

[11] This is argued from the perspective of the Athenian tragedians' appropriation of the non-Athenian heroes Oedipus, Heracles, and Orestes in E. Hall (1997*b*).

[12] Perlman (1976); Baslez (1986).

[13] It is one the virtues of the essays edited by Malkin (2001) that they emphasize the plurality, variety, and mutability of the consciousness of 'Greekness' and the identities that were invoked as its opposites, both synchronically across the Greek-speaking world and diachronically over time. See esp. Malkin's introduction, 1–28, and the discussion of Herodotus by Rosalind Thomas (ch. 7).

can be argued that Persia and Egypt were controlled through archaic and classical Greek image-making in preparation for their conquest by Greeks from further north, in Macedon.[14]

The stage presentation of the ethnic alien satisfied not only Athenian and imperial ideological requirements, but also whatever sentiments were espoused by the democratically selected judges who awarded Aeschylus the first prize in 472 BC with the tetralogy including *Persians*. Yet Rhodes's recent critique of the currently fashionable view that Athenian tragedy is in essence a democratic art form has led me to modify some thinking. Several of the key Greek ideals at stake in *Persians*—freedom of speech, protection under the law, and the accountability of magistrates—were indeed exclusive neither to Athens nor to democracies,[15] even if they happened to be particularly prominent in Athenian self-definition at the time when the *dēmos* was in power. That these ideals were not inherently objectionable to non-democrats is suggested by the early revival of *Persians* in Syracuse commissioned by the tyrant Hieron.[16] Indeed, the traditional dating of the first tragedies means that they were established under a tyrant, Peisistratus, even if he was an unusually populist one.[17] Yet we have no parallel case against which to measure the Athenian achievement in tragic theatre: no other state, democratic or otherwise, ever challenged its claim to supremacy in this genre, at least until Hellenistic times. Although tragedy began to be exported to the decidedly undemocratic kingdom of Macedon after 413, we will never know what a tragic canon that was developed from scratch in a classical Greek tyranny or oligarchy would have looked like, although Euripides' genealogical compliment to the Macedonian royal house in his fragmentary *Archelaus* offers clues.[18] In my view it is incontrovertible, moreover, that barbarians would have been portrayed differently in Athenian tragedy if the Persians had succeeded in returning Hippias to power as a result of Xerxes' invasion.

[14] See Vasunia (2001), esp. 245–61.

[15] Rhodes (2003), 116. A similar case, but using rather different arguments, is made independently by Carter (2002). I am grateful to Professor Rhodes for drawing my attention to the latter article.

[16] See Taplin (1999), 41.

[17] Cartledge (1997), 3; see Rhodes (2003), 107 n. 15. For a different perspective, which stresses tragedy's focus on elite ruling-class families, see Griffith (1998), 23–30.

[18] On which see the edition by Harder (1985); E. Hall (1989), 180.

Over the last fifteen years the discipline of Classics has assimilated into mainstream thinking the seismic intellectual and ideological shifts of the late 1960s to mid-1980s.[19] It has stopped deriding feminism and gender studies and accepted their premises, for the most part wholeheartedly; it has begun tentatively to wrestle with its own implications in the history of empire and racist thinking, and to see the relevance of the contemporary notion of 'multiculturalism' to the study of ancient societies;[20] it has modified its initial passion for too-simple binary structuralism; it flirted with deconstruction only to return to an insistence upon the need for historical contextualization. It also discovered Bakhtin's views on speech genres and Italian Narratology, both of which would have been useful in the analysis of the representation and suppression of barbarian voices in ancient drama.[21] Since 1989, several books and articles have appeared which I fervently wish had been published earlier because they would have supplemented, supported, or refined my own thinking. A few have made me seriously question aspects of my approach to the cultural construction of ethnicity; on the other hand, a small group has made me think that I must have stated the case with insufficient clarity or trenchancy (see the sections below on Identity and on Gender). But writing a new edition of a book so bound up with its particular historical moment— the Cold War circumstances under which it was written—would constitute a project overloaded with contradiction. Since the representation of ethnicity and Orientalism are matters of urgency in the third millennium, it seems more appropriate to offer an update, but a freestanding one.

Two publications of which I was shamefully unaware at the time that I completed *Inventing the Barbarian* were Page duBois's *Centaurs*

[19] See E. Hall (2004), 37–42; Leonard (2005).

[20] The way in which 'anyone today thinks about ancient Greece is inseparable from two hundred years of European colonialism . . . an Egyptian, Iranian, or Indian is going to respond very differently to Herodotus than a white European who has been raised in the Anglo-Saxon tradition' (Vasunia (2003), 96). On imperialism and (post)colonialism see also e.g. Goff (2005); Vasunia (2001); on multiculturalism see especially Levine (1992); Dougherty and Kurke (2003), 2–6.

[21] See Branham (2001); de Jong (1991) and (2001); de Jong, Nünlist, and Bowie (2004). On the struggle for narrative control in texts by Afro-Americans see the brilliant work of Stepto (1979).

and Amazons: Women and the Pre-History of the Great Chain of Being,
and Suzanne Saïd's article 'Grecs et barbares dans les tragedies
d'Euripide: le fin des différences?'[22] The first makes important points
about the way that the polarization of Greek and Barbarian was
grafted onto a pre-existing 'grammar' of oppositions and analogies
(many of them gendered) in Greek mythical cosmogony, anthropology, and aetiology; the second attempts to understand a single
tragedian's negotiations with the category *barbaros*, and as such
would have provided an important stimulus to my own analysis of
some Euripidean passages. It is not so clear that it would have been
advantageous to have read the one volume then available of Martin
Bernal's *Black Athena: The Afroasiatic Roots of Classical Civilization,
The Fabrication of Ancient Greece 1785–1985*; this had been
published in 1987, which could have been just in time to affect the
contents of *Inventing the Barbarian*. On the whole I think it was
better that I remained unaware of it at the time; not because I think it
is a bad book—on the contrary, it makes a convincing case for the
invention by some Enlightenment thinkers of ancient Greece in the
image of their own ancestors. But I would certainly have
been sidetracked from my own argument by feeling the need
to engage with Bernal, who emphasizes the importance of
the category of biological ethnicity even while attacking some of its
worst consequences in human history; this is a radically different
version of left-wing thinking from my own approach, which emphasizes the ideological and social construction of ethnic difference and
consciously avoids discussing the 'true' genetic makeup of any members of the human race, past or present.[23] On the other hand, if I had
read Bernal I would have been warned about the un-detonated bombs
littering the publishing arena that I was so naively about to enter;
I had far too little sensitivity towards the tension surrounding race
issues in North America.

Indeed, chief among the many publications that it would have
been good to have read in the 1980s is Henry Louis Gates's *Figures in
Black: Words, Signs and the Racial Self* (1987), which is the most
sophisticated discussion in existence of the issues involved in the
literary representation of race and slavery. Whether on the social

---

[22] duBois (1982); S. Said (1984).   [23] See E. Hall (1992).

potency of metaphor, the complexities of the representation of agency and subjectivity, or the relationship between genres and social hierarchies, Gates coruscates continuously.[24] I would also have learned a great deal from Anouar Abdel-Malek's seminal article 'Orientalism in Crisis', published as early as 1963, fifteen years before Edward Said's *Orientalism* brought such ideas into mainstream Anglo-American academic discourse and thereby to my personal attention.[25] Abdel-Malek brilliantly juxtaposed the considerable positive achievements in the field of traditional 'Oriental Studies' with its problematic objectification and essentialist conception of the human beings and human discourses that constituted its field of study. Above all, he drew attention to the implication of traditional Classics in the crisis even of meaning in the word 'Orientalism'. Classics paid attention to Greek and Roman cultures that had been 'reborn' in the sixteenth century, while preferring to see the achievements of the 'Orient' as past and dead, thus ignoring the very vital presence of Arabic language, literature, and culture in the contemporary world. If I had read this article before I began research, I think I would have been so alarmed by its implications for the sheer ideological potency of the project on which I was embarking that I might have rethought my plans altogether.

From a theoretical perspective it is regrettable that I had not in 1989 discovered Alain Grosrichard's virtuosic *Structure du sérail: La Fiction du despotisme Asiatique dans l'Occident classique* (1979; Eng. trans. 1998), partly because it demonstrates so persuasively the importance of the fantasy of oriental despotism to the era of the Enlightenment, which was the very period at which the basic political structures of modernity emerged, along with the bourgeois western subject and the particular shape of his conscious identity.[26] More importantly, however, Grosrichard's work was the first to regard the exercise of documenting and analysing cultural fictions and fantasies of the Orient as a serious intellectual business. Grosrichard is convinced, as a thoroughgoing (although not usually explicit) disciple of

---

[24] Equally suggestive are the explorations of the centrality of the race and slavery issues to the 19th-cent. foundation texts of North American literary narrative in Stepto (1979) and Gardner (1998).

[25] Abdel-Malek (1963); Said's *Orientalism* was first published in 1978.

[26] See also Nippel (2002), 304–10.

Jacques Lacan, that the very efficacy of ideas often lies in their fantasized correlatives: fantasy, however far removed from material or documentable reality, often explains how political mechanisms of enmity or control can operate.[27] The 'serious' western discourses centred on Liberty, Equality, and Masculinity partly operate through the pleasurable fiction of the oriental sexual paradise. Fantasy dressed up in fiction or performed mimesis offers *pleasure*, and thus appeals to its consumers in their role as subjects of desire, a role which reinforces their status as *political* subjects. It is in the intersection between our capacity for enjoyment—aesthetic and/or libidinal—and our political subjectivity as citizens that fantasies such as the luxurious oriental court find their most effective sphere of action. The author of an introduction to the recent translation of Grosrichard's work into English, Mladen Dolar, argues that behind every political concept there may lurk such a 'phantasmic kernel' which makes it function through mental *enjoyment*.[28]

The last decade has seen a corresponding advance in the sophistication of the scholarly understanding of the relationships between slavery, sexuality, and pornography, and of the aesthetic reflections of the fetishization in the eighteenth to nineteenth centuries of the ethnically different and subordinated body of the slave from the imperial colonies.[29] Much of this work suggests questions that might fruitfully be asked of ancient texts: the most extended and detailed sex scene in ancient literature takes place between a free man and a female domestic slave, from the free man's perspective.[30] Saharan sands and sexual fantasies, especially in cinema, have borne a particularly profound relationship to imperialism in North

---

[27] On the Lacanian correlation between enjoyable fantasy and political organization, see esp. Stavrakis (1999).

[28] See Grosrichard (1998), p. xi. Slajov Žižek, a controversial Slovenian philosopher who draws on both Marx and Lacan, signalled the real focus of the argument in his instant philosophical classic on the way that popular culture shapes political belief, *For they Know Not What They Do* (2002 [1991]), through its subtitle *Enjoyment as a Political Factor* (see also above, Ch. 1, pp. 5–6).

[29] See e.g. Marcus Wood (1999) and (2002), esp. 87–140 and 181–254.

[30] This is the encounter between the slave girl Palaestra and Lucius, the hero of the Greek *Ass* novel attributed to Lucian (7–10), which is much more physical and realistic than the corresponding scene in Apuleius' *Golden Ass*. See further E. Hall (1995).

Africa; thus, closely related to the savouring of pleasure in the consumption of political ideas, is the last item written before 1989 that would undoubtedly have altered the actual course of my argument: the Antillean psychiatrist Frantz Fanon's article 'Algeria unveiled'. This was first published in 1959 at the height of the Algerian struggle for independence, a cause to which Fanon was passionately committed.[31] As an exploration of how one material item can come to symbolize a whole nexus of issues in the power relation between colonizer and colonized, this article remains unsurpassed either in the penetration of its insights or the lucidity and grace of its expression. The veil or *haïk*, as seen by the eyes of the westerner, conceals alluring objects of fantasy—untold beauty to be ravished—but also implies the fearsome danger, plots, and secret resistance, which demand unveiling and extirpation. This is bound up with the personification of the land of Algeria as a mysterious, dark, female to be enjoyed, subdued, and possessed.

BARBARIANS ANSWER BACK

The most prescient feature of Fanon's article was, however, that it examined the veil as a contested symbol, from the perspective of both sides in the Algerian war: his readings are conducted from the viewpoint of the imperial Frenchman, the French woman, the Algerian man, and above all the Algerian woman. Recent reappraisals of 'Orientalism' under the British empire have been stressing how much colonial subjects shaped the ideology of their imperial masters, rather than focusing exclusively on Orientalism as a one-way process.[32] Investigations of the images of the barbarian in the works of Byzantine authors are beginning to be balanced by studies of the Arab perception of Byzantium.[33] Analogously, the most exciting development from the perspective of the ancient Greeks' experience of non-Greek cultures has been the growing insistence that the

[31] See Fanon (1997).
[32] See e.g. Codell and Macleod (1998), esp. the Introduction (1–10).
[33] See esp. El Cheikh (2004).

'barbarians' were active agents and participants in the production of Mediterranean and Near Eastern culture. An outstanding recent article by Ian Moyer, for example, has urged that Herodotus' accounts of the Egyptian past need to be reappraised in the light of the dynamic presentation and mediation of that past as developed by Egyptians more or less contemporary with him; the priority now is to recognize the agency, rather than the passivity, of Herodotus' Egyptian inform-ers.[34] Johannes Haubold has also argued persuasively that the Persian kings appropriated Greek mythology and history in their own propa-ganda, and that the fifth-century meanings imposed, for example, on the *Iliad* may well reflect Persian as well as Athenian cultural inter-vention.[35] Although I was indeed concerned in both *Inventing the Barbarian* and the commentary on *Persians* to emphasize the extent to which, for example, Egyptian literature or the Persian royal family's own self-representations were reflected in Greek perceptions,[36] I was not equipped to do this with any degree of expertise, as Sancisi-Weerdenburg pointed out in an undeservedly charitable review.[37] In any case, in the 1980s and early 1990s it still seemed overwhelmingly necessary to demonstrate the potency of the *Greek* ideological agenda behind Greek thinking about ethnicity, and the unreliability of both their imaginative constructions and their empirical observation, how-ever self-evident this may all now seem to younger scholars, born at least a decade after the murder of Martin Luther King.

Yet western discourse about the Orient does now need to be reassessed as just one component in a dynamic and unceasing ex-change between the two, rather than a view from one side of a conceptual wall; as Whitby has shown, Greek elites in and around the north-west regions of the Persian empire cultivated close and warm relationships with the courts of the King and his satraps.[38]

---

[34] Moyer (2002).

[35] Haubold (forthcoming *a*); in another paper (forthcoming *b*), he looks at what bridging the Hellespont might have meant from the perspective of the new leader of a Persian regime, attempting both symbolically and militarily to reinforce and validate his claim to empire. I am grateful to Dr Haubold for his advice on this section.

[36] See e.g. E. Hall (1989), 94, 158–9, 206.

[37] Sancisi-Weerdenburg (1993).

[38] Whitby (1998). For the importance of reading the Persian and Babylonian sources when reconstructing the slightly later period of Alexander the Great's con-quests, see Lendering (2004).

There were, moreover, large numbers of individuals living in ethnically complicated civic communities, above all in the Black Sea and Asia Minor, whose input into the Athenocentric classical Greek sources on Asia has rarely been systematically investigated, at least not using the type of up-to-date theoretical models which have recently been developed by societies actually forged in interaction, such as the large Anglo-Indian community in India,[39] or indeed the sophisticated anthropological and sociological models of ethnicity that Jonathan Hall has recently applied to the more mainstream Greek evidence.[40] One work that would have helped me to see the possibilities of this approach, had it been published earlier, would have been the third chapter of Pericles Georges's *Barbarian Asia and the Greek Experience*.[41] Georges makes an original attempt to see Persian manoeuvres in operation behind the ideas about Persia and reports of Persian deeds that appear in Greek sources. His emphasis is less on what the Greek image of Persia tells us about Greek self-definition, than on the dialectical interpenetration of culture and especially propaganda. The Persian kings and their satellites used Greek intermediaries through whom they communicated with the Greek-speaking public, whether under their jurisdiction in Asia or in free Greek cities to their west, and undoubtedly tried to present themselves in ways that would have appealed to Greek sensibilities. Georges's approach kept attention on far more of the humans involved in the generation of ethnic identity in the fifth-century Aegean than did my own Athenocentric and literary focus.

More recently, Amélie Kuhrt has argued that the interplay of Greeks and Iranians was 'an intricate one, and by no means unidirectional', and that progress could be made towards understanding how the Greeks' eastern neighbours saw the Greeks.[42] Indeed, the evidence she accumulates suggests that the antithesis between Greek and barbarian which was imposed on the world by Athenians and their allies in the early fifth century essayed a violently binary

---

[39] See Moore-Gilbert (1986), ch. 27; Macfie (2000), 7. For an excellent study of 'shades of Greekness' amongst the populations of Roman Asia Minor, see however Spawforth (2001).

[40] See Jonathan Hall (1999) and (2001).

[41] 'Tabula Rasa: The Invention of the Persians', in Georges (1994), 47–75.

[42] Kuhrt (2002), 8.

over-simplification of hazy entities: the enormously diverse Aegean
and Near Eastern spheres need to be visualized, instead, 'as a mosaic
of highly individual and distinctive cultures, which had overlapped
and interacted more and less intensely over several thousand years'
even by the eighth century BC.[43] The essays collected by Irad Malkin,
studying ancient perceptions of Greek ethnicity (2001), includes
explorations of what both the Achaemenids and the Jews made of
the Greeks and Greekness.[44] Parts II and III of Pierre Briant's monu-
mental *Histoire de l'empire perse* (1996), available in English translation (2002), are now also required reading for anybody interested in
the authentic self-representations of the Persian royal family and
court officials, whose curious Greek-speaking theatrical surrogates
sang and danced so outlandishly together on Aeschylus' Athenian
stage.

THE BARBARIAN SPECTATOR?

Anyone embarking on a study of ethnicity in the classical Athenian
theatre would now be fortunate enough to have access to the astonishing new papyrus of Simonides' poem about Plataea (*POxy* 3965).
This offers an elegiac account of the defeat of the barbarians in a
battle of the Persian Wars which can make some claim to rival
Aeschylus' *Persians* in scope if not quite scale. It also demonstrates
the subtlety of interplay between history and myth that was possible
in the early fifth century, above all in drawing connections between
the defeat of Troy and the repulse of Xerxes.[45] Indeed, it would now

[43] Ibid. 9–10.

[44] Sancisi-Weerdenburg (2001); Gruen (2001); see also the sophisticated study by
Rajak (2000).

[45] The new Simonides papyrus also made possible the identification as Simonidean of another previously published papyrus (*POxy* 2327). They were first brought
together and published under the name of their author in the second edition of vol. ii
of M. L. West's *IEG* (1992*b*). There is a large amount of extremely useful scholarship
on the Plataea poem, including much new material exploring the cultural shaping of
the conflict with the barbarians, in Boedeker and Sider (2002). This also includes an
excellent translation of the fragments by Sider (2002), 13–29, and, on the mutual
assimilation of the narratives of the Trojan and Persian wars, especially Boedeker
(2002), 155–8; Rutherford (2002), 40–4; P.-J. Shaw (2002).

be possible to widen considerably the brief of any discussion of theatrical foreigners in terms of drawing inferences from the representation of barbarians, both mythical and quotidian, in drama;[46] the situation has improved even more in the case of the visual arts, above all Attic pottery.[47] It would also be possible to investigate more fully the presence of 'real' barbarians in Attica. Over the last few years several fascinating publications have studied evidence for non-Greeks offered by inscriptions on gravestones, nomenclature, and references in 'real-world' texts such as Thucydides' mention of a suburb—or ghetto—known as 'Phrygioi' in Athens (Thuc. 2.22.2).[48] The evidence for individual non-Athenian residents of Attica has been assembled in a single volume.[49]

It is now a matter of urgency to reassess the theatrical texts from the perspective not only of the indigenous Athenian citizen spectator, but the potential spectator of metic or servile status from Thrace, Scythia, Phrygia, Lydia, Syria, and all the other territories from which the Athenians drew their slaves: what did the barbarian who lived in Athens think—if anything—about the portrayal of ethnic issues on the public stage? There has, moreover, been increased scholarly interest during the last decade in fifth- and fourth-century performances beyond the city-centre of Athens. In Attic deme theatres, the opportunities for watching revived plays became ever more numerous: even Kollytos, a deme in the heart of the city centre, had incorporated drama into its local festival programme by the 370s.[50] By 380 centres of theatrical

---

[46] See the elegant literary interpretations of the place of ethnicity in Euripides' *Hecuba* produced in the early 1990s by C. P. Segal (1990) and Zeitlin (1991). For ethnographic material in tragedy and comedy see e.g. the useful discussion of tragedy and comedy in Tuplin (1996), 133–6 and 141–52, esp. 144–5 on the material connected with the 'persistent subtext of Persian parallels' in *Acharnians*.

[47] There is a useful overview of the Athenian visual image of the foreigner in Lissarrague (1997). See also, besides the extensive evidence in the articles on 'barbarian' mythical figures in *LIMC*, M. Miller (1997) on Persians in classical Greek art; M. Miller (1988) on Midas; Rein (1996) and Roller (1999) on the Greek iconography of Phrygian cults; M. Miller (2000) on Busiris.

[48] See e.g. M. Miller (1997), 81–5 with table 3.c; Tuplin (1996), 132–77, who points out that Miller tends to assume that Persian names suggest dead Greeks who had been given fashionably Persian names rather than dead Persians; Bäbler (1998); De Vries (2000), 339–41; Hagemajer Allen (2003). I am very grateful to P. J. Rhodes for help on this issue.

[49] Osborne and Byrne (1996).

[50] See Csapo (forthcoming), Hall (forthcoming *b*).

activity had mushroomed elsewhere in mainland Greece–at Corinth, the Isthmus, Eretria, and Phigaleia.⁵¹ Performances in more far-flung theatres are attested from as early as the 460s in Sicily, and from 413 onwards in Macedon and Megale Hellas, as well as on temporary stages erected in market-places by travelling players;⁵² in such cases it becomes impossible for the modern scholar to exclude low-status spectators from ancient performance spaces. By Plato's day, reactionary males began to deplore the fact that not only women and children, but also 'the entire crowd' (*ton panta ochlon*) now all had their opinions on tragedy, and were influenced by it (Plato, *Laws* 7.817b–c, see also above p. 165 n. 65).

In Athens, amongst the resident foreigners classified as 'metics', there were undoubtedly individuals with a barbarian upbringing, or if they had been born in Athens (like the 'Egyptian' Athenogenes discussed below) an ethnic identity informed by barbarian parentage and possibly bilingualism. Metics may have been present in some numbers at drama competitions, at least at those held at the Lenaea, where they were even allowed to fund choruses.⁵³ They are not known to have been excluded from at least *watching* plays at the Dionysia. Moreover, although evidence is thin on the ground (not least, presumably, because a naturalized citizen would be unlikely to want to draw attention to foreign origins), it was at least possible for a metic to become a citizen. The issue of naturalization in classical Athens is admittedly beset by problems and controversy. The situation changed several times (especially after Pericles' citizenship law of 451 BC). In addition, it is not always clear whether the ancient evidence that a slave who was freed (of which there are plenty of examples) is also implying that he was enrolled in a deme and received the full rights of a citizen, and the ability to pass them to legitimate offspring. Freed slaves tend to disappear from the historical record. Indeed, it is partly their singularity that adds the frisson to the remarkable stories of the banker Pasion (father of the orator Apollodorus), who acquired Athenian citizenship after using his status as metic to confer generous benefactions upon the city, and his 'bought' slave Phormio, said to speak with a strong foreign accent, who was manumitted by his master, and eventually also

⁵¹ See above, p. 29 and n. 55.   ⁵² Taplin (1999), 38.
⁵³ D. M. Lewis (1968), 380.

naturalized. But Pasion, also, had originally been neither metic nor citizen; he was himself once a slave, probably from Phoenicia.[54] It seems most unlikely that such a publicly prominent figure never attended a theatrical performance once he had become a citizen: the only questions are how often he had attended in his earlier lives, and whether his changes in status were as atypical as some scholars have asserted. Any ex-slave who became a citizen would have been well advised not to draw too much attention to his lowly past.

Indeed, the participation of both slaves and ex-slaves in the consumption of classical Greek theatre is a topic that deserves more consideration. Some scholars have argued that Socrates is only talking hypothetically when in *Gorgias* he describes tragedy as a form of rhetoric that aims solely at giving pleasure, as much to slaves, women, and children as to the male and free (502b–d). But Theophrastus implies that by the later part of the fourth century, at least, it was standard practice for any Athenian citizen who could afford it to be attended by a personal slave who placed the cushion on his seat at the theatre (*Char.* 21.4), as well as for the habitual sponger to trick other people into subsidizing a seat at the theatre for his children's *paidagōgos* (*Char.* 9.5). Much earlier, in the late fifth century, there were almost certainly state slaves such as the Scythian archers present at the Dionysia, because one of their official roles was the regulation of crowd behaviour at large gatherings of people in public spaces. They may not have paid close attention to the performances, but the question of their responses, especially when they were themselves impersonated in comedy, can scarcely be dismissed altogether.[55] Slaves were often skilled musicians: we simply do not have the evidence to prove whether or not an attested slave *aulētēs*, known to have been active in Athens in 415 BC, had ever experienced the representation of any barbarian character in any of the performance arts.[56]

[54] For the colourful careers of Pasion and Phormion, see the testimonia and discussion in M. J. Osborne (1981–3), iii. 48–9 and 55; Bers (2003), 'Introduction'.

[55] On the Scythian archers, see further, Ch. 8, pp. 232–5. There is some suggestion that even in the fifth century the eight official slaves attached to the Council sat in the theatre with the Five Hundred whom they served, in the prestigious seating section called, in Aristophanes' *Birds* (794), the *bouleutikon*. See especially Goldhill (1994), 364.

[56] Hikesios, of unknown ethnicity: see Andocides 1.12; Osborne and Byrne (1996), 338, no. 7724.

The most important group, however, is constituted by the slaves who were emancipated as a reward for rowing alongside Athenian citizens. Xanthias in Aristophanes' *Frogs* (405 BC), whose slave role is unprecedented in its development and authority, certainly constitutes an aesthetic reaction to the very recent emancipation and almost certainly naturalization of a large number of male Athenian slaves—many of whom may have been non-Greeks—in recognition of their contribution as rowers in the battle of Arginusae the previous year.[57] The sheer scale of the chaos and crisis in Athens in 406, along with the acute shortage of manpower, made even the desperate expedient of the mass enfranchisement of slaves seem, for once, acceptable. The Old Oligarch was probably exaggerating when he claimed that Athenian slaves were impossible to distinguish from free men in Athens by their clothes and appearance (1.10), but the passage may illuminate the comparative ease with which former slaves could, at least at Athens, assume new roles as citizens. There is, moreover, little reason to suppose that the new citizens enfranchised by Arginusae were not actually yet present in the audience at the première of *Frogs*: indeed, several of the lines in the dialogues involving Xanthias and in the parabasis seem consciously designed to cultivate their applause (33–4, 190–2, 693–9).[58] And their responses to, for example, the humiliation of Dionysus in the flogging scene (605–73), would have differed considerably from the reactions of those who had never experienced slavery.

The opportunities to react to theatre were not, of course, restricted to actual full performances at festivals. Plays needed to be rehearsed for weeks—indeed months—before performances, and were much discussed after them. Speeches from tragedy were, by the time of Aristophanes' *Clouds* (1371–2), being recited at symposia; scenes from drama, or myths regularly enacted in drama, were painted on

[57] See *Frogs* 31–4, 693–4; Xenophon, *Hellenica* 1.6.24; Hellanicus 4 *FgrH* fr. 171, and the other testimonia assembled and discussed in M. Osborne (1981–3), iii. 33–7; Dover (1993), 43–50; Peter Hunt (2001).

[58] Although some scholars have been reluctant to believe that the Arginusae slaves can have become fully naturalized Athenian citizens, the evidence offers no reason to doubt this, as the majority of recent scholars, following the detailed arguments of M. Osborne (1981–3), iii. 33–7, 181, are agreed. See e.g. Cartledge (1993), 92–3, and Peter Hunt (1998), 92–3, with bibliography.

the vases from which slaves served their masters, and Sian Lewis has recently reminded us that vase-paintings were 'an open form of communication, available to every gaze', and their meanings were therefore construed in the minds of slaves as well as those of free people.[59] It is of course impossible to be sure how an individual metic or slave might have responded to Aeschylus' savage Egyptian herald in *Suppliants*, to Euripides' obtuse Crimean monarch Thoas, or to the loyal pedagogue in Sophocles' *Electra*. But that does not mean that we should avoid asking the question. If the male slave from Colchis who was sold at Athens in 414/13 ever witnessed, or heard about, a production of Euripides' *Medea*, or even saw a vase on which this tragedy was painted, can his reactions to her and her nurse have been identical to those of an Athenian Greek?[60] The largest group of barbarian slaves at Athens came from Thrace: at least one Thracian slave, Sosias, was in a position of some importance as *epistatēs* of other slaves working in the mines, in 420 BC; this was just four or five years after the Thracian king Polymestor's shocking scenes in Euripides' *Hecuba*, and probably the famous *Tereus* by Sophocles, in which another Thracian monarch had raped and mutilated a freeborn Athenian princess.[61] The playscripts of Athens only acquired their multiplicity of original meanings at the point that they were realized in the mind of each spectator, even if the vast majority of these spectators, like the authors, were indeed free and enfranchised *politai*.

The largest category of non-Greeks in Athens was undoubtedly constituted by slaves. Indeed, it is difficult to over-stress the intimacy of the connection in the ancient mind between ethnic difference and suitability for slavery; the idea may have reached its most developed theoretical exposition in the first book of Aristotle's *Politics*, but it is implicit in much of the discussion of slavery prior to that. It is certainly an issue, for example, in Plato's *Lysis*, where Socrates

[59] Sian Lewis (1998/9), 74. As she trenchantly states (p. 75), 'all members of the household must be potential viewers (and interpreters) of the scenes, whether or not they could read, or even understand Greek'.

[60] The Colchian was a slave belonging to Cephisodorus, a wealthy metic (*IG* I³. 421.44, no. 7782 in Osborne and Byrne (1996), 341).

[61] For Sosias, whose owner was Niceratus Cydantides, see Xenophon, *Poroi* 4.14 and Osborne and Byrne (1996), 109, no. 2585.

emphasizes that a young citizen boy has less liberty than a slave. Indeed, he is ruled by a slave in the form of his *paidagōgos*: Socrates remarks that it is a terrible thing for a free man (*eleutheros*) to be ruled by a *doulos* (208c–d). At the end, he remembers (223a–b),

there arrived the *paidagōgoi* of Lysis and Menexenus, like supernatural beings (*daimones tines*), bringing with them the boys' brothers; they called out to them, telling them it was time to be off, for it was already late. At first both we and the bystanders tried to drive them off, but they took no notice of us at all, and became annoyed and carried on calling out in their barbarian speech (*hupobarbarizontes*). They seemed to us to have become a bit tipsy at the Hermaia.

The elevated Greek conversation is thus contrasted with the drunken barbarisms of the boys' slave-class minders, theatrically presented like *daimones* suddenly appearing on stage: the word used of their speech implies that they had a pronounced foreign accent. If these semi-barbarian *paidagōgoi* could move freely around the town, and attend an obscure festival of Hermes, who is to say that they were necessarily excluded completely from any of the public festivals of Dionysus?[62]

It is always a struggle to remind ourselves of the ubiquity of slaves in classical Athens, and what must have been the theatregoer's almost daily experience of dealing with individuals who were both not Greeks and almost completely powerless.[63] It is only over the last fifteen years that theoretical models have even begun to be developed for investigating the nature of the relationship between the large-scale use of slaves in Mediterranean antiquity, and the aesthetics that underlay Greek and Roman cultural products.[64] The boundary between Greek and barbarian was less a 'vertical' curtain encircling

[62] For a collection of other passages mentioning or assuming the presence of slaves in Platonic dialogues, see Gera (1996). A rather different note is struck by the former slave Epictetus, who implies around the end of the 1st cent. AD that runaway slaves would be likely to try to evade recapture by mingling amongst the audience at the performance of a play (*Discourses* 1.29.9).

[63] A point made with sustained passion in P. duBois (2003); see now the Athenian letter, probably from a slave boy to his mother, discussed in Edward Harris (2004).

[64] The relationship between slavery and literary form and content has however been taken seriously of late, in e.g. P. W. Rose (1992); Thalmann (1998); Fitzgerald (2000); some of the essays in Joshel and Murnaghan (1998); McCarthy (2000); Keith Bradley (2000).

the areas of the Mediterranean and Black Sea mainly populated by Greek-speaking communities than, in Athens at least, a 'horizontal' slicing across the heart of the community, both within the city walls and beyond them in more rural demes. Slavery imposed an intellectual pressure on the class of owners, forced to create elaborate rationales to justify the everyday conviction that one ethnic group was either naturally, or culturally, more slavish than another (see below).[65] The level of emotional pressure that slavery imposed both on slaves and on masters is most devastatingly illustrated by the assumption in Plato's *Republic* that the slaves of a rich man would instantly kill him, together with his wife and his children, if they were given the opportunity to do so (*Republic* 9.578d–79c). The property confiscated by the state from the Athenian metic Cephisodorus in 425 BC (*IG* I³. 421) remains one of the most eloquent reminders of the type of slave being transferred from one owner to another in classical Athens at the time when Euripides and Sophocles were writing their tragedies.[66] Among his possessions, he had counted women, men and children from Thrace, Caria, Syria, Scythia, Lydia, and elsewhere. This ethnic mixture would have been approved by the venerable Athenian in Plato's *Laws*, who regarded it is an important principle of slave management to keep apart slaves who could speak the same barbarian language (*Laws* 6.776). Thinking harder about the cultural resonance of each ethnic label in classical Athens would also be desirable: although dating from the later part of the fourth century, it is fascinating to find Theophrastus, for example, say that a sign of the man of petty ambition (*mikrophilotimia*) is that he wants to impress people by choosing an African slave to attend him on public outings (*Char.* 21. 4).

One of the problems with investigating Athenian slaves is that they themselves left little easily perceptible trace on the prime texts which constitute our understanding of everyday reality, for example forensic oratory, since slaves could not litigate in person (see Ch. 12, pp. 377, 383). But the tensions surrounding ethnic difference, which can be an explosive issue in theatrical texts, are indeed well

---

[65] There has been some exciting work recently on the 5th-cent. intellectual pyrotechnics on ethnicity and their reflection in e.g. Herodotus: see esp. Rosalind Thomas (2000).

[66] The inscription is translated in Austin and Vidal-Naquet (1977), 283–4, no. 75.

illustrated by some ancient legal speeches. Athenian comedy cracks jokes at the expense of what are said to be 'Egyptian' businessmen, the purveyors of drugs and fragrances, for example an Egyptian perfumier named Deinias mentioned in a fragment of Strattis.[67] But the comic poets could only win laughs by poking the finger at 'Egyptian' merchants because of attitudes inherent in their audiences, which had themselves been nurtured by poetic and theatrical images since as least as early as Aeschylus' *Suppliants*. The cunning Egyptian tradesman became, through a combination of 'real-life' experiences and culturally transmitted images, a vivid, instantly recognisable member of the theatrical cast of Athens. It is hardly a surprise, therefore, that the identical stereotypes, with their concomitant prejudices, should be exploited by the speech-writers should an Egyptian or person of actual or alleged Egyptian descent ever become involved in litigation. In Isaeus' fifth oration, Melas (whose name, 'the black one', may also be ethnically significant) is labelled 'The Egyptian' every time he is mentioned, in order to ensure that the jury never forgets that they are not dealing with an Athenian Greek (Isaeus 5.7, 8, 40).[68]

An Egyptian perfumier is to be found in the 'real' context of a speech by the orator Hyperides (oration 3), probably composed around 330 BC. This speech was famous enough in antiquity for the author of the treatise *On Sublimity* attributed to Longinus to cite it as an example of its author's fabled charm in oratory on a small scale (34.4) The plaintiff, who appears to be called Epicrates (although the problematic state of the text renders this identification uncertain), is conducting a private prosecution for damages against Athenogenes, a perfumier resident in Athens. Athenogenes is said to be 'Egyptian' (although his name may well mean that he had been born in Athens, and he may have lived there all his life).[69] The

[67] See T. Long (1986), 58, 80, 110.

[68] On the stereotype of the cunning Egyptian see also E. Hall (1989), 123; Whitehead (2000), 287; Demosthenes 21.163 provides a rhetorical reference to a metic suggestively labelled 'the Egyptian, Pamphilos'; for a discussion of what we would call 'racist' invective in the Athenian law courts, see Whitehead (1977), 112.

[69] For a succinct discussion of all the evidence concerning this speech, the metics who conducted trade in perfume, and of the proper name Athenogenes, see now the excellent commentary on Hyperides by Whitehead (2000), 265–71, 287–8. There are several attested Egyptian tradesmen in Athens, including one Hermaios, during the fifth and fourth centuries: see Osborne and Byrne (1996), 11 (nos. 214–22).

plaintiff alleges that 'the Egyptian' tricked him into buying a business which was already badly in debt. Since there was actually a written contract between the two, which had been agreed without any duress and in front of witnesses, the plaintiff is skating on thin ice in bringing the prosecution; everything had to depend 'on the presentation of the two individuals concerned'.[70] The version of events relayed by the Athenian citizen Epicrates (who seems to have delivered the speech himself) runs as follows: Athenogenes owned three perfume businesses. One of them was run for him by a slave called Midas whose two sons (also slaves of Athenogenes) acted as his assistants.[71] Epicrates became infatuated with one of the two boys. Athenogenes tricked him into buying not only the boy, but the business, the father, and the brother, by sending one Antigone, a *hetaira* with whom he had himself once been sexually involved, to 'persuade' the hapless Epicrates. The lovelorn Epicrates was so desperate to get his hands on the boy that he consented, and finalized the agreement, unaware that with the business came considerable debts, all mention of which had been omitted from the document.

In this speech Epicrates relies on arousing sympathy from his fellow Athenian jury by impugning the character of the non-citizen. He casts himself as the credulous but honest and honourable victim of an alien's cunning, thus appealing to his compatriots' shared prejudices. The tone is set in his attack on Antigone, the prostitute and accomplice in fraud (3): 'what do you think she has in mind now she has taken as her partner Athenogenes: a speech-writer and marketeer fellow (*agoraios*), and to cap it all an Egyptian?' (*to de megiston, Aiguption*).[72] The implications of the defendant's ethnic origins are thus seen as telling the jury more about his character and the likelihood of his guilt even than his dodgy choice of female associate, or his communication skills.

Such few factual details as can be extracted from the speech imply that Athenogenes really was a force to be reckoned with. He was well established, having two generations of perfume vendors behind him

---

[70] Whitehead (2000), 269; see also MacDowell (1978), 140.

[71] The name Midas probably suggests Phrygian origin: see Strabo 7.3.12.

[72] Translation from Whitehead (2000), 272.

(19); he had owned three perfumeries until the sale to his prosecutor. He had avoided fighting at Chaeronea (28–9), and had previously found his way into the civic administration at Troezen (33). He probably wrote his own speech in his defence (3). Egyptian metics as a group had indeed by this date established themselves comfortably at Athens; they had recently been officially allowed to establish a cult of Isis there. But the significance of the speech lies in the prejudices to which Epicrates believes he can appeal, especially the prejudices held towards such a prosperous 'barbarian' metic. Athenogenes is accused of the cunning stereotypically imputed to Egyptians (*deinotēs*, 13) and of mendacity (*pseusamenos*, 14). The speaker adds three further types of culpable behaviour very often 'exported' in the Greek imagination to the barbarian world: brazen effrontery (*anaideian*, 23), the moral degradation implied in the adjective *ponēros* (31), which it is emphasized is 'true'—*homoios*—to his (Egyptian) self, and especially great cruelty (*ōmōs*, 32).

The rhetorical strategy is to argue that the Athenians have been nurturing a snake in their own civic bosom. Although it is factually entirely irrelevant to the case in hand, the speaker reminds the jury that the daughters of this alien had been nurtured on the prosperity provided by them, the citizens (29). The 'debt' which the Egyptian had thus incurred had been betrayed when he had defected to Troezen rather than fight at Chaeronea (28–9). In order to emphasize his point, Epicrates orders the recitation of the law decreeing that no metic could leave the city in time of war. But, implies Epicrates, the draft-dodging metic has become a sinister entrepreneur in the political sphere as well as in commerce. At Troezen he had hitched his wagon to the traitor Mnesias, and won an appointment as a magistrate despite his barbarian provenance. The unspoken implication is that Athenogenes is the 'enemy within', whose success at Troezen may yet be repeated at Athens. By arousing fear of his opponent Epicrates, therefore, uses the strongest possible weapon against his adversary: today it would undoubtedly be classed as incitement of racial hatred. And yet by arousing fear of his opponent, a prosperous metic, he also invites *us* to ask what on earth Athenogenes might have made of the Egyptians whom he may well have had an opportunity to see represented on stage.

IDENTITY AND IDENTIFICATION

Those who are inclined to perceive 'liberal' and cosmopolitan texts and subtexts in classical Athenian theatre should remember that the men who sat on the juries, and to whose tastes and prejudices Hyperides' insidious rhetoric is directed, were the same men who formed the core of the Athenian theatre-going public. Reading Hyperides' third oration offers a useful reminder of the potency of the ethnic stereotypes circulating within the Athenian adult male population. Yet several reviewers of my earlier work have objected to what they see as my exaggeration or over-simplification of the ethnocentric bias of the Greeks in general and of Aeschylus' *Persians* in particular.[73] The stern reviewer in *Journal of Hellenic Studies* judged that my edition relentlessly looks in Aeschylus' text for 'grist' to its 'ideological mill'. It 'has a serious flaw' in being conditioned by the 'contemporary fashion that may be called anti-occidentalism, the dangerous myth that western culture is inherently and uniquely racist, imperialist and chauvinist'.[74] I do indeed think that western culture has always been racist, imperialist, and chauvinist, but not uniquely so. Every single known human society thus far has been both xenophobic and chauvinist, but this is not inherent—we can *imagine* a multicultural society which is neither. The reviewer's opinion is legitimate, and internally consistent. His only mistake is to regard himself as free from any ideological agenda of his own; but this view is compromised by his use of the term 'anti-occidentalism', a transparent gloss for a much more contemporary political concept, and a very specific and potent one: Orientalism.

In answer I would actually underline even more emphatically my view that the best way to read the *effect* of the play on fifth-century Athenian sources would be to see what they made of it at the time. The evidence, in Aristophanes' *Frogs*, at least, suggests that its

---

[73] e.g. Rosenbloom (1998), 38. It is worth remembering that the ancient Greek imagination could generate a myth in which even *birds* could respect the difference between Greeks and barbarians; on the island Diomedeia in the Adriatic, the local birds allow all Greeks to visit Diomedes' shrine, but kill barbarians who disembark there ([Aristotle], *De Mirabilibus* 79 = 836^{a}8–18).

[74] Sommerstein (1998a), 211–12.

patriotic undertow was widely acknowledged: Aeschylus claims that
the play always made its audiences yearn for victory over their
enemies (1026–7). Another way to explore the effect the play might
have had is to investigate its emotional register, which is dominated
explicitly by terms expressing terror, hate, and longing for the dead.
Yet my emphasis on looking at emotional signals when conducting
an exercise in cultural hermeneutics has led at least one other scholar
to question my interpretation from another trajectory altogether. In
The Emptiness of Asia, Thomas Harrison agrees that the import of the
play in its original context was self-congratulatory.[75] His objections
are, rather, to my view of how this may have operated psychologically.

Unlike Harrison, I recognize that the play as a whole enacts a
prolonged crescendo of ritual mourning. Sociologically speaking, an
act of collective sympathy in a cultural, performative context creates
its primary bond less with the sufferer than between the fellow
sympathizers; this was certainly the case with the group identities
sustained by the affective power of middlebrow expressions of communal sympathy in American Cold-War representations of Asia.[76]
Acknowledging that a particular audience had an affective response to
a representation of suffering need not entail acknowledging that the
audience felt remotely sorry for the real sufferer undergoing representation, especially when he was hundreds of miles away in Persep-
olis or Susa. For this reason, while I do not share the premise of
Kuhns's analysis of *Persians* (published in 1991) as poetically repli-
cating the universally constituted human psyche's propulsion
through the different stages of mourning, it is worth reading because
Kuhns does justice to the dynamic emotional details accumulated in
the play.[77] Similarly, the part of the interpretation to which Harrison
objects most is when he says that Hall 'falls back' on a psychological
explanation when discussing the cognitive experience of an Athenian
audience when *Persians* was performed.[78] I suggested that the
Athenians could 'feel' two different things at once—jubilation and

[75] Harrison (2000), 9, describes the relationship between our studies of *Persians* in
slightly different language.
[76] See Christina Klein (2003), 100–42.
[77] Kuhns (1991), 11–34.
[78] T. Harrison (2000), 104–5.

remembered pain—while 'projecting' their pain onto Persia. The process of psychological projection entails the casting of an image of one's own desires and experiences onto the blank 'screen' constituted by another individual's psyche. Projection is what is happening when a child who is afraid of a parent assumes (as the child inevitably will unless s/he acquires, and is able to draw inferences from, experiences to the contrary) that *all* children are afraid of a parent. Projection is a key process in psychoanalysis, where a patient's own desires and assumptions can be dissected with the analyst after they have been brought to consciousness through controlled and observed projection. Projection is the process at work when, after I have had a hard day, it strikes me forcibly that *my husband* looks like he needs a drink.[79]

This initially difficult idea appears self-evident to those who have studied or experienced formal psychoanalysis, but often strikes non-believers as silly psychobabble. Even less consensual is the notion, distrusted or not comprehended by most commonsensical empirico-positivist Anglo-Saxon critics, that an experience can be *dialectical*. It was Heraclitus who first articulated the philosophical principle of the dialectical unity of opposites—'that one or other apparent opposition is actually a unity in dynamic tension'.[80] The notion is now usually illustrated by the example of the North Pole and the South Pole, which constitute both opposites and an indivisible unity; it has been an elementary concept in Continental philosophy since Hegel, and is a linchpin of Marxist cultural theory.[81] If the mental effort can be made to see how the excitement of victory only meant so much to the Athenian survivors of the Persian Wars *because* of the degree of loss and terror which had accompanied it—that the two emotional registers of triumph and misery constituted opposites in a unity as indivisible as the North and South poles—an understanding can

---

[79] See the first definition offered under the heading of 'projection' in Reber and Reber (2001), 570: it is a symbolic process 'by which one ascribes one's own traits, emotions, dispositions, etc. to another person'. Typically, this projection implies 'an accompanying denial that one has these feelings or tendencies'.

[80] Wardy (2002), 4 (a fascinating reading of Plato's *Symposium* from the starting-point of Heraclitus' proposition of unity-in-opposition).

[81] For an example of the fruitful use of the concept in decoding the paradoxical language of Greek mystery cult, see Seaford (2003).

emerge of what *Persians* may have meant to its first audience.[82] The
Athenians really could subliminally address their own battle trauma,
pain, bereavement, and humiliation, while feeling delight in revenge
and victory; the way to do it was by watching their hated invader,
who had smashed up their city and slaughtered their fathers, sons
and brothers, going through loss and humiliation. Even war films
made in the UK and the USA in the 1950s permit expressions of
terror and sorrow on German and Japanese faces,[83] but this hardly
means that much prominence was given in the minds of many people
in the UK or USA watching these films (who had felt some terror and
sorrow themselves) to contemplating profundities such as the
universality of human suffering. It would be to the credit of the
audiences if they had dwelt on these humanist abstractions, but any
conversations with battle-scarred Britons born in the 1920s suggest
that it is most unlikely.

Another area where the dialectical principle can help to illuminate
the way that the barbarian functioned in the Athenian imagination is to
acknowledge that one ethnic group or nation-state can feel what may
initially seem entirely inconsistent and contradictory emotional responses towards another one.[84] The Athenians certainly hated the
Persians after the 480 invasion; the more democratically minded of
them without a doubt despised the more obsequious aspects they
discerned in the Persian court and administrative hierarchies, and
feared that the Persians might once again attempt to support a non-
democratic government in Athens. Yet the Persian monarchy was
conceptually *inseparable* from aspects of the Asian lifestyle that not

---

[82] I am full of admiration for the subtle study of kings in Greek tragedy, including
Xerxes, by Griffith (1998), who is similarly interested in the illumination which
psychological theory can bring to the study of the impact made by ancient drama.
He rightly emphasizes that theatrical performances invite members of their audiences
'to adopt different subject positions' (39), and actually require a degree of psychological 'splitting' in terms of the subjects with whom they identify during a play. But,
as he acknowledges, these phenomena 'are notoriously difficult to track and analyse
empirically in any detail' (*ibid.*).

[83] For a fascinating filmography of Word War II combat movies until the early
1960s, see Basinger (2003), 275–302; on the depiction of Germans, see also 24–6,
260–1; for Japanese, ibid. 28–9, 32–3, 55–6, 124–5, and esp. 147–54, on *The Sands of
Iwo Jima* (1949), whose cast included real veterans of combat.

[84] There are some perceptive remarks on the issue of Greek and Athenian hatred
for Persia in Tuplin (1996), 153–4.

only impressed the Athenians, but made them feel distinctly aspir-
ational if not actually envious. As Margaret Miller has shown, Persian
material culture—art, metalwork, and textiles—had a significant impact on taste, clothing, and design in classical Athens, especially but not
exclusively in wealthy elite circles. The process may more accurately be
described as adaptation than imitation, but it is undeniable.[85] The form
and decoration of Attic grave monuments also seems to have been
influenced by the perception of Persian and other barbarian memorials
to the dead.[86] There have been some important works published
recently which have advanced our understanding of the way that
Athenians used 'coded' comparisons of particular activities and indeed
individuals with different types of barbarian; one example is the sympotic conceit of 'drinking like a Scythian' (see also Ch. 8, p. 237).[87]

An illuminating parallel to this bifurcated vision is offered by
British views of France during the eighteenth century, for much of
which the two countries were furiously at war somewhere on the
planet, whether the battles were fought in the Netherlands, North
America, Canada, or India. Between the Act of Union in 1707 and the
French Revolution, the British increasingly defined themselves as
Protestant, masculine, mercantile, enlightened, modern, and anti-
monarchical against their rivals and 'Others' just over the Channel,
thought to be festering in a Catholic, effeminate, feudal, reactionary,
and despotic ancient regime.[88] English literature of this period displays a tension between artistic admiration for French cultural
achievements and artistic models (exhibited in the self-regarding
acknowledgements of French sources in, for example, the prologues
and prefaces to English dramas), and a profound anti-French prejudice of a political and ideological nature.[89] Denunciations of French
social mores and political institutions sit everywhere alongside the
wholesale import and imitation of French manners, vocabulary,
delicacies, fashions, ceramics, interior design, music, poetry, and
fiction. In ethnic contexts, hatred and fear can coexist beside envy
and emulation without any of the difficulties many classical scholars
have supposed.

[85] M. Miller (1997), 135–258; see also the remarks of Tuplin (1996), 173–6; Cohen (2001).
[86] K. H. Allen (2003).
[87] Lissarrague (1997).
[88] Colley (1992).
[89] Hall and Macintosh (2005), 33–8.

GENDER AND ETHNICITY IN INTERACTION

British masculinity routinely defined itself in opposition to perceived Continental (Italian and Spanish as well as French) effeminacy, and one aspect of the argument presented in *Inventing the Barbarian* that would not be changed is its account of the role of gendered thinking in the construction of ethnic difference. In Classics and Ancient History circles this notion has—somewhat bafflingly—proved controversial, and thus seems to require clarification. Aeschylus' *Persians*, first performed in 472 BC, is not the source of the earliest scene in western theatre concerning which substantial information is available. That honourable position in theatre history is held by the opening of the play on which *Persians* was based, Phrynichus' *Phoenician Women*. The iambic prologue of this drama was delivered by a barbarian eunuch putting out cushions on seats for a meeting of Persian imperial magistrates (*tois tēs archēs paredrois*), while informing his spectators that Xerxes had already been defeated.[90]

This information is passed down to us in exactly eighteen ancient Greek words.[91] The impression is that even in the earliest known fifth-century playwrights, a certain repertoire of images still familiar today already defined the Orient.[92] The cushions for the magistrates introduce the customary trope of softness, luxury, and plentiful textiles; the meeting is for magistrates of *empire* (*archē*): the status of eunuch compromises the masculinity of the East, as well as drawing attention to its practice of cruel bodily mutilations. The lines in this primordial theatrical scene were spoken by a Greek actor pretending not only to be Not Greek, but Not Genitally Intact, either.

---

[90] The hypothesis to Aeschylus' *Persians*, which claims to be quoting a work on plotlines by an ancient scholar named Glaucus (see E. Hall (1996*a*), 105–6). This is perhaps the late 5th-cent. Glaucus of Rhegium, author of the treatise *On Poets* which heavily informed Plutarch's influential *On Music*. On Glaucus and other early literary historians, see Ford (2002), 139–40.

[91] *plēn ekei eunouchos estin aggellōn en archēi tēn Xerxou hēttan, stornus te thronous tinas tois tēs archēs paredrois.*

[92] It must be acknowledged that John MacKenzie (1995) has argued with considerable cogency that Said's theory of Orientalism in the period of European Imperialism was excessively binary and simple. MacKenzie argues that Orientalism was endlessly protean, as often consumed by admiration and reverence as by denigration and depreciation. But certain key elements in the Oriental fantasy have proved remarkably tenacious from Ctesias to the twentieth-century cinema; and, as I argue above, hostility and admiration can be as co-existent, indeed as co-dependent, as the North and South Poles.

Phrynichus' eunuch invites our curious gaze; he represents a symbol of the actor's art, of the mutable sexual identity at the core of the western theatrical tradition.[93] Even some of the earliest sources on tragic actors imply that they were perceived to be less than fully male.[94] This effeminized, mutilated, servile figure is a theatrical fantasy born out of conflict and triumph: he oversees historically a period of struggle for imperial control of the Aegean. The scenic, poetic, and histrionic effort to which the Athenian citizens put themselves in the aftermath of the Persian Wars was central to the development of their social imagination.

Although most reviewers approved of my emphasis on the reliance of ancient ethnic thinking on categories of gender,[95] a few distinguished scholars (all, as it happens, male) have objected to it explicitly. In his fascinating book *From Melos to My Lai* the Vietnam veteran Larry Tritle argues that 'feminist literary theory' vanquished my ability to listen to the authentic experience recorded in the play.[96] It would have been helpful of Alison Keith to have published her excellent study of gender categories in Roman epic, which has met widespread approval, thirteen years earlier.[97] I would like to have been able to draw on the subtle problematizing of the elision of gendered and ethnic heterogeneities in Lisa Lowe's *Critical Terrains*, published in 1991.[98] Even more particularly, I wish that I had known about Joan Scott's brilliant work on gender as an analytical category in the analysis of historical experience, initiated in an article published in 1986, which has been taken very seriously even by conservative Modern Historians.[99] Yet even the weight of Scott's authority

---

[93] Case (1985); Solomon (1997), 2.

[94] See Ch. 10, pp. 309–10 on the perceived effeminacy of members of the tragic acting profession, and E. Hall (2002*a*), 22–3 on the practice of genital ligature by male performers who wished to sing at a high register.

[95] See e.g. Bakewell (1997).

[96] Tritle (2000), 111 n. 34; see also 107 n. 19. This is a fair criticism, at least from Tritle's perspective. I remain unhappy, however, at being represented as someone who underestimated the impact that being a Persian war survivor would have had on Aeschylus, since this—especially the death of his brother as a result of a terrible wound inflicted at Marathon—is something that I have been almost alone amongst *Persians* scholars in stressing. See e.g. E. Hall (1996*a*), 3, 14.

[97] A. M. Keith (2000), esp. chs. 1 and 3.

[98] Lowe (1991), esp. 1–29 and 75–101.

[99] Joan W. Scott (1986), elaborated in Joan W. Scott (1988).

might have made little difference to those Ancient Historians who think that the investigation of imagery, semantic complexes, and metaphorical structures 'goes too far' when it comes to reconstructing the realities of experience. A scholar either think it matters that in *Persians* there are serial images of defeated or lamenting barbarian women, some of them in bedroom environments, or s/he will not. S/he either thinks that the traces of psychological experience recorded in imaginative and fictional sources have an important place in the records of 'real' history, or that they should be excluded from it. My own view is that imagery of this kind can be the most important of all tools in uncovering ideological currents, since, like myth, it 'transforms history into nature'.[100] I have, with reluctance, come to the conclusion that this still needs spelling out in rather more detail.[101]

It is not controversial to acknowledge that there was an asymmetry of power in Greek culture between men and women. Athenian men controlled their wives and daughters sexually and economically, and deprived them of political agency. Nor can it be any more regarded as debatable that the hierarchical duality of the human species came to inform other conceptual hierarchies and polarizations. The Pythagorean table of opposites, 'an explicit expression... of much older Greek beliefs',[102] opposed man, light, right, and good to woman, darkness, left, and evil (Aristotle, *Met.* 1.986ª22–6). Male supremacy over the female was considered to be natural and right; sexual relations were conceived as hierarchical, with man coming out on top.[103] By drawing a parallel between male and female and the relationship between Greek and barbarian, Greek ascendancy over non-Greek cultures was 'naturalized' and thus legitimized.[104]

The Greeks' use of the possession of women, and victory over them, as metaphors for the defeat of Asia is one historically specific

[100] Barthes (1973), 129; MacDonald (1987), 3; Hausman (1989), 10.

[101] An earlier version of the remainder of Section 5 of this chapter was first published as part of an earlier publication: E. Hall (1993), 118–27.

[102] Geoffrey Lloyd (1966), 49.

[103] Halperin (1990a), 266.

[104] For the canonical study of the conceptual overlap and interplay between the Greek male's different 'Others', see Cartledge (1993). It was, of course, not only non-Greek territories that became conceptually feminine in relation to Athenian imperialism; on the complexities of gender symbolism in Eupolis' comedy *Demes*, see the excellent study by Rosen (1997a), esp. 158–9, 170.

example of a widespread tendency in human history for categories of gender to articulate ideas about warfare.[105] Men active in peace movements have often been maligned as effeminate cowards. When Woodrow Wilson was reluctant to take the USA into World War I, Teddy Roosevelt accused him of 'lack of manhood'.[106] In military training, even where women are recruited alongside men, gendered insults litter the language used both to stimulate aggression and to identify the enemy.[107] The idea (and, historically, all too often the practice) of rape has been a key trope for victory.[108] When warfare concerns the conquest of territory, the land itself is often metaphorically feminized, and the winning of new domains conceptualized as sexual union.[109] One of the imperial reliefs from the Sebasteion at Aphrodisias, for example, depicts a muscular Claudius standing triumphantly over the prostrate figure of Britannia. He pulls her loosened hair and prepares to strike the death-blow with his spear: she, semi-naked, struggles to prevent her dress from slipping off her shoulder. On another relief Nero, equally muscular, supports the naked, slumping figure of Armenia, her hair spilling over her shoulders, between his wide-striding legs.[110] It was customary for America to be represented as female in the late sixteenth-and early seventeenth-century discourses of the European conquerors. In iconography Europe is male, and stands over the relaxed and/or naked figure of the New Continent. America may by turns appear as a dangerous Amazon, an erotic seductress inviting penetration, or a modest maiden shyly giving up her virginity.[111] In Ben Jonson's drama *Eastward Ho* (1605), the song performed in the tavern by Seagull, the sea captain, begins, 'Come, boys, Virginia longs till we share the rest of her maidenhead'.[112]

[105] Porter (1986), 232.

[106] Wiltsher (1985), 172; MacDonald (1987), 21.

[107] MacDonald (1987), 16.

[108] Porter (1986), 232; Dougherty (1993), 61–2, 64–9, 75–6, 85–8, 88–9; Dougherty (1998). On the feminization of the defeated in early Greek literature, see Vermeule (1979), 99–105. Seamus Heaney's poem *Act of Union*, a poem about British imperialism in Ireland (in Heaney 1975) ironically subverts the traditional *topos*.

[109] Kolodny (1973); Porter (1986), 232; Dougherty (1998).

[110] R. Smith (1987), 115–20, with pls. 14 and 16.

[111] Hulme (1985), 17.

[112] Act III, scene iii.15 in the edition of Van Fossen (1979), 127. *Eastward Ho* resulted from Jonson's collaboration with George Chapman and John Marston. See also Carr (1985), 46.

Such imagery holds no surprises for students of the ancient poetics of colonization. Raping a virgin and marrying a maiden are metaphors for sacking a city.[113] Siege or foundation myths often revolve around a pivot involving the sexual union, whether through rape or marriage, of a Greek hero or male Olympian with a female.[114] The Hesiodic *Catalogue of Women* provides a mythical *aition* for Greek colonization of the eastern Mediterranean by tracing back to Io, impregnated by Zeus, the genealogies of numerous barbarian peoples in North Africa, Egypt, and the Levant. The cyclic epics provided other paradigms of colonization in their reports of Greek heroes' fleeting sexual encounters with foreign women on distant shores.[115] In Pindar's 9th *Pythian*, the colonization of Libya is symbolized by both Apollo's seduction of the athletic Cyrene, and Alexidamus' marriage to the daughter of the Libyan Antaeus. The possession of new-found territory is illustrated by the metaphorical possession of women.

Non-Greek, defeated, and female were therefore categories that, through metaphor, became elided. Since woman was the ancient Athenian's primary 'other' and, with barbarian slaves, the most immediate object of his power, he used her as an image for the ethnically alien, transferring from the asymmetrical power-relation embedded in her difference from the patriarchal male to the sphere of international power struggle.[116] This affects the narratives recounting the Persian Wars. First, the oppositions man–woman and rapist–raped are transferred to the non-Greek relationship; Greek ascendancy over Persia is made to appear 'naturally' sanctioned. Second, the ambivalence towards woman's otherness, as source and symbol of desirability, danger, and potential anarchy, is transferred onto the foreign culture against which war continued to be waged for years after 472 BC. This process contributed to the ideological project by which Athenian imperialism sought to weaken Persian influence; it helped to perpetuate the notions of panhellenism and its corollary, the 'barbarian peril'.[117]

---

[113] Hanson (1990), 326.   [114] Zeitlin (1986), 124–5.
[115] Rougé (1970), 309–10.   [116] Cartledge (1993).
[117] Perlman (1976); Baslez (1986).

The male–female polarity has subsequently conditioned most European conceptualizations of the non-European, but of all Europe's 'others'—Africa, America, Australasia—the one most systematically feminized has always been the Orient.[118] Asia has been 'routinely described as feminine, its riches as fertile, its main symbols the sensual woman and the despotic . . . ruler'.[119] Herodotus' Asiatic tyrants—their feminine ways, their transgressive women, their eunuchs, and their luxury—created an implied reader who was not only victorious, but also emphatically Greek, self-disciplined, and masculine. In *Persians* Aeschylus trapped the oriental court inside the theatre of Dionysus, where its cast presented a tableau, as in many Athenian tragedies (except those set at Athens), in which the court is portrayed as lacking a phallic authority figure—an adult male hand steering the rudder of government.[120] The males in the play are the senescent chorus, the dead Darius, and the (largely) absent Xerxes. The text also combines numerous implications of the bereft, the erotic, the soft, and the threnodic, which work cumulatively, and often subliminally, to create the impression of a 'female' continent, vulnerable to Greek 'male' domination. The idea is conveyed that virtually the entire military has been wiped out.

It still seems to me that the West did and does routinely define its relationship with the East as sexual, conceiving the West as the male, penetrative agent.[121] Yet it would have been beneficial to have explored in more depth what such a metaphorical sexual act might mean in ideological terms. It has been argued, for example, that what makes the routine myth of oriental effeminacy necessary is the apprehended virility and fertility of Arab men. Since the advent of Islam, at any rate, polygamy, large families, the masculine power and sexual potency of the Prophet himself—all this has paradoxically become transformed by Orientalist psychological imperatives into a tabu on taking that very sexuality seriously.[122] The phallic Orient is

[118] See the elegant remarks of Briant (2002), 202–3 on the relationship between the Graeco-Roman myth of Persian decadence and the perceived femininity of the Persian court.
[119] Hartog (1988), 330–9.
[120] E. Hall (1997*b*), 103–9.
[121] See above all E. Said (1975), in Macfie (2000), 93.
[122] E. Said (1975), in Macfie (2000), 95; E. Said (1985), 23; for some of the earlier examples of this process, see Daniel (1960), 144–6, 242–3, 267, 355–8.

symbolically castrated. It is, as Said says of exactly this paradox of
representation, 'in the logic of myths, like dreams, exactly to welcome
radical antitheses. For a myth does not analyze or solve problems.
It represents them as already analyzed.'[123] On this account, it becomes important to fuse a reading of the Orient as unmanned with
an apprehension of what it meant to an Athenian to have seen his
homeland penetrated and ravaged by a large and hostile army of
powerful men with terrifying military hardware.

For, in Aeschylus' *Persians*, the dominant image of Asia construes
her as a woman in mourning. She is either a fruitful, maternal figure
(see below) or a young wife, aching with desire for her bridegroom.
The slaughtered Persians are mourned by their parents, but also by
their wives, who pass the days 'in long-drawn-out grief' (63–4). The
marriage beds of Persia are filled with tears brought on by yearning
(*pothos*) for husbands (133–4); the grieving Persian widows, who
have sent forth the partners of their beds, are left alone to think
'man-desiring thoughts' (*pothōi philanori*, 134–9), The chorus recall
how once before, after Marathon, the beds of the Persian wives were
left empty of men (288–9). In the great central dirge, the audience
hears how the 'softly wailing' Persian women long to see again their
recent bridegrooms, to enjoy the 'pleasures of luxuriant youth' on
'soft-sheeted' nuptial couches; instead, however, they must mourn in
insatiable lamentation (541–5).

The alternative female image personifies the Earth of Asia (*chthōn
Asiatis*), who put forth her male children like flowers (59–62), but
has now fallen to her knees in prostration (929–30); Susa is a mother
in mourning (946). An entirely consistent view of Asia, as a fertile but
soft and feminine continent, is presented in the treatise *On Airs,
Waters, Places*, attributed to Hippocrates and probably an authentic
fifth-century work. It connects the diversity of physiology and medical conditions in different human communities with the climate and
environment to which they are subject. From chapter 12 onwards the
writer embarks on a systematic comparison of Asiatics and Europeans. In Asia, he says, everything grows beautiful and large, and the
character of Asiatics is gentle: it is the temperate climate which causes
these characteristics (12.7–16). Since Asia suffers extremes of neither

---

[123] E. Said (1985), 23.

drought nor cold, it enjoys plentiful harvests of both wild vegetation and cultivated crops; its cattle are the sturdiest to be found (12.24–35). Fine natural development is also to be found in the humans there, who are of fine physique and uniform size (12.35–8). But there is a disadvantage, the treatise argues, in this natural wealth: it is impossible for a temperate zone to engender courage, endurance, industry, and high spirits, i.e. the characteristics that define the European, who is bred and tested in a harsh and changeable climate. Indeed, the Asiatics, whose cowardice and sloth are environmentally determined, will always, inevitably, be ruled by the principle of pleasure (12.40–4).

The uniformity of the seasons in Asia is said to lead its inhabitants to lack courage. They are subject to none of the physical changes that harden humans to passion and action (16.3–12). The political constitutions (*nomoi*) of Asiatics are a contributory factor, it is argued, for people have no motivation to improve their lot if ruled by monarchical masters (16.16–33). At this point the writer is suggesting two independent reasons for the inherent passivity of the Asiatic temperament: one from *physis* (the natural environment), and one from *nomos* (political constitutions). But, taken as a whole, the treatise demonstrates that these two factors interconnect; the Asiatic temperament *gives rise* to such forms of government, which would never be tolerated by the rugged individualists of Europe. To explain the unequal size of Europeans, even within a single city, the writer invokes the speed at which the foetus forms in the womb. Its forms by a process of coagulation; changes of season disturb the speed of the process, leading to variations in individuals' size. In Asia, where the temperature is alleged to remain stable, people are all the same size. More significantly, however, the changes of season while the foetus is in the womb also affect character, for shocks to the mind caused by changing environmental conditions engender wildness and independence, whereas uniformity imparts slackness and cowardice. The theories here developed, during the fifth century, thus represent the earliest attempt to base the superiority of Greek culture on arguments from natural science.[124] The Asiatics whose roles were played on the Athenian stage were genuinely believed, at least by some spectators, to

[124] Backhaus (1976); Jouanna (1981), 11–15.

be more feminine, and more slavish, according to natural rules whose operation could be *proven scientifically.*

CHANGING WORLD, CHANGING STAGES

Finally, the recent investigation of the afterlife of Aeschylus' *Persians* has inevitably coloured attitudes to this seminal play.[125] This is possibly at the cost of some objectivity, since a clear view of what was going on in 472 BC is not *necessarily* enhanced by studying what cultural adventures have been had subsequently by a text written at that ancient date. Yet the two perspectives, if handled judiciously, can be mutually illuminating.[126] Aeschylus' *Persians* has played an indisputable role in the perpetuation of the ideological conflict between East and West that has recently re-erupted with such terrible violence. It has historically helped to reinforce the adoption by the Christian mindset of a primary Other in the shape of Islam. The third-millennial vilification of the Arab world has a long history which cannot be dissociated from the rediscovery of *ancient* Greek xenophobia and prejudices against non-Greeks in the East.

In the late Roman, early Christian, and Byzantine eras the complexities of ethnic and religious identity surpassed anything that had gone before, as notions of Greekness, 'Roman-ness' (or *Rōmaiosynē*) and Christianity were constantly contested and redefined. This process acquired a fresh intensity after the Normans attacked Byzantine territory in the late eleventh century, and the supreme Others of the medieval Byzantines became the western Christians: Anna Comnena could even call them *barbaroi*.[127] But a new world order was in gestation. The attention of the Renaissance West was first attracted back to Aeschylus through the Aldine printed edition (1518),

---

[125] See further E. Hall (2006), part of a project on cultural responses to the Persian Wars conducted with Professor P. J. Rhodes and other members of the Department of Classics and Ancient History at Durham University, resulting in Bridges, Hall, and Rhodes (2006).

[126] E. Hall (2004c).

[127] Browning (2002), 270–1. For the Arab perception of the Byzantines at this time, see El Cheikh (2004).

and Jean Saint-Ravy's influential Latin translation *Aeschyli poetae Vetvstissimi Tragoediae*, published in Basel in 1555. But these books came into a world that had changed since the triumph of Christianity, above all in the arrival as a world presence of the Ottoman Turks. It had been the first crusade of 1095 which made Islam familiar in the more northerly countries of the West.[128] Their notion of both the Prophet and the religion was thus born in triumph after the Christian taking of Antioch and Jerusalem, and gave rise to a popular image—comprising savagery, depravity, sexual profligacy, pagan darkness, and satanic evil—of astonishing tenacity. The ground was laid for the identification of Islam with the pagan ancient Persians by one strand in the medieval picture of Mahomet, in which he was seen as a *magus* of demoniacal power, operating in barbarian lands at the time of the emperor Theodosius.[129] By the time of the Renaissance it was the Turks, by now synonymous with Islam, who were regularly presented in the West as descendants of the Herodotean Scythians, and thus the heirs to the ancient Greek prejudices against the barbarians around the Black Sea. This view legitimized constant military action against them, not as a war against infidels but as an atavistic *bellum contra barbaros* with noble antique precedents: as Rodinson put it in *Europe and the Mystique of Islam*, 'to those Europeans brought up on Herodotus and Xenophon, this was an enticing notion'.[130]

It was in the context of this perception of the Ottomans that Aeschylus' *Persians* was first discovered by the European Renaissance. It was recited at an event which explicitly equated Achaemenid Persia with the Ottoman empire, thus, for the first certain time in the western tradition, seeing Aeschylus' cast members through a lens conditioned by Christian views of Islam. For in 1571 a western naval alliance, including the Venetians of the Heptanesian islands and led by John of Austria, had defeated the Ottoman fleet at the Battle of Lepanto. The performance of *Persians* took place, probably in an Italian translation, possibly in ancient Greek or in Saint-Ravy's Latin, in the private house of a member of the Venetian nobility who

[128] Southern (1962), 27–8. [129] See Metlitzki (1977), 199–203.
[130] Rodinson (1987), 36.

then ruled the Heptanesian island of Zante (Zakynthos).[131] By the time of Milton, although Aeschylean scholarship was slow to develop in the later sixteenth and seventeenth centuries, Xerxes, as ancient barbarian and imagined cultural ancestor of the Turks, can be suggestively aligned even with Satan. John Milton compares Satan's bridge from heaven to hell in *Paradise Lost* book 9 with Xerxes' Hellespontine contrivance.[132]

The Enlightenment forged a fundamental Oriental antitype that fused inherited images of the ancient Achaemenids with the contemporary picture of the Islamic Ottoman empire.[133] It was not until the 1760s that the Ottoman empire ceased to look like an immediately pressing threat to Christian civilization at large, and more like a promising pawn in Northern European superpower politics. The turning-point was the Russian–Turkish war of 1768–74, by the end of which the Austrians, and nearly everyone else, agreed that the Russians were a far worse threat to European stability than the Turks. The possibility was raised of reviving the spirit of the crusades in order to re-annexe Constantinople, whose 1453 seizure by the Turks, and its status as the capital of Islam, had remained a constant irritant at least to western Europeans.[134] Then in the second half of the seventeenth century Aeschylus suddenly became available in modern languages, and *Persians* was visualized exclusively in Ottoman terms;[135] responses to its depiction of the barbarian court were informed by countless abduction plays and operas of the eighteenth century, in which Christians are held captive at the court of a Muslim monarch, to face threats of torture and sexual slavery.[136] The best-known of these—and, despite its tawdry stereotypes, one of the least

[131] See E. Hall (1996*a*), 2; Hall and Macintosh (2005), p. 265; Van Steen (forthcoming).

[132] 'So, if great things to small may be compared, | Xerxes, the liberty of Greece to yoke, | From Susa, his Memnonian palace high, | Came to the sea: and, over Hellespont | Bridging his way, Europe with Asia joined, | And scourged with many a stroke the indignant waves.'

[133] See Valensi (1990); Grosrichard (1998); Nippel (2002), 304–10.

[134] W. Daniel Wilson (1985), 81–2.

[135] See the chalk cartoons illustrating *Persians* by George Romney, one of which is reproduced in Hall and Macintosh (2005), ch. 7, and another in Bridges, Hall, and Rhodes (2007).

[136] See the excellent discussion in W. Daniel Wilson (1985).

xenophobic taken overall—is probably Mozart's *Die Entführung aus dem Serail*, which premièred in Vienna in 1782, and in which the janissary Osmin is as greedy, gullible, sadistic, and lecherous a Muslim opponent as ever walked the stage. In English literature, the ancient Persians, just like the contemporary Ottomans, became 'the turban'd tyrant';[137] in a nineteenth-century German illustration of the battle of Marathon, the barbarian's clothes, turbans, and moustaches are indistinguishable from those worn by Turks in art contemporary with it.[138]

The fate of *Persians* as a key text in the western ideological war against Islam was sealed forever by Shelley's *Hellas*, an adaptation published in 1822 and dedicated to the Prince Alexandros Mavrokordatos, a refugee from the Turkocracy. Shelley's Preface twins the Aeschylean Greek tragic vision of the struggle for freedom with the 1821 uprising, setting the scene at Constantinople, in the seraglio of Mahmud II, who was the Ottoman sultan between 1808 and 1839. Islam becomes the open enemy of western *liberty*. In *Hellas* Shelley was unable to liberate himself sufficiently from the contemporary stereotypes of Islam, and the Christian rhetoric of the crusade, to leave the notion of a religious war back in the medieval period where it belongs.[139] The stirring politics and utopian idealism of *Hellas* are compromised by its complicity in the ideology of the Christian crusade. The notion that the greatest threat to cosmic Liberty is the Islamic faith, a notion which is still causing such problems today, was grafted onto the founding myth of western democracy by *Hellas*, and Shelley's status as canonical poet of western liberalism must mean that some of the blame for the inherited prejudices must, regrettably, be laid at his door.

Indeed, the final way in which the stage barbarian would be presented differently today from the way s/he was discussed in *Inventing the Barbarian* is connected with the radically altered historical circumstances under which intellectual work is now conducted. The scholarly perspective on the ancient stage barbarian

---

[137] See Hall and Macintosh (2005), ch. 4, pp. 264–7.

[138] The illustration, which is anonymous, is reproduced from von Rotteck (1842) in Witschel (2002), 6 fig. 2.

[139] See the perspicacious remarks of Daniel (1966), 222–3; *Hellas* is discussed in much greater detail in E. Hall (forthcoming *c*).

obviously can not be the same in 2004 as it was in 1984, when I began my doctoral research. Although nobody knew it at the time, the mid-1980s were the penultimate years of the Cold War, just before the sudden collapse of the Soviet Union and its authority in the German Democratic Republic. *Inventing the Barbarian* was published only a couple of months before November 1989, when the Berlin wall was actually breached.

Some scholars have objected to what they have perceived as the overly simple structuralism underpinning some of the analysis, which they have often paired, rather misleadingly, with Hartog's much more purist structuralism and pyrotechnical style of textual analysis in *Le Miroir d'Hérodote: essai sur la représentation de l'autre* (1980). Yet perhaps there is a similarity, if of rather a different sort than is usually alleged: the two books are both, transparently, products of the final stage of the Cold War. Their model of Self and Other was certainly inseparable from the experience of two superpowers defining themselves, and what they each felt to be their core values, against their enemy of several decades. For the Soviet Union, the key images encapsulating the West represented destitute men without jobs, homeless children, and heroin-injecting prostitutes: for the USA and western Europe, the crucial ideals of personal liberty and plentiful commodities were routinely defined against images of intellectuals being injected with sedatives, and mile-long food queues in Moscow. Now, however, since the fall of the wall and the Gulf War, all this has completely changed. The key images of the West's Other now portray breast-beatings, ululations, beheadings, amputations, beards, veils, rifles, and explosives. The role of Great Barbarian has been completely recast. How different *Inventing the Barbarian* would be today, when the image of the sinister technocratic Soviet communist has been replaced by what is presented as a far more medieval-looking and unknowable Islamic extremist, it is thus quite impossible to say.

8

The Scythian Archer in Aristophanes'
Thesmophoriazusae

In the history of comedy and light opera, the use of characters of an ethnicity different from that of the majority of their original audiences has a long and disreputable history.[1] In our own era, the representation of ethnic minorities within western states, and of members of other ethnic groups further afield, has rightly become an issue of the most profound sensitivity: it is important to remember that it is less than three decades since the grotesque conventions of the popular 'Black-and-White Minstrel Show' ceased to be broadcast on British television;[2] opera lovers are still regularly asked to sit through Monostatos lamenting what he calls his 'ugly' blackness and frustrated desire for the white—and therefore beautiful—Pamina in Act II scene 3 of *The Magic Flute*;[3] I know from direct and recent experience that children's Christmas pantomimes, at least in the North-East of England, still impersonate Native Americans,

---

[1] On ethnic stereotypes on the British imperial stage see above all Bratton et al. (1991); on North America, see Gavin Jones (1999) and Erdman (1997); there are important observations in Roberts (2000) and Floyd-Wilson (2003).

[2] This variety show, a direct descendant of the 'Nigger minstrel' routines popular in the Victorian music hall, and involving white men with black facial make-up dancing and singing with white women, was broadcast on BBC television continuously for twenty years between 1958 and 1978. Occupying a prime slot on Saturday evenings, it regularly attracted record-breaking numbers of viewers and was regarded as excellent family entertainment.

[3] 'Alles fühlt der Liebe Freuden, | Schnäbelt, tändelt, herzt und küß | Und ich sollt' die Liebe meiden, | Weil ein Schwarzer häßlich ist! | . . . | Lieber guter Mond, vergebe, | Eine Weiße nahm mich ein. | Weiß ist schön!'

Turks, Chinese, and Germans in asinine ways unlikely to facilitate international understanding.

The problem facing all writers of comedy today is simply that ethnicity, and the group identity fostered by jokes on the theme of ethnic difference, is one of the most universally exemplified forms of humour.[4] In ancient Greece, which had no such qualms about the impersonation of ethnic difference, pretending to belong to a different ethnic group was from the earliest extant comedy—*Acharnians*— onwards, a significant source of humour.[5] Sometimes this is a matter of actors playing representatives of different Greek *poleis*, for example Megarians, Spartans, or Boeotians.[6] But in *Thesmophoriazusae* the tritagonist, who had earlier in the play appeared in such histrionically extravagant roles as Agathon and Cleisthenes, faced the most demanding 'ethnic' role in the extant Greek comic repertoire:[7] for the last quarter of the play he needed to pretend to be not only unfree and untutored in theatre, but an import into Athens from the far-flung northern shore of the Black Sea.

There are several aspects of the role of the Scythian archer which render it one of the most remarkable in the drama of the period. He is the only speaking Scythian to have survived from the classical Greek theatre; Sophocles' *Scythians* (*Skuthai*), whether tragic or satyric, is known only from fragments.[8] He also represents the most important source for the Athenians' view not only of their corps of archers, but of all their *dēmosioi huperetai*, slaves owned and subsidized by the state, who performed in its service a variety of

---

[4] See Apte (1985), 108–48.

[5] For a recent bibliography, see Willi (2002*b*), 119.

[6] On which see Halliwell (1990); Colvin (1999) and (2000).

[7] On the role distribution of *Thesmophoriazusae* and its implications, see Russo (1994), 196–7.

[8] Sophocles frags. 546–52 *TgrF*; the play has been connected with the journey of the Argonauts. See A. C. Pearson (1917), ii. 185–91. If the 4th-cent. comedies by Antiphanes and Xenarchus entitled *Scythians* had survived, much more could have been said about the projection of this ethnic group in Greek drama. The ancient view of Scythia was a bipolar fusion of romanticised utopianism and censorious anti-primitivism, not unlike the conflicted picture of Native American culture in Hollywood cinema. The idea that the Scythians were well-governed (*eunomoi*) probably goes back to the Homeric Abii (*Il.* 13.6), and can be found in drama in both Aeschylus (fr. 198 *TgrF*) and Antiphanes' comedy *Misoponeros* (fr. 157 K–A). See Lovejoy and Boas (1935), 315–44; Lévy (1981); Long (1986), 9, 16–18.

duties.[9] The central argument of this chapter, moreover, will be that he is a comic response to a very particular type of role in tragedy— the villainous barbarian monarch in Euripides' innovative escape tragedies. But for many decades, indeed until the middle of the 1980s, the only aspect of this role to attract any significant attention from scholars was the element of linguistic caricature.[10]

THE LANGUAGE OF THE OTHER

This fascination with the Scythian's language was in itself under-standable, since his role represents quite the most extensive example of caricature of barbarized Greek speech to have survived from the Greek comic stage; Pseudartabas in *Acharnians* and the Triballian deity in *Birds* each deliver but a few words.[11] The fragments of Old Comedy suggest, however, that this kind of linguistic pastiche was far from uncommon. The comic poet Plato brought Cleophon's supposedly Thracian mother (alluded to in *Frogs* 679–82) onto the stage 'speaking like a barbarian' (*barbarizousan*).[12] The unidentified scene from Old Comedy portrayed by the Tarporley Painter on the 'New York Goose Play Vase' in about 400 BC actually has 'nonsense' sounds representing barbarian speech inscribed near an ugly young man's mouth.[13] Imitation of a barbarian language for comic effect was a poetic convention with a long history. The earliest clear

[9] On the Scythian archers see Plassart (1913); on the state slaves in Athens in general, Jacob (1928); Hunter (1994), 148 and (1997), 300; Gera (1996).

[10] Scholarly interest in the demeaning way in which the archer was portrayed exactly coincided with the realization that his section of the play required to be sensitively handled in performance, especially if recontextualized to the contemporary world. See below, p. 253–4.

[11] Ar. *Ach.* 100, 104; *Birds* 1572, 1615, 1628–9, 1678–9. On the Triballian god see Whatmough (1952), and, for the language and ethnic identity of the Triballians, Papazoglu (1978), 67–81.

[12] See fr. 611 K–A. The allegation that family members were barbarians finds close parallels in the lawcourt speeches: see Ch. 12, p. 373.

[13] See Taplin (1993), 31, with pl. 10.2, who thinks that the figure is 'likely to have a role like that of the Skythian 'policeman' in *Thesmophoriazousai*. He wields a rod in a threatening manner, apparently intent on beating the older, captive man whose arms are stretched over his head. Nonsense sounds (NORARETTEBO) are written in a

example is in a poem by the sixth-century iambographos Hipponax (fr. 92 *IEG*), where a woman was portrayed uttering a lewd incantation, supposedly in Lydian (*ludizousa*, 92.1), but what seems in fact to be Greek with an admixture of Lydian and Phyrgian words.[14] Subsequent to the fifth century, amongst a variety of interesting examples,[15] a particularly exciting encounter with linguistic otherness is to be found in the so-called *Charition* mime discovered on a papyrus. This mime constituted a loose parody of Euripides' *IT* and includes what must have sounded like gibberish to a Greek-speaking audience, nonsense sounds just possibly based on one of the Dravidian dialects of southern India.[16] The most notable heir to this tradition in Roman comedy is Hanno, the imposing Carthaginian of Plautus' *Poenulus*, whose role may imply that there was an extended part for a Carthaginian in the comedy's Greek archetype.[17] But the archer in *Thesmophoriazusae* is the only ancient role, as far as we know, which required its actor to represent foreign pronunciation of Greek speech for an extended period. Although this has now been appreciated by experts in linguistics, it is remarkable how little attention even the linguistic aspect of his portrayal attracted before the late 1980s, when classical scholars began to take seriously both the representation of ethnic difference and the complicated art of ancient acting.[18]

---

position that shows they are issuing from the aggressor's mouth, indicating that he is a barbarian, while the other characters on the vase say words in recognizable Greek. See further Taplin (1993), 97–8, 103.

[14] See Colvin (1999), 39–54.

[15] See the essays collected in Müller, Sier, and Werner (1992), especially the attached bibliography, Werner (1992), which addresses scholarship on foreign languages in Greek and Roman literature from 1900 onwards.

[16] The mime was published with an English translation in Page (1942), and with commentary in Cunningham (1987), 42–7 and Andreassi (2001). The dialect which it was believed had been incorporated into the mime is Kanarese: see Hultzsch (1904) and Varadpande (1981), 98–110; but compare the sceptical remarks of Page (ibid. 336), who was persuaded that the similarities in vocabulary were accidental.

[17] See Hanno's lines in 'Punic' between 930 and 1027, and Gidennis' exchange with her son at 1141–2; these passages may well be imitated from a barbarizing Carthaginian in Plautus' Greek model *Karchedonios*. See Gratwick (1971); Franko (1996), 427–9. For a sophisticated recent reading of the ethnic issues in Plautus' play, see Starks (2000).

[18] An exception was Friedrich (1919); much more recently, see esp. Brixhe (1988) and Willi (2002*b*), 143–6.

The Scythian archer is on stage for longer and has more lines to deliver than any other character in *Thesmophoriazusae* except the kinsman himself, Euripides, and the first female speaker at the festival. The strangeness of his speech is portrayed more consistently than that of other barbarizing characters in Aristophanes: the words of the Triballian god in *Birds* constitute either virtually incomprehensible sounds (1628–9), or unremarkable Greek (1572), while Pseudartabas in *Acharnians* has only two lines to deliver, of which one is 'gibberish made from Persian noises',[19] and the other, again, nearly Greek (100, 104). But the Scythian never merely utters incomprehensible nonsense supposed to signify the Scythian tongue. Instead, he persistently and consistently speaks Greek, as a second language, but strongly inflected and simplified—the sort of dialect of Greek presumably spoken by slaves imported in adulthood to Athens, whether they were addressing Greeks or fellow slaves from other ethnic backgrounds. Aristophanes may have had an ear for foreign languages, or perhaps the text represents a collaborative effort on the part of the poet and a comic actor with a particular talent for impersonating barbarian pronunciation of Greek speech.[20] A justifiable suspicion that classical Greek authors can simply never be trusted to provide any kind of information free from distortion when representing barbarians is the only reason to suppose that the text does not imitate with some fidelity the sounds made by Scythians pronouncing the Attic dialect; Aristophanes may well have had 'a fair idea of the sort of noises Persians make',[21] and Scythian was an Indo-Iranian language akin to Persian.[22] But the archer's pronunciation is rendered remarkably consistent if a very few slight changes are made to the text, which shows signs of unconscious scribal 'correction' to orthodox Attic (e.g. the unmetrical *mallon* which appears to have replaced the original *mallo* at 1005).

---

[19] M. L. West (1968), 6. Dover (1963), 8, on the other hand, had argued that Pseudartabas, far from being an Athenian impostor, is actually meant to be Persian, and that line 100 is an attempt to simulate, at least, Persian words meaning 'Iarta by name, son of Xerxes, satrap'; this interpretation has more recently been approved by e.g. Chiasson (1984).

[20] See e.g. Csapo (2002), 141–3; Long (1986), 134–7.

[21] M. L. West (1968), 6.

[22] See e.g. Meillet (1962 [1949]), 62; Lehmann (1962), 22.

The Greeks seem to have found the Scythians noisy, and their speech particularly hard on the ear:[23] Athenaeus preserves a fragment of Parmenon, a choliambic poet of about the third century BC, which equates the speech of a drunken man with that of a Scythian (*Skuthisti phōnei*, Parmenon ap. *Ath.* 5.221a, line 2). The most striking of the Aristophanic Scythian's verbal habits is that he uses no aspirates at the beginnings of his words, and substitutes *k*, *p* and *t* for *ch*, *ph*, and *th*. This differentiates him from the Triballian god and Pseudartabas, both of whom can apparently manage the aspirates with which Thracians, Illyrians, and Macedonians were believed to have problems (*Birds* 1572; *Ach.* 104).[24] The effect is heightened by his frequent omission of a final *n* before a consonant (e.g. 1096),[25] and by his problems with *r*. Perhaps *x* was thought to be a distinctively barbarian sound (cf. Xerxes, Prexaspes, Pixodarus), or even especially Scythian; it certainly occurs in a large number of Scythian proper names familiar from Herodotus, such as Lipoxias, Arpoxais, Colaxais, Araxes, Exampaeus, and Taxacis,[26] a phenomenon which may have inspired the archer's mispronunciation of 'Artemisia' as 'Artamouxia' (1201). His language is therefore likely to be have been an authentic enough imitation of Attic Greek pronounced by Scythians, or at any rate as Attic Greeks *perceived* Scythians to pronounce their language, even though it was exaggerated and transposed into iambic trimeters.[27]

Like anybody learning a foreign language at elementary stage, the archer has difficulties not only with Greek phonology, but struggles morphologically and grammatically with tense, case, and gender. A recent study by Willi has nevertheless shown that both his syntax and his vocabulary are very much less impaired.[28] He can handle hypotaxis as well as parataxis, conditionals, and imperatives. His Greek vocabulary is quite extensive, 'especially its vulgar domains';

[23] Anacreon fr. 356b.1–3 *PMG*; Ar. *Ach.* 711.
[24] Friedrich (1919), 283.
[25] In 5th-cent. Attic Greek, final *n* was normally assimilated to a following initial consonant: W. S. Allen (1968), 31–3.
[26] On the etymology of Scythian proper names see the remarks of Rostovtzeff (1922), 36–40.
[27] Friedrich (1919), 300–1, concludes that Aristophanes must have observed with some care the way that non-Greeks spoke the Attic dialect in particular. On the sometimes peculiar metre of the archer's speeches, see Rogers (1904), comment on line 1001.
[28] Willi (2002*b*), 142–9.

more importantly, he can use, even if the terminations are incorrect, certain types of 'function-word' that are crucial to effective communication and social interaction, including articles and prepositions.[29] He may be coarse and totally uncultured. But he has sufficient command of the Athenians' language to lay down the Athenian law.

THE REALITY OF THE SCYTHIAN INTERNAL OTHER

The element of linguistic caricature is, however, very far from the only interesting aspect of the archer. Besides anything else, he is, as Vogt noted forty years ago in his thoughtful book on ancient slavery, the ultimate representative of the slave class in fifth-century Athenian literature.[30] It is astonishing to discover how little interest he attracted for most of the twentieth century, even taking into account the neglect *Thesmophoriazusae* suffered until the 1980s; Stephanis's 1980 study of slaves in Aristophanes chose to avoid the archer altogether.[31] The first signs of a shift in scholarly reactions are discernible in Long's book about barbarians on the Greek comic stage, published in 1986, which devotes three pages to him, and concludes: 'He is certainly the most biting portrayal of the foreigner in Aristophanes. In him are combined the cruelty and stupidity which the Greeks felt separated the Hellene from the rest of humanity, and he is portrayed not as a good-natured joke...but as an intruder condemned to the outside.'[32]

One reason for this xenophobia was the close association in the Athenian mind of Scythia with slavery. There were probably some free Scythian metics living in Athens whose business was connected with the grain trade;[33] there were certainly domestic slaves of

---

[29] Ibid. 146.   [30] Vogt (1965), 6.
[31] Stephanis (1980).
[32] Long (1986), 107.
[33] Scythians are probably covered by Xenophon's observation that metics included 'Lydians and Phrygians and other barbarians of all kinds' (*Ways and Means* 2.3). The Black Sea grain trade is likely to have brought merchants with it; see Dinarchus 16 fr. 4 ed. Conomis (1975). It is not clear whether the war casualties of about 410 BC, whose inscribed label was 'barbarian archer', were Scythians; nor is it clear whether they were slaves or metics (Osborne and Byrne (1996), 325, no. 7452 and 341, no 7772).

Scythian extraction.[34] But the capacity in which they were undoubtedly and overwhelmingly most familiar to the Athenian theatregoer was that illustrated by *Thesmophoriazusae*, as members of the corps of archers, state slaves under the command of the prytaneion. It is impossible to date accurately their first arrival in the city; the picture has long been clouded by the extraordinary popularity in late sixth-century vase painting of the image of the Scythian squire, appearing on the fringes of mysterious military scenes involving hoplites that had little to do with contemporary Athenian reality, but were part of an aristocratic iconography which emphasized the epic resonances of hoplite warfare.[35] But the Scythian archers that appear in Aristophanes seem to have had little enough connection either with these images, or with the Scythian mercenaries that really were hired by Peisistratus,[36] except insofar as their visual impact and role as inferior 'other' were already firmly entrenched elements in the Athenian imagination. The only ancient writer to attempt to date the introduction of the state slaves to democratic Athens was Andocides, in his notoriously inaccurate résumé of fifth-century history included in *On the Peace with Sparta*. Amongst the benefits to Athens which he lists, in somewhat garbled manner, as resulting from the 'thirty years' peace' following the revolt of Euboeoa in 446, he includes the state's purchase of 300 Scythian archers (3.5). This indicates that they arrived in Athens in the middle years of the fifth century, and it has been long proposed that Pericles brought them back with him after

---

[34] The Aristophanic evidence for Scythian slaves other than the archers is slim, although the proper name 'Xanthias' may suggest either Thracian or Scythian extraction (*Ach.* 243, 259; *Clouds* 1485; *Birds* 656). A fragment of Alexis mentions a female Scythian (fr. 332 K–A; see Arnott (1996), 809). There is a solitary Scythian among the slaves, auctioned in 414 BC, who had been the property of the metic and Hermocopid Cephisodorus (*IG* 1³. 421. 42); three other specific Scythian slaves, including one named Dionysius and another named Simos, have been identified during the last fifteen years of the 5th cent. (Osborne and Byrne (1996), 295, nos. 6909–10; 352, nos. 8008–9). See also M. I. Finley (1962).

[35] In this there is general agreement, despite their otherwise divergent interpretations, between Lissarrague (1990c), esp. 239, and Osborne (2004). There may also have been a fashion amongst Athenian cavalrymen, before around 480 BC, for adopting some elements of Scythian clothing (see Tuplin (1996), 174).

[36] See Vos (1963), 68; for a sceptical discussion of the theory that Peisistratus introduced barbarian bodyguards in significant numbers, Lavelle (1992). I have not yet seen the new discussions of the archers in Braund (2005).

his expedition to the Black Sea.[37] But to this period Andocides also attributes the fortification of the Piraeus, which would accurately be placed in the decade immediately after Xerxes' invasion. Others have therefore argued that the archers appeared in the Athenian democracy in the 470s.[38]

Their number is equally obscure. Andocides uses the figures of both 300 (3.5), and, by implication, 1,200 (3.7), whereas a scholion on *Acharnians* 54 puts it at 1,000. Perhaps there were originally 300, but later four *lochoi* (perhaps four companies are implied by *Lysistrata* 451–61) consisting of 300 archers each. Unfortunately it is not always clear when writers refer to unspecified archers (*toxotai*) at Athens, for example the 1,600 mounted bowmen mentioned by Thucydides (2.13), whether the term refers to the Scythians, or is even inclusive of them.[39] For the requirements of the current argument, however, it is only really necessary to observe that the Scythian archers at Athens were numerous, that they were no innovation by the time of the production of *Acharnians* in 425 BC, and that their deployment continued well into the next century (Ar. *Eccl.* 258–9; Plato, *Prot.* 319b–c).[40]

The state archers lived in barracks, and in *Thesmophoriazusae* the Scythian's reference to fleas on his sheepskin implies that he is accustomed to living in dirty and uncomfortable circumstances (1180).[41] Their duties included assisting arrests, various forms of public service, keeping order in the courts, in addition (probably) to regular service in the Athenian army.[42] The citizens of the

[37] See the comment of Rennie (1909), on Ar. *Ach.* 54.

[38] See e.g. the remarks by Starkie (1909), on Ar. *Ach.* 54, with the schol. ad loc. Albini (1964), 60–1 argued that the archers were probably introduced during the reorganization of the Athenian army which took place in the 470s, and certainly not later than the Peace of Cimon.

[39] On this problem see the discussions of Lippelt (1910), 36–9, and Welwei (1974–7), i. 48–54.

[40] For a discussion of the likely date of the corps' dissolution see Jacob (1928), 76–7; he argues that it must have occurred in the first quarter of the fourth century, and have been caused by the city's relative poverty during that period.

[41] See Austin and Olson (2004), 341.

[42] On the arrest scene in *Thesmophoriazusae*, where the archer is acting on the orders of the magistrate in order to extend the law of the *polis* wherever necessary, even into a sacred shrine, see Naiden (2004), 77–8. For the general functions performed by the archers, see Plassart (1913), 189–95. Lippelt (1910), 37 n. 5 argues that the size of the Scythian 'police corps' means that it must inevitably have participated in military campaigns as well as in the maintenance of civic order.

Athenian democracy, whose sense of individual liberty was grounded in the idea that their own bodies were inviolable, preferred to authorize this other group, state slaves, physically to carry out (under strict supervision) all arrests, imprisonments, physical punishments, and executions.[43] This was apparently felt to be a suitable solution to the problem posed by the undesirability of authorizing any one citizen to lay a finger on any other. As an idea, it is not altogether dissimilar to the democratic ideal expressed in ethnographic myth about the citizens of Oenaria in Tyrrhenia, who were so terrified that someone might install a tyranny that they set up a government consisting of manumitted household slaves, who stepped down and were replaced annually ([Aristotle], *De Mirabilibus* 94 = 837^b33–837^a5). But the usual context in which the Scythian archers are mentioned is the Athenian Assembly, where they seem to have acted a bit like nightclub bouncers; the archer's appearance in *Thesmophoriazusae* is certainly connected with the comic identification offered in the play between the male-only Assembly and the exclusively female civic gatherings at the festival of Demeter and her daughter.[44] The archers manipulated the cord used to direct citizens loitering in the agora towards the Pnyx on Assembly days (Ar. *Ach.* 22, *Eccl.* 378–9): Pollux explains that it was by this means that the archers rounded up the Athenian citizens, under the direction of *lexiarchoi*, or 'registrars' (*Onomastikon* 8.104). In the parody of the male Assembly which comprises the first scene of *Lysistrata*, the servant whom Lysistrata instructs to set forth a shield and sacrificial offerings is a female Scythian (*Skuthaina*, 184), and so her duties perhaps correspond to the general services in the Assembly performed in reality by her male counterparts. But the specific function

[43] Austin and Olson (2004), 292, are correct in insisting that 'Athens had nothing we should recognize as a police force', and that the archers were simply used under the jurisdiction of the prytaneis in order to impose their will. The term 'policeman' in reference to Aristophanes' Scythian is therefore rather misleading.

[44] See A. Bowie (1993), 205–12. On the absence of an identifiable Athenian state Thesmophorion, and the likelihood that many spectators of *Thesmophoriazusae* would have had in mind the Thesmophorion in the city-centre deme of Melite, a cult centre situated close to the agora, see Clinton (1996), esp. 120: 'Every Athenian who watched the play...would probably have had a particular Thesmophorion in mind...and for the majority of the audience, that would be a Thesmophorion in central Athens, like the one that served Melite.'

within the Assembly for which the archers were most renowned was that of removing speakers from the platform when instructed to do so by the prytaneis.

In *Ecclesiazusae* one of Praxagora's companions poses various obstacles which the women may encounter in their bid to infiltrate the Assembly: Praxagora may be insulted (248), interrupted (256), or the archers may drag her away (258–9). The same practice is mentioned many years earlier in *Knights* (665). That this was not merely a farcical invention of comedy is confirmed by a passage in Plato's *Protagoras* (319b–c). Socrates is describing how the Assembly invites specialist experts to speak on individual policy decisions: builders advise on construction work, and shipwrights on naval matters. If anyone tries to speak who does not have the pertinent specialized knowledge, then he is mocked and shouted down until he either retires of his own accord, or 'the archers drag him away or take him down on the orders of the prytaneis' (*hoi toxotai auton aphelkusōsin ē exarōntai keleuontōn tōn prutaneōn*). It was not only speaking ignorantly or irrelevantly which merited the humiliation of being removed by the barbarian archers: the precocious Glaucon, who though less than twenty years of age was always hogging the *bēma* and delivering long-winded speeches, was regularly dragged away (Xen. *Mem.* 2.6.1). Drunkenness or quarrelling also earned forcible expulsion from the Assembly (*Eccl.* 142–3).

STAGING THE SKUTHAI IN *LYSISTRATA*

Scythian archers were actually represented on Aristophanes' stage in at least three of his extant plays, *Acharnians*, *Lysistrata*, and *Thesmophoriazusae*, and mentioned in others:[45] the whip-holding slaves on whose assistance Aeacus can call in *Frogs*, as superintendent of civic order in Hades, have distinctly Scythian-sounding names (Ditylas, Sceblyas, and Pardocas, 608). The scholia on this passage actually say

---

[45] On the comic sources for the archers' duties in the Assembly, see also Rhodes (2004a), 224–7.

that they are the names of 'slaves or barbarian archers'.[46] Often such roles would have given trainee or mediocre actors the chance for a moment of significant action (unless we are to toy with the unlikely possibility that state slaves might play 'themselves' in certain types of civic scene in Old Comedy): in *Acharnians* they are mute, and simply remove Amphitheus from the Assembly on an order from the prytanis (54). Similarly, in Eupolis' *Taxiarchoi* one character, perhaps Phormio, orders one of the archers to bring a female forward and put her up for sale (fr. 273 K–A). It is therefore possible that whenever the poets of Old Comedy laid their scenes in the Assembly or in contexts modelled upon it or corresponding to it, such as the opening of *Lysistrata*, or indeed showed figures who held authority in the state authorizing the arrest of troublemakers, it was conventional for archers to make brief appearances in the roles of mute 'extras' or accessories. In his *Demes*, for example, Eupolis resurrected four deceased Athenian leaders, each of whom gave a speech: that the venue was the Assembly is suggested by the word *dēmēgorein* in a papyrus fragment (fr. 99.23 K–A). The comic poet Plato wrote a play in which a *proxenos* was connected with an instruction to tie up a dog with an iron chain (fr. 22 K–A), which might have been addressed to an archer. Cratinus apparently punished his staged state miscreants by the same method as Aristophanes' prytanis ordered the archer in *Thesmophoriazusae* to employ on Euripides' kinsman (*pros sanisin edesmeuonto pollakis, hōs kai Kratinos dēloi*, Cratinus fr. 366 K–A = Σ *Thesm.* 940), and the obvious candidate for carrying out the punishment is a Sythian archer.

It is likely enough, therefore, that Scythian archers appeared in relatively unimportant roles as 'extras' in a fair number of comedies, but in *Lysistrata* and *Thesmophoriazusae* they are prominent throughout extended sequences. In *Lysistrata* they are under the jurisdiction of the *proboulos*, one of the magistrates appointed after the Sicilian disaster of 413 BC to introduce 'measures beneficial to the state' (Σ *Lys.* 421, Thuc. 8.1.3), and their function is to aid the repression of anyone arguing for peace.[47] The insurgent women

---

[46] See Sommerstein (1996*b*), 208–9.

[47] See Long (1986), 104. Perhaps one reason why Aristophanes used Scythians on stage as brutal law-enforcers was that such a role comically subverted their reputation in utopian writing for being peaceable and well-governed ideal primitives (see n. 8 above).

have barricaded themselves into the Acropolis, and the *proboulos* arrives, accompanied by some Scythian archers, apparently four in number (453). They are armed with crowbars (424) with which to prise open the gates obstructing the magistrate's entry, but are conspicuously slow to follow orders. This may because Aristophanes wishes to portray them as generally dense and indolent, or perhaps because they were known to have difficulty in understanding Greek (426–9). Orders to the archers in the theatre are habitually prefaced by an insulting remark, often connected with the caricatured stereotype which suggests that they were believed to make a habit of gazing around absently.[48] Just as the archer in *Thesmophoriazusae* is rebuked for slouching (930), and the *Skuthaina* in the opening scene of *Lysistrata* for her vacuous stare (*poi blepeis*, 184), so the *proboulos* here reprimands one of his archers for gaping in search of a tavern (426–7). This rebuke also feeds off the Scythians' long-standing reputation as an ethnic group for unusually heavy drinking.[49]

As Lysistrata and the other women who have occupied the Acropolis open the gates and emerge from them, a sequence begins in which the effect is achieved by wholesale role reversal. The *proboulos* orders each of the four archers in succession to arrest each of the four women, all of whom respond with threats of violent retribution (433–48). If the minatory behaviour of the archer in *Thesmophoriazusae* is anything to go by, such threats were to be expected of these allegedly most brutal of all barbarians, employed precisely for their powers of physical restraint, rather than from their female opponents. In desperation, the *proboulos* orders his minions to close ranks and charge, but Lysistrata retorts that she has four companies of warlike and armed women with which to oppose them (453–4). The attributes to be expected in the barbarians are thus transferred to the women. In the ensuing scuffle, Lysistrata's forces drag their

---

[48] This is not to say that comic rebukes for gawping are confined to Scythian slaves; see Menander's *Dyskolos* 441, with the comment ad loc. of Handley (1965). But Stone (1981), 45 and 289 discusses the possibility that the Scythian archers in comedy did indeed wear a special gaping mask.

[49] Anacreon fr. 356b 1–3 *PMG*; Plato *Laws* 1.637d7, e2; [Arist.], *Probl.* 3.7 = 872^{a}3. This reputation may have found at least some material support in the very large number of Greek wine jars found by archaeologists in Scythian territory; see e.g. Minns (1913), 49; Kocybala (1978).

adversaries along the ground, strike them and verbally abuse them (459–60). The audience have already watched the chorus of Athenian citizens being drenched with water (381), but the humiliation of total defeat in hand-to-hand fighting is reserved for the Scythians who represent the long arm of the *proboulos'* law. Lysistrata instructs her women not to strip the archers of their arms (461), which implies that they are lying prostrate, and are perhaps even supposed to be dead. If so, their corpses may have remained littering the stage as material proof of the women's invincibility throughout the long scene in which the *proboulos* receives his lesson in the art of gentler government (i.e. until 613).

In Ehrenberg's brief discussion of the Scythian archers he draws the conclusion that their existence 'was generally accepted without grumbling, and without any feeling of humiliation'.[50] But the evidence surely implies something rather different; indeed the references to the archers in other sources imply that humiliation, shame, and indignity were important components of the social ritual of being dragged away from the platform in the Assembly. The unpopular speaker is in each case *mocked* by his peers while the archers remove him (Plato, *Prot.* 319c: *katagelōsi kai thorubousin*; Xen. *Mem.* 2.6.1: *katagelaston onta*). Secondly, all the comic instances include a remark either explicitly disparaging the archers' status or protesting against the maltreatment. Just as Philocleon was in *Wasps* outraged at being mishandled by his own three barbarian slaves (439), so Lysistrata objects to being touched by a public slave, a *dēmosios* (436), and Praxagora vows that she will not be 'grabbed around the waist' in the Assembly (*Eccl.* 260). Dicaeopolis objects to the way in which Amphitheus is treated (*Ach.* 56–7), and the chorus of *Acharnians* say that they were reduced to tears at the sight of the ageing Thucydides being dragged away by the archers (*Ach.* 706–7).[51] Thirdly,

[50] Ehrenberg (1951), 175.

[51] Ehrenberg (ibid.) seems anxious to play down the significance of this passage. Thucydides, he writes, 'merely arouses pity because of his age, and it is even possible that the "bowman" here mentioned was an advocate alleged to be of Scythian origin'. But even if this suggestion is correct, surely Aristophanes' use of expulsion from the platform as a metaphor to suggest that Thucydides was savaged verbally in a lawsuit by an advocate with allegedly Scythian blood or manners would in no way diminish the force of the chorus' statement. On the contrary, it would demonstrate that the

the most convincing evidence that harassment by the archers was disliked and resented by those citizens who suffered it is that, in all three plays in which archers appear, the success of the scenes is predicated upon the audience sharing a sense of group identity with the onstage Athenians actually being roughly handled, and in both *Lysistrata* and *Thesmophoriazusae* much ethnocentric humour is derived from the Athenian characters' reciprocal humiliation of their barbarian adversaries.

It is, moreover, possible that the prevailing political atmosphere in Athens at around the time of the oligarchic coup has something to do with the prominence of the archers in both *Lysistrata* and *Thesmophoriazusae*: they may have been particularly unpopular at this time. Although archers also made brief appearances as 'extras' in *Acharnians*, Eupolis' *Taxiarchoi*, and possibly other comedies of the period, there is no evidence that they were ever treated at such length or suffered such indignities as they did in *Lysistrata* and *Thesmophoriazusae*, and certainly not that they ever had speaking parts elsewhere. There are no signs even of the experiment being repeated in the 'second' Aristophanic *Thesmophoriazusae*, which is usually supposed to have been produced a few years later.[52] Since the surviving play was first produced, like *Lysistrata*, in 411, then the poet's decision to humiliate the archers in distinctive scenes in both his plays of that year raises the suspicion that they had been unusually active and conspicuous under the *probouloi* in the tense and chaotic atmosphere of the city in the period after the disaster in Sicily. Perhaps their unpopularity was reaching a peak in the spring of 411, when those with oligarchic aspirations had already begun to silence the democratic opposition and to embark upon a campaign of terror (Thuc. 8.66). Nobody knows how far those in power could commandeer the archers in the service of their own political purposes, especially at a

ritual of shame—and concomitant pity—undergone by the archers' victims in the Assembly was a familiar enough phenomenon to be deployed in a metaphorical sense.

[52] But see the plausible attempt by Butrica (2001) to place the lost play no later than the Lenaea festival of 423. It seems to have been very different, with a prologue delivered by the minor divinity Calligeneia, and no sign (at least in the exiguous evidence) of a barbarian archer. On Eupolis' play see now Storey (2003), 246–60.

time when the usual mechanisms of public scrutiny and accountability of magistrates were not working effectively.

Many scholars agree with Sommerstein in approving the old hypothesis that *Lysistrata* was produced at the Lenaea of 411 and *Thesmophoriazusae* at the Dionysia a few months later:[53] the tension at the time of the later festival would presumably have been proportionately more acute, and indeed the conspicuously apolitical character of *Thesmophoriazusae* is usually put down to anxiety on Aristophanes' part.[54] If Aristophanes was reluctant to address politically sensitive issues, in particular the plan to restrict the privileges of citizenship to a select 5,000 men, then his choice of uncontroversial female and barbarian targets could be seen as a prudent decision taken with an eye to getting his play selected for performance, and subsequently to his own safety. The possibility, however, should also be kept in mind that the archers had recently been earning a degree of notoriety which was to prove highly suggestive to the dramatic creativity of Aristophanes, resulting in their ruthless caricature in both his plays of 411. The unpopularity of the archers at this time is certainly implied by what happened just a little later, as soon as the oligarchs fell from power.

Aristarchus, general under the Four Hundred, whose activities in this office met with disapproval elsewhere in Old Comedy (Eupolis fr. 49 K–A), was the most ardent opponent of the democracy and the most zealous amongst the oligarchs to overthrow it (Thuc. 8.90, 92; Xen. *Hell.* 2.3.46). After the oligarchs were deposed, his final act of treachery was to escape to the Athenian garrison at Oenoe on the Boeotian frontier, and outrageously to betray it the Boeotians (Thuc. 8.98). When he eventually returned to Athens he was executed.[55] Thucydides tells that he took with him on this dangerous mission, when his very survival was at stake, 'some of the most barbaric of the

---

[53] Sommerstein (1977), following von Wilamowitz-Moellendorff (1893), ii. 343–52, and Dover (1972), 169–71. For further discussion and bibliography, see Austin and Olson (2004), pp. xli–xliv. But *Lysistrata* is decidedly panhellenic in focus, which might suggest a Dionysia audience, and there is merit in the reservations expressed by McLeish (1980), 28: he thinks that *Thesmophoriazusae*, which 'deals with purely local matters, and is full of private jokes and specialized humour', may have been better suited to the Lenaea.

[54] H. Hansen (1976), 66; Sommerstein (1977), 124.

[55] See Lycurgus, *In Leocr.* 115. For the evidence concerning Aristarchus, see Kirchner (1901–3), i. 113–14.

archers' (*toxotas tinas tous barbarōtatous*, ibid.). Most commentators have assumed that the archers whom the oligarch Aristarchus took with him to Oenoe were Scythian state slaves.[56]

PARATRAGIC ESCAPOLOGY: THE BARBARIAN DETAINER

Yet the most important reason why Aristophanes chose the Scythian archer to be the final victim of Euripides' and his kinsman's baiting is very theatrical, and very precise: it is because his role is a comic response to the parts played by duped male barbarians in Euripidean escape plays. The whole structure of *Thesmophoriazusae* is of course reminiscent of the ancient theme of Greek heroes escaping from non-humans or non-Greeks by means of their superior intelligence. In the *Odyssey*, the escape from the Cyclopes, whom Austin and Vidal-Naquet long ago styled 'the barbarians of the golden age', is effected through Odysseus' guile.[57] Primitives and barbarians were no doubt frequently outwitted by Greek heroes in satyric drama, if Euripides' *Cyclops* is typical of that genre.[58] The same poet experimented with the idea in his tragedies, for the basic plot of *Iphigenia among the Taurians*, *Helen*, and *Andromeda* was escape from the barbarian or monstrous.[59]

---

[56] There is just a possibility that these were Iberian rather than Scythian archers. Two fragmentary lines of Aristophanes' *Triphales* mention some Iberians—possibly fictive Iberians in a dramatic chorus—in connection with one Aristarchus, apparently a *chorēgos* who may or may not be the same man as the oligarch (fr. 564 K–A): Sophocles wrote an *Iberians*, and an individual named Aristarchus had acted as *chorēgos*: see J. K. Davies (1971), 48. The hypothesis anyway rests upon another one—the possible presence of Iberian mercenaries at Athens, which in turn depends on whether fulfilment ever came to Alcibiades' intention to bring some such back from Sicily in the event of a victory there (Thuc. 6.90).

[57] Austin and Vidal-Naquet (1977 [1973]), 202.

[58] See Sutton (1980), 119, 145–51. Indeed, Austin and Olson (2004), 339, suggest that the archer scene 'is best understood as a sort of satyr play which rounds out the Euripidean tetralogy' in the second half of the comedy constituted by the parodies of *Palamedes*, *Helen*, and *Andromeda* respectively.

[59] On the motif of escape in Homer and the tragedians see Matthiessen (1964), part II, 93–143; E. Hall (1989), 122–3; Wright (2005).

What features of setting and plot development are shared by the two extant Euripidean escape tragedies, *IT* and *Helen*? They are both set in a distant, exotic, and frightening locale, the Tauric Chersonese and Egypt respectively. They are both written dominantly from the perspective of their prologist Greek heroine, Iphigenia or Helen, stranded unwillingly by the edict of the gods in this farflung location. They each contain an emotional *anagnōrisis*, a recognition of the said stranded heroine by her Greek rescuer, Orestes/Menelaus. The *peripeteia* in both cases arises from a distinctive scene in which a violent barbarian male, Thoas/Theoclymenus, is deceived in a tense but humorous demonstration of the superiority of the Hellenic brain over barbarian brawn; in both cases the deception relates to what are presented as peculiarly Greek customs—the purging of matricidal miasma, or funeral rites at sea. In neither play does the barbarian male whose chief function is to be duped appear until late in the proceedings—*IT* 1153, *Helen* 1165. The whole premise of each plot is escape through tactics, *mēchanai*, successfully implemented only at the last minute. The final action sees the vanquished barbarian villain fulminating in frustration and determined to chase and recapture the escapers.

These essential articulations of *IT* and *Helen* (almost certainly a later play than *IT* and modelled closely upon it) are precisely those of *Thesmophoriazusae*.[60] It is set in an exotic locale, the 'other', female world of the Thesmophoria festival, an analogue of the *barbaros gē* in which Euripides loved to set his tragedies. It is written from the viewpoint of the 'victim', the kinsman stranded in this dangerous place; although frequently discussed in connection with Aristophanes' other two plays where women are temporarily in control,[61] it is entirely different in that its hero is set in opposition to them from the beginning. *Thesmophoriazuzae*, moreover, would have been a very different play had it opened with a meeting of women stating their case for the improvement of their city's situation. It

---

[60] On the similarities between the two plays, and their relative dating, see Matthiessen (1964), 1–63; he concludes that *IT* was first produced after 416 but before 412. While I am inclined to believe that *IT* is the earlier play, I can, however, see little justification beyond the rather overworked metrical arguments for any certainty on this issue.

[61] e.g. in Whitman (1964), ch. 6, 200–27, 'War between the sexes'.

also includes an *anagnōrisis* in which the stranded heroine, impersonated by the kinsman, is recognized by her Hellenic rescuer, Euripides/Menelaus. The reversal arises from a scene involving the deception of an uncouth barbarian male—the Scythian archer, in a demonstration of the superiority of Hellenic intelligence over barbarian physical strength: the deception involves the deployment of a peculiarly Greek invention and ritual, the performance of tragic drama, with which the barbarian is unfamiliar and to which he is not emotionally or cognitively susceptible. The Scythian captor who replaces the women as detainer of the kinsman is like Thoas and Theoclymenus in that he does not physically appear until relatively late in the proceedings (929). The premise of the whole plot is escape from captivity by implementation of *mēchanai* successfully accomplished only at the last minute. The closing scene sees the frustration of the barbarian and his determination to pursue and recapture his victim.

The comedy, therefore, is not only a repository of close parodies from various tragedies,[62] but in its overall structure is closely modelled on the familiar escape-from-the-barbarian type of plot which Euripides had made his own, with a stage barbarian villain who had become a familiar member of the theatrical cast of Athens.[63] The play's similarity with *Cyclops*, where a clever Greek escapes from the savage giant in faraway Sicily, has also been noted.[64] If we knew more about Euripides' *Andromeda*, moreover, the scheme into which its plot fitted might well be found to be extremely similar.[65] It was set in the barbarian land of Ethiopia, and opened with the audience's attention focused on the heroine.[66] The immediate danger was

---

[62] On which see, among others, Harold W. Miller (1946); Rau (1975), 343–4.

[63] There may also be a conscious (although certainly not emphasized) level on which the ritual myth underlying the Thesmophoria—Persephone's abduction by Hades and eventual (partial) release—is burlesqued in the play. See Tzanetou (2002), who argues (p. 351) that the archer corresponds to the figure of Hades in this scenario, and the kinsman to Persephone.

[64] Ussher (1978), 197–8; Seaford (1984), 49.

[65] The fragments of *Andromeda* have been edited conscientiously by Bubel (1991) and, along with the fragments of the Roman plays on her theme, rather more perfunctorily by Klimek-Winter (1993).

[66] See *Σ* Ar. *Thesm.* 1065 = Eur fr. 114 *TgrF*; Webster (1967), 192–3; Gibert in Collard, Cropp, and Gibert (2004), 156.

presented to her by a sea monster (whose role the archer in *Thesmo-phoriazusae* has sometimes been supposed to replace).[67] But An-dromeda, like the kinsman in *Thesmophoriazusae*, may have been attended by barbarian (Ethiopian) guards,[68] and the play also almost certainly involved the barbarian king Cepheus. He (or at least the speaker of fr. 141 *TgrF*) obstructed Perseus' plans to marry his daughter and had to be overcome before the Greek hero and his bride could implement their getaway to Argos.[69] In the essential features of exotic setting, detainment, intrigue, escape, and the victory of a Greek hero over the monstrous/barbarian, *Andromeda* too adumbrated the plot of *Thesmophoriazusae*.[70]

The whole plot direction of *Thesmophoriazusae* represents comic travesty of an innovative type of dramatic plot, the category of escape-tragedy especially associated with Euripides, and in the cases of *Helen* and *Andromeda* (as well, probably, as *IT*), with plays very recently performed; it is also possible that *Cyclops*, the escape-theme satyr drama, was a recent memory, and that it (or other satyr dramas with similar plots) had contributed to the invention of Euripidean escape-tragedy.[71] Aristophanes' reason for replacing the female cap-tors at the festival with the gullible and thuggish barbarian begin to become clear—they are primarily to do with comic commentary on the recent evolution of tragedy. If in a tragedy you were detained by the mythical Egyptian, Pontic or Ethiopian state apparatus, your senior captor would obviously be the King of that region. But if

---

[67] Zeitlin (1981), 190.

[68] Webster (1967), 193.

[69] See the discussion of Gibert in Collard, Cropp, and Gibert (2004), 136.

[70] Aristophanes' interest in the barbarian element in tragedy is further evidenced by his comic references to Egyptian ethnography and language in the *Helen* parody (*Thesm.* 857, 922), and by the titles of his lost *Danaids* and *Phoenissae*. For his comic exploitation of 'barbarian' cries and dances in Aeschylean tragedy, see also *Frogs* 1028 with E. Hall (1989), 132–3, and fr. 696B.3 K–A.

[71] On the vexed question of the date of *Cyclops* see Sutton (1980), 108–20. Ussher (1978), 193 n. 5, 204, seems to approve the suggestion of Marquart (1912), 51–2, that *Cyclops* was actually produced in 412 in group with *Helen* and *Andromeda* and one other unidentified tragedy, making at least three escape plots in one tragic produc-tion. But *Cyclops* simply defies all attempts at precise dating; the similarities in the type of plot can be just as well explained by thinking in terms of the impact made by certain types of satyric narrative pattern stimulating Euripides' inventiveness in tragic plot construction.

you were detained by the Athenian state, you would be placed in the custody of the archers: Aristophanes' *Thesmophoriazusae* lends Euripidean escape dramas his own inflection by grafting them onto a background constituted by contemporary Athenian reality. The archer is the comic substitute for Euripides' male barbarian captors of recent productions—Thoas, Theoclymenus, and probably Cepheus or his minions, and possibly the Sicilian Cyclops. The poet took the time-honoured theme of Greeks tricking the represen-tatives of supposedly inferior cultures, parodied before his audience's eyes tragedies set in foreign parts, and, in the paratragic fantasy he had created, replaced the stereotypical barbarian villain with the 'most barbaric' of foreigners to be found in contemporary Athens.

For after the failure of the stratagem by which the kinsman has failed to escape captivity by pretending to be Helen awaiting rescue in Euripides' *Helen*, Euripides disappears (927), and the prytanis enters, summoned by Cleisthenes, and followed by a Scythian archer. At this stage the archer does not speak: indeed, he is probably played by a mute 'extra'. He is instructed to go and bind the kinsman to a plank and guard him (932), apparently in preparation for execution by the horrible means called *apotumpanismos*: the kinsman is actually in mortal danger.[72] The Scythian's duties thus correspond with the 'ordering of public places' attributed to the archers;[73] the legal pro-cedure dramatized here seems to be what was called an *aphēgēsis*, in which a magistrate could make an arrest on the instigation of a private citizen.[74] On his return, bringing with him the kinsman (now bound to the plank), he is played by the same actor who had

---

[72] See Austin and Olson (2004), 294. Todd's detailed discussion of *apotumpanismos* (2000) adds this scene in *Thesmophoriazusae* to the other textual and archaeological evidence, including the seventeen skeletons extracted from a mass grave at Phaleron in 1923, with iron cramps around their necks, wrists and ankles, to which fragments of wood were still adhering (see Keramopoullos (1923)). Todd (p. 35) concludes that it is not certain whether victims of *apotumpanismos* died from exposure or from the garrotting process suggested by the tightening of the kinsman's neckbands at *Thesm.* 1001–6.

[73] See Pollux 8.131–2. His presence in the Assembly is also thematically linked with the parody, earlier in the comedy, of the ceremonies performed at the opening of meetings of the Assembly. See Haldane (1965).

[74] The victim was pinned to a plank and suspended upon it until he died; it is specified as a punishment for defiling a sanctuary also at Hdt. 7.33. See Austin and Olson (2004), 294–5.

taken the roles of the effeminates Agathon and Cleisthenes,[75] and was therefore required to display considerable expertise at both vocal special effects and presumably caricatured gait and deportment. If the archer carried the kinsman single-handedly, the actor must have been strongly built; the visual impact of his long, loose hair, his distinctive patterned costume,[76] whip (1125), short-sword (1127) and archery equipment (1197) was no doubt suitably intimidating.[77] In a scene reminiscent of the opening of *Prometheus Bound* and possibly Sophocles' *Andromeda*,[78] he cruelly tightens the peg which secures his captive's bonds (1005), for the Scythians were thought to be savage to their victims (see e.g. Hdt. 5.62–3). But he is lazy and irresponsible too, and disappears to fetch a mat to sleep on: although this is typically unreliable behaviour for a comic slave,[79] it is interesting to compare Hippocrates' scientific description of the Scythians as fat and sluggish (*De Aër.* 20).

The archer's departure leaves the stage clear for the first part of the parody of Euripides' *Andromeda*.[80] Since the moment when the women's suspicions were aroused against the kinsman, the stage has been successively transformed in the audience's imagination into two foreign settings familiar from Euripides' tragedies: the Greek camp at Troy in the *Palamedes* parody (769–71), and the island of Pharos in Egypt (850–928). Aristophanes now translates his spectators to Ethiopia, yet another *gē barbaros*, the favourite term of Euripides, here repeated by his parodist (1098). The kinsman

---

[75] See Russo (1994), 196–7; Dearden (1976), 100.

[76] There are surprisingly no certain representations of Scythian archers in Attic art of the late 5th cent., but a good idea of the outfit they would have worn can be gained from the proliferation of Scythians on vases from *c.* 530–490 BC. For descriptions of their appearance see Vos (1963) and Räck (1981), 10–13. On their hair, von Wilamowitz-Moellendorff (1927), comment on *Lys.* 448; Stone (1981), 289.

[77] Ehrenberg (1951), 175 may be correct in thinking that the archers' whips 'were an invention of comedy'; perhaps Aristophanes derived the notion from the story of the Scythians who fought their own rebellious slaves with whips (Hdt. 4.33–4). The short-sword (*xiphomachaira*) mentioned in *Thesmophoriaze* (1127) was identified by Jacob (1928) with the dagger (*egcheiridion*) which Herodotus said the Scythians carried (7.64). The distinctive Scythian sigma-shaped bow was composite and excited much attention, being very different from the Greek segmented version. See e.g. Agathon fr. 4.3 *TgrF.*

[78] See Webster (1967), 193.

[79] References are assembled in Austin and Olson (2004), 310.

[80] It is not clear exactly when he re-enters; see H. Hansen (1976), 181.

comprehends the hint of Euripides, who has previously made a brief appearance disguised as Perseus (1010–11), and the two relatives commence what must have been a close parody of scenes from the tragedy. But there can have been no Scythian state slave in *Androm-eda*, and much of the humour is therefore derived from incongruous references to the *Skuthēs*, whose ethnic label alone in this context creates bathos. Thus 'Perseus' caps an address to the chorus lifted verbatim from the tragic prototype with the ridiculous query, 'How can I elude *the Scythian*?' (1016–18). 'Andromeda' claims in a long lyric passage, almost entirely in tragic diction, that '*the Scythian*' has bound him, to offer a feast for the crows (1026).[81]

Besides its barbarian setting, its popularity (cf. *Frogs* 52–4), and the recentness of its production in 412, *Andromeda* lent itself to Aristophanes' purpose particularly on account of its 'Echo' scene. The comic poet has brought onto the stage a speaking barbarian, and has paid special attention to his accent. The unusual scene with 'Echo' grants him the opportunity precisely to extend the linguistic joke, for when the archer returns to the stage with his mat (1081), 'Echo' mercilessly repeats every single mispronounced phrase he utters.[82] Along similar lines is the word play in the next sequence, where the archer misunderstands the reference of 'Perseus' to the Gorgon's head (1101–2), and hears instead 'Gorgias's head'.[83] Such mis-hearings are common enough in comedy, but the Scythian's inadequate grasp of Greek allows the poet to stretch the joke. For 'Gorgon' the archer now hears 'Gorgo', a female monster with whom children were threatened (see Strabo 1.2.8, 19). The archer's barbar-ian ethnicity has thus helped to determine not only the choice of scene from *Andromeda*, but the type of joke created to lampoon it.

'Andromeda' has only two short interjections in this sequence, Aristophanes here preferring 'to rely on the farcical expressions of

[81] Cf. the way in which *Skuthēs* becomes an implicitly derogatory—even abusive—label in the orators: e.g. Aeschines 3.172 and Dinarchus 1.15 (both in reference to Demosthenes).

[82] No Aristophanic Greek, however extreme his frustration, is so repetitively foul-mouthed (1097, 1109, 1111, 1133, etc.)

[83] It has been argued that the Gorgias here mentioned is not, for once, the famous sophist, but there is also a pun on Gorgias/Gorgon at Plato, *Symp.* 198c, where the sophist is certainly meant.

the Scythian guard'.[84] But this source of the comic effect is subtler than this might imply. The two worlds of the imaginary Ethiopia and the 'real' Athens, the kinsman's feminine charade and his masculine 'real' identity, young love and earthy sexuality, the rival genres of tragedy and comedy, are all verbally framed and juxtaposed in the elevated and banal diction of 'Perseus' and 'the Scythian' respectively. The archer can never be persuaded to participate in the tragic fantasy: when on one occasion he appears to use a feminine participle of the kinsman (1109), he is merely muddling up his grammatical genders in his customary manner (cf. *kalē to skēma*, 1188). Indeed, in a play so dependent upon sexual ambiguity and transvestism,[85] it is only Euripides, the professional wordsmith, who always uses the correct gender for each actor in accordance with the mythical roles he has conjured up for them to play. Euripides' ability to write delicately differentiated roles is here given a comic re-reading.

The kinsman tries to follow suit, but occasionally slips out of Euripides' illusory world, for example when he uses a masculine ending for himself in one of 'Andromeda's' speeches (1022–3). But the archer is never for a moment beguiled. Again, 'Andromeda's' utterances in this sequence are in respectably tragic diction, 'Perseus' wavers between the tragic and demotic styles, but the archer refuses to abandon his boorish patois. He cannot play roles, even those created for him by the master role-writer, Euripides. This is no virgin, he states, but a wicked old man (1111). On the solemn avowal of 'Perseus' that he wishes to enjoy nuptial bliss with 'Andromeda' (1122), the Scythian allows him a concession: he can bore a hole through the back of the plank and enjoy anal intercourse with him (*pugizein*, 1123–4).[86] Thus by his rejection of fiction, his 'rational' insistence on the difference between appearance and reality, his dispersal of the tragic illusion, the archer reveals that he is going to

---

[84]   Rogers (1904), comment on lines 1107–8.

[85]   On which see above all the pathbreaking study by Zeitlin (1981); also H. Hansen (1976), 174, 178–9; Taaffe (1993), 76.

[86]   It is just possible that this specific obscene idiom was associated with the Greek talked by Black Sea archers. Robin Osborne draws my attention to a graffito of about 500 BC on the exterior of a black-glaze cup from Olbia, which reads, 'Who wants to fuck, let him first deposit ten arrowheads and then bugger [*pugizetō*] Hephaistodoros' (L. DuBois (1996), no. 31).

be much harder to deceive than his counterparts in satyr play or tragedy—the Cyclops, Thoas, or Theoclymenus.

'Perseus' begins once more a paratragic speech, with a line perhaps taken from *Andromeda*, 'Alas, what shall I do? To what words can I turn?' (1128).[87] But he rejects the idea of implementing further words, for barbarians are simply not receptive, he now sees, to *logoi* (1129). This is a standard topos in rhetoric about the distinctions between the Greek and barbarian character found in the mouths of Euripidean characters, especially xenophobes (see *Hec.* 1129–31). But the inference is more profound: this barbarian is not susceptible to a particular type of *logoi*, the words out of which drama and dramatic roles were constituted and in which they were articulated. For drama, of course, was felt by Greeks to be a peculiarly Hellenic art. It is this feature above all others which distinguishes and alienates him from the Athenian citizen body, whether in the audience, in the chorus, amongst the actors playing on the stage, or even the roles that they were assuming. Niall Slater has shown how the slaves in the comic theatre of Plautus are able to control other characters, including socially powerful free members of the slave-owning classes, because their understanding of the conventions of theatre, above all asides and role-playing, is not only infinitely superior, but grants them executive power over the evolution of the plot analogous to that of the playwright.[88] But this could not be further from the situation in *Thesmophoriazusae*, where it is beginning to become clear that the real victim in Aristophanes' comedy is to be the solitary, philistine foreigner. Everyone else shares at least the ability to participate in the paratragic experience. Aristophanes confirms this analysis by making 'Perseus' continue (1130–2):

> 'To feed slow wits with novel subtleties (*kaina prospherōn sopha*)
> Is effort vainly spent'. No, I must bring to bear
> Some other scheme, more suited to this man.[89]

---

[87] Nauck (1889) believed that 1128–9 were both lifted from *Andromeda*, and printed them consecutively as Eur. fr. 139. Rau is sceptical but agrees that both lines at least sound Euripidean (Rau (1967), 88); Kannicht in his new *TgrF* vol. v, and Gibert in Collard, Cropp and Gibert (2004), 165, both reject them.

[88] Slater (1985*b*).

[89] Translated by Sommerstein (1994), 129.

The first of the three Greek lines here is lifted, slightly altered, from yet another Euripidean tragedy where the contrast between Greek and barbarian mores had been explored (*Medea* 298).[90] But there is a sting in the comic poet's tail, for the archer's 'slow wits' lie precisely in his refusal to be taken in by the scheme which 'Perseus' had instigated. Common sense has defeated fantasy. Euripides must find another strategy which makes no intellectual or cultural demands on the Scythian, since he can apparently only be defeated on a physical level.[91] In an extraordinary *volte-face* the chorus suddenly agrees to forgive Euripides (1170): the Greeks—indeed Athenians—have speedily forgotten their internal quarrels, forged an alliance, and on a comic plane exposed the supposedly indissoluble conflict cause by ethnic difference which, in Plato's more serious but equally chauvinist formulation, inevitably supersedes internecine strife (*Rep.* 5.470c–d). At the end of the play the chorus even assists its former adversaries, Euripides and the kinsman, by giving false directions to the archer (1218–24), but for the time being they indicate that it is for Euripides to deal with the barbarian threat (1171: *ton barbaron de touton autos peithe su*).

The second—and this time successful—tactic which Euripides now introduces has met with mixed responses over the last century and a quarter. The pious Benjamin Bickley Rogers wrote that this *mēchanē*, which befits 'the gross and licentious character of the Scythian, is itself so gross and licentious as to cast a dark shadow over the concluding scenes of the play'.[92] The red-blooded Whitman, on the other hand, felt that after all the homosexuality and transvestism in the comedy the archer's unabashed maleness was positively 'refreshing'.[93] Hansen's somewhat more complex reading contrasts the goal

[90] See the remarks of Pucci (1961), 382; Rau (1967), 88–9.

[91] Rau (1975), 356, who writes: 'Dieses grössere und komödienhafte Mechanema ist die parodistische reductio ad absurdum der euripideischen Rettungsmechanemata.'

[92] Rogers (1904), comment on line 1132. The archer, however, is only given six obscenities to utter, in comparison with the kinsman, whose role as *bōmolochos* dictates that he deliver thirty-two (Euripides has only two). But the kinsman's obscene sentiments tend to be wittier and involve word-play, whereas the archer's are crude and direct. See de Wittak (1968), 63.

[93] Whitman (1964), 224.

of the Thesmophoria (fertility) with the actual sterility of the characters portrayed, and argues that the apparently 'normal' sex presented at the denouement is still 'sex of the commercial sort and not
productive'.[94] Such views of course fail to do justice to Aristophanes'
inventiveness. The Scythian, as an alien, is excluded from the cere-
bral, imaginative, and conspiratorial experience of paratragedy, and
must of necessity be deceived on a gross and carnal level. In tragedy,
barbarians are duped through their religious sensibilities and super-
stition. In satyr play the appropriate weapon is, predictably, alcohol.
In comedy, it follows, barbarians should be tricked by the means
pertinent to the phallic humour of the genre: barbarians, moreover,
were conveniently reputed (even by some characters in Euripides
such as Hermione at *Andromache* 170–80) to be, as a genus, sexually
depraved.[95]

In *Frogs* Euripides is accused of poetically dealing in *pornai*,
prostitutes like Phaedra and Stheneboea (1043). It is probably in
connection with this type of allegation that Aristophanes, in a moment of inspiration, makes Euripides himself take on the role and
disguise of a procuress. He brings on Elaphion and Teredon, his
dancing girl and *aulētēs* (1172, 1175);[96] their names provide a contrast with the nameless barbarian,[97] repeatedly called simply *ho
Skuthēs*, for his behaviour is determined, in the crude prosopography

[94] H. Hansen (1976), 179.

[95] Curiously, however, the characteristics of the Scythians in the ancient ethnographic tradition did not include excessive libidinal drive: the Hippocratic *On Airs,
Waters, Places* observes, quite apart from the specific case of the effeminate Scythian
'Anaries', that since men of Scythian ethnicity wore trousers and spent a considerable
amount of time in the saddle, they were unusually prone to impotence (21–2).

[96] Some scholars, including Rogers (1904; comments on lines 1174 and 1203),
have not believed that Euripides brought on an extra aulete of his own, but that
Teredon was the theatrical aulete, now explicitly included in the action. See, however,
the editions of Coulon and van Daele (1946), 68, and Austin and Olson (2004), 337,
with the discussion of Taplin (1991), 40.

[97] Bobrick (1991), 14 argues that the name Elaphion is connected with the
alternative denouement of the Euripidean *Iphigenia in Aulis* in which Iphigenia was
rescued by Artemis and a deer substituted on the sacrificial altar. She bafflingly does
not address the problem posed to this argument by the date of the première of *IA*
(405 BC) either here or in her other article on *Thesmophoriazusae*, Bobrick
(1997), 182.

of comedy, by his ethnicity alone. When he awakens (1176), his irritation is soon assuaged by the suitably barbarian-sounding Persian nome Teredon plays on his *aulos* (1175), and by Elaphion's gyrations;[98] she then sits on his knee while he applauds both her physique and, excitedly, his own priapic response to it (1185, 1187–8).[99] Now Euripides has seen that his horny victim will do anything in order to consummate his passion, and in the moment of imminent victory makes him exchange what else but the very emblem of his ethnic provenance—his bowcase (1197).[100] The Scythian at last leaves the stage with the dancer, leaving Euripides and his kinsman free to make good their escape.

The crude strategy has therefore succeeded where the clever tactic (*kaina sopha*, 1130) had failed. The play's last laugh is not on Agathon, nor Cleisthenes nor Euripides and his kinsman, nor even on the women of Athens, but on the dense and uncouth barbarian. The escape from the foreigner, which began as a fantasy in the *Helen* parody, and culminated in the deception of the comic counterpart of Euripides' thuggish barbarian villains, has at last been effected. The archer's lust is quickly satiated, for only nine lines after his exit he reappears to find his charges have vanished (1210). In a final glance at Euripides' escape-dramas, in this case *Iphigenia in Tauris,* the chorus now colludes with its former opponents against the outsider (1218–24):[101] the Scythian's reasoning powers in the end desert him

[98] Austin and Olson (2004), 340, suggest that the music was perhaps 'wantonly sensual', thus fitting the description implicit in Teredon's name, which means 'ship-worm', suggestive of the intricate, winding nature of the melodic line.

[99] For speculative reconstruction of the obscene but 'probably unrecoverable visual joke' at 1187–8, where the archer seems to address his own phallus, see Slater (2002), 303 n. 105.

[100] The spelling *subinē*, adopted in the Budé edn. (1946), is tempting, since it provides the pun with the obscene *katabinein* at 1215.

[101] Aristophanes had been struck by *IT,* for he parodied it elsewhere (*Lemnians,* fr. 373 K–A); in what looks like a reminiscence of that play, the chorus here tells the archer to pursue his victims along the opposite route to that which they had actually taken (1218–21), just as in *IT* the chorus told the second Taurian messenger to seek Thoas elsewhere, and pointed him in the entirely wrong direction (1294–301). This is not, however, the view taken by Ussher (1978), 204, who thinks either that this type of search scene was a 'stock-in-trade' of comic writers, or that Aristophanes is imitating, rather, the chorus' similar ruse at *Cyclops* 680–3.

completely and he is finally routed. As the chorus remarks, it is time for everyone to go home (1228–9).

The Scythian archer's role demanded an actor specializing in the impersonation of foreign speech, and in bringing to life a series of fairly predictable and certainly stereotypical traits in the barbarian character who inhabited the theatre of the Athenian public mind. In the 'para-Athens' portrayed in Aristophanic comedy—that unique parallel universe, a synthesis of fantasy and recognizable details from contemporary civic life—the Scythian *toxotēs* was one of the safest of all targets: beside his barbarized Greek, his most obvious attributes are cruelty, sloth, aggression, verbal abusiveness, libidinousness, and philistine failure to understand the protocols of either the tragic or the paratragic stage. Evidence adducible from other Greek literature may concur with many facets of this artificial Scythian *persona*, this fascinating but profoundly chauvinist role. But he remains by far the most important evidence for the Athenians' unsympathetic verdict on the representatives in their city of his ethnic group. It is scarcely surprising that by 1989 (the year, coincidentally, that the earlier version of this chapter first appeared), the African-American poet Rita Dove was publishing a poetic record of her sickened reaction to the presentation of the Scythian archer as an uneducated black American policeman, in a university production of a translation by William Arrowsmith.[102] Her poem opens, memorably:

> The eminent scholar 'took the bull by the horns',
> Substituting urban black speech for the voice
> Of an illiterate cop in Aristophanes' *Thesmophoriazusae*.
> And we sat there.

Substituting the appearance and speech of the descendant of a slave in the North American context had shockingly revealed the full extent of the ancient comedy's ethnocentrism, as well as the extent of insensitivity possible in the work of an educated theatrical writer,

---

[102] See now the remarks of Gamel (2002*a*), 473–4, on the impossibility, for a modern producer or adapter of the play 'in an era sensitive to racist stereotypes', of retaining the archer in the way that Aristophanes wrote the role.

whether ancient or modern. In the Greek original, the orchestrated collusion of actor, acted character, chorus, and audience in the inspection, deception, and humiliation of the outsider—a poetic lynching of a type without parallel even in Greek comedy—must ultimately speak for itself.[103]

[103] It was first published in Dove's collection *Grace Notes* (1989), 49–50. In a brilliant but as yet unpublished paper, which she has been kind enough to let me see, Deborah Roberts first drew Classicists' attention to Dove's poem 'Arrow'. Roberts's discussion suggests that the way Arrowsmith 'translated' the role of the barbarian archer was, given the historical context, demeaning, since it situated 'the urban black as other in relation to Aristophanes' text. The poet's narrative makes plain the irony of any talk of "celebrating differences"' (Roberts (2000), 9). See also Scharffenberger (2002), 456–60 and n. 45. Dove has confirmed to me by email that the poem was a direct reaction to a performance at the University of Arizona in 1986–7 of William Arrowsmith's (unpublished) adaptation of *Thesmophoriazusae* as *Euripides Agonistes*.

9

Drowning Act: The Greeks, Swimming, and Timotheus' *Persians*

Lord, Lord! Methought what pain it is to drown!
What dreadful noise of waters in mine ears!
What ugly sights of death within mine eyes!
Methought I saw a thousand fearful wrecks;
Ten thousand men that fishes gnawed upon.

> (The Duke of Clarence describes his prophetic dream in
> *Richard the Third*, I. iv).

INTRODUCTION

The presence of flamboyant Asiatics in the Athenian theatre and social imagination gave rise, towards the end of the fifth century, to ever more elaborate types of actorly mimesis. In this chapter the argument turns to a type of performance so close to stage acting that in practice the differences (besides the absence of a mask) may have been negligible: rendition of an original composition on a sensational theme by a solo singer, to his own citharodic accompaniment.[1] For with the advent of the New Music, which used melody and tonal effect in unprecedentedly mimetic ways, both performances by auletes and citharodic dithyrambs became ever more theatrical.[2]

---

[1] For a suggestive account of the mimetic delivery style required by a performer of Timotheus' *Persians*, see Herington (1985), 151–60.

[2] See especially Csapo (2004*b*), 215–16, who points out that Aristotle 'lumps the nome and dithyramb together with tragedy and comedy in classifying mimetic arts which use all the modes of musical mimesis' (*Poet.* 1447[b]24–7, 1454[a]30–1).

These musicians increasingly used their bodies to imitate the actions being described in the piece, and could even wear appropriate costumes.[3]

The single example of the genre of citharodic nome of which a substantial set of poetic fragments survives is the dithyrambic *Persians* by Timotheus, who originally came from Miletus but made an incalculable impact on late fifth-century Athenian musical and dramatic culture. His song replays the old patriotic theme of the Greek victory over the Persians at Salamis, and seems to have cleverly blended the idea of that naval victory with Timotheus' hopes for the supremacy of his innovative new aesthetics; at its conclusion (196–201) it annexes the god of both the victory song and the musical old guard, Pythian Apollo, 'as the divine patron of the New Music'.[4] But the concern of this chapter is with exploring the aria's portrayal of the battle of Salamis, and in particular the different barbarian roles that Timotheus and subsequent performers were required to assume when performing it.[5] These included Xerxes, the epitome of oriental despotism, in the throes of humiliation and despair. But the Xerxes section of the aria was preceded by (amongst other things) the impersonation of a common barbarophone Phrygian sailor undergoing a protracted death. The type of death being suffered by the Phrygian is of crucial importance to the cast of the fifth-century male Athenian mindset: he is flailing, choking, and gasping as he drowns at Salamis, for, unlike the water-confident citizens of Athens, he has never learned to swim.

SWIMMING IN ETHNIC SELF-DEFINITION

Before turning to Timotheus' drowning Phrygian, one of the most flamboyant of all the roles ever played by an ancient Greek performer,

---

[3] See esp. Csapo (2004*b*), 212–16; Aristotle complains about vulgar auletes who wheel about in imitation of a discus (*Poet.* 1461[b]30), and one is supposed to have worn effeminate shoes and a yellow ritual gown when performing a song that required the projection of a komastic identity (Suda s.v. 'Antigeneides').

[4] See the brilliant interpretation by P. Wilson (2004), 305.

[5] Csapo (2004*b*), 214, speaks in terms of the 'role-playing' required by performers of the New Music.

it is illuminating to reflect on the history of swimming and drowning in celebrations of ethnic achievement. Scholars have recently been stressing the importance of memorials to the Persian wars in the cult centres and sanctuaries visited by Pausanias in the second century AD.[6] When he visited Delphi, he saw a dedication made hundreds of years before, in the aftermath of the archetypal Greek victories over the barbarians (10.19.1). The Delian League, he says, made a dedication to Skyllis the diver and his daughter Hydne, whom he had instructed in his craft. Pausanias reports that the pair had worked for the Greek cause against the Persians during the storm at Pelion; they had dragged up the fleet's anchor lines and moorings to complete the havoc. Pausanias implies that a statue of Skyllis was still there to be seen, although Hydne had been removed by Nero. Thus swimming and diving achievements had for centuries been celebrated in the panhellenic context of the Delphic sanctuary as symbolic of Greek victory over the barbarians.

From as early as the Assyrian sculptures which portray the King's defeated enemies floundering in the water,[7] swimming and diving have frequently been implicated in the formation of ethnic and national identities, and the discourses of military conflict and imperialism. The ability to swim has usually (although not quite invariably) been seen as a reason for ethnic pride.[8] The image of drowning enemies recurs in cultural celebrations of victory in war. Although, for example, swimming is only mentioned in four passages of the Bible, its connection with Jewish victory over ethnically different groups underlies two of them. In the first book of the apocryphal Maccabees the Jewish commander Jonathan swam the

[6] This is an underlying theme of Arafat (1996), and several of the essays in Alcock, Cherry, and Elsner (2001). See also the Introduction to Bridges, Hall, and Rhodes (2006).

[7] See the illustrations collected in Ralph Thomas (1904), 78–87.

[8] The Middle Ages seem to constitute an exception, in that there is evidence that swimming was denigrated in some genres of literature. It was not normally required of Charlemagne, Roland, and other knightly heroes of romances and *chansons de geste* (see Orme (1983), 31). Indeed, it was something imputed to the un-Christian Saracen Palomydes, in contrast with Tristram, who has worsted him in battle, Palomydes abandons his horse (a most unknightly thing to do) and engages in a swim across a river, an escapade painted in slightly ridiculous colours. See Thomas Malory's 15th-cent. translation of the *Roman de Tristran*, in Vinaver (1947), 441.

Jordan with his men to escape the Syrian army (1 Maccabees 9.48), 'but the enemy did not cross the river in pursuit'. In Isaiah 25.11, on the other hand, the people conceptualized as swimming are the Moabites, the hostile tribes across the river Jordan, who are envisaged as failing to escape, like a swimmer losing the struggle to keep afloat. It is predicted that the Lord will trample Moab under his feet 'as straw is trampled in a midden. In it Moab shall spread out his hands as a swimmer spreads his hands to swim, but shall sink his pride with every stroke of his hands'.[9]

Equally good examples can be found in the heroic swimming feats of Roman myth and history. These are usually performed in military contexts where differentiation from an ethnically different enemy is an issue; the favoured venues are rivers, rather than the sea, where Greek and Norse swimming heroes prefer to exhibit their skill. The feats of Roman swimmers are often rendered even more arduous by the masochistic accumulation of extra impediments or hazards—especially the carrying of heavy arms or the evasion of a barrage of missiles. The most outstanding example is Plutarch's description of the swimming feat of the warrior Quintus Sertorius, performed while he was serving in Gaul against the Cimbri and the Teutones in 105 BC. He swam the Rhone unaided, wounded, wearing his breastplate, carrying his shield, and opposed by a strong current: 'so sturdy was his body and so inured to hardship by training' (*Vit. Sert.* 3).

Virgil seems to have identified the manly skill of swimming in frigid conditions as something contributed to Roman culture by the indigenous inhabitants of Italy, rather than by the Trojans whom Aeneas led there from Troy.[10] Numanus, Turnus' brother-in-law, boasts that their 'hardy race brings its sons to the rivers early, and hardens them to the frost and the waters' (*Aen.* 9.603–4). The two heroic swims of the *Aeneid* are both performed by indigenous Italians. The ninth book closes with the Rutulian Turnus, after putting up a valiant struggle against the Trojans, leaping headlong in full armour into the Tiber,

---

[9] See also the stream 'deep enough to swim in' in Ezekiel 47, and the people who swam to shore when the ship carrying St Paul was wrecked off the island of Malta (Acts 27.42–4). Josephus escaped a shipwreck, and with the help of God performed an epic swim to safety when several others were drowned (*Life* 15). I am most grateful to Tessa Rajak for this and other references.

[10] See Orme (1983), 5.

and returning to his comrades on the opposite bank (9.815–18). Diana recalls that the Volscian Metabus, driven out by his own people, attached his baby daughter Camilla to his spear, shot her safely across the torrential Amasenus, and then leapt into the river himself (11.565). They both safely reached the other side.

In accounts of the early history of Rome it is clear that swimming is symbolic of Roman supremacy over other peoples. In Livy (2.10) it is over the Etruscans: Horatius Cocles, after defending the bridge,

With a prayer to Father Tiber to bless him and his sword, plunged fully armed into the water and swam through the missiles, which fell thick about him, safely to the other side, where his friends were waiting to receive him.

Cloelia escaped from Porsenna to Rome by swimming across the same river (Livy 2.13). Silius Italicus records that Scipio, the champion of Roman supremacy in Spain, Africa and the Hellenistic East, used to train his Campanian troops by personally showing them how to hurl stakes, leap over trenches, and 'stem the billows of the sea with his breastplate on' (*Pun.* 8.551–4). Sons of upright champions of Roman ideals had no need to take recourse to the type of handbook on swimming mentioned by Ovid (*artem nandi*, *Tristia* 2.485–6): Cato the Elder undertook the education of his son in enduring extremes of temperature and swimming 'lustily through the eddies and billows of the Tiber'; it is significant that the very next element of the boy's education here enumerated was the reading of Cato's own *History of Rome*, in order to implant knowledge of 'his country's ancient traditions' (Plut. *Vit. Cat.* 20.5–6). Augustus, similarly, is said to have taught Gaius and Lucius their letters, the art of swimming, and other *rudimenta* (Suetonius, *Augustus* 64).[11]

Romanness and swimming became tangled up with the use of gender as well as of ethnicity in the depiction of historical figures. 'Manly' ones are said to have been powerful swimmers, while those

---

[11] The text of this passage has elicited controversy. Many editors have preferred to read *et litteras et notare*. But *natare* is surely protected by the interest in the emperor's swimming skills evinced elsewhere, and by the Greek proverb (discussed below, pp. 263–4), 'neither letters nor swimming'. See Trankle (1984), 102–4. I would add that the proverb was certainly known at Rome in the form of a Greek iambic line quoted in Seneca's *Controversiae* 9.14.8. The witty Asilius Sabinus said to the mother of Domitius, an idle consul who spent his time building baths and practising declamation, 'first diving, then letters' (*prōton kolumban, deuteron de grammata*).

characterized as weak and effeminate are not. Julius Caesar was reputed to have been a particularly remarkable swimmer, and his most famous feat is explicitly in the context of Rome's most important enemy of the period—the Egyptians. At Alexandria in 48–7 BC he was compelled by them to withdraw from a bridge; he leapt into the sea in order to swim to the safety of a ship. Suetonius (1.64) claims that the swim extended over 200 paces (which means nearly 300 metres) and that Caesar dragged his cloak behind him in his teeth lest the enemy acquire it as a trophy.

Plutarch's version is even more elaborate and more explicitly implies that Caesar's swim was a 'manly' triumph over an effeminate barbarian adversary. Hostilities ensued at Alexandria after the queen's emergence from a carpet and Caesar's discovery that Potheinus the eunuch was hatching a plot against him. The swim was performed during a battle at Pharos, with 'the Egyptians sailing against him from every side'. But despite the missiles flying at him, Caesar was supposed to have held many papers in his hand, and to have refused to let them go, holding them above the water and swimming with only one arm (*Vit. Caes.* 49.3–4). It is difficult not to contrast this with Plutarch's report that Antony was outfaced by the swimming feat of one of Cleopatra's own men, performed in the same location (Plut. *Vit. Ant.* 29). And the allegedly effeminate Caligula, although an enthusiastic actor, singer, and dancer, is alleged by Suetonius to have been unable to swim a single stroke (*Caligula* 54).

In the context of nineteenth- and twentieth-century imperialism, swimming (like other sports) became transparently connected with racist and nationalist discourses.[12] Sprawson's excellent book on the history of swimming demonstrates that during the nineteenth-century heyday of the British empire, London looked upon itself as the capital not only of half the world, but as the capital of swimming.[13] The achievement of Matthew Webb, the first Channel swimmer, who arrived in Calais on 25 August 1875, was perceived not only as repeating an ancient gesture of superiority over France, but

---

[12] Zeigler (1968), 33, 58–9.
[13] Sprawson (1992), ch. 1. The book was brilliantly reviewed by Richard Jenkyns in *The New Yorker*, 5 April (1993), 104–7. See also Sanders (1925), esp. 566.

as scoring a national victory of 'old' British virtues over those of the youthful America, since Webb had beaten the American Paul Boyton in the race to perform this particular feat.[14]

In order to counter the numerous travellers' tales of prodigious swimmers amongst outlying tribes of their empire, the Victorian texts passionately argued that white men were inevitably superior 'natators'. A history of the sport, first published in 1868, entitles an entire section 'Foreigners Better than English?'[15] A manual by a famous champion devotes its conclusion to discrediting the rumours that 'the piccaninnies are often in a manner amphibious', and declares there to have been 'no instance of any foreigner civilised or uncivilised whose achievements in the water surpass those of the British in the same element'.[16] Captain Webb himself, who had made it his business to inspect at first hand the native swimmers of Port Natal in South Africa, could reassure his readers that 'as far as swimming goes none of the black people that I have ever seen approach [*sic*] a first-class English swimmer'.[17]

It was in the early years of the twentieth century that the German swimmer emerged as a national symbol and expression of Aryan manly vigour. In the quest to discover the Aryan heroic swimmer's ancestry, some makers of Nazi ideology looked to the German tribes mentioned in Roman authors. Excellent candidates were the cold-hardened Suebi, who wore few clothes and swam in their local rivers, the Germani, who practised unisex bathing and could escape even from the mighty Caesar by swimming across the Rhine (Caesar, *Gallic Wars* 6.1, 6.21, 1.53), and Batavi, who specialized in swimming across rivers with horses and equipment (Tacitus, *Histories* 4.12).[18]

---

[14] See Williams (1884), 2–5; Elderwick (1987), 50.

[15] Ralph Thomas (1904),133–6.

[16] Steedman (1867), 263, 85.

[17] Elderwick (1987), 18; Webb (1875), 64.

[18] I am grateful to Greg Woolf for pointing out to me that an unnamed Batavian auxiliary, serving under Hadrian in AD 117 by the Danube, performed a swimming feat so remarkable that an inscription was erected nearby to commemorate it: 'This is I . . . the first and strongest amongst one thousand of the Batavi. I was able (how, let Hadrian be judge) to swim across the wide waters of the deep Danube with all my arms; and while a weapon from a bow hung in the air fell, I transfixed it with an arrow and broke it, I whom no Roman nor barbarian, no soldier with a javelin nor Parthian was ever able to outdo . . .' (*CIL* iii.1, no. 462).

Others referred Aryan supremacy in the water back to the great swimming heroes of Norse and Anglo-Saxon epic: Egil in *Egil's Saga*, Kjartan and Bolli in *The Laxdale Saga*,[19] semi-historical Norwegian kings in the *Heimskringla*,[20] and above all Beowulf. In the course of his epic Beowulf undertakes no fewer than three swimming feats, including the crossings from southern Sweden to Lapland,[21] and from Frisia to Sweden.[22]

Hitler, on the other hand, like his cinematic propagandist Leni Riefenstahl in her *Olympiad*, made to celebrate the 1936 Olympic games, preferred to draw the imagery of the German swimmer and diver from an invented version of the ancient Greeks, especially the Spartans.[23] This was partly in emulous response to the plan earlier conceived by Japanese leaders to define their country in the world's eyes as a nation of invincible swimmers; they had orchestrated a challenge at the 1932 Los Angeles games, with a training regime inspired by Samurai mythology, which had resulted in victories in five out of the six events then possible.[24] National leaders have subsequently encouraged the celebration—even embellishment—of their own heroic swimming feats; in the case of Mao Zedong, it was 'The Great Swim' on the Long March to Beijing in 1966. Saddam Hussein in 1995 staged a re-enactment of his legendary swim across the Tigris, originally executed during his escape from an unsuccessful attempt in 1959 to assassinate Abdul Karim Qassim, then Iraqi prime minister.

[19] Palsson and Edwards (1976), 78–102; *Egil's Saga* even includes a woman swimmer in the form of the slave sorceress Thorgerd Brak (ibid. 201, 95). For *The Laxdale Saga* see Press (1964), 103–4, 132–4.

[20] Orme (1983), 15.

[21] Beowulf tells Unferth of his self-inflicted swimming ordeal, performed in chain-mail alongside Breca, when they were youths: 'I had more strength in the sea and difficulties to face in the waves than any other man... We had a tough naked sword in our hand as we swam off into the ocean—we intended to protect ourselves against whales... So we remained at sea for the duration of five nights until the swell, the surging waters, the most freezing weather and darkening night drove us apart.' Eventually, after a heroic battle with nine water-monsters, all of which he had killed, Beowulf was carried along the coast by the floodtide into the land of the Finns, i.e. Lapland (*Beowulf* 8.530–9.580, as translated in Bradley (1982), 425–7).

[22] *Beowulf* 23.2359–68 in Bradley (1982), 473.

[23] Sprawson (1992), 217–18.

[24] Ibid., ch. 8.

Such an implication of swimming in the discourses of ethnic identity and ethnic pride was also clearly discernible in the archaic and classical periods of ancient Greek culture. The next section will argue that Greek sources on swimming and diving show that these activities played a part in the cultural production of the Greek sense of ethnic identity and superiority. It is this conclusion which can profoundly illuminate one of the most exciting and unfairly neglected of all ancient texts: the lengthy papyrus fragment of Timotheus' *Persians*. The impact of a large portion of it has never been properly understood or appreciated for the simple reason that classical Greek feelings about swimming have never been brought to bear upon it.

SWIMMING IN ANCIENT GREEK AUTHORS

A classical Athenian who wanted to express the concept of ignorance of the most rudimentary aspects of education might well have used a proverb attested by Plato's Athenian in the *Laws*: the outstandingly ignorant person is one who knows 'neither letters nor swimming' (3.689d3, *an kai to legomenon mēte grammata mēte nein epistōntai*). The compilers of proverbs in later antiquity were insistent that this one defined ignorance (*amathia*): the *Suda* explains the proverb as applying to 'those who are totally ignorant' (*epi tōn ta panta amathōn*, s.v. *mēte nein*). The defect of ignorance was of course often attributed in Greek discourse to barbarians, a sign of the failure to achieve the cardinal Hellenic virtue of wisdom or intelligence (*sophia* or *xunesis*);[25] ignorance (*amathia*) is named as the vice correlative to the virtue of intelligence in Plato's *Republic* (4.444b7–8). Lack of education or understanding is often a feature of the Greeks' stereotypical portraits of barbarians;[26] indeed, in Aristophanes' *Clouds* the adjective 'barbarian' is found in tandem with the adjective 'ignorant' (492). The

[25] The others, as defined in e.g. Plato, *Resp.* 4.427e10–11, were self-restraint, manly courage, and justice (*sōphrosunē, andreia, dikaiosunē*): see further Kunsemüller (1935).

[26] See E. Hall (1989), 121–3.

lexicographer Diogenianus expanded the definition of ignorance in his discussion of the famous proverb by saying 'for in Athens they learned letters and swimming from childhood'.[27]

An anonymous commentator on the *Progymnasmata* by the rhetorician Aphthonius of Antioch went further, and offered an explanation of the reasons why the classical Athenians required these two fundamental skills:

The Athenians in the olden days used to instruct their own children in literacy and in swimming. The first was on account of their laws, and the second on account of battles at sea.[28]

This comment is supported in some of the (scanty) references to swimming in classical times, which tend to appear in the context of marine military operations: at Syracuse, for example, the Athenians sent down divers to destroy the stakes which the Syracusans had placed under water (Thuc. 7.25, cf. 4.26). Moreover, Greek texts imply on several occasions that victories in sea-battles were partly a result of the Greeks' ability to swim as compared with the barbarians' ignorance of this elementary skill. Despite the apparently well-known proverb, however, Greek texts have surprisingly little to say about swimming or indeed diving, at least outside a couple of obvious contexts such as Oppian's famous discussion of sponge-cutting divers in his *Halieutica* (2.434–53, 5.612–74). It is argued (correctly) in the Aristotelian *Problems* that it is easier to swim in seawater (23.13), and one of the three Aristotelian *Problems* devoted to diving matters (32.2–5) fascinatingly reveals that there was an established practice by which air could be sent down to divers in a bucket lowered by force (presumably covered or upside down). This implies a fairly highly developed science of diving, which enabled its practitioners to stay below water for considerable lengths of time (32.5).

Perhaps mobility in the water was considered so entirely necessary and normal by most Greeks that its importance was self-understood. It was, apparently, a familiar and integral aspect of Athenian life, passed on privately between family members rather than in any

[27] Leutsch and Schneidewin (1839), i. 278.
[28] Walz (1835), 44–5: *hoi gar Athēnaioi to palaion tous heautōn paidas grammata kai nēchesthai exepaideuon; to men dia tous nomous, to de dia tas naumachias.*

public or institutional arena.[29] This might well explain why the sources tend to remark only on the surprising and exceptional: dazzling feats of swimming prowess, or conversely the inability to swim. It is almost certainly significant that Plutarch makes a point of remarking that Alexander the Great, whose claim to being Greek was such a hotly contested issue, could not swim. This is the only distinctive instance of this inability, on the part of a Greek male, reported in ancient authors.[30] When his Macedonian troops hesitated to advance on the city of Nysa because of a deep river, he halted on the bank and berated himself. 'Most miserable man that I am, why have I not learned to swim?' (Plut. *Vit. Alex.* 58.4). That it was considered eminently desirable to be able to swim is, if not explicitly stated, then certainly widely implied. A legal text suggests that shipwreck, if near enough to land, would result in the survival of at least some of the crew (Dem. 34.10); despite the loss of twenty-five Athenian ships and crews in the chaos at Arginusae, a few men nevertheless managed to get safely to shore.[31]

General familiarity with both diving and swimming is also suggested by the type of metaphor drawn from the activity in tragedy and philosophy. In one context, the Argive king Pelasgus is—perhaps significantly—trying to work out a strategy for dealing with the problematic presence in Greece of a large number of barbarians. He says that there is need of profound thought, 'like a diver descending into the depth' (Aesch. *Suppl.* 408; see also Theseus' figure of speech at Eur. *Hipp.* 822–4). Philosophical texts reveal that diving was sometimes used in metaphors connected with 'plumbing depths' of intellectual obscurity,[32] and swimming for evading counter-arguments. Thus in the *Republic* Socrates is trying to persuade Glaucon of his controversial views on women and children. To express the difficulty of the philosophical challenge he chooses an analogy from swimming. 'Whether someone falls into a small swimming-pool (*eis*

---

[29] Gardiner (1930), 93.

[30] Couch (1933–4), 610 n. 5.

[31] Xen. *Hell.* 1.6.34. I am very grateful to Stephen Todd and Paul Cartledge respectively for these two references.

[32] The references are collected by Johansen and Whittle (1980), 326; see also Ginouvès (1962), 110 n. 3.

kolumbēthran mikran), or into the middle of the largest sea, he must still swim all the same (*homōs ge nei ouden hētton*). When Glaucon agrees, Socrates continues: 'So we too must swim (*kai hēmin neusteon*), and try to get safely out of the argument, in the hope that a dolphin will pick us up, or that some other means of salvation will appear' (*Republic* 5.453d5–11).

One of the reasons why swimming figures so little in Greek authors may be because it was not treated as a formal competitive sport such as those performed at public games. This may have been because, unlike combat sports, equestrian sports, and running on land, swimming does not seem to have been a standard part of public military training.[33] The sources suggest that swimming was a skill most Greek men learned in childhood from another male member of their household. But the great sixth-century boxer Teisander is said, in much later antiquity, to have used long-distance swimming as part of his general preparations (Philostratus, *Gymn.* 43), and competitions in swimming were not entirely unknown. Both sources for swimming races place them in Dionysiac contexts, which might have had some obscure cultic relevance to Dionysus' connection with sea-voyages, arrival from the sea, and dolphins.[34] Pausanias reports that at Hermione swimming or diving competitions were held, along with a boat-race and musical contests, at the shrine of black-goat Dionysus (2.35.1); and in Nonnos' *Dionysiaca* the god allows Ampelos to beat him at wrestling, sprinting, and in a swimming race across the river Pactolus (11.43.55). A little later in the same text, Kalamos and Karpos also engage in a complicated biathlon involving a sprint down the bank of the Maeander, swimming across it, and then sprinting back up the other bank (11.400–30).

---

[33] A very late Roman text of the 4th or 5th cent. AD suggests that some Roman recruits received training in swimming (Vegetius, *de Re mil.* 1.10): *Natandi usum aestivis mensibus omnis aequaliter debet tiro condiscere. Non enim semper pontibus flumina transeuntur, sed ut cedens et insequens natare cogitur frequenter exercitus.*
[34] In the Homeric *Hymn to Dionysus* the sailors, terrified by the god, leap into the sea but are transformed into dolphins (51–3); see also Ovid, *Met.* 3.572–691. Pausanias recounts another suggestive story concerning the wooden face or mask (*prosōpon*) of Dionysus, worshipped on Lesbos after Methymnian fishermen had hauled it up from the sea in their nets (10.19.2).

The literary and historiographical evidence may be scanty, but it nevertheless firmly suggests that the ability to swim, and endurance in the water, were from the archaic era that enjoyed Homeric epic onwards regarded as desirable accoutrements of Greek manhood. Swimming and diving are both implicated in the *Iliad*'s account of the Achaean victories over Troy. In battlefield rhetoric Patroclus paints a vivid word-picture of a nimble diver leaping overboard 'even in choppy, heaving seas'; this is in his ironic 'compliment' to his Trojan victim Cebriones, who has fallen from his chariot: 'apparently there are divers even among the Trojans', he sarcastically concludes (*Il.* 16.746–9). The Trojans later driven into the river by Achilles die horribly (21.10–16), swimming this way and that, tossed in the whirlpools (*enneon entha kai entha, elissomenoi peri dinas*). Their plight is likened to that of a swarm of locusts driven towards a river by a scorching fire. The stream of the deep-swirling Xanthus chokes and resounds with the cries of men and horses. The Trojans can therefore apparently swim, but not well enough to survive.[35]

Odysseus, on the other hand, does survive. His first really impressive physical feat in the *Odyssey* is the forerunner of many heroic swims in the European tradition, whether by Horatius or Julius Caesar or Beowulf, or even the legendary Welsh swimmers Cei and Dylan.[36] After his raft breaks up he struggles in the water for more than forty-eight hours until he is washed up on Scheriē (*Od.* 5.312–63). Although the scarf Leucothea gave him is an indispensable aid, the text makes it clear that Odysseus is a remarkable swimmer. When he sees land after being buffeted in the water for two days and two nights, 'he swam (*nēche*) on in eager hope that his feet would tread dry land again' (5.399). When a billow attacks him near the rocky shore, Athena sharpens his wits, and (5.438–44)

he struggled forth from the line of breakers thundering against the shore, then swam outside it (*nēche parex*) ... And when in his swimming (*neōn*) he came abreast of a flowing river, where he thought the ground best to land on, being clear from rocks and sheltered from winds besides, he hailed the outflowing stream as a god and prayed to him in his heart.

---

[35] See van Esveld (1908), 7.

[36] See Jones and Jones (1949), 107 (Cei's nine-day underwater swim), and 63–4 (Dylan's leap into the sea, resulting in him being renamed 'Sea son of Wave').

This episode has been called 'the most beautiful description of swimming in world literature'.[37] It also put swimming prowess on the list of required accomplishments for many ideal figures of western manhood thereafter. It is awareness of this that led Apollonius, whose project entailed frequent ironic debunking of the epic tradition, to bestow the exceptional swim in his *Argonautica* on the foolish Boutes. Rather than swimming hard to survive and return home to wife and homeland, Boutes is enchanted by the song of the Sirens, plunges from the Argo into the dark swell, and attempts to swim aross to their island of Anthemoessa (4.912–19). Fortunately for him he is rescued by Aphrodite.

Besides Odysseus, a few other Greek heroes are credited with legendary feats in the water. Bacchylides describes Theseus jumping from the stern of his ship in order to salvage Minos' golden ring, his visit (admittedly facilitated by dolphins) to Poseidon's palace, and his triumphant return to the surface (17.81–122). Greek folklore (and indeed a lost tragedy by Aeschylus) told of Glaucus the fisherman, who some said became an immortal sea-dweller after eating a special kind of grass, although rationalists claimed that he was simply an exceptional swimmer who could stay at sea for days on end.[38] The Locrian Ajax seems traditionally to have been a fine swimmer (see below, p. 281), but most famous of all were Leander's serial swims over the Hellespont to visit his lover Hero. These seem to have been enacted on the Hellenistic tragic stage, and were recounted in an epic of Hellenistic date (*SH* 951). They were mentioned by Virgil in his *Georgics* (3.258–63) and elaborated by Ovid (*Heroides* 18–19). They were enacted in a flooded Colosseum in order to celebrate its opening in AD 80 (Martial, *Lib. Spect.* 25), narrated definitively in Musaeus' late Greek epyllion *Hero and Leander*, which became an extremely influential poem in the Renaissance, and famously emulated by Lord George Byron on 3 May 1810.

---

[37] Mehl (1931), 848: 'Die schönste Schwimmschilderung des Weltschrifttums'. The exact location of the swim was discussed in antiquity: see Pausanias 5.25.3.

[38] Both versions of Glaucus' story are preserved in Palaephatus, *On Unbelievable Things* 27, in Festa (1902), iii.2, 35–7. One tragedy in the tetralogy with which Aeschylus was victorious in 472 BC (also including *Persians*) was a play about Glaucus, just possibly connecting him with the Persian wars: see E. Hall (1996a), 11.

BARBARIANS WHO CANNOT SWIM

There was a tradition that one of the reasons for the Persians' defeat at the battle of Marathon had been that they fell into a marshy lake there (Paus. 1.32.6), a story in accordance with the three passages in fifth-century historiographical literature which assert or imply that while most adult Greek males knew how to swim, 'barbarians' generally did not. In terms of understanding Timotheus' histrionic enactment of the drowning Phrygian, the most important passage occurs in Herodotus' account of the battle of Salamis (8.89). He informs his readers that in addition to the death of Ariabignes, Xerxes' brother, there were many fatalities amongst other famous men from Persia, Media, and the countries allied to them. Herodotus continues,

There were also Greek casualties but not many, for most of the Greeks could swim, and those who had lost their ships, provided they were not killed in the actual fighting, swam over to Salamis. Most of the enemy, on the other hand, being unable to swim (*neein ouk epistamenoi*), were drowned.

This idea reiterates a theme already stated in Herodotus' account of the storm which had wrecked Mardonius' fleet on Athos during the previous Persian invasion (6.44). Herodotus reports that it was claimed that around 300 ships were wrecked, with a loss of 20,000 men. He continues:

The sea in the neighbourhood of Athos is full of monsters, so that those of the ships' companies which were not dashed on the rocks were seized and devoured. Others, unable to swim (*neein ouk epistamenoi*), were drowned; others again died from cold.

The last passage involved the Athenian historian Thucydides writing about the Thracian mercenaries whom the Athenians had sent back to their homeland as a result of their financial crisis. After being characterized by Thucydides as one of the 'most bloodthirsty of peoples' on account of the atrocities they committed at Mycalessus, including butchering all the pupils at the largest local school (7.29), the barbarous Thracians are caught up with by the Thebans, who

took away their booty, struck terror into them, and drove them down to Euripus and the sea, where the boats that had brought them were lying at anchor. Most of those who were killed were killed while embarking, since they did not know how to swim (*oute epistamenous nein*), and the crews, when they saw what was happening on shore, anchored their ships out of range of the arrows.   (7.30)

The Thracians lost 230 out of 1,300 men. So Greek proficiency at swimming, especially as a means of escape from a shipwreck or sea-battle, was regarded not only as an asset, but as a marker of ethnic difference and a source of ethnic pride.

There was until recently a long-standing scholarly tendency to believe the ancient sources and accept that knowledge of swimming amongst the (allegedly) less athletic and wholesome non-Greeks was indeed a rarity. In the 1930s, Couch solemnly argued that the ancient Asiatics' inability to swim could be explained by their generic aversion to nudity, alleged, for example, by both Herodotus (1.10.3) and Thucydides (1.6.5).[39] But the biblical citations discussed above show that at least among Jewish 'barbarians' swimming was regularly practised; moreover, the pre-Talmudic Rabbinic literature of Palestine, in a formulation highly reminiscent of the Athenian proverb 'neither letters nor swimming', enjoins Jewish fathers to teach their sons to swim as well as to study.[40] And the Macedonians led by Alexander during the siege of Tyre in 332 BC encountered difficulties on account of the skill of Tyrian divers, who cut through the ropes holding their ships in place (Arrian, *Anab.* 2.21.6). The important point is not whether the Greek sources are true or false, but that they consistently implied that knowledge of swimming was widespread, and that Greeks were proud of their expertise in the water. Such cases as the feats of Odysseus and Skyllis were deeply embedded in the collective Greek-speaking imagination, encoded in the panhellenic self-definitions constituted by the corpus of heroic literature and art.

TIMOTHEUS' *PERSIANS*

With Timotheus of Miletus, the composer of a number of famous long poems, this part of the book addresses one of the few authors of

[39] Couch (1933–4), 611.
[40] *Tosefta* 114 paragraph 1.29, 71. I am hugely indebted to Tessa Rajak for locating this important reference.

the classical period who contributed some important roles to the Athenian theatrical imagination, but who was not himself of Athenian descent or citizen status. This poet's dates are approximately 450 to 360 BC. He was chiefly studied in the ancient world, and has until recently been almost exclusively studied in the modern, as a pivotal figure in the history of Greek music;[41] his creations spanned the era when both dithyrambic poets (i.e. writers of choral songs, sung to the *aulos*) and citharodic poets (i.e. writers of solo lyrics sung to the cithara, although even these are sometimes confusingly labelled 'dithyrambs' or 'nomes') were abandoning strict verse structures and paying much more attention to melody, variety, and modulations. The influence of these developments is apparent in the increased sophistication of the lyric monodies in late Euripides (see Ch. 10).[42] Timotheus' polymetric songs seem to have achieved the status of 'classical' music in the ancient world's musical repertoire.

His *Persians* was believed to have been performed at the Nemean games two centuries after its composition (see below). Polybius implies that Timotheus was a canonical poet amongst the Arcadians of the second century BC (4.20.8–9), for he says that the boys there were all trained in singing, particularly the songs of Philoxenus and Timotheus. As late as Nero's time a Greek epigrammatist ridicules a citharode named Hegelochus who sang a work called *Nauplius*, almost certainly the aria of that name attributed to Timotheus (Lucilius in *AP* 9.185). But until the early twentieth century Timotheus' *Persians*—perhaps his most celebrated work in antiquity—survived in a few tiny fragments quoted by other ancient authors. Quite suddenly, a much clearer idea of its contents was supplied by a remarkable papyrus of the fourth century BC, probably even antedating Alexander the Great, and thus the oldest surviving Greek book.[43] This ancient document contains roughly the last third of the poem (*PBerol* 9865).

It was discovered by the German archaeologist Ludwig Borchardt, who was excavating a Greek cemetery near one of the pyramids at

---

[41] See e.g. under 'Timotheus' in the index to M. L. West (1992*a*).

[42] See e.g. Webster (1967), 17–20.

[43] So Watzinger (1905), 8–15; for a detailed discussion of the actual circumstances in which the papyrus was found, and their implications, see van Minnen (1997), 247–9.

Abusir, north-west of Memphis, during excavations by the Deutsche Orient-Gesellschaft, on February 1 1902. The papyrus, which is written in an aesthetically pleasing Ionian hand, seems originally to have been owned by one of the Hellenomemphites, Ionian Greeks who had settled in the Egyptian delta in the archaic period, and had been transferred to Memphis by the pharaoh Amasis in the mid-sixth century BC.[44] It thus constitutes very striking evidence for the spread of Greek culture in Egypt even during the classical period, and for 'the worldwide popularity of the New Poetry represented by Timotheus in what must be regarded as an outpost of Greek culture'.[45] Even before Alexander, Timotheus' *Persians* clearly had reverberations for Greek-speakers wanting to maintain their cultural identity in a barbarian environment.[46] The importance of the papyrus was recognized as soon as it was discovered, and Wilamowitz was asked to edit it.[47] The poem began its modern life, as it had been used in the ancient world, in a ceremony with strong ethnic and national reverberations when it was presented to the Prussian Kaiser, Wilhelm II. In his memoirs, Wilamowitz recalls his visit to the palace at Potsdam, the address he delivered, his lunch (also attended by the empress), and his inability to speak quite as submissively in conversation as his status-conscious emperor would have liked.[48]

PLUTARCH, TIMOTHEUS, AND GREEK ETHNIC IDENTITY

In the early years of the twentieth century the poem caused a sensation in palaeographical, musicological, and metrical circles. Numerous articles by distinguished philologists appeared almost

[44] See van Minnen (1997), 249.

[45] Ibid. 248.

[46] For an interesting comparison, see Meriani (2003), esp. 17, who argues that the traditions surrounding the music theorist Aristoxenus reflect a vigorous debate about the 'Old' versus 'New' music of Greece in Tyrrhenian Posidoneia in the late 4th cent. BC.

[47] von Wilamowitz-Moellendorff (1903). There are much more recent editions by Janssen (1984) and Hordern (2002).

[48] von Wilamowitz-Moellendorff (1930), 310–11.

immediately and in several waves thereafter.[49] But the Timothean poem's contribution to the cultural depiction of non-Greek peoples, in particular Asiatics, was almost entirely overlooked. Timotheus does not even appear in the *index* to Broadhead's mammoth edition of Aeschylus' *Persians*, which was published in 1960.[50] For scholars nurtured on the classical Greek lyric poetry of Pindar, Bacchylides, and the tragedians, the poem was and apparently still is, artistically speaking, a profound disappointment:[51] the standard reaction before the Second World War was an aesthetic horror at the strange, colourful diction of the poem and the sound-world it creates, which was often explicitly identified by conservative classical scholars with what they saw as the worst excesses of the Modernist poets of their own time.[52] Yet, even before the discovery of the papyrus, a certain amount was already known about the poem. Three of the half-a-dozen fragments which had survived as quotations in ancient authors were preserved by Plutarch, in contexts where the focus is on the collective Hellenic identity, and, more specifically, on Greek freedom and independence.

The most famous citation occurs in Plutarch's biography of Philopoemen. In 206 BC, when he was general of the Achaean League, Philopoemen had utterly defeated the Spartans and rendered the Achaeans virtually independent of Macedon. Having been resonantly entitled 'the last of the Greeks' by an unnamed Roman (1.4), Philopoemen is depicted by Plutarch at the celebration of the Nemean Games in the following year, 205 (1.11). He displayed his phalanx, which performed tactical moves 'before the assembled Greeks'. Then, during the citharodic competition, he entered the theatre just as the singer Pylades was singing the opening of the *Persians* by Timotheus (perhaps even the opening line, depending on the precise meaning of

---

[49] See e.g. Croiset (1903); Reinach (1903); Gildersleeve (1903); Keil (1913); Ebeling (1925).

[50] Broadhead (1960).

[51] See e.g. Kenyon (1919), 5: Timotheus 'contradicts in every respect the ideals of Hellenic art and taste'. See also C. P. Segal's influential dismissal of the poem in his discussion of 5th-cent. lyric in Segal (1985*a*), 243. But his reading, which incorrectly states that there are groups of Persian women in the poem, suggests that he had not consulted it closely.

[52] See e.g. Winter (1933), 212–13: 'In its riot of noise it is not unlike a poem by Vachel Lindsay, and exemplifies completely the poet's boast of modernism'; the poem's 'horrors are indicative of an era of poor taste as well as of a poor poet'.

enarxasthai): 'Fashioning for Greece the great ornament of freedom' (*kleinon eleutherias teuchōn megan Helladi kosmon* = fr. 788 *PMG*). Immediately 'all the spectators turned their eyes towards Philopoemen, and the Greeks broke into joyful applause, since in their hopes they were recovering their ancient prestige, and in their confidence coming close to the spirit of those earlier days'.[53] We may never know the identity of the original grammatical subject of the word 'fashioning' in the first line of Timotheus' poem; we cannot even be absolutely sure that it was sung at the Nemean games in 205. The important points are, however, that it clearly opened with the *idea* of Hellenic freedom, and that Plutarch felt that his readership knew enough about the song and its celebration of Greek collective identity to include it in his own portrayal of this ethnic hero, the 'last of Hellenes'.

The second fragment quoted by Plutarch occurs in the *Life of Agesilaus*, in an equally Hellenocentric, indeed triumphalist context—albeit one complicated by Plutarch's meditations on the self-destructive patterns inherent in Greek history.[54] The Spartan hero has sailed to fight The Barbarian 'on behalf of Hellas' (6.1), and has routed Tissaphernes, 'an abominable man, and most hateful to the Greeks' (10.3). We are told that he has spent two years in the field, and that the people of Asia have much to say about his definitively Hellenic virtues of self-restraint (*sōphrosunē*), piety, and moderation (*metriotēs*, 14.1). Plutarch then turns to the emotions Agesilaus had aroused in the eastern Greeks, for whom it was most gratifying (14.1)

to see the Persian viceroys and generals, who had long been insufferably cruel, and had revelled in wealth and luxury, now fearful and obsequious before a man who went about in a paltry cloak, and at one brief and laconic speech from him conforming themselves to his ways and changing their

---

[53] Translated by Perrin (1921).

[54] See Pelling (1989). The undoubted triumphalism of the 'Salamis spirit' in the quotations from Timotheus in the lives of both Philopoemen and Agesilaus interact with these biographies' complex reflections on the glorious self-harm which the Greeks had repeatedly inflicted upon themselves. In the story of Agesilaus it is self-defeating jealousy that tore the Greeks apart, and Philopoemen, although a Greek 'freedom-fighter', is not able to secure freedom for his country, since, as 'last of the Greeks' he embodies both their brilliance and the internecine contentiousness. I am grateful to Professor Pelling for discussing this issue with me.

dress and mien; insomuch that many were moved to cite the words of Timotheus, 'Ares is lord; Greece has no fear of gold'.[55]   (= fr. 790 *PMG*)

This anecdote is particularly interesting because it includes the eastern Greeks of Ionia in the sense of collective Hellenic identity. It is however another source, a compilation of proverbs, which explicitly refers the line to Timotheus' *Persians*, before adding that the poem enjoyed enormous popularity at Athens and that this particular line was quoted proverbially in Menander's *Thaïs*.[56]

TIMOTHEUS' DYING BARBARIAN

The final Plutarchean passage comes from *How Young Men Should Listen to Poetry* (11), where Plutarch is discussing the beneficial effects of battle exhortations in Greek literature. After two quotations from Homer (*Iliad* 16.422, 13.122), which Plutarch praises for the way in which they encourage valour, he adds that a further excellent example is furnished by the opening of the exhortation to the Greeks in Timotheus' *Persians* (= fr. 789 *PMG*): 'Worship honour, the helpmate of battling valour'. This fragment must have been delivered in direct speech by a Greek leader—probably Themistocles—thus setting up an internal dialogue between the voices of the courageous Greeks and those of the vanquished barbarians. For the papyrus section of the poem only includes direct speech delivered by non-Greek speakers.

Citharodic arias like *Persians* were conventionally composed in a series of seven sections, of which the centrepiece and climax was the fifth section, the *omphalos*, or central narrative (Pollux 4.66). The papyrus of *Persians* opens during the *omphalos*, probably near its opening, making the battle of Salamis and its immediate aftermath the central interest of the poem.[57] The battle of Salamis has of course been constantly reinvoked as a canonical reference point by those celebrating uprisings against enemies perceived as imperialist

---

[55] Translated by Perrin (1917).
[56] Zenobius Athous 2.47; Menander fr. 167 K–A.
[57] See Croiset (1903), 327–8.

aggressors—from Rome's association of Salamis with Actium, to the defeat of the Ottomans at Lepanto, of Napoleon in the Nile, or even the moral victory scored by the Irish republicans at Easter in 1916.[58] When this chapter was first being researched, a theatrical adaptation of Aeschylus' *Persians* made the ancient sea-battle stand unequivocally for the bombardment of Iraq in 1991; when the chapter was prepared for publication in its final form, a second important adaptation drew equally unmistakeable parallels between Salamis and the 2003 invasion of Iraq.[59] But the description of this particular mother of all sea-battles was of course already a standard topic in Greek culture; the poem's forerunners included not only Phrynichus' tragedy *Phoenissae*, Aeschylus' *Persians* and Herodotus' *Histories*, but also Simonides' *Sea-battle* (*Naumachia*, frr. 532–5 *PMG*),[60] which is in its own way as important as the new Simonidean elegy on Plataea (see Ch. 7, pp. 196–7). Depending on the date of Timotheus' poem, which was probably composed towards the end of the fifth century, Salamis texts may also have included Choerilus' epic *Persica*, and the source of the anonymous tragic fragment 685 *TgrF*, which seems to have been part of a lament for Darius performed by barbarians.[61]

The surviving part of Timotheus' central narrative focuses successively on four episodes during the sea-battle. The episodes, taken together, confirm Plutarch's diagnosis that this was a patriotic, indeed triumphalist, popular classic.[62] Timotheus' portrait of the barbarians suffering and dying at Salamis is replete with images and terminology drawn from the 'vocabulary of barbarism', the orientalist discourse which had been developed in Greek culture

---

[58] On Napoleon see Hall and Macintosh (2005), ch. 10; on the Irish connection see Macintosh (1992), 189; for an overview see Hall (forthcoming *c*).

[59] See E. Hall (forthcoming *c*).

[60] For the (relatively) new papyrus fragments of this poem, see Parsons (1992).

[61] On which see E. Hall (1996*a*), 8. The place and date of the première of Timotheus' *Persians* have been hotly contested; see e.g. Bassett (1931) and Hose (1993). Hansen's suggestion (1984) of the Mounichia festival in 410/9 BC is as plausible as any. For a recent and agnostic survey of the debate, see Hordern (2002), 15–17.

[62] See the fascinating study of van Minnen (1997), esp. 257, who argues that it would have held particular significance for the mid-4th cent. Hellenomemphite community in whose cemetery the papyrus was found, since at this time the Persians were incessantly trying to re-establish their hold on Egypt after it had regained its independence.

from at least as early as Aeschylus' tragic *Persians*. A key theme, for example, is extravagant displays of lamentation, regarded as inappropriate, at any rate in men, in fifth-century Athens.[63] Some barbarians have drowned, for the sea 'swarmed with bodies (sunlight-)robbed from failure of breath, and the shores were laden with them' (94–7).[64] Others are stranded naked on the sea headlands, 'with shouts and tear-shedding wailing, breast-beating wailers', who are 'gripped by dirge-like lamentation' (98–103, see also 139). At the point where the flight of the barbarian force is checked, just before Timotheus (or whoever was performing the poem) began to sing in the voice of Xerxes himself, there is detailed evocation of the excessive lamentation in which these barbarians indulged, after casting down their spears (166–72):

> Their faces were torn by their nails; and they rent their well-woven Persian dress about their breasts, and a high-pitched Asian wailing was attuned to the many-tongued lament, and the whole of the King's entourage clamoured as they gazed in fear on the coming disaster.

The barbarians take up abject physical positions of supplication; the third barbarian voice impersonated in direct speech by the Greek singer of *Persians* belongs to a man who addresses his words to the Greek grasping him by the hair, 'writhing and clasping him around the knees' (140–6)—offering the performer ample opportunity for suiting his gestures to his song. The King himself also had also 'fallen to his knees and maltreated his body' when he recognized that he had been defeated (176).

The servile attitude of the barbarians towards their king is conveyed by the use of obeisant vocabulary, certain items of which, by Timotheus' day, had been canonized for several decades in the register of orientalist discourse; the third barbarian voice refers to Xerxes as 'my master' (*emos despotēs*, 152); he also addresses the Greek whom he supplicates by the painfully reverential 'father'

---

[63] On the association of Persia with excessive displays of lamentation see e.g. E. Hall (1996*a*), 168–9.

[64] In this and all the following citations the text used is fundamentally that of Denys Page in *Poetae Melici Graeci*, as revised and translated by David Campbell in the new Loeb *Greek Lyric*, v (1993), 90–111. The numeration in both is the same.

(*pater*, 154), a word not thus used by a Greek after Homer, but one of the words used by Aeschylus' *Persians* in respect of Darius (*Pers.* 663, 671).

The second barbarian voice to which Timotheus exposed his audience is a collective one; it is the voice of a group including both Mysians and Lydians, who sing to us jointly like a tragic chorus. This section of direct speech is introduced by a pathetic narrative describing the barbarian fleet in headlong flight. Every ship was broken against one shoal or another (88–90); the barbarians' teeth are knocked out as they dash against their own oars (91–3); the sea was swarming, and the shores were heavy with those drowned and bereft of breath (94–7). It is against such a pictured backdrop that the huddled barbarians find their collective voice, sitting on shores, naked, freezing and weeping (98–101). Their song is a lament for their homelands and an appeal to the Asiatic Mother goddess for salvation; they know that the only fate they can expect is death. Each of them will either have his throat cut by the iron weapon of some Greek warrior, or die of exposure to the 'ship-wrecking' north wind—Boreas, the old enemy of the Persians (121–38).[65]

The third barbarian voice belongs to an inhabitant of Celaenae, a city in Phrygia; his entreaty, with its appended monologue, is presented as one amongst many similar speeches being delivered simultaneously (140–61):

Whenever some steel-bladed Greek seized and carried off an inhabitant of rich-pasturing Celaenae bereft of his fighting powers, he would carry him off dragging him by the hair; and he, embracing his knees, would beseech him, interweaving Greek speech with Asian, shattering his mouth's seal in piercing cry, tracking down the Ionian tongue: 'How me speak you, and what thing speak? Never again I come back. This time my master, he brung me here to this place; but from now on no more, father, nor more I come again here for fight: I sit still. I no come here to you. I go over there to Sardis, to Susa, Ecbatana dweller. Artimis, my great god, will guard me to Ephesus.

This section of direct speech is quite unlike the previous two, in which the diction, however baroque, did not apparently attempt to imitate either the sounds of a barbarian language, or solecistic Greek.

---

[65] Boreas was supposed to have helped the Greeks to defeat the Persians at Artemisium, and to have received a shrine in gratitude (Hdt. 7.189).

But in this section Timotheus launches into a linguistic caricature of a type avoided completely in tragedy except, perhaps, in the case of the Phrygian eunuch in Euripides' *Orestes*, although his Greek is infinitely better than Timotheus' suppliant from Celaenae.[66] The text that is most strongly reminiscent of this passage comes, rather from Old Comedy: it is the barbarizing Scythian archer's tortured Greek in Aristophanes' *Thesmophoriazusae* (on which see Ch. 8). The introduction to the speech even announces programmatically that this is to be this typical barbarian's medium of expression: 'interweaving Greek speech with Asian' (146–7).

Other composers and poets associated with the New Music reveal a penchant for Oriental themes and effects.[67] Timotheus, it seems, is not only exhibiting his own mastery of the poetic diction of different poetic and dramatic genres, but trying for pleasing variety in his impersonation of dying barbarians: the closeness of the technical parallel in an Aristophanic play implies that the impact of this passage, at any rate, was actually designed to be pleasurable if not humorous. The errors in the Greek mark every line; besides the peculiar word order, there are mistakes in number, case, ending, voice, and choice of preposition. It is likely, as Hordern remarks, that 'as a citizen of Miletus, Timotheus would clearly be more familiar than an Athenian with the kinds of error' western Asiatics were likely to make when speaking Greek.[68] But this voice also demonstrates how generic the Asiatic barbarian of mimetic poetry had become by the end of the fifth century BC;[69] it represents an amalgam of numerous different sub-groups. Celaenae is in Phrygia, but this barbarian apparently lives in both Lydian Sardis and Persian Susa, while worshipping Artemis of Ephesus. The citharodic performer must impersonate this synthetic barbarian as he grovels at some victorious Greek's knees, his hair tightly gripped in a Greek fist. The appeal that he makes to the audience's patriotic sentiments is

---

[66] See Reinach (1903), 72; E. Hall (1989), 38–54.

[67] Hordern (2002), 123–4 lists, amongst others, the dithyrambic *Nanis* by Licymnius of Chios, which related the story of Cyrus' capture of Sardis, and the *Mysians* and *Syrus* by Timotheus' great contemporary dithyrambist, the paradigmatic exponent of the new musical style, Philoxenus of Cythera.

[68] Hordern (2002), 38.

[69] See above nn. 66–7.

surely not all that sophisticated: he even deflects any potential pathos by the humorous impact of his solecisms.

The fourth and last barbarian voice to be heard is that of Xerxes himself (178–96). A description of the defeated monarch immediately after he had witnessed the naval engagement was of course a staple ingredient of Salamis narratives; what is remarkable about this one, owing as much as it does to the battle of Salamis narratives in Aeschylus and Herodotus, is the use of direct speech. Timotheus' Xerxes is not only given the opportunity to articulate his feelings in *oratio recta*: he can express himself in correct Greek. In high tragic style he laments the destruction of his men and his ships by the Greek navy, and the grief now falling upon the land of Persia. He concludes by summoning his four-horsed chariot (the chariot or other luxurious vehicle being one of the most conventional features of Xerxean narratives), and concludes his speech with words that imply, as so often, the alleged Persian obsession with wealth. His orders his 'countless riches' to be brought out to his wagons (191–2), and his tents to be burned, so that the Greeks may not profit from his fortune (*ploutou*, the last word he utters, at 195).[70]

The Salamis section of the poem, before the poet's *sphragis* in which his own voice is prominent, and the brief four-line epilogue, now concludes with a brief return to view the glorious Greek army; with predictable piety they set up trophies to Zeus, and sing a paean to Apollo accompanied by a high-stepping dance (196–201). Timotheus has attempted to display his command of several different literary ways of representing the ethnically other. The narrative is jerky and inconsistent in style, pace and tone: its syncopation and heterogeneity mark it out as an early and conscious attempt at the artificial stylistic variety known as *poikilia*.[71] Basil Gildersleeve demonstrated his rare feeling for the tonal effects in Greek poetry in his judgement that 'ibis-like, Timotheos has swallowed and digested all the departments of Greek poetry, epic, lyric, dramatic'.[72]

[70] The importance of Aeschylus' *Persians* to this section is appreciated by van Minnen (1997), 251.

[71] Reinach (1903), 62. Segal (1985*a*), 243, says that the nome anticipates 'the worst traits of Hellenistic poetry'.

[72] Gildersleeve (1903), 233.

DROWNING IN DEFEAT

With the variegated nature of Timotheus' poetic representation of the ethnically other in mind, it is now time to return, at last, to his first speaking barbarian. The longest and most detailed picture in this surviving part of the poem portrays a man in the process of drowning. His specific ethnic origin from within Asia is uncertain, and depends on the way that lines 40–1 are reconstructed, especially the meaning of the word beginning *hamerodromoi-*. If he was described as something like 'lord of the land of people who can run a long way in a single day', then it probably means that he was understood as coming from Persia, of which the high-speed courier system had been made famous by Herodotus' description (8.98).[73] In the stichometry of *Poetae Melici Graeci* his episode is forty-six lines long—the time it takes him to drown. There are of course other drowning scenes in ancient literature. In Musaeus' epyllion *Hero and Leander* it takes Leander twenty-two dactylic hexameters to expire (309–30), but the entire description is quite different because this romantic hero is a superlative swimmer. So is the Locrian Ajax in Quintus of Smyrna's *Posthomerica,* who after the wreck of the Greek fleet cleaves the salty waves with his sinewy arms, endowed 'with all the strength of a tireless Titan' (14.550); he swims indomitably through mountain-high waves, thunderbolts, and earth tremors until Poseidon has to resort to killing him with the weight of an entire uprooted mountain (14.588–9). Timotheus' barbarian therefore provides the most vivid, physiologically detailed and extended account of a drowning in ancient literature.[74] Not only does he speak intermittently, but his words are enclosed between sections of narrative, describing in the most gruesome and dramatic terms his struggles in the water. It is as though his face repeatedly emerges from the water, splutters a few words, before disappearing again after considerable thrashing to catch another desperate breath.

---

[73] E. Hall (1989), 121–3.

[74] It is, of course, brief in comparison with the novel *Pincher Martin* by William Golding (1956), of which all two hundred pages are structured around one man's experience of drowning.

Such histrionic representations of persons undergoing physical and psychological disturbance seem to have been one of Timotheus' hallmarks, for amongst the other citharodic titles we encounter *The Madness of Ajax*, and the infamous *Birth-Pangs of Semele*. It was noted in quite another context (Ch. 4, p. 93), that Semele's perinatal sufferings as she produced Dionysus were made worse by Zeus' ceraunic intervention. According to a character quoted in Athenaeus, Timotheus' Semele 'could not have made more noise if she had given birth to a stage-carpenter instead of a god' (*Deipn.* 8.352a = *PMG* fr. 792). Timotheus' *Elpenor* must have offered potential for impersonating a man drunk, falling from a roof, and reappearing as a ghost in the underworld (fr. 779 *PMG*); his *Cyclops* certainly dealt with the theme of inebriation (fr. 780 *PMG*); his *Nauplius* included an evocation of a storm (fr. 785 *PMG*); the first-person sequences of his *Niobe* included one where the performer sang in the sinister persona of Charon, calling on the newly dead to board his ferry (fr. 786 *PMG*). This trend towards mimesis of the aurally sensational may have been traditional in instrumental music; the *Pythikos Nomos* depicted in its music the struggle between Apollo and the serpent at Delphi.[75] It was certainly an established trend in late classical music, according to Plato's objections to music that imitates the sounds made by thunder, winds, hail, axes, pulleys, trumpets, pipes, panpipes, and even sheep and bird noises' (*Resp.* 3.397a; cf. *Laws* 2.699b–670a). An aulos-player named Dorion was noted for the musical representation of a storm in his composition entitled *Nauplius*, and the destruction of the Persian fleet at Salamis must have presented Timotheus with a wonderful opportunity for similar mimetic display.[76]

It has long been recognized that Timotheus' nome is heavily dependent on Aeschylus' *Persians*.[77] But it has not been noticed that Timotheus' emphasis on drowning is an Aeschylean motif. One of the recurrent images in both the play's messenger speeches and its choral odes pictures barbarian men, defeated by Greeks, struggling in the seawater, or choking the sea-straits and knocking against the shore. It is widely accepted that the play as a whole, from the parodos onwards,

---

[75] Pollux 4.84; Strabo 9.3.10; see Hordern (2002), 38.

[76] Hordern (2002), 38–9; on Dorion see M. L. West (1992), 369 and n. 4; Theopompus *FgrH* 115 F 236; Athen. *Deipn.* 8.337c–338a.

[77] For a collection of close verbal parallels, see Croiset (1903), 330–5.

implies that the Persians were powerful on land, but tempted fate by trying to extend their supremacy to the sea. But the actual descriptions of barbarians struggling in the water have received little attention. This is probably because Aeschylus does not explicitly use words denoting drowning or swimming, choosing instead elaborate periphrases and metaphors. 'The shores of Salamis and all the coastline are filling up with corpses of men wretchedly destroyed,' laments the messenger (272–3); the chorus responds in words which (despite textual corruption) plainly painted a picture of bodies, encased in gorgeous Persian robes, bobbing up and down in the swirling water (275–7). The messenger offers a catalogue of the watery demises of important barbarians: Artembares 'is buffeted' against the coast (303); Dadaces 'leapt lightly' from his ship (305); Tenagon 'roams' the seawashed coastline (306–7). The sea became invisible, with the beaches and reefs brimming with corpses (419–21; see also 567–8, 966); many more barbarians met their death by drowning in the Strymon when it suddenly melted beneath their feet: lucky was the man whose breath (*pneuma*) was quickest to leave his body (506–7). None of Aeschylus' drowning barbarians articulates his death throes with the help of direct speech; his Xerxes' speech from the safety of the shore is put into *oratio obliqua* (469–70). But Timotheus puts even his version of Xerxes' lament into direct speech.[78] This was one of Timotheus' typically innovatory strokes; as a citharodic performer, he had to impersonate more or less directly any characters who used the first person singular. He has thus made his song not only more entertaining, but the psychological experience of listening to it more immediate, more powerful, and, to Greek patriotic sentiments, more deeply satisfying. One of the reasons why Greek audiences enjoyed this poem so much was because they themselves could swim.

The first barbarian is introduced through a section of narrative describing the assault on the Persian navy of numerous Greek missiles, repeated rammings, arrows falling on limbs, and burning fire-darts (5–28); the result of this violent onslaught is that 'the emerald-haired sea had its furrow reddened by the drops of naval blood, and shouting mingled with screaming prevailed' (31–4). It is against this backdrop of violence, cacophony, and gore that the first

---

[78] Xerxes' lament is, indeed, one of the few sections of the poem ever to have received any critical commendation, from e.g. Segal (1985), 243.

barbarian is introduced. The text at this point is lacunose, but it is apparent that the poem concentrated on his physical struggle in the water. I can find only one suggestion in all the secondary literature published prior to the first version of this chapter that the significance of this had been noticed at all; in 1925 Ebeling noted that our man 'like most Asiatics is not a swimmer', thus apparently drawing on an early twentieth-century western European ethnic stereotype, rather than an ancient Greek one.[79] Yet Timotheus' character is emphatically no swimmer: he is beating the water with his arms (44–5), is being buffeted (*theinome*[*nos*, 46), and is unable to find a way to escape (47). He then says something in direct speech, including an appeal to a male god, possibly Poseidon (50).

Further narrative ensues. It is difficult to reconstruct, but certainly remarks upon the drowning man's pallor (56). Another brief section of direct speech may have commenced here, in which case its theme was the victim's sensations of being tossed around in close confinement (56–9). At line 60 the quality of the text improves, and from this point onwards the problems are more of interpretation than legibility. The barbarian is floundering in the bloodied brine, and a section now commences which narrates in gruesome detail his struggle for breath and the impotent rage which overwhelms him (60–71):

and whenever the winds dropped in one place to attack in another, water devoid of Bacchus rained down with foam and poured into his alimentary vessel; and as the surging brine bubbled over from his mouth, with shrill distorted voice and wits deranged, sated by it all, he would make threats gnashing his teeth in anger against the sea, the destroyer of his body.

On the point of expiry, the barbarian is now given one last speech, in which he curses this same lethal sea. In very few words Timotheus manages to cram several significant events in what, by his time, was already the canonical narrative of the Persian invasions. The barbarian reminds the sea that it had already been yoked in a flaxen fetter (72–4, a reference, of course, to Xerxes' bridge over the Hellespont), and threatens it with a forthcoming punishment: his king will once more stir up the sea and enclose it (76–8). This looks like a prediction of Xerxes' attempt to build a bridge from Attica to Salamis after the battle (Hdt. 8.97). This drowning barbarian is aware that it is his king who has brought him to his death in Greece, but with the servility and respect for hierarchy long stereotypical of Persians in the Greek imagination, he remains loyal and respectful (see 76).

He concludes by execrating the sea, which he calls 'hateful thing of old' (79–80). The ancient hatred was the result of the several famous disasters inflicted upon the Persians' fleets during the wars: the wreck of Mardonius' fleet off Athos, and of course Artemisium, the place closely associated, in contrast, with the brilliant swimming of the Greek diver Skyllis (see below). The curse of the sea is the barbarian's last recorded words; his episode closes with yet another grim description of the drowning process, and yet stops just short of his demise (82–5): 'He spoke in distress from his choking and spat out a grim froth, belching from his mouth the deep-sea brine.' It has been suggested that 'his end is omitted as likely to rouse our pity for the wrong side'.[80] This seems to me unlikely: it is part of Timotheus' mimetic technique to focus serially upon the experiences of individual figures. This episode is followed, as we have seen, by two similar sequences which give direct speech to a chorus of barbarians stranded, awaiting death on the beach, and to a desperate Phrygian begging his adversary to spare his life. Each one of the voices anticipates and laments its owner's impending death; but none of them actually dies in the poem. Timotheus is lacing together a series of visually and aurally colourful vignettes, freezing in his listeners' imaginations the last, miserable minutes of various barbarians' lives, their *Todesangst*.[81] By denial of closure this procedure leaves an even greater psychological impact on his audience. For a listener to Timotheus' *Persians*, the barbarians await death forever.

SWIMMING FOR VICTORY

The poetic image of a barbarian, forever frozen in his drowning moments in Timotheus' classic song, has, of course, a direct antitype in the Greek cultural imagination and in particular its apprehension

---

[80] Edmonds (1927), 317 n. 1.   [81] Keil (1913), 134.

of the major battles of the Persian wars. The gasping, floundering, spewing barbarian is the negative counterpart, the reverse image, the 'Other' of Skyllis the Greek diver (also known as Skyllias or Skyllos), silently gliding deep in the still waters beneath the waves at Artemisium, whose notice in Pausanias was discussed above. That Greek expertise in the water was conceived as an important contributory factor in the archetypal victory over barbarism in the Persian wars is demonstrated beyond question by this memorable figure, first mentioned in Herodotus (8.8). He was a native of the Macedonian town of Scione, and, according to the historian, the most accomplished diver of his day. Originally siding with the Persians, he salvaged treasure for himself and for his masters after the wreck at Pelion. But he deserted to the Greeks and was able to give them invaluable information. Herodotus reports that many anecdotes circulated about Skyllis, including the rumour that he had swum underwater all the way from Aphetae to Artemisium, a distance of approximately ten miles.[82] Herodotus does not believe in this feat, any more than in other, unspecified tall stories (*alla pseudesi ikela*).

Besides' Pausanias' description of the Delian League's dedication to Skyllis at Delphi, there is other testimony to the continuing popularity of his story in the poetry and visual arts of antiquity. Later Greeks delighted in being reminded of this watery hero of the Persian wars.[83] An iambic poem by Aeschrion of Samos, which was addressed to the sea-divinity Glaucus, alleged that he had fallen in love with Hydne (Athen. *Deipn.* 7.29e). Pliny records that an artist named Androbius 'painted Scyllus cutting through the anchor-cables of the Persian fleet' (*NH* 35.139). An epigram by Apollonides in *The Garland of Philip* is dedicated to the diver:

Scyllus, when the long fleet of Xerxes was harassing all Hellas, invented sea-fighting from the depths (*buthiēn heureto naumachiēn*, 2), swimming under Nereus' secret shallows, and cut the ships' moorings from anchor. So Persia, with all her men, slipped landward in silent perishing—Themistocles' first enterprise.[84]

---

[82] H. A. Harris (1972), 112.

[83] Couch (1945–6). This article was written at the close of World War II, and inspired by a United Press despatch on the allegedly astonishing performance of the American forces' underwater demolition teams (UDTs).

[84] Translation taken from Gow and Page (1968), i. 143.

It is of course entirely unimportant whether or not the story had any basis in truth, as was already perceptively remarked as early as 1886.[85] The reasons for thinking the story may be fictitious include Herodotus' scepticism about Skyllis' abilities, the suspicious similarity of his name with 'Scylla', and of his daughter's with both the Homeric word 'daughter-of-the-sea' (*halosudnē*), an epithet of Thetis (*Il.* 20.207, see also *Od.* 4.404), and with the word for 'water' (*hudōr*). What the existence of the Skyllis tradition does confirm, however, is that the Greeks felt a cultural pride in their prowess in the water, and a conviction that it was one of the many features that signified their superiority over non-Greek peoples and enabled them to beat them in sea-battles. This had been demonstrated for all time in the canonical victories over the Persians in the heyday of Greek supremacy at the dawn of the classical period. The same conviction surely underlies the drowning barbarian's histrionic appearance in Timotheus' famously patriotic *Persians*.

Such concepts are culturally transferable and have proved tenacious in European narratives of maritime warfare. The seventeenth-century educationalist Henry Peacham in 1622 reported the following contribution made by Englishmen to the engagements of 1588 with the Spanish Armada:

> Gerrard and Harvey, two gentlemen of our own nation ... in the fight at sea swam in the night-time and pierced with augers or suchlike instruments the side of the Spanish galleons and returned safe back to the fleet.[86]

Peacham was not the only English writer of the seventeenth century to draw the parallel between the defeat of the Spanish Armada and the battle of Salamis: Thomas Rymer, indeed, drew up (albeit with some irony) detailed plans for a tragedy modelled on Aeschylus' *Persians*, but set in the court of King Philip II of Spain, at the time of the defeat of his Armada by Elizabeth I's navy.[87] This patriotic English story about Gerrard and Harvey was in all likelihood inspired by and modelled on the famous ancient story, and served almost identical cultural purposes.

---

[85] Hauvette (1886).
[86] Peacham (1622), 180–1; see the edition by Heltzel (1962), 139–40.
[87] Rymer (1693), on which see Hall and Macintosh (2005), 266.

10

Singing Roles in Tragedy

CLASS ACTS

At the moment that he assumed his role, the ancient actor also began to mediate the dichotomy between the real, material world inhabited by his audience and the fictional world of the play, to preside over imaginative journeys through space and time. But it was not the silent physical presence of the actor so much as his *voice* which provided the indispensable conduit connecting reality and psychic experience. Epictetus, a shrewd observer of theatre, observed at around the turn of the second century AD that the voice was the only part of an actor's 'real' self that remained when he erased his physical presence behind a costume and mask (*Discourses* 1.29.6). Yet material reality could only become fully *transformed* through the production of incorporeal sound from the actor's fleshly body; air physically propelled through the actor's torso, throat and head mutated into language, poetry, ideology, and culture. When the ancient actor opened his mouth, beneath his sculptured, painted mask, and forced the air from his lungs through his larynx, teeth and lips, it was his voice that allowed matter to become mind, art, and emotion, and the carnal, biological body to meet the metaphorical body politic.[1]

When a dramatist designed a tragic role, one of the most important decisions that he needed to make was about the mysterious phenomenon that we call vocality. This decision concerned the type of poetry that the actor would be required to deliver. Some cast members in tragedy sing and some do not. This chapter brings

---

[1] For a suggestive introduction to the considerable body of philosophical work on the voice, especially in literature and theatre, see Durand (1977).

together several of the previous strands of argument in the book by exploring the links connecting the theatrical representation of gender, class, or ethnic difference with histrionic vocal performance. This exploration takes the form of an enquiry into the politics as well as the aesthetics of tragic solo singing. There is all too little external evidence about the cultural or psychological impact made within the dominantly spoken medium of tragedy by actors who burst into lyric, accompanied by the music of the *aulos*. But one invaluable text does address the issue of the social ramifications of tragic solo song:

Why do choruses in tragedy sing neither in the hypodorian nor in the hypophrygian mode? ... both these modes are inappropriate to the chorus, and more suitable to the actors on the stage. For those on stage are imitating heroes, and in the old days only the rulers (*hēgemones*) were heroes, while the rest of the people (*hoi de laoi*), to whom the chorus belong, were ordinary human beings (*anthrōpoi*). ([Aristotle], *Problems* 19.48)

Two features of this *Problem* have previously attracted interest. The first is its conception of the contribution made by choruses to tragedy, for the author proceeds to distinguish the active role of the characters on stage from the relative passivity of the chorus. The other feature, cited by musicologists, is its evidence for the aural effects of the different musical modes.[2] Yet the *Problem* also offers evidence for views of social class in tragedy. It states that 'in the old days' there were social distinctions within tragedy. Moreover, it implicitly acknowledges that those social distinctions were related to musical expression. In tragedy of the old days the *anthrōpoi*, of whom the chorus were a part, were to be distinguished from the rulers (*hēgemones*), and this distinction explains why different kinds of songs are given to each different type of person. This chapter takes a hint from this *Problem*, and thinks about actor's song in tragedy from a perspective conditioned by sensitivity to the social identity of the characters represented as singing.

---

[2] For the text as evidence for the chorus in tragedy see e.g. the comments in Flashar (1967), 625–6, who is surely correct in suggesting that this is the original source of A. W. von Schlegel's influential notion of the chorus as ideal spectator ('ideale Zuschauer'); on the modes see M. L. West (1992*a*), 183–4.

In the earliest surviving tragedy, Aeschylus' *Persians*, the only cast member with a claim to heroic status never speaks a single iambic trimeter. This makes him unique amongst the important characters in the extant remains of the genre. Xerxes and the chorus briefly exchange lyric anapaests (908–30),[3] before he launches the antiphonal dirge which will last until the end of the play. Xerxes' role thus consists exclusively of briefly introducing and then abjectly singing fifteen increasingly wild lyric stanzas with his chorus of elderly Persians. Yet it seems never to have been observed that the voice of the great theatrical King of Persia is only heard performing in a vocal medium quite distinct from speech.

If we travel forwards perhaps a century to what is probably the last extant Greek tragedy to be written, the *Rhesus*, we find another actor dressed up in the mask and clothes of an unnamed Muse.[4] She appears in the theatrical machine with the corpse of her Thracian son, over whom she sings a monodic lament (*Rhesus* 895–903, 906–14). The Muse is an immortal practitioner of the art of singing itself, who once competed, as she tells us, against the bard Thamyris (917–25). She is also the first character to sing a monody in this particular play, and the earliest known immortal with a tragic monody. That immortals in fifth-century tragedy hardly ever sing lyrics is in itself a suggestive expression of classical Athenian theology and ideology—a performed differentiation between gods and mortals.[5] Yet nobody seems to have been interested in the ramifications of this emotional

---

[3] On the thorny issue of the vocal delivery of anapaests, see the following section, 'Vocal Techniques'.

[4] The text of the play offers no support for the identifications of the Muse made by either the author of the first hypothesis (who calls her Calliope), or by Aristophanes of Byzantium, who in the third hypothesis specifies Terpsichore. In his edition, however, Ebener (1966), 114, follows Aristophanes. See also above, Ch. 6, p. 176.

[5] Hera, disguised as a (human) mendicant priestess, may have performed the lyric hexameters, preserved on a papyrus, which have been attributed to both Aeschylus' *Xantriai*, and to his *Semele* or *Hydrophoroi* (Aeschylus fr. 168.16–30 *TgrF*). On the possible connection of the disguise with this startling 'monody' entry see Taplin (1977), 427. Dionysus in *Bacchae* (also disguised as a mortal) delivers a few lyric utterances in the 'earthquake' amoibaion with the chorus following the second stasimon (between 576 and 603). It is intriguing that both Polyphemus and Silenus, who are immortals of a kind, can sing lyric metres in satyr drama (*Cycl.* 503–10, Aeschylus' *Dictyulci* fr. 47a.799–820 *TgrF*); see also n. 74 below on Argus in Sophocles' *Inachus*.

singing theophany of the Muse in *Rhesus*.[6] Still less thought has been given to its implications for the development of the performative dimension of tragedy in the fourth century.[7]

Ancient Greek music, however, has exerted a fascination. Attention has been paid to music as a topic of discussion in ancient authors, including the tragedians.[8] Studies and performances of ancient Greek music enjoyed a vogue in the late nineteenth to early twentieth centuries,[9] and reconstructions can now be purchased on CD.[10] In 1933 Friedrich Marx published an article on Greek tragic music in which he argued, among other things, that a relic of its music is to be heard in the *Volga Boat Song*.[11] In the 1951 MGM movie *Quo Vadis*, directed by Mervyn LeRoy, the composer was Miklós Rózsa, an historian of music interested in recreating the authentic melodies of antiquity. He persuaded Peter Ustinov (Nero) to perform the 'Song of Seikilos', a dirge which was inscribed, with musical notation, on a stele in Caria of the first century AD.[12]

---

[6] In his influential book *The Authenticity of the Rhesus of Euripides* (1964), William Ritchie needed to minimize the extraordinary nature of this scene, because he was arguing that the tragedy was an authentic work of Euripides. But even he conceded that the monody was unique according to the categories of position in the drama and physical elevation of the performer: 'The monody of *Rhesus* is unique in its position in the drama. In no other surviving tragedy do we find a monody in the exodos and in the mouth of a *deus ex machina*' (p. 340).

[7] Certainly by the 2nd cent. BC the role of the god Dionysus in *Bacchae* could be realized as a sung *aisma*, with kithara accompaniment, by the star performer Satyrus of Samos: Dittenberger (1960), no. 648B. See Gentili (1979), 27–8; Eitrem, Amundsen, and Winnington-Ingram (1955), 27. There is little on actor's song during the classical period in the study of Greek actors by Ghiron-Bistagne (1976); see now E. Hall (2002*a*).

[8] See e.g. Moutsopoulos (1962).

[9] For bibliography see e.g. Stumpf (1896), 49 n. 1. In his edition of Aristoxenus, Henry Macran records with touching candour the disappointment felt at an experimental comparison of foreign and ancient Greek music organised at Trinity College, Dublin: 'It was the unanimous verdict... that...the Greek hymn stood quite alone in its absolute lack of meaning and its unredeemed ugliness' (Macran (1912), 2).

[10] A recent book on Greek music optimistically boasts a 'Discography' as well as a 'bibliography': Anderson (1994), 239.

[11] F. Marx (1933).

[12] See Palmer (1975), 38–40. For a transcription of this surviving four-line example of ancient Greek music, see M. L. West (1992*a*), 301–2. It was fortunate for *Ben-Hur* (1959) that Rózsa threatened to resign when instructed to insert the tune of *Oh come, all ye faithful* into the part of his (Oscar-winning) score that accompanied the nativity scene.

The parodos of Aeschylus' *Persians* was performed (to music written by M. L. West) at the Triennial Meeting of the Greek and Roman Societies in Oxford in August 1995, thus definitively proving the superiority of comedy over tragedy. Yet this perennial curiosity about ancient Greek music has not been accompanied by the level of interest in the form of vocal delivery of tragic poetry which, since the publication of Taplin's *The Stagecraft of Aeschylus* (1977), has attended upon the *visual* dimensions of the genre.

An obscure ancient grammarian named Diomedes said that we should sing Greek lyric poetry when we read it, even if we do not know or cannot remember the tune.[13] It is not clear how this should be done, beyond raising the pitch of our voice on accented syllables.[14] But Diomedes' recommendation suggests that the difference between sung and spoken verse was so powerfully perceived that even an invented melody would help the reader to recover the experience of a sung lyric poem. Yet a modern student coming to Greek tragedy would not easily be able to practise the imaginative reading Diomedes prescribes. She probably knows that choral odes were sung. She may also know that some parts of some actors' roles were sung. But unless she takes a course in advanced Greek metre she will not be able to decide which those sung bits are. Even then she will be so confused by the terminology of choriambic anaklasis and the resolved lyric prokeleusmatic that she will lose sight of the performance wood for the forest of metrical trees. Translations rarely indicate which sections were sung, and Greek texts, while engaging in complex colometry, fail to convey the most crucial information from a performative perspective, that is, which bits were sung to musical accompaniment. Thus most individuals coming to Greek tragedy are deprived of one of the most important hermeneutic tools in deciphering its expressive logic: it is inconceivable that a similar state of ignorance would be allowed to apply to the texts of, say, William Shakespeare.[15]

---

[13] *dei meta melous anagignōskein*: Hilgard (1991), 21.19–21. Diomedes' advice appears in his commentary on a passage in Dionysius of Thrace's *Ars Grammatica* where it is recommended that lyrics be read *emmelōs*, and laments in an abandoned and dirgelike manner: Uhlig (1983), p. 6, para. 2.8–11.

[14] So suggests Lionel Pearson in his edition of Aristoxenus (1990), p.xlix.

[15] I am not, of course, suggesting that scholars have dismissed the importance of understanding actor's song in tragedy. But it is unarguable that in the English- and

Already in the fifth century actor's song was regarded as worthy of comment. In Aristophanes' *Wasps* Philocleon leans out of a window to perform a burlesque of a tragic song (316–33), perhaps originally delivered by Danae in a tragedy where she was shut up in her tower.[16] Euripides' songs, both monodic and choral, made a huge impact.[17] In *Thesmophorizausae* Euripides' in-law parodies Andromeda's monody in her Euripidean name-play (1015–55), and the instant popularity of *Andromeda* may partly have been caused by brilliant acting in the tragic scene where Echo replicated Andromeda's singing.[18] Moreover, in *Frogs* songs are one of the only two features of tragedy (the other is the prologue) to be examined at length. On Dionysus' invitation Euripides promises to show that Aeschylus was a repetitive song-writer (*melopoion*, 1249–50). Subsequently, in Aeschylus' parody of Euripides' music (see below), the song 'from the stage' (*apo skēnēs*), or 'actor's song', is subjected to thorough analysis.

When a dimension of tragedy has been neglected by scholars, it usually transpires that Aristotle was not interested in it, either. Tragic song is no exception. Aristotle's theoretical writings on both poetry and rhetoric articulate a prejudice against delivery (*hupokrisis*) and the performative dimensions of both theatrical and oratorical texts.[19] Yet even Aristotle regards song-writing as a more important enhancement of tragedy than spectacle (*Poet.* 6.1450b 15–16). Aristotle, furthermore, despite his attempts in the *Poetics* to divest tragedy of its ideological function and performative dimension,[20] nevertheless drops a clue about the ideological ramifications of song. This clue attests as clearly as the later *Problem* quoted at the outset to a

French-speaking scholarly worlds, at least, infinitely more has been published on, say, the *agōn*.

[16] See Rau (1967), 150–2; MacDowell (1971), 176.

[17] Testimony abounds to the popularity of Euripidean songs (see Michaelides (1978), 117–19), although it is often not clear whether choral odes or actors' songs (or both) are indicated. See, for example, Plutarch's report that some Athenians in Sicily saved themselves after the disaster at Syracuse in 413 BC by singing some songs (*melē*) by this poet (*Vit. Nic.* 29); in Axionicus' *Phileuripides*, fr. 3 K–A, a character speaks about people who hated all but Euripidean lyrics. In Strattis fr. 1.1 K–A (from *Anthroporestes*) the speaker seems to say that he doesn't care about the songs (*melē*) of any poets except Euripides, although the point of comparison is not clear.

[18] See Gilula (1996), 163–4.

[19] See Ch. 12, pp. 356–9.

[20] See Taplin (1977), 24–6; E. Hall (1996*b*).

perception that choice of spoken versus sung self-expression for represented characters in performed *mousikē* was intertwined with perceptions of social roles.

The clue is in ch. 15, which offers two examples of inappropriateness in characterization. The first is Odysseus's lament (*thrēnos*) in the *Scylla*, probably the dithyramb by Timotheus to which Aristotle later refers in connection with *aulos*-playing.[21] We are not told why Odysseus' lament was inappropriate, but the example is paired with that of 'Melanippe's speech' (*rhēsis*). This almost certainly means Melanippe's famous (iambic spoken) repudiation of misogynist rhetoric in Euripides' *Melanippe Desmōtis* (fr. 494 *TgrF*), 'Men's criticism of women is worthless twanging of a bowstring and evil talk', etc.[22] Odysseus' sung lament, and Melanippe's spoken diatribe, are thus 'inappropriate' when judged by a criterion implicated in the discourse of gender and its representations. But was Odysseus' *thrēnos* inappropriate because he was a man, or because he was a high-status hero, or a Greek, or all of these?

Aeschylus' Xerxes is a man with a *thrēnos* if ever there was one: the implications of his speechlessness for the tragic encrypting of Persia through performative mode have not penetrated the scholarly consciousness. *Why* does he not speak? (his words are kept in *oratio obliqua* in the messenger speeches, too).[23] Is it because he is *a* barbarian, or rather because as King of Persia and erstwhile invader of Hellas he is *The* Barbarian? Is it because of the ritual orientation of his scene, which is a funerary *kommos*, albeit with no corpses? Given the ubiquitous association of funerary lamentation with women in Greek thought, is it a formal strategy which effeminises him through genre, vocal delivery and choice of metre? Is it because he is emotionally disturbed, like Polymestor, another intemperate barbarian male given a wild song in Euripides' *Hecuba*? Could Xerxes have sung if he were a slave? In the *Life of Sophocles* (6) it is said that the tragedian took account of his actors' abilities when composing his tragedies: does Xerxes' unusual role suggest the availability of a

---

[21] *Poet.* 15.1454ᵃ29–30 and 26.1461ᵇ29–32 = *PMG* fr. 793. On *Scylla* in relation to other songs by Timotheus, see also Ch. 9, p. 282.

[22] Translation from Lefkowitz and Fant (1992), 14.

[23] e.g. 365–71, 469–70. See E. Hall (1996*a*), 363.

performer with a remarkable singing voice,[24] a factor which may have been involved in the creation of the elaborate arias in Euripides' *Orestes*?[25] It has even been suggested that the relative dearth of actors' lyrics in Euripides' *Bacchae* and *IA* is a result of these plays' supposed composition in Macedonia, where there might have been a lack of operatic talent.[26]

Although a fine Oxford doctoral thesis on Euripidean monody was written by Jane Beverley,[27] such questions have hitherto been insufficiently aired. There are several reasons for the oversight. The first is the complexity of the terminology: it is rarely possible to distinguish with confidence between a 'kommos', an 'amoibaion' and a 'monody with interruptions', even if we could be sure that the ancients really cared about such definitions.[28] Another problem is the ambiguity of the evidence about actor's song (to be reviewed briefly in the next section), especially concerning so-called 'recitative' performance of metres neither iambic nor lyric. This confusion was already apparent in the Renaissance and was creatively implicated in the birth of European opera: the founding fathers in Italy toward the end of the sixteenth century imagined all of Greek tragedy to have been sung.[29]

Yet the most important explanation for the neglect of the socio-aesthetic ramifications of tragic song is to be sought, rather, in the history of classical scholarship itself. During the twentieth century there was an estrangement between formalist analysis of tragedy and anthropologically informed studies promoting the erasure of the

---

[24] See Pintacuda (1978), 31. On the evidence that actors were selected for the power of their voices see Hunningher (1956), 303–38.

[25] See M. L. West (1987*a*), 38; E. Hall (1989), 119, 210; Damen (1990), 141–2.

[26] A. S. Owen (1936), 153. Owen further develops his theory that musical roles were composed according to an actor's talent at singing: he suggests, for example, that when a role only uses one lyrical metre (e.g. Creon's dochmiacs in *Antigone*), it could be entrusted 'to an actor with only limited musical ability' (p. 150).

[27] The contents of this paper were first delivered as 'Mad, sad, and foreign voices: why characters sing in Greek tragedy' at an interdisciplinary theatre seminar run by Patricia Fann at St Cross College, Oxford, in May 1990. I subsequently read Jane Beverley's excellent chapters on *Ion* and *Phoenissae* in her Oxford D.Phil. dissertation (1997), and heard her discussion of Theseus in *Hippolytus*. I take confidence from the fact that we came quite independently to similar conclusions.

[28] See Barner (1971), 277–9.

[29] See E. Hall (2002*b*), 430–1.

distinction between what used to be called 'art' and 'reality'. The German-speaking philological tradition long produced important books about the formal and metrical elements of tragedy; they have titles like *Monolog und Selbstgresprach: Untersuchungen zur Formgeschichte der griechischen Tragödie*, or *Stasimon: Untersuchung zu Form und Gehalt der griechischen Tragödie*, or (more recently) *Die Bauformen der griechischen Tragödie*.[30] The French and Americans (at least since the 1960s), on the other hand, have written about gender, polis group identity, democracy, myth, and the interpenetration of cultural artefacts such as plays and vase-paintings with the more overtly civic discourses.[31] In Britain until extremely recently scholars at Oxford largely read the analytical Germans, while those at Cambridge preferred the synthetic French.[32] Tragic studies would benefit from a flirtation between the metrical, analytical school and the society-oriented synthetic approach, especially if it resulted in offspring recognizing that both form itself, and the codes by which tragedians selected form, are ideologically and politically determined and conditioned.[33]

VOCAL TECHNIQUES

Attempts to reconstruct the vocal delivery of a classical Greek tragic actor when singing his lyrics are no longer fashionable. Gone are the days when scholars compared the effect of Greek tragic anapaests with that of the recitative in Handel's operas or the overtures to Schumann's *Manfred* and Beethoven's *Egmont*;[34] nobody today would (in print) ask whether Greek tragic song more closely

[30] Schadewaldt (1926), Kranz (1933), and Jens (1971) respectively.

[31] Although three of the few discussions of actor's song in tragedy are in nineteenth-century French: Gevaert (1875–81), ii. 501–62; Décharme (1893), 522–40; Masqueray (1895).

[32] The book in which the approach to tragic song is most nearly consonant with this proposal is actually in Italian: Pintacuda (1978).

[33] On the ideological implications of the trilogic form see Peter Rose (1992), 185–97. The classic synthesis of the position developed in Marxism and Critical Theory, that literary form is ideologically conditioned, remains Jameson (1971).

[34] Greenwood (1953), 138–9; Stumpf (1896), 73.

resembled the declamatory 'ranting' of the nineteenth-century actor or the Catholic priest intoning the liturgy; it would be a fruitless diversion to enquire, with Kathleen Schlesinger's book on the *aulos*, 'Would the songs sung by a Greek tragic chorus remind us of the choir of St. Paul's or of the peasant in the uplands of Andalusia?'[35] There is no way to achieve an 'archaeology of ears' and scrape away the barnacles of our culturally determined emotional and aesthetic responses in order to replace them with those of an ancient audience.[36]

It is, however, certain that the voice of the ancient actor needed to be loud. It has even been suggested that the convention of the mask survived because it allowed the singer to concentrate on the production of sound at the expense of facial expression.[37] A popular ancient anecdote demonstrated the primitivism of barbarians by reporting some Spanish natives' terrified reaction to their first ever experience of a tragic actor's huge singing voice; in one source the actor, an unnamed itinerant *tragōidos* of Nero's time, is said to have selected a song from Euripides' *Andromeda*.[38] There is also evidence that the training of an actor's voice was severe ([Aristot.] *Probl.* 11.22): Pollux reports that the comic actor Hermon, a contemporary of Aristophanes, once arrived late at the theatre because he had been doing his vocal exercises (*Onomastikon* 4.88).[39] Yet it is impossible now to recover the tension of the vocal chords, the control of the air supply, and the quality of the noise emitted by ancient tragic actors. Allegations that they used the bass register, rather than the higher pitch of the tenor, are insubstantiable.[40] Although Euripides tells his in-law to speak in a convincingly feminine way at the Thesmophoria (*tōi phthegmati | gunaikieis eu kai pithanōs, Thesm.* 267–8), we do not

---

[35] Helmholtz (1885), 238; Schlesinger (1959), p.xvii.

[36] For a chastening discussion of the ease with which modern Western-centred aesthetic and artistic concepts and judgements can creep into the study of the music of other cultures see the ethnomusicologist Alan Merriam (1964), ch. 13, 259–76.

[37] Hunningher (1956), 326–8.

[38] Eunapius fr. 54, in Dindorf (1880–1), i. 246–8. There is another version in Philostratus, *Vita Ap.* 5.9. Lucian, *How to Write History*, 1, locates the story in Abdera. Here the actor Archelaus' performance of *Andromeda* caused an epidemic whose symptoms included sweats, fever, nosebleeds, and crazed singing of monodies from this tragedy!

[39] See Hunningher (1956), 324, 329.

[40] e.g. Gevaert and Vollgraff (1901–3), ii. 204–5.

even know for certain whether classical Greek actors sang in a style comparable with what we call 'falsetto' when they performed lyrics in female and juvenile roles,[41] let alone whether they distinguished the voices of young virgin girls from those of mature women.[42]

Ancient Greek's clear distinction between long and short syllables even makes it probable that singing and speaking were not so widely separated from one another as in most modern European languages.[43] Moreover, in later antiquity even iambic speeches could be performed to music. By the third century the performance of drama had changed significantly, and the movement seems to have been inexorably toward increasing the amount of song. Fourth-century sources already attest to the emergence of professional actors like Neoptolemus and Theodorus, who went on tour as distinguished protagonists, stagers of revivals, and virtuoso performers (Theodorus, for example, was a specialist in female roles).[44] Hellenistic theatre practice increasingly focused on the performance of individual tragic speeches, scenes, and arias, often set to new music by specialist *tragōidoi*. Such actors are attested, for example, by the inscription of the Delphic *Soteria* regarding the make-up of theatrical companies in the first fifty years of the third century BC. These singing *tragōidoi* offered virtuoso performances (*epideixeis* or *akroaseis*), accompanied by cithara or aulos, of both lyric and dramatic texts. Several papyri containing the songs sung at such recitals, with musical notation, have been preserved. These can tell us some interesting things about the types of melodic line, musical intervals,

---

[41] See Pintacuda (1978), 31. The ancients did discuss the phenomenon of the breaking adolescent male voice: the Hippocratic *Coän Prognoses* 1.321 says it happened in a boy's thirteenth year. It was thought standard for boys and men to sing with the voices an octave apart ([Aristot.] *Probl.* 19.39).

[42] Ancient medical texts attest to a belief that women's voices became lower in pitch when they lost their virginity: see Hanson and Armstrong (1986). Some ancient actors and chorusmen avoided sexual intercourse and ejaculation, or practised penile ligature or infibulation, in order to preserve the tessitura and quality of their voices: see further E. Hall (2002a), 23–4. In much more recent times it has sometimes been asserted that larynx size is related to sexual activity (so that prostitutes are supposed to speak in low voices), and promiscuity to endanger the singing careers of sopranos and tenors: see Ellis (1929), 101–2; Baron (1986), 73–4.

[43] See the 'Epilogue—Speech and Song', in Monro (1984), 113–26; L. Pearson (1990), p.xxix.

[44] Dem. 19.246. See Dihle (1981), 29–31; Easterling (1999).

and ornamentation in the delivery of which such *tragōidoi* were specialists.[45] By the Roman imperial period Lucian complains that tragic actors of his day chant iambic trimeters and sing even messenger speeches (*De Salt.* 27, see also Suetonius, *Nero* 46). But mercifully we can be fairly sure that an iambic trimeter still meant spoken enunciation in democratic Athenian tragedy.[46]

In Aristotle's *Poetics* the philosopher claims that iambics were substituted for trochaic tetrameters in tragedy after dialogue had been introduced, because the iambic is the metre most suited to speech (*malista . . . lektikon*); he adds that we most usually drop into iambics in our conversation with one another, whereas we seldom talk in hexameters (4.1449a19–28). In the *Rhetoric* (3.1408b24–6) the same perception is articulated in a manner which even brings social class into the picture: 'Iambic speech is the very rhythm of the masses (*hē lexis hē tōn pollōn*), which is why, of all metres, people in conversation speak iambics'. On the other hand, sounding completely natural when speaking iambic trimeters was a skilled accomplishment. Aristotle says that Theodorus' ability to do so distinguished him from other actors, and that it was only possible after Euripides had composed iambics consisting of everyday vocabulary (*Rhet.* 3.1404b18–25). Aristoxenus, the musicologist writing in the late fourth century, has a clear criterion for distinguishing speech from song. He held that speech was continuous, whereas song moved in discrete intervals. This theory, according to the arithmetician Nicomachus five hundred years later, was first originated by the Pythagoreans (*Encheiridion harmonikēs*, p. 4); Nicomachus adds that if the notes and intervals of the speaking voice are allowed to become separate and distinct, the form of utterance turns into singing.

Aristoxenus' stipulation of the essential nature of the speech/song dichotomy is suggestive for tragedy precisely because he brings emotion into the equation. Movement between the high and the low positions of the voice happens both when we speak and when we sing, but the movement is not of the same kind:

[45] See Sifakis (1967), 75–9, 156–65; Gentili (1979), 22–7; more recent references and bibliography in E. Hall (2002*a*), 18–21.

[46] There is one late piece of evidence that iambic trimeters could be sung already in the classical period. The second sophistic text *On Music* attributed to Plutarch (1140f–41a) claims that the tragedians 'took over' from Archilochus the practice of accompanying some of their iambics with music, and even singing some of them.

continuous motion we call the motion of speech, as in speaking the voice moves without ever seeming to come to a standstill...Hence in ordinary conversation we avoid bringing the voice to a standstill, unless occasionally forced *by strong feeling* (*dia pathos*) to resort to such a motion; whereas in singing we act in precisely the opposite way, avoiding continuous motion and making the voice become, as far as possible, absolutely stationary. The more we succeed in rendering each of our voice-utterances one, stationary, and identical, the more correct does the singing appear to the ear.[47]   (*El. Harm.* 1.9–10)

This distinction may illuminate the testimony that jurors in Athenian courts complained that men who delivered defence speeches poorly were guilty of 'singing' them (*aidein*, Aristophanes fr. 101 K–A): perhaps strong feeling made defendants lose the 'continuous motion' of speech and resort to the songlike 'stationary' intonation which we would call 'whining'.[48]

Besides iambics, lyrics, and anapaests, other types of genre and metre made occasional appearances. Sophocles' biographical tradition claims that he sang himself in his *Thamyris*, on account of which he was portrayed playing the lyre in the Painted Stoa (*Vita* 5, Sophocles T Ha). A fragment of *Thamyris* consisting of two dactylic lines with heroic content show that hexameters were performed (fr. 242 *TgrF*). The mythical lyre-player Amphion sang in similar vein in Euripides' *Antiope* by accompanying his own hexameter monody (fr. 182a *TgrF*),[49] and the numerous other plays where mythical bards took roles suggest that citharodic hexameter performances were more familiar features in tragedy than our extant remains imply.[50] Another atypical song is constituted by Andromache's

---

[47] Translated by Macran (1912). On Aristoxenus see also Ch. 9, p. 272 n. 46, and the excellent recent discussion of his important place in the development of Greek musical theory, by Meriani (2003).

[48] This might also explain why, according to the MSS of Aristophanes' *Clouds*, Strepsiades, who asked his son to speak (*lexai*) some Aeschylus, uses the verb *aidein* of the Euripidean rhesis from *Aeolus* which Pheidippides actually performed (1371). Perhaps Strepsiades wants to characterise his son's delivery as whining. Dover (1968), 255, may thus be losing the point of the joke in emending away the verb 'sang' here on precisely the ground that in Greek you do not normally 'sing' a 'speech'.

[49] Webster (1970), 168.

[50] Orpheus was a central character in Aeschylus' lost *Bassarids*; Aeschylus as well as Sophocles composed a play named *Thamyris* dramatizing the singing competition between this bard and the muses; Euripides' *Hypsipyle* portrayed the citharode

threnodic elegiacs in Euripides' *Andromache* (103–116), a metre whose uniqueness to extant tragedy led it to form part of the evidence Page used for his case that the play's first production was in Argos.[51]

Besides tragic portions that were almost certainly spoken (i.e. iambic trimeters) and those which were sung (lyric metres), there is the probability of a distinct third form of delivery. This mode of delivery is called 'speaking to musical accompaniment', 'chanting', 'intoning', 'reciting', 'recitative', or even 'singing', depending on which book you happen to be reading. Although there is some suggestion that trochaic tetrameters fell into this category, the metrical unit with which this type of delivery is most commonly associated is the anapaest (basically,$\smile\smile-$). The anapaest was thought to be a descendant of the Spartan military marching songs (*embatēria*) of poets such as Tyrtaeus (e.g. *PMG* 856.6, 857).[52] It was associated with processions and a synchronised military pace,[53] although Parker has warned against subsuming all 'recitative' anapaests in tragedy under the label 'marching anapaests'.[54] It is conventional to draw a distinction between so-called 'marching' or 'recitative' anapaests and 'melic' anapaests (which are more likely to have been fully 'sung'). But this distinction is in practice often wobbly: it is based on the *extent* of Doricism and, more importantly, resolution, so that some passages of allegedly sung anapaests in tragedy are 'scarcely distinguishable rhythmically from recitative'.[55] The distinction certainly needs sociological investigation, since high status is likely to be a prerequisite of more 'lyric' anapaests,[56] but the primary focus of this chapter is actors' lyrics.

Euneus, who founded an Athenian clan of musicians; his *Antiope* also featured a full-scale debate between lyre-playing Amphion and his brother Zethus about the benefits which poets confer on a community (see above and P. Wilson (1999–2000)). On the use of the cithara in tragedy see also Koller (1963), 165–73.

[51] See further note 117 below.

[52] Cole (1988), 169 (see also 117,118), goes so far as to describe anapaestic systems as 'part of the Doric heritage of tragedy'.

[53] See Raven (1968), 56–61; M. L. West (1987*b*), 29, 48–9.

[54] L. P. E. Parker (1997), 56–7.

[55] Ibid. 57.

[56] Webster (1970), 117, suggests that 'melic' anapaests were originally processional, like 'marching' anapaests, but that their special features were a result of their performance specifically at funerals.

The anapaest was clearly conceived in a different way from lyrics in tragedy, for the significant reason that slaves like the nurses in *Medea* and *Hippolytus* are given (recitative) anapaests with some regularity, whereas with two extraordinary exceptions low-status characters never sing lyrics (see below, pp. 304–8). On the other hand, there are reasons to believe that all anapaests in tragedy were accompanied by the *aulos* and that their delivery was nearer to song than to speech. A scholion on Aristophanes' *Wasps* 582 states that in tragic *exodoi* the aulete used to play the *auloi* while leading the members of the chorus in procession.[57] Since anapaests (unlike iambics) followed a musical line different from the natural pitch of the tonal Greek language,[58] their delivery cannot have sounded identical to ordinary speech. They were therefore probably performed in a manner which can legitimately be denoted by the verbs 'intone' or 'recite'.

There is a frustrating notice in the Byzantine treatise *On Tragedy* dating from around AD 1300, probably to be attributed to Michael Psellos, and containing information in part deriving from Hellenistic sources.[59] It describes a mode of utterance in tragedy different from either song or recitative (par. 9): 'There are some other things classified along with tragic music and metre, such as ... *anaboēma* ('crying aloud'?) ... *anaboēma* is very nearly like singing but something between song and *katalogē*'. Although the author specifies a form of musical delivery close to singing called *anaboēma*, he creates confusion by distinguishing it from the utterance called *katalogē*, which is not necessarily musical. The picture is further complicated by the use in the classical period of the verb *katalegein* to designate the type of delivery which should probably be associated with anapaests, although the text which supports this view is a comment on the effect created by *aulos* accompaniment of tetrameters. In Xenophon's *Symposium* 6.3 Hermogenes offers to converse with Socrates to *aulos* music, 'just like Nikostratos the actor *katelegen*

---

[57] That in comedy anapaests (at least in parabaseis) were accompanied by the *aulos* is suggested by a scholion on Aristophanes' *Birds* 682.

[58] Pötscher (1959).

[59] It is surprising, for example, that the author seems to know something about the arcane genre of satyr drama, for he says that it allowed of more (presumably *extra metrum*) interjected shouts (*epiphthegmata*) than did tragedy: see Browning's edition (1963), 79.

tetrameters to the *auloí*. Thus it is safest to assume that *kataloge*
means a form of utterance more marked and less 'smooth' than
speech, more estranged from natural conversation, but not necessarily approaching song.[60]

Suggestive testimony occurs in the pseudo-Aristotelian *Problem*
19.6, which says that it is difference—'unlikeness'—of delivery which
creates an emotional effect. The *Problem* asks why the form of
delivery called *parakataloge*, when in (or 'inserted into') the songs,
is tragic:

> Is it because of the contrast involved (*dia tēn anōmalian*)? Contrast is
> emotive in situations of great misfortune or grief; regularity (*to homales*)
> is less conducive to lamentation.

The meaning of *parakataloge* here is disputed. Is it 'intoned recitative,
to instrumental accompaniment'? Does it refer to the anapaestic
introductions which often precede lyrics (e.g. those introducing Xerxes' *kommos*)?[61] Or is it a reference to the insertion of a different kind
of metrical form and/or vocal delivery into a song *after* its commence-
ment? A further possibility is that the 'anomaly' is not between types
of metre and vocal delivery, but signifies the discrepancy between the
music of the accompanying *aulos*, which raises the expectation of
sung delivery, and the actual recitation or spoken utterance in(serted
into) the song.[62] But this problematic *Problem* does make it plain that
the ancients were sensitive to the differences between lyric song and
other types of vocal delivery, and that the dissimilarity was
perceived to create the emotional effects appropriate to tragedy.
'Unlikeness', lack of uniformity in noise/and or metre, in itself performed a function generative of tragic emotion and meaning.

To summarize: iambic trimeters were originally spoken and
sounded closer to ordinary speech than other metres; lyric song
sounded less smooth and continuous than speech; lyrics sounded

---

[60] This was the conclusion reached by Pickard-Cambridge (1988), 156–64. See
also Christ (1875), 163, 166 (which remains an impressive collection of evidence).

[61] Other examples in L. P. E Parker (1997), 57.

[62] So Flashar (1967), 602: the *anōmalia* 'bestand in dem Widerstreit von spra-
chlicher Deklamation und musikalischer Begleitung'. It would help if we knew more
about the musical theorist Damon's principle of 'similarity' (*homoiotēs*), on which see
W. D. Anderson (1966), 40.

emotional; the *contrast* between tragic song and an inexactly understood but different third type of tragic vocal delivery (distinct from
both lyric song and from unaccompanied speech) was in itself
emotionally effective. So without getting bogged down in the recitative controversy, or in the distinctions between species of lyric verse,
let us instead focus on the suggestive notion of emotive contrast, and
take the 'unlikeness' of lyric song to other types of delivery as the
benchmark for a sociological review of tragic actors' song.

SONG AND STATUS

The metrician Paul Maas once formulated a principle in relation to
Greek tragedy:

Characters of lower status (except the Phrygian in *Orestes*) have no sung
verses, but they do have anapaests, like the nurse in *Hippolytus*, or hexameters, like the old man in the *Trachiniae*.[63]

Characters of low social status in Greek tragedy, said Maas, do not
sing lyrics. In tragedy, in other words, song is a performed marker of
high social status. 'Status' hides inexactitude: nearly everyone who
sings tragic lyrics is royal. From Aeschylus' Xerxes, Cassandra, Electra, and Orestes, through Sophocles' Electra, Heracles, and Antigone,
through to Euripides' Phaedra, Helen, Creusa, and Ion, it is almost
always a marker of royalty inherited by blood. It signifies privilege
both by birth status and by emotional role within the play. A conceptual boundary thus existed between tragic roles which could
involve singing and those which could accommodate anapaests but
not lyrics. An informative passage is the exchange between the chorus
and Rhesus' charioteer in the *Rhesus*. After Rhesus' murder, the
charioteer arrives to announce it, himself badly wounded, and
performs a passionate exchange (728–53). Yet as charioteer and

---

[63] 'Personen niederen Standes (ausgenommen den Phryger in Orestes) erhalten
keine Singverse, wohl aber Anapäste, wie die Amme in Hippolytos, oder Hexameter,
wie der Alte in den Trachinierinnen'. Maas (1929), para. 76, p. 20, trans. Lloyd-Jones
(1962). Maas's principle was much more recently brought to the notice of a wide
English-speaking audience by Lloyd-Jones's translation of this book.

underling, he is given anapaests for the purpose where a high-status character who had been injured and bereaved would typically have been given lyrics.[64]

Lyric metres are a marker of birth status: slaves in Greek tragedy can sing—indeed they sing often—provided that they were freeborn. One of the pervasive vaguenesses about slaves in tragedy is implicit in Maas' formulation: he would undoubtedly say that slaves cannot sing. It is true that slaves by birth (with one possible major exception, the Phrygian eunuch in Euripides' *Orestes*) do not get given lyrics. It would astonish us all if a tragedy were to turn up in which even an important servant like Cilissa in *Choephoroe*, the Corinthian shepherd in *OT*, or the *paidagōgos* in *Ion* or in either *Electra* sang lyrics, let alone an insignificant attendant.[65] But in the frequent tragic situation where the once free have been enslaved (for example, Hecuba and Andromache in both *Hecuba* and *Troades*, Ion, and Hypsipyle), their aristocratic birth ensures that they retain the 'privilege' of lyric self-expression into their life of servitude. Indeed, Hypsipyle explicitly contrasts the menial song she sings to the baby Opheltes with the songs she once sang as mistress of her house on Lemnos.[66] Thus the conventions surrounding tragic song only respect what Aristotle's *Politics* book 1 would define as 'natural' class boundaries imposed at birth.

In a scene in Aristophanes' *Frogs* discussed above in Chapter 6 (pp. 173–4), Euripides' Muse is summoned onto the stage (1305–7). Her (current) social status is not high, which makes this personification of Euripidean lyric consonant with *Frogs*' portrayal of Euripides as a poet of unheroic individuals (959), colloquial speech (978–9), and 'democratized' tragedy in which women and slaves speak as

[64] An undated tragic performance attested by a papyrus with musical annotation shows that in later antiquity a character whose status as underling is confirmed by their use of the vocative *despoti* could certainly sing an emotional speech to their mistress: see Eitrem, Amundsen, and Winnington-Ingram (1955), 10. But the low-status singer, interestingly, is still using anapaests.

[65] A lonely exception is Østerud (1970), who seems unaware of Maas's hypothesis, and perversely argues that these lyric iambics are more suited to the character of the nurse in *Hippolytus* than to Phaedra.

[66] Fr. I ii 9–16, in Cockle (1987), 59 = fr 752f.9–14 *TgrF*. On Hypsipyle's song for Opheltes see also Wærn (1960), 6–7, who regards it as a song to *entertain* awake children rather than a lullaby; the intimacy of the scene is well brought out by Pache (2004), 100–2.

much as 'the master of the house' (949–52).[67] From line 1331 onwards Aeschylus sings in the manner he explicitly ascribes to Euripides' monodies (*ton tōn monōidiōn diexelthein tropon*, 1330), while adopting a female persona that Dover says must be, like the unpersonable Muse, 'of low social status':[68] his evidence is that she sings of going to the market to sell flax (1350–1). Yet she is certainly no household slave: she has her own attendants (*amphipoloi*), whom she instructs to light her lamps and fetch her water (1338). This parody of a Euripidean singing character has unheroic, domestic concerns and may have to work herself. But there is no evidence that she contravenes Maas' principle. Like Euripides' Electra in *Electra*,[69] Hypsipyle,[70] and Ion, she may have fallen on hard times and is singing while she works or in an impoverished context. But there is no evidence that she is 'of low social status' by birth.

So the free/unfree class boundary is respected even in Aristophanes' parody of solo actors' singing in Euripides' controversial 'democratized' tragedy. Thus one of the ways in which a tragic playwright evoked the social universe instantiated in his plays was by implementing a taboo on slaves by birth breaking into lyric metres. This tragic phenomenon was presumably not a reflection of the realities of Athenian life. There is no reason to suppose that lyric music was not sung in classical Athens as often by slaves as by the free; indeed, there is some evidence that in elitist quarters singing was regarded as a banausic activity unfit for the *eleutheros*. Aristotle, at any rate, argued that the Spartans had got it right (*Politics* 8.1339^{a}41–^{b}10): they acquire good taste and the art of judgement by listening to others. Free men, rather than learning to perform themselves, might instead

[67] On this passage see E. Hall (1997*b*).
[68] Dover (1968), 358. On the Muse of Euripides see further Ch. 6, p. 173.
[69] The audience will already have this iconoclastic play in mind, since Aeschylus has quoted it in the foregoing parody of Euripidean choral lyric (Eur. *El.* 435–7 = *Frogs* 1317–18).
[70] The Muse of Euripides is given potsherds to play (*ostrakois*, 1305), almost certainly in direct parody of the castanets or rattle (*krotala*) Hypsipyle had played to the baby Opheltes as she sang to him in Euripides' *Hypsipyle* fr. 752f.9 *TgrF* (see note 50 above). See also the quotation of *Hypsipyle* (fr. 752 *TgrF*) at *Frogs* 1211–13. Since *Hypsipyle* was performed between 412 and 407 (*Σ* Ar. *Ran.* 53 says it was performed with *Phoenissae* and *Antiope*), it would have been relatively fresh in the mind of any regular theatre-goer at Athens in 405 BC.

enjoy the fruits of another's study. Here Aristotle raises the example of the poets' portrayal of Zeus:

The poets do not depict Zeus as playing and singing in person. In fact we regard professional performers as belonging to the lower classes, though a man may play and sing for his own amusement or at a party when he has had a good deal to drink.

Even pre-tragic poets do not portray many immortals as singing (with the important exceptions of Apollo and the Muses), which in itself may illuminate the dearth of lyric singing by divinities in tragedy before the *Rhesus*. The *Homeric Hymn to Apollo* (189–206) may be relevant here: the Muses sing, several female and youthful divinities dance, Apollo plays the cithara, while Zeus and Leto *watch*, perhaps because they are older and more dignified.

Aristotle's view is contentious and extreme. When it comes to humans, other sources confirm that citizen men were expected to sing in the context of the symposium. The repertoire of well-known songs for performance after the paean and libations included the compositions of the great lyric poets, extracts from tragedy, and lyrics from comedy. Although lengthy virtuoso performances may have been restricted to guests with musical skills above the average, every participant was probably expected to perform a stanza as he held the myrtle branch.[71] In Theophrastus' *Characters* a sign of the surly (*authadēs*) man is that he 'always refuses to sing, perform a speech, or dance' at symposia (15.10).[72] It is in a travesty of a sympotic context that Polyphemus drunkenly sings solo in Euripides' satyric *Cyclops* (503–10).[73] But Polyphemus is hardly a cultured individual, and the text of the *Characters* elsewhere indicates that singing was not something a refined man would indulge in at whim: type of song, context, and *dignity* were critical.

---

[71] Pellizer (1990), 179; L. P. E. Parker (1997), 3–4.

[72] In his *Inachus*, which was almost certainly a satyr play, Sophocles gave the many-eyed herdsman Argus a sung entrance (*aidonta auton eisagei*, fr. 281a TgrF).

[73] Ar. *Clouds* 1355–8, 1364–72; *Wasps* 1222 with schol. *ad loc*; Xen. *Symp.* 7.1, where Socrates leads the singing. According to Cicero, Themistocles' refusal to play the lyre at feasts earned him the reputation of being *indoctior* (*Tusc. Disp.* 1.2.4). See Ussher (1960), 133.

Singing Roles in Tragedy

It was one thing to sing a skolion to fellow symposiasts that had
been composed by, say, Timocreon of Rhodes. It was quite another to
commit to memory the songs associated with lower-class entertainments such as conjurors' shows (*thaumata*). These were apparently
favoured by children, and featured females playing the aulos and
dancing (Xen. *Symp.* 2.1). In the *Characters* the man who does his
learning too late, the *opsimathēs*, attends these shows repeatedly in
order to learn the songs off by heart (*ta aismata ekmanthanein*, 27.7).
Perhaps, as Ussher suggests, the songs were like those composed by
the 'poets of shameful songs' with whom Philip of Macedon sur-
rounded himself, and to which he was said to be addicted.[74] Singing
in an inappropriate public context is criticized in the Theophrastan
definition of the *agroikos*, the 'boor', a term which elsewhere is found
in tandem with terminology defining the *aneleutheros*:[75] the boorish
man is liable 'to sing (*aisai*) at the baths' (*Char.* 4.14).[76]

LYRIC FEMININITY

For the parody of Euripidean monody in *Frogs* the singing persona
whose identity Aeschylus assumes is a woman. In Aeschylus female
singers (Hypermestra[?], Antigone and Ismene, Cassandra, Electra, Io)
outnumber male (Xerxes, Orestes). Singing in Euripides seems to be a
female (and barbarian) prerogative: with a few exceptions (notably
Theseus in *Hippolytus*, see below), lyric utterance tends to
be associated especially with women (Phaedra, Electra, Hecuba, Andromache, Cassandra, Polyxena, Evadne, Helen, Andromeda, Hypsipyle,
Creusa, Jocasta, Antigone, Iphigeneia in both her plays, Agave). Singing
males include the barbarians Polymestor and the eunuch in *Orestes*, the

---

[74] Ussher (1960), 230. On the performances called *thaumata* see also Isocr.,
Antidosis 213.
[75] In Aristophanes fr. 706 K–A the man who is both *agroikos* and *aneleutheros*
cannot speak in a dignified way in public.
[76] This view to be found articulated elsewhere: Artemidorus asserts that it is not a
good thing to sing at the baths (1.76), and the barbarous Triballians are said to behave
in an ill-bred way in the baths (*Etymology* s.v. *Triballoi*). See also Seneca *Ep.* 56.2
(*et illum cui vox sua in balneo placet*), Petronius, *Sat.* 73, Ussher (1960), 61–2.

children of the heroines of *Alcestis* and *Andromache*, the youths
Hippolytus and Ion, and the aged Peleus in *Andromache* and Oedipus
in *Phoenissae*.[77] In Sophocles the protagonist, regardless of gender, is
given lyrics when in physical pain or extreme emotional turmoil: Ajax
sings a great lament, which Sophocles ironically prefaces with the
information that this hero regarded high-pitched lamentation as 'unmanly' (317–20). Heracles sings in *Trachiniae*, and so do Oedipus,
Antigone, Creon, Electra and Philoctetes (although the brevity of
Oedipus' lyric musical utterances in *OC* has been attributed to his
identity as an old man, who could not be expected 'at the very close
of his life to sing with the necessary vigour').[78] But Aeschylean and
Euripidean singers are generally the 'others' of the free Greek man in his
prime.[79]

A tendency to gender song as feminine is apparent in ancient (and
more modern) thought,[80] from the symbolism embodied in the Muses,
to Aristides Quintilianus' schematization, which he attributes to 'the
ancients', whereby melody is the female partner in bringing music to life
and rhythm is the male partner (1.19).[81] But if the Hibeh
Papyrus' fragmentary treatise on musical modes is indeed a contemporary's response to the fifth-century musical theorist Damon, who
came from the Attic deme of Oa, then the masculinity specifically of
tragic actors and their singing had been impugned by the early fourth

[77] Oiax probably sang a lament for his brother, entailing both dactylo-epitrites and
anapaests, in Euripides' lost *Palamedes*: see frr. 588 and 588a *TgrF*.
[78] Owen (1936), 152: Owen's article discusses Sophoclean actors' songs in detail.
Neither actor's song nor its socio-political dimension receives much attention in W.
C. Scott (1984) and (1996), which discuss the metrical design of Aeschylean and
Sophoclean drama.
[79] Barner (1971), 314, agrees that Aeschylean and Euripidean singers sing for
similar reasons and are similar theatrical types. The main difference is, of course,
that Aeschylean singers all sing during exchanges with the chorus. But it is just
possible that the paradosis may give us a distorted view of Aeschylean song: according
to Philostratus' *Life of Apollonius of Tyana* 6.11.219c, one of Aeschylus' improvements
to tragedy was that he 'invented dialogues for the actors, discarding the long
monodies' (*to tōn monōidiōn mēkos*).
[80] Segal (1994).
[81] Ed. Winnington-Ingram (1963): *tines de ton palaiōn ton men rhuthmon arren
apekaloun, to de melos thēlu* etc. The theory is dependent on the Aristotelian view of
mammalian reproduction: 'feminine' melody is formless, lifeless and inactive material which needs to be shaped and put in order by the active 'masculine' principle of
rhythm, thus producing music (*De Gen. An.* 2.4. 738^{b}20–8; see Ch. 6, p. 177).

century: it is denied that the enharmonic mode can bestow bravery on
tragic actors, for they are not 'a manly lot'.[82]

Ritual, especially ritual lament, cannot be left out of the equation.
A few tragic songs delivered by actors are work songs (Ion) or
perverted wedding songs (Cassandra in *Troades* and Evadne in *Suppliant Women*). But the ancients seem to have believed that most
tragic songs were fundamentally threnodic.[83] The ritual lament
which informs so many tragic songs had traditionally been a female
obligation.[84] But the Platonic Socrates' gendered objection to tragic
performance in book 10 of the *Republic* (also discussed, from a
different perspective, above Chs. 3 and 5, pp. 67 and 163–4) is crucial
here. He argues that tragedy encourages types of behaviour and
emotional expression which are inappropriate in a man and only
befit a woman; particularly reprehensible and 'feminine' is indulging
in the pleasurable experience of watching heroes in distress
delivering long speeches or singing and beating themselves' (*aidontas
te kai koptomenous*, Plato, *Republic* 10.605c10–e2). Plato is presumably thinking specifically of tragic lamentation – the combination of
song and gesture denoted by the noun *kommos*. The passage is
suggestive because singing (*aidein*) has entered the vocabulary referring to tragic behaviour inappropriate in men; this will resurface, as
we have seen, in Aristotle's distinction between Odysseus and Melanippe in the *Poetics*.

Famous performances of tragedy in later antiquity usually involve
female singing roles. The actor who terrified the barbarians in Spain
was performing a song of the Euripidean Andromeda.[85] At the
beginning of the Christian era there was a performance of Euripides'
Hypsipyle, by the Argive actor Leonteus, in front of Juba II of
Mauretania (Athen. *Deipn.* 8.343e–f).[86] Leonteus' performance was

---

[82] Grenfell and Hunt (1906), pt. 1 no. 13, pp. 45–58, col ii. For a more contemporary English translation see W. D. Anderson (1966), 147–9. On Damon of Oa, who
was the earliest analytical theorist of the relationship between music, psychology and
behaviour, see now Wallace (2004).

[83] So the scholiast on Eur. *Andr.* 103 ('A monody is the song of a character doing a
thrēnos'), and the Suda's gloss of *monōidein* as *to thrēnein*: 'for all the songs from the
stage in tragedy are properly *thrēnoi*'.

[84] Especially Foley (1993).

[85] See p. 297 n. 38.

[86] See Cockle (1987), 41.

so poor that King Juba composed an epigram to reprove him. In it Juba picked on the actor's *voice*: Leonteus had been eating too many artichokes.[87] Juba says that his own vocal gifts had been ruined by over-eating, but that Bacchus used to love his voice (*gērun*), a term which, along with the cognate verb *gēruō*, is often found in contexts to do with expert *singing*. To have the voice of Orpheus is to have a *gērus* (Eur. *Alc.* 969); in Pindar *gēruein* is regularly the term used of the performance of lyric poetry; the middle form *gēruesthai* often means, absolutely, 'to sing'.[88] It was Leonteus' failure in the role of Hypsipyle which provoked this epigram on the interrelationship of vocal performance and diet, so outstanding vocal form was thought to be required for the role of Hypsipyle. The papyri confirm that her role was a heavily musical one not dissimilar to that of Euripides' Helen, and certainly an inspiration behind Aristophanes' parody of Euripidean actors' lyrics in *Frogs*.[89]

Another example is provided by Plutarch's report of the death of Crassus (*Vit. Crass.* 33.2–4). The head of the slaughtered Roman general was brought into the presence of the Parthian king Orodes on an occasion when a tragic actor (*tragōidiōn hupokritēs*), Jason of Tralles, performed 'the part of Euripides' *Bacchae* which is about Agave' (*aiden Euripidou ta peri tēn Agauēn*). Jason handed his 'Pentheus' costume to one of the chorus, and seized Crassus' head. Assuming the role of the frenzied Agave, and using Crassus' head as 'a grisly prop',[90] he sang the words from her lyrical interchange with the chorus, 'We bear from the mountain a newly cut tendril to the palace, a blessed spoil from the hunt' (*Bacch.* 1169–71). This delighted everyone. But when the dialogue was sung where the chorus asks, 'Who killed him?', and Agave responds, 'mine was this privilege' (1179), the actual murderer sprang up and grabbed Crassus' head, feeling that these words were more appropriate for him to utter than for Jason. The distinctive sung exchange of *Bacchae*, where

---

[87] For other ancient sources on the effect of certain dietary items on the voice see Flashar (1967), 546.

[88] *Hymn. Hom. Merc.* 426 and *Theocr.* 1.136 (of birdsong), Pind. *Isthm.* 1.34, Eur. *Hipp.* (of Phaedra, who is delivering lyric anapaests in contrast with her nurse's recitative anapaests), Aesch. *Suppl.* 460.

[89] See above, nn. 66, 70.

[90] Braund (1993), 468–9.

Agave's sung utterance over Pentheus' head represents Bacchic *mania*, was thus a party-piece in antiquity.[91]

Or take Euripides' *Electra*. Plutarch records that after the battle of Aegospotami, at which Athens lost the Peloponnesian war in 404 BC, the Theban Erianthus proposed to raze Athens to the ground and sell the Athenians into slavery. But the city was saved by one Phocion at a banquet where Lysander and the other allied generals were assembled: he performed the parodos (*tēn parodon*) of Euripides' *Electra*, which begins with the female chorus' address to the distressed princess: 'O Electra, daughter of Agamemnon, I have come to your rustic court...' (167–8). This song is shared with a soloist: Electra responds to the chorus in this first strophe, lamenting her shabbiness and her absence from Hera's festivals (175–89). Phocion is thus supposed by Plutarch to have performed Electra's sung lament.[92] The evocation of Electra's pitiable plight affected the generals; they connected it with the parlous state in which Athens found herself, and decided against destroying the city (Plut. *Vit. Lys.*15.2–3). Plutarch therefore remembers a female tragic role which we know was distinguished by its pathetic singing. Perhaps the same applied to the actor Polus' celebrated rendition of Sophocles' *Electra* (another role characterised by extensive song), in which he 'method acted' by utilising his 'real living grief (*luctu*) and lamentations (*lamentis*)', as he handled the urn containing the ashes of his own dead son (Aulus Gellius 6.4, see above, Ch. 2, p. 18).

Electra has a singing role in all four plays involving her by all three tragic poets. This raises the possibility that certain mythical characters were more likely than others to be made to sing by the tragedians. Clytemnestra, unlike Electra, never seems to sing lyrics, although Aeschylus in *Agamemnon* gives to her (as to Athena in *Eumenides*)

---

[91] On the variety of dramatic entertainments offered at dinner parties, especially in the Roman imperial era, see C. P. Jones (1991).

[92] Diodorus (16.92) reports that a tragic actor famous for the power of his voice (*megalophōnia*) sang at another important symposium with military overtones, held by Philip of Macedon the night before his assassination. Neoptolemus (on whom see also the references Stephanis (1988), 321–2, no. 1797) was ordered to choose a piece pertinent to the King's planned expedition against Persia. Unfortunately it is not clear whether his song was originally designed to be delivered by a male or female character, nor, indeed, whether it was from a monody or a choral lyric (*TgrF* vol. ii, no. 127). See Easterling (1999).

anapaestic lines in an exchange with the chorus.[93] Parker has remarked that Clytemnestra here subverts expectation precisely by failing to use even lyric anapaests: 'in this aberrant specimen of the genre the dead man's wife, instead of joining in the lament, uses recitative anapaests'.[94] Perhaps anapaests could be recited in a grand and declamatory manner more suitable than lyric song for indomitable masculinized females.[95] It is striking that tragedy's other 'manly' female, Euripides' Medea, is likewise given anapaests but never lyric song:[96] the emasculated Jason, on the other hand, is likely to have performed a monody in a lost tragic *Medea* performed before 421 BC, possibly by the dramatist Morsimus (29 fr. 1 *TgrF*). Clytemnestra does not even sing lyrics in Euripides' *IA*, where as a morally unimpeachable grief-stricken mother, listening to her daughter's heart-rending monody, she had certainly found a suitable occasion (Clytemnestra's introductory anapaests: 1276–8. Iphigeneia's anapaests and monody: 1279–310).

Were Hecuba and Andromache famous as singing characters? Certainly their roles in *Trojan Women* were renowned for their emotive potential. In his *Life of Pelopidas* (29.4–6) Plutarch describes the legendary cruelty of Alexander of Pherae, the fourth-century tyrant who killed his own uncle; he used to bury enemies alive, or encase them in the hides of wild animals and set his hunting dogs on them. But at a production of *Trojan Women* he was forced to leave rather than let the people see him weep 'at the sorrows of Hecuba and Andromache'. He subsequently sent a message to 'the actor' (*tragōidon*) to say that his departure was no reflection on the actor's performance (*agōnizesthai*). These two female characters, of course, are both singing roles in *Trojan Women* and in other tragedies, perhaps an inheritance from their performance of dirges for Hector in the twenty-fourth book of the *Iliad*.

Certain female characters seem almost pre-programmed to sing (Electra, Hecuba, Iphigeneia, Cassandra). With others there is no

---

[93] On which see Peretti (1939), 181.

[94] L. P. E. Parker (1997), 57.

[95] This notion is certainly latent in Pintacuda's discussions of both Clytemnestra and Medea (Pintacuda (1978), 114, 171–3).

[96] What Euripides might have done is shown by the song Ennius seems to have given Medea at some point during the crisis over the death of the children (fr. 282 in Vahlen (1903), 70).

consistency, and the choice of speech or song may partly depend on the extent of the 'interiorization' of a woman's character in an individual play, for monodists, especially in Euripides, tend to be deeply self-absorbed and self-referential.[97] Helen, who also performs a lament in *Iliad* 24, stands out in Euripides' *Trojan Women* as the only woman in Troy who does *not* sing: Hecuba, Cassandra, and Andromache are lyric roles, but this cynical rhetorician of a Helen is confined to the iambic trimeter. What a difference, therefore, in the play of but a few years later, Euripides' *Helen*, where the heroine can hardly be stopped from lyric expression, at least in the first third of the drama (164–78, 191–210, 229–52, 348–85).

If singing wild dirges impugned a man's masculinity, the question arises of the extent to which tragic heroes with laments are effectively 'effeminized'. There can be little doubt that this applies to Xerxes. He may even sing in a high pitch, like the Phrygian eunuch in *Orestes*, whose 'chariot melody' (1384) was in the high-pitched Phrygian mode: the same actor who played the eunuch almost certainly took the part of Electra, who in turn was almost certainly required to sing in a high-pitched voice (Dion. Hal. *Comp.* 11).[98] The pseudo-Aristotelian *Problem* 11.62 asks, 'Why do children, women and eunuchs and old men speak in a shrill voice (*phtheggontai oxu*)?' The dirge in *Persians* may even announce both the high pitch of melody to which the dirge is sung (it is 'Mariandynian', 937), and the type of instrument (a Mariandynian *aulos*, traditionally of high pitch) used to accompany it.[99] If this is correct, then the actor singing Xerxes will indeed be performatively confirming the earlier implications that he is effeminate, including the statement of the messenger that he was given to wail (*kōkuein*) in a shrill manner designated by the term *oxu*—that is, lamenting in a high-pitched voice appropriate to a woman.[100]

Barbarian males are often given song (see below), but in extant tragedy and in the fragments (e.g. of *Erechtheus*) adult Athenian men, with the exceptions of Theseus in *Hippolytus*, and Sophocles'

[97] See Damen (1990), 134–5.

[98] See the references in note 42 above. The Phrygian in *Orestes* was certainly regarded as a eunuch in later antiquity: see Terentianus Maurus, *de Metris* (2nd cent. AD), 1960–2.

[99] See the scholion on *Pers.* 917 and Comottie (1989), 33.

[100] See E. Hall (1996*a*), 143.

Salaminian Ajax, do not sing lyrics. Was it felt appropriate that the mythical ancestors of the hosts at the City Dionysia should maintain the appearance of dignity by sticking to the iambic trimeter? In *Hippolytus*, however, Theseus delivers some lyric lines after the discovery of Phaedra's death (between 817 and 851). But he might actually be the exception who proves the rule, because the pattern of his delivery is two lyric lines alternating repeatedly with two iambic trimeters. The lyrics never run away with him, as it were, but are restrained by the repeated insertion of iambic (and thus probably spoken) lines.[101] This metrical pattern is frequently found in epirrhematic scenes, where choral song alternates with actor's spoken trimeters or *vice versa*. It is also common in female–male 'duets', where women have lyrics while their performance partners mostly have iambic trimeters. Examples are the recognition scenes in *IT*, *Helen* and in Sophocles' *Electra*, where Electra sings, Orestes speaks, and she fails to persuade him to join her (except for a lone bacchiac at 1280) in the feminine emotional self-expression of which her lyrics are the vehicle.[102] In Euripides' Theseus a similar struggle between lyric and iambic, between song and speech, is located within one individual.

ALIEN ARIAS

There are only three possible exceptions to Maas's principle. They are the Phrygian eunuch in Euripides' *Orestes,* the Egyptian herald in Aeschylus' *Suppliants*, and the nurse in Sophocles' *Women of Trachis*. To argue backwards, Deianeira's nurse almost certainly does not sing: the slightest of emendations restores her to spoken iambic trimeters.[103] But there is little doubt that the Egyptian herald sings. The Danaids have been terrified by the sight of their cousins rowing into shore. Between 825 and 871 there is a long lyric sequence,

---

[101] Schadewaldt (1926), 147–51, makes some sensitive comments on the unusual metrical structure of Theseus' monody.
[102] Willink (1989), makes some perceptive remarks on these 'recognition' duets in 46–7. On singing in Sophocles' *Electra* see Webster (1970), 173–4.
[103] See L. D. J. Henderson (1976); Easterling (1982), 183.

heavily corrupt, and marked by remarkable words and phrases. Internal evidence proves that the Danaids cannot sing several of the groups of lines (836–42, 847–53, 859–65). They are having an interchange with an opponent who threatens them with extreme violence, including decapitation. Immediately afterwards, an aggressive herald sent by the sons of Aegyptus speaks in iambic trimeters to both the chorus of Danaids and to Pelasgus, and he is the most likely candidate for the lyric utterances.

Critics have long been tempted to invent a chorus of Egyptians here, in order to remove the alleged problem of a low-status singing character.[104] But the Danaids' consistent use of the singular to designate their adversary, and the extreme rarity in tragedy of interchanges between two choruses, make this secondary chorus theory quite unnecessary. Many scholars now infer that the Danaids' singing adversary is the solo herald.[105] Perhaps Henderson was correct to argue that the status of heralds had always been ambivalent: neither servants nor equals of kings.[106] But it may be more important that the singer is a barbarian. His lyrics represent anger and uncontrolled physicality. His lyrics are not work song, wedding song, or lament: he sings because he is violent and because he is not Greek. He is in a tradition of singing stage *barbaros* going back at least to Aeschylus' Xerxes,[107] and forward to Euripides' Phrygian eunuch, and the barbarian characters given *oratio recta* within Timotheus' flamboyant Salamis aria, his *Persians*.[108] It may also be significant that the same actor who played Danaus must have performed the herald's role; the playwrights may have exploited the distinctive timbre of a particular actor's voice in establishing links between the characters he took in a play. Pavloskis has suggested that in *Suppliant Women* the

[104] e.g. Maas (1929). The singing herald is replaced with a chorus by Johansen and Whittle (1980), a decision they try to justify at iii. 171–4.

[105] e.g. Popp (1971), 242; Taplin (1977), 217, is rightly dismissive of the subsidiary chorus theory.

[106] L. D. J. Henderson (1976).

[107] And almost certainly beyond Aeschylus to Phrynichus. Nothing is known of the cast of Phrynichus' *Sack of Miletus*, but the eunuch who spoke the iambic prologue of his *Phoenissae* (fr. 8 *TgrF*) may have sung later, and the play must have included members of the Persian royal family.

[108] On which see Ch. 9, pp. 277–80.

duplication suggested the foreign character of both Danaus and the herald, in contrast with the Greek Pelasgus.[109]

Yet it is debatable how far the herald's language characterized him as a *barbaros*: some have thought that the actual noises are supposed to replicate barbarian speech, or a barbarian accent on Greek speech similar to the caricatured Scythian pronunciation used by the archer in Aristophanes' *Thesmophoriazusae*.[110] It is more likely that an exotic type of utterance was implied symbolically by certain features. These include the recurrent word-doubling (836, 838, 839, 842, 860, 861, 863—also a feature of the exodos of *Persae*), the syntactical strangeness of the verbless sentence of 838–42, and the exoticism of *barin* and *ichar*.[111] The Phrygian slave in Euripides' *Orestes*, whatever he owes to the 'New Music' of Timotheus (see Ch. 9), helps to protect this Aeschylean exception to the exclusion of low-status singers, since he, likewise, is an overwrought male barbarian. Non-Greekness seems to prompt an Athenian tragedian to think in terms of song; it may be significant that Greeks thought that in barbarian tyrannies there was no secure distinction between slave and free.

Polymestor may offer a closer parallel to the Egyptian herald and to the Phrygian than has been appreciated. He is a ruler of sorts and as such might be expected to sing a 'blind' scene, but even his status as king is ambivalent: Euripides took pains to make him a barbarous Thracian horseman (710), who lives in the mountains without a polis, and who has no claim to aristocratic birth. He is only once called 'king', and then it is by Agamemnon in a fit of cynical flattery (856). He is, however, called 'barbarian' and 'you there', and no fewer than nine times he is just 'the Thracian', which subliminally associates him with one of the commonest slave ethnic names in Athens.[112] As a violent barbarian male,[113] whose ethnicity is compounded by physical agony, the poet's decision to make him sing becomes almost over-determined. Collard's account of Polymestor's monody is one

---

[109] Pavloskis (1977–8), 116. For arguments along similar lines see also Damen (1989).

[110] Garvie (1969), 56–7. On the Scythian archer's voice, see Ch. 8, pp. 227–31.

[111] Johansen and Whittle (1980), iii. 174.

[112] E. Hall (1989), 109–10.

[113] I do not understand why the only moderately substantial published study of monody in tragedy classifies Polymestor as a Greek (Barner (1971), 262–3).

of the more perceptive descriptions in existence of a tragic song, and one of the few discussions of monody in the English language:[114] 'His crippling physical pain is conveyed by theatrical entry on all fours ...and a changed mask now all bloody...Irregular shrieks of agony and despair; cries of hate; broken, illogically ordered thought, mostly phrased as imploring questions; staccato delivery (the monody has no connective particles between clauses whatsoever).'[115] This last asyndetic feature is unimaginable in spoken iambic trimeters, and is reminiscent of Aristotle's objection to lack of connection in the speech of the orator, which he says is a reprehensible habit borrowed from actors (*Rhet.* 3.1413[b]).

THE POLITICS OF FORM

One of the most significant issues ever raised by Vernant was the need to examine the processes whereby Athenian tragedy *transformed* reality while assimilating it into its own medium—what cultural materialists would call the processes of artistic 'mediation': 'No reference to other domains of social life... can be pertinent unless we can also show how tragedy assimilates into its own perspective the elements it borrows, thereby quite transmuting them'.[116] It is important to be aware of the particular codes and conventions conditioning such processes of transformation, and then to ask what those codes reveal about the society operating them. Work of this kind has been done on the *content* of the tragedies: we now understand better how issues of concern to the democratic city-state are examined by temporal location in the heroic mythical past. But what I hope this chapter has shown is that insufficient attention has been paid to the relationship of

---

[114] An important exception is also by Chris Collard, namely, his review of the bibliography on monody and analysis of Evadne's song in his edition of *Suppliant Women* (1975), ii. 358–62. There are also some excellent points made in the account of the imagery in Euripidean monody in Barlow (1986*a*), 43–60, and of its diction and style in Barlow (1986*b*). L. P. E. Parker (1997), 514–18, offers an admirably succinct review of the metrical features of Euripidean monody.

[115] Collard (1991), 187.

[116] In Vernant and Vidal-Naquet (1988), 31.

tragedy's aural *form*—its actors' musical and metrical performance codes—to the society which produced it.

Even from this cursory look at some actor's songs some interesting results have emerged. Song versus speech was both an emotionally and an ideologically laden distinction. Singing in the fifth-century theatre seems to be a human, rather than divine, form of self-expression. Solo song is affected by social status, for it distinguishes rulers from 'ordinary people', and individuals born into slavery from those enslaved by misfortune. Solo song is also implicated in tragic distinctions determined by gender: Plato's Socrates had more to complain about in Sophocles (where male protagonists regularly *aidein* and *koptesthai*) than in Euripides, where they do not. Song could imply barbarian ethnicity. Besides Sophocles' Ajax, Athenians tend not to sing, except in the case of Theseus' half-hearted lament in *Hippolytus*. Certain characters (especially virgins like Electra) seem almost pre-programmed to sing in tragedy while others (especially the 'manly' matrons Clytemnestra and Medea) do not. Female tragic roles with important sung elements seem to have been particularly popular choices as star turns in later antiquity.

Tragic song and metre, therefore, are not to be separated from the sociology of tragedy, and what is relevant to the sociology of tragedy is relevant to the sociology of the polis. Acknowledging the ideological implications of mode of delivery and metrical form begs further questions, not least relating to Athenian imperialism. Tragedy is a remarkably inclusive genre, with a sponge-like ability to attract to and contain within itself other genres inherited from other parts of the Greek-speaking world. This feature must have ideological implications for a city-state setting itself up in the sixth century as the cultural centre of the Greek-speaking world, and in the fifth as the leading imperial power. A way of looking at tragedy could be to see it as not only *aesthetically* 'Panhellenizing', but effectively as imperialism expressed on the level of genre.

Athens had no distinctive poetic genre of its own, despite the Peisistratean attempts to hegemonize Homeric epic. The Dorians had choral lyric and anapaestic marching songs, the eastern Aegean had monody, the Ionians had iambos: in tragedy the Athenians invented an inclusive new genre which assimilated them all. Many of the types of delivery of both speech and song associated with other

Greek-speaking communities, and to be heard all over Hellas, now
came to be appropriated and heard in composite performances in the
theatre of Dionysus at Athens. It may even be the tragedians could
pay far more explicit compliments to other (friendly) communities
by their inclusion of certain genres of song than we are remotely
aware.[117] Thus when Aeschylus chose to effeminize the great King of
Persia through *kommos* and to prevent him from using the
'rational' discourse of iambic speech, his decision may have been
literally 'consonant' with the same fifth-century imperial Athenian
version of the world which in tragedy produced metrical and musical
Panhellenism performed on the level of genre. As Diomedes the
grammarian said, there is much to be learnt by singing lyrics as we
read them, even though we do not know the tragedian's original tune.

[117] Long ago Denys Page implicitly argued that genre, form, and ideology were
inseparable. According to his view of Euripides' *Andromache*, choice of metrical form
and sung performance were inextricably bound up with Athenian politics and its
imperial programme. He argues that *Andromache* was first produced at Argos at a
time when Athens was seeking to secure Argive support against Sparta. The grounds
are that (i) there was a tradition of 'Doric threnodic elegy' at Argos, of which the
Argive poet Sakadas was the chief representative poet; that (ii) the play was not
produced at Athens (so a scholion on line 445); and that therefore (iii) the elegiacs
sung by Andromache strongly suggest an Argive first production, and constitute a
sung compliment, by inclusion of a genre unusual in tragedy, to the Argive poetical
tradition: Page (1936), 223–8.

11

Casting the Role of Trygaeus in Aristophanes' *Peace*

A GIFT FOR AN ACTOR

Few indeed are the surviving ancient Greek dramas where the name of the leading actor who first realized the protagonist's role is known to us. The earliest example is almost certainly that of Apollodorus, the comic actor who in 421 BC first played Trygaeus, the leading part in Aristophanes' *Peace*. This is recorded, along with the information that the play was beaten into second place by Eupolis' *Flatterer* (*Kolax*), in a single transmitted source: the third of the four ancient hypotheses to *Peace* which have been preserved in the learned codex Venetus Marcianus 474 (line 441). Some might not regard the information either as one hundred per cent reliable or as remotely important.[1] But provisionally bestowing the name Apollodorus on the actor who first played Trygaeus might encourage us to reconstruct concretely the way the splendid role was brought to life. Vinegrower and lunatic, saviour and trickster, beetle rider, aerial adventurer, cosmic diplomat, and bridegroom—Trygaeus is all of these. He is also a substitute for Nicias and a congener of Dionysus. This chapter argues that his role *represents* the art of socially useful comedy; as such it includes, within the comic role, a fascinating range not only of theatrical roles (including Bellerophon and Silenus), but of poetic genres, forms, metres, quotations, and styles of vocal delivery. This certainly would have been a fitting role for an actor whose name meant 'gift of Apollo', gift of the divine president of Helicon.

---

[1] See e.g. Olson (1998), 65–6. An exception is Russo (1994), 146: 'the Apollodorus named by the Argument . . . was the first actor of *Peace*'.

Although 'pacifist' is an unhelpful term in discussing Aristophanes, if only because it arose in the late nineteenth century in order to designate a political principle incomprehensible to the fifth-century mindset,[2] Trygaeus is undoubtedly an advocate of peace. He is an example of ancient pagan creativity in response to the need for *positive* cultural expressions of that desirable circumstance. This contrasts with the dearth of pacific imagery in the western post-Renaissance cultural encyclopaedia, lamented, for example, by Marina Warner in reaction to the American bombing of Libya in 1986: with the exception of the Old Testament's symbolic iconography of the dove and the olive twig, most western monuments to peace, like the Cenotaph in London, only define it passively and negatively. The idea of peace 'seems difficult to seize without referring to the absence of war, and thus making war present as a standard'.[3] But from as early as the pastoral imagery in Homeric similes,[4] the town at peace on Achilles' shield in the *Iliad,* and the depiction of peasant farming in Hesiod's *Works and Days,* the Greeks enjoyed a rich repertoire of images for the activities of peace-time.[5] A favoured theme of choral lyric, in a paean by Bacchylides (fr. 4.61–80 Snell-Maehler) Peace was described as bringing wealth, songs, festivals, and sacrifices; in tragedy, Euripides had made the chorus of his *Cresphontes* praise Peace, who brings in her train wealth, songs, and revelry ((39) Eur. fr. 453 *TgrF*).

Comedy took up the theme enthusiastically. In Aristophanes' *Farmers* of 424 BC, the activities of peace-time included a bath, a good meal, and drinking of the new vintage.[6] In the subsequent version of his *Peace,* Aristophanes presented his audience with a dialogue between Eirene and Georgia, the personification of agriculture (fr. 294 K–A).[7] In the surviving version, the core symbol of peace is viticulture, as inherently Dionysiac as theatre itself: an Attic red-figure kalyx-krater which may well have been influenced by the play, and which dates from the decade following it, depicts a blissful nocturnal scene with Dionysus attended by Himeros, a satyr named 'Sweet-Wine' or 'Wine-Enjoyer' (*Hēduoinos*), and maenads

---

[2] See Durvye (2002), 83.   [3] Warner (1986).   [4] See Duchemin (1960).

[5] On the importance of Hesiod to the ancient conceptualization of the peace-war antithesis, see Zampaglione (1973), 26–7.

[6] Fr. 109 K–A. On such lyrical scenes in the Greek poets, see Harriott (1986), 126–7.

[7] See Stafford (2000), 187–8.

including *Opōra*, Dione, and a recumbent Eirene, torch and drinking horn in hand.[8] But in *Peace* the battle for peace is more verbally sophisticated than its equation with grape-harvesting might imply; it is formulated as a battle between literary genres, with heroic epic identified as the enemy. Even Ionian *iambos* and Aesopic fable are, within the opening sequence, enrolled in the service of Trygaeus' mission.[9] If art is to be understood as a product of a particular society at a particular time, criticism must involve 'illuminating some of the ways in which various forms, genres, and styles . . . come to have value ascribed to them by certain groups in particular contexts'.[10]

Perhaps it is a modern failure to understand the idea of peace as *an activity* which led to *Peace* suffering worse twentieth-century scholarly neglect than most of Aristophanes' works,[11] for other times and other places had estimated it differently. After the Renaissance rediscovery of Greek drama, *Peace* was spectacularly performed at Trinity College, Cambridge, as early as 1546.[12] The play probably lies behind the figure of Irene, borne aloft in the procession at the coronation of James I, 'her attire white, semined with stares, her hair loose', even though she also carried the Judaeo-Christian dove and olive wreath.[13] A recent study by Michelakis has shown how *Peace* was staged at painfully appropriate moments in twentieth-century history; in Greece in 1919, Switzerland in 1945, and in a Parisian adaptation during the Algerian war (1961).[14] It was influentially directed by Peter Hacks in East Berlin to denounce the Cold War (1962), a production subsequently revived more than once in that tense city: the final scene featured Trygaeus teaching a *Friedenslied* to a young neo-fascist paramilitary.[15] Trygaeus has also enjoyed a

---

[8] Vienna 1024 = ARV^2 1152.8; no. 11 in Simon (1986); fig. 25 *a* and *b* in Stafford (2000), who discusses this and other late fifth-century Athenian visual images of Eirene ibid. 188.

[9] See Rosen (1984).

[10] Wolff (1981), 7.

[11] The publication of Olson's substantial edition in 1998 has already done much to encourage *Peace* studies.

[12] Boas (1914), 17; Michelakis (2002*b*), 115.

[13] She was flanked by Plutus and Esychia, with Enyalius beneath her feet. See Herford, Simpson, and Simpson (1941), 97.

[14] Michelakis (2002*b*).

[15] Riedel (1984), 145.

certain popularity in France, where he has traditionally been called 'Lavendange', and has been identified as the ancestor of famous French roles including Molière's con-man Scapin, and valet Sganarelle in *Don Juan*; Aristophanes has been seen as a forerunner of indigenous French writers—Rabelais, Voltaire, and Giraudoux—in having advocated peace in a comic medium.[16] In academic circles, until very recently, Trygaeus was nevertheless sidelined in comparison with most heroes of Old Comedy.

Yet his opening stunt, in which he rises into the air on the back of a giant dung-beetle, is the most fantastic in Aristophanes.[17] His mount is truly 'carnivalesque', a riotous combination of the tragic with the scatological.[18] The stunt is more extended and arduous than many scholars have appreciated. Trygaeus appears, rising on the beetle, at approximately lines 80–1 (*meteōros airetai*), and plunges into an agitated anapaestic sequence, which implies that the beetle is either resisting being steered, or that the actor tried to convey that impression. What a challenge this presented to Apollodorus can only be appreciated by an imaginative exercise. Without even considering the fact that Trygaeus is involved in an elaborate parody of tragic diction, music, and acting style, he is swaying around astride 'a counter-weighted beam balanced on a pole slightly higher than the central portion of the skene', a beam which probably required a crew of several men to move it vertically or pivot it around its fulcrum.[19] Moreover, the text implies that Trygaeus actually remains suspended in mid-air throughout the entire sequence 82–179, which makes it by far the longest crane scene in fifth-century drama.[20] Even if he alights at 102, and delivers the para-tragic iambic dialogue with his slave and his daughters from the roof, he must remount his malodorous steed once again at 154, and resume his hazardous ascent reciting anapaests derived from Euripides'

[16] See the essays by Revel-Mouroz (2002), 102 and Durvye (2002), 85.
[17] See Casari (2002), 43. It was still familiar to several late antique rhetors: see see Olson (1998), 84.
[18] Francesco de Buti, the author of a 14th-cent. commentary on Dante, argued that the goat had symbolized tragedy because its regal appearance from the front, crowned with horns, had a counterpart in its naked, filthy backside. See Eagleton (2003), 13; Casari (2002), 45.
[19] Mastronarde (1990), 268–72, 290–4; Olson (1998), 83.
[20] See Mastronarde (1990), 293, with the remarks of Olson (1998), 88.

Bellerophon.[21] And hazardous it is: not only does he become distracted, pointing out an individual in a latrine far away in the Piraeus (164–5), but something goes wrong with the operation of the crane. The beetle starts nose-diving at 158, and Trygaeus is rocked so hard that his body becomes bent double at 173–5, requiring the actor to break all dramatic illusion and tell the crane operator to pay better attention.[22] Apollodorus must have been relieved when he discovered that his descent to earth did not require him to remount (725–6).

PEASANT AND SAVIOUR

Trygaeus shares with other Aristophanic heroes his Athenian citizenship. Yet he is less urban and more exclusively associated with the countryside even than his nearest parallel, Dicaeopolis. As he informs Hermes, he is a peasant from Athmonon, a skilled vine-grower, and a man who usually avoids conflict (190–1). His extra-mural deme, which lay far north-east from the city centre at the foot of Mount Pentelikon, was no doubt chosen because of its excellent vines;[23] it may also already have housed the cult of Aphrodite Ourania that was reputed, in Pausanias' day, to have been of extreme antiquity (1.14.7),[24] and the play associates peace with renewed erotic opportunities (884–908).[25] Trygaeus knows and loves the farming business: he is well-versed in the prices of honey (253–4). His own raven fig-tree was cut down by Spartans marauding in Attica (628–9), ending his rural

---

[21] Frr. 307–8 *TgrF*. See Rau (1967), 89–97; Collard in Collard, Cropp, and Lee (1995), 119.

[22] Slater (2002), 116–19 is one of the few scholars to have appreciated exactly what the scene entailed in acting terms.

[23] On the fertility of Athmonon and its excellent vines see Frazer (1913), 413–14; for Trygaeus' relationship with the countryside and what it represented ideologically see esp. N. F. Jones (2004), 203–6.

[24] On Aphrodite Ourania at Athens see Halperin (1990*a*), 260 and n. 6; according to Xen. *Symp.* 8.9–10 there were two separate altars for Aphrodite, and the one for Ourania is the venue for particularly important rituals. According to a late source (Artemidorus 2.37), Aphrodite Ourania is propitious for marriages, partnerships, and the birth of children; she also indicates good luck for farmers.

[25] Whitehead (1986), 207; see also the interpretation of Vilardo (1976). Perhaps Athmonon had a reputation for public-mindedness and encouraging particularly

idyll (569–81). But he is a householder with responsibilities, just prosperous enough to own two slaves (181). He has hungry daughters (115–53), but must be a single parent; his freedom to marry *Opōra* at the end of the play suggests that he is a widower.

As an opponent of war Trygaeus resembles Dicaeopolis and Lysistrata.[26] After the successful recovery of Peace, he is hailed as a paradigmatic good citizen (*politēs*, 911–14), and even in the language of encomia as 'saviour' (914, see also 1035–6, an epithet primarily of Zeus).[27] But he is exceptional amongst Aristophanic heroes in that he represents the whole of the assembled city, inviting identification with virtually all Athenians present. He is humane, altruistic, and self-sacrificial (364–75); he is only self-interested insofar as his self-interest coincides with that of his fellow Athenians and Greeks.[28] For he is also the most Panhellenic of all Aristophanes' heroes,[29] leading a chorus consisting of members of numerous Greek states in the retrieval of Peace.[30] Trygaeus enacts in the realm of comic fiction the events of the past few months preceding the play, the present in which his audience found themselves, and even their immediate future under the Peace of Nicias, shortly to be ratified.

NICIAS' SHADOW

Peace does not develop any explicit identification of Trygaeus with Nicias, probably on account of the unflattering nature of the established comic image of this politician—Nicias had been portrayed as a

---

attentive practice of ritual in its demesmen: a 4th-cent. inscription (from the year 325/4) reports that six named individuals holding the office of *merarchos* were praised and crowned by the deme for their zeal and efficiency in supervising sacrifices and discharging other public duties (*IG* 2². 1203; see Whitehead (1986), 140, 376.

[26] Thiercy (1986), 207.

[27] See also the term *zēlōtos* (1038); on these epithets see Zimmermann (1985), 180–1.

[28] See Moulton (1981), 864; Casari (2002), 45.

[29] See 59, 93 ('I fly on behalf of all Greeks'), and 105; on Trygaeus' Panhellenism see also Thiercy (1986), 210–11; Harriott (1986), 122.

[30] On the problem of the chorus's unusually fluid identity, which is at times more Athenian and at others more Panhellenic in emphasis, see especially Sifakis (1971*b*), 32 and Hubbard (1991), 241–2; McGlew (2001) offers a different approach.

slavish attendant of Cleon in *Knights*, and handicapped by unusually timid gait in a play by Phrynichus (fr. 62 K–A). Yet *Peace* is tied more closely than any other Aristophanic work to its immediate historical situation. Trygaeus' achievement, unlike Dionysus' recovery of Aeschylus in *Frogs*, or the reconciliation between Athens and Sparta effected by Lysistrata, is uniquely no fantasy: it is a direct comic analogue of what was being enacted in reality.[31] Nicias, moreover, is the only contemporary politician of any significance, dead or alive, never satirized in the play, which must be connected with his advocacy of peace in the months leading up to its production.

When Apollodorus donned the mask of Trygaeus at the Dionysia in 421 BC, the Peloponnesian War was a decade old. The previous summer had seen the Athenians defeated in the terrible battle of Amphipolis. But Cleon and Brasidas, the generals on both sides, had died as a result of this confrontation, leaving the way at last open for peace negotiations between Athens and Sparta (Thuc. 5.16.1). These continued throughout the winter (Thuc. 5.17.2). By the time of the Dionysia, in the month of Elaphebolion, the terms of a treaty had been agreed. Two aspects of this diplomatic procedure are central to *Peace*. First, the treaty was ratified, according to Thucydides, 'immediately after the City Dionysia' (*ek Dionusiōn euthus tōn astikōn*, 5.20.1), which probably means that the festival ended on the 13th of the month, and the Athenian assembly met on the 14th to elect the delegation which would go to Sparta, where the truce was ratified a few days later (Thuc. 5.18–19). *Peace* was therefore performed just days before peace was inaugurated in reality, and in front of an audience from numerous Greek cities profoundly interested in the collective ceasefire. Secondly, the first clause of the Peace of Nicias was itself concerned with the right of all individuals to attend sanctuaries, oracles, and *festivals*:

With regard to the sanctuaries held in common, everyone who so wishes shall be able, according to the customs of his country, to sacrifice in them and visit them and consult oracles in them and attend the festivals in them (*theōrein*) in safety   (Thuc. 5.18.1).

[31] Thiercy (1986), 207; Newiger (1980), 233–4. I am mystified by the connection drawn by McGlew (2002), 76 (see also McGlew (2001)), between 'the Athenian general Trygaeus' and Lamachus.

The mute character *Theōria*, whom Trygaeus bestows upon the Athenian *prutaneis* (887–91), is thus simultaneously a reference to the vastly increased right to enjoy attending festivals to be assured by the imminent treaty, and a self-conscious comment on the occasion at which the play is performed. It is in keeping with the emphasis on *theōria* that the joys of peace, when eventually they begin to become a reality in the play, not only include the festivals which Trygaeus promises to transfer to Hermes (418–20, see below), but trips to the Brauron festival and the Isthmian games (874, 879); the metaphorical equivalence of sex and athletics is subsequently elaborated at length (894–904).

NAMING TRYGAEUS

Trygaeus' name is suggestive of a well-known proverb, *erēmas trugan*, 'to strip unwatched vines', used of one who is bold where there is nothing to fear—an opportunist: Aristophanes was aware of the saying, for it appears both in *Wasps* (634, see *Σ* ad loc.), which preceded *Peace*, and later in *Ecclesiazousae* (886). Trygaeus' opportunistic ruse, when he discovers that the gods have migrated, leaving Olympus without a ruler (207–9), is to bribe its last remaining guardian, Hermes. He promises that in future it will be in Hermes' exclusive honour that the Athenians will hold their festivals of the Panathenaea, the Mysteries, the Dipolieia and the Adonia (416–20); all the States will worship him in cult (421–2). Trygaeus caps this promise with a gift of a gold libation-bowl (424). Trygaeus is certainly clever; while tricking the god of trickery himself, he plays in an Odyssean manner with the name *miarōtatos* (184–8, see *Knights* 336–7), and orchestrates the chorus' piteous entreaties (384–401).[32]

His identity as a vine-grower is also expressed in Trygaeus' name. The verb *trugaō* meant 'I gather in a crop', including a crop of grapes.

---

[32] On Trygaeus' assimilation of Hermes' role as trickster, especially as portrayed in the *Homeric Hymn to Hermes*, see Bowie (1993), 140–1.

Trygaeus himself uses the verb after handing *Theōria* to the chairman of the *prutaneis*: the citizens will know what a hero he is when they 'gather in the crop' (*hotan trugat*, 909–12). Here the verb may have what Taplin calls the 'fescennine' metaphorical sense which it clearly bears in the closing wedding song:[33] there the chorus sing that they will *trugan* Peace the bride (1339–40). They are clearly thinking of a male sexual action, whether the dominant image is plucking grapes, prodding them, or squeezing them in a basket.[34]

Trygaeus' name also almost certainly associates him with satyrs in the Athenian imagination. The noun *trux* means 'unfermented wine' (Ar. *Clouds* 50), 'must', 'lees' or dregs' (Ar. *Plut.* 1085); a fragment of Aristophanes' *Farmers* (*Georgoi*), which was performed before *Peace* either in 424 or at the 421 Lenaea, praises doing things with *trux* as a peactime pleasure (fr. 111 K–A). A *trugoipos* was a wine-making apparatus in which grapes were trodden, consisting of a basket set in a further container, sometimes a spouted trough (Ar. *Plut.* 1087). The *trugoipos* is mentioned in *Peace* (535). But in fifth-century vase-paintings, when such activities as squashing grapes in a *trugoipos* were depicted, the agents are conventionally satyrs.[35] Trygaeus' name probably had associations with a cult title of the satyrs' divine master, Dionysus, whose festivals are conspicuously omitted from those offered by Trygaeus to Hermes. The term *protrugaios* is later found as an epithet of Dionysus, meaning 'presiding over the vintage' (Achilles Tatius 2.2, see also Ael. *VH* 3.41); Hesychius glosses *protrugaia* as 'a festival of Dionysus and Poseidon'; *theoi protrugaioi* are mentioned by Pollux (1.24). Bowie's discussion, informed by ritual structuralism, suggests that the term already had Dionysiac connotations in fifth-century Athens, perhaps audible in Trygaeus' name; there are also 'many possible echoes' of the Athenian Anthesteria in

---

[33] Taplin (1983), 333. The reading of the *exodos* of *Peace* by Calame (2004), 173, implies that an important resonance of Trygaeus' name is 'young bridegroom'.

[34] On the sexual connotations of Trygaeus' name see Thiercy (1986), 208, and Ioannidi (1973). On the sexual promise inherent in the hope of peace, cf. *Ach.* 263, 277–8 and Edmunds (1980), 6.

[35] See e.g. the representation of satyrs involved in wine-making on a mid-5th cent. red-figured column krater (*ARV*[2] 569, no. 39), with the remarks of Sparkes (1975), 135; in Athenian black-figure depictions of cropping and treading grapes, the figures are also almost invariably satyrs rather than humans: see especially Carpenter (1986), 91–3.

the play.[36] Trygaeus' marriage to *Opōra* perhaps finds a plausible parallel in the *hieros gamos* of Dionysus enacted at that festival.[37]

If not quite Dionysus' surrogate, Trygaeus is certainly his disciple. As a vine-grower his craft-deity is of course Dionysus, by whom he swears oaths (443); in one instance the vocative suggests that he turns to face the statue of Dionysus Eleuthereus, brought into the theatre earlier in the festival (267).[38] A Dionysiac picture is also suggested by Trygaeus' epiphany from behind the *skēnē*, accompanied by *Opōra* and *Theōria* (819),[39] he is leading an entourage similar to the scene on the Attic red-figure vase discussed above. Yet Trygaeus' name is more than generally Dionysiac, since it bears specifically *theatrical* overtones. The names of Aristophanes' dominant citizen characters, whether Just-City, Sausage-seller, Cleon-Lover, Cleon-Hater, Companion-Persuader, Optimist, Army-Dissolver, Fair Victory, or Speech-Act, make direct reference to their owners' roles. Trygaeus' name is undoubtedly related to the poetic genre in which its owner is a hero: namely, *trugedy*, 'wine-song'. This term was used as early as *Acharnians* to mean 'comedy' (499), just as *trugōidoi* in *Wasps* denotes comic poets (650, 1537). *Trugedy* is a type of comedy taking its name from a pun on *tragōidia*; to the word for 'song' (*ōidē*) was prefixed the root common to *trugaō* (gather in a crop of grapes), *trux* (unfermented wine), and *trugē* (vintage).[40]

Ancient commentators tried to explain how comedy came to find such a nickname as tragedy. Guesses included the notion that actors smeared their faces with wines lees, that new wine was given as a prize, and that comedy was performed at the season of the vintage.[41] It is more likely that, as Taplin suggests, the term is an invention of comedy itself, perhaps even coined for the purposes of *Acharnians* in

[36] Bowie (1993), 148 and n. 87; at 138 Bowie tentatively proposes that 'his name, derived from *truge*, points to the grape-harvest and perhaps also comedy's comic name for itself, *trugoidia*'.

[37] Bowie (1993), 146–50; Edmunds (1980), 20–1, who also refers to the parallel of Demeter's union with the hero Iasion (Homer, *Od.* 5.125–8; Hesiod, *Theog.* 969–74). For other attempts to explain features of the play by appealing to ritual structures, see Thiercy (1986), 307–10, who argues that when Trygaeus returns to earth he has undergone a rejuvenation analogous to those experienced by initiates into Mysteries.

[38] Sharpley (1905), 82.

[39] On whom see Newiger (1957), 108–11.

[40] See Ghiron-Bistagne (1973).

[41] See *Σ* Ar. *Ach.* 499–500, Athen. 2. 2.40b, and LSJ s.v. *trugōidia.*

425 BC, when its earliest certain use is documented.[42] Aristophanes created a neologistic pun on it in *Clouds*, where he forms *trugodaimōn*, meaning 'comic poet', by fusing *kakodaimōn* and *trugōidos* (296). The familiarity of the term by 421 is thus certain, regardless of the date of the lost play in which Aristophanes first coined the dazzling composite term 'trugedic-poetic-musical' (*trugōidopoiomousikē* [*technē*], fr. 333 K–A), or of his *Gērytades*, in which he sent poets of tragedy, trugedy, and cyclic hymns to the underworld in order to find Poetry.[43]

The audience of *Peace* had previously been entertained by a variety of self-conscious discussions, within drama, of poetry and its functions. Indeed, they were by now well versed in comedy's conventions of self-analysis. In the dialogue with Hermes, it transpires that Cratinus has recently died, unable to cope with the sight of a wine-jar being smashed (702–3). This joke cannot have failed to have reminded the audience of Cratinus' *Putinē*, victorious at the Dionysia in 423, in which *Kōmōidia* herself had appeared. She was the wife of Cratinus, but had left him because of his addiction to alcohol, in particular to his wine-flask, personified as the 'other woman'. In this play Cratinus had been unable to write comedy any more because of an excess of wine.[44] In the notion of trugedy, conversely, Aristophanic comedy's relationship with wine is seen as constructive and generative.

In Chapter 6 it was seen that it was not only in Cratinus' *Putinē* that Old Comedy reflected upon poetic abstractions by staging them. Aristophanes could have followed Cratinus' practice and introduced a female personification of comedy: if Cratinus could give a role to *Kōmōidia*, Aristophanes could have staged *Trugōidia*. He certainly introduced a personification of Poetry in his *Poiēsis*.[45] Trygaeus is somewhat different. His name delicately associates him with his genre, of which he seems to be rather some kind of practitioner or agent than a personification. Yet although Trygaeus is characterized occasionally as something approximating to a dramatic actor (see below), the name Trygaeus is still less concrete than would have been

---

[42] Taplin (1983), 331.   [43] See Ch. 5, pp. 175–6.

[44] See the excellent study by Rosen (2000).

[45] In Pherecrates' *Cheiron*, similarly, the character *Mousikē* described to the chorus the succession of wrongs which she had received at the hands of a succession of poets. See above, pp. 181–3.

suggested by the actual name *Trugōidos*: that would have had to mean 'trugedian'—that is, either 'trugic poet' or 'trugic actor'.

Evidence that when Athenians heard the name *Trygaeus* they would have been prompted to think of *trugedy* can be invoked from the formation of their proper names. Aristophanes could have called his hero by the attested proper names Trugias or Trugēs, from the same root; but he did not.[46] He chose to use a form which suggested that the name was *an abbreviated compound*. For Greek names fell into three basic categories: they were names taken from adjectives or ordinary nouns (*Purrhos*, *Leōn*), or they were compounds (*Patrokleēs*), or abbreviations of compounds (*Patroklos*).[47] Abbreviations of compounds were frequent and important; when Athenian men had sons, they often used an abbreviated form of their father's compound names, or of their own; everyone knew this and would automatically connect the abbreviated name of the child with the full compound.

One of the suffixes used in Attica in the creation of abbreviated compounds was *–aios* (as in *Trugaios*). According to the reverse index of the *Lexicon of Greek Personal Names* vol. ii (Attica), in the fifth century one Aristaios is the father of Aristōnumos, in the fourth an Aristaios is the father of Aristomachos, and in the third one Agathaios is the son of Agatharchos. In the following century a Charitaios appears as the son of a Chariklēs.[48] This evidence is sufficient to support the argument that an Athenian audience would assume that *Trygaeus* was an abbreviated form of a compound with *trug*; on consulting Professor Anna Davies, she wrote that the evidence from other names is 'sufficient to guarantee that an Athenian public would be capable of linking a name Trygaeus with a supposed name Trugōidos', although of course this does not mean that they *certainly* made the connection.[49] There are very few known compounds with *trug*- that *Trygaeus* could have been 'short for', especially as early as the fifth century, besides the *trugoipos* mentioned in the play itself. By far the

---

[46] See the references in Sommerstein (1985), 138.

[47] It was also possible to lose the second element entirely and add (or even not add) another suffix, as in Aleximachos becoming Alexis or Alexeus.

[48] Osborne and Byrne (1994).

[49] Personal letter from Professor Anna Morpurgo Davies, January 1997.

most likely candidate, especially in the context of recent comedy, would have to be *Trugōidos* ('Trugedian').

TRYGAEUS THE TRUGEDIAN

If Trygaeus is in some sense the offspring of 'Trugedian', this illuminates his special expertise and distinctive manner of achieving his goals—primarily through his knowledge of dramatic poetry and skill at performing it. The term *trugedy*, formed on analogy with the word *tragedy*, makes a strong link between the comic and tragic genres. One possibility is that *trugedy* meant a type of comedy which played extensively with tragedy; this entailed not only quoting tragedy and creatively using tragic archetypes, as Dicaeopolis does with Euripides' *Telephus* in *Acharnians*, and Lysistrata with his Melanippe,[50] but being distinctively *paratragic*. There is evidence that prior to *Acharnians* it was epic, rather than tragedy, which had been the mainstay of parody in Old Comedy (for example, recently, in Cratinus' *Dionysalexandros*, which seems to have offered a major parody of the Trojan war); Michael Silk argues that Aristophanes' almost exclusive interest in tragedy was a significant innovation.[51] *Trugedy* might then mean comedy which *utilized* tragedy, and this could describe *Peace*, with its stunning stunt drawn from *Bellerophon*. Trygaeus' name would then be saying something about trugedy's *assimilation* of tragedy to the comic genre.[52]

But there is another possibility. Taplin has argued that in *Acharnians* trugedy may refer, more ambitiously, to comedy with a serious purpose and a claim to the role of civic teacher, as at *Acharnians* 499–500;[53] in this case, by calling his hero *Trygaeus*, Aristophanes was proposing an embodiment or practitioner of his own socially useful

---

[50] Foley (1988), esp. 47. Corbato (1975) suggests that *Peace* may draw on the treatment of peace in Aeschylus' *Aitnaiai*.

[51] See Silk (1993); on *Dionysalexandros* and the Trojan war, Luppe (1966).

[52] At least one tragedian was supposed to have shared Trygaeus' occupation, at least in his youth: Aeschylus was said to have decided to become a tragedian after he had fallen asleep when looking after a vineyard, and been given this career direction by Dionysus, who visited him in a dream (Paus. 1.21.3).

[53] Taplin (1983), 333.

comedy. Trygaeus may not theorize about trugedy, but that may be because at no point is he identified with the authorial persona of his poet. When Dicaeopolis talks about trugedy in *Acharnians*, it is as Aristophanes, speaking as 'who in fact I am' (441): Edmunds is probably correct in arguing that it would have been much more difficult for Dicaeopolis 'to make assertions about the nature of comic poetry' when speaking in character.[54]

Trygaeus is not only emblematic of a certain type of theatre: he is also a versatile theatrical actor. His project, to use tragedy and satyr play to win Peace for Greece, is initiated under the influence of a form of inspired madness denoted by the term *mania* (54, 65), a Dionysiac condition. It may be connected with the melancholic surfeit of bile which seems to have affected the psyche of Euripides' Bellerophon;[55] it is not dissimilar to Philocleon's madness, discussed in *Wasps* (114, 1496). Yet, unlike these forms of mental illness, Trygaeus' *mania* is beneficial to both himself and his society.[56] Trygaeus characterizes his own project as a *tolmēma neon* (94), a 'daring new feat'. It is an unprecedented act of daring that takes Trygaeus to Olympus in order to remonstrate with frightening divinities, but the 'new feat' has also been interpreted as the bold project of reinstating the utopian age enjoyed by Hesiod's golden race of men—a godlike existence, free from care, delighting in festivals, *hēsuchia*, and food which grew spontaneously (*Erg.* 109–19). This motif had certainly become popular in contemporary Old Comedy, for example in Eupolis' *Chrusoun Genos* and Teleclides' *Amphictyones* (fr. 1 K–A).[57] But Trygaeus' 'new feat' could equally be a programmatic and self-referential notion. Perhaps it is connected to the identity of actors; just possibly Apollodorus had been lead actor in *Acharnians*, whose peace-loving hero Dicaeopolis had dared a previous *tolmēma*.[58] Or perhaps the feat is simply that in

---

[54] Edmunds (1980), 11. Some scholars have speculated that Aristophanes himself played Dicaeopolis: for discussion and bibliography see Slater (1989), 78–80.

[55] Σ *Iliad* 6.202a; see Riedweg (1990), 49–50; Olson (1998), 81.

[56] Bowie (1993), 138.

[57] Moulton (1981), 103–5, exploring a suggestive remark about Trygaeus' homecoming as marking the return of the golden age in Frye (1957), 177. On utopianism in Old Comedy see Manuel and Manuel (1972); Farioli (2001), 274–5; on Eupolis' play, Storey (2003), 266–77.

[58] Cassio (1985), 105–18. On the level of pure speculation, Apollodorus could even have been the son of the leading actor in *Acharnians*.

Peace Aristophanes is introducing a new hero who fights mostly through *poetry*.

During much of the play Trygaeus is creatively engaged with tragedy, satyr play, and epic (see further below). Dicaeopolis may conduct a rural Dionysia within the frame of a comedy played at the Dionysiac festival of the Lenaea, and thus make the dramatic performance in which he figures, as Edmunds has put it, 'itself a metaphor for the process it describes'; the audience of *Acharnians* is 're-educated in the metaphors that underlie the Dionysiac festival in which they are now participating as spectators'.[59] But this applies also to Trygaeus, who orchestrates his own and the other characters' negotiations with competitive displays of poetry. It is Trygaeus who takes all the initiatives in shifting dramatic registers. There is not a genre of dramatic poetry in which he is not proficient in the leading role: as Bellerophon, as Silenus in a satyr play, and as the supreme Dionysiac comic hero Trygaeus, vine-grower of the deme of Athmonon, who, in a scene-type typical of Old Comedy,[60] sees off the variety of braggart-type (*alazōn*) personages representing impediments to his plan.[61]

SPECTATOR INTEGRATION AND METAFESTIVAL

This trugedic context can illuminate the play's exceptional number of cases of 'audience participation'.[62] The prominence of audience 'integration' has been given a political interpretation by Cassio, who maintains that there is a tendency to pick on the Ionian allies present, which reinforces the propaganda that figured Athens as their mother-city.[63] It is indeed likely that there was a more *international* Greek

---

[59] Edmunds (1980), 36.   [60] Moulton (1981), 83.

[61] Plutarch, *Life of Cimon* 13.5 reports that an altar of Eirene had been erected after the Peace of Callias; but Deubner (1959), 37–8, doubts whether there was ever an official cult of Eirene earlier than by 374. For a detailed recent discussion of the evidence for Athenian worship of Eirene, see Stafford (2000), 173–7. Cartledge (1990), 60, suggests that Eirene is cleverly linked by Aristophanes to the cult of Athena, by being given momentarily the label *lusimachē*, which happened to be the name of the priestess of Athena Polias at the time.

[62] Dover (1972), 134.

audience present at the 421 Dionysia than for several years, almost certainly including Spartans as well as Ionians. But there has never been much stress on the insistency with which the play's strong interest in the boundary between play and audience is focused on its hero.[64]

Slater has argued that theatrical self-consciousness in *Peace* differs from that in Aristophanes' three preceding plays (*Acharnians, Knights*, and *Wasps*), which shifted the audience's attention to the notion of performance in other venues, such as the Assembly and the courts of law. In *Peace*, the self-reflexivity is emphatically related to the here and now of the theatre of Dionysus, and what Trygaeus is doing in this context.[65] This apprehension fits the notion that Trygaeus is a hero who effects his aims not through politics nor rhetoric but through poetic performance of diverse kinds. Trygaeus is certainly aware to an unusual degree of the mechanics of the theatre, admonishing the crane operator in the vocative to be careful as he rises to Olympus (*mēchanopoie*, 174). When he hands over the mute character *Theōria* to the Councillors sitting in the front row (881–908), he strikingly crosses the physical boundary between actors and audience. There is also a consistently high level of direct address of, or reference to, the audience by the actors, especially by Trygaeus himself (e.g. 50–61, 64–78, probably 263 and 286, 292–300). These phenomena include jokes resulting from the problem of suggesting within the limited illusionist capacities of a theatre the physical journey between Olympus and Athens (725–6, 819–20). There is castigation of thieves who lurk near the stage-building (*skēnē*, 730–1), and references to the stewards whose job was to keep order in the theatre (*rhabdouchoi*, 734). Characters speculate about what individual members of the audience (*theatai*) are thinking and saying (43–8, 543–4, 545–51). Eirene herself refuses to

---

[63] Cassio (1985). See also Thiercy (1986), 142–3.

[64] It does not significantly progress understanding simply to label 'metatheatre' anything which has to do with such a fundamental social dimension of a particular form of theatre as the nature of its relationship with, and involvement of, the spectators and therefore the wider community. See further Ch. 4, pp. 105–11. On the relationship between actors and community in medieval Mystery and subsequently Morality plays, which involved extensive audience address and integration, see e.g. Righter (1962), 13–42.

[65] Slater (2002), ch. 6, esp. 130–1.

address the *theatai* or anyone else at all except (silently) Hermes—prompting the 'interpretation' scene (658–83);[66] during this she turns her head from the audience, but it does later become apparent that the very first question she asked was connected with drama—that is, how Sophocles was faring (695). Other passages in *Peace* which integrate the spectators into the action include the sequence where they are pelted with grain at the sacrifice (962–5), Trygaeus' generous offer not actually to sacrifice the sheep in order to save the (unidentified) *chorēgos* some money (1022), and subsequently the hero's invitation to the spectators to share the offals with him and his slave (*age dē, theatai, deuro susplanchneuete* | *meta nōin*, 1114–1116). So Trygaeus has some unusually overt and self-conscious negotiations—even by the standards of Old Comedy—with his trugedic play's theatrical status.

The play is obsessively interested in festivals,[67] and especially in the City Dionysia. Most importantly, there occurs on one occasion a total confusion, unique in Old Comedy,[68] of what scholars used to call the art–life boundary. This is in the chorus' invitation to the audience at 815–18 'to thrust aside wars and dance with me your friend … and celebrate the festival along with me' (*met' emou sumpaize tēn heortēn*). It is not possible to be sure here whether the chorus mean the festival within the play (celebrating the reinstatement of Peace), or the City Dionysia extraneous to the play (the prelude to the ratification of peace), so it is legitimate to assume that they mean both. Secondly, when *Theōria*—'the right of spectating at public festivals'—is first sniffed by Trygaeus (529–35), he smells 'harvest-time (*opōra*), entertaining, Dionysia festivals, *auloi*, tragedies, songs by Sophocles, Euripidean diction … ivy, and the wine-strainer'. The 'Peace of Trygaeus' brings with it the Dionysia,

---

[66] Kassel (1983) discusses the *topos* of the voiceless statue, and suggests that it was Alexandrian taste that most approved of presentations of dialogues with statues; there may, however, have been a talking statue of Hermes in a comedy by Plato Comicus (see fr. 204 K–A).

[67] More recent interpreters of the play have seen that self-consciousness about the notion of festivals—meta*festival*—is one of its central focuses. See e.g. the extended discussion of *Theōria* in the two chapters of Reckford (1987) devoted to *Peace*, esp. 15: 'How can we understand Aristophanes' plays adequately when we ourselves disregard holidays?'

[68] Dover (1992), 59.

tragedy, Dionysus' plant, and the wine-making equipment which resonates so audibly with Trygaeus' own proper name. The play's assimilation of tragedy and satyr play, and explicit discussion of tragedy and dithyramb, could thus be seen as part of its own implicit salute to the role of the theatre in establishing Peace in Athens. It is even possible that there is also a structural shape assimilated from the festival of the City Dionysia. The play's structure could be designed to reflect that of the drama competition itself—that is, of the shape taken by a day at the Dionysiac competition during that period of the war. It seems that the tragedies and satyr drama of one poet were staged in the morning, followed by comedy in the afternoon. Although Luppe and others have questioned this structure, it would nevertheless be broadly reduplicated in the shape taken by Trygaeus' discovery, rescue, and implementation of Peace.[69] This play could be seen as a fictive compression, played out within the autonomous comedic world constituted by the alternative, even virtual, city portrayed in Old Comedy—'Para-Athens', as it is sometimes labelled— of the experience of a day at the Dionysia.

TRAGEDY AND SATYR PLAY

In the sequence between the satyric and the comic movements Trygaeus tells of the dithyrambic poets he met on his way down to earth (829–31), and we do not know how the dithyrambic choral competitions fitted into the festival's daily drama programme at this time. But this does not affect the possibility that one of the deep structures underlying the drama is the ordering of activities at the Dionysia: Aristophanes could be lending to history, as it takes place, a shape informed by the triadic sequence tragedy-satyr-play-comedy.[70] The opening movement sees Trygaeus, the hero of the play, flying to heaven on a dung-beetle in a powerful parody of

[69] Luppe (1972); but see the responses of Mastromarco (1975) and the remarks of Slater (1999), with bibliography in 351 n. 1; Csapo and Slater (1995), 107.

[70] See below for the presence in the final, comedic section, of two sequences of hexameter feuding, between Trygaeus and the oracle-monger Hierocles (1063–114) and Trygaeus and Lamachus' little son (1270–83, 1286–9, 1292–3).

Euripides' *Bellerophon* in which the hero flew on the winged horse Pegasus. This conception is similar to Dicaeopolis' use of the Euripidean role of Telephus in *Acharnians*. Rau points out that Bellerophon had *finished* with the chimaera in Euripides' play, just as Trygaeus, as we are told on more than one occasion (e.g. 313–14), including the parabasis (751–9), has already disposed of the Cleon-monster, long since dead.[71] Trygaeus tells us, as he ascends, that his intention is to question Zeus, and an interrogation of Zeus is not an improbable motive for Bellerophon in the tragedy.[72] The whole sequence is opened by explicit commentary on what is going on by one of Trygaeus' slaves. He tells the other slave that he is going to explain the plot to 'the children and the youths and the men and the important men and even these 'men beyond men' here (*huperēnor-eousin* (53)—see further below); his master is mad (*mainetai*) in a new way (*kainon tropon*), for all day long he looks at the heavens, and with his mouth agape 'like this' he upbraids Zeus (50–60).

The slave must here imitate tragic acting style, perhaps representing the effect of the angle taken by the mouth hole in a tragic actor's mask during an imprecation of heaven.[73] He also points out the rows of people sitting in the theatre, their status increasing with their proximity to the orchestra, climaxing with those of such high status that they enjoyed the right to sit on the very front row (*prohedria*).[74] This direct description of the audience implies a striking flourish of gesture and/or posture. The range of skills that would be expected of a leading *tragōidos* is certainly displayed by Trygaeus. Like (for example) Medea, Trygaeus is first heard booming out from indoors, while the slave asks the audience, in the plural, whether they can *hear* (*akouete*) the kind of mania from which Trygaeus is suffering (65).[75] Like Medea (for example), Trygaeus has access to the theatrical *mēchanē*. Trygaeus' daughter suggests that he should have ridden on Pegasus rather than the beetle, 'so as to appear more like a tragic hero in the eyes of gods' (*tragikōteros*, 134), and warns him not to fall off, thus becoming lame and providing Euripides with a plot for

---

[71] Rau (1967), 406.   [72] Sommerstein (1985), 139.

[73] See Paley (1873), 11, who compares Aeschylus, *Septem* 422, *thnētos ōn eis ouranon*, etc.

[74] See Paley (1873), 11; Olson (1998), 78.

[75] On the parallels with *Medea* see Rau (1967), 91, and Harriott (1986), 121.

tragedy (*kai tragōidia genēi* (148; see Ch. 2, pp. 36–7). The children's appeal to their departing father also makes use of Euripides' *Aeolus*.[76] Trygaeus then rebukes the crane operator (*mēchanopoie*) in an absurd clash of registers (172–6), demanding that the audience see through the identities of both Bellerophon and Trygaeus to the actor, communicating with another theatre worker.[77] At the house of Zeus, an opposition between tragedy and epic is implied in the altercation with Polemos, the personification of war, as well as the dialogue with Hermes. In response to the Iliadic diction of their Olympian opponents (see below and e.g. Hermes' poetic term *amaldunthēsomai*, 'I will be made soft'; cf. *Iliad* 7.463), the chorus and Trygaeus use other phrases and indeed quotations from tragedies, probably including *Heracles* (976–7) and the Aeschylean *Prometheus* (319–20).[78] Such has been tragedy's contribution to the peace process.

In the scene where Peace is rescued, the play closely resembles a satyr-drama, the type of play which routinely followed tragedies at the fifth-century Dionysia (see Ch. 5, pp. 149–51), and which had previously informed some famous comedies, including Cratinus' *Dionysalexandros*, which had featured a chorus of satyrs.[79] The hauling of a cult object from hiding, inherited from much earlier ritual precedents, was a familiar satyric theme.[80] Aeschylus' *Sisyphus*, which staged Sisyphus pushing up his stone from the underworld, explicitly likened him to a dung-beetle rolling a ball of dung (fr. 223 *TgrF*, actually quoted by Σ *Peace* 73b).[81] In Aeschylus' *Dictyulci*, satyrs hauled the chest containing Danae out of the sea, and the hauling scene in *Peace* is certainly partially modelled on that satyric prototype. The parodos of *Peace* is instigated by Trygaeus' summons (296–8), 'You peasants and merchants and carpenters and craftsmen and immigrants and foreigners and islanders come hither, all you people, as quickly as you can'. This is modelled on the invitation in *Dictyulci* to

[76] Rau (1967), 92; Harriott (1986), 122. On *Aeolus* see also Ch. 3, pp. 74–6.
[77] See Thiercy (1986), 141.   [78] See Olson (1998), 127.
[79] T i.42 K–A = *POxy* 663, col. ii, 42, with Bakola (2005). The satyrs somehow helped Dionysus-Paris (i.e. Pericles) to escape arrest: see recently McGlew (2002), 46–56.
[80] On the ritual antecedents of the hauling scene, with fascinating vase images, see Adrados (1972).
[81] Harriott (1986), 124.

'all peasants, vine-diggers...and shepherds', and probably other groups, to aid in the hauling of the chest.[82] Trygaeus has thus virtually turned into Silenus, the satyr-choreographer who directed the hauling scene in the episode's Aeschylean prototype.[83] The chorusmen spontaneously burst into dance steps, a malady which has been diagnosed as satyric 'auto-orchestrism' (322–36), also manifested in the satyrs of Sophocles' *Trackers* (fr. 314.229–30 *TgrF*) and implied in *Cyclops*.[84] Moreover, Trygaeus needs to order the chorus to keep their noise down, lest they waken Cleon in Hades (318–19); the chorus of *Trackers* are rebuked for their din by the nymph Cyllene, lest they waken Hermes.[85] The chorus of Aristophanes' *Peace* are thus temporarily assuming the role of satyrs, and Trygaeus, like Silenus, simultaneously encourages and disciplines them.

TRYGAEUS AND LYRIC

Yet in the continuosly shifting refraction of the traditions of poetry through the comic prism of *Peace*, it is choral lyric that comes to the fore in the predominantly dactylo-epitrite metre of the strophic pair concluding the parabasis (775–96 = 797–818). The appropriation of such lyric to the cause of peace extends to sustained allusion to Stesichorus' *Oresteia* (775–80, see Stesichorus fr. 33 *PMG*). The Stesichorean material in the strophe is an address to the Muse on the topic of the joys of peace—weddings of gods, banquets of men, and the festivities of the blessed, 'for these have been your chosen themes from the start' (775–80); in the antistrophe Stesichorus' authority is invoked to confirm that it is peaceable songs that the wise man is obligated to sing (797–800). Stesichorus, of course, was traditionally credited with having issued warnings against violence and tyranny, advocating peace, and, moreover, being the son of

---

[82] Sommerstein (1985), 147. On *Dictyulci*, see further above, Ch. 5, pp. 158–60.

[83] On the representation of Silenus in satyr drama generally, see now Krumeich, Pechstein, and Seidensticker (1999), 164–5 with references.

[84] See Zimmermann (1996); cf. *Birds* 305–6, *Frogs* 386–9, and esp. *Plutus* 288–9; Seaford (1984), 193–4.

[85] On satyric prancing and dancing generally, see Ch. 5, n. 10.

Hesiod, who later becomes a significant ancestral figure in Trygaeus' mission (see below).[86]

The lyric theme is continued into the ensuing dialogue between Trygaeus and his slave; Trygaeus reports that on his way down he encountered the souls of dithyrambic composers, 'flitting about collecting ideas for some preludes of the air-haunting-swiftly-soaring kind';[87] the language here recalls two separate Pindaric images of the poet: as a bird who sings winged songs (*Nem.* 3.80–3; see also Bacchylides 3.96–8), and as a bee who flits between flowers collecting the honey of the Muses (*Pyth.* 10.53–4). This accumulation of lyric metre, quotation, and imagery reaches a climax with Trygaeus' claim that he actually encountered the katasterized Ion of Chios; he has been renamed for his own famous dithyramb, 'Dawnstar' (835–7),[88] whose opening line sang of the star that 'heralded the sun' (fr. 6 *PMG*)—a suitable allusion for a hero about to inaugurate a new golden age, and indeed to get married. For in a splendid climax to the parabasis, Trygaeus re-emerges triumphantly with his new female attendants, and announces his imminent marriage to *Opōra*; here the metres in which the chorus responds to him are telesilleans and reizianums, which in Sappho fr. 141.1 were clearly associated with weddings (856–67 = 909–21).

The two key images of Peace in the cultural encyclopaedia of archaic and classical Greece were farming and weddings; it seems almost inevitable that the farmer Trygaeus should also be a bridegroom. The remainder of the play consists of an extended wedding preparation, but continues its serial examination of poetic genres and their respective relationships to war and peace. Trygaeus may temporarily have acted the parts of Bellerophon in a tragedy and Silenus in a satyr drama, but is fundamentally a comic—or rather, a *trugedic*—hero, and the play's finale re-establishes the primacy of that genre. Tragedy identified the problem, satyr play solved it, choral lyric has provided a collective

---

[86] See Aristotle, *Rhet.* 2.1393^{b}8, 2.1394^{b}15–^{a}1; Conon *FgrH* 26 F 1.42, and further references in M. L. West (1971), esp. 303 n. 1. Hesiod was said to be the father of Stesichorus in Aristotle's *Constitution of Ochomenus*, quoted in Tzetzes, *Life of Hesiod* p. 39 ed. Colonna (1983); also by Proclus on Hesiod, *Erg.* 271, and in the *Suda*, s.v. Stesichorus. Thanks to Peter Wilson for help with these valuable references.

[87] Translation by Sommerstein (1985), 830–1.

[88] See Leurini's edition of Ion of Chios (1992), 111–12 fr. 84.

transition into the joyous new world where Peace reigns; now Trygaeus interacts with his slave throughout the scene in which the cult of peace is installed (819–1126). The motifs in this episode are predominantly comic—play around the sacrifice, foolery with food,[89] discussion of somatic functions, audience participation, extended sexual innuendo (894–904), and the intrusion of the oracle-monger Hierocles. There follow the arms-dealer and the two little boys who are guests at Trygaeus' wedding. The poetic struggle filtered through the comic lens now becomes Hesiodic *versus* heroic martial epic and its associated symbols, especially the shield.

This confrontation of Hesiodic and Homeric poetics is also the comedy's most agonistic feature. Trygaeus is physically violent only once (against Hierocles, 1119); unlike the oratorical Dicaeopolis and Sausage-Seller he is not rhetorically argumentative. His part requires the performance of no rhetorical agon, no sophistical monologue, no speech to perform in a civic arena.[90] This might be a theatrical response to the suspension of public business during the Dionysia (Dem. *Against Meidias* 10).[91] Trygaeus' festive world is not concerned with the law courts: as he tells Hermes, he brings no malicious accusations and is no busybody (191). While the play's 'toning down of the agonistic element' has been noted, the dimension that has always been said to replace it has been an unusually intense engagement with choral lyric.[92] But even the central, Stesichorean panel of the play transmutes into a denunciation of theatrical practitioners—Carcinus, Morsimus, and Melanthius—whose mediocrity excludes them from Trygaeus' banquet (781–95, 802–14). Thus to focus exclusively on the play's response to the lyric tradition, at the expense of the rich use of hexameter as well as theatrical verse, is to miss Trygaeus' far-reaching vocal and poetical point.[93]

---

[89] For a recent discussion of the importance of food and feasting in *Peace*, see Compton-Engle (1999).

[90] Blistein (1980), 222–3; Thiercy (1986), 208; Moulton (1981), 84–5; Murphy (1938); Slater (1989), 82.

[91] See Csapo and Slater (1995), 105–6, 112.

[92] Moulton (1981), 84; see also Harriott (1986), 127.

[93] There are no equivalents in the surviving Aristophanic plays of the heroic (as opposed to oracular, melic or recitative) hexameters in *Peace*: see John Williams White (1912), 149; Pretagostini (1995), 166–70. Thanks to Eric Handley for help on this question.

TRYGAEUS AND HEXAMETER POETRY

In the second half of the play the actor playing Trygaeus needed to demonstrate an altogether different type of virtuosity. Trygaeus can also fight bellicosity through epic: epic becomes ammunition for advocates of both war and peace. Choice of diction has even much earlier in the play insinuated an association between martial epic and the opponents of peace: the term Trygaeus' slave used for the 'arrogant supermen' in the theatre (53) was the Homeric *hyperēnoreousin* (see e.g. *Iliad* 4.176), and Trygaeus applied to Polemos the resonantly epic epithet *talaurinos*, 'wearing a huge leather shield' (241).[94] In the play's negotiation with hexameter poetry, there are important resonances in terms of other comedies that are unfortunately almost inaudible today. The fragments of other poets of Old Comedy show that comic burlesques of passages of Hesiod and Homeric catalogues were a recognized, if not particularly common, element in comedy's repertoire: Pherecrates' *Cheiron*, a play with a strong interest in poetics, included a thirteen-line hexameter parody of Hesiod (fr. 162 K–A), while Hermippus spoofed the catalogue convention with a hexameter list of remarkable wines and their provenances (fr. 63 K–A).[95] Moreover, Cratinus' *Archilochoi*, an earlier play than *Peace*, had discussed the relationship between the poetry of Archilochus and Homeric epic, included at least one imposing hexameter (fr. 7 K–A), and probably staged an opposition between advocates of Homer and of Hesiod respectively.[96] A similar opposition comes to inform the second half of *Peace*. In three separate encounters Trygaeus is presented as the adversary of martial epic, but in slightly different ways.

At 1063 Hierocles embarks on hexameters, in which he utters dire oracular warnings against the making of peace. But in this metre Trygaeus, it appears, can give as good as he gets. Here the notion of the battle between peace and war begins to be formulated in terms of

[94] In the *Iliad* the epithet *talaurinos* is used (e.g. 5.289) of Ares exclusively; it was applied to Lamachus in *Acharnians* (964).

[95] See also Cratinus' *Seriphioi* frr. 222–4 K–A.

[96] See especially the remarks of Diogenes Laertius 1.12, who quotes *Archilochoi* fr. 2 K–A, and Bizzaro (1999), 13–26. The comedy was probably produced in about 430 BC. See also Teleclides' comedy *Hesiodoi* (fragments 15–24 K–A).

Homeric epic and its martial emphasis.[97] When Hierocles asks what oracle has given him the authorization to make this sacrifice, Trygaeus answers in a patchwork of phrases from both the *Iliad* and the *Odyssey* (1090–4), with one exception: there is an entirely novel line (1091). In order to explain what worshipping Peace might entail, Trygaeus has to extemporize, to become a rhapsodic innovator. He manipulates the tradition of martial epic to allow it to express a more Hesiodic sentiment: 'They chose Peace for themselves, and installed her with a sacrifice' (*Eirēnēn heilonto kai hidrusanth' hiereiōi*).

To a dominantly ancient Athenian audience, the idea of creative elaboration in hexameters, in a competition against another performer, will have suggested the panhellenic festivals to which the Peace of Nicias would renew access, including the Pythian games, at which poetic *agōnes* had long been held.[98] But musical competitions had become extremely popular in Attica in the mid-fifth century;[99] the rhapsodic confrontation in *Peace* will also have brought to mind the Panathenaea, where rhapsodes competed in the performance of epic; indeed, according to the rules for the competition attributed to Hipparchus, they officially performed, like Hierocles and Trygaeus, 'by exchange and by cue' (*ex hupolēpseōs ephexēs*, [Plato], *Hipparchus* 228b–c). It has recently been argued that this allowed for a far greater degree of improvisation by individual rhapsodes, up until the moment of the pre-arranged 'cue' for handover, than has often been allowed.[100]

The confrontation of Hesiod and Homer is one of several oppositions with which the play reinforces the fundamental Peace/War antithesis. A sensory example is the olfactory contrast between the malodorous dung balls fed to the beetle, while War is still in the ascendant, and the delicious fragrance wafting from the recovered Eirene's statue.[101] Gendered symbolism also plays a role, since Peace is represented by pacific females: Trygaeus' daughters, *Theōria* and *Opōra*, and the Hesiodic entourages of Graces (41, 797–800), Seasons

---

[97] See the excellent discussion of Collins (2001), esp. 22–3.

[98] See Rutherford (2004), 74.

[99] It has recently been stressed that the building of the Periclean Odeion in Athens had been a response to the need to accommodate 'the musical contests burgeoning across Attica' (P. Wilson (2004), 285).

[100] On the poetic struggle battle between different types of hexameter—oracular and epic—see e.g. Blistein (1980), 96.

[101] See Assoun (2002), 109.

(456–7), and Muses. War, on the other hand, is represented by pairs of bellicose males with epic associations: Polemos and Kudoimos, the sons of Lamachus and Cleonymus, and Ares and Enyalios (456–7). Polemos is not himself named in Homer, but rather in Pindar (fr. 78.1 S-M, as the father of the personified war-cry), Heraclitus (22 B 53 D–K), and in Aristophanes' own *Acharnians* (978–87). But in *Peace* he uses blatantly Homeric language, such as 'abject' in his opening line (*polutlēmones*, 236; see *Il.* 7.152).[102] Kudoimos is indeed an Homeric figure, an associate of Ares (*Iliad* 5.593).

Peter Green has described Aristophanes' project in *Peace* as a celebration of the 'precarious' treaty 'cobbled up' in 421, by composing 'a topical play lambasting Athenian arms-profiteers'.[103] The second male arrival to prove an impediment to Peace, the arms dealer (accompanied by a mute helmet-maker and spear-maker), is furious because the advent of peace in Greece will ruin his business (1212–13).[104] There ensues a comic perversion of a Homeric arming scene. But the items of armour are not fitted on the hero. Instead, each weapon the arms dealer and his colleagues offer for sale is itemized, described, becomes the butt of Trygaeus' humour and is ultimately rejected. One of the items is a cuirass, which Trygaeus sets down on the floor and attempts to use as a chamber-pot (1224–36). The joke is considerably extended and may require that the spectators recall a heroic painting, dependent on a cyclic epic about the Trojan war, at Delphi. The scene may have been designed to bring to mind Polygnotus' famous painting of the Sack of Troy (a scene derived from the epic of that name), which adorned the Cnidian *Lesche* at Delphi.[105] In the picture, according to Pausanias, the child Glaucus (son of Theano and Antenor) sat on a hollow breastplate (10.27.1). It helps here to

---

[102] Homeric diction in the course of the play's heteroglot manipulation of different styles of poetic diction in the service of social causes is also used by the Peace lobby to *derogate* bellicose leaders: men in power act like 'lions' at home, however cowardly in battle, sing the chorus at 1189.

[103] P. Green (2004), 86.

[104] P. Green (2004), 86 n. 13, points out that the theme of arms supply creates an opportunity for a joke at the expense of Sophocles' father, who owned a shield factory, and is now said to be desperate for cash (698–9).

[105] Mark I. Davies (1980). For a surviving example of a 5th-cent. bronze muscle cuirass, from Ruvo in southern Italy (British Museum GR 1856.12–26.614), see Everson (2004), p. 141 fig. 51. Thanks to Rosie Wyles for this reference.

envisage the flared and hollow form of the cuirass, which from the front, at least, bore distinct similarities to a child's potty (*amis, ouranē*).[106] When Trygaeus takes his seat on the corselet, he may therefore spoof the tradition of heroic mural painting and thus of heroic martial epic. Davies's theory is lent support by the other jokes requiring familiarity with famous artists and works of visual art in the play. These include a discussion of Pheidias intended to call to mind his statue of Athena in the Parthenon (615–18),[107] and a reference to the statue of Pandion, one of the eponymous heroes (1183).

The final threat to Peace comes in the form of the two little boys, sons of bellicose generals, who have come to be guests at Trygaeus' wedding, and want to practise their songs. At this wedding, there is to be held a musical *agōn* more suggestive of a panhellenic festival than a private party.[108] The first boy launches straight into the opening hexameter of the cyclic *Epigoni*, 'The deeds of younger arms I sing' (1270), and ignores Trygaeus' furious interruption. He doggedly continues with a quotation consisting of lines from the *Iliad*, 'And when, advancing against each other, they were at close quarters, they dashed together their bucklers and their centre-bossed shields' (1273–4). Trygaeus asks him to stop going on about shields, but he continues with another Iliadic line, 'and then together rose men's cries of pain and triumph' (1276). Again Trygaeus interrupts, this time swearing by his favourite god, Dionysus, with a joke, once again involving shields, about 'centre-bossed' cries of pain (1277). When the boy expresses confusion about what exactly he *should* be singing about, Trygaeus decides to *compete* with him by improvising two lines parodying epic metre and style (1281–2), 'Thus they feasted on oxen (and this sort of thing): They had breakfast set before them, and whatever is most pleasant to taste'. Finally, the boy responds (1283–4) with a couplet only very slightly

---

[106] See e.g. the large 6th-cent. child's potty found in the agora area, with its rounded upper section and flared base, which originally encased the receptacle, in Lang and Eliot (1976), 240–1 fig. 125.

[107] This joke is connected with Pheidias' supposed indictment for embezzling precious materials used in the construction of the statue of Athena Parthenos: see Plutarch's *Life of Pericles* 31–2, and Frost (1964).

[108] See the excellent discussion of the fusion in the exodos of *Peace* of traditional *hymenaion* form with Dionysiac elements in Calame (2004), 172–6; Zimmermann (1985), 185–88, stresses the importance of the theme of the return to the fields in the hymeneal lyric elements.

adapted from one delivered by Homer in the *Contest of Homer and Hesiod* (107–8), a contest which Hesiod wins.

The surviving manuscript text of the *Contest* stems from a fourth-century work, the *Mouseion* of Alcidamas, a pupil of Gorgias. The contest does not encompass the entire poem, but, rather, lines 62–214; this episode, and the fundamental idea of an *agōn* between verses of Homer and verses of Hesiod, are both certainly of earlier origin.[109] The agenda underlying the text of the *Contest* is complicated; although Hesiod wins because his poetry is wiser and more socially useful, the poetry of Homer is given a surprisingly positive presentation, despite his ultimate defeat.[110] In a subtle essay, Rosen has recently shown that such an *agōn* is an indisputable undertext of the competition in poetry—and wisdom—between Aeschylus and Euripides staged in Aristophanes' *Frogs*.[111] Richardson, who believes that the *Contest* dates to the sixth century, saw that the situation at the end of *Peace* also replicates the situation in the *Contest*: in both texts a bellicose advocate of Homeric epic is vanquished in rhapsodic competition against a man whose hexameters advocate peace and husbandry.[112]

Another critic of Homer, Xenophanes, had decades earlier objected to the singing of songs about battles and *stasis* at symposia (fr. 1 *IEG*); Anacreon had also rejected poems about conflict and tearful war on such occasions (fr. 2 *PMG*). But the boy will not desist from uttering martial Iliadic verses; Trygaeus dismisses him, only to have to dispense, more quickly, with Cleonymus' son. His choice of sympotic song is Archilochus' famous elegy about throwing away his shield in the war against the Saians (1295–1301)—shields again. This plan is rejected by Trygaeus in language tinged with epic formulae, probably a direct parody of Alcaeus (fr. 6 *PLF*). Archilochean martial elegy has

---

[109] O'Sullivan (1992), 85.   [110] See Rosen (1997*b*), 473–6.

[111] Rosen (2004), 297–314; previous scholars who have noted the likelihood of the Homer–Hesiod *agōn* as a prototype for *Frogs* include O'Sullivan (1992), 87 n. 143; Cavalli (1999), 105.

[112] Richardson (1981), 2. For this dating see also Schadewaldt (1942), 64–6; Hess (1961), 7–26. The presence of the *Contest* behind the competition in *Peace* can be accepted even on the more cautious chronology of Graziosi (2001), 62–9, who argues that the *Contest* fits well with 5th-cent. literary concerns; she assembles cogent arguments from enjambment, phrasing, and punctuation in the hexameter quotations in *Peace* for seeing the whole exchange there as using and subverting lines that were not only already familiar, but which had already been linked to Homer and Hesiod respectively.

no place in his plan.[113] Trygaeus has trumped the oracle-monger's bellicose hexameters with peaceable ones, made fun of visual arts painting martial epic, shown himself able to improvise hexameters in combat with the *Iliad*, in a sequence almost certainly intended to remind the audience of the content (and conclusion) of the *Contest of Homer and Hesiod*, and located himself in the tradition of those who proscribed martial themes at symposia by his exclusion of Archilochean elegy. Is Aristophanes laying claim to following in Hesiod's footsteps rather than Homer's, and representing in Trygaeus the advocacy of peace and symbolic representation of the peasantry previously associated with the author of *Works and Days*? Is Aristophanes saying that his new socially concerned and peace-oriented parody of more serious drama was effectively the new rival of Homer?

THE SIGN OF THE SHIELD

The Hesiodic divinity Peace is represented in the comedy by a beautiful statue of a maiden, a *korē*, passive femininity in aestheticized form.[114] Trygaeus' longing for peace is an erotic impulse, the impulse lovely statues of females could elicit in their viewer (see Ch. 4, pp. 131–3).[115] Peace is addressed by Hermes as the 'most shield-band-hating' of females (662, *ō gunaikōn misoporpakistatē*), a suggestive neologism which supports the view that the primary symbol throughout the play of Peace's adversary, War, is the shield. Shields provide by far the most numerous puns in *Peace* (at least seventeen instances), and the speed at which they occur accelerates. In the second version of *Peace*, the list

---

[113] Bonanno (1973–4) discusses the epic/Alcaeic resonances of Trygaeus' response. Harriott (1986), 127, argues that the Archilochus is rejected because the poem is 'escapist' in tone.

[114] The decision to portray her as a statue won derision from other comic playwrights: see Eupolis fr. 62 K–A and Plato Comicus fr. 86 K–A. For a discussion of her likely appearance—she may have resembled the nubile personifications of the Meidias painter—see Stafford (2000), 187 and n. 68; an alternative view—that she required little more than a peplos draped round a pole with a mask affixed—is expressed by Slater (2002), 123.

[115] For a psychoanalytical reading of the comedy which stresses the importance of desire—erotic and otherwise—to its scenography, see Assoun (2002), esp. 107–8.

of armour in the scene with the arms-dealer was supplemented by a shield (fr. 306 K–A): this may have been added because of the plethora of shield jokes in the rest of the play.

Shields were topical. After the Athenian victory at Pylos in 425 BC, Cleon had brought 298 Peloponnesian hostages (including 120 Spartans) to Athens in triumphal procession (Thuc. 4.21.2). There are comments in Aristophanes' *Farmers, Clouds,* and *Knights* about these unfortunate captives.[116] Cleon had also ordered Spartan shields to be hammered to the walls of the Stoa Poikile, inscribed with the words, 'Athenians, from the Lakedaimonians, [taken] from Pylos'. Pausanias commented upon them (1.15.5): one has turned up.[117] It has been argued recently that Cleon also had Pylian shields displayed on the bastion of the Nike temple, transforming it 'into a gleaming tower of bronze—a spectacular trophy indeed', in the very sightline of spectators in the theatre of Dionysus, and visible all the way from the Piraeus to the Kerameikos.[118] These tokens of victory illuminate Aristophanes' choice of the shield as the material symbol of the aggressive imperialism he associated with Cleon and his supporters. Shields are also used to attack the generals and politicians who forced peasants to fight, but turned out themselves to be cowardly shield-droppers (1186). The notorious *rhipsaspis* Cleonymus is attacked three times, the last instance during the stage appearance of his own son (446, 673–5, 1298–9 = Archil. fr. 5 *IEG*). The shield, therefore, operates as a key sign in the symbolic code by which the audience identifies the 'anti-peace' politicians at Athens. The delights of returning to peace are also imagined in terms of shields. In the hauling scene, the chorus cry, 'I'm glad, I'm happy, I fart, I laugh, *at having escaped from my shield*' (335–6). They pray that every man who helps in the tug-of-peace '*may never again take up a shield*' (438), and that pro-war shield retailers be attacked by brigands (447–8).

The shield brought with it a telling symbolic heritage. It is not just that in *Acharnians* Dicaeopolis had Lamachus' shield inverted so that he could vomit into it (585–6). The shield was the most privileged bearer of *ekphraseis* in epic, and Achilles' shield portrays two contrasting

---

[116] See Panagopoulos (1985), 51–4.

[117] See Lang and Eliot (1976), 255–6 with fig. 134, and the photograph in Witschel (2002), 8, fig. 6.

[118] Schultz (2003), 49, 51.

communities, one at war and one at peace. The marriage feast of Trygaeus and *Opōra* at the play's conclusion draws on one of the peace scenes in speaking of a banquet, of the hymenaion, of torches and of dancing (1316–59). But Trygaeus and the chorus of peasant-farmers are also the animate, theatrical descendants of the vine-growers portrayed in the community at peace. Indeed, the verb *trugaō* makes its sole appearance in the *Iliad* during this description (18.561–6):

And on it he also put a vineyard heavily laden with clusters, a fair one made of gold. The grapes were black, and throughout the vines were set up on silver poles. And he drove around it a trench of cyanus, and around that a trench of tin. One single path led to it, by which the vintagers visited it, whenever they gathered the vintage (*hote trugoōien alōēn*).[119]

Aristophanes' dramatization of Dionysiac amity, with its bridegroom hero Trygaeus and its key image of the shield, thus owes a powerful associative debt to the towns at peace in epic ecphrases.

CONCLUSION

The role of Trygaeus is politically uncompromising, thematically complex, poetically resonant, and histrionically demanding. The actor Apollodorus had theatrically to shadow Nicias, and to continue the work of Dicaeopolis. Trygaeus is a comic representative of the vine-growers of Attica and of Greek peasants everywhere.[120] He is a trickster and opportunist, perhaps personifying a figure in a popular proverb. He shares features with Dionysus, the god of vines and of drama, and with the *archōn* who played the part of Dionysus at the Anthesteria. His name suggests penetrative heterosexual sex from a male perspective, an activity for which Peace will increase opportunities. He is connected

---

[119] See also the pseudo-Hesiodic *Aspis* (which is probably of later date than Aristophanes, but drew on traditional material and formulae): the root *trug-* occurs twice within three lines in the description of Heracles' shield (291–5): 'Some were holding reaping hooks and were gathering in the vintage (*hoi d' etrugōn oinas*), while others were taking from the reapers (*hupo trugētērōn*) white and black clusters off the long rows of vines which were heavy with leaves and silver tendrils.'

[120] On the 'universal' dimension of Trygaeus' status as countryman, see Moulton (1981), 110–11.

with the satyrs who trample the grapes in the *trugoipos* with which he also shares part of his name. He is also closely related to Trugedy, a term by which poets in the late 420s often described comedy. If not quite a personification, he is certainly an offshoot and *agent* of trugedy, a practitioner of the trugedic art.

Trygaeus is a theatrical performer, sometimes overtly conflated with the actor beneath his own mask: he can recite tragic anapaests (82–101, 154–72), sing lyric dactyls (119–23), and knows his Euripides intimately. He can also play the part of Silenus in a satyr play, orchestrating a chorus of quasi-satyric dancers; he knows about dithyrambs and lyric. He can see off enemies in true comic style, perhaps even demonstrating a knowledge of poetry's visual counterpart, painting. In the second half he metamorphoses into a rhapsode, who can extemporise from hexameter cues, and gives better than he gets in parody of martial epic in dactylic hexameters. He is also configured in this scene as Hesiod, fighting against Homer in the traditional contest between them, Finally, his name and its association ultimately make him the literary descendant of the very vine-growers on epic shields, the primary representatives of towns at peace in pre-theatrical poetry.

In Plato's *Republic* Socrates argues that a dramatist cannot be proficient at writing both tragedy and comedy. Nor can the same performers be simultaneously rhapsodes and actors. Even more specifically, Socrates then suggests that the same actors are not capable of performing in both tragedy and comedy (3.395a2–b1). Yet Socrates might have been given food for thought by both Trygaeus and Apollodorus, at least for the hectic hour or two it took to discharge the role. Trygaeus is a comic hero who can perform tragedy and satyr drama, and can improvise epic hexameters into the bargain. The primary weapon which Trygaeus deploys in his war on war is not violence or rhetoric or verbal abuse, but poetry; this agent of trugedy and trugedic performer is not only the happiest of Aristophanes' heroes, as one of his few previous admirers called him,[121] but the only one whose peculiarly pacific heroism is fundamentally grounded in his association with Apollo's gift, the art of poetry.

---

[121] Thiercy (1986), 215: 'C'est le héros le plus heureux de tout le théâtre d'Aristophane.'

12

Lawcourt Dramas: Acting and Performance in Legal Oratory

THE ATHENIAN CAST OF LITIGANTS

In Aristophanes' *Wasps* the actor playing the role of the addicted juror Philocleon delivers a pseudo-legal speech in defence of jury attendance. He lists the types of entertaining performances he can expect to witness in court (562–70):

> I can listen to the defendants letting forth every manner of voice (*pasas phōnas hientōn*) in order to get acquitted ... Some bewail their poverty and exaggerate their plight ... Others tell us stories or a funny Aesopic fable; others crack jokes to make me laugh and put me in a good mood. And if these means don't persuade me, they drag in their little children by the hand forthwith, girls and boys, who cower together and bleat in chorus ...

Even more outlandish litigators' presentations than these are subsequently envisaged by Philocleon; recitations from tragedy, *aulos*-recitals, and competitions in rhetorical entreaty by rival suitors for the hand of a rich heiress. This is a comic, biased, and exaggerated account of the proceedings in the Athenian *dikastērion*.[1] But nobody in Aristophanes' audience would have found it amusing had it borne no relation to reality. It isolates three kinds of social performance—pathetic lamentation, humorous joke-telling, and verbal contest—which are reminiscent of other kinds of public performance in

---

[1] On the relationship of the characterisation of Philocleon to the Athenian jurors in reality, see the wise remarks of Carey (2000), 198–203.

Athens: tragedy, comedy, and the rhetorical debate (*agōn*) common to both theatrical genres.

In classical Athens a similar shape and overall character—what social anthropologists call *isomorphism*—characterized dramatic festivals, athletics competitions, meetings of the assembly, and court cases.[2] They had all developed out of the tradition of the aristocratic competition, the *agōn*. Indeed, the litigants sometimes describe the trial in which they are engaged as an *agōn* (Ant. 6.9, Lys. 9.3). Hansen has compared the ancient Athenian lawsuit to 'a play with three characters, all amateurs: the citizen who brought the charge, the magistrate who prepared the case and presided over the court, and the jury who heard the case and gave the judgment'.[3] The shape of the actual trial, however, implies a rather different analogy with drama in which both defendant and prosecutor learn roles, and enact an *agōn* in front of the jurors, who represent either the listening, responsive chorus, or the audience, rather than an individual role. It is with developing this analogy that this chapter is chiefly concerned.

Trials all involved a small number of individuals competing in front of an audience, often a very large audience, of citizens: Demosthenes compares the assessment of an orator's skill with the judgements passed on playwrights, choruses, and athletes (18.318–19). The analogy between athletics and the law is occasionally reflected in the metaphors used by the speech-writers (e.g. wrestling and boxing, Aeschin. 3.205–6), but the analogy between drama and litigation is closer. Dramatic contests shared with legal trials not only such formal aspects as performance before an audience and judgement by a democratically selected jury, but subject-matter as well. Crime, and the problem of what to do with the criminal, were the topics which had to be addressed by both the dramatist and the writer of forensic speeches. Each had to create convincing roles to be played by his major players, and the roles needed to be believable in terms of their family's histories, both in and out of the legal arena, just as in tragedy the hero's parentage and ancestry can be a decisive

---

[2] Garner (1987), 3. For an important study of 'the interplay of political rhetoric and drama' in Athenian society, which came independently to some very similar conclusions as this discussion, by a rather different, comparative anthropological route, see Ober and Strauss (1990).

[3] Hansen (1991), 180. See also the remarks of Whitehead (2000), 8.

factor in his presentation.[4] Moreover, as Rubinstein has stressed, each litigant often acted as part of a larger group whose interests he represented and on whose support he could call; in these *sunēgoroi* he had, effectively, a cast of supporting actors.[5] The main difference between drama and the law is that, for the courts, two different authors usually wrote the scripts—the two leading actor's separate but interacting 'parts'—instead of one.

It is nothing new to discuss the influence of the legal practices of the Athenians on their drama. It has long been remarked that examples of set-piece trial scenes survive from some of the very earliest extant tragedies. The lost plays of Aeschylus' tetralogic *Danaids* included a trial at Argos; the *Oresteia* reaches its climax with Orestes' acquittal at the court of the Areopagus. Scholars have long recognized the impact on drama made by the development, under the democracy, of legal language, concepts, and procedure, and especially by the advent of the teachers of rhetoric.[6] But the relationship between the dramatic and the legal practices of the Athenians was of course dialectical, and the development of drama had an impact on the direction taken by forensic oratory. This chapter aims to demonstrate, by stressing the affinities between legal trials and dramatic productions, that the manner in which forensic speeches were *performed* was as important to their success as their intellectual content and their literary merit. Rhodes has recently argued that we must be careful not to exaggerate the 'irrelevance' of the material presented at trials. It is true that the ancient Athenians, who defined jurisprudential 'relevance' rather more widely than is usual today, did require the speeches delivered in their courts to deal primarily with the legal issues, and the majority of the surviving examples stick fairly closely to the allegations, evidence, and facts which are under

---

[4] Rhodes (2004*b*), 141: 'frequently the particular episode which has given rise to the formal charge is part of a larger story, a man's involvement with the oligarchy of the Thirty, or a family feud.'

[5] Rubinstein (2000), esp. 24–75.

[6] See A. D. Thomson (1898); Gernet (1917); Else (1959); L. Pearson (1962), 90–135; Duchemin (1968); Eden (1980) and (1986), 7–23; Buxton (1982); Goebel (1983); Ober and Strauss (1990), esp. 259–69; Bers (1994); Halliwell (1997), which contains some extremely sophisticated points about the antagonistic nature of tragic rhetoric and its self-consciousness of its own status as persuasive tactic; Wise (1998), 119–68; Pelling (2005).

dispute.[7] But it remains important that we assess the legal speeches as the written records of performances by individual litigants who not only needed to 'keep to the point', but also to compete in the delivery of polished speeches, before responsive audiences, in an emotionally charged social context.

By the last quarter of the fifth century, at any rate, the caricature of verbal styles favoured by individual politicians suggests that Athenian citizens were able to appreciate quite subtle stylistic differences between speeches, and to have developed a fairly elaborate critical language for their comparative evaluation.[8] Some of the speeches are sophisticated in structure and internal ring composition.[9] Yet stylistic and structural effects create no 'live' impact without adequately competent delivery. Some ancient theorists were well aware that the spontaneous performance and delivery of all species of oratory played a bigger part in the effectiveness of the persuasion than the contents of the speeches themselves. A papyrus fragment preserves part of a treatise, probably dating from the early fourth century, which recommends not only using 'common phrases not written ones' in addresses to the jury, but feigning memory loss in order to create an ingénue and spontaneous effect.[10] Much of the treatise *On the Sophists* by Gorgias' pupil Alcidamas, indeed, is devoted to arguing that the ability to extemporize makes for more effective persuasion, in *all* social situations, including the *dikastērion*, than the ability to write an elegant oration (9):

For who does not know that to speak on the spot is a necessary thing for those who speak in the public assembly, for those who go to law, and for those who make private transactions? And often unexpectedly opportunities

---

[7] See Rhodes (2004*b*), a fascinating survey of the proportions of 'relevant' and 'irrelevant' material in the extant speeches; it produces the interesting result (p. 155) that speeches delivered by a litigant's *synēgoroi* (supporters), e.g. Lysias 14, were more inclined 'to gravitate to the irrelevant end of the spectrum'.

[8] See C. T. Murphy (1938), and especially the excellent, detailed study in O'Sullivan (1992), 106–50.

[9] See recently Worthington (1996*b*).

[10] *POxy* 410, ed. Grenfell and Hunt (1903), col. i.5–7 (*mē gegrammenais dokēi chrēsthai* [*tis*], *alla idiōtikais*); col. iv.114–23 ([*hoi*]*on gar mē epibe*[*bō*]*leukēmen all' autoschediazen to epilelasthai*). The treatise is of particular interest not only because of its early date (see Winter (1933), 257), but also because it is in Doric and may represent a trace of the Sicilian rhetorical tradition founded by Tisias and Corax.

for actions fall in one's way, at which times those who are silent will seem to be contemptible, but we see those who speak being honoured by the others as if having intelligence that is godlike.

This treatise was for centuries extraordinarily overlooked by historians both of Athens and of rhetoric. Sure evidence of this neglect is the fact that until 1990 the only available English translation was in an obscure location and even obscurer diction.[11] With the occasional outstanding exception, even the idiosyncratic nature of Alcidamas' own style within the treatise, and his remarkable imagery, attracted little scholarly interest. This is proof in turn that modern scholarship, until the early 1990s at any rate, failed to take the spontaneous and performative dimensions of classical Greek forensic rhetoric seriously.[12]

  The lack of interest in the importance of performance in the Greek courtroom may partly be Aristotle's responsibility. From the moment when he relegated music and spectacle to last place in his discussion of the constituents of tragedy (*Poet.* 6.1450^{b}15–20), until at least the 1970s, critics underestimated the importance of the performative aspects even of ancient drama, and the participatory role of the theatrical audience. The practice of awarding prizes to *chorēgoi* and actors, for example, was almost completely ignored in comparison with the interest expressed in the prizes won by dramatic poets. A similar attitude applied to forensic oratory, partly because Aristotle's *Rhetoric* emphasizes performative aspects of public speaking, '*how* to speak' (*hōs dei eipein*), far less than '*what* to speak' (*ha dei legein*), i.e. content, arrangement, and style.[13] Aristotle does not regard delivery as an elevated subject of inquiry; indeed, it is 'vulgar' (*phortikon*). He rather grudgingly concedes, however, that the study of delivery is indispensable, since 'the whole business of rhetoric is concerned with appearances'.[14] For every ancient legal speech, however extensively it was edited, circulated, and studied subsequently to the trial,[15] was originally conceived and designed as an act to be orally

[11] van Hook (1919); but see now Matsen (1990).
[12] There is an outstanding analysis of the treatise in O'Sullivan (1992), esp. 32–62. See also O'Sullivan (1996), 126–7 and the perceptive remarks of Ford (2002), 233–5.
[13] 3.1403b16. See Sonkowsky (1959), 258–9.
[14] 3.1404a1–8; see E. L. Hunt (1961), 64–5.
[15] Isoc. 4.11; see Usher (1976), 37–8.

performed. It was judged at the time of delivery not in terms of its 'literary' merit, but in terms of the effectiveness with which the speaker communicated with his audience, in this case consisting of jurors and bystanders (*perihestēkotes*).[16] Alcidamas compares the relationship between written speeches and the experience of a performed oration to that between lifeless works of visual art and living bodies, while conceding that animate creatures (and therefore performed orations) are less beautiful than their polished 'copies' (*De Soph.* 27–8; see also Ch. 4, p. 121).

There are problems involved in using the published versions of the speeches. They may differ greatly both from those originally prepared and from those spontaneously delivered, interreactively with the audience, on the actual day of the trial.[17] The speeches must often have been adapted in performance, and probably rewritten before circulation.[18] The editing procedure, moreover, in an attempt to give the impression that the litigant had achieved the ideal of speaking 'temperately' (*metriōs*), may often have sought to eliminate from the speeches precisely the more theatrical aspects of forensic verbal display. Aristotle says that clauses that are poorly connected, and the frequent repetition of the same word, are verbal phenomena which are used by rhetoricians in public debate, but 'rightly disapproved in written discourse' (*Rhet.* 3.1413^b). Yet there is some evidence internal to the speeches which can be used to reconstruct the nature of the litigants' actual performances. This chapter assembles some of this evidence, and supplements it with material from sources such as drama and philosophical works from the same historical period as the classical forensic speeches, but the anachronistic reading back of evidence on delivery from later antiquity has generally been avoided. The results have been organized under headings suggested by the metaphorical conceptualization of the litigant as an actor performing a role as a member of the cast of the social drama of

---

[16] On the trial audiences at Athens see esp. Lanni (1997). The importance of performance in contemporary trials, especially in summation speeches, has been stressed by e.g. Kurzon (1986) and Walter (1988), two fascinating discussions to which I was alerted by Wise (1998), 141.

[17] See Lämmli (1938), 17–57; Lavency (1964), 183–94; Dover (1968), 168–70; Todd (1990*b*).

[18] Worthington (1991).

Athens, his platform (*bēma*) as a stage (*skēnē*), the court as a theatre, and the whole procedure of the legal trial as a dramatic experience.

THE STAGE

Drama and trials shared a context: both were enacted in public spaces in the civic heart of the city; actors performed in the open air, just like litigants in murder cases, who were required to plead their cases under the open sky.[19] Legal speeches, like tragedies and comedies set in the city, refer to important civic and religious sites in the immediate proximity—the prison (Dem. 24.131), or the propylaea (Dem. 24.184).[20] Modern actors often stare into the darkness of an auditorium, but ancient actors, like ancient litigants, could see their audience in the daylight. Unfortunately we know little about the physical appearance of any of the classical Athenian courts (just as we know surprisingly little about the nature of the performance space in the sanctuary of Dionysus before the first stone building was erected), even though there are traces of several buildings which archaeologists have identified as likely sites. If more evidence were available it might be that the parallels between the physical contexts in which plays and trials were performed would be even clearer.[21] Jurors seem to have taken their seats, as they did at the theatre, in rows at varying distances from the rostra;[22] in one Demosthenic oration the speaker says he has decided not to write a family tree on a *pinax* because those sitting at a greater distance would be at a

[19] See the discussion in Parker (1983), 122.

[20] For a discussion of what is known about the exact location of the Athenian state prison, and attempts to identify its remains, see V. Hunter (1997), 298–9 and the appendix at 319–23.

[21] Boegehold (1995), 10–16 and 43–50 and 91–113 discusses the relevant structures and likely sites in and near the agora, on the Areopagus and (in the case of the so-called Palladion) beyond the city walls. It seems clear that many trial spaces were defined by enclosing fences originally made of wood, perhaps later of metal. See *Wasps* 385, 552, 830, 844, and the rest of the testimony compiled and discussed in Boegehold (1995), 195–201.

[22] On seating arrangements in the Assembly's meeting-place on the Pnyx as well as in the courts in relation to those in the theatre, see especially Ober and Strauss (1990), 238 and n. 3.

visual disadvantage (Dem. 43.18). The term *prohedria* was used to designate sitting on the front bench, exactly as it was in the theatre (Epicrates fr. 11 K–A).

Thought was given to the exploitation of the platform(s). If you were secretly in league with the man publicly perceived as your opponent (a type of conspiratorial scenario far from unimaginable in ancient Athens), you would sit in silence on your platform while your supposed antagonist but secret colleague delivered his speech from the other one (Dem. 48.31), two litigants colluding in a whole-sale dramatic illusion. An exciting strategy was to put one's opponent on the platform and attempt to embarrass him by interrogation (Lys. 12.24, see Ar. *Ach.* 687–8). Technically speaking, information elicited from an opponent in court was not even admissible as evidence, since he could not have an action for perjury brought against him.[23] But such interrogations must have influenced juries, because the strategy receives serious attention in ancient handbooks on rhetoric (e.g. Anaximenes, *Rhet. ad Alex.* 36.1444b 9–21), importantly implying that spontaneous verbal combat and repartee took precedence over formalities.

By the end of the trial the platform might become crowded. Political allies were often introduced in large numbers to vouch for their performer's good name; indeed, Rubinstein has argued persuasively that the competitions enacted in the courts of law were often competitions between rival teams, or ensembles, rather than rival individuals.[24] It was also customary to arrange one's family, especially children, on the platform in a social display (see e.g. Dem. 21.99, Aeschin. 2.152). Although parodied by Aristophanes and condemned by Socrates (*Wasps.* 568–740, Plato, *Apol.* 34c), failure to produce family members might cast doubt on the unity of one's household.[25] Interestingly it is a tragedy, and an early one, which best describes the demeanour suitable for children soliciting social approval and sympathy from the platform. When in Aeschylus' *Suppliants* the asylum-seeking Danaids are about to supplicate Pelasgus, their father instructs them to look modest, piteous, and humble, and to speak the kind of words that elicit pity, neither harshly nor at excessive length (191–203).

---

[23] See Bonner and Smith (1938), ii. 122.   [24] Rubinstein (2000).
[25] Lavency (1964), 80.

STAGECRAFT

Much of the pleasure to be gained from being a spectator, whether in the court or the theatre, is derived from suspense and surprise. A skilled orator might plan a case so as to exploit the 'dramatic' potential of the courtroom. Herodotus relates, for example, that when Miltiades was tried in the Assembly in 489 BC he had been wounded (fatally, as it turned out); throughout the trial he lay pathetically silent on a stretcher in full view of the people, like a tragic hero dying on the stage, while his friends spoke on his behalf.[26] The silences of the principal actors were of course an effective technique in tragic drama, especially in Aeschylus.[27]

In Antiphon's speech *On the Choreutēs* ('chorus-dancer') we hear that Philocrates had gone before a heliastic court which was scheduled to hear, on the following day, a case brought by the chorusman. Philocrates pre-emptively counter-attacked the chorus-dancer by charging him with the murder of his brother; the chorusman immediately presented himself to the court in order to defend himself against this serious charge (6.21–2). The whole procedure was presumably spontaneous in so far as the case had not even been registered for trial, and was designed to prejudice the chorusman's chances in the trial which *had* been arranged.[28]

An even more 'dramatic' scene occurs in Isocrates' report of a previous trial (18.53–4). Callimachus was an enemy of Cratinus. So he and his brother-in-law had hidden a female slave, and prosecuted Cratinus in the court of the Palladion for killing her by the sensational means of crushing her head. Only after they had testified to her death, testimony corroborated on oath by no fewer than fourteen individuals, did the man they were falsely accusing feel the theatrical moment was right to present her, alive, in court. Alcestis-like, the silent revenant was returned to the stage from the dead, a theatrical coup combining intense emotional relief with a slightly sinister, even spine-chilling aura. The fourteen corroborators were presumably bribed into bearing false witness: a character in Aristophanes' *Storks* said, 'If you prosecute

---

[26] Hdt. 6.136; see Bauman (1990), 18.   [27] See Taplin (1972).

[28] For a discussion of the rival strategies adopted in this case, see Gagarin (2002), 139–46.

one lawless (*adikos*) man, then twelve others who serve him for their supper swear against you in court' (*antimarturousi*, fr. 437 K–A).

Athenian drama refers several times to the mythical Helen's ruse of saving her life by revealing her breasts to Menelaus (e.g. Eur. *Andr.* 628, Ar. *Lys.* 155). Clearly modelled on this archetypal episode is the story about Phryne, the beautiful Ephesian courtesan accused of impiety, defended by her lover Hyperides, and acquitted. The pseudo-Plutarchean *Lives of the Ten Orators* (849e) and Athenaeus (13.590e) both claim that it was Hyperides—an orator whose cleverness was much admired by his contemporaries (see Timocles frags. 4 and 17 K–A)—who revealed her breasts to the jury while weeping piteously himself.[29] A fragment of Posidippus, a third-century comic poet much nearer to Hyperides' time, seems to confirm that something memorable went on at Phryne's trial (*Ephesian Woman*, fr. 13 K–A), although in his version Phryne herself tearfully supplicated every jury member in turn.[30] Whatever the truth of these pleasurable anecdotes, they do at least confirm that such spectacular and titillating tactics were not beyond the imagination of the ancient courtgoer. Indeed, a scene in Herodas' second mime, in which a beautiful prostitute's body is displayed to a jury, is probably a parody of the type of scene which was thought to have characterized the Athenian courts of law. Battarus the brothel-keeper delivers an oration which parodies an Attic prosecution speech. He accuses a ship-owner of assaulting Myrtale, one of the women who worked in his brothel, whom he produces in court in order to detail not only her torn clothing, bruises and scars, but her enticing nether regions (2.65–78). It used to be thought that this plotline was specifically a parody of the Phryne story, but it is far more likely to be a distinctly theatrical reaction to the histrionic nature of the displays of battered bodies during trials at Athens in the classical heyday of legal oratory.[31]

From sex to violence: Demosthenes can envisage a scene in which he is attacked on the platform itself by Meidias' friend Blepaeus the

[29] An egregious example of 'extra-rational proof'; see Kennedy (1963), 253. On Hyperides' reputation in his own day, see Whitehead (2000), 10–11; for a brilliant discussion of the sources and strategies used by the author of the *Lives of the Ten Orators*, see now Pitcher (2005).

[30] On Hyperides' role in the trial of Phryne, see in general Cooper (1995).

[31] So Cooper (1995), 314–15.

banker (21.215–17); Aeschines, histrionic as ever, titillates his audience by unusually offering to permit his slaves to be tortured in court during his allotted time (this may not have been a serious practical possibility);[32] he caps this offer with the invitation to his fellow citizens to rise up and execute him on the spot if the slaves should not corroborate his testimony (2.126). Even suicide during or immediately after a trial seems to have been well within the realms of possibility. Paches, at least according to Plutarch, did actually stab himself to death in 426 BC when facing the shame of a possible conviction (*Vit. Nic.* 61, *Vit. Arist.* 26.3). In one Demosthenic speech the jurors are begged to acquit the defendant, for the sake of his mother; if they do not, he will kill himself (57.70). It is probably relevant that conviction in this particular case would have entailed the humiliating personal catastrophe of being sold into slavery. Trials may have been theatrical and entertaining, but individual Athenians' lives and livelihoods were often at stake, and the sheer desperation of some of the 'actors' emanates even from their carefully crafted speeches; even more telling are the curse tablets that have been discovered in which litigants attempted to enlist supernatural powers in order to wreck their opponents' cases, just as the Erinyes in *Eumenides* attempt to use 'binding magic' coercively against Orestes in order to determine the outcome of his trial.[33]

THE AUDIENCE

An important article by Victor Bers two decades ago assembled the testimony to the influence that the shouts and other noises made by jurors and bystanders might have had on the outcome of an ancient

[32] For the scholarly debates surrounding the torture of slaves to elicit evidence, see Gagarin (1996). A slave is tortured offstage in Euripides' *Ion* (1214), and another is threatened with torture in *OT* (1154, see E. Hall (1997*b*), 113–16). The staging of slave torture in classical tragedy did not go unnoticed in antiquity, since the Suda (s.v. 218 = 15 *TgrF* T i) provides evidence for a tradition that the fifth-century Neophron was the first dramatist to have introduced such a scene.

[33] See Boegehold (1995), 55–7. About twenty-five lead tablets relating to late 5th- and early 4th-cent. trials have been identified. On the Erinyes' binding song, see the brilliant study of Faraone (1985).

Athenian trial.[34] In Plato it is said that these noises, collectively designated as 'din' (*thorubos*, *Laws* 9.876b1–6), arise in assemblies, theatres, military encampments, and lawcourts (*Rep.* 6.492b5–c1). From this it can be inferred that the well-documented noises emitted by theatrical audiences were also customary in the *dikastēria*. These noises are characterized by the censorious Athenian of Plato's *Laws* as whistling or hissing (*surrigx*, see also Dem. 18.265, 21.226), the uncouth shouts of the mob (*amousai boai plēthous*), and handclapping (*krotoi*) to signify approval (*Laws* 3.700c1–4). Demosthenes testifies to an abusive sound denoted by the verb *klōzein* (21.226): it is defined in Harpocration as an inarticulate mouth noise used by audiences when they wanted to get an actor thrown off stage (s.v. *klōzete*). Such intimations of disapproval might be supplemented by heel-drumming (Pollux 4.122). Pollux records a day when an audience's hissing drove off one comic actor after another (4.68); Plutarch even claims that tragic actors needed the support of a claque in the theatre (*Quomodo adulator* 63a). Such noises were regarded by Plato as having been taken to such extremes that they had established over the poets a 'dictatorship of the spectatorship' (*theatrokratia*, *Laws* 3.701a 3).

Bers argues that although there was no affirmative entitlement in Athenian law for a juror to shout at a litigant, trials were in practice an extremely noisy and participatory business, far more than is indicated by the edited forms of the speeches which survived. Aristotle's *Rhetoric* strangely neglects *thorubos*, although there is a brief account of the demagogue Androcles dealing with it in the assembly (2.1400[a]9–14). In order to manage *thorubos* a speaker needed to be able to think on his feet and adapt his argument around unforeseen developments: this was perceived by Alcidamas, the brilliant advocate of the art of extemporization (*autoschediasmos*, see above).[35]

During the dog's trial in *Wasps*, the prosecuting dog is interrupted by the juror Philocleon (912). Noisy juror participation is also suggested by references and apparent cues within the speeches. Speakers beg the audience to refrain from interrupting them;[36] speakers incite the jurors to interrupt their opponents. Jurors make

[34] Bers (1985).   [35] *De Sophistis* 3, 22; see Kennedy (1963), 172–3.
[36] See e.g. Hyp. *Lyc.* fr. 2 with the comments in Whitehead (2000), 96–7.

their wishes known and speakers comply (Dem. 23.18–19). Jurors assume emotional roles themselves when they are said (whether descriptively or prescriptively) to become angry (Dem. 58.13); they become imperious, and summon individuals to the platform (Hyp. 1.20). A fragment of Aristophanes' *Farmers* says that jurors interrupt those delivering poor defence speeches with the criticism that they are 'singing' or 'chanting' their speeches (*aidein*, fr. 101 K–A);[37] comedy attests to the use of murmuring to impede a speaker (*hupokrouein*, Alexis fr. 33 K–A). There were interchanges between speakers and jurors reminiscent of audience participation in a twenty-first-century children's pantomime. Is Timarchus a lover or a prostitute, Aeschines asks the jury: his subsequent remarks imply that they chorus 'a prostitute' in response (1.159). Is Aeschines a 'friend' or merely on the payroll of Alexander: 'on the payroll' they cry in unison (Dem. 18.52). Their unscripted response becomes evidence in itself: 'You hear what they say' (*akoueis ha legousin*), remarks Demosthenes.

Bers also points out that *thorubos* could have been deafening (as it must have been at theatrical competitions) when multiples of five hundred jurors (plus the one extra juror required to create an odd number) were present (Andocides 1.17, Lys. 13.35);[38] the shouting of spectators in such cases must also have been difficult to distinguish from the shouting of the jurors themselves. The author of the *Rhetorica ad Alexandrum* (probably Anaximenes) differentiates the management of interruptions by jurors from that of the *thorubos* of the mass of the audience (*to plēthos*, 18.1433^{a}14–20). Homicide defendants were permitted to withdraw into exile after their first defence speeches (Ant. 5.13, Dem. 23.69); their decisions must have rested on the degree of sympathy they perceived in the jurors. This would have had to be deduced from their *thorubos* and general demeanour: scowling jurors are mentioned at *Wasps* 623–7. The orchestration of shouting and juror reaction was therefore an essential aspect of

[37] For a discussion of what this might mean in terms of vocal enunciation, see Ch. 10, p. 300 n. 48.

[38] This is not the place to engage in the notorious controversy caused by the conflicting ancient accounts of the size of jury panels; scholars now use figures between 251 and 2501. See Hansen (1991), 187; Todd (1993), 83 with n. 10; Whitehead (2000), 8.

rhetorical strategy, and in practice trials were spontaneous affairs in which the opinion of the jury could have been swung unpredictably in one direction or the other, depending almost entirely on the atmosphere created in the heat of the moment.

THE PROTAGONISTS

The social group which furnished the dramatic cast for the Athenian law-courts was similar to the one which provided the cast for the theatrical productions. Isocrates' pupils and followers included the prominent fourth-century tragedians Astydamas, Aphareus, and Theodectes.[39] The speech-writers, as well as the politically active men who jostled for influence in the assembly and the courts, came from the same high-profile public families which produced poets, actors, and dancers. There are frequent mentions of the men in such professions who are friends of litigants or their speech-writers, spend time at their houses, drink with them, and share their women. Timarchus sold his house to Nausicrates the comic poet, and it was later bought by Cleaenetus the chorus-master (Aeschines 1.98). Satyrus the comic actor was on the notorious embassy to Philip (Aeschines 2.156–7); Lysias the sophist had allegedly been the lover of Metanaera, one of Neaera's colleagues; in Corinth two of Neaera's supposed clients were the poet Xenocleides and Hipparchus the actor ([Dem.] 59.21, 26). The men who battled in the law-courts, and those who wrote speeches for them, also lived and breathed the theatre: although probably incorrect, it was not an inherently implausible tradition which held that Antiphon had written tragedies himself ([Plut.] *Lives of the Ten Orators* 833c).[40] The assumption that there was considerable cross-fertilization between tragic and legal rhetoric is underlined by the anecdote preserved by Aristotle that this same Antiphon's famous speech in his own defence (see further below) was praised by the tragedian Agathon, earning Antiphon's

[39] See A. D. Thomson (1898), 9–20 n. 2; Webster (1956), 67; E. Hall (forthcoming *c*).

[40] Antiphon was a very common name, and the logographer was sometimes confused with the early 4th-cent. tragedian with the same name who was executed by Dionysius of Syracuse. See Gagarin (2002), 7 with n. 13, 38 with n. 14.

grateful response that the praise of a single expert is worth more than the approbation of many ordinary men (*Eudemian Ethics* 3.5).

The significance of poetry in the training of the ancient rhetor is clear from the quotations appearing in the rhetorical handbooks, not only for illustrating the importance of quoting poetic maxims, but for illustrating stylistic devices (see e.g. the way in which Euripides is quoted at *Rhet. ad Alex.* 18.1433^{b}11–14). Aristotle's *Rhetoric* abounds in illustrations drawn from Homer and the tragic poets, assuming of the apprentice speech-writers who formed its readership a wide and intimate knowledge of poetry.[41] Aristotle approves of the deployment of poetry in the courtroom, and supplies anecdotes concerning poems as a form of proof (*Rhet.* 1.1375^{b}25–1376^{a}2); poetry was apparently used by both Socrates and his opponents at the philosopher's trial.[42] It therefore comes as something of a surprise how infrequently direct quotations of poetry appear in the extant corpus of speeches.[43]

Direct quotations from poetry seem to have presented a challenge to inexperienced speakers, since they only appear in those texts which were delivered by logographers themselves. Indeed, it is Aeschines, a former tragic actor, whose extant works most frequently include quotations from poetry. He does not hesitate to recite long passages of poetry,[44] one quotation from Homer running up to eighteen lines (1.149 = *Iliad* 23.77–95).[45] Nothing, however, can outstrip the extravagance of Lycurgus' 55-line performance of Praxithea's great patriotic speech from Euripides' *Erechtheus* (*In Leocr.* 100). It is very likely that Lycurgus used the poets in his other speeches, for Hermogenes reports that 'he digresses many times into myths and stories and poems';[46] in his speech against Menesaichmos, or 'Delian speech', he seems to have taken the opportunity to recount the story

---

[41] See North (1952), 6–8; Bolgar (1969), 37–8. On quotations of both poetry and historical paradigms, see Ober and Strauss (1990), 250–5; on the ways in which the study of Homer, in particular, benefited any speech-writer in democratic Athens, see Ford (1999), esp. 232–9.

[42] See Xen. *Mem.* 1.2.56–8; Dorjahn (1927), 59.

[43] Assembled by Perlman (1964), 162–5.

[44] In Aeschines' case it is particularly unlikely that he would have needed the clerk to recite poetry for him, a possibility envisaged by Dorjahn (1927), 92.

[45] For the importance of Homeric undertexts to Aeschines 1 (*Against Timarchus*), see the brilliant study by Ford (1999).

[46] *Peri ideōn* 2.389; see Dorjahn (1927), 88.

of Abaris and the Hyperboreans.[47] Jurors enjoyed such mythic and poetic material. Philocleon says that if the famous tragic actor Oeagrus should ever find himself playing the role of a defendant in court, the jurors would refuse to allow him to be acquitted until they had heard him deliver the very finest speech from the tragedy *Niobe* (*Wasps* 579–80): plays with this title are attributed to both Aeschylus and Sophocles.[48]

Aristotle's famous tripartite division of rhetoric defines deliberative rhetoric as looking to the future and urging expedience, epideictic rhetoric as looking to the present and urging honour, but legal rhetoric as looking to the past and urging justice.[49] This definition confirms the connection between tragedy and legal rhetoric, for tragic drama, like law-court speeches, deals with the past, and its subject-matter addresses alleged crime, proof, culpability or innocence, judgement, and punishment. Yet in practice the distinction between the three categories of rhetoric is frequently blurred (as the writer of the *Rhetorica ad Alexandrum* observed, 5.1427^{b}33–4), for the relationship between law and politics was much closer than it is today.

Public performances against rivals, in the setting of the law-courts, were used by Athenians to regulate conflicts and control social relations.[50] Accusations were laid in order to promote the interest of particular families.[51] The *dikastērion* 'was not only a juridical and theatrical space, but also and essentially a politically defined arena',[52] an arena for the constant combative social performances engaged in by prominent men.[53] These ambitious Athenians delivered speeches which not only addressed themselves to the case in hand, but also contained material which Aristotle would have categorized as 'symbouleutic' or 'epideictic'. The speaker, aspiring to the role of leader of his city, may deliberate about its best course of action; he may calumniate his opponent while cataloguing his own noble ancestors

---

[47] See the discussion of the fragmentary evidence in Conomis (1961), 145–6.
[48] MacDowell (1971), 210–11, thinks that the Aeschylean *Niobe*, rather than the Sophoclean, is most likely to be meant, because it is discussed at *Frogs* 912.
[49] *Rhet.* 1.1357^{a}36–^{b}29. See Baldwin (1924), 14–15.
[50] See R. Osborne (1985), 52.   [51] See Wilcox (1945), 175.
[52] See Cartledge, Millett, and Todd (1990), 42.
[53] See Wilcox (1942), 135; Perlman (1963), 342–3.

and his performances of civic liturgies. This procedure is at times analogous less to a modern trial than to the televised debates between the candidates for the presidency of the USA before an election.[54]

The candidate who wins the American presidential election is usually the one whose appearance has been most attractive, whose spontaneous verbal performance has been the most engaging, and who has managed to tap into the public's collective consciousness by a judicious blend of laughter, tears, arousal of fear, and soupy patriotism. Approximately the same recipe would have been prescribed by any competent teacher of rhetoric in classical Athens. A trial was a one-off business; although its outcome was affected by the opponents' social status, reputation, previous public performances, and precursory propaganda campaigns,[55] as well as the evidence placed before the jurors for evaluation, the spontaneous performances on the actual day that the two collided in public were, besides the inherent strength of each case, the most crucial factor.

For ancient jurors liked to be entertained. One of the reasons Philocleon gives for his love of the lawcourts is the sheer pleasure of the experience of attending them (*Wasps* 550–1). Legal speeches often express the desirability of brevity (Lys. 23.1), and a fear of wearying or boring the jurors (*enochlein*, Lys 24.21; *diatribein*, Isaeus 7.43). Hyperides was commended for not only avoiding tedium in his speeches, but doing so without resorting to exaggeratedly histrionic tactics ([Plut.] *Lives of the Ten Orators* 850a–b); his lightness and fluency in storytelling were particularly appreciated ('Longinus', *De Subl.* 34.2). Aeschines says that Leodamas gave him more pleasure than Demosthenes (he was *hēdiōn*, 3.139), although he would say that, wouldn't he?

DELIVERY (*HYPOKRISIS*)

When asked what were the three most important things in oratory, Demosthenes is supposed to have said, 'delivery, delivery, delivery' ([Plut.] *Lives of the Ten Orators* 845a). Although this anecdote is

[54] For illuminating analyses of which see Benoit and Wells (1996); Benoit, Hansen and Tillery (2003).

[55] See Dorjahn (1935), 274–95.

probably fictional, it underlines the important truth that a well-written speech can never have been in itself enough to impress a jury. Thrasymachus gave advice on delivery in his treatise on arousing pity (Ar. *Rhet.* 3.1404ᵃ): Theophrastus, who regarded delivery as the 'most important aspect of persuasion' (*megiston ... pros to peisai tēn hupokrisin*, fr. 712 ed. Fortenbaugh (1992)), devoted an entire work to the subject (Diog. Laert. *Vitae* 5.48). The word *hupokrisis* of course also denoted the art of the actor, the *hupokritēs*.[56] Aristotle recognized a similarity between theatrical and rhetorical delivery (*Rhet.* 3.1403ᵇ 24–30), and vocal training by the time of the Hellenistic schools was certainly dominated by the declamation of poetry.[57] The anecdote which related how Demosthenes was trained by the actor Satyrus in the delivery of speeches by Sophocles and Euripides may, again, not be literally true (Plut. *Vit. Dem.* 7; [Plut.] *Lives of the Ten Orators* 844–5). But it expresses a truth about the way in which ancient speakers learned both the art of delivery and mnemonic techniques; the latter, a speciality of the sophist Hippias (Plato, *Hipp. Min.* 368d), were already well developed by the end of the fifth century.[58]

In Aristophanes' *Knights* the Paphlagonian is pouring contempt on the sausage-seller's pride in his own forensic oratory. The sausage-seller may win some trifling case against a resident foreigner, but only by abstaining from alcohol and staying up at night to repeat the speech over and over again, reciting it to himself in the street, and wearying his friends by rehearsing his performance in front of them (347–9). For although there was no official requirement for litigants to deliver their speeches off by heart,[59] which might have been impossible for the inexperienced or incompetent, successful performance at a trial was undoubtedly facilitated by the ability to deliver the speech, like an actor, from memory. Memorization was regarded as difficult (Alcidamas, *De Soph.* 18); anecdotes about 'drying up', like Labes, the jaw-locked canine defendant in Aristophanes' *Wasps* (945), can be used to humiliate an opponent (Aeschines 2.34–5). Yet it was important, however much work had gone into committing the speech to memory, to lend an *impression* of spontaneity. Many speeches contain formulaic phrases

[56] See Ghiron-Bistagne (1976), 115–19.   [57] See Krumbacher (1924).
[58] See North (1952), 11 and n. 54; Yates (1966), 29; Blum (1969), 40–55.
[59] See Usher (1976), 36.

designed to signal extempore composition, such as 'really, I can't contain myself' (Din. 1.15), or 'I nearly forgot to mention this' (Dem. 21.110), the latter in Demosthenes' *Against Meidias*, which was probably never even delivered.[60]

Speech-writers took account of their clients' skill in declamation. Depending on their client's grasp of oratory, for example, they utilized varying degrees of hiatus. Hiatus entails the use of a word ending with a vowel, followed by another word beginning with a vowel; it requires a special physical effort from the speaker, and lends an explosive emphasis to the second word. Demosthenes uses hiatus with dazzling effect at the end of important cola or in order to punctuate a string of direct questions. When writing for less competent speakers, however, he uses far less hiatus.[61] Another challenge was presented by long sentences, which required great control of the vocal chords and lungs, unless they were broken down into distinct cola and parentheses; Hermogenes actually distinguishes between sentences which can be broken down into short cola, and the type of vocally demanding period, with a single colon (*monokōlos periodos*), which was so arranged that its meaning required a single movement through from beginning to end (*Peri Heureseōs* 4.3). Virtuoso passages, anger, and climaxes attract long *monokōla* (Dem. 30.30, 35–6), and are frequently followed by the reading of evidence in order to allow the speaker a rest. As Demosthenes matured, he made much greater demands upon himself in the speeches written for his own delivery. But in the first speech against Aphobus, written so as to cast the client in the role of a self-confessedly inexperienced litigant and public speaker (27.2), the sentences are short and the cola not only manageable but designed to sound like natural, unscripted speech.[62]

Aristotle strongly asserted that the volume and the pitch of the voice needed to be modulated in accordance with the emotional response it was meant to elicit.[63] Yet in practice a loud voice always seems to have been an advantage in an orator, just as actors were usually praised for the sheer size of their voices, their *megalophōnia*.[64] An opponent may

---

[60] See MacDowell (1990), 27.   [61] Pearson (1975*a*).

[62] Pearson (1975*b*), 215–18.

[63] *Rhet.* 3.1403^{b}27–32; see Fortenbaugh (1986).

[64] See Haigh (1889), 246–7.

certainly be forced into suggesting that a loud voice implies a violent and unscrupulous nature, or alternatively into deriding its sound as 'shrieking' or 'roaring' (*kraugē*, Dem. 40.53, Isae. 6.59, Hyp. 5 col. 12).[65] The elderly politician (not the historian) Thucydides notoriously 'dried up' when required to defend himself in court against the vigorous verbal onslaughts of the much younger Cephisodemus (*Wasps* 946–8); the chorus of *Acharnians* remembers sadly that when Thucydides was less advanced in years, he could easily have 'shouted down with his roaring' even three thousand noisy archers (*kateboēse... kekragōs*, 711; see Ch. 8, pp. 238–9 and n. 51).

The importance attached to vocal training is best exemplified by the case of the ex-actor Aeschines. Having formerly put his beautiful speaking voice to work in the performance of tragic poetry, he was able to point out to the jury that Demosthenes, in contrast, sounded shrill, unpleasant, and strained (*oxeia kai anosios phōnē*, 2.157; *tonos tēs phōnēs*, 3.21). Demosthenes came up with several lines of counter-attack which reveal the extent to which he was threatened by his opponent's fine delivery. He claims that Aeschines was never a good actor at all, but used to be driven from the stage by theatrical *thorubos* (19.337). He tries to make Aeschines' delivery appear absurd, by char-acterizing it as a loud noise developed in Aeschines' youth when he had assisted his mother at initiation rites and adopted the type of vocal technique used by women in incantations (*ololuzein*, 18.259). Demos-thenes accuses Aeschines of having gone to law simply in order to indulge in 'verbal exhibitionism' and 'speechifying' (*logōn epideixis*, *phōnaskia*, 18.280). He reminds the jury that Aeschines has never been appointed to deliver an oration at the public funeral, *despite his lovely voice*, and claims that the reason for excluding him from this office was that people deemed it inappropriate for such a solemn speech to be delivered in the feigning, tearful voice of an actor (*mēde tēi phōnēi dakruein hupokrinomenon*, 18.285–7). He constantly uses references to Aeschines's vocal gifts, keeping the listeners' attention fixed on the medium, rather than the message, of his rival.[66] The issue of Aeschines' voice, says Aeschines, threatened to take over the substance of the

---

[65] On 'booming' delivery in the orators, see Worman (2004), 8–10.
[66] On the way that voices and performance styles become a focus of the actual argument between Aeschines and Demosthenes, see above all Easterling (1999).

argument: a passage in his *Against Ctesiphon* predicts that Demosthenes will soon go so far as to compare Aeschines with the sirens, whose lovely voices bring men to destruction, because the smooth flow of his words (*eurhoia*) and natural ability have always ruined those who listened to him (3.228). No such brilliantly suggestive mythical analogy actually appears in Demosthenes' extant speeches; unless Aeschines himself dreamt up the image, Demosthenes must either have omitted it spontaneously after his sweet-voiced opponent had defused its power by this pre-emptive strike, or he edited it out for publication.

In Aeschylus' *Suppliant Women* the barbarizing Egyptians state their fear of the prejudice held by Greeks against anyone speaking with a foreign accent (972–4). Chapters 8 and 9 above explored two important cases of linguistic caricature of barbarians in comedy and citharody. Legal speeches also display a prejudice against barbarian inflections in public speech; this becomes particularly important in cases where the defendant has been accused of not being a full-blooded Athenian citizen. Eubulides used against Euxitheus, for example, the claim that his father had a non-Attic accent; Euxitheus tells a story that sounds somewhat implausible (and is perhaps, therefore, the more likely to be true) about his father being sold into slavery as a war captive, and sent abroad, where he picked up an alien accent and started to sound foreign (*xenizein*, Dem. 57.18). In Apollodorus' prosecution of Phormio the defendant needed to have an advocate perform the whole defence for him, because he had originally been a slave, and had never learned Greek well enough to speak before the Athenians. He is accused of 'solecizing' (Dem. 36.1; see 45.30, 81, and above, Ch. 7, pp. 198–9).

A brisk pace seems to have been desirable. In Eupolis' *Demes*, part of the brilliance of Pericles' delivery seems to be attributed to the speed at which he spoke: he is likened to a sprinter who leaves his competitors standing at the starting-line (Eupolis fr. 102 K–A). The physical strain of speaking without amplification must not be underestimated. An opponent is said to have 'over-exerted himself' (*huper-diateinomenon*, Dem. 25.1), and Lysias, in a speech he delivered himself, at one point says that he is going to hand over to his witnesses on the ground that he needs a rest (12.61).

The exertion was not only verbal. Demosthenes seems to have used gestures effectively, for Aeschines needed to make fun of them; his opponent, he complains, had 'wheeled round in a circle on the platform' to emphasise a point (3.167). Demosthenes in turn complains that Aeschines had been mimicking his diction and gestures (*rhēmata kai schēmata mimoumenos*), as if the fate of Hellas rested on a hand movement (18.232). Yet there are disappointingly few references to gesture in the speeches, and they are usually derogatory.[67] This is because gesture, at least in excess, was disdained. Theophrastus was said to have 'indulged in' gestures (Athen. *Deipn.* 1.21a–b). It was thought that in the days of Themistocles and Pericles it had been the custom to speak with the arm inside the cloak, whereas in the fourth century everyone's arm protruded (Aesch. 1.25; see also [Arist.] *Ath. Pol.* 28.3). But removing the cloak, and excessive physical movement were certainly disapproved of, if Aeschines' caricature of Timarchus in the assembly is anything to go by: he is said to have cast off his cloak and jumped around half-naked like a gymnast, his body so foul with drunkenness that right-thinking men covered their eyes (Aesch. 1.26).

THE CAST OF CHARACTER

'It is the demeanour (*tropos*) of the speaker which persuades, rather than his speech (*logos*)', said a character in Menander's *Hymnis* (fr. 362.7 K–A). A large part of successful persuasion came down to characterization. The outcome of a case must frequently have depended not on the discovery of the actual truth or falsity of the two versions of events rendered, but on their competitive plausibility. This was in turn dependent on the credibility of those rendering them—that is, on the competitive realization in terms of the portrayal of *ēthos* of the rhetoricians' principle of *eikos*, or likelihood.[68] Winning a case required the adoption of a believable character, and the ability to sustain the role under the stress entailed by public

---

[67] The Romans of course developed the use of gesture into a fine science. On the discussions in Cicero and Quintilian, see Graf (1991); Gunderson (1998), with bibliography.

[68] On which see recently the discussion of Schmitz (2000), with bibliography.

performance. Every litigant and every corroborative speaker needed to convince the jury that his character (*ēthos*) was authentic. The ancient speech-writer, no less than the modern advocate, was like a dramatic director who had to inculcate into his cast, his troupe of social actors, the version of events which he wished to present to the public. He had to train them in their roles. As the early fourth-century Athenian general Iphicrates was supposed to have said when defeated by one of Aristophon's orators, 'my opponents' actor is better, but the superior play is mine'.[69] The case might be jeopardized if any member of the legal cast forgot his lines, or failed to persuade the jury of the authenticity of the dramatic character that he had assumed.

The handbooks describe techniques whereby speech-writers could construct for the clients a plausible personality, an *ēthos*, through their language: Aristotle states that the character must be credible, inspire confidence in the jury, and be appropriate to the individual speaker's age, gender, and ethnicity (*Rhet.* 1.1356ª1–13, 3.1408ª25–31). This is almost identical to his prescription in the *Poetics* that tragic characterization must conform with gender and status (1454ª16–25): it would be implausible, for example, for a female to be characterized as either courageous or intelligent. It was Lysias who was regarded by the literary critics as the supreme exponent of character construction (*ēthopoiia*) in oratory,[70] and indeed his high-minded Euphiletus, his gallant Mantitheus, and his humorous but humble invalid in 1, 16 and 24 respectively are powerfully individualized through their language and attitudes. In the case of legal oratory, *ēthopoiia* has been the subject of several distinguished studies.[71] The manipulation of verbal style and ornamentation in the rhetorical portrayal of character to be found in poetry and epideictic prose, as well as logography, has also, more recently, begun to attract

[69] *beltiōn men ho tōn antidikōn hupokritēs drama de toumon ameinon* (Plut. *Mor.* 801f = *Precepts of Statecraft* 5). Du Cann (1980), 78, reports a similar modern rhetorical flourish, when the Treasury Counsel at the Old Bailey concluded his opening thus: 'I have set the stage for you, Members of the Jury. The scenery is in place. Let me ring up the curtain and the play begin.' The effect of the theatrical metaphors was demolished by the retort of the Defending Counsel: 'And have your actors learned their lines?'
[70] Dio. Hal. *De Lysia* 8–9; see Devries (1892); Usher (1965).
[71] See Süss (1910); Sattler (1957); Morford (1966); Russell (1990). On Demosthenes 54 (*Against Conon*), see especially Carey and Reid (1985), 73–4.

attention.[72] But it is important to stress that this chapter has little interest in the truth or falsity of any of the 'facts' or personalities in the ancient legal speeches. Although a skilled speech-writer such as Lysias would presumably develop his characterization of a particular litigant in a manner designed to emphasize the client's 'real' personality (at least if it were an attractive one),[73] all that can be inferred from the texts is that every figure presented to the Athenian courts was, in an important sense, a fictive character invented by a professional writer of speeches. Each surviving specimen of legal oratory constitutes one side of a performed dramatic dialogue, a conflict of roles, where the words of another speech-writer, composed for the presentation of the opponent's case, are usually lost to us forever.

THE CAST (*TOU DRAMATOS PROSŌPA*)

When a poet redesigned a myth for the tragic contests he was at liberty, besides the protagonists, to people his cast very much as he liked. In Euripides' *Orestes*, for example, the poet chose to have a messenger speech about an attack on Helen delivered neither by her nurse nor a *paidagōgos* of Orestes, but by a flamboyant Phrygian eunuch.[74] Analogously, a speech-writer could choose whom to bring in to participate, at least within certain limits defined by the evidence required to prove his case. Part of the fun of being a spectator at a trial must have lain in waiting to see who was to be introduced into the cast of characters. Demosthenes' speeches demonstrate extremely creative manipulation of casts: he sometimes asks for a particular individual to stand up in court to be identified, thus creating an exciting split-second when everyone looks all around the building in order to see which one of the audience is directly implicated in the trial (e.g. 21.95; see also Hyperides fr. 55). Much work remains to be done in this area,[75] although the usual function of the 404 witnesses

---

[72] See e.g. Worman (2002), 17–40.   [73] See Bonner (1922), 101.

[74] See Ch. 2, p. 50. The choice of cast-member in both theatrical and legal contexts will partly have been a response to the talent available.

[75] See Humphreys (1985*b*) and (1985*c*).

produced in the extant orations was to corroborate what the speaker had already said so far.[76] What follows is the briefest of surveys of a few of the most theatrical cast members in the legal texts; they are not all official witnesses.

Dinarchus understands the opportunities for evocation of pathos provided by the small child, and when trying to arouse pity for Didymus brings his infant into the court, calling him by the emotive diminutive *paidion* (fr. 21). In his speech against Neaera, Apollodorus turns his venom against her daughter Phano, who had married the *archōn* and with him undergone the sacred marriage at the Anthesteria. Apollodorus has the imagination to bring into his drama the very herald who had waited upon Phano when she had administered the oath of chastity to the venerable priestesses. Both herald and oath are absolutely irrelevant to the questions of Neaera's ethnicity and claim to citizen status. But by introducing the herald into the cast, and making him read out an oath which says 'I live a holy life and am pure and unstained by all else that pollutes and by intercourse with men', the narrative underscores Neaera's own alleged sexual profligacy, which has occupied so much of the speech ([Dem.] 59.78).

A speech attributed to Demosthenes, bringing an indictment against Aristogeiton, catalogues the failings of this notorious orator, who has already served time in gaol for the debts he had inherited from his father. To crown his exercise in malicious character assassination, the speaker claims that during a quarrel which had taken place in the prison, Aristogeiton had bitten off the nose of another inmate; the speaker crowns this bizarre allegation by actually producing the gruesome spectacle of a Noseless Convict in court (25. 61–2).[77] Slaves could not give evidence in court. But they could be used as mute exhibits, like the silent extras and servile attendants of tragedy. Cratinus produced the very slave woman he was alleged to have killed (Isoc. 18-53–4), and in Demosthenes 37.46 an old slave named Antigenes is exhibited to public view in order to show that he was physically incapable of committing an assault on Pantaenetus—a visual refutation of the opponent's argument.

[76] See Todd (1990*a*), 23.
[77] On Aristogeiton's career as a prisoner, see V. Hunter (1997), 305.

THE 'MASKS'

The proof for which the feeble old Antigenes was produced relied on his appearance alone; one of Aristotle's six elements of tragic drama is *opsis*, the visual dimension. The litigant's thespian ability was different from the actor's, for in the absence of a mask he was required to use his facial expressions in order to convey the personality and arouse the emotions (*pathē*) his case required. The eyes were carefully used. A fragment of Theophrastus' *On Delivery* underlines the value of moving the eyes and altering their expression; a speaker whose gaze remains fixed on a single point is as ineffective as 'an actor with his back turned' (fr. 713 ed. Fortenbaugh (1992)). Speeches also suggest the importance of making eye contact with the jurors: Andocides tells his witnesses to look straight at them (1.18, see also Aesch. 1.121, 63; Dem. 18.283). The facial expressions of the jurors, which signified their likely reactions, were not only an important element in the visual aspect of a trial, but sometimes played a part in the explicit terms of the debate (e.g. Dem. 25.1).

Anyone who has ever been to court understands the power of physical appearance. Treatises from later antiquity stress that the rhetor should cultivate a manly and dignified image.[78] The speeches written in the classical period imply that for men good looks were certainly an asset. Hyperides comments on the poor impression made by excessive thinness (2 fr. 21); Alcibiades stresses that he was won contests in physique (*euandria*, Andoc. 4.42), which were held at the Panathenaea (Anaxilas fr. 8 K–A; [Arist.] *Ath. Pol.* 60.3). Arguments from physiognomy are not unknown:[79] an unattractive appearance may be used as evidence of bad character (Andoc. 1.100), and sometimes a litigant needs to ask the jury to *disregard* someone's good looks, on the ground that they mask an evil interior. The accuser of Theomnestus, for example, claims that the taller and more youthfully handsome (*neaniai*) his opponents are, the more the jury should suspect them (Lys. 10.29).

Beauty in women was more easily turned to their disadvantage, for myth had long authorized its equation with destructive power in the stories of Pandora and Helen. Neaera was actually in attendance at

---

[78] See Gleason (1990), 398–415.   [79] See Hesk (1999), 220–1.

court when Apollodorus brought his case against her, for there are deictics throughout referring to her directly. 'This woman here', he says repeatedly, to keep the jurors' attention fixed on her ([Dem.] 59.44, 50, 64, 115). He also stresses her beauty. Near the end of the speech he asks the jurors to take a good look at her appearance (*opsis*) before passing judgement (115).[80]

THE COSTUMES

Clothing is a vital aspect of visual persuasion. Modern lawyers advise prostitutes to dress up in staid frocks like provincial Sunday-school teachers; vagrants required as witnesses are lent well-cut, respectable suits.[81] When the baby Hermes makes his defence speech before Zeus in the *Homeric Hymn to Hermes*, he appeals to his visually obvious lack of strength, saying he was born but yesterday, and that he therefore 'bears no resemblance to a cattle-rustler, a strong man' (377); while he delivered his speech he kept shooting sidelong glances and deliberately 'kept his swaddling bands on his arm, and did not cast them away' (388). Clothing thus becomes part of the god of cunning's argument from probability. Likewise, the actors in the ancient legal dramas needed to wear suitable costumes for the roles that they were assuming. Subdued clothing commanded respect: in a speech against Conon the plaintiff Ariston tries to undermine the good impression made by sombre apparel. He says that his opponent is supported by three grey-haired men, whom he points out sitting in court. By day they put on sour looks and pretend to 'play the Spartan' (i.e. the moral and abstemious type),[82] wearing single-soled shoes

---

[80] Neaera's presence is accepted even by Goldhill (1994), 359, in the course of a fascinating and lucid argument which, however, perhaps presses a little too hard the case for the exclusion of women from the courts.

[81] Lindi St Claire, a prominent brothel-keeper and campaigner for the decriminalization of prostitution, went to the High Court on a tax evasion charge in 1987, wearing a suit and pillbox hat. She lost the case. In 1990 she took it to the Court of Appeal, announcing that she would be wearing leather and carrying whips. 'This time', she said, 'I won't pretend to be what I'm not' (*The Independent*, 15 May 1990, p. 1).

[82] See L. B. Carter (1986), 72.

and short Laconian cloaks.[83] Yet beneath this deceptive clothing they 'leave no form of wickedness or indecency untried' (Dem. 54.34).

Litigants should not appear too shabby, unless, like Cephisodotus (Isaeus 5.11), or Lysias' invalid (24), poverty was an essential component of their case. The invalid seems to have made a special sartorial effort, because he carefully mentions that he has to use two sticks, and explicitly asks the jury to believe their own eyes rather than the words used by his opponent (24.12, 14). Even in cases where poverty did not need to be proven, an ostentatiously modish appearance risked arousing the jury's prejudices. Lysias 16 was written for Mantitheus, a young man of the knight census class. He pleads with the jury not to take exception to him because he favours the long hair fashionable among his social peer group. Don't judge me on my *opsis*, he asks, but on my deeds (*erga*, 6.18.19).

Clothing could suggest ways in which to insult an opponent: Demosthenes 19.314 portrays Aeschines striding round the *agora* puffing out his cheeks, with his cloak trailing round his ankles. The ethical significance is not altogether clear, although *episurontes*, 'trailing one's robes', is sometimes a metaphor for slipshod language (Dem. 20.131). Demosthenes, on the other hand, is alleged by Aeschines to wear such effeminate mantles and soft shirts that, if they were handed round the jury, they would be unable to tell whether they were male or female clothing (1.131).

Cases that involved alleged violence might require the display of bodily scars. A litigant needed to ensure that any scars resulting from an assault were conspicuous, at least on the day when he first went in to lodge his complaint (Dem. 47.41); it helped to be seen being driven around in a litter, incapacitated by an alleged wound (Lys. 4.9). There are accusations which show that it was well understood that people might actually wound themselves in order to take someone else to court: Aeschines says that Demosthenes has inflicted a thousand gashes on his own head, which is not a head 'but an investment' (3.212). But if a plaintiff's wounds had healed up by the time of the trial (or, indeed, if he had never received any in the first place), medical experts could always be produced in court to testify to the injuries' previous existence (Dem. 40.33, 54.12, 36).

[83] See Plato Comicus fr. 132 K–A.

DEPORTMENT

Gait was construed ethically by the Greeks. Menelaus' delicate gait is remarked upon in Euripides' *Orestes*, a play in which it is implied that this Spartan has gone native in Asia, and become orientalized and tyrannical.[84] In Aristotle's *Physiognomics* the gait of a man with a short, quick step is diagnosed as indicating that his was the type of character who starts a project well, but has no staying power (6.813a).[85] In a lost comedy by Phrynichus, the politician Nicias was ridiculed for the timidity of his gait (*hupotageis ebadizon*, fr. 62 K–A). Servility of character was thought to be indicated by uncoordinated walking (*badizein arruthmōs*, Alexis fr. 265 K–A). Early impressions last: how a person approached the platform to speak could be decisive in determining a jury's response to his words. 'Leap up' (*anapēdan*) is used derogatively (Aesch. 1.71, 3.169), just as it was in reference to leaping up in a disorderly manner (*akosmōs*) in the assembly (Ar. *Eccl.* 438–9; Cratinus fr. 378 K–A).[86] The platform should be approached in a restrained and sober manner (*sōphronōs*, Aeschines 3.2). In his speech against Timarchus, Aeschines predicts that a general will appear in support of the defence, and caricatures him proleptically as mounting the rostrum with a self-conscious air and head held high, as if to claim that he is a graduate of the wrestling-school, and a philosopher (1.132). Particularly intriguing is the ethical significance of Nicoboulos' gait; jurors were asked to suspect him on the ground that he was a 'fast-walking, loud-talking, cane-carrying' moneylender (*tacheōs badizei, kai mega phtheggetai, kai baktrian phorei*, 37.52). The ethical import of the fast walking may perhaps be illuminated by comparison with the contemporary Greek noun *tachypodarakias*, which signifies something like the English 'fancy footworker', a shifty and extremely untrustworthy 'operator'.

[84] 349–51; see E. Hall (1989), 81, 210 n. 33; Bremmer (1991).
[85] For later Greek ideas about the relationship between gait and qualities of character, see Gleason (1990), 392–3.
[86] See Rhodes (2004a), 233 n. 23.

THE MESSENGER SPEECH (NARRATIVE)

Both tragedy and legal speeches examine, in a public arena, actions which have happened away from the public gaze. Just as violent deeds in tragedy nearly always take place within or away from the household, but the public assessment of them is conducted outside the palace or tent, so legal speeches expose to the public the most intimate secrets of family and personal life. The social experience of the collective visualisation of a violent, pathetic, or criminal action is very similar indeed to the shared aesthetic experience of imagining Heracles murdering his wife and children, Deianeira stabbing herself to death, or the struggle between Theseus and the Thebans over the kidnapped daughters of Oedipus.

There are also more specific structural affinities between forensic and tragic narratives. The narratives in the legal speeches tend to involve no more than three figures in the action being narrated at any one time, even when the case involves a large cast and complicated plot.[87] Holding on to the movements and motives of more than three individuals becomes almost impossible for an auditor, and it is reminiscent of the three-actor convention. Moreover, participants in the stories recounted in legal narratives often use sentences of identical length in reported interchange, which is strikingly suggestive of tragic stichomythia. Often the speech-writer elevates the verbal register in order to mark the importance of the section; in tragedy epic vocabulary and phraseology often appear in the messenger speech.

In narrative the speaker could do things forbidden by the conventions of the court, such as recount speeches by people who could not be witnesses themselves. Using direct speech enabled the litigant temporarily to re-enact the performances delivered in previous trials, or to assume the persona of one of the cast members of the forensic drama.[88] He needed, therefore, to be able to act his own public persona in the process of assuming the role of another individual. Just as in the theatre male actors impersonated women, in the law-courts female

[87] See e.g. Dem. 32 and 36, with Pearson (1975*b*), 222 and n. 21.
[88] See the fascinating survey of the different types of direct speech, and the stylistic registers they adopt, in Bers (1997), 129–217.

utterances were often delivered in direct speech to great effect, since women could not normally be used as witnesses. Men took on female roles on the forensic stage, as they did in the theatre, when it suited them to do so.[89] Perhaps the best example is in the Lysianic *In Diogeiton*. The speaker enacts in *oratio recta* the powerful speech of Diodotus' widow on behalf of her children.[90] If recast in the iambic trimeter it could be imported more or less directly into a suppliant scene in a tragedy. It effectively turns the jurors into recipients of the widow's supplication and entreaty, even though there are reasons for doubting that she ever did give a speech of exactly this kind.[91]

In Lysias 1, of course, direct speech is used in several interchanges involving Euphiletus and various women—his young wife, an old woman, and a domestic slave girl. These encounters build up the complication of the plot, and enhance both the plausibility and excitement of the narrative. The alleged adulterer himself is given no direct speech in the reporting of events, for Lysias does not want him to have a defined personality that might elicit sympathy; his role is solely to personify all that threatens decent Athenian patriarchs. The scenes with the women, and the silence of Eratosthenes, serve to throw the last piece of direct speech into profound and memorable relief. It is in a different, more elevated semantic register, and uttered by Euphiletus himself, as he stands over Eratosthenes before executing him, improbably announcing 'with all the formality of a judge pronouncing sentence',[92] 'it is not I who shall kill you, but our city's laws' (26).

THE TRIAL AS TRAGEDY

This discussion has examined one of the ancient Athenians' several 'metaphorical extensions of drama into the realm of social relations and their performance', an expression borrowed from Herzfeld's

---

[89] See Halperin (1990*a*), 290. Goldhill (1994), 357–60 (but see above n. 80).

[90] 32.15–17; see Albini (1952), 189.

[91] 'The account of this meeting makes it sound very staged, almost as if she had been given a script ... these children suffered precisely because their mother was not strong-minded and independent': so Foxhall (1996), 149, at the conclusion of an excellent analysis of this mysterious affair.

[92] Usher (1965), 105.

description of the engagement of the male villagers of Glendi in twentieth-century Crete in constant, competitive social displays.[93] But this metaphor is not altogether an anachronism, since the affinity between legal and tragic public performances in classical Athens was sensed at the time, and often reflected explicitly in the metaphors and analogies used by the speech-writers themselves. Lycurgus made a client say about someone, perhaps Demades, that he would attempt to play parts that required superior skills in tragic acting than he actually possessed (fr. 3);[94] Meidias' family life, averred Demosthenes, was 'like a tragedy' (21.149); Hyperides' client Lycophron accuses his opponent of 'writing tragic phrases' (1.12);[95] his client Euxenippus describes the various allegations made by Olympias as belonging in the tragic theatre (*tas tragōidias autēs kai tas katēgorias, Eux.* 26). The analogy with tragedy also pervades the speeches in other, slightly more subtle ways.

Jurors wanted to be entertained; absorption and comprehension of information became problematic when the issues were complicated, the evidence detailed, or the legal terms too specialized and technical. Demosthenes complains that jurors may not be intelligent enough to follow an argument (23.97), Demades comments on the difficulty involved in following arguments (1.1), and in a fragment of Aristophanes a young man derides his father for having an inadequate grasp of legal terminology (fr. 233 K–A). But in the consciousness of any half-educated Athenian there was embedded a cast of characters derived from the shared virtual world of myth, a code by which he organized his perceptions of the world; the speakers in the courts introduced mythical and theatrical parallels to themselves or their opponents in order to furnish a memorable and familiar analogy which would stick in the jurors' minds when detailed evidence might be lost on them.[96]

---

[93] Herzfeld (1985), 10.

[94] *tous heterous tragōidous agōnieitai* (preserved by Harpocration). The interpretation given here derived from Didymus, who explained the quotation as 'a saying which referred to people who seek to adapt themselves to a role beyond their powers' (Burtt (1954), 141).

[95] See further Whitehead (2000), 130–1; P. Wilson (1996), 321 with n. 58.

[96] See Aristot. *Rhet.* 3.1416b 26–9; Perlman (1964), 157.

The exempla may be derived from Homeric epic. Aeschines claims that his opponents will use the Homeric friendship between Achilles and Patroclus in order to justify the conduct of Timarchus (1.141). But usually it is tragedy which supplies the mythical archetypes for the actors of the Attic courts of law; as Ober and Strauss have put it, for Athenian orators, 'tragedy held a particular appeal as a cultural paradigm'.[97] Demades and Lycurgus both deploy Erechtheus' daughters, portrayed in Euripides' *Erechtheus* as sacrificing themselves for Athens, as exemplars of patriotism (Demades 1.37; *In Leocr.* 98–100). A speech by Hyperides, rhetorically characterizing the opponent as insane, produces the analogy of Orestes, one of the most famous of all tragic madmen (*Lyc.* 7);[98] this comparison immediately precedes one with the hero of burlesque epic, 'Margites, the biggest fool of them all' (7). Antiphon wrote a speech in which a man prosecutes his step-mother for poisoning his father, and it implies that she is like the most famous tragic husband-slayer, Clytemnestra (Antiphon 1.17). This sly allusion suggests that the speaker is an Orestes, offering the woman up, as in Aeschylus' *Eumenides*, to the jurors of Athens. They are thus encouraged to vote, like Athena in that play, in the speaker's favour.[99] The case, if authentic, would have been heard, like that of Aeschylus' Orestes, before the court of the Areopagus; if, on the other hand, it is a demonstration piece designed to teach aspiring logographers how to write a prosecution speech, the use of the mythical allusion becomes all the more significant: this is how a speech-writer created material when the stakes were high in a murder trial.

Andocides describes Callias' allegedly colourful private life. Callias is supposed to have been married to a mother and her daughter simultaneously, and to have fancied the grandmother to boot (1.129). What ought we to call such a man, asks Andocides: Oedipus or Aegisthus? Here the analogies are inaccurate, since neither

---

[97] Ober and Strauss (1990), 247.

[98] The name *Oreste]s* here is a supplement to the papyrus, but one based on the discernment of the trace of an initial *omicron*, which makes Orestes a more likely choice than the other mythical madmen, Heracles and Ajax (Whitehead (2000), 122). See also the apparently proverbial mad Orestes adduced at Ar. *Ach.* 1166–8; Isaeus 8.3, 44.

[99] Gagarin (1997), 116, and (2002), 146, considers that other parts of the same speech were also designed to bring the *Oresteia* to mind.

Oedipus nor Aegisthus slept with three generations of biologically related women, although Jocasta was indeed both mother and grandmother to Oedipus. The point is that one dysfunctional or abnormal tragic family was as good as any other when it came to furnishing ammunition to cast against an opponent's domestic arrangements. The mythical parallels are left engraved upon the jury's imagination, suggesting that Callias has transgressed the most basic socio-sexual tabus.[100]

THE REVERSAL (*PERIPETEIA*)

Once the speeches had been delivered, the jurors voted immediately, using the urns that were part of the theatrical scenery, standing on or very close to the *bēma* (Dem. 19.311). In the Athenian court there was no delay for consultation with fellow jurors or for private reflection before the actual verdict was delivered.[101] The drama of each trial was therefore enacted, like an individual tragedy, without an intermission. In theatrical terms, the *peripeteia* occurred immediately after the debate scene (*agōn*). When the penalty was heavy, litigants often adopted the personae of tragic heroes, stressing the danger in which they found themselves (Dem. 57.1), and their emotions of fear and anger (Demades 1.5). Supporters are asked to speak in order to save the defendant's life (Aeschines 2.142). Apollodorus says that it brings him pleasure to relate to a sympathetic audience the terrible wrongs he has suffered at the hands of Phormio, in language clearly modelled on the tortured hero's words to the chorus of the Aeschylean *Prometheus Bound* (Dem. 45.1; see *PV* 637–9).

Trials were sometimes turned into generic contests between two types of tragic plot. A defendant may beg the jury to save him, and thus turn the trial's drama into an escape plot (Dem. 57.1; Demades 1.5). Plaintiffs may characterise the jury as avengers,[102] and attempt to turn the trial into an emotionally satisfying revenge tragedy (Lysias 13.1). The jurors may be called, invitingly, the 'agents of justice' (*dikē*,

---

[100] See Taplin (1993), 62.   [101] See MacDowell (1978), 251–2.
[102] See Missiou (1992), 177–9.

Dem. 25.11). Like the tragic chorus, they are simultaneously observers and participants. As Aeschines puts it, they are the judges of his words, but *he* is the spectator (*theatēs*) of their deeds (i.e. of their verdict, 1.196).

THE TRIAL AS COMEDY

In the passage from *Wasps* with which this chapter began, Philocleon cited laughter as one of the pleasures of jury service. Some litigants 'tell us stories or a funny Aesopic fable; others crack jokes to make me laugh and put me in a good mood'. This book has looked at performances in the tragic, satyric, dithyrambic and rhapsodic as well as legal arenas, but it perhaps should be concluded, like a day at the Dionysia, within the comic sphere. One feature which trials shared with comedy more closely than with tragedy was certainly the tendency of litigants to appeal to antecedent, if not quite to precedent, by discussing the success or failure of previous lawsuits, including ones in which they had themselves appeared.[103] This self-conscious sense that the current performance was part of a larger continuum of serial public displays, with a history, conventions, and expectations of its own, is not at all unlike the way that the poets of Old Comedy make their characters refer to previous performances of comedy, at previous Dionysiac festivals.

There are, unfortunately, very few examples of funny stories of the kind Philocleon says he enjoys. It may be that this was precisely the kind of material which the speech-writer edited out of his oration before its text came to be published.[104] One Aesopic fable is, however, credited to Demosthenes: the story of the ass's shadow. This was a proverbial example of a ridiculously petty dispute to take to court (see Aristophanes fr. 199 K–A); with this in mind, Demosthenes' approximate contemporary Archippus composed a comedy entitled *The Ass's Shadow*. The orator is said to have introduced the silly tale into a speech in order to retrieve the attention of a listless and

---

[103] On actual arguments from precedent in Athenian law, see Lanni (2004).
[104] See Bonner (1922), 103.

uninterested jury.[105] The ancient rhetoricians were aware that laughter is a potent oratorical weapon; wit and humour receive due attention in the handbooks.[106] The aspiring speech-writer was certainly expected to be familiar with comic texts in addition to more serious poetry, for passages from comedy are sometimes used in the handbooks to illustrate rhetorical tactics and stylistic devices (e.g. Anaxandrides fr. 67 K–A, quoted by Aristotle to illustrate the use of wit achieved through metaphor, *Rhet.* 3.1411^{a}18).

The hostile laughter of vilification which constituted a large part of ancient court-room humour usually functioned, as it does today, by establishing a sense of 'in-group' consciousness that binds one of the litigants and the jurors, thus estranging his opponent from the group. The question is simply which of the two jurors becomes the group's leader, the prime mover in mockery, and which becomes alienated from it. In some passages, ancient legal rhetoric thus reveals a much stronger affinity with comedy than with tragedy.[107] The ridicule meted out in Old Comedy has much in common with the language of socio-political abuse in the legal texts. One commonplace of both genres, for example, is the allegation that someone is unable to speak Athenian Greek, a failure which calls his claim to citizen status into question (see above p. 373 and e.g. Eupolis fr. 99 K–A, where it is alleged that a demagogue cannot 'talk Attic'— *attikizein*—convincingly).

The prominent public figures who were most likely to be lampooned in comedy were the same men who engaged in litigation against one another; the stereotypes summoned up in the law-courts must have drawn upon the same aspects of individuals' public reputations as did their comic characterizations. Socrates is supposed to have claimed that his poor public image was a creation of the comic poets (Plato, *Apol.* 18b–d, 19b–c, 23c–d), probably in allusion

---

[105] *Σ* Ar. *Wasps* 191; see B. B. Rogers (1915), 28–9.

[106] See e.g. Aristot. *Rhet.* 3.1412^{a}26–^{b}4, and the distinction Demetrius draws between lofty pleasantry and vulgar buffoonery (*On Style* 3.128; 5.262); M. A. Grant (1924).

[107] See Harding (1994), although Halliwell (1991), 286, offers some interesting remarks on the tragic *topos* of fear of hostile laughter. See especially his remarks on the light shed on the function of laughter in comedy and in the courts by Dionysus' plan in *Bacchae* to lead the transvestite Pentheus through the streets of the town, in order to display him for the laughter of the people (854–5).

to his portrayal in Aristophanes' *Clouds*.[108] Philippides, the defendant in Hyperides 2, was also sent up in comedy (Athen. *Deipn.* 6.230c; 238c); the comic poet Timocles wrote a *Neaera* (Athen. *Deipn.* 13.567e); Blepaeus the banker, mentioned in Demosthenes' *Against Meidias* (21.215–17), was attacked in comedy on the ground of his excessive wealth (Alexis fr. 229 K–A). Timarchus, says Aeschines in his speech against him, had recently been lampooned in comedies at the rural Dionysia (1.157), which suggests that his forensic portrayal as a failed rent-boy may owe much to comic caricature. But Timarchus allegedly intended to get his own back by the subversively comic—even satyric—ruse of displaying Aeschines' own erotic poems in public (Aesch. 1.135).

Humour is culturally and historically relative, and it is often difficult to assess the tone and likely impact of particular passages, especially where subtle irony or assumption of parodic speech registers is involved. There are, however, some transparently obvious bids for jury laughter.[109] One of Demosthenes' clients, defending himself in a suit concerning land drainage, asks what he is supposed to do with all the surplus water that has accumulated on his land; 'Will the plaintiff insist that I drink it?'[110] A fragment of Lysias (fr. 1) explores, to hilarious effect, the gap between the behaviour which might be expected of a former pupil of Socrates, reputedly much given to discussing the nature of virtue, and his 'actual' character as an incurable borrower of money and failed perfumier. Isaeus 4.7 contains an amusing characterization of the excessive displays of bereavement evinced by litigants in a dispute over a will.

The papyrus text of Hyperides' speech in defence of Lycophron, a cavalryman, horse-breeder, and alleged *homme du monde*, reveals that he is currently accused of seducing a freeborn Athenian woman. This trial seems to have been consciously formulated as a genre battle between the rival dramatic modes of tragedy and comedy. The opponent is characterized as one who uses *tragic* phrases (*tragōidias grapsai*, 1.12), while Hyperides deploys strategies appropriated from the contrasting theatrical genre. Lycophron would hardly have been

---

[108] See Henderson (1990), 301–5.
[109] See the remarks on laughter as an aim of rhetoric in Halliwell (1991), 287–91.
[110] 55.18; see also 55.4, Lysias 1.36, 7.1, 7.14, 16.5, Bonner (1922), 100.

likely to assault Charippus' wife at her wedding given the presence of two wrestlers (one of them her own brother), 'acknowledged to be the strongest men in Greece' (1.6). And anyway, he says, adultery is not a habit that it is advisable to begin above the age of fifty (1.15)! There is extant, however, another forensic speech which was probably delivered in Lycophron's support at the same trial; the speaker would have been one of his friends (*POxy* 1607).[111] Here the tactic is to undercut the *prosecution's* use of comedy by labelling it as vulgar (*kordakizōn kai gelōtopoiōn*, 7), and claiming that it has debased the solemnity of the proceedings. As Halliwell points out, the accepted potency of laughter as a medium in which enmities may be pursued sat alongside an emphatic 'recognition of its dangers to the social fabric of the polis'.[112] Consequently, complaints about the threat laughter posed were as frequent as bids for laughter; Demosthenes laments that he has been the victim of the wit of both Aeschines and Philocrates (19.23, 46). Aeschines attacks Timarchus for his use of bawdy insinuation (1.80, 84), although he is himself responsible for scatological colloquialisms at Demosthenes' expense.[113]

CONCLUSION

Athenian legal speeches are a prime site for revealing the extent to which the experience of theatre had penetrated social life and public discourse. The texts reveal affinities with dramatic 'parts' in terms of the context in which they were performed, the relationship between speakers and audiences, the enactment of roles constituted by fictive identities which even extended to the attention paid to appearance, costume, use of the eyes, gait, deportment, and demeanour. It also affected the ways in which the courtroom, the witnesses, and other 'extras' in the legal cast were exploited and orchestrated. The cast of

---

[111] On the vexed question of the authorship of the second speech in defence of Lycophron, see Whitehead (2000), 86–9.
[112] Halliwell (1991), 287.   [113] 2.44; see Maxwell-Stuart (1975).

characters which the jurors had encountered in the theatre—sexual deviants, murderers, longsuffering victims of tyrannical abuse in tragedy, rent-boys in comedy—affected the way that roles were conceived in the courts of law, and the ways in which they were performed.

One reason for prosecuting a rival was to furnish an opportunity for competing against him in public, and successful performance at a trial required almost identical skills to those required by the dramatic actor: stamina, exciting delivery, charismatic presence, vocal virtuosity, memorization, and the ability to relate to and control the audience, hold its attention, and arouse its emotions. Other criteria than these must of course have influenced the outcome of a trial. The speech made by the oligarch Antiphon in defence of his life, according to Thucydides at any rate, was the best of its kind in living memory (8.68.2). The section preserved on papyrus has shown the audacity and intellectual bravura of which he was capable.[114] But the circumstances in Athens after the fall of the short-lived oligarchy meant that no speech could ever have secured his acquittal.[115]

The evidence accumulated in this survey, however, indicates that we should approach the ancient Athenians' legal texts, as we approach their theatrical ones, only after conceding that we have lost almost all access to one of the most significant dimensions of the ancient event in which they were delivered: the trial was a theatrical and competitive performance between Athenian citizens attempting to persuade an audience of the authenticity of the roles they had publicly assumed. This statement by Richard Martin on the importance of the notion of performance to our understanding of epic poetry is as pertinent to the drama of Athens, to its legal oratory, and indeed to the whole of this book:

---

[114] For the fragments of Antiphon's own defence speech, *On the Revolution*, see Gagarin (1997), 102–3. Antiphon dared the high-risk strategy of arguing that he would never have wanted to subvert the democracy, because 'under the democracy I have long been the one with power because of my skill with words' (translation taken from Gagarin and MacDowell (1998), 91–2).

[115] Gagarin (2002), 161–4, esp. n. 78, emphasizes the complexity of Antiphon's sophistical argumentation, especially in comparison with the more straightforward and direct pleas made by Andocides on his own behalf in Andocides 1 and 2.

timing, gesture, voice inflection, tempo, proximity to the audience, the past relation of a particular performer with his . . . audience, the setting . . . are factors that determine the meaning of the actual words spoken by a performer as much if not more so than the literal meaning of the words themselves. That is to say that it is the performance, not the text, which counts.[116]

[116] Martin (1989), 7.

Afterword

The first chapter of this volume considers a range of metaphors that have been used to describe the relationship between the real, everyday world of the classical Athenians and the fictional worlds that they staged in their dramas. One of the aptest images is also one of the oldest (in post-Renaissance terms), since it is one produced by mid-nineteenth-century Dialectical Materialism (which we call 'Marxist theory', although Marx himself hated the label). This image compares the relationship borne to material reality by the world created in art and discourse with the relationship borne to an element in its solid or liquid form by a chemical sublimate of the same element. One appropriate example is the opaque gas used to entrance and mystify the audiences in theatres ('dry ice'), which is related in this way, as a sublimate, to blocks of frozen carbon dioxide. Both the vaporous contents of the human psyche that become expressed in the arts, and the solid, empirically tangible contents of the world, are constituted by the identical element, which nevertheless undergoes ceaseless mutations in and out of its different presentations.

Critical labour at the coal-face of literature and culture often consists of an unselfconscious response to findings. This critic commonly feels as though she is groping around wildly and intuitively on autopilot. But it may be helpful to reflect retrospectively on the different types of theory that have informed the individual questions asked in each of the foregoing chapters since, as the Introduction also suggests, no single theoretical model can ever be sufficiently nuanced to illuminate every aspect of the vast and complex interface between Athenian life and Athenian theatrical fictions. A case can be made for brazen theoretical and methodological eclecticism in approaching individual types of role, subject-matter, and theatrical convention, and in drawing distinctions between the way that each of them frames the contiguities and disjunctions between the invented and the materially existent worlds.

Chapter 2 draws on theories ultimately developed in Performance Studies, as it turns to ancient actors–the men whose presence and vocality physically effected the alchemical transformation of the Athenian theatre of Dionysus into the different places and times in which ancient dramas were set, from mythical Egypt to the Black Sea, from Hades to Cloudcuckooland. The discussion considers several different ways in which the concept of the enacted *role* bridged the 'real' world inhabited on the one hand by the actor and his audience, and on the other by the conjured world of the drama: it looks at the evidence for the actual, material papyrus scripts from which actors learned their fictional parts, and explores the penetration of the great canonical roles into psychological and social arenas far beyond the theatre. The classical Athenians thought rather differently from the way we do today about what happened in a theatre when an actor took on his enacted identity: lacking any word for 'role', the ancient Greeks seem to have conflated the actor more powerfully than we do with the character whose role he assumed. This intense perception of the identity of the actor and his role created some notable consequences: it offered Plato the opportunity to claim that an actor inevitably *turned into* the type of person whose role he imitated; it also meant that ancient people had powerful dreams, recorded by the oneirocritics, that predicted the dreamers' futures by suggesting that they had virtually metamorphosed into the mythical individuals whom they had seen being represented in theatrical performances.

A different methodological trajectory is taken in the third chapter. It starts out from the apparent inconsistency between the difficulty of accessing the psychological experience of families undergoing the arrival of a new baby in reality (a topic on which the ancient Greek sources are notoriously almost silent), and the single, indubitably public, activity in which pregnancy, birth, and the first few days after birth played a striking role: theatrical performance. The Phenomenological model of theatre suggests that theatrical mimesis has a special claim to truth value, and stresses the importance of enactment as presenting visible manifestations, or symptoms, of underlying social concerns: the evidence is therefore collected for tragic and comic domestic plots set at exactly the moment of childbirth (or the days immediately subsequent to it while the baby's paternity is yet unconfirmed), and for the popularity of acted impersonations of pregnant, labouring and post-parturient females. The stage was a place on which birthing could legitimately and pleasurably become a social matter; the ancient baby-plays—however fragmentary and elusive—constitute an important dimension of ancient collective psychology.

The real, physical items under scrutiny in Chapter 4, however, are not ancient babies but theatrical masks, cast in plaster and rags from moulds, painted with colours, and donned by actors as they assumed their roles. These masks had a particularly potent impact on the content of tragedy, by adding a significant strand of imagery to the repertoire available to the poets, who often compare their characters, especially women, with paintings and statues. The ephemeral materials from which ancient craftsmen constructed the masks that allowed male actors to make *women* visible in the theatrical cast has thus left a permanent impression on the texts of the playscripts that have survived.

By focusing on the psychological contexts in which the artwork analogies appear, the argument is developed that the visual dimension of tragic mimesis, most concretely instantiated in the lovely female mask placed over a male actor's features, was central to the way in which fifth-century audiences conceived the aesthetics of tragic theatre as a whole. The analogies with artworks thus function (somewhat like the artistic *mise-en-abyme* labelled by André Gide and beloved of Poststructuralist literary theorists) to draw attention to the collective cognitive process going on in tragedy. But they also help us to appreciate the remoteness and elevation of the heroic world which the dramatists sought to create in their tragedies; far from using explicit metatheatre, they generically *avoided* overt references to the theatre, whether as a social institution, a physical location, a material presence, or an aesthetic experience.

Chapter 5 looks at another convention–the satyr dramas which throughout the fifth century and well into the fourth constituted the final play in tragic tetralogies performed at the Athenian Dionysia. Satyr plays thus provided closure to performances of tragedy, in which the audience had often been identifying with female characters and reacting with emotions usually socially constructed as 'feminine'. This chapter examines the evidence for female roles amongst the dominantly boisterous male casts of satyr drama; it argues from a perspective informed by constructivist and psychoanalytical Feminism that one function of satyr drama was to reaffirm in its audience, at the end of the tragic productions, a masculine collective consciousness based in libidinal awareness. The viewpoint of dramatic satyrs was pointedly masculine, characterized by a hyperbolic sexual appetitiveness, and permitted both heterosexual and homosexual expression. Enjoying satyr drama's childlike, carnal, homosocial ambience brought its spectators back into the psychological gender orientation appropriate to the City Dionysia, by substituting a joyous collective male consciousness physically centred on the phallus.

The subject of Chapter 6, under the influence of Deconstruction's interest in allegory, is the phenomenon by which the poets of Old Comedy introduced into their casts allegorical figures representing poetic and dramatic abstractions. Unlike tragedy, which Chapter 4 argues was extremely reluctant to make self-conscious comments on its status as theatre, Aristophanes, Cratinus, and their colleagues brought into the view of their audiences male actors actually dressed and masked as female figures including Poetry, Comedy, Mousikē, and the Muse of Euripides; through these concrete figures the comic dramatists were able to meditate with great explicitness and self-consciousness on comedy's generic theatrical conventions and poetics. Moreover, this metatheatrical content is routinely gendered in ways that dovetailed with the comic genre's licence of (hetero)sexual aggression and presentation of gender hierarchies: the female body—pregnable, sexually abused, *available*—was something which the poets of Old Comedy discovered was good to think with when it came to understanding poetry—especially comic poetry—and its relationship with poets.

It has long been recognized that Greek tragedy repeatedly stages confrontations between members of different ethnic groups, which provided a context for extensive Athenian self-definition and indeed imperial propaganda. Chapter 7 offers an update to the model of ethnically defined self and other proposed in *Inventing the Barbarian: Greek Self-Definition through Tragedy* (Hall 1989); it surveys recent reassessments of the extent to which Athenian tragedy is definitively a democratic art form, and the insights which polemical anti-racist, Postcolonial, African American, and Feminist literary theorists can offer the reader of ethnicity in ancient drama. It also argues that although the original audiences at the premières of ancient Greek plays may have been almost exclusively free male citizens, along with their free male guests from allied states, it is becoming increasingly important to consider the potential reactions of a more diverse audience in terms both of ethnicity and of class. This reassessment is required if only by the large number of revivals and performances of the classic repertoire that were taking place, by the early fourth century, in many contexts and venues other than the major Athenian festivals.

The most barbarous barbarian in the surviving theatrical cast of Athens is the Scythian archer who in Aristophanes' *Thesmophoria-zusae* is ordered to bind Euripides' kinsman to a plank in preparation for a horrid execution. The creation of this role is a direct response to the social institution, within the democratic Athenian polis, of the corps of state slaves from Scythia who were required to perform various functions related to crowd control, arrest, and punishment within the civic administration: Aristophanes' Scythian therefore constitutes a straightforward example of a derogatory comic ethnic stereotype of the type that has attracted considerable attention, as a site where racist ideologies are affirmed, in recent Postcolonial Studies. Chapter 8 offers a detailed discussion of this role, from linguistic, aesthetic, and socio-historical perspectives, and argues that not only does the Scythian offer a safe target within the extreme ethnocentric assumptions of the Athenian comic universe, but that the drama itself presents theatre–especially the innovative recent theatre of Euripides–as an exclusive cultural process which is inherently closed to non-Greeks both intellectually and imaginatively.

Chapter 9 looks at how another artistic medium within Athens–the solo aria, to cithara accompaniment–began in the later fifth century to take on an increasingly theatrical tone. In *Persians*, a citharodic nome by Timotheus of Miletus, the star soloist was required to deliver a series of flamboyant mimetic sung imperson-ations of barbarians at the time of the battle of Salamis, including one who is drowning at the scene of the sea-battle because he cannot

swim. Drawing on the Narratological premise that there is considerable significance attached to any author's decision to lend a character
within narrative voice in direct speech, the discussion then proceeds
on a broadly Structuralist principle to argue that the drowning
barbarian Other serves to affirm his Greek audience's pride in their
own proficiency at swimming, and explores the important contribution made by a consciousness of superior skills in the water to the
Athenian and wider Greek definitions of Self.

The theoretical model underlying the tenth chapter, which is also
concerned with solo singing, is the notion (widely associated with the
Marxist-Formalist critic Fredric Jameson) that literary *form* is as
ideologically conditioned and charged as literary style or content.
This chapter looks at the solo lyrics sung by actors in Athenian
tragedy, and argues that the conventions underlying dramatists'
decisions to make a particular character sing or not are profoundly
implicated in the gendered, ethnocentric, and class-conscious socio-
political hierarchies which governed the world of Athenian reality.
Furthermore, Athenian drama, which appropriated and absorbed
into itself a wide variety of metres and types of poetry associated
with places all over the Greek-speaking world, can be seen as Athenian imperialism performed on the level of genre.

The political dimension of literary form is also important in
Chapter 11, which examines the role of the protagonist Trygaeus in
Aristophanes' *Peace* from the perspective of his actor. This procedure
demonstrates the wide variety of poetic metres and media in which
he was required to perform, in a particularly flamboyant example of
what Formalist critics would call Old Comedy's highly 'inclusive'
status as genre: it has absorbed into its overarching structure numerous other genres of poetry. This insight in turn reveals that Aristophanes is creating an ideologically charged taxonomy of poetic
genres, in which martial epic is opposed to Hesiod, Stesichorus,
and all types of theatrical poetry. Semiotically speaking, the object
which welds this poetic and symbolic antithesis to the real world of
politics and history is the shield–a recurring symbol and image in the
play, the site in epic poetry of contrasting scenes of war and peace,
and the material object which the warmonger Cleon had taken from
the Spartans and hammered to important buildings in the city
centre.

The methodology in the final chapter is more straightforwardly inter-generic, in that it takes the conventions and content of the fictional worlds created in the theatre, and sees how they came to affect the conventions and content of the more 'real'—but nevertheless highly performative—world of the Athenian law-courts. The study was originally inspired by the Social Anthropological proposal that institutions within the same community often develop 'isomorphically' (that is, take on similar shapes, practices and modes of expression). From the physical layout of the courtroom space, to style of vocal delivery, orchestration of 'cast' members, attention given to costume, deportment, and gesture, mythical analogies, and emotional reactions, the experience of the juror witnessing the speeches of litigants at an Athenian trial was in manifold ways similar to his experience as a spectator at the theatre. Like all dimensions of Athenian society, the shape of litigation, as a result of the institution and experience of the drama competitions, came to be cast, during the classical period, in an increasingly theatrical mould.

Consolidated Bibliography

ABDEL-MALEK, ANOUAR (1963), 'Orientalism in crisis', *Diogenes* 44, 104–12, reproduced in Macfie (2000), 47–56.

ABEL, LIONEL (1963), *Metatheatre: A New View of Dramatic Form.* New York.

ADAMS, ALICE E. (1994), *Images of Childbirth in Science, Feminist Theory, and Literature.* Ithaca and London.

ADRADOS, FRANCISCO R. (1972), 'Los coros de la "Paz" y los "Dictiulcos" y sus precedentes rituales', *Studi classici in honor di Quintino Cataudella* i. 173–236. Catania.

AITCHISON, JEAN (1994), *Words in the Mind: An Introduction to the Mental Lexicon* (second edition). Oxford.

ALBINI, U. (1952), 'Lysia narratore', *Maia* 5, 182–90.

—— (1964) (ed.), *Andocide, De Pace, Introduzione e Commento.* Florence.

ALCOCK, SUSAN E., CHERRY, JOHN F., and ELSNER, JAS (2001) (eds.), *Pausanias : Travel and Memory in Roman Greece.* Oxford.

ALLEN, KATARZYNA HAGEMAJER (2003), 'Becoming the "Other": attitudes and practices at Attic cemeteries', in Dougherty and Kurke (2003), 207–36.

ALLEN, W. SIDNEY (1968), *Vox Graeca.* Cambridge.

ANDERSON, W.D. (1966), *Ethos and Education in Greek Music* (Cambridge, Mass.).

—— (1982), 'Euripides' *Auge* and Menander's *Epitrepontes*', *GRBS* 23, 165–77.

—— (1994), *Music and Musicians in Ancient Greece.* Ithaca, NY, and London.

ANDREASSI, MARIO (2001) (ed.), *Mimi greci in Egitto. Charition e Moicheutria.* Bari.

ANTONACCIO, CARLA (2003), 'Hybridity and the cultures within ancient Greek culture', in Dougherty and Kurke (2003), 57–74.

APTE, MAHADEV L. (1985), *Humor and Laughter: an Anthropological Approach.* Ithaca, NY.

ARAFAT, K. W. (1996), *Pausanias' Greece: Ancient Artists and Roman Rulers.* Cambridge.

ARNOLD, THOMAS (1874), *The History of the Peloponnesian War.* 8th edn. Oxford.

Arnott, W. Geoffrey (1996) (ed.), *Alexis: The Fragments*. Cambridge.

—— (2000) (ed. and trans.), *Menander*, vol. iii. Cambridge, Mass. and London.

Arnould, Dominique (1981), *Guerre et paix dans la poesie grecque de Callinos a Pindare*. New York.

Arrowsmith, W. (1968), 'Conversion in Euripides', in J. R. Wilson (ed.), *Twentieth Century Interpretations of Euripides' Alcestis*, 31–6. Englewood Cliffs, NJ.

Arthur, Marilyn (1973), 'Early Greece: the origins of the western attitude toward women', *Arethusa* 6, 1–58.

Assoun, Paul-Laurent (2002), 'Eros et Polemos: la comédie de la paix', in Rochefort-Guillouet (2002), 107–14.

Austin, C., and Douglas Olson, S. (2004) (eds.), *Aristophanes' Thesmophoriazusae*. Oxford.

Austin, M., and Vidal-Naquet, P. (1977 [1973]), *Economic and Social History of Ancient Greece. An Introduction*. Eng. trans. of French 2nd edn. London.

Babbitt, Frank Cole (1936, trans.), *Plutarch's Moralia*, vol. iv. Cambridge, Mass. and London.

Bäbler, B. (1998), *Fleissige Thrakerinnen und wehrhafte Skythen. Nichtgriechen im Klassichen Athen und ihre archäologische Hinterlassenschaft*. Stuttgart and Leipzig.

Backhaus, W. (1976), 'Der Hellenen-Barbaren-Gegensatz und die hippokratische Schrift *peri aeron hydaton topon*', *Historia* 25, 170–85.

Baier, Thomas (1999*a*), ' "On ne peut faillir en l'imitant": Rotrous *Sosies*, eine Nachgestaltung des plautinischen *Amphitruo*', in Baier (1999*b*), 203–37.

—— (1999*b*) (ed.), *Studien zu Plautus' Amphitruo*. Tübingen.

Bakewell, Geoff (1997), review of E. Hall (ed. 1996), *Aeschylus' Persians*, *Bryn Mawr Classical Review* 8.9, 849.

Bakola, Emmanuela (2005), 'Old Comedy disguised as satyr play: a new reading of Cratinus' *Dionysalexandros* (P.Oxy. 663)', *ZPE* 154, 46–58.

Baldwin, C. S. (1924), *Ancient Rhetoric and Poetic*. New York.

Ballaira, Guglielmo (1974) (ed.), *'Seneca'. Ottavia*. Turin.

Banton, Michael (1965), *Roles: an Introduction to the Study of Social Relations*. New York.

Barker, Andrew (2004), 'Transforming the nightingale: aspects of Athenian musical discourse in the late fifth century', in Murray and Wilson (2004), 185–204.

Barker, F. (1985) (ed.), *Europe and its Others: Proceedings of the Essex Conference on the Sociology of Literature*. Colchester.

BARLOW, SHIRLEY (1982), 'Structure and dramatic realism in Euripides' Herakles', *G&R* 29, 115–25.

—— —— (1986a), *The Imagery of Euripides*. 2nd edn. Bristol.

—— (1986b), 'The language of Euripides' monodies', in J.H. Betts, J.T. Hooker, and J.R. Green (eds.), *Studies in Honour of T.B.L. Webster* vol. i, 10–22. Bristol.

BARON, DENNIS (1986), *Grammar and Gender*. New Haven and London.

BARNER, WILFRIED (1971), 'Die Monodie', in Jens (1971), 277–320.

BARRETT, W.S. (1964) (ed.), *Euripides, Hippolytos*. Oxford.

BARTHES, R. (1973), *Mythologies* (Eng. trans.). London.

BASINGER, JEANINE (2003), *The World War II Combat Film: Anatomy of a Genre*. Middletown, Conn.

BASLEZ, M.-F. (1986), 'Le péril barbare, une invention des Grecs?', in C. Mossé (ed.), *La Grèce ancienne*, 284–99. Paris.

BASSETT, S. E. (1931), 'The place and date of the first performance of the *Persians* of Timotheus', *CP* 26, 153–65.

BASSI, KAREN (1998); *Acting Like Men: Gender, Drama and Nostalgia in Ancient Greece*. Ann Arbor, Mich.

BATES, WILLIAM NICKERSON (1930), *Euripides: A Student of Human Nature*. New York.

BAUCHHENSS-THÜRIEDL, CHRISTA (1986), 'Auge', *LIMC* iii.1, 45–51. Zurich and Munich.

BAUMAN, R. A. (1990), *Political Trials in Ancient Greece*. London and New York.

BEKKER, I. (1824–5) (ed.), *Photii Bibliotheca*. 2 vols. Berlin.

BENOIT, W. L., and WELLS, W. T. (1996). *Candidates in Conflict: Persuasive Attack and Defense in the 1992 Presidential Debates*. Tuscaloosa, Ala.

BENOIT, W. L., HANSEN, G. J., and TILLERY, R. M. (2003), 'A meta-analysis of the effects of viewing presidential debates'. *Communication Monographs* 70, 335–50.

BENTLEY, ERIC (1964), *The Life of the Drama*. New York.

BENVENISTE, E. (1932), 'Le sens du mot κολοσσός et les noms grecs de la statue', *Rev. Phil.* 6, 118–35.

BENZ, LORE (1999), 'Dramenbearbeitung und Dramenparodie im antiken Mimus und im plautinischen *Amphitruo*', in Baier (1999b), 51–91.

BERGER-DOER, GRATIA (1990), 'Kanake', *LIMC* V.1, 950–1. Zurich and Munich.

BERGK, THEODORE (1838), *Commentationum de reliquiis comoediae atticae antiquae libri duo*. Leipzig.

BERNAL, MARTIN (1987), *Black Athena: The Afroasiatic Roots of Classical Civilization. The Fabrication of Ancient Greece, 1785–1985*. London.

BERS, V. (1985), 'Dikastic *thorubos*', in Paul Cartledge and David Harvey (eds.), *Crux: Essays in Greek History presented to G. E. M. de Ste. Croix*, 1–15. London.

—— (1994), 'Tragedy and rhetoric', in Worthington (1994), 176–95.

—— (1997), *Speech in Speech: Studies in Incorporated Oratio Recta in Attic Drama & Oratory*. Lanham, Md., Boulder, Colo., New York, and London.

—— (2003) (trans.), *Demosthenes, Speeches 50–59*. Austin, Tex.

BEVERLEY, E. JANE (1997), 'The dramatic function of actors' monody in later Euripides'. D.Phil thesis, Oxford.

BIERL, ANTON (1990), 'Dionysus, wine, and tragic poetry: a metatheatrical reading of P. Köln VI 242a = *TgrF* II F646a', *GRBS* 31, 353–403.

BIRT, T. (1907), *Die Buchrolle in der Kunst*. Leipzig.

BIZZARO, FERRUCIO CONTI (1999), *Poetica e Critica Letteraria nei Frammenti dei Poeti Comici Graeci* [= *Speculum* 21]. Naples.

BLISTEIN, ADAM D. (1980), 'The nature and significance of the protagonists in the fifth-century comedies of Aristophanes', Ph.D. Thesis, Yale.

BLUM, H. (1969), *Die antike Mnemotechnik* (= *Spudasmata* 15). New York.

BOADEN, JAMES (1831–2) (ed.), *The private correspondence of David Garrick : with the most celebrated persons of his time and now first published from the originals and illustrated with notes and a new bibliographical memoir of Garrick*. 2 vol. London.

BOARDMAN, JOHN (2004), 'Unnatural conception and birth in Greek mythology', in Dasen (2004), 147–58.

BOAS, F. (1914), *University Drama in the Tudor Age*. Oxford.

BOBRICK, ELIZABETH (1991), 'Iphigenia revisited: *Thesmophoriazusae* 1160–1225', *Arethusa* 24, 67–76.

—— (1997), 'The tyranny of roles: playacting and privilege in Aristophanes' *Thesmophoriazusae*', in Dobrov (1997), 177–97.

BOEDEKER, D. (2002), 'Paths to heroization at Plataea', in Boedeker and Sider (2002), 148–63.

BOEDEKER, D. and SIDER, D. (2002) (eds.), *The New Simonides: Contexts of Praise and Desire*. Oxford.

BOEGEHOLD, ALAN (1995), *The Lawcourts at Athens: Sites, Buildings, Equipment, Procedure, and Testimonia* [= *The Athenian Agora* vol. xxviii]. Princeton, NJ.

BOGREN, L. Y. (1989), 'Pregnancy symptoms in the expectant male', *Journal of Psychometric Obstetrics and Gynaecology*, suppl. 10.

BOLGAR, R. R. (1969), 'The training of elites in Greek education', in R. Wilkinson (1969), *Governing Elites: Studies in Training and Selection*, 23–49. New York.

BONANNO, MARIA GRAZIA (1973–4), 'Aristoph. *Pax* 1301', *Mus. Crit.* 8–9, 191–3.

BONNER, R. J. (1922), 'Wit and humour in Athenian courts', *CP* 17, 97–103.

—— and SMITH, G. (1938), *The Administration of Justice from Homer to Aristotle.* Chicago.

BORCHHARDT, J. (1983), 'Bildnisse Achaimenidischer Herrscher', in H. Koch and D.N. Mackenzie (eds.), *Kunst, Kultur, und Geschichte der Achämenidenzeit unr ihr Fortleben,* 207–23. Berlin.

BORNSTEIN, M., HAYNES, O., PASCUAL, L., PAINTER, K., and GALPERIN, C. (1999), 'Play in two societies: pervasiveness of process, specificity of structure', *Child Development,* 70, 317–31.

BOVON, A. (1963), 'La representation des guerres perses et la notion de barbare dans la 1è moitié du Ve siècle', *BCH* 87, 579–602.

BOWIE, ANGUS (1993), *Aristophanes: Myth, Ritual and Comedy.* Cambridge.

BRADLEY, KEITH (2000), 'Animalizing the slaves: the truth of fiction', *JRS* 90, 110–25.

BRADLEY, S. A. J. (1982) (trans.), *Anglo-Saxon Poetry.* London and Melbourne.

BRANHAM, R. BRACHT (2001) (ed.), *Bakhtin and the Classics.* Evanston, Ill.

BRATTON, J. S., CAVE, R. A., GREGORY, B., HOLDER, H., and PICKERING, M. (1991), *Acts of Supremacy: The British Empire and the Stage, 1790–1930. Manchester and New York.*

BRAUND, D. (1993), 'Dionysiac tragedy in Plutarch, *Crassus*', *CQ* 43, 468–74.

—— (2005) (ed.) *Scythians and Greeks: Cultural Interactions in Scythia, Athens and the Early Roman Empire.* Exeter.

BREMMER, J. (1983), 'The importance of the maternal uncle and grandfather in archaic and classical Greece and early Byzantium', *ZPE* 50, 173–86.

—— (1991), 'Walking, standing, and sitting in ancient Greek culture', in Bremmer and Roodenburg (1991), 15–35.

—— and ROODENBURG, H. (1991), (eds.), *A Cultural History of Gesture.* Oxford and Cambridge.

BRIANT, PIERRE (1996), *Histoire de l'Empire perse de Cyrus à Alexandre.* Paris, translated into English by Peter T. Daniels as *From Cyrus to Alexander: A History of the Persian Empire.* Winona Lake, Ind. 2002.

—— (2002), 'The Greeks and Persian decadence', in T. Harrison (2002), 193–210. Originally published in 1989 as 'Histoire et idéologie: les Grecs et la "décadence perse" ', in M.-M. Mactou and E. Geny (eds.), *Mélanges P. Lévêque,* ii. 33–47. Bésançon.

BRIDGES, EMMA, HALL, EDITH, and RHODES, P. J. (2007) (eds.), *Cultural Responses to the Persian Wars: Antiquity to the Third Millennium.* Oxford.

BRIXHE, C. (1988), 'La langue de l'étrange non grec chez Aristophane', in R. Lonis (ed.), *L'Étranger dans le monde grec,* 113–38. Nancy.

BROADHEAD, H. D. (1960) (ed.), *The Persae of Aeschylus*. Cambridge.

BROMMER, F. (1937), *Satyroi* (Wärzburg).

—— (1959), *Das Satyrspiele* (Berlin).

BRONFEN, E. (1992), *Over her Dead Body: Death, Femininity, and the Aesthetic*. Manchester.

BROWNING, ROBERT (1963), 'A Byzantine treatise on tragedy', in L. Varcl and R. F. Willetts (eds.), *Geras: Studies Presented to George Thomson on the Occasion of his 60th Birthday*, 67–81. Prague.

—— (2002), 'Greek and others: from antiquity to the Renaissance', in T. Harrison (2002), 257–77. Originally published as ch. 2 of Robert Browning, *History, Language and Literacy in the Byzantine World*. Northampton, 1989.

BROWNMILLER, S. (1973), *Against our Will: Men, Women, and Rape*. New York.

BRYSON, NORMAN (1981), *Word and Image: French Painting of the Ancien Régime*. Cambridge.

BUBEL, FRANK (1991) (ed.), *Euripides, Andromeda* [= *Palingenesia* 34]. Stuttgart.

BURKE, KENNETH (1965), 'On Human Behavior Considered Dramatistically', in his *Permanence and Change*, 274–94. Indianapolis.

BURKERT, W. (1979), *Structure and History in Greek Mythology and Ritual*. Berkeley, Los Angeles, and London.

—— (1985), *Greek Religion* (Eng. trans.). Oxford.

BURNETT, A. P. (1971), *Catastrophe Survived: Euripides*. Oxford.

BURNS, ALFRED (1981), 'Athenian literacy in the fifth century BC', *Journal of the History of Ideas* 42, 371–87.

BURNS, E. (1972), *Theatricality: A Study of Convention in the Theatre and in Social Life*. London.

BURTT, J. O. (1954) (trans.), *Minor Attic Orators*, vol. ii. London.

BUTRICA, JAMES (2001), 'The lost *Thesmophoriazusae* of Aristophanes', *The Phoenix* 55, 44–76.

BUXTON, RICHARD (1982), *Persuasion in Greek Tragedy: A Study of Peitho*. Cambridge.

CALAME, CLAUDE (1986), 'Facing otherness: the tragic mask in ancient Greece', *History of Religions* 26, 125–42.

—— (2004), 'Choral forms in Aristophanic comedy: musical mimesis and dramatic performance in classical Athens', in Murray and Wilson (eds.), 157–84.

CAMPBELL, JOSEPH (1968), *The Masks of God: Creative Mythology*. London.

CAMPO, LUIGI (1940), *I Drammi satireschi della Grecia antica*. Milan.

CAREY, C. (2000), 'Observers of speech and hearers of action: the Athenian orators', in Taplin (2000), 192–216.

CAREY, C. and REID, R. A. (1985), (eds.), *Demosthenes: Selected Private Speeches*. Cambridge.

CARPENTER, THOMAS H. (1986), *Dionysian Imagery in Archaic Greek Art*. Oxford.

CARR, H. (1985), 'Woman / Indian: the American and his others', in Barker (1985), ii. 46–60.

CARRADICE, IAN (1995), *Greek Coins*. London.

CARTER, D. M. (2004), 'Was Attic tragedy democratic', *Polis* 21, 1–24.

CARTER, L. B. (1986), *The Quiet Athenian*. Oxford.

CARTLEDGE, PAUL (1990), *Aristophanes and his Theatre of the Absurd*. Bristol.

—— (1993), *The Greeks: A Portrait of Self and Others*. Oxford.

—— (1997), 'Deep plays: theatre as process in Greek civic life', in Easterling (1997), 3–35.

—— MILLETT, P., and TODD, S. (1990) (eds.), *NOMOS: Essays on Athenian Law, Politics and Society*. Cambridge.

CASARI, JACQUES (2002), 'La lutte pour la paix dans le théâtre d'Aristophane', in Rochefort-Guillouet (2002), 36–45.

CASAUBON, I. (1605), *De Satyrica Graecorum poesi, & Romanorum satira libri duo* (Paris), reproduced in facsimile with an introduction by P. E. Medine, New York 1973.

CASE, SUE-ELLEN (1985), 'Classic drag: the Greek creation of female parts', *Theatre Journal* 37, 317–27.

CASSIO, A. C. (1985), *Commedia e Partecipazione: la Pace di Aristofane*. Naples.

—— (2002), 'The language of Doric comedy', in Willi (2002), 51–83.

CAVALLI, MARINA (1999), 'La *Rane* di Aristofane: modelli tradizionali dell'agone fra Eschilo ed Euripide', in F. Conca (ed.), *Ricordando Raffaele Cantarella. Miscellanea di Studi*, 83–105. Bologna.

CAVELL, STANLEY (1969), *Must We Mean What We Say?* New York.

CHALK, H. (1962), 'Arete and bia in Euripides' *Herakles*', *JHS* 82, 7–18.

CHAMBERS, E. K. (1930), *William Shakespeare: A Study of Facts and Problems*. Oxford.

CHAPIN, CHESTER (1955), *Personification in Eighteenth-Century Poetry*. New York.

CHARITONIDIS, S., KAHIL, L., and GINOUVÈS, R. (1970), *Les Mosaïques de la maison du Ménandre a Mytilène*. Bern.

CHIASSON, Ch. C. (1984), 'Pseudartabas and his eunuchs. *Acharnians* 91–122', *CP* 79, 131–6.

CHRIST, WILHELM (1875), 'Die Parakataloge im griechischen und römischen Drama', *Abhandlungen der philosophisch-philologischen Classe der königlichen bayerischen Akademie der Wissenschaften* 13.3, 153–222 (Munich).

CIPOLLA, PAOLO (2003) (ed.), *Poeti minori del dramma satiresco, testo critico, traduzione e commento* [= Supplementi di Lexis, XXIII.]. Amsterdam.

CLINTON, KEVIN (1996), 'The Thesmophorion in central Athens and the celebration of the Thesmophoria in Attica', in Robin Hägg (ed.), *The Role of Religion in the Early Greek Polis*, 111–25. Stockholm.

CLOUGH, E. (2004), 'In search of Xerxes: images of the Persian King', Ph.D. Diss., Durham.

COCKLE, W. E. H. (1975), 'The odes of Epagathus the choral flautist: some documentary evidence for dramatic representations in Roman Egypt', *Proceedings of the XIVth International Congress of Papyrologists*, 59–65. London.

—— (1983), 'Restoring and conserving papyri', *BICS* 30, 147–65.

—— (1987) (ed.), *Euripides, Hypsipyle. Text and Annotation based on a Re-Examination of the Papyri*. Rome.

CODELL, JULIE F., and MACLEOD, DIANNE SACHKO (1998) (eds.), *Orientalism Transposed: The Impact of the Colonies on British Culture*. Aldershot and Brookfield, Vt.

COHEN, B. (2000) (ed.), *Not the Classical Ideal: Athens and the Construction of the Other in Greek Art*. Leiden.

—— (2001), 'Ethnic identity in democratic Athens and the visual vocabulary of male costume', in Malkin (2001), 235–74.

COLE, SUSAN GUETTEL (1993), 'Procession and celebration at the Dionysia', in Ruth Scodel (ed.), *Theater and Society in the Classical World*, 25–38. Ann Arbor, Mich.

COLE, THOMAS (1988), *Epiploke: Rhythmical Continuity and Poetic Structure in Greek Lyric*. Cambridge, Mass., and London.

COLES, R. A. (1968), 'A new fragment of post-classical tragedy from Oxyrhynchus', *BICS* 15, 110–18.

COLLARD C. (1970), 'On the tragedian Chaeremon', *JHS* 90, 22–34.

—— (1975) (ed.), *Euripides' Supplices*. Groningen.

—— (1991) (ed.), *Euripides' Hecuba*. Warminster.

—— CROPP, M. J., and LEE, K. H. LEE (1995) (eds.), *Euripides: Selected Fragmentary Plays*, vol. i. Warminster, Wilts.

—— —— and GIBERT, J. (2004) (eds.), *Euripides: Selected Fragmentary Plays*, vol. ii. Oxford.

COLLEY, LINDA (1992), *Britons: Forging the Nation, 1707–1837*. New Haven, Conn., and London.

COLLINGE, N. E. (1958–9), 'Some reflections on satyr-plays', *PCPS* 185, 28–35.

COLLINS, DEREK (2001), 'Improvisation in rhapsodic performance', *Helios* 28, 11–27.

COLONNA, ARISTIDE (1983) (ed.), *Opere di Esiodo.* Turin.

COLVIN, S. (1999), *Dialect in Aristophanes and the Politics of Language in Ancient Greek Literature.* Oxford.

—— (2000), 'The language of non-Athenians in Old Comedy', in Harvey and Wilkins (2000), 285–98.

COMOTTI, GIOVANNI (1989), *Music in Greek and Roman Culture* (Eng. trans. of original 1979 Italian edn.). Baltimore and London.

COMPTON-ENGLE, GWENDOLYN (1999), 'Aristophanes' *Peace* 1265–1304: food, poetry and the comic genre', *CP* 94, 324–8.

CONOLLY, JOY (2001), 'Reclaiming the theatrical in the second sophistic', *Helios* 28, 75–96.

CONOMIS, N. (1961), 'Notes on the fragments of Lycurgus', *Klio* 39, 72–152.

—— (1975) (ed.), *Orationes Dinarchi cum fragmentis.* Leipzig.

COOPER, CRAIG (1995), 'Hyperides and the trial of Phryne', *The Phoenix* 49, 303–18.

CORBATO, CARLO (1975), 'Una ripresa Eschilea nella *Pace* di Aristofane', in *Studi Triestini di Antichità in Onore di Luigia Achillea Stella,* 323–35. Trieste.

CORNFORD, FRANCIS MACDONALD (1907), *Thucydides Mythistoricus.* London.

COUCH, H. N. (1933–4), 'Swimming among the Greeks and barbarians', *CJ* 29, 609–12.

—— (1945–6), 'Swimmers in warfare', *Classical Weekly* 39, 34–5.

COULON, VICTOR ET VAN DAELE, HILAIRE (1946) (eds.), *Aristophane,* vol. iv. Paris.

COYNE, MICHAEL (1998), *The Crowded Prairie: American National Identity in the Hollywood Western.* London.

COZZOLI, ADELE-TERESA (2001) (ed.), *Cretesi / Euripide; introduzione, testimonianze, testo critico, traduzione e commento.* Pisa.

CRANE, MARY THOMAS (2001), 'Male pregnancy and cognitive permeability in *Measure for Measure*', in *Shakespeare's Brain: Reading with Cognitive Theory,* 156–77. Princeton and Oxford.

CROISET, MAURICE (1903), 'Observations sur *Les Perses* de Timothée de Milet', *REG* 16, 323–48.

CROPP, MARTIN (1986), 'Heracles, Electra and the *Odyssey*', in Martin Cropp, Elaine Fantham, and S. E. Scully (eds.), *Greek tragedy and its legacy: essays presented to D.J. Conacher,* 187–99. Calgary.

CSAPO, ERIC (1997), 'Riding the phallus for Dionysus: iconology, ritual, and gender-role de/construction', *Phoenix* 51, 253–95.

—— (2002),'Kallipides on the floor-sweepings: the limits of realism in classical acting and performance styles', in Easterling and Hall (2002), 127–47.

—— (2004*a*), 'Some social and economic conditions behind the rise of the
acting profession in the fifth and fourth centuries BC', in C. Hugoniot,
F. Hurlet, and S. Milanezi (eds.), *Le statut de l'acteur dans l'Antiquité grecque
et romaine*, 53–76 [= Collection Perspectives Historiques 9]. Tours.

—— (2004*b*), 'The politics of the new music', in Murray and Wilson (2004),
207–48.

—— (forthcoming), *Actors, Icons and Entrepeneurs*. Oxford.

—— and SLATER, W. J. (1995), *The Context of Ancient Drama*. Ann Arbor,
Mich.

CUNNINGHAM, I. C. (1987) (ed.), *Herodas: Mimiambi*. Leipzig.

DAHRENDORF, RALF (1998), '*Homo sociologicus*: on the history, significance
and limits of the category of social role', in Uta Gerhadt (ed.), *German
Sociology*, 128–49. New York [Eng. trans. of his 'Homo Sociologicus:
Versuch zur Geschichte, Bedeutung und Kritik der Kategorie der sozialen
Rolle', in Dahrendorf (ed.), *Pfade aus Utopia. Arbeiten zur Theorie und
Methode der Soziologie*, 128–83. Munich, 1958].

DALE, A. M. (1954) (ed.), *Euripides' Alcestis*. Oxford.

DAMEN, MARK (1989), 'Actor and character in Greek tragedy', *Theatre
Journal* 41, 316–40.

—— (1990), 'Electra's monody and the role of the chorus in Euripides'
Orestes 960–1012', *TAPA* 120, 133–45.

DANIEL, NORMAN (1960), *Islam and the West: The Making of an Image*.
Edinburgh.

—— (1966), *Islam, Europe and Empire*. Edinburgh.

DASEN, VÉRONIQUE (2004) (ed.), *Naissance et petite enfance dans l'Antiquité.
Actes du colloque de Fribourg, 28 novembre-1er décembre 2001* [=Orbis
Biblicus et Orientalis 203]. Fribourg.

DAVIDSON, JOHN (2003), 'Carcinus and the temple: a problem in the Athenian theatre', *Classical Philology* 98, 109–22.

DAVIES, J.K. (1971), *Athenian Propertied Families*. Oxford.

DAVIES, MARK I. (1980), 'Commodes and cuirasses: Aristophanes' *Peace*
and a Polygnotan painting' (abstract of paper delivered at 81st meeting of
the AIA), *AJA* 84, 203.

DAVIS, NATALIE ZEMON (2000), *Slaves on Screen: Film and Historical Vision*.
Cambridge, Mass.

DAVIS, TRACY C., and POSTLEWAIT, THOMAS (2003) (eds.), *Theatricality*.
Cambridge.

DE JONG, IRENE (1991), *Narrative in Drama: The Art of the Euripidean
Messenger Speech* [= *Mnemosyne* suppl. 117]. Leiden.

de JONG, IRENE (2001), *A Narratological Commentary on the Odyssey.* Cambridge.

—— NÜNLIST, R., and BOWIE, A. (2004) (eds.), *Narrators, Narratees, and Narratives in Ancient Greek Literature,* vol. i [= *Mnemosyne* suppl. 257]. Leiden.

DE KERCKHOVE, DERRICK (1979), 'Sur la fonction du théâtre comme agent d'intériorisation des effets de l'alphabet phonétique à Athènes au Vᵉ siècle', *Les Imaginaires II,* 10/18, 345–68.

DE LAURETIS, TERESA (1987), *Technologies of Gender: Essays on Theory, Film, and Fiction.* Bloomington and Indianapolis.

DE MAN, PAUL (1984), *The Rhetoric of Romanticism.* New York.

DE VRIES, K. (2000), 'The nearly other: the Attic vision of Phrygians and Lydians', in Cohen (2000), 338–63.

DE WITTAK, Th. M. (1968), 'The function of obscenity in Aristophanes' *Thesmophoriazusae* and *Ecclesiazusae*', *Mnemosyne* 21, 357–65.

DEAN-JONES, LESLEY ANN (1994), *Women's Bodies in Classical Greek Science.* Oxford.

DEARDEN, C. W. (1976), *The Stage of Aristophanes.* London.

DÉCHARME, P. (1889), 'Le drame satyrique sans satyres', *REG* 12, 290–9.

—— (1893), *Euripides et l'esprit de son théâtre.* Paris.

DEDOUSSI, CHRISTINA (1965) (ed.), *MENANDROU SAMIA.* Athens.

DEMAND, NANCY (1994), *Birth, Death and Motherhood in Classical Greece.* Baltimore and London.

DEUBNER, L. (1959), *Attische Feste.* Hildesheim.

DEVRIES, W. (1892), *Ethopoiia: A Rhetorical Study of the Types of Character in the Orations of Lysias.* Baltimore.

DIHLE, A. (1981), *Der Prolog der 'Bacchen' und die antike Überlieferungsphase des Euripides-Textes.* Heidelberg.

DILLON, MATTHEW (1999), 'Post-nuptial sacrifices on Kos (Segre, *ED* 178) and ancient Greek marriage rites', *ZPE* 124, 63–80.

—— (2002), *Girls and Women in Classical Greek Religion.* London and New York.

DINDORF, L. (1880–1) (ed.), *Historici Graeci Minores.* Leipzig.

DITTENBERGER, G. (1960), *Sylloge Inscriptionum Graecarum,* 4th edn. Hildesheim.

DOBROV, GREGORY (1995) (ed.), *Beyond Aristophanes: Transition and Diversity in Greek Comedy.* Atlanta.

—— (1997) (ed.), *The City as Comedy: Society and Representation in Athenian Drama.* Chapel Hill, NC, and London.

—— and Urios-Aparisi, Eduardo (1995), 'The maculate muse: gender, genre and the *Chiron* of Pherecrates', in Dobrov (1995), 139–74.

DONOVAN, BRUCE E. (1969), *Euripides Papyri*, vol. i, *Texts from Oxyrhynchus* [= *American Studies in Papyrology* 5]. New Haven and Toronto.

DORJAHN, A.P. (1927), 'Poetry in Athenian courts', *CP* 32, 85–93.

—— (1935), 'Anticipation of arguments in Athenian courts', *TAPA* 66, 274–95.

DOUGHERTY, CAROL (1993), *The Poetics of Colonization: From City to Text in Archaic Greece*. Oxford.

—— (1998), 'Sowing the seeds of violence: rape, women, and the land', in Wyke, 267–84.

—— and KURKE, L. (2003) (eds.), *The Cultures within Ancient Greek Culture: Contact, Conflict, Collaboration*. Cambridge.

DOUGLAS, MARY (1975), 'Couvade and menstruation', in her *Implicit Meanings: Essays in Anthropology*, 60–72. London.

DOVE, RITA (1989), *Grace Notes: Poems*. New York and London.

DOVER, K. J. (1963), 'Notes on Aristophanes' *Acharnians*', *Maia* 15, 6–25.

—— (1966) (ed.), *Aristophanes' Clouds*. Oxford.

—— (1968), *Lysias and the Corpus Lysianicum*. Berkeley and Los Angeles.

—— (1972), *Aristophanic Comedy*. London.

—— (1978), *Greek Homosexuality*. London.

—— (1992) (ed.), *Aristophanes' Frogs*. Oxford.

DU CANN, RICHARD (1980), *The Art of the Advocate*, rev. edn. Harmondsworth.

DuBOIS, LAURENT (1996), *Inscriptions Grecques Dialectales d'Olbia du Pont*. Geneva.

DuBOIS, PAGE (1982), *Centaurs and Amazons: Women and the Pre-History of the Great Chain of Being*. Ann Arbor, Mich.

—— (1988), *Sowing the Body: Psychoanalysis and Ancient Representations of Gender*. Chicago.

—— (2003), *Slaves and Other Objects*. Chicago and London.

DUCAT, J. (1976), 'Fonctions de la statue dans la Grèce archaïque: kouros et kolossos', *BCH* 100, 239–51.

DUCHEMIN, J. (1960), 'Aspects pastoraux de la Poésie homérique: les comparaisons dans l'Iliade', *REG* 73, 362–415.

—— (1968), *L'AGŌN dans la tragédie grecque*, 2nd edn. Paris.

DUNN, FRANCIS (1997), 'Ends and means in Euripides' *Heracles*', in D. H. Roberts, Francis M. Dunn, and Don Fowler (eds.), *Classical Closure: Reading the End in Greek and Latin Literature*, 83–111. Princeton.

DURAND, RÉGIS (1977), 'The disposition of the voice', in M. Benamour and C. Caramello (eds.), *Performance in Postmodern Culture*, 99–110. Milwaukee and Madison, Wis. Repr. in Timothy Murray (1997), 301–10.

Durvye, Catherine (2002), 'Le rire et la paix', in Rochefort-Guillouet (2002), 75–85.

Eagleton, Terry (2003), *Sweet Violence: the Idea of the Tragic.* Oxford.

Easterling, H. J., and Easterling, P. E. (1962) (trans.), *The Clouds of Aristophanes.* Cambridge.

Easterling, P. E. (1982) (ed.), *Sophocles' Trachiniae.* Cambridge.

—— (1985), 'Anachronism in Greek tragedy', *JHS* 105, 1–10.

—— (1997*a*) (ed.), *The Cambridge Companion to Greek Tragedy.* Cambridge.

—— (1997*b*), 'A Show for Dionysos', in Easterling (ed.), 36–53.

—— (1997*c*), 'Form and performance', in Easterling (ed.), 151–77.

—— (1997*d*), 'From repertoire to canon', in Easterling (1997*a*), 211–27.

—— (1999), 'Actors and voices: reading between the lines in Aeschines and Demsothenes', in Goldhill and Osborne (1999), 154–66.

—— (2002), 'Actor as icon', in Easterling and Hall (2002), 327–41.

—— and Hall, E. (2002) (eds.), *Greek and Roman Actors: Aspects of an Ancient Profession.* Cambridge.

Ebeling, Herman Louis (1925), 'The Persians of Timotheus', *AJP* 46, 317–31.

Ebener, D. (1966) (ed.), *Rhesos. Tragödie eines unbekannten Dichters.* Berlin.

Eden, K. (1980), 'The influence of legal procedure on the development of tragic structure', Diss. Stanford.

—— (1986), *Poetic and Legal Fiction in the Aristotelian Tradition.* Princeton.

Edmonds, J. M. (1927) (ed.), *Lyra Graeca* vol. iii. London and New York.

Edmunds, Lowell (1980), Edmunds, 'Aristophanes' Acharnians', in J. Henderson (ed.), *Aristophanes: Essays in Interpretation*, 1–39 [= *YCS* 26].

Edwards, Catharine (2002), 'Acting and self-actualisation in imperial Rome', in Easterling and Hall (2002), 377–94.

Ehrenberg, V. (1951), *The People of Aristophanes*, 2nd edn. Oxford.

Eitrem, S., Amundsen, L., and Winnington-Ingram, R. P. (1955) (eds.), 'Fragments of unknown Greek tragic texts with musical notation (P. Oslo inv. no. 1413)', *SO* 31, 1–87.

El Cheikh, Nadia Maria (2004), *Byzantium Viewed by the Arabs* [=Harvard Middle Eastern Monographs, 36]. Cambridge, Mass.

Elderwick, David (1987), *Captain Webb: Channel Swimmer.* Studley.

Ellis, Havelock (1929), *Man and Woman*, 2nd edn. Boston.

Else, Gerald F. (1957), 'The origin of Τραγωιδια', *Hermes* 85, 17–46.

—— (1958), ' "Imitation" in the fifth century', *CP* 53, 73–90.

—— (1959), 'ΥΠΟΚΡΙΤΗΣ', *WS* 72, 75–107.

Enk, P.J. (1953) (ed.), *Plauti Truculentus*, 2 vols. Leiden.

—— (1964) 'Plautus' *Truculentus*', in C. Henderson (ed.), *Classical, Mediaeval and Renaissance Studies in Honour of Berthold Louis Ullman*, i. 49–65. Rome.

ERDMAN, HARLEY (1997), *Staging the Jew: The Performance of an American Ethnicity*. New Brunswick, NJ.

ERIKSON, ERIK H. (1963), *Childhood and Society*, 2nd edn. New York.

EVERSON, T. (2004), *Warfare in Ancient Greece: Arms and Armour from the Heroes of Homer to Alexander the Great*. Stroud.

FANON, FRANTZ (1997), 'Algeria unveiled', in Timothy Murray (1997), 259–73. First published in English in the translation of Haakon Chevalier in *A Dying Colonialism*, 35–67. New York 1967.

FANTHAM, ELAINE (1982) (ed.), *Seneca's Troades. A Literary Introduction with Text, Translation and Commentary*. Princeton.

FARAONE, C. A. (1985), 'Aeschylus' *humnos desmios* [*Eum.* 306] and Attic judicial tablets', *JHS* 105, 150–4.

FARIOLI, MARCELLA (2001), *Mundus alter. Utopie e distopie nella commedia greca antica*. Milan.

FARRELL, JOSEPH, and SCUDERI, ANTONIO (2000) (eds.), *Dario Fo: Stage, Text, and Tradition*. Carbondale and Edwardsville, Ill.

FAVORINI, ATTILIO (2003), 'History, collective memory, and Aeschylus' *The Persians*', *Theatre Journal* 55.1 [= *Special Issue on Ancient Theatre*], 99–111.

FEENEY, D. (1993), 'Towards an account of the ancient world's concepts of fictive belief', in C. Gill and T. P. Wiseman (eds.), *Lies and Fiction in the Ancient World*, 230–44. Exeter.

FESTA, N. (1902) (ed.), *Mythographi Graeci*. Leipzig.

FIGES, KATE (1998), *Life after Birth: What Even your Friends Won't Tell You about Motherhood*. London.

FINKELBERG, MARGALIT (1998), *The Birth of Literary Fiction in Ancient Greece*. Oxford and New York.

FINLEY, J. H. (1967), *Three Essays on Thucydides*. Cambridge, Mass.

FINLEY, M. I. (1962), 'The Black Sea and Danubian regions and the slave trade in antiquity', *Klio* 40, 51–9.

FITZGERALD, W. (2000), *Slavery and the Roman Literary Imagination*. Cambridge.

FLASHAR, HELLMUT (1967) (trans.), *Aristoteles Problemata Physica*. Berlin.

FLORY, S. (1980), 'Who read Herodotus' *Histories*?', *AJP* 101, 12–28.

FLOYD-WILSON, MARY (2003), *English Ethnicity and Race in Early Modern Drama*. Cambridge.

FO, DARIO (1974), 'Culture populaire et travail militant: Dario Fo et le collectif La Commune', *Cahiers du cinéma* 250, 11–25.

FOLEY, HELENE P. (1981*a*), 'The conception of women in Athenian drama', in Foley (1981*b*), 127–67.

FOLEY, HELENE P. (1981*b*) (ed.), *Reflections of Women in Antiquity*. London and New York.

—— (1985), *Ritual Irony: Poetry and Sacrifice in Euripides*. Ithaca, NY.

—— (1988), 'Tragedy and politics in Aristophanes' *Acharnians*', *JHS* 108, 33–47.

—— (1993), 'The politics of tragic lamentation', in Sommerstein *et al.* (1993), 101–43.

—— (1994) (ed.), *The Homeric Hymn to Demeter*. Princeton.

—— (2001), *Female Acts in Greek Tragedy*. Princeton and Oxford.

—— (2003*a*), 'Mothers and daughters', in Neils and Oakley, 113–37.

—— (2003*b*), 'Choral identity in Greek tragedy', *CP* 98, 1–30.

FORD, ANDREW (1999), 'Reading Homer from the rostrum: poems and laws in Aeschines' *Against Timarchus*', in Goldhill and Osborne (1999), 231–56.

—— (2002), *The Origins of Criticism: Literary Culture and Poetic Theory in Classical Greece*. Princeton.

FORTENBAUGH, W. W. (1986), 'Aristotle's Platonic attitude towards delivery', *Philosophy and Rhetoric* 19, 242–54.

—— et al. (1992) (eds.), *Theophrastus of Eresus: Sources for his Life, Writings, Thought and Influence*, vol. ii. Leiden.

FOWLER, BARBARA HUGHES (1989), *The Hellenistic Aesthetic*. Bristol.

FOWLER, ROBERT (1998), 'Genealogical thinking, Hesiod's *Catalogue*, and the creation of the Hellenes', *PCPS* 44, 1–20.

FOXHALL, LIN (1996), 'The law and the lady: women and legal proceedings in classical Athens', in L. Foxhall and A. D. E. Lewis (eds.), *Greek Law in its Political Setting: Justifications not Justice*, 133–52. Oxford.

—— and SALMON, JOHN (1998) (eds.), *Thinking Men: Masculinity and Self-Representation in the Classical Tradition*. London and New York.

—— and STEARS, KAREN (2000), 'Redressing the balance: dedications of clothing to Artemis and the order of life stages', in Moira Donald and Linda Hurcombe (eds.), *Studies in Gender and Material Culture*, 3–16. Basingstoke.

FRAENKEL, E. (1950) (ed.), *Aeschylus' Agamemnon*. Oxford.

FRANKO, GEORGE FREDRIC (1996), 'The Characterization of Hanno in Plautus' *Poenulus*', *AJP* 117, 425–52.

FRAZER, J. G. (1913), *Pausanias's Description of Greece*, 2nd edn., vol. ii. London.

FRIEDRICH, J. (1919), 'Das Attische im Munde von Ausländern bei Aristophanes', *Philologus* 75 (ns 29), 274–303.

FRONTISI-DUCROUX, F. (1984), 'A miroir du masque', in C. Bérard and J.-P. Vernant, *La cité des images: Religion et société en Grèce antique*, 147–61. Lausanne and Paris.

—— (1995), *Du masque au visage: aspects de l'identité en Grèce ancienne.* Paris.

—— (1996), 'Eros, desire, and the gaze', Eng. trans. by Nancy Kline, in Kampen (1996), 81–100.

FROST, FRANK J. (1964), 'Pericles and Dracontides', *JHS* 84, 69–72.

FRYE, NORTHROP (1957), *Anatomy of Criticism: Four Essays.* Princeton.

—— (1965), *A Natural Perspective: the Development of Shakespearean Comedy.* New York and London.

—— (1976), *The Secular Scripture: A Study of the Structure of Romance.* Cambridge, Mass.

GABELMANN, H. (1984), *Antike Audienz- und Tribunalszenen.* Darmstadt.

GAGARIN, MICHAEL (1996), 'The Torture of Slaves in Athenian Law', *CP,* 1–18.

—— (1997) (ed.), *Antiphon: The Speeches.* Cambridge.

—— (2002), *Antiphon the Athenian: Oratory, Law and Justice in the Age of the Sophists.* Austin, Tex.

—— and MacDOWELL, D. M. (1998) (trans.), *Antiphon and Andocides.* Austin, Tex.

GAMEL, MARY-KAY (2002*a*) (ed.), *Performing/Transforming Aristophanes' Thesmophoriazousaï* [= *AJP* Special Issue 123.3]. Baltimore.

—— (2002*b*), 'From *Thesmphoriazousai* to *The Julie Thesmo Show*: adaptation, performance, reception', in Gamel (2002*a*), 465–99.

GARDINER, E. NORMAN (1930), *Athletics of the Ancient World.* Oxford.

GARDINER, S. (1606), *A booke of angling, or fishing: Wherein is shewed, by conference with scriptures, the agreement betweene the fishermen, fishes, fishing of both natures temporall, and spirituall.* London.

GARDNER, JARED (1998), *Master Plots: Race and the Foundation of an American Literature, 1787–1845.* Baltimore and London.

GARNER, R. (1987), *Law and Society in Classical Athens.* London and Sydney.

GARTON, C. (1972), *Personal Aspects of the Roman Theatre.* Toronto.

GARVIE, A. (1969), *Aeschylus' Suppliants: Play and Trilogy.* Cambridge.

GATES, HENRY LOUIS (1987), *Figures in Black: Words, Signs, and the Racial Self.* New York and Oxford.

GELLRICH, MICHELLE (2002), 'Medea hypokrites', *Arethusa* 35, 315–37.

GENTILI, BRUNO (1979), *Theatrical Performances in the Ancient World: Hellenistic and Early Roman Theatre.* Amsterdam and Uithoorn.

—— (1983), 'Oralità e scrittura in Grecia', in M. Vegetti (ed.), *Oralità Scrittura Spettacolo,* 30–52. Turin.

GEORGES, PERICLES (1994), *Barbarian Asia and the Greek Experience.* Baltimore.

GERA, D.L. (1996), 'Porters, Paidagogoi, Jailers, and Attendants: Some Slaves in Plato,' *SCI* 15, 90–101.

GERNET, L. (1917), *Recherches sur la développement de la pensée juridique et morale en Grèce.* Paris.

—— (1981*a*), *The Anthropology of Ancient Greece.* Eng. trans. by J. Hamilton, S. J. Nagy and B. Nagy. Baltimore.

—— (1981*b*), ' "Value" in Greek myth', in R. L. Gordon (ed.), *Myth, Religion and Society: Structuralist Essays*, 111–46. Cambridge.

GEVAERT, F. A. (1875–81), 'La musique dans le drame grec', in his *Histoire et théorie de la musique dans l'antiquité.* Ghent.

—— and VOLLGRAFF, J. C. (1901–3) (eds.), *Les Problèmes musicaux d'Aristote.* Ghent.

GHIRON-BISTAGNE, PAULETTE (1973), 'Un calembour méconnu d'Aristophane', *REG* 86, 285–91.

—— (1976), *Recherches sur les acteurs dans la Grèce antique.* Paris.

GIDE, ANDRÉ (1996), *Journal*, vol. i (1887–1925) ed. Éric Marty. Paris.

GILDERSLEEVE, BASIL (1903), 'The *PERSAI* of Timotheos', *AJP* 24, 222–36.

GILL, C. (1988), 'Personhood and personality: the four *personae* theory in Cicero, *De Officiis* I', *Oxford Studies in Ancient Philosophy* 6, 169–99.

GILMAN, C. P. (1911), *The Man-made World; or, Our Androcentric Culture.* New York.

GILULA, D. (1996), 'A singularly gifted actor', *Quaderni di Storia* 44 (1996), 159–64.

GINOUVÈS, R. (1962), *Balaneutiké: Recherches sur le bain dans l'antiquité grecque.* Paris.

GLEASON, M. (1990), 'The semiotics of gender: physiognomy and self-fashioning in the second century C.E.', in Halperin, Winkler, and Zeitlin (1990), 398–415.

GOEBEL, G. H. (1983), 'Early Greek Rhetorical Theory and Practice: Proof and Arrangement in the Speeches of Antiphon and Euripides', Ph.D. Diss. Univ. of Wisconsin (Madison).

GOFF, BARBARA E. (2005) (ed.), *Classics and Colonialism.* London.

GOFFMAN, ERVING (1959), *The Presentation of Self in Everyday Life.* Garden City, NY.

GOLDEN, MARK (1986), 'Names and naming at Athens: three studies', *ECM* NS 5, 245–69.

GOLDER, HERBERT (1992), 'Visual meaning in Greek drama: Sophocles' *Ajax* and the art of dying', in Fernando Poyatos (ed.), *Advances in Nonverbal Communication: Sociocultural, Clinical, Esthetic, and Literary Perspectives*, 323–60. Amsterdam.

GOLDHILL, SIMON (1984), *Language, Sexuality, Narrative: the Oresteia.* Cambridge.

—— (1986), *Reading Greek Tragedy.* Cambridge.

—— (1987), 'The Great Dionysia and civic ideology', *JHS* 107, 58–76.

—— (1994), 'Representing Democracy: Women at the Great Dionysia,' in Osborne and Hornblower (1994), 347–69.

—— (1998), 'The seductions of the gaze: Socrates and his girlfriends', in Cartledge, Millet, and von Reden (1998), 105–24.

—— (2004), *Aeschylus. The Oresteia,* 2nd edn. Cambridge.

—— and OSBORNE, ROBIN (1994) (eds.), *Art and text in Ancient Greek Culture.* Cambridge.

GOLDING, WILLIAM (1956), *Pincher Martin.* London.

GOLDMAN, MICHAEL (1975), *The Actor's Freedom: Toward a Theory of Drama.* New York.

—— (2000), *On Drama: Boundaries of Genre, Borders of Self.* Ann Arbor, Mich.

GOLDMAN, L. R. (1998), *Child's Play: Myth, Mimesis, and Make-Believe.* Oxford and New York.

GOMME, A. W., and SANDBACH, F. H. (1973), *Menander. A Commentary.* Oxford.

GORDON, R. L. (1981) (ed.), *Myth, Religion and Society: Structuralist Essays.* Cambridge.

GOW, A. S. F., and PAGE, D. L. (1965) (eds.), *The Greek Anthology: Hellenistic Epigrams,* 2 vols. Cambridge.

—— (1968) (eds.), *The Greek Anthology: The Garland of Philip,* vol. i. Cambridge

GRAF, F. (1991), 'Gestures and conventions: the gestures of Roman actors and orators', in Bremmer and Roodenburg (1991), 36–58.

GRANT, M. A. (1924), *The Ancient Rhetorical Theories of the Laughable.* Madison, Wis.

GRATWICK, A. S. (1971), 'Hanno's Punic speech in the *Poenulus* of Plautus', *Hermes* 99, 25–45.

GRAZIOSI, BARBARA (2001), 'Competition in wisdom', in Felix Budelmann and Pantelis Michelakis (eds.), *Homer, Tragedy and Beyond: Essays in Honour of P.E. Easterling,* 57–74. London.

GREEN, J. R. (1990), 'Carcinus and the temple: a lesson in the staging of tragedy', *GRBS* 31, 281–5.

—— (1994), *Theatre in Ancient Greek Society.* London.

—— (1995a), 'Oral tragedies? A question from St. Petersburg', *QUCC* NS 51, 77–86.

GREEN, J. R. (1995*b*), 'Theatrical motifs in non-theatrical contexts on vases of the later fifth and fourth centuries', in Alan Griffiths (ed.), *Stage Directions: Essays in Ancient Drama in Honour of E.W. Handley,* 93–121. London.

—— and ERIC HANDLEY (1995), *Images of the Greek Theatre.* London.

GREEN, PETER (1973), *A Concise History of Ancient Greece to the Close of the Classical Era.* London.

—— (2004), *From Ikaria to the Stars: Classical Mythification, Ancient and Modern.* Austin, Tex.

GREEN, R. L. (1957), *Two Satyr Plays. Euripides' Cyclops and Sophocles' Ichneutai,* trans. with introd. Harmondsworth.

GREENWOOD, L. H. G. (1953), *Aspects of Euripidean Tragedy.* Cambridge.

GREGORY, JUSTINA (1999), *Euripides' Hecuba: Introduction, Text & Commentary.* Atlanta.

GRENFELL, B. P., and HUNT, A. S. (1903) (eds.), 'Rhetorical treatise', *The Oxyrhynchus Papyri* no. 410, iii. 26–31.

—— (1906 eds.), *The Hibeh Papyri.* London.

GRIFFITH, MARK (1995) 'Brilliant dynasts: power and politics in the *Oresteia*'. *CA* 14, 62–129.

—— (1998), 'The King and eye: the rule of the father in Greek tragedy', *PCPS* 44, 20–84.

—— (2002), 'Slaves of Dionysos: satyrs, audience, and the ends of the *Oresteia*', *CA* 195–258.

GROSRICHARD, ALAIN (1998), *The Sultan's Court: European Fantasies of the East,* trans. Liz Heron with an introd. by Mladen Dolar. London and New York. Originally published in 1979 as *Structure du sérial: La Fiction du despotisme Asiatique dans l'Occident classique.* Paris.

GRUEN, E. (2001), 'Jewish perspectives on Greek culture and ethnicity', in Malkin (2001), 347–73.

GUM, COBURN (1969), *The Aristophanic Comedies of Ben Jonson: A Comparative Study of Jonson and Aristophanes.* The Hague and Paris.

GUNDERSON, E. (1998), 'Discovering the body in Roman oratory', in Wyke (1998), 169–89.

GURD, SEAN ALEXANDER (2005), *Iphigeneias at Aulis: Textual Multiplicity, Radical Philology.* Ithaca, NY.

GUTZWILLER, KATHRYN (2000), 'The tragic mask of comedy: metatheatricality in Menander', *CA* 19, 102–37.

HAGEMAJER ALLEN, K. (2003), 'The cultures within', in C. Dougherty & L. Kurke (eds.), *Ancient Greek Culture: Context, Conflict, Collaboration,* 207–36. Cambridge.

HAIGH, A. E. (1889), *The Attic Theatre.* Oxford.

HAIGHT, W., WANG, K., FUNG, H., WILLIAMS, K., and MINTZ, J. (1999), 'Universal, developmental and variable aspects of young children's play: a cross-cultural comparison of pretending at home', *Child Development*, 70, 1477–88.

HALDANE, J. A. (1965), 'A scene in the *Thesmophoriazusae*', *Philologus* 109, 39–46.

HALL, EDITH (1989), *Inventing the Barbarian: Greek Self-Definition through Tragedy*. Oxford.

—— (1990), 'The changing face of Oedipus and the mask of Dionysus', *Cambridge Review* 111, 70–4.

—— (1992), review of Laurence Boswell's production of Euripides' *Hecuba* at the Gate, Notting Hill, *TLS* 4668, 20.

—— (1993), 'Asia unmanned; images of victory in classical Athens', in J. Rich and G. Shipley (eds.), *War and Society in the Greek World*, 107–33. London.

—— (1995), 'The ass with double vision: politicizing an ancient Greek novel', in D. Margolies and M. Ioannou (eds.), *Heart of a Heartless World: Essays in Cultural Resistance in Honour of Margot Heinemann*, 47–59. London.

—— (1996a) (ed.), *Aeschylus' Persians: Edited with Introduction, Translation and Commentary*. Warminster, Wilts.

—— (1996b), 'Is there a polis in Aristotle's *Poetics*?', in M. Silk (1996), 295–309.

—— (1997a), 'Electra's baby in Euripides', *Omnibus* 33, 17–20.

—— (1997b), 'The sociology of Athenian tragedy', in Easterling (1997), 9–126.

—— (1998), 'Literature and performance', in Paul Cartledge (ed.), *The Cambridge Illustrated History of Ancient Greece*, 219–49. Cambridge.

—— (2002a), 'The singing actors of antiquity', in Easterling and Hall (2002), 3–38.

—— (2002b), 'The ancient actor's presence since the Renaissance', in Easterling and Hall (2002), 419–34.

—— (2004), 'Towards a theory of performance reception', *Arion* 12, 51–89.

—— (2006), 'Aeschylus' *Persians* via the Ottoman Empire to Saddam Hussein', in Bridges, Hall, and Rhodes (2006).

—— (forthcoming a), 'Tragedy personified', in J. Elsner, S. Goldhill, H. Foley, and C.S. Kraus (eds.), *Visualising Tragedy*. Oxford.

—— (forthcoming b), 'Greek Tragedy 430–380 BC', in R. Osborne (ed.), *Anatomy of Cultural Revolution*.

—— and MACINTOSH, F. (2005), *Greek Tragedy and the British Theatre 1660–1914*. Oxford.

—— —— and TAPLIN, O. (2000) (eds.), *Medea in Performance 1500–2000*. Oxford.

—— —— and WRIGLEY, A. (2004) (eds.), *Dionysus since 69: Greek Tragedy at the Dawn of the Third Millennium*. Oxford.

HALL, JONATHAN M. (1999) *Hellenicity: Between Ethnicity and Culture*. Chicago and London.

—— (2001), 'Contested ethnicities: perceptions of Macedonia within evolving definitions of Greek identity', in Malkin (2001), 159–86.

HALLAM, E., and STREET, B. V. (2000) (eds.), *Cultural Encounters: Representing Otherness*. London.

HALLIWELL, S. (1990), 'The sounds of the voice in Old Comedy', in E.M. Craik (ed.), *'Owls to Athens': Essays on Classical Subjects Presented to Sir Kenneth Dover*, 69–79. Oxford.

—— (1991), 'The uses of laughter in Greek culture', *CQ* 41, 279–96.

—— (1993), 'The function and aesthetics of the Greek tragic mask', *Drama* 2 [= N. W. Slater and B. Zimmermann (eds.), *Intertextualität in der griechisch-römischen Komödie*], 195–211. Stuttgart.

—— (1997), 'Between public and private: tragedy and Athenian experience of rhetoric', in Pelling (ed.), 121–41.

HALPERIN, D. M. (1990*a*), 'Why is Diotima a woman?', in Halperin, Winkler and Zeitlin (1990), 257–308.

—— (1990*b*), *One Hundred Years of Homosexuality and Other Essays on Greek Love*. New York and London.

—— WINKLER, J. J., and ZEITLIN, F. I. (1990) (eds.), *Before Sexuality: The Construction of the Erotic Experience in the Ancient Greek World*. Princeton.

HAMILTON, R. (1984), 'Sources for the Athenian amphidromia', *GRBS* 25, 243–51.

—— (1992), *Choes and Anthesteria: Athenian Iconography and Ritual*. Ann Arbor.

HANDLEY, ERIC (1965) (ed.), *The Dyskolos of Menander*. London.

HANSEN, H. (1976), 'Aristophanes' *Thesmophoriazusae*: theme, structure, and production', *Philologus* 120, 165–85.

HANSEN, M.H. (1991), *The Athenian Democracy in the Age of Demosthenes*. Oxford.

HANSEN, O. (1984), 'On the date and place of the first performance of Timotheus' *Persae*', *Philologus* 128, 135–8.

HANSON, A. E. (1990), 'The medical writers' woman', in Halperin, Winkler and Zeitlin (1990), 309–38.

—— (1991), 'Continuity and change: three case studies in Hippocratic gynecological therapy and theory', in Sarah B. Pomeroy (ed.), *Women's History and Ancient History*, 73–110. Chapel Hill, NC, and London.

—— (1994), 'A division of labor: roles for men in Greek and Roman births', *Thamyris* 1, 157–202.

HANSON, A., and ARMSTRONG, D. (1986), 'The virgin's voice and neck: Aeschylus, *Agamemnon* 245 and other texts', *BICS* 33, 97–100.

HARDER, A. (1985) (ed.), *Euripides' Kresphontes and Archelaos* [= *Mnemosyne* suppl. 87]. Leiden.

HARDIE, ALEX (2004), 'Muses and mysteries', in Murray and Wilson (2004), 11–37.

HARDING, P. (1994), 'Comedy and rhetoric', in Worthington (1994), 196–221.

HARDWICK, LORNA (2005), 'The comic in the tragic: parody and critique in modern productions of Euripides' *Hecuba*', in Mieke Kolk (ed.), *The Performance of the Comic in Arabic Theater*, 306–15. Amsterdam.

HARRIOTT, ROSEMARY (1986), *Aristophanes: Poet and Dramatist*. London and Sydney.

HARRIS, EDWARD M. (2004), 'Notes on a lead letter from the Athenian agora', *HSCP* 102, 157–70.

HARRIS, EDWARD M., and RUBINSTEIN, LENE (2004) (eds.), *The Law and the Courts in Ancient Greece*. London.

HARRIS, H. A. (1972), *Sport in Greece and Rome*. London.

HARRISON, A. R. W. (1968), *The Law of Athens*, vol. i. Oxford.

HARRISON, THOMAS (2000), *The Emptiness of Asia: Aeschylus' Persians and the History of the Fifth Century*. London.

—— (2002) (ed.), *Greeks and Barbarians*. Edinburgh.

HARRISON, TONY (1991), *The Trackers of Oxyrhynchus*, 2nd edn. London.

HARTOG, F. (1988), *The Mirror of Herodotus: The Representation of the Other in the Writing of History*. Berkeley, C. Eng. trans. of original French version (1980).

HARVEY, DAVID (2000), 'Phrynichos and his Muses', in Harvey and Wilkins (2000), 91–134.

—— and WILKINS, JOHN (2000) (eds.), *The Rivals of Aristophanes: Studies in Athenian Old Comedy*. London and Swansea.

HAUBOLD, JOHANNES (forthcoming *a*), 'Xerxes' Homer', in Bridges, Hall, and Rhodes.

—— (forthcoming *b*), 'Beyond the bitter river: Xerxes, the Greeks, and the bridging of the Hellespont'.

HAUSMAN, CARL R. (1989), *Metaphor and Art*. Cambridge.

HAUVETTE, A. (1886), 'Un épisode de la seconde guerre médique', *RPh* 10, 132–42.

HAVELOCK, CHRISTINE MITCHELL (1995), *The Aphrodite of Knidos and her Successors: A Historical Review of the Female Nude in Greek Art*. Ann Arbor, Mich.

HAVELOCK, ERIC A. (1982), *The Literate Revolution in Greece and its Cultural Consequences*. Princeton.

HEANEY, SEAMUS (1975), *North*. London.

HEAP, A. (1998), 'Understanding the young men in Menander', in Foxhall and Salmon (1998), 115–29.

—— (2002–3), 'The baby as hero: the role of the infant in Menander', *BICS* 46, 77–123.

HEDREEN, G. M. (1992), *Silens in Attic Black-figure Vase-Painting*. Ann Arbor.

HELMHOLTZ, HERMANN L. F. (1885), *On the Sensations of Tone as a Physiological Basis for the Theory of Music*, 2nd Eng. edn. London.

HELTZEL, V. B. (1962) (ed.) *Henry Peacha: The Complete Gentleman, The Truth of Our Times and The Art of Living in London*. Ithaca, NY.

HENDERSON, J. (1990), 'The *dēmos* and comic competition', in Winkler and Zeitlin (1990), 271–313.

—— (1991 [1975]), *The Maculate Muse: Obscene Language in Attic Comedy*, 2nd edn. New York and Oxford.

HENDERSON, L. D. J. (1976), 'Sophocles' *Trachiniae* 878–92 and a principle of Paul Maas', *Maia* 28, 19–24.

HENRICHS, A. (1994–5), 'Why should I dance? Choral self-referentiality in tragedy', *Arion* 3, 56–111.

HERFORD, C. H., Simpson, Percy, and Simpson, Evelyn (1941) (eds.), *Ben Jonson*, vol. vii. Oxford.

HERINGTON, JOHN (1985), *Poetry into Drama: Early Tragedy and the Greek Poetic Tradition*. Berkeley, Los Angeles, and London.

HERRICK, B. M. T. (1955), *Tragicomedy*. Urbana, Ill.

HERZFELD, M. (1985), *The Poetics of Manhood: Contest and Identity in a Cretan Mountain Village*. Princeton.

HESK, JONATHAN (1999), 'The rhetoric of anti-rhetoric in Athenian oratory', in Goldhill and Osborne (1999), 201–30.

—— (2000), *Deception and Democracy in Classical Athens*. Cambridge.

—— (2003), *Sophocles: Ajax* [Duckworth companions to Greek and Roman tragedy]. London.

HESS, KONRAD (1961), *Der Agon zwischen Homer und Hesiod, seine Entstehung und kulturgeschichtliche Stellung*. Basel.

HIGGINS, R. A. (1954), *Catalogue of the Terracottas* [British Museum Publications]. London.

HILGARD, A. (1991) (ed.), *Scholia in Dionysii Thracis Artem Grammaticum* (= *Grammatici Graeci* Part 1 vol. iii). Leipzig.

HILLMAN, J. (1983), *Healing Fiction*. Tarrytown, NY.

HOFFMANN, HERBERT (1977), 'Sexual and asexual pursuit: a structuralist approach to Greek vase-painting', *Royal Anthropolological Institute of Great Britain and Ireland Occasional Paper* 34. London.

HOMAN, SIDNEY (1981), *When the Theater Turns to Itself: The Aesthetic Metaphor in Shakespeare*. Lewisburg, London, and Toronto.

HORDERN, JAMES (2002) (ed.), *The Fragments of Timotheus of Miletus*. Oxford.

HORN, H. (1972), *Mysteriensymbolik auf dem Kölner Dionysosmosaik*. Bonn.

HORNBY, RICHARD (1986), *Drama, Metadrama, and Perception*. London and Toronto.

HOSE, MARTIN (1994), 'Response' to Hall (1993), in H. A. Khan (ed.), *The Birth of the European Identity: The Europe–Asia Contrast in Greek Thought, 490–332 B.C.* Nottingham Classical Literature Studies, v. 2.

—— (1996), 'Fiktionalität und Läge: Über einen Unterschied zwischen römischer und griechischer Terminologie', *Poetica* 29, 257–74.

HOWE, T. P. (1959), 'The style of Aeschylus as satyr-playwright', *G&R* 6, 150–65.

HUBBARD, T. K. (1991), *The Mask of Comedy: Aristophanes and the Intertextual Parabasis*. Ithaca, NY.

HUDDILSTON, JOHN H. (1898), *The Attitude of the Greek Tragedians towards Art*. London.

HUEFFNER, F. (1894), *De Plauti Comoediarum Exemplis Atticis*. Göttingen.

HUGONIOT, C., HURLET, F., and MILANEZI, S. (2004) (eds.), *Le Statut de le'actuer dans l'Antiquité grecque et romaine*. Tours.

HUIZINGA, JOHAN (1938), *Homo Ludens*. Haarlem.

HULME, P. (1985), 'Polytropic man: tropes of sexuality and mobility in early colonial discourse', in Barker (1985), ii. 17–32.

HULTZSCH, E. (1904), 'Zum papyrus 413 aus Oxyrhynhus', *Hermes* 39, 307–11.

HUMPHREYS, S. C. (1985*a*), *The Discourse of Law* (= *History and Anthropology* 1.2). London.

—— (1985*b*), 'Law as discourse', in Humphreys (1985*a*), 241–64.

—— (1985*c*), 'Social relations on stage: witnesses in classical Athens', in Humphreys (1985*a*), 313–69.

HUNNINGHER, B. (1956), *Acoustics and Acting in the Theatre of Dionysus Eleuthereus* (= *Mededelinger der koninklijke Nederlandse Akademie van Wetenschappen, afd. Letterkunde* 19.9). Amsterdam.

HUNT, E. L. (1961), 'Plato and Aristotle on rhetoric and rhetoricians', in R. F. Howes (ed.), *Historical Studies on Rhetoric and Rhetoricians*, 19–70. Ithaca, NY.

HUNT, PETER (2001), 'The slaves and the generals of Arginusae', *AJP* 122, 359–80.

—— (1998), *Slaves, Warfare, and Ideology in the Greek Historians*. Cambridge.

HUNTER, RICHARD (1979), 'The comic chorus in the fourth century' *ZPE* 36, 23–38.

—— (1983) (ed.), *Eubulus: The Fragments*. Cambridge.

HUNTER, VIRGINIA (1994), *Policing Athens: Social Control in the Attic Lawsuits, 420–320 B.C.* Princeton.

—— —— (1997), 'The prison of Athens: a comparative perspective', *The Phoenix* 51, 296–326.

HUYS, MARC (1995), *The Tale of the Hero who was Exposed at Birth in Euripidean Tragedy.* Leuven.

IGNATIEFF, MICHAEL (1998), *The Warrior's Honor: Ethnic War and the Modern Conscience.* New York.

IMMERWAHR, HENRY R. (1964), 'Book rolls on Attic vases', in C. Henderson (ed.), *Classical, Mediaeval and Renaissance Studies in Honour of Berthold Louis Ullman*, i. 17–48.

—— (1973), 'More book rolls on Attic vases', *Antike Kunst* 16, 143–7.

IOANNIDI, H. (1973), 'A propos de l'article ci-dessus "un calembour méconnu d'Aristophane"' [by P. Ghiron-Bistagne] *REG* 86, 292–3.

JACOB, O. (1928), *Les Esclaves publics à Athènes.* Paris.

JAKOBSON, ROMAN (1987), 'The statue in Pushkin's poetic mythology', Eng. trans. by John Burbank (of an essay originally published in Czech in 1937), in K. Pomorska and S. Rudy (eds.), *Jakobson's Language and Literature*, 318–67. Cambridge, Mass. and London.

JAMESON, F. (1971), *Marxism and Form: Twentieth-Century Dialectical Theories of Literature.* Princeton.

—— (1981), *The Political Unconscious: Narrative as a Socially Symbolic* Act. London.

—— (1990), *Signatures of the Visible.* New York and London.

JANKO, RICHARD (1981), 'The structure of the Homeric hymns: a study in genre', *Hermes* 109, 9–24.

JANOV, ARTHUR (1983), *Imprints: The Lifelong Effects of the Birth Experience.* New York.

JANSSEN, T. H. (1984) (ed.), *Timotheus' Persae.* Amsterdam. Eng. trans. of original Dutch edn. (1976).

JENKYNS, RICHARD (1993), review of Sprawson (1992), in *The New Yorker*, 5 April 104–7.

JENS, W. (1971) (ed.), *Die Bauformen der griechischen Tragödie.* Munich.

JOHANSEN, H. FRIIS, and WHITTLE, EDWARD W. (1980) (eds.), *Aeschylus, The Suppliants.* Copenhagen.

JOHNSTON, SARAH ILES (1995), 'Defining the dreadful: remarks on the Greek child-killing demon', in M. Meyer amd P. Mirecki (eds.), *Ancient Magic and Ritual Power*, 361–87. Leiden.

—— (1997), 'Corinthian Medea and the cult of Hera Akraia', in James J. Clauss and Sarah Iles Johnston (eds.), *Medea*, 44–70. Princeton.

Jones, C. P. (1991), 'Dinner Theater', in William Slater (ed.), *Dining in a Classical Context*, 185–97. Ann Arbor, Mich.

Jones, Gavin (1999), *Strange Talk: The Politics of Dialect Literature in Gilded Age America*. Berkeley and London.

Jones, Gwyn, and Jones, Thomas (1949), *The Mabinogion*. London.

Jones, Nicholas F. (2004), *Rural Athens under the Democracy*. Philadelphia.

Jones, W. H. S. (1909), *Malaria and Greek History*. Manchester.

Joshel, Sandra R., and Murnaghan, Sheila (1998) (eds.), *Women and Slaves in Greco-Roman Culture*. London.

Jouan, F. (1981), 'Réflexions sur le rôle du protagoniste tragique', *Théâtre et Spectacles dans l'Antiquité*, 63–80. (Actes du colloque de Strasbourg). Amsterdam.

Jouanna, P. (1981), 'Les causes de la défaite des barbares chez Eschyle, Hérodote, et Hippocrate', *Ktema* 6, 3–15.

Kabbani, Rana (1986), *Europe's Myths of Orient: Devise and Rule*. London.

Kahil, L. (1988), 'Harpyiai', *LIMC* iv.1, 445–50.

—— (1994), 'Phineus I', *LIMC* vii.1, 387–91.

Kampen, Natalie Boymel (1996) (ed.), *Sexuality in Ancient Art*. Cambridge.

Kashima, Yoshihisa, Foddy, Margaret, and Platow, Michael J. (2002) (eds.), *Self and Identity: Personal, Social, and Symbolic*. Mahwah, NJ, and London.

Kassel, R. (1983), 'Dialoge mit Statuen', *ZPE* 51, 1–12.

Katsouris, Andreas G. (1975), *Tragic Patterns in Menander*. Athens.

Keil, Bruno (1913), 'Zu den Persern des Timotheos', *Hermes* 48, 88–140.

Keith, A. M. (2000), *Engendering Rome: Women in Latin Epic*. Cambridge.

Kennedy, G. (1963), *The Art of Persuasion in Greece*. Princeton.

Kenyon, F. G. (1919), 'Greek papyri and their contribution to classical literature', *JHS* 39, 1–15.

Keramopoullos, A. D. (1923), *Ho Apotumpanismos*. Athens.

Kern, Otto (1922) (ed.), *Orphicorum Fragmenta*. Berlin.

Keuls, Eva C. (1975), 'Skiagraphia once again', *AJA* 79, 1–16, reproduced in her *Painter and Poet in Ancient Greece* (Stuttgart and Leipzig, 1997), 107–44.

—— (1978), *Plato and Greek Painting*. Leiden.

—— (1985), *The Reign of the Phallus: Sexual Politics in Ancient Athens*. Berkeley, Los Angeles and London.

Kierkegaard, Søren (1987). *Either/Or*, Part I, ed. and trans. Howard V. Hong and Edna H. Hong [= *Kierkegaard's Writings*, iii] (Princeton); originally published as *Enten/Eller: Et Livs-Fragment udgivet af Victor Eremita* (Copenhagen, 1843).

KING, HELEN (1983), 'Bound to bleed: Artemis and Greek Women', in A. Cameron and A. Kuhrt (eds.), *Images of Women in Antiquity*, 109–27. London and Sydney.

KING, HELEN (1998), *Hippocrates' Woman: Reading the Female Body in Ancient Greece*. London, and New York.

KINKEL, G. (1872), *Euripides und die bildende Kunst*. Berlin.

KIRCHNER, J. (1901–3), *Prosopographia Attica*. Berlin.

KLEIN, CHRISTINA (2003), *Cold War Orientalism: Asia in the Middlebrow Imagination, 1945–1961*. Berkeley, Los Angeles, and London.

KLIMEK-WINTER, RAINER (1993) (ed.), *Andromedatragödien. Sophokles, Euripides, Livius Andronikos, Ennius, Accius; Text, Einleitung und Kommentar*. Stuttgart.

KNOX, PETER E. (1995) (ed.), *Ovid, Heroides: Select Epistles*. Cambridge.

KOCYBALA, A. X. (1978), 'Greek Colonization on the North Shore of the Black Sea in the Archaic Period'. Diss. Pensylvania.

KOEHNEN, L. (1969), 'Eine Hypothesis zur Auge des Euripides und Tegeatische Plynterien', *ZPE* 4, 7–18.

KOGAN, STEPHEN (1986), *The Hieroglyphic King: Wisdom and Idolatry in the Seventeenth-Century Masque*. London and Toronto.

KOLLER, HERMANN (1963), *Musik und Dichtung im alten Griechenland*. Bern and Munich.

KOLODNY, A. (1973), 'The land as woman: literary convention and latent psychological content', *Women's Studies* 1, 167–82.

KONSTAN, DAVID (1990), 'The anthropology of Euripides *Kyklōps*', in Winkler and Zeitlin (1990), 207–27.

—— (1993), 'Premarital sex, illegitimacy, and male anxiety in Menander and Athens', in Alan Boegehold and Adele Scafuro (eds.), *Athenian Identity and Civic Ideology* (Baltimore 1993), pp. 217–35; adapted version in David Konstan, *Greek Comedy and Ideology* (New York, and Oxford, 1995), 141–52.

KÖRTE, A. (1935), 'Euripides' Skyrier', *Hermes* 69, 1–12.

KOSSATZ-DEISSMANN, A. (1997), 'Tragoidia', *LIMC* 8.1, 48–50.

KOVACS, D. (1994), *Euripidea. Mnem.* Suppl. 132. Leiden, New York and Cologne.

KÖVES-ZULAUF, THOMAS (1990), *Römische Geburtsriten*. Munich [= *Zetemata* 87].

KRANZ, W. (1933), *Stasimon: Untersuchung zu Form und Gehalt der griechischen Tragödie*. Berlin.

KRAUS, C. S. (1998), 'Dangerous supplements: etymology and genealogy in Euripides' *Heracles*', *PCPS* 44, 137–57.

KRUMBACHER, A. (1924), 'The Voice Training of Orators in Antiquity up to the Time of Quintilian' (Eng. trans.). Diss. Cornell.

KRUMEICH, RALF, PECHSTEIN, N., and SEIDENSTICKER, B. (1999) (eds.), *Das griechische Satyrspiel*. Darmstadt.

KUHNS, RICHARD (1991), *Tragedy: Contradiction and Repression*. Chicago and London.

KUHRT, AMÉLIE (2002), ' "Greeks" and "Greece" in Mesopotamian and Persian Perspectives', [= *The Twenty-First J. L. Myres Memorial Lecture*]. Oxford.

KUNSEMÜLLER, O. (1935), *De Herkunft der platonischen Kardinaltugenden*. Diss. Erlangen, repr. New York (1979).

KURKE, LESLIE (1991), *The Traffic in Praise: Pindar and the Poetics of Social Economy*. Ithaca, NY.

KURZON, DENNIS (1986), *It is Hereby Performed: Explorations in Legal Speech Acts*. Amsterdam.

LADA-RICHARDS, ISMENE (2002), 'The subjectivity of Greek performance', in Easterling and Hall (2002), 395–418.

—— (2003), ' "A worthless feminine thing"? Lucian and the "optic intoxication" of pantomime dancing', *Helios* 30, 21–75.

LÄMMLI, F. (1938), *Das attische Prozessverfahren in seiner Wirkung auf die Gerichtsrede*. Paderborn.

LANATA, G. (1963), *Poetica Preplatonica*. Florence.

LANDY, ROBERT J. (1993), *Persona and Performance: The Meaning of Role in Drama, Therapy, and Everyday Life*. New York and London.

LANG, MABEL, and ELIOT, C. W. J. (1976), *The Athenian Agora: A Guide to the Excavation and the Museum*, 3rd edn. rev. H. A. Thompson. Athens.

LANNI, ADRIAAN (1997), 'Spectator sport or serious politics? *Hoi periestēkotes* and the Athenian lawcourts', *JHS* 117, 183–9.

—— (2004), 'Arguing from 'precedent': modern perspectives on Athenian practice', in Harris and Rubinstein (2004), 159–71.

LAPE, SUSAN (2004), *Reproducing Athens: Menander's Comedy, Democratic Culture, and the Hellenistic City*. Princeton and Oxford.

LARSON, JENNIFER (1995), *Greek Heroine Cults*. Madison, Wis.

LASSERE, F. (1973), 'Le drame satyrique', *RFIC* 101, 273–301.

LAVELLE, B. M. (1992), 'Herodotos, Skythian archers, and the *doryphoroi* of the Peisistratids', *Klio* 74, 78–97.

LAVENCY, M. (1964), *Aspects de la logographie judiciaire attique*. Louvain.

LE GUEN, B. (2001), *Les Associations de technites dionysiaques à l'époque héllenistique*, 2 vols. Nancy.

LEFKOWITZ, MARY (1981), *The Lives of the Greek Poets*. London.

LEFKOWITZ, MARY R. and FANT, MAUREEN B. (1992), *Women's Life in Greece and Rome: A Source-book in Translation*, 2nd edn. London.

LEHMANN, W. P. (1962), *Historical Linguistics. An Introduction*. New York.

LEITAO, DAVID D. (1998), 'Male pregnancy rituals in the Greco-Roman world' *Humanities Magazine* 16, 117–37.

LENDERING, JONA (2004), *Alexander de Grote. De Ondergang van het Perzische Rijk*. Amsterdam.

LEONARD, MIRIAM (2005), *Athens in Paris: Ancient Greece and the Political in Postwar French Thought*. Oxford.

LESSING, GOTTHOLD EPHRAIM (1836 [1766]), *Laocoon; or, The Limits of Poetry and Painting*, Eng. trans. by W. Ross. London.

L'ESTRANGE, ROGER (1692), *Fables, of Æsop and other eminent mythologists: with morals and reflexions*. London.

LEURINI, L. (1992) (ed.), *Ionis Chii: Testimonia et Fragmenta*. Amsterdam.

LEUTSCH, E. L., and SCHNEIDEWIN, F. G. (1839) (eds.), *Paroemiographi Graeci*. Göttingen.

LEVINE, MOLLY (1992), 'Multiculturalism and the Classics', *Arethusa* 25, 215–20.

LÉVY, E. (1981), 'Les origines du mirage scythe', *Ktema* 6, 57–68.

LEWIS, D. M. (1968), 'Dedications of phialai at Athens', *Hesperia* 37, 368–80.

LEWIS, SIAN (1998–9) 'Slaves as viewers and users of Athenian pottery,' *Hephaistos* 16–17, 71–90.

LiDONNICI, LYNN R. (1995), *The Epidaurian Miracle Inscriptions*. Atlanta.

LIGHTFOOT, JANE (2002), 'Nothing to do with the *technitai* of Dionysus?', in Easterling and Hall (2002), 209–37.

LINDBERGER, ÖRJAN (1956), *The Transformations of Amphitryon*. Stockholm.

LINDERS, T. (1972), *Studies in the Treasure Records of Artemis Brauronia found in Athens*. Stockholm.

LINDSAY, A. D. (1976) (trans.), *Plato: The Republic*. London.

LINKE, K. (1977) (ed.), *Die Fragmente des Grammatikers Dionysios Thrax*, in *Sammlung griechischer und lateinischer Grammatiker*, vol. iii. Berlin and New York.

LIPPELT, O. (1910), 'Die griechischen Leichtbewaffneten bis auf Alexander den Grossen', Diss. Jena.

LISSARRAGUE, FRANÇOIS (1987), *Un flot d'images: une esthétique du banquet grec*. Paris.

—— (1990*a*), 'The sexual life of satyrs', Halperin, Winkler, and Zeitlin (1990), 53–81.

—— (1990*b*) 'Why satyrs are good to represent', in J. J. Winkler and F. I. Zeitlin (eds.), *Nothing to do with Dionysos?*, 228–3. Princeton.

—— (1990*c*), *L'Autre Guerrier: archers, peltastes, cavaliers dans l'imagerie attique*. Paris and Rome.

—— (2002), 'L'immagine dello straniero ad Atene', in S. Settis (ed.), *I Greci*, vol. ii [= *Definizione*], 938–58. Translated into English as 'The Athenian image of the foreigner', in T. Harrison (2002) 101–24.

—— (2003), 'Satiri tra le donne', in Paul Veyne, François Lissarrague, and Françoise Frontisi-Ducroux, *I misteri del gineceo*, 171–90. Editori Laterza, Rome and Bari. [Translation by Barbara Gregori of original French edition, *Les Mystères du gynécée*, Éditions Gallimard (1998).]

LLOYD, G. E. R. (1966), *Polarity and Analogy: Two Types of Argumentation in Early Greek Thought*. Cambridge.

LLOYD-JONES, HUGH (1979), *Aeschylus: Oresteia. Agamemnon*, ed. with trans. and notes. London and Dallas, Tex.

—— (1981), 'Notes on P. Turner 4 (Aristophanes, *Poiesis*)', *ZPE* 42, 23–5.

—— (1983) (ed.) 'Appendix: fragments published since 1930', in Herbert Weir Smyth (trans.), *Aeschylus* vol. ii. Cambridge, Mass., and London.

LOBEL, E. (1941), 'No. 2161, Aeschylus, *Diktuoulkoi*', *The Oxyrhynchus Papyri* 18, 9–13.

LONG, TIMOTHY (1986), *Barbarians in Greek Comedy*. Carbondale and Edwardsville, Ill.

LONSDALE, STEVEN H. (1993), *Dance and Ritual Play in Greek Religion*. Baltimore and London.

LORAUX, NICOLE (1981), *Les Enfants d'Athéna*. Paris.

—— (1995), *The Experiences of Tiresias: The Feminine and the Greek Man*, trans. Paula Wissing. Princeton.

LOVEJOY, O., and BOAS, G. (1935), *Primitivism and Related Ideas in Antiquity*. Baltimore.

LOWE, LISA (1991), *Critical Terrains: French and British Orientalisms*. Ithaca, NY.

LUCAS, D. W. (1950), *The Greek Tragic Poets*. London.

LUMPKIN, K. (1933), *The Family. A Study of Member Roles*. Chapel Hill, NC.

LUPPE, W. (1966), 'Die Hypothese zu Kratinos' *Dionysalexandros*', *Philologus* 110, 169–93.

—— (1972), 'Die Zahl der Konkurrenten an den komischen Agonen zur Zeit. des Peloponnesischen Krieges', *Philologus* 116, 53–75.

LYONS, DEBORAH (1997), *Gender and Immortality: Heroines in Ancient Greek Myth and Cult*. Princeton.

MAAS, P. (1929), *Griechische Metrik*, = A. Gercke and E. Norden (eds.), *Einleitung in die Altertumswissenschaft* vol. 1.7 (Leipzig and Berlin). Translated into English as *Greek Metre* by Hugh Lloyd-Jones (Oxford, 1962).

MACCARY, W. THOMAS (1973), 'The comic tradition and comic structure in Diphilos' *Kleroumenoi*', *Hermes* 101, 194–208.

MacDonald, Sharon (1987), 'Drawing the Lines—Gender, Peace and War: an introduction', in S. Macdonald, Pat Holden and Shirley Ardener (eds.), *Images of Women in Peace and War: Cross-cultural and Historical Perspectives*, 1–26. Basingstoke.

MacDowell, D. M. (1971) (ed.), *Aristophanes' Wasps*. Oxford.

—— (1978), *The Law in Classical Athens*. London.

—— (1990) (ed.), *Demosthenes, Against Meidias*. Oxford.

Macfie, A. L. (2000) (ed.), *Orientalism: A Reader*. Edinburgh.

Macintosh, Fiona (1992), 'When Gael joins Greek', *Books Ireland*, October, 189–91.

—— (2000), 'Introduction: the performer in performance', in Hall, Macintosh, and Taplin (2000), 1–31.

Mack, Rainer (2002), 'Facing down Medusa (an aetiology of the gaze)', *Art History* 25, 571–604.

MacKenzie, John (1995), *Orientalism: History, Theory and the Arts*. Manchester.

MacLeod, C. W. (1982), 'Thucydides and Tragedy', *Classicum* 8, 1–10.

——, 'Euripides' rags', in *Collected Essays*, 233–4. Oxford.

Macran, Henry (1912) (ed.), *The Harmonics of Aristoxenus*. Oxford.

Maidment, K. (1941), *Minor Attic Orators*. Cambridge, Mass.

Malkin, Irad (2001) (ed.), *Ancient Perceptions of Greek Ethnicity*. Cambridge, Mass., and London.

Manakidou, Flora (1993), *Beschreibung von Kunstwerken in der hellenistischen Dichtung: ein Beitrag zur hellenistischen Poetik*. Stuttgart.

Manchester, William (1979), *Goodbye, Darkness: A Memoir of the Pacific*. New York.

Manuel, F. E., and Manuel, F. P. (1972), 'Sketch for a natural history of paradise', *Daedalus* (Winter), 84–90.

Marenghi, G. (1959), 'Tra cruces ed emendationes', *Maia* 11, 320–5.

Maresca, Thomas (1993), 'Personification versus allegory', in Kevin L. Cope (ed.), *Enlightening Allegory*, 21–39. New York.

Marquart, R. (1912), 'Die Datierung des euripideischen Kylops', Diss. Halle.

Marranca, Bonnie, and Dasgupta, Gautam (1999) (eds.), *Conversations on Art and Performance*. Baltimore.

Marshall, C. W. (1994), 'The rule of three actors in practice', *Text & Presentation* 15, 53–61.

—— (1999), 'Some fifth-century masking conventions', *G&R* 46, 188–202.

—— (2001), 'The costume of Hecuba's attendants', *Acta Classica* 54, 127–36.

—— (2004), '*Alcestis* and the ancient rehearsal process (P.Oxy. 4546)', *Arion* 11.3, 27–45.

MARTIN, RICHARD (1989), *The Language of Heroes: Speech and Performance in the Iliad*. Ithaca, NY and London.

MARX, F. (1933), 'Musik aus der griechischen Tragödie', *Rhein. Mus.* 82, 230–46.

MARX, KARL, and ENGELS, FRIEDRICH (1956–68), *Werke*, 40 vols. Berlin.

MASQUERAY, PAUL (1895), *Théorie des formes lyriques de la tragédie grecque*. Paris.

MASTROMARCO, G. (1975), 'Guerra peloponnesiaca e agoni comici in Atene', *Belfagor* 30, 469–73.

MASTRONARDE, DONALD (1990), 'Actors on high: the skene roof, the crane and the gods in Attic drama', *CA* 9, 247–94.

MATTHIESSEN, KJELD (1964), *Elektra, Taurische Iphigenie und Helena and Untersuchungen zur Chronologie und zur dramatischen Form im Spätwerk des Euripides* [= *Hypomnemata* 4]. Göttingen.

MATSEN, P. P. (1990), 'Alcidamas, *Concerning those who write written speeches, or Concerning Sophists*', in P. P. Matsen, P. Rollinson and M. Sousa (eds.), *Readings From Classical Rhetoric*, 38–42. New York.

MAURIZIO, LISA (2001), 'Performance, hysteria, and democratic identities in the Anthesteria', *Helios* 28, 29–41.

MAUSS, MARCEL (1985), 'A category of the human mind: The notion of person; the notion of self', in M. Carrithers, S. Collins and S. Lukes (eds.), *The Category of the Person*, 1–25. New York & Cambridge. Eng. trans. of an essay first published in 1938 and available as 'Une catégorie de l'esprit humain: La notion de personne, celle de "Moi" ', Mauss, *Sociologie et anthropologie* (Paris, 1950).

MAXWELL-STUART, P. G. (1975), 'Three words of abusive slang in Aeschines', *AJP* 96, 7–12.

MCARDLE, PAUL (2001), 'Children's play', *Child: Care, Health and Development* 27.6, 509–14.

MCCARTHY, KATHLEEN (2000), *Slaves, Masters & The Art of Authority in Plautine Comedy*. Princeton.

MCGLEW, JAMES F. (2001), 'Identity and ideology: the farmer chorus of Aristophanes' *Peace*', *Syllecta Classica* 12, 74–97.

—— (2002), *Citizens on Stage: Comedy and Political Culture in the Athenian Democracy*. Ann Arbor, Mich.

MCLEISH, K. (1980), *The Theatre of Aristophanes*. London.

MEAD, G. H. (1913), 'The social self', *Journal of Philosophy, Psychology and Scientific Methods* 10, 374–80.

MEHL, E. (1931), 'Schwimmen', *RE* suppl. 5, 847–64. Stuttgart.

MEIJERING, R. (1987), *Literary and Rhetorical Theories in Greek Scholia*. Groningen.

MEILLET, A. (1962), *Introduction a l'étude comparative des langues indo-européennes*, 8th edn. Paris.

MERIANI, ANGELO (2003), *Sulla Musica Greca Antica: Studi e Ricerche*. Salerno.

MERRIAM, ALAN (1964), *The Anthropology of Music*. Chicago.

METLITZKI, DOROTHEE (1977), *The Matter of Araby in Medieval England*. New Haven and London.

MEYER, E. (1884–1902), *Geschichte des Alterthums*. Stuttgart and Berlin.

MICHAELIDES, SOLON (1978), *The Music of Ancient Greece: An Encyclopaedia*. London.

MICHELAKIS, PANTELIS (2002*a*), *Achilles in Greek Tragedy*. Cambridge.

—— (2002*b*), 'Mise en scène de *La Paix* d'Aristophane', in Rochefort-Guillouet (2002), 115–17.

MILLER, HAROLD W. (1946), 'Some tragic influences in the *Thesmophoriazusae* of Aristophanes', *TAPA* 77 (1946), 171–82.

MILLER, MARGARET (1988), 'Midas as the Great King in Attic fifth-century vase painting', *Antike Kunst* 31, 79–88.

—— (1997), *Athenians and Persians in the Fifth Century BC: A Study in Cultural Receptivity*. Cambridge.

—— (2000), 'The myth of Bousiris: ethnicity and art,' in Cohen (2000), 413–42.

MILLER, P., and GARVEY, C. (1984), 'Mother-baby role play: its origins in social support', in I. Bretherton (ed.), *Symbolic Play: The Development of Social Understanding*, 101–30. New York.

MINNS, E. H. (1913), *Scythians and Greeks*. Cambridge.

MISSIOU, A. (1992), *The Subversive Oratory of Andokides*. Cambridge.

MONRO, D. B. (1894), *The Modes of Ancient Greek Music*. Oxford.

MOORE, TIMOTHY J. (1998), *The Theater of Plautus: Playing to the Audience*. Austin, Tex.

MOORE-GILBERT, B. J. (1986), *Kipling and Orientalism*. London.

MORAW, SUSANNE (2002), *Die Geburt des Theaters in der griechischen Antike*. Mainz.

MORENO, J. L. (1946), *Psychodrama*, vol. i. Beacon, NY.

MORFORD, M. P. O. (1966), '*Ethopoiia* and character-assassination in the *Conon* of Demosthenes', *Mnemosyne* 19, 241–8.

MORIZOT, YVETTE (2004), 'Offrandes à Artémis pour une naissance. Autour du relief d'Achinos', in Dasen (2004), 159–70.

MOSSMAN, JUDITH (1991), 'Plutarch's use of statues', in M. A. Flower and M. Toher (eds.), *Georgica: Studies in Honour of George Cawkwell* (=*BICS* suppl. 58), 98–119. London.

—— (1995), *Wild Justice: a Study in Euripides' Hecuba*. Oxford.

Most, G. W. (2000), 'Generating genres: the idea of the tragic', in Mary Depew and Dirk Obbink (eds.), *Matrices of Genre: Authors, Canons, Society*, 15–35. Cambridge, Mass., and London.

Moulton, Carroll (1981), *Aristophanic Poetry* (= *Hypomnemata* 68). Göttingen.

Moutsopoulos, E. (1962), 'Euripide et la philosophie de la musique', *REG* 75, 396–452.

Moyer, Ian S. (2002), 'Herodotus and an Egyptian mirage: the geneaologies of the Athenian priests', *JHS* 122, 70–90.

Muecke, Frances (1982), 'A portrait of the artist as a young woman', *CQ* 32, 41–55.

Müller, Carl Werner, Sier, Kurt, and Werner, Jürgen (1992) (eds.), *Zum Umgang mid fremden Sprachen in der griechish-römischen Antike* [= *Palingenesia* 36]. Stuttgart.

Müller, Dietram (1974), *Handwerk und Sprache: Die sprachlichen Bilder aus dem Bereich des Handwerks in der griechischen Literatur bis 400 v. Chr.* Meisenheim am Glan.

Mulvey, Laura (1975), 'Visual pleasure and narrative cinema', *Screen* 16.3, 6–18.

—— (1989), *Visual and Other Pleasures*. Basingstoke and London.

Murphy, C. T. (1935), summary of 'Quae Ratio inter fabulas satyricas et comoediam antiquam intercedat', Diss. Harvard, in *HSCP* 46, 206–9.

—— (1938), 'Aristophanes and the art of rhetoric', *HSCP* 49, 69–114.

Murray, Gilbert (1936), *Greek Poetry and Life: Essays Presented to Gilbert Murray on his Seventieth Birthday*. Oxford.

Murray, Penelope (1996) (ed.), *Plato on Poetry*. Cambridge.

Murray, Penelope, and Wilson, Peter (2004) (eds.), *Music and the Muses: The Culture of 'Mousikē' in the Classical Athenian City*. Oxford.

Murray, Timothy (1997) (ed.), *Mimesis, Masochism, & Mime: The Politics of Theatricality in Contemporary French Thought*. Ann Arbor, Mich.

Nagy, G. (1989), 'Early Greek views of poets and poetry', in George A. Kennedy (ed.), *The Cambridge History of Literary Criticism*, i. 1–77. Cambridge.

—— (1996), *Poetry as Performance: Homer and Beyond*. Cambridge.

Naiden, F. S. (2004), 'Supplication and the law', in Harris and Rubinstein (2004), 71–91.

Nauck, A. (1889) (ed.), *Tragicorum graecorum fragmenta*. 2nd edn. Leipzig.

Nédoncelle, M. (1948), '*Prosopon* et *persona* dans l'antiquité classique', *Revue des Sciences Religieuses* 22, 277–9.

Neils, Jenifer (2003), 'Children and Greek religion', in Neils and Oakley (2003), 138–61.

NEILS, JENIFER and OAKLEY, JOHN H. (2003), *Coming of Age in Ancient Greece: Images of Childhood from the Classical Past*. New Haven and London.

NESSELRATH, H.-G. (1995), 'Myth, parody, and comic plots: the birth of gods and Middle Comedy', in G.W. Dobrov (ed.), *Beyond Aristophanes: Transition and Diversity in Greek Comedy*, 1–27. Atlanta.

NEWIGER, HANS-JOACHIM (1957), *Metafer und Allegorie: Studien zu Aristophanes*. Munich.

—— (1980), 'War and peace in the comedy of Aristophanes', in J. Henderson (ed.), *Aristophanes: Essays in Interpretation*, 219–327 [= *YCS* 26].

NEWSOM, ROBERT (1994), 'Doing duality once more', *Narrative* 2.2, 140–51.

NIELSEN, INGE (2002), *Cultic Theatres and Ritual Drama: A Study in Regional Development and Religious Interchange between East and West in Antiquity*. Aarhus.

NIETZSCHE, F. (1972 [1872]), *Die Geburt der Tragödie*, in *Nietzsche. Werke*, ed. G. Colli and M. Montinari, Part III vol. i, 5–152. Berlin and New York.

NIGHTINGALE, ANDREA WILSON (1995), *Genres in Dialogue: Plato and the Construct of Philosophy*. Cambridge.

NIPPEL, WILFRIED (2002), 'The construction of the "Other" ', in T. Harrison (2002), 278–310. Originally published in S. Setti (ed.), *I Greci*, vol. i [= *Noi e I Greci*], 165–96. Turin.

NIXON, P. (1938) (trans.), *Plautus*, vol. v (Loeb Classical Library). Cambridge, Mass.

NOLLÉ, J., and WENNINGER, A. (2001), 'Themistokles und Archepolis: eine griechische Dynastie im Perserreich und ihre Mänzprägung', *Jahrbuch für Numismatik und Geldgeschichte* 48/9 [1998/9], 29–70.

NORTH, H. (1952), 'The use of poetry in the training of the ancient orator', *Traditio* 8, 1–33.

OBBINK, DIRK (2001), 'Euripides, *Alcestis* 344–82 with omissions', *The Oxyrhynchus Papyri* 67, 19–22 and pl. 2.

OBER, J., and STRAUSS, B. (1990), 'Drama, political rhetoric, and the discourse of Athenian democracy', in Winkler and Zeitlin (1990), 237–70.

O'HIGGINS, LAURIE (2003), *Women and Humour in Classical Greece*. Cambridge.

OLMOS, RICARDO (1986), 'Eileithyia', *LIMC* 3.1, 685–99. Zurich and Munich.

OLSON, S. DOUGLAS (1998) (ed.), *Aristophanes' Peace*. Oxford.

—— (2002) (ed.), *Aristophanes' Acharnians*. Oxford.

ORME, NICHOLAS (1983), *Early British Swimming, 55 BC–AD 1719*. Exeter.

OSBORNE, M. J. (1981–3), *Naturalization in Athens*, 4 vols. Brussels.

—— and BYRNE, S. (1994) (eds.), *A Lexicon of Greek Personal Names* (general editors P. M. Fraser and E. Matthews), vol. ii, *Attica*. Oxford.

—— —— (1996), *The Foreign Residents of Athens: An Annex to the Lexicon of Greek Personal Names: Attica* (= Studia Hellenistica 33). Leuven.

OSBORNE, R. (1985), 'Law in action in classical Athens', *JHS* 105, 40–58.

—— (1993), 'Competitive festivals and the polis: a context for dramatic festivals at Athens', in Sommerstein et al. (1993), 21–37.

—— (1994), 'Looking on—Greek style. Does the sculpted girl speak to women too?', in I. Morris (ed.), *Classical Greece: Ancient Histories and Modern Archaeologies*, 81–96. Cambridge.

—— (1996), 'Desiring women on Athenian pottery', in Kampen (1996), 65–80.

—— (2004), 'Images of a warrior on a group of Athenian vases and their public', in Clemente Marconi (ed.), *Greek Vases: Images, Contexts, and Controversies*, 41–54. Brill, Leiden and Boston.

OSBORNE, R., and HORNBLOWER, S. (1994) (eds.), *Ritual, Finance, Politics: Athenian Democratic Accounts Presented to David Lewis*. Oxford.

ØSTERUD, SVEIN (1970), 'Who sings the monody 669–79 in Euripides' *Hippolytus*?', *GRBS* 11 (1970), 307–20.

O'SULLIVAN, NEIL (1992), *Alcidamas, Aristophanes and the Beginnings of Greek Stylistic Theory* [= *Hermes* Einzelschr. 60]. Stuttgart.

—— (1996), 'Written and spoken in the first sophistic', in Worthington (1996), 115–27.

OWEN, A. S. (1936), 'The date of Sophocles' *Electra*', in Gilbert Murray (1936), 145–57.

PACHE, CORINNE ONDINE (2004), *Baby and Child Heroes in Ancient Greece*. Urbana, Ill., Chicago.

PAGE, D. L. (1936), 'The elegiacs in Euripides' *Andromache*', in Gilbert Murray (1936), 206–30.

—— (1942) (ed.), *Greek Literary Papyri*, vol. i (Cambridge, Mass., and London).

PALEY, F. A. (1873) (ed.), *The "Peace" of Aristophanes*. Cambridge.

PALFREY, SIMON, and STERN, TIFFANY (forthcoming), *Shakespeare in Parts*. Oxford.

PALMER, CHRISTOPHER (1975), *Miklós Rózsa: A Sketch of his Life and Work*. London and Wiesbaden.

PALSSON, H. and EDWARDS, P. (1976) (trans.), *Egil's Saga*. Harmondsworth.

PANAGOPOULOS, ANDREAS (1985), 'Aristophanes and Euripides on the victims of war', *BICS* 32, 51–62.

PAPAZOGLU, FANULA (1978), *The Central Balkan Tribes in Pre-Roman Times*. Amsterdam [= trans. of original Serbo-Croatian edn., Sarajevo (1969)].

PARK, ROY (1969), ' "Ut pictura poesis": the nineteenth-century aftermath', *Journal of Aesthetics and Art Criticism* 28.2, 155–65.

PARKER, L. P. E. (1997), *The Songs of Aristophanes* (Oxford).

PARKER, ROBERT (1983), *Miasma: Pollution and Purification in Early Greek Religion*. Oxford.

PARSONS, PETER (1992) (ed.), 'Simonides, Elegies', *Oxyrhynchus Papyri* 59, 4–50.

PAVLOSKIS, ZOJA (1977), 'The voice of the actor in Greek tragedy', *CW* 71, 113–23.

PAXSON, JAMES (1994), *The Poetics of Personification*. Cambridge.

PEACHAM, HENRY (1622), *The Compleat Gentleman*. London.

PEARSON, A. C. (1917) (ed.), *The Fragments of Sophocles*. Cambridge.

PEARSON, L. (1962), *Popular Ethics in Ancient Greece*. Stanford, Calif.

—— (1975*a*), 'Hiatus and its purposes in Attic oratory', *AJP* 96, 138–59.

—— (1975*b*), 'The virtuoso passages in Demosthenes' speeches', *The Phoenix* 29, 214–30.

—— (1990) (ed.), *Aristoxenus. Elementa Rhythmica*. Oxford.

PELLEGRINI, A. D., and BOYD, B. (1993), 'The role of play in early childhood development and education: Issues in definition and function', in B. Spodek (ed.), *Handbook of Research on the Education of Young Children*, 105–21. New York.

PELLEGRINI, A. D., and PERLMUTTER, J. C. (1989), 'Classroom contextual effects on children's play', *Developmental Psychology*, 25.2, 289–96.

PELLING, C. B. R. (1989), 'Plutarch: Roman heroes and Greek culture', in M. Griffin and J. Barnes (eds.), *Philosophia Togata: Essays on Philosophy and Roman Society*, 199–232. Oxford.

—— (1997) (ed.), *Greek Tragedy and the Historian*. Oxford.

—— (2000), *Literary Texts and the Greek Historian*. London.

—— (2005), 'Tragedy, rhetoric, and performance culture', in Justina Gregory (ed.), *A Companion to Greek Tragedy*, 83–102. Oxford.

PELLIZER, EZIO (1990), 'Sympotic entertainment', in O. Murray (ed.), *Sympotica: A Symposium on the Symposium*, 177–84. Oxford.

PENDER, E. E. (1992), 'Spiritual pregnancy in Plato's *Symposium*', *CQ* 42, 72–86.

PETERSEN, LEIVA (1939), *Zur Geschichte der Personifikation in griechischer Dichtung und bildender Kunst*. Würzburg.

PERETTI, AURELIO (1939), *Epirrema e tragedia*. Florence.

PERLMAN, S. (1963), 'The politicians in the Athenian democracy of the fourth century BC', *Athenaeum* ns 41, 327–55.

—— (1964), 'Quotations from poetry in Attic orators of the fourth century BC', *AJP* 85, 155–72.

—— (1976), 'Panhellenism, the polis, and imperialism', *Historia* 25, 1–30.

PERRIN, B. (1917), *Plutarch's Lives*, vol. v. Loeb edn. Cambridge, Mass., and London.

—— (1921), *Plutarch's Lives*, vol. x. Loeb edn. Cambridge, Mass., and London.

PERTUSI, A. (1959), 'Selezione teatrale e scelta erudite nella tradizione del testo di Euripide', *Dioniso* 19, 111–41.

PETERSEN, E. (1911), 'Zu Aischylos' *Agamemnon*', *Rheinisches Museum* 76, 1–37.

PETERSEN, LEIVA (1939), *Zur Geschichte der Personifikation in griechischer Dichtung und bildender Kunst.* Wärzburg.

PHILIPP, HANNA (1968), *Tektonon Daidala: Der bildende Känstler und sein Werk im vorplatonischen Schrifttum.* Berlin.

PHILLIPS, JANE E. (1985), 'Alcumena in the Amphitruo of Plautus: a pregnant lady joke', *CJ* 80, 121–6.

PICKARD-CAMBRIDGE, A. W. (1988), *The Dramatic Festivals of Athens*, 3rd edn., rev. with suppl. by J. Gould and D. M. Lewis. Oxford.

PIERCE, KAREN F. (1998), 'Ideals of masculinity in New Comedy', in Foxhall and Salmon, 130–47.

PIAGET, J. (1967), *Six Psychological Studies.* New York.

PINGIATOGLOU, SEMELI (1981), *Eileithyia.* Wärzburg.

PINTACUDA, MARIO (1978), *La Musica nella tragedia Greca* (Maggio).

PIRENNE-DELFORGE, V. (2004), 'Qui est la Kourotrophos athénienne?', in Dasen (2004), 171–85.

PITCHER, LUKE (2005), 'Narrative technique in *The Lives of the Ten Orators*', *Classical Quarterly* 55, 217–34.

PLASSART, A. (1913), 'Les archers d'Athènes', *REG* 26, 151–23.

PODLECKI, A. J. (1999), *The Political Background of Aeschylean tragedy.* 2nd ed. London.

POE, EDGAR ALLAN (1846), 'The philosophy of composition', *Graham's Magazine*, April, reprinted in James A. Harrison (1965) (ed.), *The Complete Works of Edgar Allan Poe*, vol. 14, 193–208. New York.

POHLENZ, M. (1954), *Die griechische Tragödie*, vol. i, 2nd edn. Göttingen.

POLLITT, J. J. (1974), *The Ancient View of Greek Art.* New Haven and London.

POPP, HANSJÜRGEN (1971), 'Die Amoibaion', in Jens (1971) 221–75.

POPPO, E. F., and STAHL, J. M. (1883) (eds.), *Thucydides, De bello peloponnesiaco libri octo.* 2nd edn. Lepizig.

PORTER, R. (1986), 'Rape—does it have a historical meaning', in Tomaselli and Porter (1986), 216–36.

POSTLEWAIT, T., and DAVIS, TRACY C. (2003), 'Theatricality: an introduction', in Davis and Postlewait (2003), 1–39.

PÖTSCHER, W. (1959), 'Die Funktion der Anapästpartien in der Tragödien des Aischylos', *Eranos* 57, 79–98.

PRÉAUX, C. (1957), 'Ménandre et la société athénienne', *CE* 32.63, 84–100.

PRESS, MURIEL (1964) (trans.), *The Laxdale Saga.* London.

PRETAGOSTINI, ROBERTO (1995), 'L'esametro nel dramma attico del V secolo: problemi di "resa" e di "riconoscimento"', in Marco Fantuzzi and Roberto Pretagostini (eds.), *Struttura e storia dell'esametro Greco*, 163–91. Rome.

PROPP, VLADIMIR (1958), *Morphology of the Folktale*, ed. with introd. by S. Pirkova-Jakobson, trans. by L. Scott. Bloomington, Ind.

PUCCI, P. (1961), *Aristofane ed Euripide. Ricerche metriche e stilistiche*. Rome.

—— (1977), 'Euripides: the monument and the sacrifice', *Arethusa* 10, 165–95.

PUCHNER, MARTIN (2003) (ed.), *Tragedy and Metatheatre*. New York.

RÄCK, W. (1981), *Zum Barbarenbild in der Kunst Athens im 6. und 5. Jahrhundert v. Chr.* Bonn.

RAJAK, TESSA (2000), *The Jewish Dialogue with Greece and Rome: Studies in Cultural and Social Interaction* [= *Arbeiten zur Geschichte des antiken Judentums und des Urchristentums*, vol. 48]. Leiden.

RAVEN, D. S. (1968), *Greek Metre: an Introduction*, 2nd edn. London.

RAU, PETER (1967), *Paratragodia: Untersuchung einer komischen Form des Aristophanes* (*Zetemata* 45). Munich.

—— (1975), 'Das Tragödienspiel in den 'Thesmophoriazusen', in H.-J. Newiger (ed.), *Aristophanes und die alte Komödie*, 339–56. Darmstadt.

RAWSON, BERYL (2003), *Children and Childhood in Roman Italy*. Oxford.

REBER, ARTHUR S., and EMILY REBER (2001), *The Penguin Dictionary of Psychology*, 3rd edn. London and New York.

RECKFORD, KENNETH J. (1987), *Aristophanes' Old-and-New Comedy*, vol. i. Chapel Hill, NC.

REESON, JAMES (2001) (ed.), *Ovid's Heroides 11, 13 and 14: A Commentary* [*Mnem.* Suppl. 221]. Leiden, Boston and Cologne.

REHM, RUSH (1994), *Marriage to Death: The Conflation of Wedding and Funeral Rituals in Greek Tragedy*. Princeton.

REIN, M. J. (1996), 'Phrygian matar: emergence of an iconographic type', in E. N. Lane (ed.), *Cybele, Attis and Related Cults: Essays in Memory of J.J. Vermaseren*, 223–37. Leiden, New York, and Cologne.

REINACH, T. (1903), 'Les Perses de Timothée', *REG* 16, 62–83.

RENNIE, W. (1909) (ed.), *The Acharnians of Aristophanes*. London.

REVEL-MOUROZ, MARIANNE (2002), 'La puissance créatrice de la poésie de la paix', in Rochefort-Guillouet (2002), 98–106.

REVERMANN, MARTIN (1999–2000), 'Euripides, tragedy and Macedon: some conditions of reception', *ICS* 24–5, 451–67.

—— (forthcoming), 'The competence of theatre audiences', *JHS*.

REY, ALAIN (1995) (ed.), *Dictionnaire historique de la langue Française*. 2nd edn., 2 vols. Paris.

RHODES, P. J. (2003), 'Nothing to do with democracy: Athenian drama and the polis', *JHS* 123, 104–19.

—— (2004*a*), 'Aristophanes and the Athenian Assembly', in D. L. Cairns and R. A. Knox (eds.), *Law, Rhetoric and Comedy in Classical Athens* [Studs. D. M. MacDowell], 223–7.

—— (2004*b*), 'Keeping to the point', in Harris and Rubinstein (2004), 137–58.

RHODES, P. J., and OSBORNE, ROBIN (2003) (eds.), *Greek Historical Inscriptions, 404–323 BC, Edited with Introduction, Translations, and Commentaries.* Oxford.

RICCIARDELLI, G. (2000), 'Mito e *Performance* nelle associazioni Dionisiache', in M. Tororelli Ghidini, A. Storchi Marino, and A. Visconti (eds.), *Tra Orfeo e Pitagora*, 265–84. Naples.

RICHARDSON, N. J. (1981), 'The contest of Homer and Hesiod and Alcidamas' *Mouseion*, *CQ* 31, 1–10.

RIEDEL, V. (1984), *Antikerezeption in der Literatur der deutschen demokratischen Republik.* Berlin.

RIEDWEG, C. (1990), 'The 'Atheistic' Fragment from Euripides' Bellerophontes (286 N[2])', *ICS* 15, 39–53.

RIGHTER, ANNE (1962), *Shakespeare and the Idea of the Play.* London

RILEY, KATHLEEN (2001), review of Simon Armitage's *Mister Heracles*, *Oxford Magazine* 189, 11–12.

—— (2003), 'Browning's Versions: Robert Browning, Greek Tragedy and the Victorian Translation Debate', *Literature and Aesthetics*, 13, 51–66.

—— (2004), 'Reasoning Madness: The Reception and Performance of Euripides' Herakles'. D.Phil. thesis. Oxford.

RINGER, MARK (1998), *Electra and the Empty Urn: Metatheater and Role Playing in Sophocles.* Chapel Hill, NC, and London.

RITCHIE, WILLIAM (1964), *The Authenticity of the Rhesus of Euripides.* Cambridge.

ROBB, KEVIN (1994), *Literacy and Paideia in Ancient Greece.* New York and Oxford.

ROBERTS, DEBORAH (2000), 'The drunk and the policeman: Arrowsmith, convention, and the changing context of twentieth-century translations', Paper delivered at PAMLA.

ROCHEBLAVE-SPENLÉ, ANNE-MARIE (1962), *La notion de rôle en psychologie sociale: étude historico-critique.* Paris.

ROCHEFORT-GUILLOUET, SOPHIE (2002) (ed.), *Analyses & réflexions sur Aristophane, La Paix.* Paris.

RODINSON, MAXIME (1987), *Europe and the Mystique of Islam*, Eng. trans. by Roger Veinus of *La fascination de l'Islam. Les étapes du regard occidental sur le monde musulman. Les études arabes et islamiques en Europe* (Paris, 1980).

ROGERS, B. B. (1902) (ed.), *The Frogs of Aristophanes*. London.
—— (1904) (ed.), *The Thesmophoriazusae of Aristophanes*. London.
—— (1915) (ed.), *The Wasps of Aristophanes*. London.
ROLLER, L. E. (1999), *In Search of God the Mother: The Cult of Anatolian Cybele*. Berkeley, Los Angeles and London.
ROSE, H. J. (1958), *A Commentary on the Surviving Plays of Aeschylus*, vol. ii. Amsterdam.
ROSE, PETER (1992), *Sons of the Gods, Children of Earth: Ideology and Literary Form in Ancient Greece*. Ithaca, NY, and London.
ROSEN, RALPH (1984), 'The Ionian at Aristophanes *Peace* 46', *GRBS* 25, 389–96.
—— (1997a), 'The gendered polis in Eupolis' *Cities*', in Dobrov (1997), 149–76.
—— (1997b), 'Homer and Hesiod', in Ian Morris and Barry Powell (eds.), *A New Companion to Homer*, 463–88. Leiden, New York, and Cologne.
—— (2000), 'Cratinus' *Pytine* and the construction of the comic self', in Harvey and Wilkins (2000), 3–39.
—— (2004), 'Aristophanes' *Frogs* and the *Contest of Homer and Hesiod*', *TAPA* 134, 295–322.
ROSENBLOOM, DAVID (1998), 'Review of Edith Hall (ed.) Aeschylus: *Persians*', *Prudentia* 30, 35–41.
—— (2002), 'From Poneros to Pharmakos: Theater, Social Drama and Revolution at Athens, 428–404 BCE', *Classical Antiquity*, 21.2, 283–346.
—— (2005), *Aeschylus' Persians* [Duckworth Companions to Ancient Tragedy]. London.
ROSENMEYER, PATRICIA E. (1991), 'Simonides' Danae fragment reconsidered', *Arethusa* 24, 5–29.
ROSIVACH, VINCENT J. (1998), *When a Young Man Falls in Love: The Sexual Exploitation of Women in New Comedy*. London and New York.
ROSTOVTZEFF, M. (1922), *Iranians and Greeks in South Russia*. Oxford.
ROUGÉ, J. (1970), 'La colonization greque et les femmes', *Cahiers d'histoire* 15, 307–17.
ROUSSEAU, G. S., and PORTER, ROY (1989) (eds.), *Exoticism in the Enlightenment*. Manchester.
ROUX, G. (1960), 'Qu'est-ce qu'un κολοσσός?', *REA* 62, 5–40.
RUBIN, S., and WOLF, D. (1979), 'The development of maybe: the evolution of social roles into fantasy roles', in E. Winner and H. Gardner (eds.), *Fact, Fiction and Fantasy in Childhood*, 15–28. San Francisco.
RUBINSTEIN, LENE (2000), *Litigation and Cooperation: Supporting Speakers in the Courts of Classical Athens* [= *Historia* Einzelschr. 147]. Stuttgart.
RUCK, C. (1976), 'Duality and the madness of Herakles', *Arethusa* 9, 53–5.

RUSSELL, D. A. (1990), '*Ēthos* in oratory and rhetoric', in C. B. R. Pelling (ed.), *Characterization and Individuality in Greek Literature*, 197–212. Oxford.

RUSSO, CARLO FERDINANDO, (1994), *Aristophanes, an Author for the* Stage, rev. and expanded edn., trans. Kevin Wren, of *Aristofane, autore di teatro*. (Florence 1962).

RUTHERFORD, I. (2002), 'The new Simonides: towards a commentary', in Boedeker and Sider (2002), 33–54.

—— (2004), '*Choros heis ek tēsde tēs poleōs* (Xen. *Mem.* 3.3.12): song-dance and state-pilgrimage at Athens', in Murray and Wilson (2004), 67–90.

RYMER, THOMAS (1693), *A Short View of Tragedy, its Original, Excellency, and Corruption*. London.

SAID, EDWARD (1975), 'Shattered myths', in Nasser H. Aruri (ed.), *Middle East Crucible*, 41–7. Wilmette, Ill.

—— (1978), *Orientalism*. London.

—— (1985), 'Orientalism reconsidered', in Barker (1985), i. 14–27.

—— (2003), 'A window on the world', *The Guardian Review*, 2 August, 4–6.

SAÏD, SUZANNE (1984), 'Grecs et barbares dans les tragedies d'Euripide: le fin des différences', *Ktema* 9. 27–53. Eng. trans. in T. Harrison (2002), 62–100.

SALLER, RICHARD P. (1993), 'The social dynamics of consent to marriage and sexual relations: the evidence of Roman comedy', in Angeliki E. Laiou (ed.), *Consent and Coercion to Sex and Marriage in Ancient and Medieval Societies*, 83–104. Washington, DC.

SANCISI-WEERDENBURG, H. (1993), review of E. Hall (1989), *Gerion* 11, 373–85.

—— (2001), '*Yaunā* by the sea and across the sea', in Malkin (2001), 323–46.

SANDERS, H. A. (1925), 'Swimming among the Greeks and Romans', *CJ* 20, 566–8.

SATTLER, W. (1957), 'Concepts of ethos in ancient rhetoric', *Speech Monographs* 14, 55–68.

SCAFURO, ADELE (1990), 'Discourses of sexual violation in mythic accounts and dramatic versions of "The Girl's Tragedy" ', *Differences* 2.1, 126–59.

—— (1997), *The Forensic Stage: Settling Disputes in Graeco-Roman New Comedy*. Cambridge.

SCHACHTER, ALBERT (1981), *Cults of Boiotia*, vol. i (*BICS* suppl. 38.1). London.

SCHADEWALDT, WOLFGANG (1926), *Monolog und Selbstgresprach: Untersuchungen zur Formgeschichte der griechischen Tragödie*. Berlin.

—— (1942), *Legende von Homer den fahrenden Sänger*. Leipzig.

SCHARFFENBERGER, ELIZABETH (2002), 'Aristophanes' *Thesmophoriazousai* and the challenges of comic translation: the case of William Arrowsmith's *Euripides Agonistes*', in Gamel (2002), 429–63.

SCHENKL, H. (1916) (ed.), *Epicteti Dissertationes ab Arriano digestae.* 2nd edn. Leipzig.

SCHLESINGER, KATHLEEN (1959), Schlesinger, *The Greek Aulos: A Study of its Mechanism and of its Relation to the Modal System of Ancient Greek Music.* London.

SCHMID, W. (1934), 'Der Hinzutritt des Satyrspiels', in W. Schmid and O. Stählin, *Geschichte der griechischen Literatur* vol. i.2, 79–86. Munich.

SCHMIDT, MARGOT (1967), 'Dionysien', *Antike Kunst* 10, 70–81.

—— (1998), 'Komische arme Teufel und andere Gesellen auf der griechischen Komödienbähne', *Antike Kunst* 41, 17–32.

SCHMIZ, THOMAS A. (2000), 'Plausibility in the Greek orators', *AJP* 121, 47–77.

SCHÖNE, ANGELIKA (1987), *Der Thiasos: eine Ikonographische Untersuchung äber das Gefolge des Dionysos in der attischen Vasenmalerei des 6. und 5. Jhs v. Chr.* Göteborg, Sweden.

SCHRIJVERS, P. H. (1976), 'O Tragoedia tu labor aeternus: étude sur l'élégie III, 1 des Amores d'Ovide', in J. M. Bremer, S. L. Radt, C. J. Ruijgh (eds.), *Miscellanea Tragica in honorem J.C. Kamerbeek*, 405–24. Amsterdam.

SCHULTZ, PETER (2003), 'The Stoa Poikile, the Nike temple bastion and Cleon's shields from Pylos: A note on Knights 843–859,' *Numismatica e antichità classiche* 32, 43–62.

SCOTT, JOAN WALLACH (1986), 'Gender: A Useful Category of Historical Analysis,' *American Historical Review*, 91 (1986), 1053–75.

—— (1988), *Gender and the Politics of History.* New York.

SCOTT, W. C. (1984), *Musical Design in Aeschylean Theater.* Hanover and London.

—— (1996), *Musical Design in Sophoclean Theater.* Hanover and London.

SCUDERI, ANTONIO (2000), 'Updating antiquity', in Farrell and Scuderi, 39–64.

SEAFORD, RICHARD (1984) (ed.), *Euripides' Cyclops.* Oxford.

—— (1994), *Reciprocity and Ritual: Homer and Tragedy in the Developing City-State.* Oxford.

—— (2003), 'Aeschylus and the unity of opposites', *JHS* 123, 141–63.

SEALE, DAVID (1982), *Vision and Stagecraft in Sophocles.* London and Canberra.

SEDGWICK, W. B. (1960) (ed.), *Plautus, Amphitruo.* Manchester.

SEGAL, C. (1982), 'Tragédie, oralité, écriture', *Poétique* 50, 131–54.

Consolidated Bibliography 443

—— (1984), 'Greek tragedy: writing, truth, and the representation of the self', in Harold D. Evjen (ed.), *Mnemai: Classical Studies in Memory of Karl K. Hulley*, 41–67. Chico, Calif.

—— (1985*a*), 'Choral lyric in the fifth century', in P. E. Easterling and B. M. W. Knox (eds.), *The Cambridge History of Classical Literature*, i. 222–44. Cambridge.

—— (1985*b*), 'Greek tragedy: writing, truth and the representation of the self', in H. D. Evjen (ed.), *Mnemai. Classical Studies in Memory of Karl K. Hulley.* 41–67. Chico, Calif.

—— (1986), *Pindar's Mythmaking: The Fourth Pythian Ode.* Princeton.

—— (1990), 'Violence and the other: Greek, female and barbarian in Euripides' *Hecuba*', *TAPA* 120, 109–31.

—— (1993), *Euripides and the Poetics of Sorrow: Art, Gender, and Commemoration in Alcestis, Hippolytus, and Hecuba.* Durham, NC, and London.

—— (1994), 'The gorgon and the nightingale: the voice of female lament and Pindar's twelfth *Pythian Ode*', in Leslie C. Dunn and Nancy A. Jones (eds.), *Embodied Voices: Female Vocality in Western Culture*, 17–34. Cambridge.

—— (1997), 'On the fifth stasimon of Euripides' *Medea*', *AJP* 118, 167–84.

SEIDENSTICKER, B. (1979), 'Das Satyrspiel', in G. A. Seeck (ed.), *Das Griechische. Drama*, 204–57. Darmstadt.

—— (2003), 'The chorus in Greek satyrplay', in Eric Csapo amd Margaret C. Miller (eds.), *Poetry, Theory, Praxis: The Social Life of Myth, Word and Image in Ancient Greece*, 100–21. Oxford.

SHAPIRO, H. A. (2003), 'Fathers and sons, men and boys', in Neils and Oakley (2003), 84–111.

SHARP, THOMAS (1825), *A dissertation on the pageants or dramatic mysteries anciently performed at Coventry, by the trading companies of that city.* Coventry.

SHARPLEY, H. (1905) (ed.), *Aristophanous Eirene = The Peace of Aristophanes.* Edinburgh and London.

SHAW, BRENT D. (2001), 'Raising and killing children: two Roman myths', *Mnemosyne* 54.1, 1–77.

SHAW, P.-J. (2002), 'Lords of Hellas, old men of the sea', in Boedeker and Sider (2002), 164–81.

SHIPP, G. P. (1979) (ed.), *P. Terenti Afri Andria.* New York (repr. of edn. originally published in Oxford (1960)).

SIDER, D. (2002), 'Fragments 1–22 W²: text, apparatus criticus, and translation', in Boedeker and Sider (2002), 13–29.

SIER, KURT (1992), 'Die Rolle des Skythen in den *Thesmophoriazusen* des Aristophanes, in Mäller, Sier and Werner (1992), 63–84.

Sifakis, G. M. (1967), *Studies in the History of Hellenistic Drama*. London.
—— (1971*a*), 'Aristotle, *E.N.* IV, 2, 1123a 19–24, and the comic chorus in the fourth century', *AJP* 92, 410–32.
—— (1971*b*), *Parabasis and Animal Choruses*. London.
—— (1979), 'Boy actors in New Comedy', in G. W. Bowersock, W. Burkert and M. J. Putnam (eds.), *Arktouros: Hellenic studies presented to Bernard M. W. Knox on the occasion of his 65th birthday*, 199–208. New York and Berlin.
Silk, Michael (1993), 'Aristophanic paratragedy', in Sommerstein et. al. (1993), 477–504.
—— (1996) (ed.), *Tragedy and the Tragic: Greek Theatre and Beyond*. Oxford.
Simon, Erika (1986), 'Eirene', *LIMC* iii.1, 700–5. Zurich and Munich.
Slater, Niall W. (1985*a*), 'Vanished players: two classical reliefs and theatre history', *GRBS* 26, 333–44.
—— (1985*b*), *Plautus in Performance*. Princeton.
—— (1988), 'The fictions of patriarchy in Terence's *Hecyra*', *CW* 81.4, 249–60.
—— (1989), 'Aristophanes' apprenticeship again', *GRBS* 30, 67–82.
—— (1990), 'The idea of the actor', in Winkler and Zeitlin (1990), 385–95.
—— (1999), 'Making the Aristophanic audience', *AJP* 120, 351–68.
—— (2000), 'Dead again: (en)gendering praise in Euripides' *Alcestis*', *Helios* 27, 105–21.
—— (2002), *Spectator Politics: Metatheatre and Performance in Aristophanes*. Philadelphia.
Smith, Eric (1984), *Dictionary of Classical Reference in English Poetry*. Woodbridge, Suffolk.
Smith, R. R. R. (1987), 'The imperial reliefs from the Sebasteion at Aphrodisias', *JRS* 77, 88–138.
Smith-Lovin, Lynn (2002), 'Roles, identities, and emotions: parallel processing and the production of mixed emotions', in Kashima, Foddy, and Platow (2002), 125–43.
Smyth, H. W. (1957) (trans.), *Aeschylus*, vol. ii, with an appendix by H. Lloyd-Jones. Cambridge, Mass., and London.
Snell, B. (1964), *Scenes from Greek Drama*. Berkeley and Los Angeles.
Solomon, A. (1997), *Re-Dressing the Canon: Essays on Theatre and Gender*. London.
Solomos, A. (1961), *Ho Zōntanos Aristophanēs. Apo tēn epochē tou ōs tēn epochē mas*. Athens.
Sommerstein, Alan H. (1977), 'Aristophanes and the events of 411', *JHS* 97, 112–26.

—— (1985) (ed.), *Aristophanes' Peace.* Warminster.

—— (1994) (ed.), *Aristophanes' Thesmophoriazusae.* Warminster.

—— (1996*a*), *Aeschylean tragedy.* Bari.

—— (1996*b*) (ed.), *Aristophanes' Frogs.* Warminster.

—— (1998*a*), review of E. Hall (ed.), *Aeschylus: Persians, JHS* 118, 211–12.

—— (1998*b*), 'Rape and young manhood in Athenian comedy', in Foxhall and Salmon, 100–14.

—— (2002), *Greek Drama and Dramatists.* London.

—— Halliwell, Stephen, Henderson, Jeffrey, and Zimmermann, Bernhard (1993) (eds.), *Tragedy, Comedy and the Polis: Papers from the Greek Drama Conference, Nottingham, 18–20 July 1990.* Bari.

SONKOWSKY, R.P. (1959), 'An aspect of delivery in ancient rhetorical theory', *TAPA* 90, 256–74.

SONTAG, SUSAN (1994), *Against Interpretation.* Vintage edition of original Dell paperback, with author's preface, published in 1967.

SÖRBOM, G. (1966), *Mimesis and Art.* Uppsala.

SOURVINOU-INWOOD, CHRISTIANE (1994), 'Something to do with Athens: tragedy and ritual', in Osborne and Hornblower (1994), 269–90.

—— (2003), *Tragedy and Athenian Religion.* Lexington.

Southern, SIR RICHARD WILLIAM (1962), *Western Views of Islam in the Middle Ages.* Cambridge, Mass.

SPARKES, B. A. (1975), 'Illustrating Aristophanes', *JHS* 95, 122–35.

SPAWFORTH, A. (2001), 'Shades of Greekness: A Lydian case study', in Malkin (2001), 375–400.

SPRAWSON, CHARLES (1992), *Haunts of the Black Masseur: The Swimmer as Hero.* London.

STAFFORD, EMMA (2000), *Worshipping Virtues: Personification and the Divine in Ancient Greece.* London and Swansea.

STANISLAVSKI, CONSTANTIN (1961), *Creating a Role,* Eng. trans. Elizabeth Reynolds Hapgood. New York.

STARKIE, W. J. M. (1909) (ed.), *The Acharnians of Aristophanes.* London.

STARKS, JOHN H. (2000), '*Nullus me est hodie Poenus Poenior*: balanced ethnic humor in Plautus' *Poenulus*', *Helios* 27, 163–86.

STAVRAKIS, YANNIS (1999), *Lacan and the Political.* London and New York.

STEEDMAN, CHARLES (1867), *Manual of Swimming.* Melbourne and London.

STEFFEN, W. (1971), 'The satyr-dramas of Euripides', *Eos* 59, 203–26.

STEGGLE, M. (forthcoming), 'That scurrilous. carping comedian: Aristophanes in the English Renaissance', in E. Hall and A. Wrigley (eds.), *Aristophanes in Performance: Birds, Peace, Frogs.* Oxford.

STEHLE, EVA (2002), 'The body and its representations in Aristophanes' *Thesmophoriazousai*: where does the costume end?' *AJP* 123, 369–406.

—— (2004), 'Choral prayer in Greek tragedy: euphemia or aischrologia?', in Murray and Wilson (2004), 121–55.

STEINER, DEBORAH (1994), *The Tyrant's Writ: Myths and Images of Writing in Ancient Greece*. Princeton.

—— (1995), 'Eyeless in Argos: a reading of *Agamemnon* 416–19', *JHS* 115, 175–82.

—— (2001), *Images in Mind: Statues in Archaic and Classical Greek Literature and Thought*. Princeton and Oxford.

STEINER, WENDY (1982), *The Colors of Rhetoric: Problems in the Relation between Modern Literature and Painting*. Chicago.

—— (1988), *Pictures of Romance: Form against Content in Painting and Literature*. Chicago and London.

STEPHANIS, I. E. (1980), *Ho Doulos stis Kōmōdies tou Aristophanē*. Thessaloniki.

—— (1988), *Dionysiakoi Technitai*. Herakleion.

STEPHENS, S. A. (1981), 'Aristophanes, Ποίησις', in *Papyri Greek and Egyptian, edited by Various Hands in Honour of Eric Gardner Turner*, 23–5. London.

STEPTO, ROBERT BURNS (1979), *From Behind the Veil: A Study of Afro-American Narrative*. Urbana, Ill. and London.

STERN, TIFFANY (2000), *Rehearsal from Shakespeare to Sheridan*. Oxford.

—— (2004), *Making Shakespeare: From Stage to Page*. London and New York.

STEVEN, M. R. G. (1933), 'Plato and the art of his time', *CQ* 27, 149–55.

STOL, M. (2000), *Birth in Babylonia and the Bible: Its Mediterranean Setting* [*Cuneiform Monographs* 14]. Groningen.

STONE, LAURA M. (1981), *Costume in Aristophanic Comedy*. New York.

STOREY, I.C. (2003) (ed.), *Eupolis. Poet of Old Comedy*. Oxford.

STOTHARD, PETER (2005), 'Hit me here, and here, and here', *Times Literary Supplement* 5324, 15 April, 18.

STRAUSS, BARRY S. (1993), *Fathers and Sons in Classical Athens: Ideology and Society in the Era of the Peloponnesian War*. Princeton.

STUMPF, H. C. (1896), 'Die pseudo-Aristotelischen Probleme äber Musik', *Abhandlungen der königlichen Akademie der Wissenschaften zu Berlin*, no. 3, 1–85.

SÜSS, W. (1910), *Ethos: Studien zur älteren griechischen Rhetorik*. Leipzig.

SUTTON, D. F. (1974), 'Aeschylus' *Amymonē*', *GRBS* 15, 193–202.

—— (1980), *The Greek Satyr Play*. Meisenheim am Glan.

—— (1987), 'The theatrical families of Athens', *AJP* 108, 9–26.

SVENBRO, JASPER (1990), ' 'The interior voice': on the invention of silent reading, in Winkler and Zeitlin (1990), 366–84.

TAAFFE, LAUREN K. (1993), *Aristophanes and Women*. London.

TALMER, JEREMY (2003), 'A new *Persians* offers insight on new imperialism', *The Villager* 73.3 (June 18–24).

TAPLIN, OLIVER (1972), 'Aeschylean silences and silences in Aeschylus', *HSCP* 76, 57–97.

—— (1977), *The Stagecraft of Aeschylus*. Oxford.

TAPLIN, OLIVER (1978), *Greek Tragedy in Action*. London.

—— (1983), 'Tragedy and Trugedy', *CQ* 33, 331–33.

—— (1986), 'Fifth-century tragedy and comedy: a synkrisis', *JHS* 106, 163–74.

—— (1991), '*Auletai* and *auletrides* in Greek comedy and comic vase-paintings', *Quaderni ticinesi di numismatica e antichità classiche* 20, 31–48.

—— (1993), *Comic Angels and Other Approaches to Greek Drama through Vase-Painting*. Oxford.

—— (1996), 'Comedy and the tragic', in Silk (1996), 188–202.

—— (1999), 'Spreading the word through performance', in S. Goldhill, and R. Osborne (eds.), *Performance Culture and Athenian Democracy*, 33–57. Cambridge.

—— (2000) (ed.), *Literature in the Greek and Roman Worlds: A New Perspective*. Oxford.

—— and Peter Wilson (1993), 'The "aetiology" of tragedy in the *Oresteia*', *PCPS* 39, 169–80.

THALMANN, WILLIAM G. (1998), *The Swineherd and the Bow: Representations of Class in the* Odyssey. Ithaca, NY, and London.

THIERCY, PASCAL (1986), *Aristophane: fiction et dramaturgie*. Paris.

THOMAS, RALPH (1904), *Swimming*, 2nd edn. London.

THOMAS, ROSALIND (1989), *Oral Tradition and Written Record in Classical Athens*. Cambridge.

—— (2000), *Herodotus in Context: Ethnography, Science, and the Art of Persuasion*. Cambridge.

—— (2001), 'Ethnicity, genealogy, and Hellenism in Herodotus', in Malkin (2001), 213–33.

THOMSON, A. D. (1898), *Euripides and the Attic Orators: A Comparison*. London and New York.

THOMSON, GEORGE (1966) (ed.), *The Oresteia of Aeschylus*. 2nd edn. Prague.

TODD, S. (1990*a*), 'The purpose of evidence in Athenian courts', in Cartledge, Millett, and Todd (1990), 19–39.

TODD, S. (1990*b*), 'The use and abuse of the Attic orators', *G&R* 37, 159–78.

—— (1993), *The Shape of Athenian Law*. Oxford.

Todd, S. (2000), 'How to execute people in fourth-century Athens', in Virginia Hunter and Jonathan Edmondson (eds.), *Law and Social Status in Classics Athens*, 32–51. Oxford.

Tomaselli, S., and R. Porter (1986) (eds.), *Rape: An Historical and Social Enquiry*. Oxford.

Trankle, Hermann (1984), 'Zu drei Stellen von Suetons Augustusvita', in *Filologia e Forme Letterarie* 4 (= *Studi offerti a Francesco della Corte*), 95–104. Urbino.

Travlos, J. (1971), *Pictorial Dictionary of Ancient Athens* (Eng. trans.). London.

Trendall, A. D. and Cambitoglou, A. (1983), *The Red-Figured Vases of Apulia* suppl. I (= *BICS* suppl. 42). London.

—— and Webster, T. B. L. (1971), *Illustrations of Greek Drama*. London and New York.

Tritle, Larry (2000), *From Melos to My Lai: War and Survival*. London.

Tuplin, C. (1996), *Achaemenid Studies* (= *Historia* Einzelschriften xcix). Stuttgart.

Turner, E. G. (1962*a*), 'Euripides, *Cresphontes*', *The Oxyrhynchus Papyri* 27, 73–81.

—— (1962*b*), 'Hypotheses of Euripides' *Alcestis* and *Aeolus*', *The Oxyrhynchus Papyri* 27, no. 2457, 70–3.

Tzanetou, A. (2002), 'Something to do with Demeter: ritual and performance in Aristophanes' *Women at the Thesmophoria*, in Gamel (2002), 329–67.

Uhlig, G. (1983) (ed.), *Dionysii Thracis Ars Grammatica* (= *Grammatici Graeci* Part 1 vol. i). Leipzig.

Usher, M. D. (2002), 'Satyr play in Plato's *Symposium*', *AJP* 123, 205–28.

Usher, S. (1965), 'Individual characterization in Lysias', *Eranos* 63, 99–119.

—— (1976), 'Lysias and his clients', *GRBS* 17, 31–40.

Ussher, R. G. (1960) (ed.), *The Characters of Theophrastus*. London.

—— (1977), 'The other Aeschylus: a study of the fragments of Aeschylean satyr plays', *Phoenix* 31, 278–99.

—— (1978) (ed.), *Euripides' Cyclops, Introduction and Commentary*. Rome.

Vahlen, J. Vahlen (1903) (ed.), *Ennianae Poesis Reliquiae*. Leipzig.

Valakas, Kostas (2002), 'The use of the body by actors in tragedy and satyr-play', in P. Easterling and E. Hall (eds.), *Greek and Roman Actors: Aspects of an Ancient Profession*, 69–92. Cambridge.

Valensi, L. (1990), 'The making of a political paradigm: the Ottoman state and Oriental despotism', in A. Grafton and E. Blair (eds.), *The Transmission of Culture in Early Modern Europe*, 173–203. Philadelphia.

van Esveld, W. H. C. (1908), 'De balneis lavationibus Graecorum'. Diss. Amersfoot.

Van Fossen, R. W. (1979) (ed.), *Eastward Ho. George Chapman, Ben Jonson, John Marston*. Manchester and Baltimore.

van Hook, LaRue (1919), 'Alcidamas versus Isocrates: the spoken versus the written word', *CW* 12, 89–94.

van Minnen, Peter (1997), 'The performance and readership of the *Persai* of Timotheus', *Archiv für Papyrusforschung* 43, 246–60.

Van Steen, Gonda (2006), 'Enacting History and Patriotic Myth: Aeschylus' *Persians* on the Eve of the Greek War of Independence', in Bridges, Hall, and Rhodes (2006).

van Straten, F. T. (1981), 'Gifts for the gods', in H. S. Versnel (ed.), *Faith, Hope and Worship: Aspects of Religious Mentality in the Ancient World*, 65–151. Leiden.

Varadpande, M. L. (1981), *Ancient Indian and Indo-Greek Theatre*. New Delhi.

Vasunia, Phiroze (2001), *The Gift of the Nile: Hellenizing Egypt from Aeschylus to Alexander*. Berkeley, Los Angeles and London.

—— (2003), 'Plutarch and the return of the archaic', in A. J. Boyle and W. J. Dominik (eds.), *Flavian Rome: Culture, Image, Text*, 369–89. Leiden.

Vedder, U. (1988), 'Frauentod-Kriegertod im Spiegel der attischen Grabkunst den 4. Jhr.v.Chr.', *MDAI(A)* 103, 161–91.

Verducci, F (1985), *Ovid's Toyshop of the Heart: Epistulae Heroidum*. Princeton.

Vermeule, Emily (1979), *Aspects of Death in Early Greek Art and Poetry*. Berkeley and London.

Vernant, J.-P. (1982), 'La belle mort et le cadavre outragé', in G. Gnoli and J.-P. Vernant (eds.), *La Mort, les morts dans les sociétés anciennes*, 45–76. Cambridge and Paris.

—— (1988), *Myth and Society in Ancient Greece*, Eng. trans. New York.

—— and Vidal-Naquet, P. (1988), *Myth and Tragedy in Ancient Greece*, Eng. trans. Janet Lloyd. New York.

Verrall , A. W. (1905), *Essays on Four Plays of Euripides*. Cambridge.

Vilardo, Massimo (1976), 'La forma della comicità nella *Pace* di Aristofane', *Dioniso* 47, 54–81.

Vinaver, E. (1947) (ed.), *The Works of Thomas Malory*, vol. i. Oxford.

Vogt, Joseph (1965), *Sklaverei und Humanität* [*Historia* Einzelschriften 8]. Wiesbaden.

von Blumenthal, A. (1939), (ed.), *Ion von Chios: die reste seiner Werke*. Stuttgart and Berlin.

von Reden, Sitta and Goldhill, Simon (1999), 'Plato and the performance of dialogue', in Simon Goldhill and Robin Osborne (eds.), *Performance Culture and Athenian Democracy*, 257–89. Cambridge.

VON ROTTECK, CARL (1842), *Bilder-Gallerie zur allgemeinen Weltgeschichte.* Karlsruhe and Freiburg.

VON SCHLEGEL, A. W. (1840), *A Course of Lectures on Dramatic Art and Literature,* 2nd edn., trans. John Black. London.

VON WILAMOWITZ-MOELLENDORFF, Ulrich (1893), *Aristoteles und Athen.* Berlin.

—— (1903) (ed.), *Timotheus. Die Perser.* Leipzig.

—— (1927) (ed.), *Aristophanes Lysistrate.* Berlin.

—— (1929), 'Sepulcri Portuensis imagines', *Stud. Ital.* 8, 89–100, rep. in *Kleine Schriften* vol. 5.1 (1935), 523–32. Berlin.

—— (1930), *My Recollections 1848–1914,* trans. G. C. Richards. London.

VOS, M. F. (1963), *Scythian Archers in Archaic Attic Vase Painting.* Groningen.

WÆRN, INGRID (1960), 'Greek lullabies', *Eranos* 58, 1–8.

WALKER, R. J. (1919) (ed.), *The Ichneutae of Sophocles.* London.

WALLACE, ROBERT W. (2004), 'Damon of Oa: music theorist ostracized?', in Murray and Wilson (2004), 249–67.

WALTER, BETTYRUTH (1988), *The Jury Summation as Speech Genre.* Amsterdam.

WALZ, C. (1835) (ed.), *Rhetores Graeci,* vol. ii. Stuttgart, Täbingen, and London.

WARDY, ROBERT (2002), 'The unity of opposites in Plato's *Symposium*', in David Sedley (ed.), *Oxford Studies in Ancient Philosophy,* 1–62. Oxford.

WARNER, MARINA (1985), *Monuments and Maidens: the Allegory of the Female Form.* London.

—— (1986), 'Images of Peace', *The Listener* 15/2957 (24 April), 26.

—— (1987), *Monuments and Maidens: the Allegory of the Female Form.* London.

WATZINGER, C. (1905), *Griechische Holzsarkophage aus der Zeit Alexanders des Grossen.* Leipzig.

WEBB, MATTHEW (1875), *The Art of Swimming.* London.

WEBSTER, T. B. L. (1939), 'Greek theories of art and literature down to 400 BC', *CQ* 33, 166–79.

—— (1956), *Art and Literature in Fourth Century Athens.* London.

—— (1967), *The Tragedies of Euripides.* London.

—— (1970), *The Greek Chorus.* London.

—— *Monuments Illustrating New Comedy* (1995) 3rd edn., rev. and enlarged by J. R. Green and Axel Seeberg. London.

WEHRLI, FRITZ (1953) (ed.), *Herakleides Pontikos* [= *Die Schule des Aristoteles, Texte und Kommentar vol.* vii]. Basel.

—— (1969) (ed.), *Die Schule des Aristoteles*, 2nd edn., vol. ix. Basel and Stuttgart.

WEISS, CARINA (1986), 'Eos', *LIMC* iii.1, 747–89.

WELWEI, K.-W. (1974–7), *Unfreie im antiken Kriegsdienst*. Wiesbaden.

WERNER, JÜRGEN (1992), 'Bibliographie', in Mäller, Sier, and Werner (1992), 233–52.

WERRE-DE HAAS, M. (1961) (ed.), *Aeschylus' Dictyulci* (Leiden).

WEST, M. L. (1968), 'Two passages of Aristophanes', *CR* NS 18, 5–8.

—— (1971), 'Stesichorus', *CQ* 21, 302–14.

—— (1987*a*) (ed.), *Euripides' Orestes*. Warminster.

—— (1987*b*), *Introduction to Greek Metre*. Oxford.

—— (1992*a*), *Ancient Greek Music*. Oxford.

—— (1992*b*), *Iambi et Elegi Graeci*, vol. ii. 2nd edn. Oxford.

WHATMOUGH, J. (1952), 'On Triballic in Aristophanes' (*Birds* 1615)', *CP* 47, 26.

WHINCOP, THOMAS (1747), *Scanderbeg, or, Love and liberty: a tragedy; to which are added, a list of all the dramatic authors with some account of their lives, and of all the dramatic pieces ever published in the English language, to the year 1747*. London.

WHITBY, M. (1998), 'An international symposium? Ion of Chios fr. 27 and the margins of the Delian League', in Edward Dabrowa (ed.), *Ancient Iran and the Mediterranean World* [= Uniwessytet Jagiellonski Studies in Ancient History 2, proceedings of an international conference in honour of Professor Józef Wolski], 207–24. Krakow.

WHITE, JOHN WILLIAMS (1912), *The Verse of Greek Comedy*. London.

WHITE, ROBERT J. (1975), *Artemidorus, The Interpretation of Dreams: Oneirocritica*. Park Ridge, NJ.

WHITEHEAD, DAVID (1977), *The Ideology of the Athenian Metic*. Cambridge.

—— (1986), *The Demes of Attica: A Political and Social Study*. Princeton.

—— (2000) (ed.), *Hypereides. The Forensic Speeches*. Oxford.

WHITMAN, C. (1964), *Aristophanes and the Comic Hero*. Cambridge, Mass.

WILCOX, S. (1942), 'The scope of early rhetorical instruction', *HSCP* 53, 121–55.

—— (1945), 'Isocrates' fellow-rhetoricians', *AJP* 66, 171–86.

WILES, DAVID (1991), *The Masks of Menander: Sign and Meaning in Greek and Roman Performance*. Cambridge.

—— (1997), *Tragedy in Athens: Performance Space and Theatrical Meaning*. Cambridge.

—— (2000), *Greek theatre performance: An Introduction*. Cambridge.

WILLETTS, R. F. (1958), 'Cretan Eileithyia', *CQ* 8, 221–3.

WILLIAMS, GARETH (1992), 'Ovid's Canace: dramatic irony in *Heroides* 11', *CQ* 42, 201–9.

WILLI, ANDREAS (2002*a*) (ed.), *The Language of Greek Comedy.* Oxford.

—— (2002*b*), 'Languages on stage: Aristophanic language, cultural history, and Athenian identity', in Willi (2002*a*), 111–49.

WILLIAMS, HENRY (1884), *The Adventurous Life and Daring Exploits in England and America of Captain Matthew Webb: The Swimming Champion of the World.* London.

WILLINK, C. (1989), 'The reunion duo in Euripides' *Helen*', *CQ* 39, 45–69.

WILSHIRE, BRUCE (1982), *Role Playing and Identity: The Limits of Theater as Metaphor*, Bloomington, IA.

WILSON, PETER J. (1996), 'Tragic rhetoric: the use of tragedy and the tragic in the fourth century', in Silk (1996), 310–31.

—— (1999–2000), 'Euripides' tragic muse', in Martin Cropp, Kevin Lee and David Sansone (eds.), *Euripides and Tragic Theatre in the Late Fifth Century.* Special issue of *ICS*, vols. 24–5, 427–49.

—— (2000*a*), *The Athenian Institution of the Khoregia: The Chorus, the City and the Stage.* Cambridge.

—— (2000*b*), 'Powers of horror and laughter: the great age of drama', in Taplin (2000), 88–132.

—— (2002), 'The musicians among the actors', in P. Easterling and E. Hall (eds.), *Greek and Roman Actors: Aspects of an Ancient Profession*, 39–68. Cambridge.

—— (2004), 'Athenian strings', in Murray and Wilson (2004), 269–306.

WILSON, W. DANIEL (1985), 'Turks on the 18th-century operatic stage', *Eighteenth-Century Life* 9.2, 79–92.

WILTSHER, A. (1985), *Most Dangerous Women: Feminist Peace Campaigners of the Great War.* London.

WINKLER, J. J. (1990), 'The ephebes' song', in Winkler and Zeitlin (1990), 20–62.

—— and ZEITLIN, F. I. (1990) (eds.), *Nothing to do with Dionysos? Athenian Drama in its Social Context.* Princeton.

WINNINGTON-INGRAM, R. P. (1963) (ed.), *Aristidis Quintiliani de Musica Libri Tres.* Leipzig.

WINTER, JOHN GARRETT (1933), *Life and Letters in the Papyri.* Ann Arbor, Mich.

WISE, JENNIFER (1998), *Dionysus Writes: The Invention of Theatre in Ancient Greece.* Ithaca, NY.

WISEMAN, T. P. (1988), 'Satyrs in Rome: The Background to Horace's *Ars Poetica*', *JRS* 78, 1–13.

WITSCHEL, CHRISTIAN (2002), 'Athen im 5. Jh.v.Chr.–Der Historische Kontext', in Moraw (2002), 5–18.

WOLFF, CHRISTIAN (1992), 'Euripides' Iphigeneia among the Taurians: aetiology, ritual, and myth,' *Classical Antiquity* 11, 308–34.

WOLFF, H. J. (1944), 'Marriage, Law and Family Organization in Ancient Athens: A Study in the Interrelation of Public and Private Law in the Greek City', *Traditio* 2, 43–96.

WOLFF, JANET (1981), *The Social Production of Art*. London.

WOOD, MARCUS (1999), *Blind Memory: Representations of Slavery in England and America 1780–1865*. Manchester.

—— (2002), *Slavery, Empathy and Pornography*. Oxford.

WORMAN, NANCY (2002), *The Cast of Character: Style in Greek Literature*. Austin, Tex.

—— (2004), 'Insults and oral excess in the disputes between Aeschines and Demosthenes', *AJP* 125, 1–25.

WORTHINGTON, I. (1991), 'Greek oratory, revision of speeches and the problem of historical reliability', *C&M* 42, 55–74.

—— (1994) (ed.), *Persuasion: Greek Rhetoric in Action*. London and New York.

—— (1996a) (ed.), *Word into Text: Orality and Literacy in Ancient Greece* [= *Mnemosyne* 157]. Leiden, New York, and Cologne.

—— (1996b), 'Greek oratory and the oral/literate division', in Worthington (1996a), 165–77.

WRIGHT, M. E. (2005), *Euripides' Escape Tragedies*. Oxford.

WÜST, E. (1949), 'Pantomimus', *RE* XVIII 3 (1949), 833–69.

WYKE, MARIA (1998) (ed.), *Parchments of Gender: Deciphering the Body in Antiquity*. Oxford.

XANTHAKIS-KARAMANOS (1980), *Studies in Fourth-Century Tragedy*. Athens.

YATES, FRANCES A. (1966), *The Art of Memory*. Chicago and London.

ZAMPAGLIONE, G. (1973), *The Idea of Peace in Antiquity*, trans. R. Dunn. Notre Dame, Ind.

ZEIGLER, EARLE F. (1968), *Problems in the History of Physical Education and Sport*. Englewood Cliffs, NJ.

ZEITLIN, FROMA I. (1970), 'The Argive festival of Hera and Euripides' *Electra*,' *TAPA* 101, 645–69.

—— (1980), 'The closet of masks: role-playing and mythmaking in the *Orestes* of Euripides', *Ramus* 9, 51–77.

—— (1981), 'Travesties of gender and genre in Aristophanes' *Thesmophoriazousae*', in Foley (1981b), 169–217.

—— (1985), 'Playing the other: theater, theatricality, and the feminine in Greek drama', *Representations* 11, 63–94, revised versions in Winkler and Zeitlin (1990), 63–96 and Zeitlin (1996).

ZEITLIN, FROMA I. (1986), 'Configurations of rape in Greek myth', in Tomaselli and Porter (1986), 122–51.

—— (1991), 'Euripides' *Hekabe* and the somatics of Dionysiac drama', *Ramus* 20, 53–94.

—— (1993), 'Staging Dionysus between Thebes and Athens', in Thomas H. Carpenter and Christopher A. Faraone (eds.), *Masks of Dionysus*, 147–82. Ithaca, NY, and London.

—— (1994), 'The artful eye: vision, ecphrasis and spectacle in Euripidean theatre', in Goldhill and Osborne 1994, 138–96.

—— (1996), *Playing the Other: Gender and Society in Classical Greek Literature*. Chicago and London.

—— (2003), 'The Argive festival of Hera and Euripides' *Electra*', in J. Mossman (ed.), *Oxford Readings in Euripides* (Oxford 2003), 261–84 (revised version of article originally published in *TAPA* 101 (1970), 645–69.

ZIMMERMANN, BERNHARD (1985), *Untersuchung zur Form und dramatischen Technik der Aristophanischen Komödien*, vol. i. Königstein and Ts.

—— (1996), 'Der Tanz in der griechischen Komödie', *Primeras Jornadas Internacionales de Teatro Griego*, 121–32. Universitad de Valencia.

ŽIŽEK, SLAJOV (1994), *The Metastases of Enjoyment. Six Essays on Woman and Causality*. London.

—— (2002), *For they Know Not What They Do: Enjoyment as a Political Factor*, 2nd edn. London [Originally published in 1991].

ZWEIG, BELLA (1992), 'The mute nude female characters in Aristophanes' plays', in Amy Richlin (ed.), *Pornography and Representation in Greece and Rome*, 73–89. Oxford and New York.

Index

Index